ISBN 978-1-5283-1817-4
PIBN 10133107

English
Français
Deutsche
Italiano
Español
Português

www.forgottenbooks.com

Mythology Photography **Fiction**
Fishing Christianity **Art** Cooking
Essays Buddhism Freemasonry
Medicine **Biology** Music **Ancient
Egypt** Evolution Carpentry Physics
Dance Geology **Mathematics** Fitness
Shakespeare **Folklore** Yoga Marketing
Confidence Immortality Biographies
Poetry **Psychology** Witchcraft
Electronics Chemistry History **Law**
Accounting **Philosophy** Anthropology
Alchemy Drama Quantum Mechanics
Atheism Sexual Health **Ancient History**
Entrepreneurship Languages Sport
Paleontology Needlework Islam
Metaphysics Investment Archaeology
Parenting Statistics Criminology
Motivational

WYOMING REPORTS

CASES DECIDED

IN THE

SUPREME COURT

OF

WYOMING

FROM

SEPTEMBER 24, 1912, TO JULY 19, 1913

(Cases decided July 19, 1913, not included herein, will appear in the succeeding volume.)

REPORTED BY

CHARLES N. POTTER

VOL. 21

JUSTICES OF THE SUPREME COURT OF THE STATE OF WYOMING

DURING THE PERIOD COVERED BY THIS VOLUME.

———

CYRUS BEARD $\begin{cases}$ *Chief Justice to January 6, 1913.*
 Justice from January 6, 1913. $\end{cases}$

RICHARD H. SCOTT $\begin{cases}$ *Justice to January 6, 1913.*
 Chief Justice from January 6, 1913. $\end{cases}$

CHARLES N. POTTER, *Justice.*

———

Clerk, WILLIAM H. KELLY.

Attorney General, DOUGLAS A. PRESTON.

———

DISTRICT JUDGES

DURING THE PERIOD BY THIS VOLUME.

———

First District, RODERICK N. MATSON, *Cheyenne, to January 6, 1913.*

WILLIAM C. MENTZER, *Cheyenne, from January 6, 1913.*

Second District, CHARLES E. CARPENTER, *Laramie, to December 28, 1912.*

VOLNEY J. TIDBALL, *Laramie, from January 9, 1913.*

Third District, DAVID H. CRAIG, *Rawlins.*

Fourth District, CARROLL H. PARMELEE, *Sheridan.*

Fifth District, PERCY W. METZ, *Basin, from March 4, 1913.*

Sixth District, CHARLES E WINTER, *Casper, from March 3, 1913.*

CASES REPORTED

CASES CITED

OTHER CASES CITED.

REPORTS OF CASES

DETERMINED IN

THE SUPREME COURT

OF THE

STATE OF WYOMING

[October Term, 1912.]

BROWN v. COW CREEK SHEEP COMPANY.
(No. 689.)

Bills and Notes—Pleading—Written Instruments for the Unconditional Payment of Money Only—Checks—Unconditional Payment—Memoranda—Liability of Drawer—Countermanding Payment—Banks and Banking.

1. To make applicable Section 4406, Compiled Statutes 1910, providing that it shall be sufficient in an action on an instrument for the unconditional payment of money only to set forth a copy of the instrument, and to state that there is due to the plaintiff on such instrument, from the adverse party, a specified sum, which he claims with interest, the instrument must be one for the unconditional payment of money only, but it is not essential that it be negotiable.

2. In an action upon an instrument for the unconditional payment of money only, instead of pleading the legal effect and the other facts necessary in such case, it is sufficient under Section 4406, Compiled Statutes 1910, to set forth a copy of the instrument, and state that there is due to the plaintiff on such instrument from the adverse party, a specified sum, which he claims, with interest, stating also, if others than the makers of a promissory note or the acceptors of a bill of exchange are parties, the facts which fix their liability; and it is unnecessary in a pleading under

said section in an action upon such an instrument to aver consideration for the promise or order, whatever may be necessary as to the proof.

3. Where a check for a sum certain, payable to the order of a payee named, contained the additional words: "For Wilkes," and the following at the bottom of the check: "This check may not be paid unless object for which drawn is stated," and the check was signed in the name of a corporation by a person named, *held*, that the words "For Wilkes" did not import that the check was drawn otherwise than upon the general personal credit of the drawer, but, on the contrary, was merely a statement of the object for which the check was drawn, or the person or account to which the amount was to be charged, and did not impress upon the check any element of contingency or condition as to payment.

4. A statement in or upon a bill, note, or check indicating the consideration or account to be charged with the amount, does not render the payment, promise, or order conditional or affect the negotiability of the instrument, there being a clear distinction between such a statement and an order or promise to pay out of a particular fund; such distinction being usually recognized in statutes defining negotiable instruments, and in the statute of this state by the provision that an order or promise to pay out of a particular fund is not unconditional, but that an unqualified order or promise to pay is unconditional, though coupled with an indication of a particular fund out of which reimbursement is to be made, or a particular account to be debited with the amount, or a statement of the tranaction which gives rise to the instrument. (Comp. Stat. 1910, Sec. 3161.)

5. Where a check for a sum certain, payable to the order of a payee named, contained the additional words: "For Wilkes," *held*, that the direction contained in the instrument was not to pay out of a particular fund, as distinguished from an order upon the general credit of the drawer.

6. A "check" is usually defined to be a draft or order upon a bank for the payment, at all events, of a certain sum of money to a person or his order, or to bearer, and payable on demand; it is an evidence of indebtedness, and, as between drawer and payee, is equivalent to the drawer's promise to pay, although the latter may not be bound absolutely until payment has been duly demanded of the bank and refused.

7. An action may be brought upon a check by the holder against the drawer to recover the amount thereof.

8. The payment of a check may be stopped or countermanded at any time before it is actually presented and paid; but in doing so the drawer assumes the consequences of his act.

9. A check for a sum certain, payable to the order of a payee named, signed in the name of a corporation by a person named, contained the words in the body of the check: "For Wilkes," and also at the bottom of the check the following: "This check may not be paid unless object for which drawn is stated." *Held,* that, conceding the effect of the memorandum to be, as contended, to require that the object be stated, when the memorandum was complied with, the instrument, if otherwise in proper form and unqualified, would be a check, and necessarily an instrument for the unconditional payment of money, though subject to such defenses as may properly be interposed in a suit upon any instrument of that character in the hands of the one suing upon it; and that the words "For "Wilkes" were to be regarded as having been written in the check for the purpose of stating the object.

10. Any form of statement, however brief and indefinite, informing the drawer as to the matter, would be a sufficient compliance with a memorandum at the bottom of a check stating that the check may not be paid unless object for which drawn is stated.

11. As a general rule a bank is not bound to take notice of memoranda upon the margin or in the body of the check placed there for the convenience of the drawer.

12. A check for a sum certain, payable to the order of a payee named, signed in the name of a corporation by a person named, contained the words: "For Wilkes," and the following at the bottom of the check: "This check may not be paid unless object for which drawn is stated." *Held,* that the words "For Wilkes" was a sufficient statement of the object to have authorized the payment of the check by the bank on which it was drawn, and that the check on its face was an instrument for the unconditional payment of money only, within the meaning of the Negotiable Instruments Act (Comp. Stat. 1910, Secs. 3284, 3343), defining a bill of exchange and a check, authorizing, in an action upon the check, the short form of pleading prescribed by Section 4406, Compiled Statutes, 1910.

[Decided October 7, 1912.]   (126 Pac. 886.)

ERROR to the District Court, Carbon County; HON. DAVID H. CRAIG, Judge.

The action was by Ed Brown against the Cow Creek Sheep Company upon a check signed in the name of the company for the sum of $2,500. A general demurrer to the petition was sustained, and the plaintiff elected to stand upon the petition as filed. Judgment was rendered for the defendant for costs. The plaintiff brought error. The material facts are stated in the opinion.

N. R. Greenfield, for plaintiff in error.

Under the Negotiable Instruments Act (Comp. Stat. 1910, Secs. 3159, 3161), an indication of a particular fund out of which reimbursement is to be made, or a particular account which is. to be debited with the amount does not render the instrument conditional or non-negotiable. The distinction made by the decisions and by the Negotiable Instruments Act between instruments payable out of a particular fund and those which refer to such fund for reimbursement is close. but logically sound. It is clear that an instrument payable out of a particular fund is not payable "in any event," but depends for payment on the existence of the fund, and its sufficiency at the time fixed for payment. The true test is: Does the instrument carry the general personal credit of the drawer or maker, or only the credit of a particular fund? (4 Ency. L. (2nd Ed.) 89.) The check in controversy imports on its face a personal indebtedness in the sum named from the Cow Creek Sheep Company to Ed Brown, and is an absolute direction to the bank to pay that sum to Brown, or his order, at all events. without condition or limitation. It is drawn upon the general personal credit of the company. and not upon the credit of a particular fund, and it is not conditioned upon the sufficiency of any fund. In this state, where a large amount of business is transacted by agents of corporations upon the open range in dealing with live stock, checks of this character are almost invariably used, not for the purpose of designating a particular fund for payment, but that the principal may be advised from an inspection of the check of the transaction giving rise to the debt, and thereby enabled to make proper charges and credits upon the books. All such checks are drawn upon the general fund of the drawer on deposit at the bank. It is desirable and necessary that checks given upon the open range should be negotiable and have all the attributes of negotiable paper. The rule defining the requisites of negotiable instruments, though now declared by statute, is subject to a reasonable construction. It requires a strained construction and interpretation of the check in question to say that it is drawn upon a particular fund. The notation on the check is for the benefit of the drawer and not for the benefit or protection of the bank. The bank is fully protected upon paying such a check whether the principal is indebted to the payee named in the check or not. The check itself imports such indebtedness.

The memorandum upon this check stating that it may not be paid unless object for which drawn is stated, does not affect the character of the instrument. The "object" for which the check is drawn must be stated in all instances. The object of the present check was the payment of the amount named by the bank to the plaintiff out of the general fund or credit of the drawer at the bank. If that is not so, and it was necessary that there be some other statement of the object, then the words "For Wilkes" were sufficient as a statement of such object. The following cases support the contention that the instrument sued upon is negotiable: Bank v. Lightner, 74 Kan. 736, 88 Pac. 59; 118 Am. St. 353; 8 L. R. A. (N. S.) 231; Schmittler v. Simon, 101 N. Y. 554, 5 N. E. 425, 54 Am. Rep. 737; Corbett v. Clark, 45 Wis. 403, 30 Am. Rep. 763; Hibbs v. Brown, 190 N. Y. 167, 82 N. E. 1108; Siegel v. Bank, 131 Ill. 569, 23 N. E. 417, 19 Am. St. Rep. 51, 7 L. R. A. 537; Buchanan v. Wren, 10 Tex. Civ. App. 560, 30 S. W. 1077; Kirk v. Ins. Co., 39 Wis. 138, 20 Am. Rep. 39; Newton

Wagon Co. v. Diers, 10 Neb. 284, 4 N. W. 995; Bank v.
Michael, 96 N. C. 53, 1 S. E. 855; Taylor v. Curry, 109
Mass. 36, 12 Am. Rep. 661; Collins v. Bradbury, 64 Me. 37.
· If it should be conceded that the check is not negotiable.
nevertheless the petition states sufficient facts.   (Comp.
Stat. 1910, Sec. 4406; Frontier Supply Co. v. Loveland, 15
Wyo. 317; Sargent v. R. R. Co., 32 O. St. 449; Prindle v.
Caruthers, 15 N. Y. 425; Swan's Pl. & Prac., pp. 184, 186;
Scrock v. Schneider, 29 O. St. 499; 1 Bates' P. P. & F.
203-206; 2 id. 1052, 1051-1075; Gage v. Roberts, 12 Neb.
276, 11 N. W. 306; Stubendorf v. Sonnenschein, 11 Neb.
237, 9 N. W. 91; Collinwood v. Merchants Bank, 15 Neb.
118, 17 N. W. 359; Barnes v. Van Keuren, 31 Neb. 165,
47 N. W. 848; Scott v. Esterbrooks, 6 S. D. 253, 60 N.
W. 850; Watson v. Barr, 37 S. C. 463, 16 S. E. 188;
Strunk v. Smith, 36 Wis. 631; Dugan v. Campbell, 1 Ohio,
119.)

George E. Brimmer, for defendant in error.

It is conceded that it is the general custom of sheep corporations in this section of the country to have orders
issued by their agents in the form employed by the defendant company, for the purpose of advising the principal of
the transaction giving rise to the order upon a mere inspection of it. The form having been prepared for that purpose, it is manifest that the memoranda upon the order
does not state the transaction giving rise to the debt, and
does not enable the principal to debit a particular account
with the amount. Whenever the payment of a check or
order is based upon a condition or contingency it is not
negotiable. The cases cited by counsel for plaintiff in error
as supporting his proposition that the check is negotiable
are not applicable for the reason that the instrument considered was much different from that in the case at bar.
Where the instrument upon which suit is brought provides
for payment upon a contingency which may never happen,
Section 4406 does not apply.

A petition upon an instrument not negotiable must aver consideration. (Bank v. Cable, (Conn.) 48 Atl. 428; 8 Cyc. 110; 3 Ency. Forms, 4090; 1 Abbott's Tr. Br. on Pl. 332.) A petition upon an instrument which is payable out of a particular fund must aver the existence of the fund. (Thompson v. Merc. Co., 10 Wyo. 86; 8 Cyc. 136.) The order sued upon required payment out of a particular fund. (Thompson v. Merc. Co., supra; 4 Ency. L. (2nd Ed.) 87, 88, 89 and notes; Woodward v. Smith, (Wis.) 80 N. W. 440; Ehrichs v. DeMill, 75 N. Y. 370; Munger v. Shannon, 61 N. Y. 251; 11 Eng. & Am. Ann. Cas. 601-603.)

It was intended by the direction upon the check that the object must be stated to make it obligatory upon the agent signing the check to definitely set forth the particular purpose for which the order was drawn, so that payment might be refused by the bank in the event that the order was not drawn for company purposes, and to indicate to the bank the fund from which payment should be made. By implication, if not expressly, this order states that it was given to pay money owing or coming to John Wilkes. Unless the amount was owing to Wilkes, the order would not be payable, even though it had been accepted generally.

The check was based upon a contingency or condition, and is, therefore, not negotiable. (White v. Cushing, (Me.) 34 Atl. 164; Benedict v. Cowden, 49 N. Y. 396; Bank v. McCord, (Pa.) 21 Atl. 143; Stebbins v. R. R. Co., 2 Wyo. 71.) With reference to the direction upon the check for stating the object, see 1 Daniel Neg. Instr. (4th Ed.), Secs. 149, 150. The order was conditional upon a compliance by the drawer with the absolute requirements of the direction upon the check. Without such compliance the order was incomplete and uncertain, and the words "For Wilkes" instead of stating the object, merely indicated a special fund for payment.

POTTER, JUSTICE.

In the District Court a general demurrer to the petition filed in this case was sustained, and an exception was taken to that ruling. Thereupon, the plaintiff not desiring to further plead, but electing to stand upon the petition as filed, judgment was rendered in favor of the defendant for costs. The plaintiff brings the case here on error, assigning as error the ruling upon the demurrer and the entering of judgment for the defendant thereon.

The action was brought upon a check by the plaintiff as the payee named therein against the defendant as the drawer thereof. The petition alleges that the defendant is a corporation organized and existing under the laws of the State of Wyoming; that on the 23rd day of January, 1909, the defendant, by John Wilkes, its authorized agent, drew and delivered to the plaintiff a check in writing of that date, of which the following is a copy, with all credits and endorsements thereon:

No. 81.

FIRST NATIONAL BANK

RAWLINS, WYO., Jan. 23, 1909.

Pay to the order of Ed Brown $2,500 00/00 twenty-five hundred dollars.

For Wilkes.

COW CREEK SHEEP COMPANY.

By JOHN WILKES.

This check may not be paid unless object for which drawn is stated.

(left margin, vertical: COW CREEK SHEEP COMPANY)*

Following the copy of the check thus set out in the petition, it is alleged that the check was duly endorsed by plaintiff, and so endorsed was by plaintiff duly presented to the said First National Bank of Rawlins, Wyoming, for payment, but was not paid for the reason that the defendant countermanded the payment thereof and instructed said bank not to pay or honor said check; that "plaintiff is still the holder and owner of said check and no part thereof has been paid, and there is now due the plaintiff thereon from the defendant the sum of two thousand five hundred ($2,500.00), with interest on said amount at 8 per cent per annum from the 23rd day of January, 1909." These allegations are followed by a prayer for judgment in the sum of $2,500, together with costs and such other relief as may be proper in the premises.

The objections urged against the petition present the question whether the check upon which the action is founded is either a negotiable instrument or one for the unconditional payment of money, it being contended in support of the demurrer and the ruling thereon that the check is not such an instrument, and that the petition is therefore insufficient for the failure to aver consideration, and, further, that the check was drawn upon and payable out of a particular fund, making it necessary that the petition should allege in addition to the facts therein stated not only the fact of consideration, but also the existence of the particular fund from which the check was payable. The objections are based upon the words contained in the check, "For Wilkes," and the other words, apparently in the lower left hand corner, "This check may not be paid unless object for which drawn is stated." It is argued by counsel for defendant that the words "For Wilkes" constitutes the instrument an order payable out of a particular fund, and therefore not negotiable or unconditional; that the words above quoted indicating that the check may not be paid unless the object for which it is drawn is stated also operate to make the payment conditional, at least in the absence of a statement in definite terms of the object for which the check is drawn; and that the words "For Wilkes" do not amount to a sufficient statement to destroy the conditional effect of the requirement that the object be stated.

It is contended, on the other hand, that the check set out in the petition is an instrument for the unconditional payment of money, and that whether it is negotiable or not, though counsel deems it to be negotiable, the petition is suf-

ficient under Section 4406, Compiled Statutes, which provides as follows: "In an action, counterclaim or set-off
founded on an account or upon an instrument for the unconditional payment of money only, it shall be sufficient for
a party to set forth a copy of the account or instrument
with all credits and the indorsements thereon, and to state
that there is due to him, on such account or instrument,
from the adverse party, a specified sum, which he claims
with interest; and when others than the makers of a promissory note, or the acceptors of a bill of exchange, are parties, it shall be necessary to state the facts which fix their
liability."

The original New York Code contained a like provision
as to an action or defense founded upon an instrument for
the payment of money only, omitting the word "unconditional," but it was held under that Code that where the
obligation was conditional or depended upon facts outside
the instrument it was necessary to allege such additional
facts as might be necessary to show a complete, valid and
binding obligation. (Tooker v. Arnoux, 76 N. Y. 397;
Broome v. Taylor, id. 564.) The general effect of the provision and a pleading under it where applicable was declared
by the Court of Appeals of New York to be as follows:
"The section is express and imperative; it shall be sufficient to give a copy of the instrument, and to state that
there is due thereon to the plaintiff from the adverse party
a specified sum, which he claims. A complaint thus worded
implies that the plaintiff owns the instrument in some legal
manner of deriving title; that the event has happened on
which the payment depends, and the amount is expressly
stated. The defendant, by a general denial of the indebtedness, puts in issue every fact alleged, expressly or impliedly; and on the trial the plaintiff is bound to prove his
case the same as though every fact necessary to maintain
the action had been averred explicitly. Every fact which
is thus impliedly averred, may be traversed by the defendant

in the same manner as if it were expressly averred." (Prindle v. Caruthers, 15 N. Y. 425, 429.)

To authorize this form of pleading under our statute upon a written instrument, it must be one for the *unconditional* payment of money only. If it be such an instrument, then, instead of pleading its legal effect and the other facts necessary in such case, the party may set forth a copy of the instrument with all credits and the indorsements thereon, and state that there is due to him, on such instrument, from the adverse party, a specified sum which he claims, with interest; stating also if others than the makers of a promissory note, or the acceptors of a bill of exchange, are parties, the facts which fix their liability. There is no contention in this case that the necessary additional facts are not pleaded which fix the liability of the defendant as drawer of the check, if it should be held to be an instrument for the unconditional payment of money. It is not essential under Section 4406 that the instrument be negotiable, for it may be one for the unconditional payment of money only, though not negotiable, as where it is not payable to the order of the payee or any specified person or to bearer. It follows that where the instrument upon which the action, counterclaim, or set-off is founded is one for the unconditional payment of money only, whether negotiable or not, it is unnecessary, in the short form of pleading authorized by Section 4406, to aver consideration for the promise or order, whatever might be necessary as to the proof. (1 Bates Pl. Pr. Par. & F. 191; 2 id. 1232.) While, therefore, the question of the negotiability of the check may be incidentally involved, that is not the essential question in the case, since the suit is brought by the one named in the check as payee, who alleges that it was drawn and delivered to him and that he is still the owner and holder thereof.

The contention that the check is payable out of a particular fund cannot be sustained. The words "For Wilkes," do not, in our opinion, import that the check is drawn otherwise than upon the general personal credit of the drawer, but they appear, on the contrary, to be merely a statement of the object for which the check is drawn, or the person or account to which the amount was to be charged. Nor do they impress upon the check any element of contingency or condition as to payment. In Wells v. Brigham, 6 Cush. 6, 52 Am. Dec. 750, suit was brought upon an order reading as follows: "Mr. Brigham, Dear Sir: You will please pay Elisha Wells $30, which is due me for the two-horse wagon bought last spring, and this may be your receipt." In the opinion by Chief Justice Shaw, it was said: "The draft is payable at a time fixed, to-wit, on demand; on no contingency or condition, but absolutely; for a sum certain, out of no specific fund, but by the drawee generally. The fact that the draft indicates a debt due to the drawer as the consideration between drawer and drawee, does not make it the less a cash order or draft. The drawee, by his acceptance, admits such debt, and is estopped to deny it, as against the payee. * * * The statement of the origin of the debt, the purchase of a wagon, did not make it the less payable absolutely, and at all events, and not conditionally or out of a particular fund." In Ridgely Bank. v. Patton & Hamilton, 109 Ill. 479. the action was brought upon a check which directed the bank as follows: "Pay to Patton & Hamilton, for account of Lewis Coleman & Co., or order, ten hundred eighteen 23/100 dollars ($1,018 23/100)." Referring to the contention that the instrument was not a check because of the words "For account of Lewis Coleman & Co.," the court said: "We do not perceive that the presence of the words above named in the check detracts from its quality as such. They introduce nothing of contingency or uncertainty with respect to the payment, the sum payable, or person to whom it is to be paid. It still remains an order, in all its absoluteness, for the payment of a certain sum of money to the payees named, and is payable instantly on demand. The words, 'for account of Lewis Coleman & Co.,' would seem to have been inserted for the convenience of the drawers, to show the purpose for which the check was given, or

to show the equitable interest of Lewis Coleman & Co. A
bill or note, without affecting its character as such, may
state the transaction out of which it arose, or the consideration for which it was given. (1 Parsons on Notes and
Bills, 44.) The words in question seem to do no more."

In State National Bank v. Reilly, 124 Ill. 464, 14 N. E.
657, the suit was brought upon a check drawn by the clerk
of the United States District Court for the Southern District of Illinois, and countersigned by the District Judge.
Upon the check and over the direction to pay appeared the
name of the court, and the following words: "Check Number 53. Case No. 2105. In the Matter of H. Sanford &
Company, Bankrupts." Following the direction to pay the
plaintiff a stated sum of money, and in the body of the check,
were the words and figures: "being in full for the dividend
of seven-tenths per cent declared April 30, 1881, on his
claim for $31,380 proved against said bankrupt's estate."
The statute, as well as a rule of court, required such checks
to be drawn in that form, but all deposits of funds paid into
the court were in one account, notwithstanding that the deposits were so made as to indicate the case or proceeding in
which the money had been paid, and that manner of keeping
the account upon the books of the bank was held to be
proper. Concerning the character of the check above described, the court said that it was an absolute order to pay
the stated sum to the plaintiff, that it was "in the usual form
of bank check, drawn upon the general fund of the drawer,
without specifying any particular fund out of which it is
payable, and differs from such check only in the fact that
it has on its face some marginal memoranda, and also some
in the body of the check."

, In the case of the First National Bank v. Lightner, 74
Kan. 736, 88 Pac. 59, 8 L. R. A. (N. S.) 231, 118 Am. St.
353, 11 Ann. Cas. 596, the question was whether an order
was a negotiable bill of exchange, or was payable out of a
particular fund, the order reading as follows: "Hutchinson, Kan., August 10, 1903. G. W. Lightner, Offerle,

Kan.: Dear Sir—Pay to the order of the First National Bank of Hutchinson, Kansas, $1,500, on account of contract between you and the Snyder Planing-Mill Company. (Signed) The Snyder Planing-Mill Company, Per J. F. Donnell, Treasurer." The following also appeared upon the order: "Accepted:, G. W. Lightner." It was held that the order was a negotiable bill of exchange, payable absolutely, and that the words, "on account of contract," etc., did not amount to a direction to pay out of a particular fund, but merely indicated the fund to which the drawee was to look for reimbursement. Many pertinent authorities are cited and reviewed in the opinion. While conceding that similar expressions have been held to show an intention to charge a particular fund, the court say: "The weight of authority and reason support the proposition that the words amount to no more than an indication of the fund from which the drawee is to reimburse himself. The words used are substantially the same as though the order read, 'and charge to account of contract,' etc."

The conflict in the authorities does not, we think, extend to such memoranda or expressions as are found upon the check in question here, for we fail to observe any substantial resemblance between the words upon this check and those which have been held to indicate an intention to charge a particular fund with the payment of the amount directed or promised to be paid. Had there been no other explanatory memoranda upon the check, we would perceive no reason for holding that the words, "For Wilkes," indicate anything more than the purpose or consideration for which the check was drawn, or the account to be charged with the amount, but that they were intended as a compliance with the suggestion found upon the check that the object be stated is so evident, any ground for doubt that might otherwise exist concerning their meaning and effect would seem to be removed.

It has not generally been held that a statement in or upon a bill, note or check, indicating the consideration therefor, or the account to be charged with the amount, and the like, renders the payment, promise or order conditional, or affects the negotiability of the instrument. There is a clear distinction between such a statement and an order or promise to pay out of a particular fund, and this distinction is usually recognized in statutes defining negotiable instruments, as it is in our statute by the provision that an order or promise to pay out of a particular fund is not unconditional, but that an unqualified order or promise to pay is unconditional, though coupled with an indication of a particular fund out of which reimbursement is to be made, or a particular account to be debited with the amount, or a statement of the transaction which gives rise to the instrument. (Comp. Stat., Sec. 3161.) We hold, then, that the direction contained in this instrument is not to pay out of a particular fund as distinguished from an order upon the general credit of the drawer.

What has seemed a more difficult question is presented by the contention respecting the words in the lower left-hand corner of the instrument, "This check may not be paid unless object for which drawn is stated." The natural inference would be that these words were printed upon the check as part of the printed form used by the defendant company, expressing a rule to be observed by its officers and agents in drawing and issuing checks that the object or purpose of each check be stated upon its face; and counsel concede that to be the fact. Whether printed or written, the broadest effect that can reasonably be claimed for the words is that they require the object for which the check is drawn to be stated, and for the purposes of this case it may be conceded that they amount to such a requirement. If, when not complied with, that requirement, expressed as it is upon this check, should be held obligatory upon the bank and sufficient to deprive the payee of the right to demand payment, the reason therefor would not be that the instrument was payable only upon an unfulfilled condition, but rather that one of the elements necessary to give

the instrument any force is omitted; in other words, that
the instrument is not a check without the required statement of the object for which it was drawn. It is not declared that the check is payable only upon a contingency,
as that term is usually understood, viz: an event which may
or may not happen in the future, for that which is to be
done must obviously be done before delivery of the check,
and by the drawer or its agent as part of the act of drawing
and issuing it. This provision does not resemble any that
has been considered by the courts in determining whether
an instrument was payable upon a condition or absolutely,
for in each of the reported cases coming to our notice the
alleged condition was something to be done or to occur
after the instrument was delivered, and subject only to the
supposed condition the instrument was complete and required the payment of the amount stated. For example, in
Bavins v. Bank, 1 Q. B. Div. (1900) 270, it appeared that
a check directed the payment of a stated sum of money,
"provided the receipt at foot hereof is duly signed, stamped
and dated." It was held that the check was not unconditional and, therefore, not negotiable. And so in Bank v.
Gordon, 86 L. T. Rep. 574, a check was held not to be a
bill of exchange which was declared to be payable only
upon signature by the payees of a form of receipt at the
foot of the instrument. But in the case of Nathan v. Og-
dens Limited, 93 L. T. Rep. 553, a check was held to be
negotiable upon which were the words: "The receipt at
back hereof must be signed, which signature will be taken
as an endorsement of the cheque," and upon the back was
a printed form of receipt. The court said that the order
to pay was unconditional, for while the words at the foot
of the check were imperative in terms, they were not addressed to the bankers, and did not affect the nature of the
order to them. The provision we are considering has reference primarily to the manner of drawing the check.

As we view the matter, therefore, the question to be
decided in this connection is whether the instrument set out

in the petition is upon its face a check of the defendant
company, showing an obligation of the defendant to pay
the amount stated, payment having been refused by the
bank to which it is addressed. A check is usually defined
to be a draft or order upon a bank for the payment, at all
events, of a certain sum of money to a person, or his order,
or to bearer, and payable instantly on demand. It is an
evidence of indebtedness, and as between the drawer and
the payee is equivalent to the drawer's promise to pay, although the latter may not be bound absolutely until payment has been duly demanded of the bank and refused.
And an action may be brought upon the check by the
holder against the drawer to recover the amount evidenced
thereby. (Camas Prairie State Bank v. Newman, 15 Ida.
719, 99 Pac. 833, 128 Am. St. Rep. 81 & notes.) It is said
that the contract of the drawer is that the bank will pay
the amount on demand, and until demanded the drawer is
not bound. "But when this is done and shown, the check
then imports a debt from the drawer to the payee, and it
may be sued on without proving the consideration, value
received being presumed." (2 Daniel's Neg. Instr. (3rd
Ed.), Sec. 1646.) The Negotiable Instruments Act defines
a check as a bill of exchange drawn on a bank payable on
demand and the Act declares that a check must be presented for payment within a reasonable time after its issue,
or the drawer will be discharged from liability thereon to
the extent of the loss caused by the delay. (Comp. Stat.,
Secs. 3343, 3344. A bill of exchange is defined as an unconditional order in writing addressed to one person by another,
signed by the person giving it, requiring the person to whom
it is addressed to pay on demand, or at a fixed determinable
future time, a certain sum of money to order or to bearer.
(Id., Sec. 3284.) The payment of a check may be stopped
or countermanded at any time before it is actually presented
and paid, but in doing so the drawer assumes the consequences of his act.

Statutes have been enacted in some states requiring a particular statement of the consideration in certain cases, as in the case of a note given for a patent right, and in Missouri the statute required that to be negotiable a note must contain the words, "value received." Under such statutes a note containing the required statement becomes a valid and effective instrument, according to its terms, except that statutes such as those requiring a note for a patent right to state that it is given for such purpose, usually provide that the note shall be subject to the same defenses as to consideration in the hands of any holder as in the hands of the payee named in the note. But the point we wish to suggest by referring to statutes requiring a statement of consideration in any form is that when the consideration is stated as required, the instrument is effectual, and may even be negotiable, subject only to such defenses in the hands of a third party as may be provided in the statute. (Haskell v. Jones, 86 Pa. St. 173.) The memorandum in question, conceding the effect thereof to be as contended, viz: to require that the object be stated, would seem to have no greater effect than a similar statutory provision, so that when complied with, if it is otherwise in proper form and unqualified, the instrument will be a check, and necessarily an instrument for the unconditional payment of money, though subject, of course, to such defenses as may properly be interposed in a suit upon any instrument of that character in the hands of the one suing upon it.

We are not called upon to decide what the rights of the parties would be if there had been no attempt to state the object upon this check, for the provision with reference to stating the object must be considered in connection with the words, "For Wilkes," which words are to be regarded as having been written in the check for the purpose of stating the object, and we think they do tend to explain it, though they may appear indefinite and uncertain to one not acquainted with the facts. It is contended that they do not amount to a sufficient statement, since "For Wilkes" might indicate either a debt due to Wilkes, or that the money was loaned or advanced to him, or even some other consideration or purpose. It is to be observed that the requirement, if it be a requirement, is merely that the object be stated. It does not go to the extent of suggesting a particular form for stating the object, or the manner of stating it. To determine, then, what would amount generally to a statement of the object within the meaning of the requirement, and whether it is sufficiently stated upon this check, it is important that we consider the reason and purpose of the requirement. Counsel do not disagree as to that, nor do we disagree with counsel. We think that the purpose is obvious. One fact is stated by counsel which we might not otherwise know, viz: that a form of check like this is generally adopted by corporations engaged in the live stock business in the section of country in which the defendant is so engaged. And they state the purpose to be, in substance, that the company may be advised from a mere inspection of the check of the transaction giving rise to it, and to aid in making the proper charges and credits upon the books of the company. In this there is no suggestion of any public interest to be subserved, but the object is to be stated for the sole convenience of the company in whose name the check is drawn. It would seem to follow that any form of statement, however brief or indefinite, that would inform the company—the drawer—as to the matter would be sufficient. But who is to determine whether the statement upon a particular check is sufficient to convey the desired information to the drawer? Must the payee or the bank assume the responsibility of doing so? To hold, as contended, that, in order to comply with the provision as to stating the object, such object must be fully and definitely stated so as to clearly explain the consideration or transaction, or otherwise the check would be of no force or validity, might permit the drawer to avoid liability upon the instrument as a check merely upon the ground that, though the object appears to be stated in some form, it is not sufficiently stated to fully and clearly inform every one as to the actual facts of the transaction, notwithstanding that the consideration may in fact have been valid and adequate, and the drawer may fully understand the meaning and purport of the words used. It would then be perilous for the bank to pay any such check, for the drawer might question the sufficiency of any statement, and the one receiving the instrument for a valid debt might find that he had surrendered some important legal advantage, or parted with something of value in exchange for a piece of paper, the value of which depends primarily upon whether the object is stated upon it in such a clear and definite manner that anyone can understand it; a matter that might ultimately have to be determined by the courts. Yet it is not unusual for checks to contain memoranda stating the consideration, or referring to the debt for which the check is given, or the transaction giving rise to it, and the character of the check is in no way affected, as a rule, by any such memoranda. As above stated, it is expressly declared by statute that an unqualified order or promise is not conditional, though coupled with statements of the kind suggested when they do not provide for payment out of a particular fund. The only difference to be observed as to the check here is that it provides for stating the object. But we do not perceive that to be at all important when the object is in fact stated. We think it evident that the form of check set out in the petition was intended to be used in the business transactions of the company like ordinary checks, and with the same effect, requiring only that in addition to the other necessary things the check shall contain a statement of the object for which it is drawn. If the contention here made on the part of the defendant be sound, then its checks would amount to practically no value until paid in the hands of anyone, and certainly of no value for commercial purposes.

The instrument in question is an order upon a bank presumably to pay the amount stated out of funds of the defendant there deposited and subject to be drawn out by check. We have referred to the custom of placing memoranda upon checks. As a rule that is done to preserve information for the benefit of the drawer, and it may also serve as a convenient receipt showing the purpose of the payment, but that does not affect the duty of the bank, for it is a general rule that a bank is not bound to take notice of memoranda upon the margin or in the body of a check placed there for the convenience of the drawer. (State National Bank v. Dodge, 124 U. S. 333, 8 Sup. Ct. 521, 31 L. Ed. 458; State National Bank v. Reilly, 124 Ill. 464, 14 N. E. 657; Duckett v. Mechanics' Bank, 86 Md. 400, 38 Atl. 983, 39 L. R. A. 84, 63 Am. St. Rep. 513.) That principle was applied in the cases of Bank v. Dodge and Bank v. Reilly under circumstances rendering them to some extent in point upon the facts of this case, though a different question was considered. It was held in those cases that a bank upon which a check had been drawn was not bound to observe memoranda stating the particular consideration and purpose of the check, notwithstanding that the check had been issued by a public officer and under a statute requiring the consideration and purpose to be stated. The facts in the two cases were similar and the point presented the same. It appeared that the bank had been appointed as depository for the United States District Court for the Southern District of Illinois. The clerk of that court deposited the funds belonging to the registry of the court with said bank, the deposits being entered by the bank in the name of said court, and each deposit ticket, as well as the entry of the deposit in the books of the bank, containing a number which represented the number of the case or proceeding in the court in which the funds had been received. A separate account, however, was not kept of the funds received in each case, but the deposits were kept in a single account upon the books of the bank. It was held by the court in Bank v. Dodge, that the account was properly so kept, that being one of the questions in the case. Checks upon the funds deposited were issued signed by the clerk and coun-

tersigned by the district judge, each of which contained
upon its face the name of the court, the title and number of
a particular case, and the order required the payment of a
specified sum of money, stating in substance that it was in
full for a certain dividend that had been declared upon the
payee's claim proven in the case mentioned upon the check.
A large sum of money had been paid into the registry of
the court in a certain bankruptcy case and the funds so
received had been deposited in said bank by deposit tickets
stating the number of the case.   It appeared that the bank
before the presentation of certain checks in controversy for
the payment of dividends in said bankruptcy case had actually paid out on similar checks, properly signed, all the
funds which had been deposited with it to the credit of the
court, many of such checks having been drawn in cases in
which no deposits had been made.   The suits were brought
to recover the amount of the checks from the bank on the
ground that it had improperly paid checks drawn in cases
wherein no money had been deposited.   But, notwithstanding that the deposit tickets and the books of the bank opposite each deposit stated a particular number as representing the number of the case in which the money had been
received and purported to be deposited, it was held that the
bank was not required to take notice of the number and
title of the case and the purpose for which the check was
drawn in paying particular checks, and was not, therefore,
liable to pay the checks in controversy, although it had paid
out of the funds deposited to the credit of the court other
checks shown to have been drawn in cases in which no deposits had been made.

In the case of Bank v. Dodge the Supreme Court of the
United States say: "The claim on the part of Dodge is,
that it was the duty of the bank, not merely to keep the
funds of the court safely, but to refuse to honor the checks
of the court if it found that the court was drawing checks
in any particular case, according to its number, beyond the
amount deposited in the bank under that number, but we

are of opinion that the bank had a right to assume that
these memoranda of numbers in the deposits and in the
checks were merely for the convenience of the court and its
officers; and that it also had a right to presume that the
court and its officers were properly performing their duty in
distributing its trust funds. * * * The deposits being
as required, in the name and to the credit of the court, the
bank was authorized and required to honor all checks drawn
by the court, and to pay them generally out of such deposits;
and the order or check for withdrawing the money, in stating the case in or on account of which it was drawn was a
memorandum imposing no duty upon the bank, but only
operated for the convenience of the court and its officers in
keeping its accounts. The obvious purpose of the memorandum of numbers in the deposit book of the court and
upon the checks was to enable the court and the clerk to
properly keep the accounts, and that the check might operate as vouchers, showing the manner in which the moneys
in any particular case were distributed, and to enable the
clerk to show to the court that he had deposited the funds
which he had received. There is no evidence anywhere of
any intention that the bank should be controlled by the numbers in paying any check drawn upon it." The court quotes
in the opinion the statute which provided that every check
upon the funds of the court so deposited "shall state the
cause in or on account of which it is drawn."

Referring to the form of the check in the case of Bank v.
Reilly, supra, which was the same as the checks in Bank v.
Dodge, the Supreme Court of Illinois say that the check was
no doubt drawn in that form for the reason that the statute
and a similar rule of the court required that "every such
order shall state the cause in or on account of which it is
drawn," and then proceed as follows: "It cannot be known
certainly why every such order should contain these things
or this particular information. Many reasons might be suggested why it should be so. First, it was an assurance from
the court to the bank that the trust funds in its custody

were being withdrawn for the use of beneficiaries, and were therefore not being misappropriated : second, it might be of advantage to the court and its officers in making up the accounts with each estate in bankruptcy pending or that had been adjudicated in the court; and third, it would be a convenient mode of obtaining vouchers from the parties receiving dividends, that would operate as a protection to the officers making such payments. What reason may have existed for so providing by statute and by rule, matters little. It is only important it is declared the check or order for withdrawing such fund shall contain the things enumerated. Without looking for the reason why it is so, the only concern is what such memoranda indicated, or what obligation, if any, there was thereby imposed upon the bank. Beyond what has already been said, that it was an assurance from the court itself, the funds were being withdrawn for a legitimate purpose, it is not perceived the memoranda, either on the margin or in the body of the check, contained anything for the guidance or information of the bank in any manner whatever, nor was the bank under any legal duty to observe such memoranda. The bank could not know, nor was it important it should know, that 'H. Sanford & Company' were the bankrupts whose estate was being administered in 'case No. 2105,' nor that the payee of the check was a creditor of such bankrupts, nor that the same was ordered to be paid him as in full of a dividend declared at a certain date, and was a certain per cent of his claim allowed against such bankrupts. These were matters exclusively within the knowledge of the court and its officers, and with which the bank had no rightful authority to intermeddle. It is well known, and the testimony is full to that point, the practice among banks paying checks of their depositors is not to observe memoranda upon such checks, but the custom is to regard them as having been made for the convenience of the drawers, and the practice in that regard, it is thought, has the sanction of law in its support."

In that case it was also said that the check was an absolute order to pay the sum of money stated.

If it was proper upon the facts of the cases above referred to for the bank to pay checks drawn upon trust funds without observing the memoranda upon the checks to determine whether any money had been deposited in the cases mentioned, there would seem to be much. less reason in this case for holding it incumbent upon the bank to observe and determine whether the words used to state the object were sufficient for that purpose. Unless such duty rested upon the bank, it might properly and it would be its duty to pay a check containing the provision aforesaid suggesting that the object must be stated, at least when the object is stated in some form which might be understood by the drawer, or one who knows the circumstances. And the bank might rightly assume, we think, that the officer or agent drawing the check had properly and sufficiently stated the object. The only reasonable conclusion, in our opinion, is that when the object appears to be stated, if not otherwise, it would not be the duty of the bank, in the absence of other specific instructions, or the payee or other holder, to inquire or determine whether the statement is such as will fully inform the company as to the transaction, and much less whether it amounts to a clear and definite explanation thereof, unless, perhaps, the object is so stated as to be manifestly fictitious or to mean nothing. For all we may know the object is stated upon the check in question in the form usually employed for that purpose by the officers and agents of the defendant company. The fact that the company countermanded payment might be taken as some indication that the act was considered necessary to prevent payment upon presentation. If the instrument be in fact without consideration, that defense is open to the drawer while the paper remains in the hands of one against whom that defense may be made. We perceive no reason for supposing that the drawer would not understand what was meant by the words. "For Wilkes," if the amount represented a valid obligation for which the check might be drawn, for it was in a position to know whether or not and for what purpose any such amount was due or properly payable by the company for or on account of Wilkes.

When it is determined that it would not only be proper, but the duty of the bank to pay the check upon presentation, unless payment has been countermanded, it follows that the check is unconditional. We, therefore, conclude that the check sued on is an instrument for the unconditional payment of money, authorizing the short form of pleading, and that it was error to sustain the demurrer. The judgment will be reversed and the cause remanded for such further proceedings as may be proper.

BEARD, C. J., and SCOTT, J., concur.

BUCKNUM v. JOHNSON.
(No. 662.)

APPEAL AND ERROR—RECORD—PRESUMPTION—PUBLIC LANDS—STATE LANDS—LEASE—APPEAL FROM STATE LAND BOARD—JURISDICTION OF DISTRICT COURT—ISSUES ON APPEAL—JUDGMENT ON APPEAL—DISPOSAL OF SCHOOL LANDS—CONTEST—PATENTS TO STATE—PRIOR VESTED RIGHTS.

1. Where, in a contest before the board of school land commissioners, the contestant sought the cancellation of a lease previously made by the board to another party, the contestant claimed to have acquired the right to a part of the land for a reservoir site; the land having belonged to the United States, and having been selected by the state in lieu of other lands, but the exact date of the state's selection did not appear in the record of the cause on appeal; Held, that the state's selection of the land would be presumed to have been made prior to the date of the lease.

2. An appeal to the District Court from the state land board is a proceeding purely of statutory origin, and brings into the District Court those questions which were or might have been raised before the board; the issues cannot be

enlarged, nor can the action be transformed into an equitable or common law action.

3. On an appeal from the state land board the District Court acts as a substitute for the board, and is limited to questions that had or may be presumed to have been passed upon by the board.

4. The statute providing for an appeal from the state land board authorizing the parties to conduct the appeal upon the original papers and affidavits or upon new and amended pleadings, and prescribing that the case shall stand for trial upon the evidence taken before the board, with a proviso that in the discretion of the court, additional evidence may be adduced on the trial, where the party desiring to introduce such evidence shall have given notice to the adverse party immediately after the perfection of the bill, of the offering of said evidence and the purport and nature thereof, and further prescribing that the case shall be heard and tried the same in all respects as civil cases are tried in said court; *Held,* that the trial upon the appeal includes the trial and determination of the issues of fact made by the pleadings, independent of the findings and determination of those issues by the board, whether such trial be had upon the evidence submitted to the board or upon new evidence as permitted by the statute.

5. The jurisdiction of the District Court on an appeal from the state land board is to try the case *de novo* on the facts, and the judgment to be rendered is not one of affirmance, reversal or modification as upon review on error, but a judgment based upon the findings of the court upon the evidence, uncontrolled by the findings of the board.

6. On an appeal to the District Court from a decision of the state board of school land commissioners in a contest seeking the cancellation of a state lease, the question to be determined by the court was the same as that which was presented to the board, viz: whether the state which had granted the lease should cancel it.

7. Where a contestant seeking the cancellation of a lease of state lands before the state land board claimed a prior vested right to a ditch and reservoir site upon the land prior to the issuance of patent to the state for the land; *Held,* that if the contestant had in fact such a vested right it would be no ground for setting aside the lease, in said contest proceeding, either by the board or by the court on appeal, for the lease would not be involved, but would be

subject to such prior vested right, and would be limited to the title conveyed to the state; whether such vested rights existed might be litigated in a proper forum and proceeding.

8. In the performance of its duties with reference to the leasing and disposal of state lands the state land board is not vested with either equitable or common law jurisdiction.

9. Where there was but one applicant for a lease to state school lands at the time a lease thereof was granted, the board was not required to pass upon any question other than the form and information contained in the application and evidence in support thereof as bearing upon the right of the applicant to the lease.

10. Where, in an application to lease state school lands, a question and the answer thereto appeared as follows: "State who, if anyone, occupies land within one mile of the tract applied for, giving section number, township and range? A. No. one," and the undisputed evidence in a contest seeking a cancellation of the lease, which had been granted upon the application, showed that the homestead of another party, including buildings, were situated within one mile of each quarter section of the land covered by the lease; Held, that it was the duty of the applicant to place the board in possession of the facts called for by the application, showing the true situation with reference to the homestead of the other party, since such information might have an important bearing on the amount of revenue obtainable for the lease, and, further, that the lease appeared to have been granted upon incorrect information as to the occupancy of such homestead.

11. The section of the statute (Comp. Stat. 1910, Sec. 618) which provides that any lease for state lands procured by fraud, deceit or misrepresentation, may be cancelled by the board upon proper proof thereof, is permissive and not compulsory, though it might be the duty of the board in a proper case to cancel a lease so procured.

12. Where the cancellation of a lease of state school lands is sought in a contest before the state board of school land commissioners on the ground that the lease was procured by fraud, deceit, or misrepresentation, in that the lessee untruthfully stated in the application for the lease that no one occupied land within one mile of the tract applied for; Held, that upon the proof submitted the board acts in a judicial capacity, and is not required to cancel the lease

unless damage to the state is shown to have been sustained in the way of rental or otherwise, where there had been no application of the contestant before the board to purchase or lease the land at the time the lease sought to be cancelled was granted.

13. In a petition filed by a third party with the state board of school land commissioners to contest a lease previously granted, petitioner claimed a preference right to the land in part on the ground of a vested water right and reservoir site. *Held,* that in the contest proceeding whether the contestant had such water right and reservoir site was a question without the jurisdiction of the board; and, further, that the cancellation of the lease was not necessary to protect any such right of the contestant existing at the time the patent had issued to the state, since the patent would be subject thereto, and the lease would be limited to the state's title.

14. Any vested right to a reservoir site upon public lands of the United States, acquired under Sections 2339 and 2340, Revised Statutes, U. S., and supplementary statutory provisions, prior to the selection and patent of such lands to the state would be protected by such statutes, independent of any recognition or want of recognition by the state land board, for the board could only deal with the title conveyed to it by the patent as construed and affected by the acts of Congress in effect at the time of the issuance of the patent.

15. Although the information furnished the state board of school land commissioners in an application for the lease of school lands with reference to the occupancy of land by other parties within one mile of the tract applied for was untrue, the board was not required to cancel said lease in a contest proceeding brought for such cancellation, in the absence of a showing that the state had been damaged by such untruthful information, or that the interest of the contestant had been injuriously affected thereby.

16. An offer to lease state land provided the state land board has the right to require the applicant to do so as a condition of recognizing certain claimed vested rights in the premises, was conditional upon the board having a right to require him to rent the land as a condition precedent to recognition of the vested right claimed, and was not an offer to pay the rental value fixed or to be fixed by the board, but tendered an issue for trial without the jurisdiction of the

board, except in so far as the alleged vested right might be considered in fixing the rental value.

[Decided November 20, 1912.]   (127 Pac. 904.)

ERROR to the District Court. Natrona County; HON. CHARLES E. CARPENTER, Judge.

Henry A. Johnson instituted a contest before the state board of school land commissioners, seeking the cancellation of a state lease granted and executed to Clark Beck April 26, 1907, which lease had been assigned by Beck to C. K. Bucknum. From the decision of the board refusing to cancel the lease, the contestant appealed to the District Court. The trial in the District Court resulted in a judgment for the contestant ordering the cancellation of the lease. The contestee, Bucknum, brought error. The material facts are stated in the opinion.

Norton & Hagens, for plaintiff in error.

The state board is vested by statute with a wide discretion with reference to leasing state lands, and the District Court, on an appeal from the board, sits as a court of review, to reverse, affirm or modify the decision of the board, and not to entirely disregard such decision as if it were vacated by the appeal. Sec. 656, Comp. Stat. 1910, must be construed and harmonized with other statutes regulating appeals from the board. Section 658 plainly indicates that appeals from the board are not to be tried *de novo,* but are to be tried upon the evidence taken before the board, the original papers and affidavits and other records in the case. Where the trial is *de novo,* the general rule, under the modern chancery practice, where the decree is vacated, is that the cause with all its incidents of pleading and evidence, is presented unchanged to the appellate court, and new issues cannot be introduced. (2 Ency. Pl. & Pr. 327; Bank v. Harvey, 16 Ia. 141; Luthe v. Luthe, 12 Colo. 429; Baier v. Humpall, 16 Neb. 127; Bishop v. Stevens, 31 Neb. 786.) Under our statute regulating this appeal the case is not tried anew as upon original process. Such an appeal differs from appeals from justice courts. The appellate proceeding seems to have been considered as a mere proceeding for review in Cooper v. McCormick, 10 Wyo. 398. (See also Baker v. Brown, 12 Wyo. 205; State ex rel. Marsh v. Board, 7 Wyo. 489; Greenwood &c. Co. v. Routt, 17 Colo. 156.)

The evidence in the case fails to show that the land was occupied by the defendant in error under any color of title, that he had any improvements thereon, or that he had exercised any control over it to the exclusion of others, or had done any work on the pretended reservoir or expended money thereon. His application for water rights do not state that the ditches did or would run through land in controversy, or that any portion of it would be irrigated, or that the proposed reservoir would include any part of it. In the notice of location of the reservoir filed with the state engineer, he does not attempt to locate the lands to be used for reservoir purposes. But if he had claimed possession of the land, or had made improvements thereon by which he could claim color of title by reason of occupancy and improvements, he obtained no right which impaired the power of congress to withdraw the land from sale, or dispose of the same to other parties. (Kimball v. Waite, 132 U. S. 35; Frisbie v. Whitney, 9 Wall. 187; Yosemite Valley Case, 15 Wall. 77; Wells v. Pennington Co., 2 S. D. 1, 39 Am. St. Rep. 759; Gibson v. Hutchings, 12 La. Ann. 545; Johnson v. Brew, 43 Am. St. 172.) The evidence does not show any bad faith on the part of the land board in selecting the land, but it does show that at the time the Beck lease was granted, the board had no knowledge of the claims or pretensions of the defendant in error to the land in controversy. The fact that an applicant owns lands within one mile of lands sought to be leased gives him no better right to a lease than any other party. (State ex rel. Marsh v. Board, 7 Wyo. 478.) If Beck had answered the question in the application as to the occupancy of land within one mile of the tract applied for by stating that

Johnson occupied land within that distance, and had described the land so occupied, there would have been no reason for the denial of Beck's application. The only restriction upon the leasing of state lands is that the board shall lease the lands for the greatest benefit to the state. There was no other application before the board when the Beck lease was granted. If the lease was granted under such circumstances as not to result to the greatest benefit to the state, the question could not be raised by defendant in error. (State ex rel. Marsh v. Board, supra.)

No amount of good faith or good intentions can give one color of title or the right of possession to the public domain. The fact that the United States land office refused to act when Johnson offered the maps of his proposed reservoir is conclusive that the state land board, when they selected the land and leased the same, were not aware that Johnson made any claim of right to possession of the land, or that he claimed any color of title. The fact that he filed his maps after the commencement of this contest proceeding is of no effect, since the title of the state vested prior to that time. The law of this case is fully covered in Caldwell v. Bush, 6 Wyo. 342, where the evidence of possession was much stronger than the evidence of Johnson's possession in the case at bar. In view of the constitutional provisions creating the land board, and the statutes governing its procedure, supplemented by the decisions of this court interpreting the same, the decision of the board should not be disturbed in the absence of fraud, or abuse of discretion on the part of the board.

No appearance for defendant in error at the time of hearing, but a brief had been filed in the cause on behalf of defendant in error by *W. R. Stoll*, April 7, 1911, then his counsel. contending substantially as follows:

On an appeal from the state land board to the District Court. it is the right of the appellant to have a trial *de novo*, but he may have a trial upon the original papers and affidavits. In this case the statute was fully complied with,

and as to the proceeding upon the trial there is no question
in this case.   No objection was interposed to the method
of the trial, and no question was raised as to the propriety
of that method.   It is the duty of the courts to correct any
abuse of discretion on the part of the land board when the
matter properly comes before it, and on appeal the proper
action for the court in order to correct such abuse is a reversal of the board's action.   The statute clearly permits
a trial *de novo,* plainly implying that the case is to be tried
as if it first originated in the court.   (2 Ency. Pl. & Pr.
324-325, 327; Ry. Co. v. Moody (Ala.), 44 So. 94; Turner
v. Mach. Co. (N. C.), 45 S. E. 781; Stetson v. Bank, 12
O. St. 577; State v. Tall (Wis.), 14 N. W. 596; Dorr v.
Birge, 5 How. Prac. 323; Jussen v. Board, 95 Ind. 567;
Beltz v. Charleston Co., 17 S. C. 586; Cox v. Lindley, 80
Ind. 327; In re. Solomon's Est., 74 S. C. 189; Reid v.
Fillmore, 12 Wyo. 72.)

Occupancy with relation to public lands, means physical
possession of the lands by some person, although there be
no record anywhere of it or color of title of the person so
occupying.   (Exploration Co. v. Gray &c. Oil Co., 112 Fed.
4; 190 U. S. 301; 47 L. C. P. 1064; Oil Co. v. Clark, 50
L. D. 550; Oil Co. v. Clarke, 30 L. D. 570; Exploration
Co. v. Oil Co., 104 Fed. 20; Oil Co. v. Oil Co., 98 Fed.
673; Oil Co. v. Miller, 97 Fed. 681; Miller v. Chrisman
(Cal.), 73 Pac. 1083; Moffat v. Gold Excav. Co., 33 Colo.
142; Weed v. Snook, 144 Cal. 439.)

One of the objects of the question in an application for
lease as to improvements and occupancy of other lands
within one mile is to ascertain whether any third party
would be interested in purchasing the same, or might have
a preference right to do so.   The lease in question should
have been cancelled because of the untruthful answer in
the application and also because there was a preference
right in the defendant in error.   The defendant in error
had a vested right to the land for a reservoir site, and this
was plainly shown by the evidence.

SCOTT, JUSTICE.

This case was originally instituted as a contest before the State Board of School Land Commissioners by Johnson, the defendant in error, on June 5, 1907, seeking the cancellation of a lease made and executed by the State to Clark Beck on April 26, 1907, and by him assigned with the approval of the board to the plaintiff in error on June 27, 1907, of the south half of the northwest quarter, the southwest quarter of the northeast quarter, the west half of the southeast quarter, the northeast quarter of the southeast quarter, and the northeast quarter of the southwest quarter of section 8, township 35 north, of range 82 west of the 6th principal meridian, and situated in Natrona County, Wyoming. The board upon hearing sustained the lease in favor of Bucknum, the assignee and plaintiff in error here, and dismissed defendant in error's contest, whereupon a motion for a rehearing was submitted by Johnson to and denied by the board and the case was appealed by him to the District Court of Natrona County. The case was tried in that court and the decision and judgment was for Johnson, the lease cancelled, and Bucknum brings the case here on error.

It was sought by Johnson to appropriate a part of the land in controversy for and as a part of a reservoir site. A part of the land included in the proposed site belonged to the United States and, as shown by the findings of the board, was selected by the state in lieu of other lands after a part of the work on the proposed reservoir was done. The exact date of the selection does not appear in the record. It must, however, be assumed to have been made prior to the date of the lease, to-wit: April 26, 1907. It appears that an application for a permit to construct the reservoir and the Johnson supply ditch therefor by Johnson was filed in the office of and approved by the State Engineer on April 5, 1901. On January 20, 1904, Johnson filed notice in such office of the completion of the reservoir, and on December 2, 1903, he filed notice in that office of the

completion of the Johnson Supply Ditch to such reservoir,
On November 29, 1904, application was made by Johnson
for permit to divert and appropriate waters for supply of
said reservoir, which application was approved by the State
Engineer and notice of the completion of this ditch was
received at the State Engineer's office on December 2, 1904,
and within the time limited by the permit. On November
29, 1904, application for permit to use water for another
proposed supply ditch for such reservoir was made to and
granted by the State Engineer, and proof of the completion
of this ditch was likewise filed in the Engineer's office
within the time limited by the permit. In addition to the
foregoing ditches, Johnson alleges and the evidence tends
to show that up to the time of instituting this contest he
had under permit, duly issued to conserve and use waters
for domestic, mining, milling and irrigation purposes in that
locality, constructed five additional reservoirs as a part of
his irrigation plan and to be used in connection with the
proposed reservoir site, the right to which is here in dispute.
It further appears that no water impounded in the proposed reservoir has been drawn therefrom for the reason
that up to the time of completing Supply Ditch No. 2 in
the latter part of December, 1906, the reservoir did not
contain sufficient water for that purpose, but since the
completion of that ditch the reservoir does contain sufficient water for irrigation purposes, and by constructing
a tunnel he will be enabled to irrigate his own land and
supply water to others in that vicinity. It thus appears
that the application of the water impounded in the reservoir for irrigation purposes has not been made.

There is some contention upon the briefs as to whether
the District Court to which the case was appealed was
vested with jurisdiction other than of review. There was
no equitable jurisdiction involved nor did the trial involve
the application of common law rules. The proceeding is
one purely of statutory origin. The appeal brought into
the District Court those questions only which were or

might have been raised before the board. The issues could not be enlarged nor could the action be transformed into an equitable nor a common law action. The District Court sat in the appeal as a substitute for the board and was limited on such appeal to questions that had or may be presumed to have been passed upon by the board. Speaking of such appeal, Section 656, Comp. Stat., says: "Said appeal shall stand to be heard and for trial *de novo* by said court," and Section 658, after providing and regulating the duties of the Commissioner, says: "The parties may conduct the appeal upon the original papers and affidavits in the case or upon new and amended pleadings, and such case shall stand for trial upon the evidence adduced before said board; *Provided,* That in the discretion of the court, additional evidence may be adduced on the trial; but the party desiring to introduce such evidence shall give notice to the adverse party or parties immediately after the perfection of the bill, of the offering of said evidence and stating the purport and nature thereof." The record shows that the statute regulating such appeal was not departed from in the matter of the trial. It was tried by the District Court upon the same pleadings and transcript of evidence sent up by the commissioner and upon additional evidence introduced upon notice duly served. It is provided by Section 660, Comp. Stat., as follows: "At the expiration of the time for the appearance of the appellees, the case is to be deemed ready for hearing; and it shall be heard and tried the same in all respects as civil cases are tried in said District Court; and an appeal from the judgment, finding and decree of said court shall lie to the Supreme Court the same in all respects as prescribed by law for appeals and proceedings in error from the District Courts to the Supreme Court of this state." This section must be construed in connection with Section 658, supra, and construing these together the conclusion seems irresistible that the trial upon the appeal includes the trial and determination of the issues of fact made by the pleadings independent of the findings and determination of those issues by the board. Whether such trial be had upon the evidence submitted to the board or upon that and new evidence in addition thereto as per-mitted under the provision of Section 658, supra, makes no difference. The jurisdiction of the District Court on the appeal is to try the case *de novo* on the facts and its judg-ment is not one of affirmance, reversal or modification, as upon review upon error, but is based upon its finding upon the evidence, and is not governed by the findings of the board; and the court is in a sense substituted for the board to determine the matter in issue upon the facts. The ques-tion to be determined by the court is the same as that which was presented to the board, viz: whether the state which had granted the lease should cancel it.

The land here in controversy was occupied as a reservoir site and permit for the use of the water therefor, under the statute and the regulation of the State Engineer thereunder, which had been duly issued prior to the date of the lease in controversy. The entire plant was in course of construc-tion, though not completed, at the time the land was selected and granted to the state. Section 2339 and Section 2340 supplementary thereto (U. S. Comp. Stat. 1901, p. 1437) are as follows:

"Sec. 2339. Whenever, by priority of possession, rights to the use of water for mining, agricultural, manufacturing, or other purposes, have vested and accrued, and the same are recognized and acknowledged by the local customs, laws, and the decisions of courts, the possessors and owners of such vested rights shall be maintained and protected in the same way; and the right of way for the construction of ditches and canals for the purposes herein specified is ac-knowledged and confirmed; but whenever any person, in the construction of any ditch or canal, injures or damages the possession of any settler on the public domain, the party committing such injury or damage shall be liable to the party injured for such injury or damage."

"Sec. 2340. All patents granted, or pre-emption or home-
steads allowed, shall be subject to any vested and accrued
water rights, or rights to ditches and reservoirs used in connection with such water rights, as may have been acquired
under or recognized by the preceding section." In addition
to the foregoing sections the Act of Congress, March 3,
1891 (U. S. Comp. Stat. 1901, p. 1570, Sec. 2477), provided for the grant of a right of way for reservoirs, canals
and ditches over public lands upon filing articles of incorporation, maps and statements in the land office. This act
was by its terms, Sec. 20, made applicable to individuals as
well as to corporations. The later Acts of Congress are
cumulative to and an enlargement of Sec. 2339, supra. (Sec.
440, Weil on Water Rights.)

In the case here it is unnecessary to enter into a lengthy
discussion of these sections of the federal statute or to determine whether Johnson had any right of way or easement
in the land or not, for if there were a prior vested right to
the ditch and reservoir site at the time of patent to the state
that of itself would be no ground for setting aside the lease,
for the latter would not be involved, but subject to any such
prior vested right. In that sense the ditch and reservoir
site do not conflict with the lease, for the latter would be
limited to the title conveyed to the state and that title would
be subject to Johnson's accrued water, ditch and reservoir
rights, if any such had accrued. Whether such rights existed as here contended or not, the question could be litigated in a proper forum and proceeding. The jurisdiction
of the land board is limited to the leasing and disposal of
the state lands. In the performance of its duties it is vested
with neither equitable nor common law jurisdiction. A contest for the right to lease land duly instituted before it, is a
statutory proceeding. In the performance of its duties it is
vested with certain discretionary powers which are limited
and circumscribed in the matter of obtaining the greatest
revenue for the lease or sale of such lands. This court said
in State v. Commissioners, 7 Wyo. 478, 489, 490, 53 Pac.

292, 295, which was a mandamus case, as follows: "The Constitution invests the board under such regulations as may be provided by law with the direction, control, disposition, and care of all state lands. (Art. 18, Sec. 3; Art. 7, Sec. 13.) A large discretion has been conferred by statute upon the board in the matter of leasing and sale of state lands. (Chaper 79, Laws of 1890, 1891.) Section 16 authorizes the board to lease any legal subdivision at an annual rental of not less than five per centum per annum on the valuation thereof fixed by the board; and Section 22 provides that 'The board shall lease all state lands in such manner and to such parties as shall inure the greatest benefit and secure the greatest revenue to the state.' Section 44 is as follows: 'The board may herein determine the claims of each person who may claim to be entitled, in whole or in part, to any land owned by this state. The decisions of the board shall be final until set aside by a court of competent jurisdiction. The board may establish such rules and regulations as in its opinion may be proper to prevent fraudulent applications being granted.' * * * * The exercise of the power conferred upon the board to lease the lands of the state in the manner and to parties which shall inure to the greatest benefit and secure the largest revenue to the state, requires judgment and discretion. No inflexible rule is laid down for the guidance of the board in those matters. The judgment and discretion to be exercised is judicial in character, and in an application for the writ of mandamus it is not proper for the court to interpose its opinion and judgment in the place of that of the board, even if the conclusion which the latter has reached upon the facts should appear to have been erroneous." The sections of the statute mentioned in that opinion are still in force though slightly modified and are embodied in Sections 609 and 615, Compiled Statutes, and are applicable by their terms to the leasing and disposal of school as well as state lands. At the time the lease here in controversy was granted there was but one applicant therefor. The board was not called upon to pass upon any questions other than the form and information contained in the application and evidence in support thereof as bearing upon the applicant's right to lease.

In the application and the evidence in support thereof by witnesses the following question appears and answer made thereto, viz: "State who, if any one, occupies land within one mile of the tract applied for, giving section number, township and range?" Ans. "No one." The evidence is undisputed that Johnson's homestead, houses and buildings are and were on the NE¼ of the SE¼ of Section 6, Tp. 35, R. 82, and 1,400 or 1,500 feet from the reservoir at the time of the application for this lease, and within one mile of each quarter section of the land covered by the lease. Mr. Johnson's evidence is uncontradicted that years before the application for the lease was made his dwelling houses had been constructed on his homestead and occupied part of the time as a home for himself and family, and that it has always been occupied either by his family or by men in his employ, and that the corrals thereon were used in working and caring for his stock. It thus appears that the land covered by Johnson's homestead was occupied by him, i. e., in his possession (Webster's New International Dictionary) for many years and was so occupied at the time of the application for the lease, yet it is stated in the application therefor that no land was occupied within one mile of the land sought to be leased. Basing Beck's and his assignee's right to the lease upon the application presented to the board, it is evident that the lease was granted upon incorrect information as to the occupancy of the Johnson homestead. It was the duty of the applicant to place the board in possession of the facts called for showing the true situation with reference to the homestead. (Sec. 609, Comp. Stat.) Such information might have an important bearing on the amount of obtainable revenue for the lease. It is provided by Sec. 618, Comp. Stat. 1910, that "Any lease for state lands procured by fraud, deceit or misrepresentation may be cancelled by the board upon proper proof thereof." It will be observed that this statute is permissive, but not compulsory, though doubtless in a proper case it would be the board's duty to cancel the lease. The proof of course must be submitted to the board, and it acts thereon in a judicial capacity. We think it not obligatory on the board to cancel the lease in controversy unless damage to the state is shown in the way of rental or otherwise to have been sustained. Johnson had no application before the board to purchase or lease the land at the time it was leased to Beck. In his petition filed with the board to contest the lease he bases a preference right in part on the ground of his water right and reservoir site. As to whether he had such water right and reservoir site was a question without the jurisdiction of the board and it appears that the object of the contest was to secure from the board a recognition of such ditch right and reservoir site and upon such recognition a cancellation of the lease. It was not necessary to cancel the lease to protect any vested water right and reservoir site existing at the time the patent issued to the state for the patent would be subject thereto and the lease from the state as already stated would be limited to the state's title. The sections of the U. S. statute, supra, were intended to and would protect such vested rights, if any, independent of any recognition or want of recognition by the board, for the latter could only deal with the title conveyed to it by the patent as construed and affected by the acts of Congress in effect at the time of the issuance of such patent. (Weil on Water Rights (3rd Ed.), Sec. 257; Chicago, B. & Q. R. Co. v. McPhillamey (Wyo.), 118 Pac. 682, 684.) Conceding that the information furnished in the application for the lease with reference to the occupancy of the Johnson homestead was untrue, then there is still an absence of showing that the state has been damaged thereby, nor has any unconditional offer or willingness on the part of Johnson been shown to pay the same or more rental than that paid by Beck or his assignee. It is true that in his petition filed with the board setting forth his grounds of contest Johnson made an offer to lease the land or any portion thereof provided such board had the right to require him to do so as a condition of recognizing his rights in the premises. As already stated, his ditch right and reservoir site vested, if at all, prior to the patent by the United States to the state and independent of any action by the board. His offer to lease was conditional upon the board having a right under the circumstances to require him to rent the land as a condition precedent to its recognition of the ditch right and reservoir site. This was not an offer to pay the rental value fixed or to be fixed by the board, but tendered an issue for trial, and not only so, but one without the jurisdiction of the board except in so far as it might enter into consideration in fixing the rental value of the land. It does not appear that any interest of the state or the contestant was injuriously affected by the apparent misrepresentation in Beck's application as to the occupancy of land within one mile of the leased tract. Johnson's contest and such application as he made to lease the land were instituted and made prior to the amendment of the statute in 1909, which statute as then amended declares a preference in case of a lease of state or school lands in favor of resident citizens of the state who reside nearest to the land applied for (Comp. Stat., Sec. 615), and the contest was decided by the board prior to the enactment of that statute. Johnson therefore could have claimed nothing in the contest under such statute, for it would not apply to him.

Our conclusion is that the state had the right to lease the land subject to Johnson's right, if any, to proceed and complete his reservoir, and whether he had such right or not is a question that could not be conclusively determined by the land board.

It follows that the judgment of the District Court declaring the lease invalid and setting it aside was error, for which the judgment should be reversed.   *Reversed.*

BEARD, C. J., and POTTER, J., concur.

MEADOWS v. ROBERTS, AS EXECUTOR.
(No. 702.)

APPEAL AND ERROR—PARTIES—SUBSTITUTION—BILL OF EXCEPTIONS—
TIME FOR PRESENTATION—STRIKING FROM FILES.

1. Where the defendant in error has died since the filing of the petition in error, the duly appointed, qualified and acting executor of his estate may be substituted as defendant in error upon motion.

2. While the statute respecting a bill of exceptions is to be liberally construed to the end that the bill, which the trial judge has deemed proper to be signed, may be sustained if possible, rather than defeated, the court cannot go so far as to disregard the plain provisions of the statute, and sustain a bill clearly not presented, for allowance in time.

3. Time was given to reduce exceptions to writing and present them for allowance until and including the first day of the next regular term, as permitted by statute; a bill was presented for allowance on the first day of said next regular term, it appearing by the certificate of the judge thereto as follows: that the bill was not then complete, in that it did not contain the transcript of the testimony given upon the trial; that permission was then given to withdraw the bill and complete the same; that the facts respecting the completion of the bill were correctly stated in the affidavit of the court reporter appearing in the record; that the bill was several months afterwards and during a later term completed and presented to the judge; that a written objection to the allowance of the bill was thereupon filed supported by said reporter's affidavit. The objection was overruled and the bill as finally presented, containing a transcript of the evidence, was allowed and signed by the judge. The affidavit of the court reporter, referred to in the judge's certificate, stated substantially that the party presenting the bill had notified said reporter a few days after the trial that a transcript of the evidence was desired, but that said party did not have the money to pay therefor; that thereafter and immediately prior to the opening of the second term of court following the trial. one of the attorneys for said party informed the reporter that a transcript of the evidence was desired, and subsequently ordered such transcript; that pursuant thereto the evidence was then transcribed; and that had such transcript been ordered in

time for that purpose the transcript would have been furnished prior to the time originally fixed for the presentation of the bill. *Held*, that, since a writing not containing the facts, or so much of the evidence as is necessary to explain the exception, is not such a bill of exceptions as the statute requires to be presented within the time allowed, the bill was not presented for allowance within the time allowed by law and fixed by the court, and that a motion to strike the bill from the record should be granted.

[Decided December 9, 1912.]   (128 Pac. 624.)

ERROR to the District Court, Crook County; HON. CARROLL H. PARMELEE, Judge.

The action was brought in the District Court by Andrew J. Parker against Ada Meadows, and from the judgment rendered in the cause the defendant brought error. Heard on motion for substitution as defendant in error of the executor of the will of Andrew J. Parker, deceased, and on motion of the substituted defendant in error to strike the bill of exceptions from the files. The material facts are stated in the opinion.

Enterline & LaFleiche and *Nichols & Nettlehorst*, for defendant in error, in support of the motion to strike the bill of exceptions.

It appears from the affidavit of the court reporter that none of the exceptions taken upon the trial or the evidence were reduced to writing until after the November, 1911, term of the court, and more than six months after the time fixed by the original order for the presentation of the bill. It further appears that the reporter was not directed to furnish said transcript of the exceptions and evidence until a few days prior to said November term, and that had a transcript been ordered in proper time it would have been furnished so that the bill could have been completed and presented within the time originally allowed. Inability on the part of the exceptant to pay for a transcript within the time fixed for the presentation of the bill of exceptions is not a legal excuse for presenting a bill not containing the evi-

dence. Where the procedure for an appeal or the taking of
a cause to an appellate court on error is fixed by statute, it
must be substantially complied with. The bill presented
within the time allowed was not a bill, since it did not contain any part of the evidence explaining the exceptions.
The facts do not bring the case within the principle decided
in Harden v. Card, 14 Wyo. 479, and hence the court was
without authority to permit the withdrawal of the bill for
completion by inserting therein the entire transcript of the
evidence, which had not been ordered within the time allowed for presenting the bill. No legal excuse is shown for
the delay in completing the bill.

Metz & Sackett, for plaintiff in error, *contra.*

When a bill of exceptions is presented, it is the duty of
the court or judge to correct it, or suggest the necessary
correction. In this case the court suggested the withdrawal
of the bill for completion, and it was finally completed as
soon as it could be done by the reporter, and then presented
to the court for signature, when it was formally allowed,
and the objections to allowance overruled. No time is fixed
by statute for signing a bill after it is presented, but the
time for allowance is largely within the discretion of the
court or judge. It is entirely proper to permit a party to
withdraw a bill for making the proper corrections. (Harden
v. Card, 14 Wyo. 495, 496.) The power of a court or judge
to settle a bill of exceptions includes the power to change,
reduce, add to, or correct a bill which has been presented.
Such power is necessarily discretionary. The purpose of a
bill of exceptions in the lower court is to put into the record
for the inspection of the court all the evidence, testimony
and matters which appeared in the court below, to the end
that the case on appeal may be heard upon the facts and the
law applicable thereto. The order of the court in this case
permitting the withdrawal of the bill and its correction by
inserting the transcript of the evidence was clearly proper
and is sustained by the decision in Harden v. Card, supra.

BEARD, CHIEF JUSTICE.

This case was submitted to this court upon two motions. One by C. M. Roberts, executor, to be substituted as defendant in error; and the other by the defendant in error to strike the bill of exceptions from the files.

It appears that since the filing of the petition in error the defendant in error, Andrew J. Parker, died, and that C. M. Roberts has been duly appointed, and is now the duly qualified and acting executor of the will of Parker, deceased. The motion to substitute is not resisted; and it appearing to be a proper case for substitution, the motion will be granted.

The motion to strike the bill of exceptions from the record is based on the ground that it was not presented for allowance within the time allowed by law and fixed by the court. The motion for a new trial was denied November 25, 1910, and at that time the defendant below, Ada Meadows, plaintiff in error, was given until and including the first day of the next regular term of the court in which to present for allowance her bill of exceptions. The next regular term of the court commenced on the third Monday in May following, being May 15, 1911. It appears by the certificate of the judge of the District Court that on May 15, 1911, the bill was presented to him for allowance; "that at that time the said bill of exceptions was not complete in that the same did not contain the transcript of the testimony given upon the trial of said cause; that permission was at that time given to the attorneys of the defendant to withdraw said bill of exceptions and to complete the same; that the facts in re- gard to said completion are correctly set forth in the affidavit of Charles L. Carter, Official Court Reporter, which said affidavit appears in this record; that the said bill of exceptions was afterwards completed and presented to me on the 5th day of January, 1912; that upon the 8th day of January, 1912, the plaintiff, by Enterline & LaFleiche, his attorneys, filed their written objection to the allowance of said bill of exceptions, supported by the affidavit of Charles L. Carter,

above referred to." The matter was argued and taken under advisement by the court, and on May 3, 1912, the objection to the allowance of the bill was overruled and the
bill as presented on January 5, 1912, containing the transcript of the evidence, was allowed and signed by the judge.
The affidavit of Mr. Carter states: "That said trial commenced on the 25th day of May, A. D. 1910, and was concluded on the 26th day of May, A. D. 1910. That a few
days after the trial of said cause and during the May, A. D.
1910, term of said court then being held in Crook County,
Wyoming, counsel for the defendant, Ada Meadows, stated
to affiant that a transcript of the evidence in said case was
desired, but that the defendant did not have the money with
which to pay therefor; that thereafter, to-wit: on or about
just prior to the opening of the November, A. D. 1911, term
of the above entitled court in and for the County of Crook,
Wyoming, W. S. Metz, one of the attorneys for the defendant, informed me at Sheridan, Wyoming, that the
defendant wanted and would pay for a transcript of said
evidence and thereafter and on or about the 17th day of
November, 1911, C. L. Sackett, one of defendant's attorneys, ordered a transcript of this evidence in said case, and
pursuant thereto I transcribed the said evidence into typewriting as appears from the transcript thereof marked Exhibit 'O,' and numbered from page 1 to page 243, inclusive." * * * * "Affiant further says that had the defendant ordered or directed him to reduce said exceptions
to writing or transcribe said evidence into typewriting, he
would have duly furnished the same to the defendant upon
being paid therefor, within the time fixed by the order of
this court for the settling and allowance of her bill of exceptions, and was ready, able and willing so to do at all
times within said period, and the fact that the said exceptions were not reduced to writing, or the said evidence
transcribed into typewriting and furnished and delivered
by me to the said defendant or her attorneys within the time
fixed and allowed by the order of the court is not due to

any fault, negligence, delay or inability on my part." We have set out at length so much of the certificate of the trial judge to the bill, and the affidavit of the reporter as are material to a determination of the question presented by the motion.

The statutes governing the preparation and presentation of bills of exceptions are as follows: (Sec. 4595. Comp. Stat. 1910): "The party objecting to the decision must except at the time the decision is made; and time may be given to reduce the exception to writing, but not beyond the first day of the next succeeding term." Sec. 4596, id.: "No particular form of exception is required, and the exception must be stated, with the facts, or so much of the evidence as is necessary to explain it, and no more, and the whole as briefly as possible." Sec. 4598, id.: "When the decision is not entered on the record, or the grounds of objection do not sufficiently appear in the entry, or the exception is to the opinion of the court on a motion to direct a non-suit, to arrest the testimony from the jury, or, for a new trial for misdirection by the court to the jury, or because the verdict, or if a jury was waived, the findings of the court, is against the law or the evidence, the party excepting must reduce his exception to writing and present it to the court, or to the judge thereof in vacation, within the time given for allowance. If true, it shall be the duty of the court, if presented in open court, or the judge of the court before whom the cause was tried, if presented in vacation, to allow and sign it, whereupon it shall be filed with the pleadings as a part of the record, but not spread at large upon the journal. If the writing is not true the court or judge shall correct it, or suggest the correction to be made, and it shall then be signed as aforesaid." A writing which does not contain the exception taken at the time the decision is made, with the facts, or so much of the evidence as is necessary to explain the exception, is not such a bill as the statute requires to be presented within the time allowed, and is no bill. In this case the writing purporting to be a bill of exception which was presented to the judge May 15, 1911, did not contain the transcript of the Reporter's notes containing these essentials, nor were they otherwise stated therein. It was not until January 5, 1912, long after the time allowed by law for the presentation of a bill, that a bill containing these essentials was presented to the trial judge. Counsel for plaintiff in error contend that the decision in Harden v. Card, 14 Wyo. 479, 491, 85 Pac. 246, 249, is applicable and should govern in this case. But the facts of the cases are not alike. In the Harden v. Card case the Official Reporter who had reported the case had died, and a transcript of his notes, made by another, of more than one-half of the evidence was contained in the bill as first presented. The court (p. 491) said: "It may be conceded that it is the duty of a party desiring to preserve his exceptions to prepare and present a bill fairly and fully setting forth the facts upon which the rulings of the court excepted to were made; and that the draft so presented should state all the evidence, as he understood it, upon which the verdict or findings were based, where the exception is to the overruling of a motion for a new trial on the ground that the verdict or findings are not supported by the evidence; and we think such a duty does rest upon the exceptant." And on page 494 of 14 Wyo., on page 250 of 85 Pac.: "The argument of counsel for defendant in error, in support of the motion, proceeds upon the theory that, when the bill was presented on the last day of the period allowed, it confessedly contained a mere fragment of the material evidence, and not all that counsel presenting it understood it should contain, or that was intended to be embodied in it. We are of the opinion, however, that we are not at liberty to give that construction to the recitals of the bill." And again, on page 495 of 14 Wyo., on page 250 of 85 Pac.: "Assuming, however, that the court or judge found on examination that, nearly one-half of the evidence had been entirely omitted from the bill, it does not necessarily follow that the party presenting it had wilfully or knowingly omitted material evidence or facts which he deemed essential to explain his exceptions." The purported bill in the present case when first presented did not contain any part of the evidence or any facts to explain the exceptions; and, as we have already stated, it was no bill, and there was, therefore, nothing upon which to base a correction. Its presentation in that condition and a request for leave to subsequently insert therein the transcript of the Reporter's notes, which had not then been made, amounted to no more than a request for additional time to prepare and present a bill, which by the express terms of the statute the court could not extend beyond the first day of the next succeeding term of the court. The failure to procure the transcript in time to be included in the bill when first presented, seems to have been because the plaintiff in error did not furnish the money necessary to procure the same. While the rule is that the statute is to be liberally construed "to the end that the bill, which the trial judge has deemed proper to be signed, may be sustained, if possible, rather than defeated," the court cannot go so far as to disregard the plain provisions of the statute and sustain a bill clearly not presented in time. Our conclusion is, that the bill of exceptions in this case was not presented for allowance within the time allowed by law and fixed by the court. and that the motion of defendant in error to strike the bill should be granted and the bill stricken from the record; and it is so ordered.   *Motion granted.*

SCOTT and POTTER, JJ., concur.

HUHN v. QUINN.
(No. 707.)

TRIAL—CHANGE OF VENUE—CHANGE OF JUDGE—EFFECT OF AFFIDAVIT OF PREJUDICE—JURISDICTION—DISTRICT COURT COMMISSIONERS—POWERS OF—"CHAMBER BUSINESS."

1. An affidavit filed by a party in a civil action, as permitted by Section 5142, Compiled Statutes, 1910, stating that said party believes that, on account of the bias and prejudice of the presiding judge of the court, he cannot obtain a fair trial, when called to the court's attention, divests the presiding judge of the court of further jurisdiction other than to call in another district judge to preside in the further proceedings and trial of the cause.

2. Under the Constitution (Article V, Section 14), which confers upon a district court commissioner the power of a judge in chambers under certain named conditions, the power of such commissioner as a subordinate officer of the court, and as to causes pending therein, is limited to such proceedings, orders, or business as might be conducted before or made or attended to by the judge at chambers, and does not include the trial of a case on its merits.

3. The provision of Section 14 of Article V of the Constitution, which authorizes the district court commissioner to take depositions and perform such other duties as shall be prescribed by law, was not intended to and does not confer upon that officer the power of a judge to preside in the trial of a case in open court.

4. The provision of Section 922, Compiled Statutes, which defines the powers of a district court commissioner, that the commissioner shall have power "to hear, try and determine all issues whenever an application shall have been made for a change of judge," does not attempt to authorize the commissioner to try the issues in the cause itself, but only the issues, if any, arising upon an application for a change of judge. Whether the power may be lawfully conferred upon such commissioner to hear an application for a change of judge and determine whether or not it shall be granted is not decided.

5. An application for change of judge includes the filing of the affidavit therefor and calling the attention of the court or judge thereto, and where the application has been so made

the judge becomes thereby divested of further authority in the matter, except to act upon the application, grant it if properly made, and call upon some other district court judge to preside in the further proceedings and trial of the cause; said judge is not thereupon authorized to direct the district court commissioner to preside in the court and hear and determine the cause.

6. Where a district court commissioner was called in by the district judge to preside in open court and hear and try a civil cause pending therein, his judgment in such case was void for want of jurisdiction, although subsequently approved by the court presided over by the district judge against whom an affidavit of prejudice had been filed prior to his directing the hearing of the case by the commissioner.

[Decided December 9, 1912.]   (128 Pac. 514.)

ERROR to the District Court, Johnson County; HON. CARROLL H. PARMELEE, Judge.

The action was brought by Ned Quinn against William Huhn, and from a judgment in favor of the plaintiff the defendant brought error. The cause was heard and decided in open court by the District Court Commissioner, who had been called in for that purpose by the District Judge, upon the attention of said judge being called to the fact that an affidavit had been filed for a change of judge on the ground alleged in the affidavit that the party filing the same could not obtain a fair trial on account of the bias and prejudice of the presiding judge of the court. After the cause had been heard and decided and judgment rendered by the District Court Commissioner, the court, presided over by the District Judge, also entered a judgment in the cause in accordance with the report and determination of the commissioner and approving and confirming in all respects the action of the commissioner. The other material facts are stated in the opinion.

Metz & Sackett, for plaintiff in error.

Under Section 5142, Compiled Statutes, 1910, the District Judge against whom an affidavit of prejudice is filed thereupon loses all jurisdiction in the cause, except to call in another District Judge to preside in the trial or further proceedings. (Baldwin v. Marygold, 2 Wis. 419; Reives v. Boyd, 7 Wis. 155; Herbert v. Beatherd, 26 Kan. 476; Smith v. State, 1 Kan. 345; People v. Hubbard, 22 Cal. 34, 37; Perkins v. McDowell, 3 Wyo. 203; Cutler v. Howard, 9 Wis. 309; Risto v. Harris, 18 Wis. 400; Bachman v. Milwaukee, 47 Wis. 435.) The Court Commissioner is not the court, nor is he the District Judge; he is an adjunct or officer of the court, without any power to render final judgment in a cause. (Mau v. Stoner, 12 Wyo. 485; State v. Ausherman, 11 Wyo. 435; State v. Finder (S. D.), 81 N. W. 959.) The District Court has no power to attach conditions to an order for a change of judge unless expressly permitted by statute. (Bentley v. Stowell, 52 N. W. 92.) This court takes judicial notice as to who are the judges of the various district courts. (Commissioners v. Shaffner, 10 Wyo. 181.) The powers of Court Commissioners are limited and cannot be extended by implication beyond the express language of the statute. Nowhere in the statute is any power granted to the commissioner to render final judgment in an action pending in the court. When the Court Commissioner presided and pretended to hear and determine this cause the District Judge was present in the county and actually holding court on the day that the commissioner heard the evidence and decided this case. This is shown by the record.

No effort was made to strike the defendant's answer from the files until after the affidavit for change of judge had been filed. If it be conceded that the court might strike the answer from the files in the absence of an affidavit for change of judge, it would be a violation of judicial discretion to refuse to permit the defendant to file an answer. The amended answer which was tendered, as well as the original answer, stated a good defense, and it was an abuse of discretion to deny the defendant the right to make any defense in the action.

Hill & Griggs, for defendant in error.

It may be conceded that had the defendant been properly in court with answer filed, and not in default, the District Judge would have had no discretion to do otherwise than to act upon the affidavit for change of judge as soon as called to his attention. The sole question here seems to be whether a defendant who is in default may disqualify the presiding judge, whose permission it is necessary to secure to permit the filing of a pleading. The defendant was not in court and had no right to file any paper in the cause without first obtaining leave of court. (Phillips Code Pl., Sec. 278; 31 Cyc. 134, 597-598; Adamson v. Bergen, 62 Pac. 629; Ry. Co. v. Linson, 18 Pac. 498; Hayward v. Goldsbury, 19 N. W. 307; Cowart v. Stanton, 30 S. E. 743; Comp. Stat., Secs. 4417-4418.) It was not an abuse of discretion to refuse the defendant leave to answer, but to have done otherwise would have been unjust to the plaintiff. (21 Ency. Pl. & Pr. 688, 689; Kent v. Upton, 3 Wyo. 43; McLaughlin v. Upton, 3 Wyo. 48; Casteel v. State, 9 Wyo. 267; Boswell v. Bliler, 9 Wyo. 277; Todd v. Peterson, 13 Wyo. 513; Cronkhite v. Bothwell, 3 Wyo. 736.) The filing of the affidavit of prejudice does not *ipso facto* divest the presiding judge of jurisdiction, but in addition to the filing of the affidavit it must be presented to the court in order to comply at all with the statute. Such an affidavit is a motion addressed to the court asking that another District Judge be called in to preside at the trial. In so far as the court must call in another judge, the motion is addressed to the court's discretion. If the mere filing of a motion would be sufficient, then no order or action on the part of the court would be necessary. It is evident that something more is necessary than merely filing the paper with the clerk. (20 Ency. Law, 1076; Wallace v. Lewis, 24 Pac. 22; Peters v. Vawter, 10 Mont. 208, 25 Pac. 428; Hoops v. Culbertson, 17 Iowa, 305.) The affidavit or motion for change of judge was, therefore, not before the court until presented to its attention, regardless of the time when it was filed. A party cannot be permitted to submit to the jurisdiction of the court by waiving his rights to object until by some particular ruling he becomes fearful that the presiding judge is not favorable to his cause, and then for the first time raise a jurisdictional question. (State v. Clifford, 118 Pac. 41.) The affidavit for change not having been presented until the defendant was in default, the change might have been properly denied. (Hull v. Wallis, 2 How. Prac. Rep. 134; Vale v. Brooklyn &c. Ry. Co., 12 Civ. Proc. Rep. 102; Spalding v. A. W. Board Co., 39 N. Y. Supp. 203.) The statute provides that the judge against whom the affidavit of prejudice is filed shall call in another District Judge to preside in the trial. The order striking the answer was a preliminary matter arising before trial, and it was proper for the regular presiding judge to pass upon it. The trial is the determination of the issue, and until the issue is framed there can be no trial. (Lipscomb v. State, 76 Miss. 253.) The position of the Court Commissioner in hearing the cause was analogous to that of a referee. Upon his report the court rendered the final judgment; hence the question as to the power of the Court Commissioner to render final judgment is not important.

Scott, Justice.

On March 11, 1911, the defendant in error as plaintiff filed his petition in the District Court of Johnson County seeking to recover from the plaintiff in error as defendant the sum of $2,692.75, with interest alleged to be due on a promissory note, and on two separate accounts for money loaned to the defendant upon his request. Summons was duly issued and served on March 13th, as appears from the return thereon and filed in the office of the clerk of that court on March 15, 1911. The time for filing an answer expired on April 8, 1911. On September 25th following, the defendant, without having obtained leave so to do, filed his answer consisting of a general denial. On October 2, 1911, the defendant filed an affidavit which, omitting the formal parts, is as follows:

"William Huhn being first duly sworn on oath states, that he is the defendant in the above entitled cause. Affiant further says he believes that on account of the bias and prejudice of the presiding judge of this court he cannot obtain a fair trial. Wherefore, defendant respectfully asks that another judge of the District Courts of this state be called to preside at the trial of said cause. Further affiant sayeth not."

On October 3, 1911, or the next day after the filing of said affidavit, the plaintiff (Quinn) filed a motion to strike the answer from the files for the reason that it was filed without leave of court and not within the time required by law. On the same day this motion was presented to and sustained by the court, both parties being represented by counsel, and the answer was stricken from the files and permission was given to the defendant to make an application for permission to file an answer upon a showing by affidavit of a good and sufficient reason for not filing his answer within the time allowed by law. Thereupon and on the same day the defendant applied to the court for permission to file and tendered an amended answer and supported his application by affidavits and the plaintiff resisted said application and filed counter affidavits. Upon hearing the court denied said application, whereupon the defendant's attorney called the court's attention to the affidavit for a change of judge which had been filed the day preceding, and withdrew his application to file an amended answer and insisted on his right to have another judge called in to try the case. The court thereupon vacated so much of the order authorizing the presentation for filing of an amended answer, such application to be supported by affidavits showing good cause for not answering within the time allowed by law. The order of the court recites that the affidavit for change of judge was then for the first time presented to the court and the case was thereupon, over the defendant's

objection, referred to the Hon. S. C. Langworthy, Court
Commissioner in and for the District Court of the County
of Johnson, who was thereupon called to hear, try and determine the cause which was set for trial in open court before said commissioner at the court house in the city of
Buffalo and County of Johnson, at two o'clock p. m. on the
4th day of October, 1911, at which time the following proceedings as shown by the journal entry were had, viz: "And
now on this October 4, 1911, came on the above entitled
matter to be heard before the court without a jury, the
Honorable S. C. Langworthy, District Court Commissioner
of Johnson County, Wyoming, presiding, pursuant to an
order of this court, made and entered this October 4, 1911,
directing the said District Court Commissioner to hear, try
and determine the issues in this case; the plaintiff appearing
in person and by Hill and Griggs, his attorneys, the defendant making no appearance herein.

"And the said court having heard the evidence, and being
now fully advised in the premises, does find that there is
due from the defendant to the plaintiff the sum of fifteen
hundred dollars principal, and five hundred seventy-five
dollars interest to the first day of the present term of this
court upon a certain promissory note given to the plaintiff
by said defendant, as alleged in said petition; that there is
likewise due from the defendant to the plaintiff the sum of
five hundred dollars principal and fifty-three and 33/100
dollars interest on account of the loan made by plaintiff to
defendant as alleged in the second cause of action of plaintiff's petition; and that there is likewise due the sum of two
hundred dollars principal and twenty-one and 33/100 dollars interest on account of the loan mentioned in plaintiff's
third cause of action; whereby the said court, the said commissioner presiding, finds that there is due and owing from
the defendant to the plaintiff, on account of the above matters, on the first day of the present term of this court the
entire sum of two thousand eight hundred forty-nine and
66/100 dollars, no part whereof has been paid.

"Wherefore, it is hereby determined by the said court, said commissioner presiding, that the said Ned Quinn, plaintiff herein, should have and recover judgment of and against the said William Huhn, defendant herein, for the sum of two thousand eight hundred forty-nine and 66/100 dollars, together with his costs herein expended, taxed at $21.70.

"Done in open court.   S. C. LANGWORTHY,
            "District Court Commissioner."

And on the same day the court entered the following judgment:

"And now on this October 4, 1911, came on the above matter to be heard upon the report and determination of the Honorable S. C. Langworthy, District Court Commissioner, and the court having read said report and determination, and being now fully advised in the premises, hereby approves the same, and said report is in all respects confirmed.

"Wherefore it is hereby ordered and adjudged by the court that Ned Quinn, plaintiff herein, have and recover judgment against the defendant, William Huhn, for the sum of two thousand eight hundred forty-nine and 66/100 dollars, together with his costs herein expended, taxed at $21.70, including $10 fees for the Court Commissioner, which is hereby allowed and directed to be taxed.

"Done in open court.   C. H. PARMELEE, Judge."

The affidavit for change of judge was sufficient to divest the presiding judge of further jurisdiction other than to call in another District Judge of the state to preside in the trial of the case, as provided by Sec. 5142, Comp. Stat., which, in so far as applicable to the question here, is as follows: "Whenever either party to a civil action in any District Court of the state shall file an affidavit in the case, stating one or more of the following causes: * * * "3. That the person making the affidavit believes that on account of the bias or prejudice, or interest of the presiding judge, he cannot obtain a fair trial. * * * The court in term or the judge in vacation shall * * * call on some other judge of the District Courts of the state to preside in the trial of the case, as hereinafter provided."

The subsequent provision thus referred to in the section is found in Section 5144 and is as follows: "That when the application is based on the first, second, third and sixth subdivisions of Sec. 5142, the judge shall call upon some other judge of the District Courts of the state to preside in the trial of the said cause, who shall proceed in the case as if it had originally been brought before him." These provisions were in force prior to the adoption of the constitution and have ever since been and are now in force (R. S. 1887, Sec. 3400; R. S. 1899, Sec. 4282) just as they appear in Secs. 5142 and 5144 as above quoted. Sec. 14, Art. V, of the constitution is as follows: "The Legislature shall provide by law for the appointment by the several District Courts of one or more District Court Commissioners (who shall be persons learned in the law) in each organized county in which a District Court is holden, such commissioners shall have authority to perform such chamber business in the absence of the District Judge from the county or upon his written statement filed with the papers, that it is improper for him to act, as may be prescribed by law, to take depositions and perform such other duties, and receive such compensation as shall be prescribed by law." By Chap. 115, Laws of 1895, which appears as Chap. 75, Comp. Stat. 1910, provision was made for the appointment and qualification of District Court Commissioners, and Section 6 of the original act, appearing as Section 922, Comp. Stat. 1910, defines the powers of such officer, among which subdivision 4 of the section is as follows: "To hear, try and determine all issues whenever an application shall have been made for a change of judge."

It will be observed that Sec. 14, Art. V, of the constitution, supra, confers upon a District Court Commissioner the power of a judge in chambers under certain named conditions. This we think limits the power of the commissioner as a subordinate officer of the court and as to causes pending therein to such proceedings, orders or business as might be conducted before, or made or attended to by the judge at chambers. Such power does not include the trial of a case on its merits, but is among those "which are exercised in preliminary, intermediate or *ex parte* matters not involving the merits of a cause—powers which may be exercised by a judge out of term, acting as a judge merely and not as a court." (11 Cyc. 623, 624; Prignitz v. Fisher, 4 Minn. 366 (Gil. 275); Pulver v. Grooves, 3 Minn. 359 (Gil. 252); Cushman v. Johnson, 13 How. Pr. (N. Y.) 495.) It should be borne in mind that "a judge at chambers is simply a judge acting out of court." (23 Cyc. 505.)

In the case here the Court Commissioner was not acting in chambers, but presided at the trial and made and entered findings in open court and as an act of the court. The provision of Section 14, Art. V, of the constitution, supra, authorizing the Court Commissioner "to take depositions and perform such other duties * * * as shall be prescribed by law," was clearly, we think, not intended to confer upon that officer the power of a judge to preside in the trial of cases in open court. Sec. 11 of Art. V of the constitution provides that "The judges of the District Courts may hold courts for each other and shall do so when required by law," and Section 12, following, provides that "No person shall be eligible to the office of judge of the District Court * * * unless he be at least twenty-eight years of age, * * * nor unless he shall have resided in the State or Territory of Wyoming at least two years next preceding his election." Sec. 5142, Comp. Stat., supra, is mandatory in terms and is in line with the constitutional provisions which construed together contemplate that no one shall be qualified to preside over a District Court except a District Judge. The commissioner as to matters pending in the court is a subordinate officer of the court. He is not a District Judge who alone possesses the power to preside over a District Court. There can be no such court in the absence of a qualified judge *de facto* or *de jure*. The Court

Commissioner is neither. The provision of Sec. 922, supra, that he may hear, try and determine all issues whenever an application shall have been made for a change of judge, when properly construed, does not attempt to authorize the commissioner to try the issues in the case itself, but only the issues, if any, arising upon the application for a change of judge. Whether the Legislature may confer upon the commissioner the power to hear such an application and determine whether or not it shall be granted need not be decided, for in this case the commissioner did not preside in the cause for that purpose. He was called in to hear and try the case. In Michigan, under a somewhat similar constitutional provision, it is held that a statute may authorize the commissioner to direct a change of venue applied for on the ground that the judge is disqualified. (Whipple v. Judge &c., 26 Mich. 342; Fellows v. Canney, 75 Mich. 445, 42 N. W. 958; Grostick v. Railroad Co., 96 Mich. 495, 56 N. W. 24.) When the application for change of judge has been made, which includes the filing thereof and calling the attention of the court or judge thereto, the judge becomes thereby divested of authority in the premises, except to act upon the application, grant it if properly made, and call upon some other of the District Judges of the state to preside in the further proceedings and trial of the case. In this case the application would seem to have been granted, but another District Judge was not called in as the statute requires. The application appearing to have been properly made, the judge was disqualified to further act in the case except as provided in Sections 5142 and 5144, Comp. Stat., supra.

We, therefore, hold that the Court Commissioner was without the power which he attempted to exercise, that the court erred in calling upon him to try the case instead of calling in one of the District Judges of the state to preside in the trial of the case as provided by Sections 5142 and 5144, Comp. Stat., and that for such error the judgment must be reversed and the cause remanded for such further

proceedings as may be proper, not inconsistent with the
views herein expressed.   *Reversed.*

BEARD, C. J., and POTTER, J., concur.

SMITH v. STONE ET AL.
(No. 694.)

PLEADING—UNCERTAINTY—DEMURRER—FRAUD—SUFFICIENCY OF AL-
LEGATION—CORPORATIONS—STOCKHOLDERS, RIGHTS OF AS TO SALE OF
CORPORATE PROPERTY—ESTOPPEL—SUIT BY MINORITY STOCKHOLDER—
SALE OF ENTIRE ASSETS OF CORPORATION BY MAJORITY STOCKHOLD-
ERS—OBJECTION BY MINORITY STOCKHOLDER—PURCHASE OF CORPO-
RATE PROPERTY BY ANOTHER CORPORATION—SUIT BY STOCKHOLDER
TO VACATE SALE—ACCOUNTING—LACHES.

1. Where a petition is indefinite and uncertain, the defect is
    ordinarily to be corrected by motion to make more definite
    and certain by amendment, and is not ordinarily a ground
    for demurrer.

2. Respecting the sufficiency of a petition, there is a distinction
    in the rules of code pleading between an entire failure to
    state a cause of action and the statement of one in an
    imperfect and defective manner, but in an action by an
    objecting stockholder to set aside a sale of the assets of
    a corporation on the ground of fraud and misconduct on
    the part of the majority stockholders, where the defect of
    indefiniteness and uncertainty in the petition relates to ma-
    terial facts concerning which the averments ought to be
    reasonably definite and certain, it may amount to a failure
    to state a cause of action rendering the petition de-
    murrable.

3. A bill or petition founded upon fraud or misconduct should
    allege with certainty and definiteness tangible facts to sus-
    tain the general averments of such fraud and misconduct.

4. Where, in an action by a minority stockholder to set aside
    the sale of corporate assets pursuant to a resolution adopted
    at an annual meeting of the stockholders, it was contended
    as one ground for vacating the sale that the stockholders
    were without authority at such meeting to consider or
    adopt the resolution for the reason that the notice of the

meeting did not specify that such matter would be considered, *Held*, that, since the statute provided as to notice of the annual meeting only that notice of the time and place of holding the same should be published, and it was provided by statute that the stockholders, or the trustees, if the certificate of incorporation so provides, shall have power to make by-laws as they shall deem proper for the management and disposition of the stock and business affairs of the company, not inconsistent with the laws of the state, and the petition did not show what provision, if any, was made in the by-laws with reference to the business that might be transacted at the annual meeting and the notice to be given at such meeting, the notice complained of may have complied in all respects with the by-laws so as to authorize the adoption of the resolution, and, hence, in that particular, the petition was indefinite and uncertain.

5. Where a minority stockholder, who was present at the annual meeting of the stockholders at which a resolution was adopted to sell the corporate property, objected to the resolution on the sole ground that the price fixed thereby was not the reasonable, fair, and market value of the property, and that by endeavor a larger price could be procured, any objection to the form of the notice of the meeting was not available to him in an action afterwards brought to set aside the sale made pursuant to such resolution, and, therefore, it was unnecessary to consider or determine whether in all cases a notice of the annual meeting which did not state that the matter of selling the property would be considered would be sufficient to authorize such a resolution as that adopted.

6. In an action by a minority stockholder to set aside a sale of the corporate property on the ground of alleged fraud and misconduct on the part of certain majority stockholders, where the petition alleged that certain stockholders were present at the meeting authorizing the sale, and that others were not present, but did not allege whether the stock of those not present was or was not legally and properly represented and voted at such meeting, *Held*, that it could not be assumed that any of the stock was not represented and voted at the meeting.

7. A petition in an action by a minority stockholder to set aside the sale of corporate property pursuant to a resolution adopted at the annual meeting of stockholders, which merely alleged, as to the adoption of the resolution for the

sale, that certain of the stockholders present "attempted" to adopt the resolution, was indefinite in that particular.

8. Although it is not within the lawful power of a majority of the stockholders of a solvent going corporation to sell its entire assets and property over the objection of a minority stockholder, unless such power is expressly conferred by law, in the absence of some exigency or a condition requiring that course to be pursued, a different rule prevails when the corporation is an unprofitable and failing enterprise; where that condition exists the majority may dispose of the corporate property and take action towards the liquidation of its affairs.

9. The fact that two corporations are controlled by the same officers or stockholders does not prevent them from dealing with each other or the purchase by one of the property of the other, unless the acts of the majority in control are fraudulent as against the corporation and complaining stockholders, but the courts will closely scrutinize a sale of corporate property effected by majority stockholders to another corporation which they control or are interested in.

10. A sale of corporate property pursuant to the vote of majority stockholders to another corporation which they control or are interested in is neither void nor constructively fraudulent, but if it is unfair to the minority, or if any unconscionable advantage of their position has been taken by the majority, it may be set aside at the suit of the minority.

11. In an action by a minority stockholder to set aside a sale of the entire corporate property made pursuant to a resolution adopted at an annual meeting of the stockholders, *Held*, that it appeared by the averments of the petition that an exigency may have arisen which would authorize the sale complained of, since upon such averments the corporation was a losing one and in a condition requiring the disposition of its property to pay its debts, and that if the sale was made it was made pursuant to certain resolutions referred to in the petition for a consideration stated in the petition for the purpose of liquidating the indebtedness of the company equaling the amount of the par value of the issued and outstanding capital stock? and *Held* further, that, in the absence of an allegation to the contrary, it was proper to assume that, if the sale was made, the said debt was paid as the result thereof.

12. In an action by a minority stockholder to set aside an alleged fraudulent sale of corporate property an allegation in the

petition that at the time of the sale certain individual defendants were associated together as partners in a firm to which the company was indebted and to which the money realized from the sale was to be paid in liquidation of said indebtedness, and that two of the individual defendants named, brothers-in-law of another named individual defendant, "and all of the said parties," were the particular holders and controlers of the corporation to which the property was sold, *Held*, that the petition was at least indefinite and uncertain as to who were meant by "all of the said parties," and that it ought not to be assumed on demurrer to the petition that any defendant, either individually or in combination with others, had a controlling or any other interest in the purchasing corporation, unless the fact was definitely alleged; and, hence, the averments to the effect that the purpose of the sale was to obtain the corporate property for less than its reasonable, fair, or market value, applied only to the said three defendants last specifically named.

13. Where, in an action by a minority stockholder to set aside the sale of the corporate property to another corporation pursuant to a resolution adopted at the annual meeting of the stockholders of the selling corporation, it was alleged that objecting stockholders stated at the meeting that a much greater price could be obtained if an endeavor was made to do so, *Held*, that said allegation had no further effect than to show that said statement was made, and did not amount to an allegation that a greater price could in fact have been obtained; it not being alleged as a fact that a greater price could have been obtained for the property and that anyone was able, ready and willing to pay a greater price for it.

14. In an action by a minority stockholder to set aside a sale of the corporate property on the ground of alleged fraud and misconduct of the majority stockholders, through the vote of whom at the annual meeting a resolution was adopted providing for the sale, *Held*, as to an allegation in the petition that objecting stockholders stated at the time of the adoption of the resolution that a much greater price than that named in the resolution could be obtained for the property if an endeavor was made to do so, that if the allegation should be considered as alleging as a fact that a "much greater" price could be obtained, said words were too indefinite under the circumstances upon which to base

general charges of fraud, since, in addition to the possible natural increase in the value of the property, the words "much greater" might imply merely a fair and reasonable profit accruing to the purchaser.

15. In the absence of fraud, the fact that a difference of opinion may have existed between the majority and minority stockholders respecting the propriety of selling the corporate property would not alone justify interference by a court of equity in an action by a minority stockholder to set aside the sale.

16. In an action by a minority stockholder to set aside a sale of the corporate property, which, if made, was made pursuant to a resolution adopted at an annual meeting of the stockholders at which the complaining minority stockholder was present, where it appeared that at the time the indebtedness of the corporation equaled in amount the par value of the issued and outstanding capital stock, and that the sale was not objected to when the resolution was adopted on the ground that there was no necessity therefor, but the objection was on the sole ground that the selling price was less than the value of the property, *Held*, that the fact alone that such selling price was less than the alleged value of the property would not authorize the legal presumption of fraud on the part of the majority stockholders and trustees, the rights of creditors not being involved.

17. It cannot be presumed, in the absence of an averment to that effect, in an action by a minority stockholder to set aside the sale of corporate property on the ground of fraud and misconduct of the majority stockholders, that the property could have been disposed of for a greater price at the time when it was found necessary to dispose of it, or that a better price could have been obtained by delaying the sale, nor can it be presumed that the stockholders and trustees by whom the sale was effected received a personal benefit or advantage, without the averment of some fact tending to show it beyond the averment of a difference between the alleged value and the selling price.

18. The corporation itself is primarily the party entitled to bring an equitable suit to set aside a fraudulent sale and transfer of all the corporate assets by the majority stockholders and trustees, and an objecting stockholder can only sue for such relief when the corporation actually or virtually refuses to sue, and his recovery in such action can be no

other than that which the corporation itself might obtain, if the case had been brought by its own officers.

19. A stockholder may be estopped from maintaining an action to set aside the sale of all the corporate property, as where he has participated or acquiesced in the transfer, or has failed for an unreasonable time to take steps to set it aside.

20. There is no inflexible rule for determining what length of time will constitute unreasonable delay in bringing an action by an objecting stockholder to set aside the sale of corporate property, but whether the delay has been reasonable or unreasonable must depend upon the facts and circumstances of each case.

21. In an action by a minority stockholder to set aside a sale alleged to have been made of all the corporate property on the ground of alleged fraud and misconduct on the part of majority stockholders and trustees, it appeared by the petition that the plaintiff was aware of the proposed sale and the circumstances and conditions thereof at the time of the annual meeting and the meeting of the trustees when the respective resolutions providing for the sale referred to in the petition were proposed and adopted on October 2, 1906, and that he took no steps to prevent the sale until April 12, 1907, when he served upon each of the trustees a notice objecting to the sale, although in the meantime he had been informed that certain instruments had been executed by the president and secretary of the company pretending to convey the property to the proposed grantee, and that the possession of the same had been transferred, and the suit to set aside the sale was not commenced until July 29, 1909, the delay in bringing suit being explained merely by the statement that a suit in the same court upon the same cause of action had been brought by the plaintiff and another against all of the present defendants except one, and that said suit had been prosecuted until September 16, 1908, when it was dismissed without prejudice, without stating the reasons for the dismissal thereof, and the defendant not a party to the previous suit was another corporation to whom the property was alleged to have been transferred by the original purchasing corporation, and further, that all of the property had been disposed of by the last purchasing corporation, the purchasers thereof not being made parties to the action nor their names disclosed by the petition. *Held,*

that, whatever the right of the selling corporation may
have been, or the plaintiff as a stockholder, to question
the validity of the sale even to the extent of demanding
its vacation, had the property remained in the possession
and control of either of the purchasing corporations,
neither the selling corporation nor the plaintiff suing on its
behalf would be entitled to a decree in the present action
setting aside the sale to the original purchasing corporation or a subsequent sale by said purchaser, since the
rights of other parties had intervened who presumably
obtained the property in good faith, there being no averments to the contrary, and no decree could be entered
which would affect their title.

22. It further appearing that the debt of the selling corporation
had been paid, and there being no offer to return the
consideration paid for the property by the original purchasing corporation, nor the showing of any means by
which it could be refunded or returned, it would be inequitable to declare the sale void or by a decree to set it
aside; all of such conditions having resulted through the
laches of the plaintiff, if at any time the corporation or
the plaintiff might have sustained an action for such
relief.

23. An allegation in a petition by a minority stockholder to set
aside the sale of corporate property on the ground of
alleged fraud and misconduct on the part of majority
stockholders, where the only allegation of profit received
by any individual defendant was that the property was
disposed of for a sum much greater than the debt of the
company to pay which the property was sold, *Held*, that
said allegation did not necessarily imply an unfair or
unreasonable profit or condition, and was not sufficient to
require an accounting by the purchaser or any of the individual stockholders who assented to the sale and were
made defendants.

24. In such an action sufficient facts not being shown to justify
a decree setting aside the sale, the mere general allegation, under the circumstances, as to the difference between
the selling price and the reasonable and market value of
the property is not sufficient to require an accounting by
either of the purchasing corporations.

[Decided December 9, 1912.]   (128 Pac. 612.)

Error to the District Court, Uinta County; Hon David H. Craig, Judge.

The material facts are stated in the opinion.

T. Blake Kennedy, for plaintiff in error.

Stating in a notice for an annual meeting of a corporation that it will be held not only for the election of trustees, but "for the transaction of such business as may properly come before the meeting," does not authorize the adoption of a resolution at such meeting providing for a sale of all of the corporate assets. (Ins. Co. v. Wescot, 80 Mass. 440.) To authorize the adoption of such a resolution at any corporate meeting the stockholders must be advised thereof in the notice calling the meeting. (Atlantic &c. Co. v. Mason, 5 R. I. 463; Jones v. Railroad, 67 N. H. 19; 10 Cyc. 327.) It appears from the petition that notice was duly given to the corporation to institute proper proceedings to protect the rights of the stockholders with reference to the sale in controversy, and the corporation having failed to commence any proceeding the action for proper relief may be maintained by the plaintiff, who is a stockholder, in his own name. (Wickersham v. Crittenden, 93 Cal. 17, 22 Pac. 788; Wright v. Oroville Co., 40 Cal. 20; Brewer v. Theater, 104 Mass. 378; State v. Holmes, 60 Neb. 39; Knoop v. Bohmrich, 49 N. J. Eq. 82; Taylor v. Exporting Co., 5 Ohio, 162; Gamble v. Water Co., 123 N. Y. 91; Barr v. R. R. Co., 96 N. Y. 444; Greaves v. Gouge, 69 N. Y. 154; Detroit v. Dean, 106 U. S. 537; Butts v. Wood, 37 N. Y. 317.)

A transaction in which a person acts at one and the same time for himself and in a fiduciary capacity must be closely scrutinized. This principle applies to transactions of directors of corporations. (Bank v. Iron Co., 97 Mo. 38; Pearson v. Ry. Co., 62 N. H. 537; Fitzgerald v. Constr. Co., 44 Neb. 463; Wardens &c. v. Rector, 45 Barb. 356; Ins. Co. v. Ins. Co., 14 N. Y. 85; Booth v. Robinson, 55 Md. 419; Hutchinson v. Mfg. Co., 57 Fed. 998; Cole v. Iron Co., 59

Hun, 217; Wilbur v. Lynde, 49 Cal. 290.) In some of these cases, and in many others, the act of controlling directors of two corporations dealing together is severely criticized. Directors of corporations are trustees for the stockholders and are held to a strict accountability. (Robinson v. Smith, 24 Am. Dec. 212; Abbott v. Rubber Co., 33 Barb. 578; Canning Co. v. Fraser, 81 Tex. 407; Butts v. Wood, 37 N. Y. 317; Flynn v. Railroad Co., 158 N. Y. 493; State ex rel. v. Holmes, 60 Neb. 39; Rabe v. Dunlap, 51 N. J. Eq. 40; Pearson v. R. Co., supra; Fogg v. Blair, 139 U. S. 118; Ryan v. R. Co., 21 Kan. 70.) A court of equity will afford relief against the misconduct, bad faith, and fraudulent actions of officers of a corporation. While the court will not presume to direct the management of a corporation, yet in the case of misconduct, bad faith, or fraud on the part of the officers, relief will be afforded to the injured party. This relief embraces injunctions, receiverships, accounting and the like, and is applicable under circumstances such as those shown in the petition in this case. See authorities supra. Delay in bringing the action is not fatal to the granting of such relief. (Fitzgerald v. Mallory, 44 Neb. 463; Montgomery v. Pickering, 116 Mass. 227; Tarlington v. Purvis, 128 Ind. 187; Foley v. Holtry, 41 Neb. 563.) Even should it appear that the plaintiff was guilty of laches, the objection could not be raised by demurrer. (Sage v. Culver, 147 N. Y. 241.)

Herbert V. Lacey and *John W. Lacey*, for defendants in error.

The allegation in the petition concerning the indebtedness of the corporation is a conclusive allegation that the company was financially embarrassed and that some action was necessary for the purpose of the payment of its liabilities. The petition clearly shows the nature of the objection made by some of the stockholders to the proposition for the sale of the corporate property, viz: that the proposed price was not the fair market value. There is, however, an entire absence of averment as to what the market value was, as well as anything to show the intrinsic character of the property such as might disclose the value. For all that appears in the petition the alleged value may have been speculative merely. The form of the objection to the sale indicates a knowledge on the part of the plaintiff and other objecting stockholders that it was necessary that the property of the corporation should be sold and the business of the company closed. There is no averment in the petition that the company ever in fact conveyed any of its property to the Crawford Land Company.

The meeting at which the resolution directing the sale was adopted was the annual meeting, making it unnecessary to embrace in the notice of the meeting a statement that the proposition for a sale of the corporate property would be considered, at least when all the shareholders are present at the meeting for the purpose of transacting generally the business of the company. The plaintiff was present at the meeting and cannot complain of the absence from the notice of specific reference to the sale of the property. (Handley v. Stutz, 139 U. S. 417; Weinburgh v. Advertising Co. (N. J.), 37 Atl. 1026; Nickum v. Burckhardt (Or.), 47 Pac. 788; Jones v. Turnpike Co., 7 Ind. 547; Hill v. Atlantic &c. Co. (N. C.), 55 S. E. 854.) The proposition for the sale was acted upon by the shareholders in the first instance. When shareholders of a corporation meet as such they act individually and represent nothing but their own shares; no shareholder stands in a fiduciary relation to any other at such a meeting, but votes for his own interest. (Hodge v. Steel Corp. (N. J.), 54 Atl. 1.) The stockholders could rightfully have ratified the sale if it had been made or directed in the first instance by the trustees, if the facts in relation to the trustees are as alleged in the petition. But the petition shows that the stockholders took the initiative and directed the trustees to make the sale. Therefore, authorities bearing upon the fiduciary relation of directors of corporations and what they may do while acting as such are not here in point. Shareholders may, in the absence of

fraud or oppression, direct the sale of the entire property of
the company when it is not prosperous and is indebted to
the full amount of its capital stock. (Ditch Co. v. Zeller-
bach, 37 Cal. 543; Phillips v. Providence &c. Co. (R. I.),
43 Atl. 598; Price v. Holcomb (Ia.), 56 N. W. 407; Timber Co. v. Watkins, 109 Fed. 101.) In the cases cited and
others, a court of equity refused to interfere under circumstances similar to those alleged in this petition. It fairly
appears from the averments that the sale complained of
was compulsory, for the purpose of paying the matured
debt of the company, which equaled the amount of its capital stock. The plaintiff, when objecting to the proposition
at the annual meeting, did not offer a higher price nor disclose that anyone was ready to purchase for a greater price
than that fixed by the resolution. Again, at the meeting of
the trustees, he merely objected on the ground that the
price was too low, without offering a higher price or showing that any other person was ready to pay more. And
after waiting three years he fails to show that a higher price
would have been paid either by himself or any other bidder.

There is no averment that those who controlled the sale
were interested in the purchasing company. The only averment in that respect is that John R. Arnold and Otto
Arnold and Charles Stone were interested in that company.
No other construction of the language of the petition in that
particular is possible, although the sentence in which the
averment appears is somewhat involved.

The plaintiff has been guilty of laches, and on this ground
alone cannot maintain the action. The property has all disappeared, as alleged, and is beyond the reach of the parties
to this suit. It is impossible, therefore, to set aside the conveyance and restore the property. But waiving that matter,
it was the duty of the plaintiff in seeking the relief prayed
for to have proceeded with diligence. (Rabe v. Dunlap
(N. J. Eq.), 25 Atl. 959; Kinne v. Webb, 54 Fed. 34;
McLean v. Clapp, 141 U. S. 429; Scheftel v. Hayes, 58
Fed. 457; Richardson v. Lowe, 149 Fed. 625; Romanoff

L. & M. Co. v. Cameron (Ala.), 33 So. 864; Dennis v. Jones (N. J.), 14 Atl. 913; Kerby v. Kerby, 57 Md. 345; Gutherie v. Lyon (Tex.), 98 S. W. 432; Dickinson v. Traction Co., 114 Fed. 232; Kessler v. Ensley Co., 123 Fed. 546; Coal Co. v. L. & T. Co., 127 Fed. 625; Corbus v. Mining Co., 187 U. S. 455.)

In this state there is no statute similar to that in New York to the effect that an objection that an action has not been commenced in time can only be taken by answer. On the contrary, under our statute, like that of Ohio, the question of the statute of limitations may be raised by demurrer where it appears upon the face of the petition that the cause of action is barred. (Sturges v. Burton, 8 O. St. 215; Commissioners v. Andrews, 18 O. St. 49; Upton v. Steele, 2 Wyo. 54; Cowhick v. Shingle, 5 Wyo. 87; Sav. Ass'n. v. Clause, 13 Wyo. 166; Bonnifield v. Price, 1 Wyo. 172.) In the absence of a statute like that in New York the question of laches in bringing an action may be raised by demurrer. (Speidel v. Henrici, 120 U. S. 377; Wilson v. Wilson (Or.), 69 Pac. 923; Dringer v. Jewett (N. J.), 13 Atl. 664; Fogg v. Price (Mass.), 14 N. E. 740; Phillips v. Piney C. & C. Co. (W. Va.), 44 S. E. 774; Taylor v. Slater (R. I.), 41 Atl. 1001; Leavenworth v. Douglass (Kan.), 53 Pac. 123; Johnson v. McKinnon (Fla.), 34 So. 272; Williams v. Soc., 1 O. St. 478; Scruggs v. Decatur M. & L. Co. (Ala.), 5 So. 440; Furlong v. Riley, 103 Ill. 628; Pearson v. David, 1 Ia. 23; Montgomery's Est. (Pa.), 3 Brewst. 306; McLung v. Sneed (Tenn.), 3 Head, 213.) The reasons for the rule requiring promptness in a suit for such relief are apparent. When there has been delay, especially when property has been sold to third parties during the delay, it is the duty of the plaintiff to show an excuse for his delay, so that the court may be informed in the first instance of the equity of his cause, for if the cause as stated does not appeal to the conscience of the court, it will be insufficient. There is more in this case than the mere lapse of time to bar the relief. There is the very element which

in every case has been said to be a reason of the greatest
strength requiring diligence, viz: the passing of the property into the hands of other persons not named in the petition.

There is no sufficient averment in the petition that the
plaintiff sought redress within the corporation. Facts not
averred in the petition are presumed not to exist. (Phillips
v. Copper Co., 86 N. Y. Supp. 200; McClure v. Warner
(Neb.), 20 N. W. 387; Ry. Co. v. Shepherd (Neb.), 58
N. W. 189; Sheridan v. Jackson, 72 N. Y. 172.) There is
a supposed protest or notice attached to the petition, which
the petition alleges was served upon each of the trustees,
but in the petition itself there is no statement of the contents of the notice. Whatever was done, therefore, by the
plaintiff in the way of demanding action by the corporation
appears only in the paper attached to the petition. The
principle is well settled that an exhibit attached to and filed
with a pleading forms no part of it and will not be considered on the hearing of a demurrer. (Johnson v. Ins. Co.,
3 Wyo. 140; Ins. Co. v. Kahn, 4 Wyo. 364.) If the resolutions for the sale of the corporate property were injurious
to the company and to the plaintiff as a shareholder, it was
the clear duty of the plaintiff to make every possible effort
within the corporation itself to obtain a rescission of the
action, first, by an appeal to the trustees and next by an
appeal to the shareholders in a meeting of shareholders.
(Hawes v. Oakland, 104 U. S. 450; Dillon Lee (Ia.), 81
N. W. 245; Ulmer v. Maine R. Est. Co. (Me.), 45 Atl. 40.)
If there was any right to rescind the sale, the right was in
the corporation. The plaintiff could only bring suit to
rescind in the name of the corporation, and in this action
he can succeed only as representing the corporation, and in
case the corporation should have succeeded in a similar
action.

He who seeks equity must do equity. This principle is
clearly applicable upon the facts here, since the plaintiff
does not offer to return the purchase price of the property

or any part of it. He seeks to set aside the sale and obtain the property itself, as well as the consideration received for it, if any sale was made. He makes no offer to return to either of the purchasing companies the consideration paid for the property. This failure on the part of the plaintiff to do or even offer to do equity bars his right of recovery. (Hinckley v. Pfister, 83 Wis. 64; Frinck v. Thomas (Or.), 25 Pac. 717; Wilcox v. San Jose &c. Co. (Ala.), 21 So. 376; Farwell v. Hanchett (Ill.), 9 N. E. 58; Weed v. Page, 7 Wis. 503; Kimball v. Cunningham, 4 Mass. 502; Gibson v. Lancaster (Tex.), 39 S. W. 1078; Hammond v. Wallace (Cal.), 24 Pac. 837; Wood v. Nichols (Wash.), 32 Pac. 1055; Reeves v. Corning, 51 Fed. 774; Stuart v. Hayden, 72 Fed. 402; Burnes v. Burnes, 137 Fed. 781; Clint v. Oil Co. (Cal.), 86 Pac. 817; Modern Woodmen v. Vincent (Ind.), 82 N. E. 475; Central &c. Soc. v. Mulford (Colo.), 100 Pac. 423; Guilfoyle v. Pierce, 109 N. Y. Supp. 924, 89 N. E. 1101.)

POTTER, JUSTICE.

This action was brought by John Smith, who alleges in the petition that it is brought on behalf of the Bear River Land & Stock Company, a corporation, and on his own behalf as a stockholder of said corporation, and on the behalf of all other stockholders who may desire to come in and be made parties to the cause and bear the expenses incurred therein. The defendants named in the petition are Charles Stone, John H. Ward, George E. Pexton, John R. Arnold, Otto Arnold, A. E. Bradbury, James Smith, J. C. Riley, Crawford Land Company, a corporation, Bear River Land & Stock Company, a corporation, and Bear River Development Company, a corporation. The petition alleges as a reason for joining James Smith and J. C. Riley as defendants that the plaintiff has been unable to procure their consent to be made plaintiffs in the cause. Each of the defendants, except James Smith and J. C. Riley, filed a separate general demurrer to the petition, and said demurrers

having been argued and submitted to the District Court
they were each sustained, the plaintiff excepting thereto.
Thereupon the further order was made in the case that the
petition be dismissed with costs assessed against the plaintiff. The case is here on error, and the general question to
be determined is whether or not the petition states a cause
of action against the defendants or either of them.

The object of the action, stated generally, is to avoid a
sale of the property and assets of the Bear River Land &
Stock Company which may have been made and which the
petition seems to assume was made to the Crawford Land
Company, a corporation, pursuant to a resolution adopted
at the annual meeting of the stockholders of the Bear River
Land & Stock Company held on the 2nd day of October,
1906, and a like resolution adopted on the same day at a
meeting of the trustees of said corporation, and also a subsequent sale of said property and assets alleged to have been
made by the Crawford Land Company to the Bear River
Development Company, and to require an accounting by
the defendants and each of them, except James Smith and
J. C. Riley, of the money received by them or either of
them from the sale of the assets of the said Bear River
Land & Stock Company and the amounts expended, and the
payment of alleged debts of said corporation.

The petition alleges that at all the times mentioned therein
each of the companies above named was a corporation existing and doing business under the laws of the State of
Wyoming; that the plaintiff is a stockholder in the Bear
River Land & Stock Company, owning 98 shares of its
capital stock; that said capital stock consists of $150,000,
divided into 1,500 shares of the par value of $100 each, of
which 765 shares have been issued and were outstanding on
the 2nd day of October, 1906, the defendant Charles Stone
holding 228 shares, the defendant Otto Arnold 1 share, the
defendant John R. Arnold 1 share, the defendant George
E. Pexton 56 shares, the defendant John H. Ward 57
shares, the defendant A. E. Bradbury 115 shares, the de-

fendant James Smith 97 shares and the defendant J. C. Riley 112 shares. That on said 2nd day of October, 1906, the Bear River Land & Stock Company was indebted to North & Stone, a co-partnership, doing a banking business in Evanston, Wyoming, in about the sum of $76,500. That the said co-partnership of North & Stone constitute, as plaintiff is informed and believes, all of the defendants, except James Smith and J. C. Riley, although in another paragraph of the petition in stating the names of the members of that firm the name of John R. Arnold is omitted. That on the 2nd day of October, 1906, the annual meeting of the stockholders of said Bear River Land & Stock Company was held in the town of Evanston, County of Uinta and State of Wyoming, "for the election of trustees for the ensuing year, and for no other purpose, and there were present at said meeting said Charles Stone, Otto Arnold, John Smith, James Smith, John R. Arnold and George E. Pexton; that the notice calling said meeting contained no notification that any other business than the election of trustees of said corporation for the ensuing year would be transacted, except that said notice stated that said meeting was called 'for the transaction of all other business as may properly come before the meeting,' and at said time the following named parties were elected as trustees for the ensuing year, to-wit: Charles Stone, John H. Ward, George E. Pexton, John Smith and John R. Arnold." That at said stockholders' meeting all the stockholders present other than John Smith and James Smith "wrongfully and against the rights of said corporation and the stockholders thereof, and with intent to defraud the same, and as plaintiff is informed and believes, and therefore alleges the fact to be, by reason of prearrangement between themselves, attempted to adopt a resolution authorizing the president and secretary of said company to sell all of the assets of said corporation, both real and personal, to the said defendant, the Crawford Land Company, for the sum of $76,500.00; that all the stockholders of the said Bear River Land & Stock

Company were not present at said stockholders' meeting,
John H. Ward and A. E. Bradbury not being present thereat, and the said plaintiff John Smith and the defendant
James Smith objected to said resolution and to the attempt
of the stockholders present at said meeting to pass any such
resolution, or to undertake to dispose of the assets of said
corporation for any such price as that mentioned in said
resolution, and notified said trustees that the price at which
they were undertaking to sell the assets of said corporation
was not the fair or market value thereof, nor the reasonable
value of the same, and that a price far in excess of that
could be procured for said property if an endeavor were
made so to do." That immediately following the adjournment of said stockholders' meeting the said Charles Stone,
John R. Arnold and George E. Pexton "wrongfully and
against the rights of said Bear River Land & Stock Company and the stockholders thereof attempted to hold a meeting of the newly elected trustees of said Bear River Land &
Stock Company, and this notwithstanding the fact that no
notice of the holding of the same or the business to be
transacted thereat had been given, and there was not present
at said pretended meeting said trustee John H. Ward; that
at said pretended meeting the said Charles Stone, John R.
Arnold and George E. Pexton wrongfully and against the
rights of said corporation and the stockholders thereof attempted and pretended to adopt a resolution authorizing the
sale of all of the assets of said corporation, both real and
personal aforesaid, for the sum of $76,500.00 to said Craw-
ford Land Company, and attempted to authorize the president and secretary of said corporation to make, execute and
deliver to said Crawford Land Company deeds and bills of
sale and all other and further instruments necessary to convey said assets to said latter company; that said John Smith
and James Smith being present at said pretended meeting
objected to said resolution and to the attempt of said trustees to dispose of the assets of said corporation, and notified
said trustees that the price at which they were undertaking

to sell said assets was not the fair or market value of the property, nor the reasonable value thereof, and that the price was far in excess of said price which could be procured for said property if an endeavor were made so to do and that the attempted act of said trustees was nothing more or less than an endeavor on their part to wrongfully dispose of the assets of said corporation to the injury of the minority stockholders to enable said trustees attempting to pass said resolution to gain and enjoy an individual and unjust advantage thereby."

That on the 2nd day of October, 1906, the said Bear River Land & Stock Company, as plaintiff is informed and believes, and therefore alleges the fact to be, was the owner of certain real estate described in the petition, "most of which said property was highly improved, and that the value of said property so belonging to said corporation was in excess of the sum of $70,000.00 and that at said time said corporation owned and possessed horses, cattle, hay, grain and other personal property of a value in excess of $55,000.00." And in another place in the petition it is alleged that the property of said corporation on said date was the reasonable and market value of $125,000.00, "which said fact was known to each of said trustees at said time." The petition further alleges upon information and belief that the defendants Stone, Ward, Pexton, Bradbury and Otto Arnold were at the time aforesaid, associated together in the banking business in Evanston, Wyoming, under the firm name of North & Stone, "and at all the time the said John R. Arnold and Otto Arnold, brothers-in-law of said Charles Stone, and all of the said parties were the particular owners, holders and controllers of the Crawford Land Company; that the said John R. Arnold was a mere nominal stockholder in the Bear River Land & Stock Company, and as a request of, and as an accommodation to the said Charles Stone, owning but one share of stock therein, and the said Otto Arnold was but a mere nominal stockholder in the said corporation at the request of, and as an accom-

modation to the said Charles Stone, owning but one share
in said corporation." That at said time "the said Bear
River Land & Stock Company was under the management
of the said Charles Stone, and that it was claimed by the
said Stone that the said company was indebted to the said
firm of North & Stone in the sum of $76,500.00; that no
money or other valuable consideration was paid by the said
Crawford Land Company to the Bear River Land & Stock
Company, and that upon the transfer to it of the entire
assets, the said Crawford Land Company conveyed all of
the assets of the Bear River Land & Stock Company to the
defendant, the Bear River Development Company, without
consideration of any kind, and that the said defendants heretofore mentioned, except the said James Smith and J. C.
Riley, were and are the stockholders, owners and controllers
of the said Bear River Development Company, and that all
of said transfers were made, as plaintiff is informed and believes, and so charges the fact to be, for the purpose of
obtaining property, worth at least $125,000, in satisfaction
of said alleged debt of $76,500.00 due to the said firm of
North & Stone, and for the purpose of defrauding the said
plaintiff, and the said James Smith and J. C. Riley out of
their interest in the Bear River Land & Stock Company.
Plaintiff is informed and believes that the said Bear River
Development Company has disposed of all of the assets to
(of) the said Bear River Land & Stock Company for a
sum much greater than the said alleged debt due to the
said North & Stone; that the acts of said stockholders of
said Bear River Land & Stock Company as such and as
trustees thereof were without any legal or proper proceedings therefor, were in violation of the rights of said corporation and the stockholders thereof, and were an endeavor to
attempt to enable a majority of the trustees of said corporation to acquire an undue and illegal advantage over the
other stockholders of said company by reason of their and
through their own acts as trustees of said company." That
the transfer from the Crawford Land Company to the Bear

River Development Company was without consideration, "but as he (plaintiff) is informed and believes both of said corporations are insolvent, and said transfer was made simply for the purpose of defrauding this plaintiff and the said James Smith and J. C. Riley and depriving them of their stock in the said Bear River Land & Stock Company and procuring for the other defendants, except the said James Smith and J. C. Riley, the said difference between the $76,500.00 and the real value of the said property, to-wit: $125,000.00."

It is further alleged in the petition that on the 12th day of April, 1907, the plaintiff caused to be served upon each of the trustees of the Bear River Land & Stock Company a notice "in words and figures as set forth in exhibit 'A' attached hereto and made a part of this complaint; but notwithstanding said notice no endeavor or effort has been made by the officers or trustees of said corporation to investigate the facts set forth in said notice, or institute any proceedings of any description to preserve and protect the interests of said company or the stockholders thereof." That the plaintiff, together with James Smith and J. C. Riley, instituted a suit in said District Court on behalf of themselves and all other stockholders of the Bear River Land & Stock Company that might choose to come in and be made parties to said action "upon the same cause of action set forth herein against all the defendants, except the Bear River Development Company, and prosecuted said suit until the 16th day of September, 1908, at which time said action was dismissed without prejudice."

The prayer of the petition is, (1) That the attempted conveyance of the Bear River Land & Stock Company to the Crawford Land Company be decreed to be void. (2) That the conveyance from the Crawford Land Company to the Bear River Development Company be set aside and held for naught. (3) That the defendants and each of them, except James Smith and J. C. Riley, be required to account to the plaintiff and all others interested who may join in the suit for the amount of money received by them or either of them from the sale of any of the assets of the Bear River Land & Stock Company and the amounts expended in the payment of alleged debts of the said company, and that the court may require the money in the hands of said defendants to be paid to the clerk of the court to be distributed pro rata to the stockholders of the said company. (4) And that upon their failure so to do judgment may be entered against them for such amounts as may be proper, and for such other and further relief as may be proper in the premises.

The petition is indefinite and uncertain in several important particulars. A defect of that kind is ordinarily to be corrected by motion to render the pleading more definite and certain by amendment, and is not ground for demurrer. We recognize the distinction in the rules of code pleading between an entire failure to state a cause of action and the statement of one in an imperfect and defective manner. But in the case of this petition the defect relates to so many material facts respecting which the averments in this kind of action ought to be reasonably definite and certain that it might properly be held, we think, to amount to a failure to state a cause of action rendering the petition demurrable. (Wheeler v. Pullman I. & S. Co., 143 Ill. 197, 32 N. E. 420, 17 L. R. A. 818.) As said in a recent similar case, "a bill founded upon fraud or misconduct which does not allege with certainty and definiteness tangible facts to sustain its general averments of such fraud and misconduct is insufficient, and cannot be sustained." (Smith v. Chase & Baker Piano Mfg. Co. (D. C.), 197 Fed. 466.) The indefinite character of many of the averments will be referred to as we discuss the propositions involved. It is sought by the petition to avoid and vacate a supposed sale of the assets and property of the Bear River Land & Stock Company, and to require an accounting by several of the defendants of the money received by them as the result of such sale. It is contended as one ground for avoiding the sale and setting it aside that the meeting of the stockholders at which

it is alleged that it was attempted to adopt a resolution
authorizing the sale was without authority to consider or
adopt such a resolution for the reason that the notice of the
meeting did not specify that such matter would be considered. The meeting referred to was the annual meeting of
the stockholders of the corporation; and presumably, there
being no allegation to the contrary, it was held at the proper
time and place. The notice stated that in addition to the
election of trustees the meeting was called "for the transaction of all other business as may properly come before the
meeting." The statute provided only that the trustees
(directors) shall be annually elected by the stockholders at
such time and place as shall be directed by the by-laws of
the company; and that public notice of the time and place
of holding such election shall be published not less than ten
days previous thereto, in the newspaper printed nearest to
the place where the operations of said company shall be,
carried on, and the election shall be made by such of the
stockholders as shall attend for that purpose, either in person or by proxy, provided one-half of the stock is represented. There was no other statutory provision with reference to the notice of the annual meeting of the stockholders
of a corporation, and no statutory provision with reference
to the business that might be lawfully transacted at such
meeting other than the election of trustees, nor was there
any other statutory provision regulating or relating to the
contents of a notice calling a meeting of the stockholders
for the purpose of considering the question of the sale of its
property. It was, however, provided by statute that the
stockholders of a corporation, or the trustees (directors)
if the certificate of incorporation so provides, shall have
power to make by-laws as they shall deem proper for the
management and disposition of the stock and business affairs
of the company, not inconsistent with the laws of the state,
and prescribing the duties of artificers and servants that
may be employed, for the appointment of all officers and
for the carrying on of all business within the objects and

purposes of the company. It is not shown by the petition what, if any, provision was made in the by-laws of the company with reference to the business that might be transacted at the annual meeting and the notice to be given of such meeting. It may be, therefore, that the notice here complained of complied in all respects with the by-laws so as to authorize the adoption of the resolution mentioned in the petition. But the plaintiff, who appears to be the only complaining stockholder, was present at the meeting and participated therein, and while he objected to the adoption of the resolution complained of it is not alleged that he made any objection to the form of the notice, or to the authority of the stockholders at such meeting to consider the question and adopt a resolution ·for the sale of all the assets and property of the corporation, at least for an adequate price. It appears by the petition that he and another stockholder who was present objected to the resolution upon the sole ground that the price at which it was provided by the resolution that the sale should be made was not the reasonable, fair and market value of the property, and that a price far in excess of that could be procured if an endeavor were made to do so. Under these circumstances any objection to the form of the notice of the meeting is not available to the plaintiff. (Thompson on Corp., Secs. 817-825.) It is, therefore, unnecessary to consider or determine whether in all cases the notice given of the meeting would be sufficient to authorize such a resolution as that which it is alleged was attempted to be adopted. With reference to such meeting it is further alleged that certain stockholders were present and that others were not present, but it is not alleged whether the stock of those who were not present was or was not legally and properly represented and voted at such meeting. It cannot be assumed, therefore, that any of the stock was not represented and voted at the meeting. Indeed the petition is indefinite respecting the adoption of the resolution mentioned, for it is merely alleged that certain of the stockholders present "attempted" to adopt the resolution.

It may be conceded that it is not within the lawful power of a majority of the stockholders of a solvent going corporation to sell its entire assets and property over the objection of a minority stockholder, unless such power is expressly conferred by law, in the absence of some exigency or a condition requiring that course to be pursued, the law being as stated in Cook on Corporations (6th Ed.), Vol. 2, Sec. 670, that a "dissenting stockholder may prevent the sale of all the corporate property where the corporation is a solvent going concern." But a different rule prevails when the corporation is an unprofitable and failing enterprise. (Id. and cases cited; Phillips v. Providence Steam-Engine Co., 21 R. I. 302, 43 Atl. 598, 45 L. R. A. 560; Price v. Holcomb, 89 Ia. 123, 56 N. W. 407.) The rule in such case is stated in Noyes on Intercorporate Relations as follows: "The general rule that a majority cannot sell the entire assets of a prosperous corporation is based upon the principle that a majority cannot control corporate powers to defeat corporate purposes. It is subject to the exception that such sale may be made as a step towards dissolution. The power of a majority to dispose of all the property of a *losing* corporation, however, is in furtherance of the purposes of the corporation and arises *ex necessitate*. When the further prosecution of the business of the corporation would be unprofitable, it is the duty, as well as the right, of the majority to dispose of its property and take action towards the liquidation of its affairs." (Sec. 111.) The fact that two corporations are controlled by the same officers or stockholders does not prevent them from dealing with each other or the purchase by one of the property of the other, unless the acts of the majority in control are fraudulent as against the corporation and complaining stockholders. (Smith v. Chase & Baker Piano Mfg. Co., supra.) "The courts will closely scrutinize a sale of corporate property effected by majority stockholders to another corporation, which they control or are interested in. Such a sale is not void nor constructively fraudulent. But if it is unfair to the minority, or if any unconscionable advantage of their position has been taken by the majority, the courts will not hesitate, at the suit of the minority, to set the sale aside. Regardless of the means employed, when it appears that 'the majority have put something in their pockets at the expense of the minority,' a court of equity will grant relief." (Noyes on Intercorporate Relations, Sec. 114.) Upon the face of the petition it appears, we think, that an exigency may have arisen which would authorize the transfer complained of in this case, for the corporation appears to have been a losing one and in a condition requiring the disposition of its property to pay its debts. While there is some uncertainty in the petition respecting the consideration of the supposed sale to the Crawford Land Company we think the only reasonable construction of the allegation is that if the sale was made it was made pursuant to certain resolutions referred to in the petition, that the consideration thereof was the sum of $76,500, and that the sale was made for the purpose of liquidating the indebtedness of the company to North & Stone, which, as will be observed from the averments of the petition, equaled the amount of the par value of the capital stock of the company which had been issued and was outstanding, and in the absence of an allegation to the contrary it is also proper to assume that if the sale was made the debt due North & Stone was paid as a result thereof. The corporation was at the time in a condition prohibiting it from borrowing more money or incurring further indebtedness without rendering the officers assenting thereto personally liable therefor, for it was then provided by statute and continues to be so provided that "if the indebtedness of any such company shall at any time exceed the amount of its capital stock, the directors of such company assenting thereto, shall be personally and individually liable for such excess, to the creditors of such company." (Comp. Stat., Sec. 3992.) It appears, therefore, we think, upon the face of the petition, that the company was not in a prosperous condition, and that there may have existed reasonable grounds, if not an absolute necessity, for a disposition of all the assets and property of the company for the purpose of satisfying its said indebtedness, and, although the fact of the indebtedness is alleged, there is an entire absence of averment to show that a necessity for the sale of the property did not then exist. Indeed the objection which it is alleged was made by the plaintiff and another stockholder, both at the meeting of the stockholders and at the meeting of the trustees, seems to have recognized that a necessity existed for such a disposition of the property of the company, for the only objection made had reference to the price or consideration mentioned in the resolution. It must be held, therefore, that the petition fails to show an absence of authority in the majority of the stockholders to adopt a resolution authorizing the property and assets of the company to be sold, unless the facts alleged are sufficient to show that a sale was made under such circumstances as to render it fraudulent against the corporation and the objecting stockholders.

A remarkable thing about the petition is that it fails to definitely allege the fact of a sale of the property and assets of the company to the Crawford Land Company. Clearly, it is not directly alleged that such a sale was made, or that the conveyances or instruments for the purpose of conveying the title to such assets and property authorized by the resolutions referred to were ever executed or delivered. That such a sale or transfer was in fact made is only inferentially alleged, if at all, by the statement in the petition, "that upon the transfer to it of the entire assets, the said Crawford Land Company conveyed all the assets of the Bear River Land & Stock Company to the defendant, the Bear River Development Company, without consideration of any kind," and the further statement that "plaintiff is informed and believes that the said Bear River Development Company has disposed of all the assets to (of) the said Bear River Land & Stock Company for a sum much greater than the said alleged debt due to the said North &

Stone," and the other statements in the petition charging
the acts of the stockholders and the trustees to be wrongful, fraudulent and illegal, which may or may not refer to
an actual sale and transfer of the assets and property of
the corporation, such statements being seemingly dependent
as to that upon the allegations respecting such a transfer
and sale. If it be assumed that such a sale was made then
the petition is further indefinite and uncertain respecting
the date of the sale and transfer of said assets and property
to the Crawford Land Company, and also as to the date of
the sale and transfer of said assets and property by the last
named company to the Bear River Development Company.
It is also uncertain whether it is alleged in the petition or
intended to be alleged that any of the individual defendants
other than John R. Arnold, Otto Arnold and Charles Stone
were the owners and controllers of the Crawford Land
Company. The allegation respecting that matter is so made
as to leave the petition open to the construction that the
individuals last above named were the only defendants who
owned and controlled the Crawford Land Company. It is
charged to be a fact that defendants Stone, Ward, Pexton,
Otto Arnold and Bradbury were associated together in the
banking business under the firm name and style of North &
Stone, "and at all the times the said John R. Arnold and
Otto Arnold, brothers-in-law of the said Charles Stone,
and all of the said parties were the particular holders and
controllers of the Crawford Land Company." Whether
by the words "all of the said parties" it was intended to
include all the defendants previously named, viz: Ward,
Pexton, Otto Arnold and Bradbury, is not clear. It is contended by counsel for defendants in error that the petition
merely alleges in this respect that the defendant Stone and
his brothers-in-law, John R. Arnold and Otto Arnold, were
the owners and controllers of said Crawford Land Company. As above stated, we think the petition is at least
indefinite and uncertain in that particular, and that it ought
not to be assumed that any defendant, either individually or

in combination with others, had a controlling or any other interest in the Crawford Land Company, unless that fact is definitely alleged. Therefore, if it be assumed that the property was in fact sold to said company, the petition is to be understood as alleging that the only defendants who were interested in and controlled such company were Charles Stone, John R. Arnold and Otto Arnold, and it follows that the allegations to the effect that the purpose of the sale was to obtain the property for less than its reasonable, fair and market value apply only to the three defendants named, so far as such allegations refer to the individual defendants.

Disregarding for the purpose of further discussion the indefinite character of the averments respecting the sale of the property, and assuming it to be alleged that the property was sold and transferred to the Crawford Land Company for $76,500 to satisfy the debt due to North & Stone, we find that the only allegation of fact furnishing any basis for the general charges of fraud connected with such sale is that the reasonable and market value of the property was $125,000, and that such fact was known at the time "to each of said trustees." It is not alleged as a fact that a greater price could have been obtained for the property either at private or public sale, although it is alleged that the objecting stockholders informed the majority stockholders and the trustees at the meetings referred to that a much greater price could be obtained if an endeavor was made to do so. That allegation goes no further than to show that such a statement was made by the objecting stockholders at the meeting of the stockholders and also at the meeting of the trustees. It does not amount to an allegation that a greater price could in fact have been obtained. There is no averment that any greater offer was made for the property or that anyone was ready, able and willing at the time to pay a greater price for it. Nor is it alleged that any of the defendants received any money or benefit as a result of the sale other than the benefit which resulted to the corporation in the payment of its indebtedness then due, except that it is alleged that the property was disposed of by the Bear River Development Company for a sum much greater than such debt. But it is not averred when that sale was made, and it might have been made a considerable time after the original sale to the Crawford Land Company, when the property had naturally increased in value, and after the purchaser had been at considerable expense in maintaining it. Beyond that the words "much greater" are too indefinite under the circumstances, in our opinion, upon which to base the general charges of fraud, for in addition to the possible natural increase in the value of the property the words "much greater" might imply merely a fair and reasonable profit accruing to the purchaser. It is apparent, therefore, we think, that the only allegation in the petition which would at all sustain the general charges of fraud is that respecting the reasonable market value of the property at the time. Whether that averment of fact would be sufficient under other circumstances to authorize a decree setting aside a sale of corporate property on the ground of fraud or to require an accounting we need not consider or determine. The question is whether upon such facts as are alleged in this petition a cause of action is stated entitling the plaintiff to the relief demanded. This is not an action as at law against officers and directors of a corporation for damages on the ground of mismanagement or fraudulent conduct in connection with the management, but the equitable jurisdiction of the court is attempted to be invoked for the purpose of restoring to the Bear River Land & Stock Company for the benefit of the stockholders the property that had been transferred or the money over and above the debt due to North & Stone received by the defendants or either of them.

In the absence of fraud the fact that a difference of opinion may have existed between the majority and minority stockholders would not justify interference by a court of equity. In Cook on Corporations, Sec. 684, it is said: "The discretion of the directors or a majority of the stockholders as to acts *intra vires* cannot be questioned by single stockholders unless fraud is involved. This proposition of law is clearly, firmly and very properly established beyond any question." In North American Land & Timber Company v. Watkins, 109 Fed. 101, 48 C. C. A. 254, decided by the U. S. Circuit Court of Appeals, Fifth Circuit, the court say: "It is a general rule that courts of equity will not interfere in questions of corporate management or policy. They are reluctant to undertake the management of private corporations, and, in the absence of fraud, usurpation, or gross negligence or mismanagement equivalent to fraud, they generally refuse to interfere, and allow the majority of the stockholders to rule, leaving dissatisfied stockholders to redress their grievances by ordinary corporate methods." And again: "When the management is not shown to be fraudulent or dishonest, and when it is a matter of opinion whether it is wise or unwise, advantageous or disadvantageous, if the acts complained of be *intra vires*, there is no authority for equity to interfere. To do so would be to place the control indirectly in the hands of the minority whenever interference removes from control the officers selected by the majority. There is certainly no presumption that a minority stockholder is right, and a majority stockholder is wrong, in opinion as to values and the management of the corporate property." In that case it was sought by a minority stockholder to enjoin a sale of lands by the corporation, and it was alleged, though indirectly, that the lands sold were worth "many times the price" for which it had been sold, but it was not averred that anyone had offered or was willing to pay more for it. Referring thereto the court said: "Barring a general and indirect assertion of its value, no facts are stated from which the court can determine its value, or that it is intrinsically worth more than the sum for which it has been sold. What it cost the company is not averred, and it may be that the sale is for a large profit on its cost. * * * If it be true that these lands are worth greatly over $3 an acre, it may be the honest opinion of the directors that it is to the company's interest to sell them for that price, no better price being now offered. * * * This is a matter of corporate policy and management. The price at which the company will sell its lands must necessarily be fixed by the directors, officers or agents of the company selected by the stockholders. A minority stockholder should not, on the facts here alleged, be aided by the court to control the action of the directors, and himself be allowed to fix the price. The substantial controversy between the complainant and the defendant corporation, as presented by his bill, is as to the sale of the lands. But for that sale, and the probability of other sales, the bill would not have been filed. The complainant thinks it greatly to the detriment of the company to sell the lands at $3 an acre. The directors think that the sale at that price is to the company's interest. In such controversy, in the absence of fraud and collusion, if the directors are acting within the power conferred on them by the charter, the courts cannot properly interfere. * * * While the courts in a proper case will protect the rights of a minority stockholder, they cannot interfere with the right of legitimate control by the officers representing a majority of the stockholders." It was alleged in the case cited as it is in this case that the complaining stockholder had stated to the officers his objection to the sale on the ground that the land was worth much more than the price named.

There are general allegations of fraud in this petition, based upon information and belief, referring to the purpose for which the transfer was made to the Crawford Land Company at the price named in the resolutions authorizing the same, and also the purpose of the transfer by the Crawford Land Company to the Bear River Development Company. The allegations are that the purpose was to obtain the property worth at least $125,000 in satisfaction of the debt of $76,500, and to defraud the plaintiff and the defendants Smith and Riley out of their interest in the corporation, and that the purpose of the transfer to the Bear River Development Company was to deprive the plaintiffs and said Smith and Riley of their stock and to procure for the other defendants the difference between the amount of said debt and the alleged real value of the property. It is not alleged, however, that either of the individual defendants profited in any way by the transaction complained of, though the object of the suit seems to be to obtain some relief as against such defendants, since each of the purchasing corporations is alleged to be insolvent. The allegations of fraud, therefore, seem to be founded upon no fact alleged in the petition except that the value of the property exceeded, as alleged, the price received for it, and that some of the defendants who had voted for and authorized the sale to the Crawford Land Company were interested in and controlled that company, and all the defendants so acting were interested in and controlled the Bear River Development Company. The allegations as to the actual value of the property are general, without the averment of any fact as to the character or condition of the real estate or the improvements thereon, the number of horses or cattle, or the amount of hay or grain, or the nature and condition of the other personal property. In view of the fact that the company was heavily indebted at the time, the indebtedness equaling in amount the par value of the capital stock that had been subscribed for and issued, and that the sale does not appear to have been objected to on the ground that there was no necessity therefor, the fact alone that the selling price was less than the value of the property as alleged cannot be held, we think, to authorize a legal presumption of fraud on the part of the majority stockholders and the trustees, the rights of creditors not being involved. It certainly cannot be presumed in the absence of an averment to that effect that the property could have been disposed of for a greater price at the time when it was found necessary to dispose of it, or that a better price could have been obtained by delaying the sale even if the situation permitted delay, a fact not alleged. Nor can it be presumed that the stockholders and trustees whose acts are complained of received a personal benefit or advantage without the averment of some fact tending to show it, beyond the averment of the difference between the value and the selling price. It was incumbent, therefore, upon the plaintiff to allege fraud to entitle him on that ground to the relief prayed for. And in view of the facts disclosed by the other averments, and the absence of allegations showing that the defendants acquired in fact any undue advantage over the plaintiff or other stockholders, it is open to serious question whether the general allegations of fraud above referred to are sufficient to entitle the plaintiff to equitable relief on the ground of fraud.

It is not necessary to determine whether the facts alleged in this petition with reference to the terms and conditions of the sale to the Crawford Land Company, the resolutions authorizing the same, the purpose thereof, and the value of the property, would render the petition sufficient to enjoin the sale had an action been timely brought for that purpose; nor whether such facts would be sufficient, without an offer to refund the purchase price, to entitle the plaintiff to a decree setting the sale aside, if the property remained in the possession or under the control of either the Crawford Land Company or the Bear River Development Company. But if it be conceded that upon the facts alleged the plaintiff would have been entitled to equitable relief avoiding the sale, if he had brought an action therefor while the property remained in the possession of either of the companies named, or could be restored to the selling company, any right to such relief has been lost through the laches of the plaintiff appearing upon the face of the petition. For such acts on the part of the stockholders and trustees as those complained of the corporation itself is primarily the party entitled to bring an equitable suit for relief, and a stockholder can sue only on behalf of the corporation when the latter either actually or virtually refuses to prosecute. In such case the recovery by the stockholder can be no other than that which the corporation itself might obtain were the case prosecuted by its own officers. (3 Pom. Eq. Juris. (3rd Ed.), Secs. 1094, 1095.) In Section 1095 Mr. Pomeroy says: "Whenever a cause of action exists primarily in behalf of the corporation against directors, officers, and others, for wrongfully dealing with corporate property, or wrongful exercise of corporate franchises, so that the remedy should be legally obtained through a suit by and in the name of the corporation, and the corporation either actually or virtually refuses to institute or prosecute such a suit, then, in order to prevent a failure of justice, an action may be brought and maintained by a stockholder or stockholders, either individually or suing on behalf of themselves and all others similarly situated, against the wrong-doing directors, officers, and other persons. * * * The stockholder does not bring such a suit because *his* rights have been *directly* violated or because the cause of action is *his* or because *he* is entitled to the relief sought; he is permitted to sue in this manner simply in order to set in motion the judicial machinery of the court. The stockholder, either individually or as the representative of the class, may commence the suit, and may prosecute it to judgment; but in every other respect the action is the ordinary one brought by the corporation, it is maintained directly for the benefit of the corporation, and the final relief, when obtained, belongs to the corporation, and not to the stockholder-plaintiff." (See also Wills v. Porter, 132 Cal. 516, 64 Pac. 896.) But a stockholder may be estopped from prosecuting such an action, as where he has participated or acquiesced in the transfer of the corporate property, or has failed for an unreasonable time to take steps to set it aside. For example, it is held that an injunction will not be granted, at the instance of a minority stockholder, to restrain a sale where such stockholder, by his laches, has permitted the interests of innocent persons to intervene so that it cannot be granted without inflicting serious injuries. There is no inflexible rule for determining what length of time will constitute unreasonable delay in bringing such an action for equitable relief, but whether the delay has been reasonable or unreasonable must depend upon the facts and circumstances of each case. (Noyes on Intercorporate Relations, Sec. 116.) "After a stockholder has knowledge of or is chargeable with knowledge of an *ultra vires*, fraudulent, or negligent act of the directors, he must institute his suit, if at all, within a reasonable time thereafter. As to what will constitute a reasonable time depends on the circumstances of the case. The length of time during which a stockholder may delay in bringing his suit varies with each case, according to the circumstances of that case. The court requires that reasonable promptness be exercised so that large investments of new money or changes in the ownership of the stock or property may not be prevented or jeopardized by an unreasonable delay on the part of a stockholder in objecting to the transaction." (Cook on Corporations (6th Ed.), Sec. 732.)

It appears by the allegations of the petition that the plaintiff was aware of the proposed sale and the circumstances and conditions thereof at the time of the annual meeting and the meeting of the trustees when the respective resolutions referred to in the petition were proposed and adopted, namely, on the second day of October, 1906, and that he took no steps to prevent the sale until the 12th day of April, 1907, when, it is alleged, he served upon each of the trustees a notice as set forth in an exhibit attached to and made a part of the petition. Without deciding whether that notice is properly a part of the petiition or not, it appears by reference to it that prior to the notice the plaintiff had been informed that certain instruments had been executed by the president and secretary of the company pretending to convey to the Crawford Land Company the title to all of the assets of the Bear River Land & Stock Company, and that the possession of all of said property had been transferred to said grantee. And this suit was not

commenced until July 29, 1909. The only explanation of
the delay in bringing suit, if it may be treated as an explanation, is found in the averment in the petition that a suit
in the same court upon the same cause of action was
brought by the plaintiff, together with James Smith and
J. C. Riley, against all the defendants, except the Bear
River Development Company, and that said suit was prosecuted until the 16th day of September, 1908, at which
time the suit was dismissed without prejudice. When that
suit was commenced is not stated, nor the reasons for the
dismissal thereof, and nearly a year elapsed between the
time of its dismissal and the commencement of the present
action. It further appears that before this action was commenced all the property had been disposed of by the Bear
River Development Company, but the purchasers are not
made parties to the action, nor are their names disclosed
by the petition. How long before the action was commenced
the property had been so disposed of does not appear, and
we have no right to assume from any averment found in
the petition, even if that would benefit the plaintiff, that
such disposition of the property occurred after the dismissal
of the former suit. Whatever the right of the corporation
may have been, or the plaintiff as a stockholder, to question
the validity of the sale even to the extent of demanding a
decree vacating it, had the property remained in the possession and control of either of the purchasing corporations, a
matter which need not be decided, it is clear that upon the
facts aforesaid the corporation or the plaintiff suing on its
behalf would not be entitled to a decree in this action setting
aside the original sale to the Crawford Land Company or
the subsequent sale to the Bear River Development Company. The rights of other parties have intervened who
presumably obtained the property in good faith, there being
no averment to the contrary, and as they are not made parties to the suit no decree to be entered herein could affect
them or their title. And, further, the debt of the corporation having been paid either by the Crawford Land Com-

pany or with the money which it paid for the property, and the property having passed out of its hands, as well as from the possession and control of the Bear River Development Company, and there being no offer to return the consideration paid for the property nor the showing of any means by which it could be refunded or returned, it would be inequitable to declare the sale void or attempt by a decree to set it aside. And this has resulted through the laches of the plaintiff, if at any time the corporation or the plaintiff might have sustained an action for such relief.

Upon the allegations of the petition the prayer for an accounting would seem to have been inserted as incidental to the relief prayed respecting a decree avoiding the sales. But treating the prayer for an accounting as separate and distinct, we think that sufficient facts are not stated to entitle the plaintiff as representing the corporation to an accounting from either of the defendants. It has already been stated that there is no averment that any individual defendant received any profit out of the transaction or transactions complained of, and that the only allegation in this respect is that the property was disposed of by the Bear River Development Company for a sum much greater than the debt due to North & Stone. But that does not necessarily imply an unfair or an unreasonable profit or advantage, and is not sufficient in our opinion to require an accounting by that company. The theory of the petition as to the situation and liability of the Bear River Development Company respecting the transactions complained of seems to be that that company occupied the same relation to the transaction as the Crawford Land Company, it being alleged that the stockholders and trustees of the Bear River Land & Stock Company, whose acts are complained of, own and control the Bear River Development Company, and that the property was transferred to that company by the Crawford Land Company without consideration. But as sufficient facts are not shown to justify a decree setting aside the sales or declaring them void, the mere general allegation, under the circumstances alleged, as to the difference between the selling price and the reasonable and market value of the property cannot be held sufficient to require an accounting by either of the purchasing corporations, and that is the only allegation even tending to indicate any unfairness in the transaction, or that anything was unfairly or unjustly received by any defendant. We conclude, therefore, that the plaintiff has not shown a right to the equitable relief demanded, and that, therefore, the demurrers were properly sustained. The judgment will be affirmed. *Affirmed.*

BEARD, C. J., and SCOTT, J., concur.

LAUGHLIN v. STATE BOARD OF CONTROL ET AL.
(No. 692.)

WATER AND WATER RIGHTS—RESERVOIRS—APPLICATION FOR PERMIT TO CONSTRUCT—PRIORITY—REQUEST FOR ADDITIONAL INFORMATION, EFFECT OF UPON PRIORITY—EFFECT OF INTERMEDIATE APPLICATION ON PRIORITY OF PREVIOUS APPLICATION HELD FOR ADDITIONAL INFORMATION—RIGHT OF APPEAL.

1. The state engineer may, by express provision of statute, require additional information before passing finally upon an application for permit to construct a reservoir.

2. The time within which to furnish additional information requested by the state engineer upon the filing of an application for permit to construct a reservoir is not limited by statute, but such information should be furnished within a reasonable time.

3. In the statute requiring the state engineer to reject an application for a permit to appropriate water when the proposed use conflicts with existing rights, the words "when the proposed use conflicts with existing rights" means rights which are prior in time to the use of the water.

4. It was not necessary, under the provisions of Sections 743 and 744, Compiled Statutes, 1910, to set forth in an application for a permit to construct a reservoir filed May 14, 1908, or to show upon the map accompanying the applica-

tion, the land intended to be irrigated from the reservoir, but if such application complied in form and contained the requirements of Section 743, it would be complete as a primary application to construct a reservoir; and if the source of supply of water was sufficient, and if the proposed use would not conflict with prior rights, or threaten to be detrimental to the public interest, the applicant would be entitled to a permit.

5. Where an application for a permit to construct a reservoir, which was filed May 14, 1908, was returned by the state engineer to the applicant for additional information concerning the supply ditch, suggesting that if the ditch required enlargement for the purpose of filling the reservoir the written consent of the ditch owners must be filed in the engineer's office before the application could be approved; that the outlet of the reservoir should be shown; and the land on which the water was intended to be used should also be filed upon, or, if filed upon, the number of the permit or the description of the land should be given, so that the reservoir can be tied to the lands for which the water is to be used, *Held,* that the information called for was not required by the statute to be stated in the application, and that the engineer could not properly require, as a condition to his approval of the application, that the land to be irrigated, or the title thereto be shown, since the necessity of such showing for primary permit was dispensed with by the provisions of Section 744, Compiled Statutes, 1910, providing that an enumeration of any lands proposed to be irrigated from the water stored in the reservoir shall not be required in the primary permit.

6. The fact that the state engineer has required additional information before approving an application for a permit to construct a reservoir, under and within the authority conferred upon him by Section 731, Compiled Statutes, 1910, will not disturb the priority of the application as of the date of its filing, if any such information properly required should be furnished within a reasonable time; but upon the furnishing of such information within a reasonable time the application will be entitled to consideration and when approved, will have priority, which priority will not be lost or disturbed by the fact that the application of another party may have been filed in the meantime before final action of the engineer.

7. Where an application for a permit to construct a reservoir filed May 14, 1908, complied with the provisions of Section 743, Compiled Statutes, 1910, which prescribed what should be set forth in such application, and the application was returned for additional information before final action upon it, it was not proper for the state engineer, upon the furnishing of the information in the form of a new application filed June 30, 1908, to reject the application merely upon the ground that a conflicting application had in the meantime been filed by another party.

8. Where the state engineer returned an application for a permit to construct a reservoir for additional information, and, within a reasonable time, another application was filed by the applicant to comply with the requirements of the engineer as to additional information, *Held,* that it should properly and in justice to the applicant be regarded as a part of the original application adding the information called for, and that the applicant's right to the permit should have been determined with reference to the date of filing the original application.

9. In an application for a permit to construct a reservoir it was not necessary to show the title to the proposed reservoir site, or that the right of way for the supply ditch had been obtained, or that the written consent of the owners of a ditch already constructed to enlarge and use it for supplying the reservoir had been secured, or what the title was to the land proposed to be irrigated, since such matters were not required to be stated in the application by the statute expressly prescribing what should be set forth therein.

10. Title to land embraced in a proposed reservoir site or the right of way for the supply ditch are matters without the jurisdiction of the state engineer or the board of control; the applicant assumes the burden of securing such title or easement as a part of the undertaking under the permit applied for, and within the time fixed by the state engineer for so doing.

11. The withholding of a permit to construct a reservoir for additional information with reference to an application which measures up to the requirements of the statute does not forfeit or postpone the right of the applicant, which took effect as of the date of the filing of such application, where such additional information, as in the present case, was filed within a reasonable time.

12. Where an application for a permit to construct a reservoir has been returned by the state engineer for additional information, the applicant is not then in a position to appeal, since the statute gives the right to appeal to an applicant feeling himself aggrieved by an adverse endorsement made by the engineer upon his application, and the withholding of the permit for additional information is not such an indorsement as the statute giving the right of appeal contemplates.

ON PETITION FOR REHEARING.

13. An application for a permit to construct a reservoir having been received and filed for record in the office of the state engineer May 14, 1908, and returned May 18, 1908, to the applicant by the engineer for additional information concerning the title to the right of way for the supply ditch, and the land proposed to be irrigated, and a showing as to the outlet of the reservoir, matters not required to be set forth in the application for the primary permit, and the applicant by a subsequent application for the same reservoir, received and filed June 30, 1908, attempted a compliance with said request for additional information, *Held*, that, considering the character of the information called for and furnished, the time taken to furnish the information was not unreasonable, and the delay was not such laches as to constitute an abandonment or forfeiture of the first application, so as to authorize the granting of a permit to another party upon an application filed June 22, 1908.

[Decided December 9, 1912.]   (128 Pac. 517.)
[Rehearing denied April 7, 1913.].   (131 Pac. 62.)

ERROR to the District Court, Albany County; HON. CHARLES E. CARPENTER, Judge.

From an order of the State Engineer rejecting an application of Lemuel L. Laughlin for a permit to construct a reservoir, the applicant appealed to the State Board of Control. From a decision of the board sustaining the decision of the engineer an appeal was taken to the District Court of Albany County, which resulted in a judgment affirming the action of the State Engineer and board and a dismissal of the appeal, and thereupon the applicant brought the case to the

Supreme Court on error. The material facts are stated in the opinion.

N. E. Corthell, for plaintiff in error.

The sole ground for denying the application of plaintiff in error was the fact that another party had filed a conflicting application between the dates of the filing of his original and amended applications. The State Engineer wrongfully assumed power to consider and determine questions involving the ownership of the land to be used for the reservoir, and to approve the permit of the second applicant in violation of the statute giving the prior right to the first applicant. Priority of appropriation dates from the filing of the application for a permit under the present statutory system. (Comp. Stat. 1910, Secs. 727-752, 739; Whalon v. Canal Co., 11 Wyo. 344; Const., Art. 8, Sec. 5.) Pending action upon an application the engineer may call for additional information to enable him to properly guard the public interests, and he is required to reject an application where there is no unappropriated water or where the proposed use conflicts with existing rights, or threatens to prove detrimental to the public interest. The statute requires the engineer also to indorse on the application his approval or rejection, and from his decision shown by such indorsement an appeal lies. "Existing rights" which would authorize, under the statute, a rejection of an application must refer to water rights, and, as each water right is in all respects subordinate to prior rights, it is not conceived that any new appropriation can impair the value of an existing one in a legal sense. No denial of an appropriation can be justified upon any other ground than that of public interest. Impairment of the value of a *private* interest or the detrimental · effect upon a private interest, are contingencies which cannot be considered by the engineer. In view of the emphatic language of the constitution, he cannot refuse a permit unless it is made to appear that the grounds of the decision complained of are such as are recognized and authorized by the constitution and statute. Prima facie, the application of

plaintiff in error should be approved, for such approval is a
matter of course unless some constitutional or statutory objection is shown to exist. (Richter v. State, 16 Wyo. 438.)

Upon careful consideration of the proper duties and province of the State Engineer, there would seem to be nothing
inconsistent in approving both applications which were presented and filed. These applications had reference to water
rights. The right to establish, maintain, construct and
operate the reservoir is another affair, which may be dependent upon the ownership of the lands, or the interest or
easement in the lands affected, and is to be acquired from
another source and in a different way than by an application filed in the office of the State Engineer. The question
of the ownership of the land to be used or affected is beyond
the engineer's jurisdiction and control. (Sowards v.
Meagher (Utah), 108 Pac. 1112.) The filing of an application for a permit in the engineer's notice is merely official
notice of the applicant's intention to accept and act upon the
offer of the state to grant water rights, which is open to all.
(Sowards v. Meagher, supra.) There is nothing in the
facts in this case which even suggests a public interest requiring a rejection of the application in question. The
terms "public interest" and "public policy" are very closely
related. The courts have found it necessary to define the
judicial meaning of "public policy," and have held that a
state can have no public policy except what is to be found
in its constitution and laws. (People v. Hawkins, 157 N.
Y. 12; Hollis v. Seminary, 95 N. Y. 166; Vidal v. Philadelphia, 2 Howard, 127.) The exercise of official discretion is controlled by law, and the qualifying words "according to law" are to be read into each statute investing the
officer with discretionary power. (Scott v. LaPorte (Ind.),
68 N. E. 278.) The supervision of the waters of the state
entrusted to the Board of Control, and somewhat to the
State Engineer, comprehends official administrative action
rather than judicial. (Farm Inv. Co. v. Carpenter, 9 Wyo.
110.) On the other hand the power to determine property

rights between conflicting claimants is not an administrative matter, but judicial. (State v. Carr, 129 Ind. 44, 28 N. E. 88; Thorp v. Woolman, 1 Mont. 168.) The state has no power to dispose of the public waters except in the matter of regulating appropriations for private beneficial use; it has no right which it can sell. (Rossmiller v. State, 114 Wis. 169, 189 N. W. 839.)

Groesbeck & Eby and *D. A. Preston,* Attorney General. for defendants in error.

The Laughlin application, which was returned for correction "for additional information," was never returned by the applicant to the engineer's office, but after an application had been filed by another party Laughlin made a second application, covering practically the same site mentioned and described in the other party's application. Therefore, the engineer rejected the Laughlin application on the ground that a permit had been granted to the other party under a prior application. Laughlin applied not for a water right, but for a reservoir site by the two applications particularly here in question. There was no compliance on his part with the reasonable request for additional information, as will appear by an examination of his second application. On the contrary, an entirely different application was made. (Weil on Water Rights (3rd Ed.), Sec. 414 and note; Pool v. Utah &c. Co., 105 Pac. 289.) It follows that the engineer and the Board of Control, as well as the District Court, faithfully applied the statutory requirements in granting the permit to the prior applicant.

There is a distinction under the provisions of the statute between an application to acquire a water right and one for a permit to construct a reservoir. It is clear that the statute with reference to reservoirs was intended to provide a rule or procedure whereby a reservoir to impound unappropriated waters might be constructed. Conceding that the construction of a reservoir is to impound waters acquired from the state the contention of opposing counsel that the engineer is limited in rejecting permits for reservoirs to cases where such denial is demanded by the public interest is not applicable. A reservoir can be constructed and filled from a private source without a permit. But if public waters are to be used the Legislature may make such rules and prohibitions as it may see fit. Had the engineer granted the same site to both parties there would have been a conflict as to existing rights, and his act would have been void. (Trade &c. Co. v. Frazer, 148 Fed. 587; Weil on W. R. (3rd Ed.), Sec. 793.) Great discretion is allowed the engineer in calling for additional information with reference to an application for a permit. (Weil on W. R., Sec. 143; Whalon v. Canal Co., 11 Wyo. 313.) Public interest demands the rejection of an application, which, if granted, will conflict with a prior grant. (Cookingham v. Lewis, 114 Pac. 91; Young v. Hinderlider, 110 Pac. 1049.) It is true that the terms "public interest" and "public policy" are closely related. They each mean the public good. Anything which tends to undermine the security for individual rights, or private property, is against public policy and public interest. (Goodyear v. Brown, 155 Pa. St. 514; Spence v. Harvey, 22 Cal. 340; Tarbell v. Rutland, 75 Vt. 347; In re. Lampson's Will, 53 N. Y. Supp. 531; Com. v. Alger, 7 Cush. 84; 2 Kent's Com. 340; Trustees v. Tatman, 13 Ill. 27; Munn v. People, 94 U. S. 121, 24 L. Ed. 84.) Therefore, when any citizen seeks to impound the public waters it becomes not only the prerogative but the duty of the engineer to ascertain whether or not the granting of a permit therefor will conflict with some prior vested interest of another citizen, and if so then to deny the permit. This the engineer did in this case, and he was legally justified, for should he have granted a permit to Laughlin it would have interfered with the right of the other applicant to whom a permit had been granted for the same reservoir site.

(On petition for rehearing.) The decision seems to leave little discretion to the State Engineer, and to give an advantage to an applicant who has not been vigilant, but has slept on his rights, while another party acting in good faith is held responsible for the laches of the former. Laughlin's second application might possibly be considered as an amended application, had no intermediate application been filed. But in view of the fact that the application of another party had been filed in the meantime a different construction should be given to the new application of Laughlin. The question is somewhat analogous to that which arises under the location of a mining claim, which can afterwards be amended when intervening rights have not accrued. The laws aid those who are vigilant, not those who sleep upon their rights. (7 Allen, 493; 2 Inst. 690.)

The engineer should be given the widest discretion under the law to make effective the mandate of the constitution that he shall have general supervision of the waters of the state and the officers connected with their distribution. The question of laches as to amended applications should be determined in the first instance by the State Engineer, and his discretion should not be disturbed unless it appears to have been grossly abused. (1 Weil on W. R., Sec. 419; 2 id., Sec. 750; 2 Kinney on Irr., pages 1282, 1283.) No judgment should have been directed, since the judgment below was based upon a motion at the close of the testimony which was granted without permitting the appellee to make any defense.

SCOTT, JUSTICE·

On May 14, 1908, an application under the provisions of Secs. 743, 744, Chap. 59, Comp. Stat., was filed in the office of the State Engineer on behalf of the plaintiff in error for a permit to construct a reservoir to be known as Lake Reservoir, for irrigation, stock water and domestic purposes, as recited therein. The application was examined by the State Engineer and that officer on May 18, 1908, returned it to the applicant for additional information. The instrument bears the following endorsement, to-wit:

"State Engineer's Office, State of Wyoming, ss.

"This instrument was received and filed for record on the 14th day of May, A. D. 1908, at 9 o'clock a. m.,

"(Signed)   CLARENCE T. JOHNSTON,
"State Engineer."

The application also has the following notation, to-wit: "Superseded by application No. 6 6/321, this being returned for correction. Witness my hand this 9th day of September, A. D. 1908.—Clarence T. Johnston, State Engineer." On June 30, 1908, another application for a permit to construct the Lake Reservoir in behalf of Laughlin was filed in the office of the State Engineer, and which application was designated by the Engineer as No. 6 6/321. The following certificate is endorsed thereon, viz: "This is to certify that I have examined the foregoing application and have returned the same without my approval for the following reasons: 'Application received on June 22nd, 1908, for administrator of the Carroll estate for same reservoir and site; permit issued therefor on this date.'

"Witness my hand this 7th day of July, A. D. 1908.

"CLARENCE T. JOHNSTON,
"State Engineer."

Laughlin appealed from the rejection of his application and the refusal of the Engineer to grant him a permit to construct said reservoir to the Board of Control, which board sustained the decision of the State Engineer, and thereafter Laughlin appealed from the decision of such board to the District Court of Albany County and upon trial the decision of the State Engineer was again affirmed and the appeal was dismissed and Laughlin brings the case here on error. In his letter of May 18, 1908, returning Laughlin's first application the State Engineer says: "We are returning herewith maps and application for the Lake Reservoir for additional information.

"It is proposed to fill this reservoir from the Little Laramie River. The ditch which fills the reservoir is not shown. If it is proposed to fill the reservoir through an existing ditch, such ditch should be enlarged for the purpose of filling the reservoir, and the written consent of the owners of the ditch must be filed in this office before the application can be approved. The outlet reservoir should be shown and the land on which the water is to be used should also be filed upon. If it is already filed upon the number of the permit or the description of the land should be given so that the reservoir can be tied in to the lands for which the water is to be used." That the State Engineer could before passing finally upon the application require additional information is expressly provided by statute.

A comparison of the applications filed in behalf of Laughlin, to-wit: the one filed on May 14, 1908, and the one filed June 30, 1908, show upon their face that they were filed in his behalf for permit to construct the same reservoir. The endorsement on the first of these applications which was made September 9, 1908, that it was superseded by the last application is not borne out by the facts. There is no pretense that Laughlin was acting in bad faith or intended to surrender any of his rights under his first application. On the contrary, the showing is that his second application was filed in response to the letter of the Engineer calling for additional information with reference to his first application.

Section 744, Chap. 59, Comp. Stat., is as follows:

"All applications under this chapter shall be subject to the provisions of Secs. 728 to 737 inclusive, and Secs. 825, 826, 827, which set forth the duties and authority of the State Engineer and provide for the protection of the rights of applicants; Provided, That an enumeration of any lands proposed to be irrigated under this chapter shall not be required in the primary permit. The party or parties proposing to apply to a beneficial use the water stored in any such reservoir shall file with the State Engineer an application for permit, to be known herein as the secondary permit, in compliance with the provisions of Secs. 727 to 737 inclusive. Said application shall refer to such reservoir for a supply of water and the State Engineer shall not approve the said application and issue secondary permit until the applicant thereunder shall show to such State Engineer by documentary evidence that he had entered into an agreement with the owners of the reservoir for a permanent and sufficient interest in said reservoir to impound enough water for the purposes set forth in said application. When beneficial use has been completed and perfected under the said secondary permit the Division Superintendent shall take the proof of the water user under such permit and the final certificate of appropriation shall refer to both the ditch described in the secondary permit and the reservoir described in the primary permit."

By Section 734 it is provided among other things that "Each application for permit to appropriate water for beneficial uses shall be accompanied by a map or plat in duplicate showing accurately the location and extent of the proposed work." Section 735 provides that "It shall be the duty of the State Engineer to examine these maps or plats and to ascertain if they agree with the description contained in the application, and when found to agree or made to agree, to approve the same, file one copy in his office and return the other approved to the party filing them." Section 737 in its present form has been in force ever since 1907 and provides, at least when the Engineer requires it, that * * * "The maps of all proposed reservoirs shall show the surface of the ground under water, and a sufficient number of lines of level shall be shown so that the contents of the reservoir or basin may be approximately determined. If the levels shall be shown by contour lines they shall be on a scale sufficiently large to show vertical levels not exceeding five feet, and with all such reservoir plans there shall be furnished a plan, on a scale of not less than one inch to four feet, showing the method of providing a wasteway for such reservoir or basin. If the State Engineer deems it necessary he may require the submission of complete plans and specifications for his approval. He may also require the filing of field notes of canal and reservoir surveys." In the application filed on behalf of Laughlin it is stated that the outlet of the proposed reservoir is located in the NE¼ of Section 31, Township 17 North, Range 74 West. Its description or that of the wasteway is by Section 737 to be shown by the plat accompanying and illustrating the proposed work. It will also be observed that the Engineer may require the submission of complete plans and specifications for his approval and the filing of field notes of the proposed reservoir. Such additional information is advisory and evidently so intended by the Legislature. The statute nowhere limits the time within which to furnish such additional information, though doubtless it ought to be furnished within a reasonable time. By Section 729 it is provided that "All applications which shall comply with the provisions of this chapter and with the regulations of the Engineer's office, shall be recorded in a suitable book kept for that purpose; and it shall be the duty of the State Engineer to approve all applications made in proper form, which contemplate the application of the water to a beneficial use and where the proposed use does not tend to impair the value of existing rights, or be otherwise detrimental to the public welfare. But where there is no unappropriated water in the proposed source of supply, or when the proposed use conflicts with existing rights, or threatens to prove detrimental to the public interest, it shall be the duty of the State Engineer to reject such application and refuse to issue the permit asked for." The words "when the proposed use conflicts with existing rights" mean rights which are prior in time to the use of the water. The requirement of a record of the application was evidently deemed necessary to preserve the right of appeal, and as it might have a material bearing if perfected upon the priorities of water rights from the same source of supply.

It was not necessary under the provisions of Sections 743 and 744 to set forth in the application or to show upon the map the land intended to be irrigated from the reservoir.

If the application complied in form and contained the requirements of the former section it was complete as a primary application to construct the reservoir and if the source of 'supply of water was sufficient and if the proposed use of the water would not conflict with the rights of prior appropriators or threaten to be detrimental to the public interest the applicant was entitled to a permit. (Sec. 729. id.) The information called for by the State Engineer's letter was not required by the statute to be stated in the application. As required by Section 743, it sets forth the applicant's name and postoffice address; the source of the water supply; the nature of the proposed use; the location and description of the proposed work; the time within which it is proposed to begin construction and the time required for the completion of the construction. It was not nor is it here claimed that the approval of the application would be detrimental to the public welfare nor was its refusal subsequently endorsed thereon placed upon that ground. The application measured up to the requirement of the statute, and was, therefore, entitled to be filed, as it was, and to be considered by the State Engineer. Conceding that such officer might require additional information before either approving or rejecting it, to enable him to properly guard the public interests, as provided by Section 731, he could not properly require as a condition to his approval that the land to be irrigated or reclaimed be shown, for the reason that the necessity of such a showing for the primary permit is dispensed with by the provisions of Section 744. above quoted. Nor would the fact that he required additional information under and within the authority conferred upon him by Section 731 disturb the priority of the application as of the date of its filing if any such information properly required should be furnished within a reasonable time; but upon the furnishing of such information within a reasonable time the application would be entitled to consideration and to be approved, if at all, with priority as of the date of its filing, and that right would not be lost or disturbed by the fact that the application of another party may have been filed in the meantime before the final action of the Engineer. It would not be proper, therefore, under such circumstances for the Engineer to reject the application merely upon the ground that a conflicting application had been afterwards filed by another party. As appears from the endorsement of the State Engineer, the application was not rejected because the information called for was not furnished, but solely on account of the subsequent application. The information seems to have been furnished in the form of another application, but since that was filed to comply with the requirement of the Engineer as to additional information, it should properly and in justice to the applicant be regarded as a part of the original application, adding information called for by the Engineer. Therefore, whatever right Laughlin had to a permit to construct the reservoir should have been determined with reference to the date of filing the original application. (Secs. 730, 750, id.)

The title to the proposed reservoir site, or the right of way for the supply ditch, or the written consent of the owners of a ditch already constructed to enlarge and use it for supplying the reservoir and the title to the land proposed to be irrigated were matters not required by the statute to be stated in this application. The application and permit-to construct the reservoir was the initial step and all other matters necessary in order to do so devolved upon the applicant within the time allowed to complete the work. (Sec. 732.) Title to the land embraced in the proposed reservoir site or right of way for the supply ditch were matters without the jurisdiction of the State Engineer or the Board of Control. The applicant assumed the burden of securing such title or easement as a part of the undertaking to construct the reservoir under the permit applied for and within the time to be fixed by the State Engineer for so doing. The application was not defective, nor does the Engineer's letter above set out so state. In that letter he expressly says: "We are returning herewith maps and application for the Lake Reservoir for additional information." The withholding of the permit for additional information with reference to an application which measured up to the requirements of the statute did not forfeit or postpone the right of the applicant which took effect as of the date of filing such application at least as above stated when such additional information was filed and we think it was so filed in this case within a reasonable time. Laughlin's application had neither been refused nor approved. There was no such endorsement made thereon when it was returned for additional information. He was not then in a position to appeal. It is provided by Sec. 733, id., that any applicant feeling himself aggrieved by the endorsement made by the State Engineer upon his application is given the right of appeal in the manner therein set forth. The statute, Sec. 730, id., contemplates either an endorsement of rejection or approval on the application and when made takes effect as of the date of its filing. There can be no other reasonable conclusion upon the facts and the statutes applicable thereto than that Laughlin's application was valid, entitled to record, and pending at the time of the filing of the application by the administrator of the Carroll estate, and for which latter application permit was granted; and that being so, Laughlin's first application will be regarded as duly recorded at the date of its filing and he was entitled to a prior right to the permit. His second application must be considered only as additional information with reference to his first application. We are of the opinion that the State Engineer, the Board of Control and the District Court of Albany County each erred in its and their judgment in not awarding to the plaintiff in error a permit in accordance with his application filed on May 14, 1908.

Involved in this proceeding are separate incidental applications in behalf of Laughlin for permits to construct a reservoir and to divert and appropriate waters of the state as follows, viz: (1) Application for permit to construct

the Laughlin Reservoir, filed for record in the office of the
State Engineer on June 26, 1908, and duly recorded; (2)
application for a permit to divert and appropriate flood waters of the Little Laramie River by means of the Laughlin
Inlet Ditch for filling the Laughlin and Lake Reservoirs,
filed and duly recorded in the office of the State Engineer
on June 26, 1908; (3) application for a permit to divert
and appropriate flood waters of the Little Laramie River
by means of the Lake Inlet Ditch for filling the Lake Reservoir, filed and duly recorded in the office of the State Engineer on June 26, 1908; (4) application to appropriate
flood waters of the Little Laramie River through Laughlin
and Lake Storage Reservoirs through and by means of
Lake Supply Ditch for irrigation purposes, duly filed in the
office of the State Engineer on June 26, 1908. There is no
endorsement of approval or non-approval upon any of these
applications. They all relate to impounding the flood waters
of the Little Laramie in the Laughlin and Lake Storage
Reservoirs with the exception of the fourth application,
which asks for a permit to apply the water to the irrigation
of certain lands described therein by conducting it to and
through the Laughlin and thence through the Lake Reservoir to such land, and depend upon the granting of a permit
for the Lake Reservoir, and these applications show that
they were a part of the same system.

The judgment is reversed and the case remanded to the
District Court of Albany County with direction to vacate
its judgment and to enter judgment awarding L. L. Laughlin, the plaintiff in error here and appellant there, the permit
applied for in his application filed May 14, 1908, and to
certify such judgment to the Board of Control and the
State Engineer with directions to vacate their ruling and to
cause the issuance of the permit to construct the Lake Reservoir in accordance with and as of the date of filing his
application for a permit, viz: May 14, 1908, and such of
the other permits applied for as would be proper in connec-

tion with such reservoir permit as and of the respective dates of filing in the office of the State Engineer.

Reversed.

BEARD, C. J., and POTTER, J., concur.

ON PETITION FOR REHEARING.

SCOTT, CHIEF JUSTICE.

The defendants in error have filed a petition for a rehearing. It is here urged as in their brief filed on the original hearing that Laughlin's application filed on May 14, 1908, was abandoned by him and superseded by his application filed on June 26, 1908. It was insisted on the former hearing and here that the last application being complete in form and not in words expressly referring to the former application must be construed as an original application independent of the former. It will be remembered that the first application, which we held sufficient in form under the statute, was received and filed for record in the office of the State Engineer, and then returned without approval or rejection to Laughlin with a request for additional information.

It is contended that an application such as this may be returned for correction or amendment, and will be allowed to be amended, provided that in the meantime no other valid application for a primary permit had intervened. The application of May 14, 1908, for the primary permit was not inherently defective. As said in the opinion filed, it "measured up to the requirement of the statute," and the Engineer called for no amendment. but for additional information with reference to the application. This was fully discussed and we need not here go over the question again.

It is contended that from May 14, 1908, to June 26, following, was an unreasonable time for Laughlin to take in order to furnish the information called for. It does not appear from the record that Laughlin expressly abandoned his first application or that he was guilty of laches in furnishing the information called for. On the contrary, considering the character of the information called for and furnished, we are unable to understand how such laches could be imputed to him as would work an abandonment or forfeiture of his first application, which was pending at the time the permit was granted to the administrator of the Carroll estate.

We are of the opinion that all of the questions presented in this application were discussed and decided in the original opinion and we adhere to the conclusion reached therein.

Rehearing denied.

POTTER and BEARD, JJ., concur.

COLLETT ET AL. v. MORGAN.
(No. 704.)

WATER AND WATER RIGHTS—APPROPRIATION—PRIORITY—ADJUDICATION—OWNERSHIP OF DITCH—BOARD OF CONTROL—JURISDICTION.

1. A desert entryman purchased in 1888 the right of way for and constructed an irrigating ditch, conducted water upon and reclaimed the land, filed a statement of appropriation of water through said ditch for said land, according to the law then in force, and also made final proof of the desert entry, but thereafter until 1897 only a small portion, if any, of the tract was irrigated. In 1901 a purchaser of the land irrigated and cultivated it by means of said ditch until 1906, when he sold to other parties, who were in possession and using the ditch and water for irrigating the land at the time of the hearing before the board of control for the purpose of adjudicating the various priorities of right to the use of water from the stream supplying said ditch. In the meantime other parties had applied to the state engineer for permits to appropriate water for other lands, without disclosing that the appropriation was intended to be made by means of the ditch aforesaid, one of said applicants having also obtained permission from the first purchaser of the ditch and the lands embraced in

said desert entry to use the said ditch and water when not used by the one granting the permission. *Held,* that, since the desert entryman, who had constructed the ditch and first appropriated the water, had complied with the law in force at the time, and reclaimed and cultivated the land, and purchased the right of way for and constructed the ditch, and the right to such water had not been declared forfeited, the grantees of the land, who were in possession of the ditch at least jointly with another party, and had been for years using it to irrigate their land, were entitled to a certificate of appropriation of water through the ditch in question, and it was error for the board of control, and the district court on appeal, to deny such certificate of appropriation.

2. In adjudicating the various priorities of rights to the use of water from a stream the board of control has no power to determine the disputed ownership or right to the use of a ditch through which appropriations are claimed to have been made by the contending parties, although, in granting a certificate of appropriation, it should appear that the party has the means of conducting the water from the source of supply to the place of application; the duties of the board of control are confined to the distribution of the waters of the state between the several appropriators, the granting of permits to use such waters for beneficial uses, to grant certificates therefor and the general supervision of such waters.

3. Where there is a dispute between two or more rival appropriators of water as to the ownership and right to the use of a ditch through which each party claims his appropriation to have been made, the question as to the ownership of the ditch cannot be finally settled by the board, but must be settled by the agreement of the parties or in a proper proceeding in a court of competent jurisdiction.

[Decided December 9, 1912.]   (128 Pac. 626.)
[Opinion modified and rehearing denied January 29,
     1913.]   (129 Pac. 433.)

ERROR to the District Court, Uinta County; HON. DAVID H. CRAIG, Judge.

The material facts are stated in the opinion.

T. S. Taliaferro, Jr., and *W. A. Muir,* for plaintiffs in error.

The property right of a ditch owner cannot be taken from him by any decree or order of the State Board of Control, nor can such owner be divested of his property in the ditch except in the manner provided by law and upon the payment of just compensation. The Board of Control has no jurisdiction to determine conflicting claims to the ownership of an irrigating ditch. (Hamp v. State, 118 Pac. 653; C. B. & Q. R. Co. v. McPhillamey, 118 Pac. 682.) The Board of Control specifically found that there had been no abandonment of the ditch on the part of Nina V. White or her successors in interest, the finding in that particular reciting that all of the parties had used the ditch in proportion to their respecive needs. It is clear that the board and court erred in denying a certificate of appropriation to the plaintiffs in error. Their right to use the ditch was clearly established, as well as the fact of the use of the water by them and their predecessors in interest.

J. H. Ryckman, for defendant in error.

No questions of law appear to be involved, and all the issues of fact were found by the Board of Control and by the District Court in favor of the defendant in error. The findings are sustained by abundant evidence, and ought not, therefore, to be disturbed by this court. There is no such thing as a water right without a ditch through which to conduct the water, and when the board found that the defendant in error had a water right, it follows that it also found that the water was diverted where the defendant in error claimed he had diverted it. While the board does not try and determine the title to lands or rights of way or easements, it does adjudicate water rights, and, therefore, must necessarily determine everything incidental thereto. The irrigation of the land of plaintiffs in error was not constant, but intermittent and spasmodic, and the board very properly found that they were not entitled to a water right

BEARD, CHIEF JUSTICE.

This case comes to this court from a decision of the District Court of Uinta County affirming the order and findings of the Board of Control in the following cases, viz: William Morgan, Sr., contestant, v. Sylvester Collett and T. K. Collett, contestees; William Morgan, Sr., contestant, v. Fred Roberts, contestee; and T. K. Collett, Sylvester Collett and Fred Roberts, contestants, v. William Morgan, Sr., contestee; and involving the adjudication of the rights of the appropriators of the waters of Bear River and its tributaries, made by said board December 21st, 1908. The facts out of which the several contests arose being substantially alike, they seem to have been considered together by the board and a single order made covering all of them, and were submitted on appeal to the District Court in the same way and are so submitted here. The evidence was taken before Pitt Covert, a superintendent of one of the water divisions of the state, and submitted in writing to the board and to the District Court. The facts as shown by the evidence are substantially as follows: In 1888 Nina V. White procured by purchase the right of way for and constructed the North Cokeville Ditch, which is the ditch in question in this case, and in the same year by means of said ditch conducted water upon and made final proof of her desert entry, consisting of the SE¼ of the SE¼ of Section 6, and the E½ of the NE¼ of Section 7, in Township 24 North of Range 119 West, in Uinta County. In the same year she filed in the office of the County Clerk of Uinta County her statement and claim of appropriation of water through and by means of said ditch for the irrigation of said lands, according to the law then in force. In the same year she conveyed to one Tanner one acre of said tract, which he irrigated from that time up to 1901, using said ditch for that purpose. In 1890, White gave Sylvester and T. K. Collett permission to use the ditch to irrigate lands lying north of the White lands. Little, if any, of the White tract, except the Tanner acre, was irrigated between 1888 or 1889 until about 1897, when one Stoner rented it, fenced it and used it for a pasture, using the ditch for watering his stock and at times turning water on a portion of it. It was so used by him for several years. In 1901, Kinney purchased the White tract, irrigated and cultivated it, using the ditch and the water therein for that purpose each year thereafter until 1906, when he sold to Sylvester and T. K. Collett and Fred Roberts, who were in possession and using the ditch and water for irrigating the land at the time of the hearing before the board. On August 26, 1904, Kinney filed an application in the office of the State Engineer for an appropriation of water for the irrigation of the White tract, which application was accompanied by letters stating that it was made to establish the right acquired or attempted to be acquired by White in 1888. The State Engineer, as stated in the findings of the board, held this application until November, 1908, "because of the complications in the ownership of the ditch," when he returned it to the engineer who had made the survey. In 1898 one Rowe made homestead entry on the W½ of the NE¼ and the SE¼ of the NW¼ of Section 7, Township 24 North, Range 119 West, and made application to the State Engineer for a permit for water to irrigate the same. This application did not disclose that it was identical with the North Cokeville Ditch. A permit was granted by the State Engineer; but Rowe never made proof of completion of the ditch or application of water to the land. He sold the land to Anderson in 1899. Anderson sold to Stoner in 1901, and Stoner sold to Wm. Morgan, Sr., in 1902. Some five or six acres of this tract was irrigated by means of the ditch in question in 1899. On June 4. 1904, Morgan, Sr., made an application for water for the Rowe tract, but without disclosing that the proposed ditch was in fact the North Cokeville Ditch. A permit was accordingly granted by the State Engineer. The evidence tends to show that in 1904, Morgan, Sr., got permission from Kinney to use the ditch and water when not used by Kinney. There is no evidence tending to show that

Rowe or any of his grantees ever purchased or acquired any interest in the ditch or the right of way for the same from White or any of her grantees, or that either of them had any right to use it except by express permission of White or her grantees or by their tacit consent, other than the attempted appropriation of it by Morgan, Sr., through his application for a permit made to the State Engineer and the granting of the same by that officer. The board further found "that the supply of Smith's Fork (the tributary of Bear River and the source of supply for the ditch aforesaid) being ample for all of these lands removes from this case any contest as to the division of the public waters of the state"; and "that the parties hereto have been using the North Cokeville, White, Morgan or Rowe Ditch jointly, alhough with some friction." The board granted a certificate of appropriation of water through said ditch to William Morgan, Sr., for his lands and denied Sylvester Collett, T. K. Collett and Fred Roberts the right to the use of any water for their respective tracts.

In so doing we think the board erred, and the District Court erred in affirming the order of the board. Nina V. White had complied with the law in force at the time she filed her statement and claim for a water right. The water had been applied to the land and the land reclaimed and cultivated thereby. Her right had never been declared forfeited nor had any attempt been made by any one or the state to do so. She had purchased the right of way for and had constructed the ditch. Her grantees, including the Colletts and Roberts, had been and were in possession of the ditch, at least jointly with Morgan, Sr., and were and had been for years using it to irrigate their lands. Why they should be denied a certificate of appropriation of water through the ditch in question, and Morgan, Sr., granted one, we are unable to see upon any principle of right or justice. The Board of Control had no power or authority to determine as between the parties the ownership or right to the use of the ditch. Its duties are confined to the distribution of the waters of the state between the several appropriators, the granting of permits to use the waters of the state for beneficial uses, to grant certificates therefor and the general supervision of such waters. Of course, in granting a certificate of appropriation, it should appear that the party has the means of conducting the water from the source of supply to the place of application. In the present case the parties were and for a number of years had been using the ditch jointly, each claiming the right to do so; and if that was considered by the board as sufficient to entitle one of them to a certificate of appropriation it was sufficient for each and all of them. There being a dispute between the parties as to the ownership and right to the use of the ditch, that question could not be finally settled by the board, but must be settled by the agreement of the parties or by a proper proceeding in a court of competent jurisdiction.

The judgment of the District Court is reversed and the case remanded with directions to set aside the decree heretofore entered in the case and to enter a decree establishing the respective rights of Sylvester Collett, T. K. Collett and Fred Roberts to the use of sufficient water to irrigate their respective parts of the White tract, not exceeding the ratio of one cubic foot of water per second of time for seventy acres. Said rights to have priority as of date July 18th, 1888, the date of the filing of Nina V. White's claim.

Reversed.

SCOTT and POTTER, JJ., concur.

ON PETITION FOR REHEARING.

BEARD, JUSTICE.

The defendant in error has filed a petition for a rehearing in this case, in which it is urged that the court erred in reversing the judgment of the District Court in toto, and that the effect of our decision is to deprive him of a water right. Such was not our intention; but we confess the language used in the opinion is subject to that construction. Counsel for plaintiffs in error did not contend, either in

his brief or oral argument, that defendant in error was not
entitled to an appropriation of water, but that the Board of
Control and the District Court erred in refusing certificates
of appropriation of water to plaintiffs in error for their
respective portions of the Nina V. White tract of land and
in determining that defendant in error was entitled to the
use of the ditch in question. We were of the opinion that
on the record presented the plaintiffs in error were entitled
to certificates of appropriation for sufficient water to irrigate their lands with date of priority as stated in the opinion
and that the Board of Control was without authority to
determine the ownership or right to the use of the ditch between the parties, and that on those questions—the only
ones urged in this court—the board erred and the District
Court erred in affirming the decision of the board, and to
that extent the judgment should be reversed. The writer
of that opinion, and of this, inadvertently failed to clearly
state the conclusions reached by the court. The last paragraph of the opinion is withdrawn and the following substituted therefor:

The judgment of the District Court is reversed in so far
as it attempts to determine the ownership or right to the use
of the ditch in question and in so far as it denies to plaintiffs in error appropriations of water; and the cause is remanded to the District Court with instructions to vacate
and set aside to that extent the judgment heretofore entered
and to enter judgment establishing the respective rights of
Sylvester Collett, T. K. Collett and Fred Roberts to the
use of sufficient water to irrigate their respective parts of
the Nina V. White tract of land, not exceeding one cubic
foot of water per second of time for seventy acres. Said
rights to have priority as of date July 18th, 1888, the date
of the filing of the Nina V. White claim therefor. The
rights of the parties in the ditch in question, whether as
owners or otherwise, being a question which the Board of
Control could not settle in this proceeding is not determined,
but is left to be settled by the agreement of the parties or

in a proper proceeding in a court of competent jurisdiction.
Plaintiffs in error will recover their costs in this court.

The opinion being thus modified, a rehearing is denied.

Former opinion modified and rehearing denied.

SCOTT, C. J., and POTTER, J., concur.

GUNNELL AND ELDER v. STATE.
(No. 650.)

JURY—IMPANELING JURY—EXHAUSTION OF STATUTORY METHOD—
OPEN VENIRE—QUASHING VENIRE—GROUNDS AND AFFIDAVIT—
CRIMINAL LAW—REFUSAL OF INSTRUCTIONS—REVIEW—NEWLY DIS-
COVERED EVIDENCE—NEW TRIAL—REVIEW.

1. When a jury is required and the statute makes no provision
   for procuring it, or where the statutory method has been
   exhausted leaving the jury incomplete, the court has the
   inherent power to cause an open venire to issue for the
   purpose of completing the jury.

2. Under the statutory provisions for procuring trial jurors
   (Chap. 80, Comp. Stat. 1910, Secs. 978-1021), jury box No.
   1 is not to be resorted to when boxes Nos. 4 and 3 have
   become exhausted in impaneling a jury in a particular
   case; the statute providing for resort to box No. 1 only
   for the purpose of completing the regular panel for the
   term or session of the court after box No. 3 has become
   exhausted.

3. Since the statute defining the qualifications of, and the
   method of procuring, trial jurors (Chap. 80, Comp. Stat.
   1910, Secs. 978-1021) makes no provision for any further
   drawing from the jury boxes after box No. 4 (containing
   the names of the regular panel for the term) and box No.
   3 have been exhausted, and, when that condition arises,
   does not provide the method of securing a jury in a particular case, the court, in such case, has the inherent power
   to order the issuance of an open venire to complete the
   jury for the case on trial.

4. Where the motion to quash a venire and set aside the jurors
   summoned thereunder by the sheriff did not charge as a
   ground that the sheriff was interested in the prosecution,

but the affidavit in support of the motion stated that the sheriff was very much interested in the prosecution and would be incompetent to serve as a juror on account of his bias and prejudice against the defendants, without stating what interest the sheriff had in the prosecution, or any facts showing bias or prejudice against the defendants or either of them, and it did not appear that the jurors who were finally selected to try the case were not fair and impartial, the motion was properly denied.

5. Refusal of requested instructions is not reviewable on error in the absence of any exception taken at the time to such refusal.

6. Where the instructions given appear to have fully and fairly stated the law of the case, and the evidence is not in the record, the refusal of requested instructions is not ground for reversal, since the court cannot say that they were applicable to the case.

7. Where the evidence is not in the record, the denial of a new trial on the ground of newly discovered evidence will not be ground for reversal on error, since the appellate court cannot determine whether the alleged newly discovered evidence would have been material or relevant, or merely cumulative, and since the rulings of the trial court must stand until error therein is made to appear.

[Decided December 21, 1912.]   (128 Pac. 512.)

ERROR to the District Court, Crook County; HON. CARROLL H. PARMELEE, Judge.

Merlyn J. Gunnell and Walter J. Elder were charged with the crime of murder in the first degree, and convicted of murder in the second degree. From the judgment entered upon the verdict they brought error. The material facts are stated in the opinion.

M. Nichols, for plaintiffs in error.

The court erred in issuing an open venire for the completion of the trial jury in the case against the objections of the defendants. The court should have ordered the drawing from the jury box containing the names of men qualified to serve as jurors. It was shown by the affidavit in support of the motion to quash the venire that the sheriff was interested in the prosecution of the defendants, and on that ground alone the motion to quash should have been sustained. The open venire is eliminated from the jury system of this state. (State v. Bolln, 70 Pac. 7.)

Although the evidence is not in the record, it sufficiently appears from the instructions given that the defendants were entitled to an instruction that before they could be convicted the jury must be satisfied of their guilt beyond a reasonable doubt; and it also appears that other refused instructions should have been given. (People v. Fuhs, 61 Cal. 527; Terr. v. Baca, 71 Pac. 460; State v. Harrison, 57 Pac. 647; State v. Mayo, 85 Pac. 251; Larrance v. People (Ill.), 78 N. E. 50.) The supplemental motion for new trial should have been granted upon the ground of the alleged newly discovered evidence. Where the effect of newly discovered evidence is doubtful or impossible to determine, a new trial should be granted. (State v. Kelleher, 87 Pac. 738.)

D. A. Preston, Attorney General, for the state.

The open venire was authorized by Section 1010, Comp. Stat. 1910, it being provided therein that if a sufficient number of jurors to try the issue is not obtained from the persons notified under an order to draw names from box No. 3, the court may make other and successive orders until a sufficient number is obtained. The order of the trial court for the open venire shows its necessity. While it is the theory of the statute that all the names of available jurors are in the jury box, it often happens that there are numerous citizens subject to jury duty whose names are not in the box. When no means are provided by statute for procuring a jury, or when the means provided have been exhausted, then the inherent power is in the court to resort to the common law method of issuing an open venire. (U. S. v. Clawson, 4 Utah, 34, 5 Pac. 689; Clawson v. U. S., 114 U. S. 477; Carter v. Territory, 3 Wyo. 193.) The case of State v. Bolln, cited by opposing counsel, presented a different question from that here involved. The very conditions exist in this case which were suggested in the Bolln case as necessary before an open venire could issue.

The affidavit in support of the motion to quash the venire merely states a conclusion of the affiant, without stating any facts showing bias or prejudice on the part of the sheriff. The sheriff is a public officer and is presumed to have properly performed his duty. (McLean v. Farmers &c., 98 Pac. 16; Terr. v. Sellers, 82 Pac. 575; Christ v. Fent, 84 Pac. 1074; Valley Tp. v. Bridge Co., 45 Pac. 560; Pentecost v. Stiles, 49 Pac. 921; Shepherd v. Mace, 82 Pac. 1046; Frost v. Comm'rs., 95 Pac. 289; McCaleb v. Dreyfus, 103 Pac. 924; Western U. Co. v. Los Angeles Co., 116 Pac. 564.)

The evidence not being in the record the court cannot pass upon the effect of the newly discovered evidence; it might be cumulative. The question of newly discovered evidence cannot be considered. (Clare v. State, 68 Ind. 17.) An exhaustive search of the record fails to disclose any instructions numbered in the manner mentioned in the brief of plaintiff in error. But in the absence of the evidence the refusal to give an instruction will not be reviewed. (12 Cyc. 872; Downing v. State, 11 Wyo. 86; Hill v. State, 43 Ala. 335; State v. Kern, 127 Ind. 465.)

BEARD, CHIEF JUSTICE.

The plaintiffs in error, Merlyn J. Gunnell, Walter Elder and Lewis Williams, were charged jointly on information filed in the District Court of Crook County with the crime of murder in the first degree. Upon the trial the jury returned its verdict finding Gunnell and Elder guilty of murder in the second degree, and Williams not guilty. Gunnell and Elder filed a motion for a new trial which was denied, judgment was entered against them, and they bring the case here on error.

The evidence is not brought up; and the rulings and decisions of the District Court complained of and presented in the brief of counsel for plaintiffs in error are: (1) That the court erred in the method of securing a jury to try the case; (2) that the court erred in refusing to give to the jury certain instructions requested by said defendants; and (3) that the court erred in not granting a new trial on account of newly discovered evidence. These assignments of error will be considered in the order above stated.

The provisions of the statute defining the qualifications of and the method of procuring trial jurors are contained in Chapter 80, Comp. Stat., and may be summarized as follows: The chairman of the County Commissioners, the County Treasurer and the County Clerk shall on the second Monday in January of each year select from the last assessment roll of the county, and make a list of the names and places of residence of all persons whom they believe to be competent and qualified to serve as trial jurors, and to certify such list to the clerk of the District Court. The clerk of the court shall write the names of those so selected on separate ballots and place them in a box known and marked "jury box number one." The persons so selected are known as regular jurors and serve for one year and until the next selection. The clerk shall also make duplicate ballots containing the names of those selected who reside within five miles of the city or town where the court is held, and place those ballots in "jury box number three." When a jury is required for a term or session of the court, the clerk, on order of the court or judge, shall draw from box No. 1 the requisite number to constitute the regular panel, which must be twenty-four or more as ordered, and those whose names are so drawn shall be summoned. If for any cause the requisite number to constitute the regular panel for that term or session of the court is not thus secured the clerk must draw from box No. 3 until the panel is completed or the ballots in that box exhausted. If the panel is still incomplete after drawing all the ballots from box No. 3, he shall then draw from box No. 1 to complete the regular panel. There are other provisions not necessary to be mentioned because not involved in the present case. When the regular panel is complete, the names of the persons constituting it shall be written on ballots and placed in "jury box number four." "When an issue of fact, to be tried by a jury is brought to trial the clerk under the direction of the court must openly draw out of the trial juror box numbered 'four' as many of the ballots, one after another, as are sufficient to form a jury." "If at any time during the trial of a cause and the empanelling of a jury therein all the regular panel of the jurors, that is, those contained in box number four, shall be exhausted, then the court shall make an order which shall be entered upon the minutes of the court, directing that such number of names as may be deemed necessary be drawn from box number three, in open court, and the clerk shall forthwith issue a summons for the persons so drawn to appear in court forthwith, and the names of such as are accepted by the court shall forthwith be placed in box number four, and shall be drawn therefrom to complete said list and such process shall continue from time to time when the names in box number four are exhausted, until a jury is obtained in the cause."

In the case at bar the record discloses that "it appearing to the court that not only the regular jury panel for the term, but also jury box number three is entirely exhausted, and it further appearing to the court that the trial jury for the said cause is still incomplete, and the court being now fully advised in the premises—it is hereby ordered that the clerk of this court forthwith issue an open venire, directed to the Sheriff of Crook County, Wyoming, therein commanding the said Sheriff to summon fifty true and lawful men from the body of the county to appear in this court at 4 p. m. of this day to complete the trial jury of said cause." The sole objections urged by counsel on this branch of the case are, that instead of directing an open venire to issue the court should have directed the clerk to draw the names of jurors to complete the jury from box number one, and that the sheriff was interested in the prosecution and was biased and prejudiced against the defendants. It will be observed that the statute provides that to complete the *regular* panel for the term or session of the court after box number three has become exhausted, resort is to be had to box number one; but such is not the case when boxes number four and three have become exhausted in impaneling a jury in a particular case. In such case the statute makes no provision for any further drawing from the jury boxes after boxes four and three have been exhausted; nor does it provide the method of securing a jury when such a condition arises. But we think it is well settled that, when a jury is required and the statute makes no provision for procuring it, or where the statutory method has been exhausted and the jury is still incomplete, the court possesses the inherent power to cause an open venire to issue for the purpose of completing the jury. It was directly so held in Carter v. Territory, 3 Wyo. 193, 18 Pac. 750, 19 Pac. 443, and Clawson v. U. S., 114 U. S. 477, 5 Sup. Ct. 949, 29 L. Ed. 179. Counsel for plaintiffs in error cites State v. Bolln et al., 10 Wyo. 439, 70 Pac. 1, as sustaining his contention that the open venire is eliminated from the system in this state. In that case the court said: "Under the method prescribed, an open venire to complete a trial jury can never issue until not only the panel for the term, but also jury box number three is entirely exhausted. And it would seem that, for completing the panel for the term, an open venire can never issue under any circumstances; for the first four boxes are intended to contain the names of all the qualified jurors of the county. From these boxes the regular panel when incomplete is, at all times, to be filled, and the open venire is thus eliminated from the system." Clearly, when the court used the last expression quoted it was speaking only of the method of securing the regular panel for the term; and by the other language used as clearly indicated that an open venire should issue to complete a jury in a particular case when jury boxes four and three were exhausted; and we so hold. It is further urged that the motion to quash the venire and set aside the jurors summoned thereunder should have been granted on account of the interest of the sheriff in the prosecution. The original motion is in the record, and an examination of it discloses that no such ground is stated therein. It is true that an affidavit in support of the motion and attached to it states that the sheriff is very much interested in the prosecution and would be incompetent to serve as a juror on account of his bias and prejudice against the defendants. But if the affidavit could be considered as presenting a question not presented by the motion, it does not state what interest the sheriff had in the prosecution, or any facts showing bias or prejudice against the defendants or either of them; nor does it appear that the jurors who were finally selected to try the case were not fair and impartial jurors.

With respect to the contention that the court erred in refusing to instruct the jury as requested by defendants, we have to say, that we have searched the record in vain for any exception taken at the time to the refusal of the court to so instruct. We have, however, considered the instructions given, which are quite lengthy and appear (in the absence of the evidence) to fully and fairly state the law of the case. The substance of many of the instructions refused was embodied in those given, and of the others we cannot say that they were applicable to the evidence, not having it before us. The same may be said with respect to the newly discovered evidence. Without knowing what evidence was produced on the trial, we cannot determine whether or not the newly discovered evidence would have been material or relevant, or whether merely cumulative. Much of it seems to be in the nature of impeaching testimony only. The trial court having heard all of the evidence could judge of these matters, and until error in its rulings is made to appear they must stand. We find no prejudicial error in the record and the judgment of the District Court, therefore, is affirmed.   *Affirmed.*

SCOTT and POTTER, JJ., concur.

DEAN v. OMAHA-WYOMING OIL COMPANY.
(No. 681.)

MINES AND MINERALS—MINING CLAIMS—OIL PLACER CLAIMS—
LOCATION—DISCOVERY—ADVERSE CLAIM—BURDEN OF PROOF—SUF-
FICIENCY OF EVIDENCE—LOCATION CERTIFICATES—AMENDED CER-
TIFICATE—RIGHT OF SUCCESSOR IN INTEREST TO FILE—ADVERSE
SUIT—EVIDENCE—PROOF OF CITIZENSHIP—APPEAL AND ERROR—
QUESTIONS NOT RAISED AT TRIAL.

1. An essential requirement of a valid location of a mining claim is that there shall be a discovery of mineral upon the ground.

2. In an adverse suit contesting the right to patent for an oil placer mining claim covering the northeast quarter of a certain section, where the defendant claimed discovery on said quarter section by a well alleged to have been sunk on the dividing line between said quarter section and the southeast quarter of the same section, Held, that the evidence of the county surveyor, who made a survey of the property after defendant's well had been sunk, tending to show that the stone marking the quarter corner on the west boundary of the section had been moved several feet south of its original location, and that said well by the government survey was several feet south of and off said northeast quarter of the section, was sufficient to support a finding in favor of plaintiff to the effect that defendant's discovery was not made within the boundaries of his claim.

3. A discovery for the purposes of location of a mining claim must be within the limits of the claim sought to be located.

4. While discovery of mineral is supposed to chronologically precede the acts locating a mining claim, such discovery may follow, instead of preceding, the acts of location, and will be good as against all who have not acquired intervening rights.

5. In an adverse suit contesting the right to patent to an oil placer mining claim, whether or not defendant had made a discovery of oil within the limits of the claim was a question of fact, and the burden of proving such discovery was upon the defendant.

6. The evidence in an adverse suit held insufficient to show discovery by defendant, where the trial court had found against him upon that issue, since it did not establish the fact that oil was found in the well sunk by defendant to

the depth of 52 feet, or, if oil was found, that it was sufficient in quantity to constitute a discovery, instead of being mere seepage; there being a substantial conflict in the evidence as to the character of the substance found in the well.

7. In an adverse suit, where it was claimed that defendant had not made a sufficient discovery, the question of the sufficiency of his discovery of mineral within the limits of the claim was for the trial court, and the evidence *held* sufficient to support a finding that discovery had not been made.

8. Where, in an adverse mining suit, the trial court found upon sufficient evidence that the defendant had not made a discovery within the limits of the claim, the defendant was not entitled to affirmative relief establishing in him the right of possession to the land in dispute.

9. Where the defendant in an adverse mining suit had made no discovery, *Held,* that he had acquired no intervening right which would prevent the plaintiff from filing an amended or additional certificate to the original location certificate of his claim.

10. The original location certificate of a mining claim and an amended certificate, if one be filed, must be construed together, and, if sufficient when so construed, the location record will be valid, although neither standing alone would be sufficient.

11. One who has succeeded to the interest of the original locators of a mining claim is permitted under Section 3459, Compiled Statutes, 1910, upon making discovery, to amend or file an additional certificate to show the date of discovery, and, having done so, will be entitled to the right of possession, where such amendment has not infringed upon rights of others existing at the time thereof.

12. Where an oil placer mining claim when originally located was properly staked and named, and otherwise properly located, except that there was no discovery, and afterwards upon making discovery, an additional certificate of location was filed stating the date of discovery, *Held*, that it was not necessary before filing the amended certificate to restake and again name the claim.

13. In an adverse mining suit, where the defendant, who was the applicant for patent, has not shown a discovery sufficient to entitle him to the right of possession, the fact that there was no proof of the citizenship of the original

locators of the plaintiff's claim did not entitle the defendant to affirmative relief.

14. A recorded certificate of a mining location is prima facie proof of the facts therein contained, in an adverse proceeding, as well as proof of compliance with the law in making the record, and the date thereof.

15. When the citizenship of the locator or locators of a mining claim is in issue in an adverse mining suit, it should be proven as any other fact in the case, and may be established by the affidavit of the party or a duly authorized agent.

16. The recital in the certificate of location of a mining claim to the effect that the original locators were each citizens of the United States and over the age of 21 years, together with other facts, may raise a presumption of such citizenship.

17. In an adverse mining suit the affidavit of plaintiff's agent to an additional certificate, which was filed after discovery to complete the record of plaintiff's claim, stated that the original locators of the claim were each citizens of the United States, and said affidavit was received in evidence without objection. *Held,* that said affidavit, in connection with the original and additional certificate, was prima facie proof of the citizenship of the original locators; the original and additional certificates together with said affidavit being the only evidence on the subject of said citizenship, and no objection having been made in the trial court that said locators were not citizens or that the fact of their citizenship was not shown.

18. In an action in support of an adverse mining claim the objection cannot be raised for the first time on appeal that the citizenship of the original locators under whom plaintiff claimed was not shown.

ON PETITION FOR REHEARING.

19. A petition for rehearing not filed within thirty days after the decision was rendered, as required by a rule of the Supreme Court, is not properly before the court for consideration; such rule having the force of a statutory enactment.

[Decided January 7, 1913.]   (128 Pac. 881.)
[Rehearing denied February 17, 1913.]   (129 Pac. 1023.)

ERROR to the District Court, Uinta County; HON. CHARLES E. CARPENTER, Judge.

This was an action brought in support of an adverse mining claim by the Omaha-Wyoming Oil Company, a corporation, against Charles W. Dean. From a judgment in favor of the plaintiff the defendant brought error. The material facts are stated in the opinion.

P. W. Spaulding and *S. T. Corn,* for plaintiff in error.

The only evidence in favor of the location under which the plaintiff below claimed was a location notice filed with the County Clerk May 18, 1901, to the effect that the ground had been located April 1, 1901. There is no proof of discovery of oil, the posting of notice, or the marking of the boundaries at any time, or of the citizenship of the locators. Nor does the location notice give the name of the claim "designating it as a placer claim" as required by statute. (Comp. Stat. 1910, Sec. 3474.) There was proof of certain so-called assessment work for the years 1902, 1903 and 1904 done on behalf of the plaintiff and its predecessors in interest, and for the year 1905 by plaintiff's lessee, but that proof is insufficient upon which to found a title or right to possession. The only possession of the plaintiff was for the purpose of doing the so-called assessment work. Defendant's title is based upon a location made October 23, 1903, and recorded January 4, 1904. He and his predecessors in interest were in possession of the ground during July, 1903, located and erected a rig thereon during August, 1903, began drilling October 8, 1903, and discovered oil on the claim on October 23, whereupon notice was posted and the claim located and staked as required by law. The discovery of oil was substantial and lasting. This well was drilled upon the boundary line between the defendant's two placer claims in a perpendicular direction downward, and was equally upon the claim embracing the land in controversy as well as the claim embracing the southeast quarter of the section, but a greater portion of the buildings and improvements were upon the land in controversy. A question having arisen in the mind of the defendant as to this division line well after plaintiff had begun operations upon the land, but before they were carried to any effect, the defendant caused a 52-foot discovery well to be drilled at another place on the land in December, 1905, and thereby again discovered oil.

That assessment work upon a mining claim without actual discovery or actual possession with diligent prosecution of the work towards a discovery is insufficient upon which to found title or right of possession is well settled. (Whiting v. Straup, 95 Pac. 855; McLemore v. Express Oil Co., 112 Pac. 59.) The requirement that the boundaries of the claim be marked upon the ground is mandatory. (Comp. Stat. 1910, Sec. 3474; 2 Lindley on Mines, Secs. 371-373.) Recording of the location notice and proof of that fact is proof only of such recording, names of the locators and the name and extent of the claim. (2 Lindley on Mines, Sec. 392.) The notice is not evidence of a discovery. (Berquist v. Copper Co., 106 Pac. 680.)

The evidence shows that several discoveries of oil were made in the well drilled on the division line between the two claims, and upon making one of such discoveries the location of the claim was completed by compliance with the statutory requirements. There can be no question of the right of the locator to apply either discovery in the well to either claim. The discovery was of sufficient extent to embrace both claims, since a portion of the well was upon each claim. The situation is analogous to a tunnel location, where there may be a discovery of as many lodes or veins as are found or cut in the tunnel. In adverse mining suits nothing is presumed, but all facts necessary to show a valid location must be proven and found by the court, for the reason that the findings and judgment are made by statute the foundation of the right to patent in the land office. The plaintiff failed to prove the facts essential to its right of possession, and the finding of the court in its favor was erroneous.

(On petition for rehearing.) The trial court found that oil was discovered as claimed in the defendant's well, though it found that the year of such discovery was 1905

instead of 1903. But it did find that these discoveries were
six months prior to the first discovery of the defendant in
error. This court, in its opinion, holds that the finding of
the trial court was sustained by evidence that defendant's
discoveries were not on the claim. That was not, however,
the finding of the lower court. On the contrary it was
found that the well was on the dividing line. This court
should have decided the question whether the discovery of
oil in a well upon a dividing line between two claims, and
partly in both claims, was sufficient upon which to base a
location, and a rehearing is asked upon the ground that the
court was evidently led into a mistake as to the grounds of
the decision below. The questions considered and decided
by the lower court were whether the defendant's location
was initiated by a trespass and therefore invalid, and
whether a discovery in a well upon the dividing line between
the two claims was sufficient to validate the defendant's
location of the claim in controversy.

B. M. Ausherman, for defendant in error.

The legal presumption in a case of this character is that
the findings and decree of the lower court are correct, and
they should not be disturbed or modified by the appellate
court unless it appears that an obvious error was committed
in applying the law, or some serious or important mistake in
the consideration of the evidence. (Warren v. Burt, 58
Fed. 101; Loan Co. v. McClure, 78 Fed. 209; North Am.
Expl. Co. v. Adams, 104 Fed. 404; Ins. Co. v. Wright, 126
Fed. 82; Development Co. v. Mitchell, 138 Fed. 285; Tilghman v. Proctor, 125 U. S. 136; 129 U. S. 512; 145 U. S.
132.) Under the statutes of this state there is no authority
for recording a copy of a location notice unless it is verified.
The location notice filed by the defendant and predecessor
were not verified or acknowledged so as to be entitled to
record. The evidence shows but one valid certificate of
location and that is the location of the claim of the plaintiff,
defendant in error here. Discovery of mineral is necessary
to a valid location. The first and only discovery of oil on

the ground in controversy was made on behalf of the "Aboriginal" claim June 28, 1906. The evidence of any alleged prior discoveries was not sufficient to establish such a discovery as the law requires. (Oil Co. v. Oil Co., 98 Fed. 673; Sharkey v. Candiani, 7 L. R. A. (N. S.) 763; Whiting v. Straup, 95 Pac. 849.) This case was decided by the trial court in accordance with the principles announced by this court in Whiting v. Straup. A location notice may refer to sub-divisions of the United States survey for the boundaries of the claim, although such a survey has never been approved. (Sharkey v. Candiani, supra; Gird v. Oil Co., 60 Fed. 531.) It is not essential that the location notice or the certificate contain any description of the stakes or other markings of boundary. The affidavit of C. A. Dorn, in connection with the certificate of location and proof for patent, admitted without objection, shows not only the United States survey of the claim, but states that substantial posts were in place at the time of posting and discovery.

Upon the evidence it is clear that no discovery was made in defendant's 52-foot well. The defendant having elected to apply the oil when first discovered in the well supposed to be on the dividing line between his two claims to the claim embracing the southeast quarter of the section, the claim embracing the ground in controversy is left without any discovery. (Phillips v. Brill, 95 Pac. 856.) But from the testimony of the County Surveyor it appears that the well was not located on the dividing line between the two quarter sections, but was altogether on the southeast quarter of the section. The only proof upon the trial as to citizenship of the locators was by way of affidavits with proper verifications, filed in the contest commenced in the United States Land Office. These papers with the adverse claim showing that the locators were and are citizens have become, without objection of counsel, a part of the evidence in the case, and is sufficient under the circumstances to show citizenship. (Lindley on Mines, Sec. 227.) The location of defendant in error was made in good faith, and it was in possession and prosecuting with due diligence its work towards discovery, and it was therefore fully protected by law against all forms of forcible, fraudulent, surreptitious, or clandestine entries and intrusions upon his possession. (Miller v. Chrisman, 73 Pac. 1083; Whiting v. Straup, supra.)

SCOTT, CHIEF JUSTICE.

On May 5, 1906, the plaintiff in error, defendant below, filed his application in the U. S. Land Office at Evanston, Wyoming, for a patent to a mineral claim known as the Goodwill No. 2 oil placer mining claim, embracing the NE¼ of Section 12, Township 15 North, of Range 118 West, inclusive of improvements thereon. On July 3, 1906, and within the 60-day period of publication of notice of the application the defendant in error, plaintiff below, duly filed its protest and adverse claim to the land embraced in the application, whereupon further proceedings in such land office were stayed to await the determination of a court of competent jurisdiction of the right of possession to said described lands and premises, and thereupon this action was commenced.

The plaintiff by its petition claims title subject only to the paramount title of the United States to the land in controversy by discovery of petroleum thereon and location thereof as the "Aboriginal" mining claim on April 1, 1901, by and through mesne conveyances from such locators and its predecessors in interest and by keeping up the annual assessment work of $100 thereon each year since such discovery and location. It also alleges that it and its lessee on June 28, 1906, made a further and additional discovery of petroleum on said claim and by virtue of this discovery notice was properly posted and an additional certificate of such location was on July 3, 1906, filed for record in the office of the County Clerk and Ex-Officio Register of Deeds of the County of Uinta, that being the county wherein the land is situated, as a further compliance with the mining laws of the United States and of the State of Wyoming. The defendant by his answer puts the averments of the petition in issue in so far as they affect plaintiff's right of possession and claims adversely the right of possession subject only to the paramount title of the United States by reason of the alleged location on October 23, 1903, by his predecessors in interest upon a discovery of petroleum thereon on or prior to said date, properly staking the ground and recording a certificate of location of the "Goodwill No. 2" mining claim, and the performance each year thereafter of the required annual assessment labor thereon. He also alleges that he and his predecessors in interest on December 23, 1905, made a further and additional discovery of petroleum on the said "Goodwill No. 2" mining claim and by virtue of such additional discovery properly posted a notice thereof on the claim and on January 3, 1906, filed a further and additional certificate of such location in the office of the County Clerk and Ex-Officio Register of Deeds of Uinta County. The plaintiff replied putting in issue the new matter alleged in the answer. The case was tried to the court without a jury and the court found generally against the defendant and in favor of and gave judgment for the plaintiff, defendant in error here, awarding it the possession of the land in dispute and that it was entitled to a patent for the Aboriginal oil placer mining claim. Motion for a new trial was made, which the court overruled, and the defendant brings the case here on error.

It is assigned as error that the finding and judgment are not supported by the evidence. It is conceded by the defendant in error in its brief that at the time of locating the Aboriginal claim, to-wit: on April 1, 1901, the land embraced therein was unoccupied public land of the United States and that no discovery of oil had been made on the claim, nor was any made until June 28, 1906, upon drilling to a depth of 468 feet. On July 2, 1906, the original notice of location of the Aboriginal claim was re-posted on the derrick over this well containing these additional words: "Further and additional discovery of petroleum, made June 28, 1906, on claim above described, by the Chicago-Wyoming Oil Corporation, Lessee." On July 3, 1906, an additional certificate of location, subscribed and sworn to by Carroll A. Dorn, setting forth that substantial posts were in position marking the boundary of said claim, giving the date of discovery, the name of the claim, the names of the original locators, the date of location, that said locators are and were citizens of the United States, the number of acres and legal description of the claim, was filed and recorded in the office of the County Clerk.

The defendant in error claimed the right of possession by mesne conveyances from the original locators of the Aboriginal claim and as such the right to file the additional or amended location certificate to the original location certificate of that claim.

One of the essential requirements of a valid location of a mining claim is that there shall be a discovery of mineral upon the ground. (Sec. 3474, Comp. Stat.; Columbia Min. Co. v. Duchess Min. Co., 13 Wyo. 244, 79 Pac. 385; 27 Cyc. 555.) It is here conceded and the evidence shows that there was no discovery of petroleum upon the land in controversy under the Aboriginal location until June 28, 1906. The plaintiff in error claims prior discovery and location of the claim as the Goodwill No. 2 by Charles O. Richardson et al., his predecessors in interest. He contends that he made a valid discovery of oil on October 23, 1903, by drilling a well which we here designate as Well No. 1 on the boundary line between this claim and an adjoining claim on the south, such line bisecting the well so drilled, and making several discoveries of oil therein, one at the depth of 498 feet, which he selected as the discovery to validate the claim for the southeast quarter of the section, while another and separate discovery of oil on October 23, 1903, in the same well at the depth of 560 feet was selected to validate the claim here in question known as the "Goodwill No. 2," recorded January 4, 1904.

The exact location of this well was in dispute. The evidence of the County Surveyor, who made a survey of the property on December 2, 1905, after the well was sunk, tends to show that the quarter corner on the west boundary of Section 12 had been moved 22.6 feet south of where it had been originally established by the United States official survey, and that this well by such government survey was 11 feet south of and off of the northeast quarter of the section. The court's finding was in favor of the plaintiff and this evidence supports such finding to the effect that such discovery was not made within the boundaries of the Goodwill No. 2 and upon the land here in controversy. A discovery for the purposes of the location of a mining claim must be within the limits of the claim sought to be located. (27 Cyc. 557.) That being the law, and the discovery not being on or within the limits of the claim, rendered the location based thereon void. (Nevada Sierra Oil Co. v. Miller (C. C.), 97 Fed. 681, 688.) The question of the rights which would obtain by reason of discovery on the dividing line between two mining claims or as to whether different discoveries in such well could be accredited to the different claims as here attempted to be done is not in view of the finding presented by this record.

The plaintiff in error concedes that the defendant in error made discovery of oil on the Aboriginal oil placer mining location and within its limits on June 28, 1906, but claims a second prior discovery on December 23, 1905, in a well which he sunk within the area in dispute on the Goodwill No. 2 to the depth of 52 feet and discovery of oil therein. As to whether or not discovery of oil was made in this well was a question of fact and the burden of proving it was upon the defendant (Costigan on Mining Law, 161; Sands v. Cruikshank, 15 S. D. 142, 87 N. W. 589), and while it may be said that discovery should chronologically precede the acts of location it may follow instead of preceding such acts, and will be held good as against all who have not acquired intervening rights. (Costigan on Min. Law, p. 160; Beals v. Cone, 27 Colo. 473, 62 Pac. 948, 83 Am. St. Rep. 92; Ervin v. Perigo, 93 Fed. 608, 35 C. C. A. 482; Lindley on Mines, Sec. 330.) It is undisputed that the well was sunk about 25 feet north of Well No. 1 heretofore referred to and on the land in controversy. It is contended by the plaintiff in error that the evidence is insufficient to support the finding adversely to his contention that the alleged discovery was sufficient to validate the location of the Goodwill No. 2. Youngburg, a witness for defendant, testified as follows:

"Q. In drilling this 52-foot hole did you speak about finding a two-foot shale?

"A. I don't know whether it was shale or sand rock. I couldn't say which.

"Q. At what depth was this?

"A. About 38 feet.

"Q. About what time in the afternoon was it you struck this?

"A. In the morning, about half-past eight.

"Q. And when did you find oil?

"A. At four o'clock.

"Q. And was this after you were through the shale?

"A. Yes.

"Q. And were you then drilling through the shale, did you say up to the time you found the oil?

"A. Yes.

"Q. And the oil was found beneath the shale?

"A. Yes.

"By the court:

"Q. What quantity of oil did you find there?

"A. We found the quantity that we could see on water.

"Q. Did you find it in such quantity that you could bail some of it out?

"A. No, we couldn't exactly bail it. We bailed the water used for drilling and in that was mixed the oil.

"Q. Then the only evidence of oil you had in the 52-foot well was the oil you saw on the water that you bailed out of the well?

"A. Yes, during the drilling.

"Mr. Ausherman.

"Q. Are you sure, Mr. Youngberg, that this was not the usual soapy substance that came from shale?

"A. I think it was not.

"Q. Do you know?

"A. Well, I couldn't state that."

This evidence did not establish the fact that there was oil found in this well, or if found that it was sufficient in quantity to constitute a discovery or was more than a mere seepage. It was found at a depth of 41 feet after drilling through a three-foot layer of shale and the well was bored to a depth of 52 feet or 11 feet beyond where the alleged oil was found. This witness could not say that it was the usual soapy substance that came with the shale or not. Another of defendant's witnesses testified practically the same and also that he was unable to swear whether it was oil or a soapy substance from shale that is found in that country. A number of other witnesses were sworn and testified for the defendant to the effect that it was oil. L. E. Nebergall, a witness for the plaintiff, testified that he had been engaged in drilling oil wells in different localities for 20 years, and that he had drilled wells in the vicinity of the NE¼ of Section 12, Township 15 North, Range 118 West, and had finished drilling the Jager oil well for the owners in the SW¼ of that section, and that from his experience and knowledge of that field the formation at that locality was not such as to disclose a finding of oil of any kind at a depth of from 60 to 100 feet and that there was no finding of oil made in well No. 1 referred to at the depth of 50 or 60 feet, as had been testified to, and that from his knowledge gained from drilling in that vicinity the first oil sand was and is at a depth of over 400 feet. That in the drilling of the Jager well on the SW¼ of said section he had taken

charge after it had been sunk 1,000 feet, and that he bailed
the first oil that ever came out of that well; that the crew
before he took charge got what they thought to be oil, but it
was shale oil, which is not oil and which is "an indication
that would sour a man to go ahead and look further." One
Petrie was sworn as a witness on behalf of the plaintiff and
testified that he had followed the oil business for 17 or 18
years and for the last three years in the Spring Valley oil
field, in which is situated the property here in controversy.
He testified from his experience that the formation he found
there contained no oil at a depth less than 60 to 100 feet.
Being asked at what depth it was found, he answered: "I
never found oil under 468 feet—that is as close to the top,
but they had shale—a shale grease, which looks quite a bit
like oil. Q. And did you find such conditions in the Spring
Valley field? Ans. Every hole I have worked on there was
shale. People who would come in the rig would say, 'You
have struck oil.' We would say, 'Not in paying quantities;
we will still go on down.' Q. And it would be nothing but
shale grease? Ans. That is all. Q. Is this shale grease
an indication of oil? Ans. No, sir."

In Nevada Sierra Oil Company v. Home Oil Company
(C.C.), 98 Fed. 673, a discovery of oil was in question and
the court said: "Mere indications, however strong, are not,
in my opinion, sufficient to answer the requirements of the
statute, which requires, as one of the essential conditions to
the making of a valid location of unappropriated public
land of the United States under the mining laws, a discovery
of mineral within the limits of the claim. Indications of the
existence of a thing is not the thing itself." It will be observed in the case here that there was a substantial conflict
in the evidence as to the character of the substance found in
the well. On the one side it was claimed to be oil, and on
the other that it was not oil, but a substance known and
denominated as shale grease. Upon this state of the evidence we can not say that the court erred in finding against
the defendant on the issue of discovery. The question of

the sufficiency of this discovery was for the trial court and there was sufficient evidence to support the finding of the court. This we think disposes of any claim of the defendant to affirmative relief establishing in him the right of possession to the land in dispute. He had acquired no intervening right which would prevent the plaintiff from filing an amended or additional certificate to the original location certificate of the Aboriginal mining claim. "The original certificate and the amendment must be construed together, and if sufficient when so construed the location record will be valid, although neither standing alone would be sufficient." (27 Cyc. 575; Duncan v. Fulton, 15 Colo. App. 140, 61 Pac. 244.) It is provided by Sec. 3459, Comp. Stat. 1910, that "Whenever it shall be apprehended by the locator, or his assigns, of any mining claims or property heretofore or hereafter located, that his or their original location certificate was defective, erroneous, or that the requirements of the law had not been complied with before the filing thereof, or shall be desirous of changing the surface boundaries of his or their original claim or location, or of taking in any part of an overlapping claim or location which has been abandoned, or in case the original certificate was made prior to March 6, 1888, and he or they shall be desirous of securing the benefit of this law, such locator or locators, or his or their assigns, may file an additional location certificate in compliance with and subject to the provisions of this chapter; Provided, however, That such re-location shall not infringe upon the rights of others existing at the time of such re-location, and that no such re-location, or other record thereof, shall preclude the claimant or claimants from proving any such title or titles as he or they may have held under any previous location." (Slothower v. Hunter, 15 Wyo. 189, 88 Pac. 36.)

The plaintiff succeeded to the interest of the original locators and upon the facts were privileged under this section upon making discovery on June 28, 1906, to amend or file an additional certificate to show the date of discovery and having done so secured the right of possession as such amendment did not, as already stated, infringe on the rights of the defendant. (27 Cyc. 550, 575; Sec. 354, 1 Snyder on Mines.)

It is urged that the amendment was not preceded by re-staking the claim, nor giving it a name. This was not necessary. (Sec. 399, Snyder on Mines.) There is evidence in the record tending to show that the claim when originally located was properly staked and named, and otherwise properly located, except that there was no discovery, and when discovery was afterward made an addition to the original certificate of location was filed. The original certificate gave the name and taking the original and additional certificate together the date of discovery was given and the claim was properly identified by name, staking, posting of notice and referred to by legal sub-division.

It is here urged that there is or was no proof of the citizenship of the original locators of the "Aboriginal" through which by mesne conveyances the company coupled with its discovery on June 28, 1906, claimed title, and that for that reason there is a failure of proof for which a new trial should have been granted. If this contention be correct it would not upon the facts entitle the defendant or applicant for the patent to affirmative relief. (Sherlock v. Leighton, 9 Wyo. 297, 309, 63 Pac. 580, 934.) In that case this court said: "Proof of citizenship in an adverse suit is required only to enable a party to recover judgment in his own favor." * * * "The absence of such proof may prevent a recovery by the one party, but it does not operate to authorize a judgment, for that reason alone, in favor of his adversary."

Upon the trial of the case there was admitted in evidence without objection the original and amendment or additional location certificate of the Aboriginal oil placer mining claim, and which latter was based upon the discovery made June 28, 1906. The first or original location certificate is recited in the additional certificate and gives the individual names of the locators followed by these words, "each being a citizen of the United States, over the age of twenty-one years." To this certificate is attached the following affidavit, viz: "The State of Wyoming, County of Uinta, ss. Carroll A. Dorn being duly sworn deposes and says that he has read the above and foregoing certificate of location; that he knows the contents thereof and that the same are true." (Signed) Carroll A. Dorn, and followed by the certificate of the notary before whom the oath was taken.

We know of no statute requiring such affidavit to give validity or to entitle an original certificate or an amendment or addition thereto to be recorded. We are, however, of the opinion that the recorded certificate of a location is prima facie proof of the facts therein contained in an adverse proceeding as well as proof of the compliance of the law in making the record and the date thereof. (Sec. 227, Lindley on Mines.) When citizenship is in issue it should be proven as any other fact in the case, id., and may be established by the affidavit of the party or a duly authorized agent. (Sec. 2321, R. S., U. S.; U. S. Comp. St. 1901, p. 1425.) The recital in the certificate to the effect that the original locators were each citizens of the United States and over the age of twenty-one years coupled with other facts might raise a presumption of such citizenship. The Supreme Court of Arizona said in Jantzen v. Arizona C. Co., 3 Ariz. 6, 7, 20 Pac. 93, 94: "It will be presumed that a man being a resident of the United States, and who has made a mining location, was a citizen of the United States, * * * when it appears that he recorded near the time a location reciting these facts. Such evidence will make out a prima facie case." In the case here Dorn's affidavit to the additional certificate, supra, though not required by the statute, was to the effect that the original locators of the Aboriginal oil placer claim were each citizens of the United States. He was plaintiff's agent and his affidavit was made in its behalf and introduced and received in evidence without objection in the trial of the case. Such affidavit in connection with the original and additional certificate was the only evidence on this subject and being unobjected to on the specific ground here sought to be raised was prima facie proof of the citizenship of such locators. Further than this no objection was made in the court below that these locators were not citizens or that the fact of their citizenship was not shown. This court held in Sherlock v. Leighton, supra, that such objection could not be raised in the appellate court for the first time, and cited O'Reilly v. Campbell, 116 U. S. 418, 6 Sup. Ct. 421, 29 L. Ed. 669. The language of the late Justice Field in delivering the opinion of the court in that case is pertinent. "It is true that the mineral lands of the United States are open to exploration and purchase only by citizens of the United States, or by those who have declared their intention to become such; and had the objection been taken in the court below that such citizenship of the plaintiffs had not been shown, it might, if not obviated, have been fatal. There is, however, nothing in the record to show that it was raised below. Proof of citizenship, in proceedings of this kind, may consist, in the case of an individual, of his own affidavit thereof, and in the case of an association of persons unincorporated, of the affidavit of their authorized agent, made upon his own knowledge, or upon information and belief. (Rev. Stat., Sec. 2321; U. S. Comp. St. 1901, p. 1425.) The objection to the want of proof of that fact, if taken below, might have been met at once, if, indeed, the plaintiffs are citizens. The rule is general that an objection which might be thus met must be taken at the trial or it will be considered as waived, except as to matters going to the jurisdiction of the court. The parties to this controversy own adjoining claims, and it is probable that the citizenship of each was known to the other, and, therefore, no proof on the subject was required. Be that, however, as it may, the objection, in actions of this kind, cannot be taken in this court for the first time." The case here seems to have been tried upon the theory that the locators were citizens of the United States and if that question was not put in issue and tried in the lower court it cannot be raised here for the first time. By failure to raise the question at the proper time and place it will be deemed to have been waived by the parties.

Other questions have been presented on the briefs, but in view of the conclusions reached upon the questions herein discussed it becomes unnecessary to consider them.

We are of the opinion that upon this record the finding and judgment of the trial court is supported by the evidence and that there is no prejudicial error shown. The judgment will be affirmed.   *Affirmed.*

POTTER and BEARD, JJ., concur.

ON PETITION FOR REHEARING.

SCOTT, CHIEF JUSTICE.

The plaintiff in error on February 7 and 8, 1913, filed petitions for a rehearing in this cause. The decision was rendered January 7, 1913 (128 Pac. 881), and the petitions were each filed more than thirty days thereafter. Rule 23 (104 Pac. XIV) of this court is in part as follows: "Application for re-hearing of any cause shall be by petition to the court, signed by counsel, briefly stating the points wherein it is alleged that the court has erred. Such petition shall be filed within thirty days after the decision is rendered * * *." Excluding the day on which the decision was rendered the petitions in this case were filed on the 31st and 32nd days thereafter. Rule 23 having been adopted by this court has the force of a statutory enactment. (Sec. 881, Comp. Stat. 1910.) In Bank of Chadron v. Anderson, 6 Wyo. 536, 48 Pac. 197, there was a petition for rehearing filed after the expiration of the time allowed by the rule. This court held that the petition for rehearing was not properly before it for consideration. We have, however, examined the questions presented and find that they were considered and determined in the opinion filed. The petitions will be denied. *Rehearing denied.*

POTTER, J., and BEARD, J., concur.

CHAPMAN v. CARROTHERS.
(No. 706.)

SALES—PAYMENT—BURDEN OF PROOF—SUFFICIENCY OF EVIDENCE.

1. In an action upon a written contract of sale to recover from the buyer the amount of certain indebtedness of the plaintiff, the seller, to a certain creditor, which the buyer had agreed to pay as part of the consideration for the sale, where the defendant in his answer admitted that on the date of the contract the plaintiff was indebted to said creditor in the amount stated in the petition, and alleged as a defense that on a subsequent date the defendant settled with the plaintiff and paid the full consideration of the contract sued on, the burden was upon the defendant to prove such settlement and payment.

2. In an action on a written contract to recover from the buyer the amount of certain indebtedness to a certain creditor of the plaintiff, the seller, which the buyer had agreed to pay as a part of the consideration for the sale, the evidence *held* insufficient to sustain the defense of settlement and payment pleaded in the answer, and therefore insufficient to justify a reversal of a judgment for plaintiff; the defendant by his answer having admitted that on the date of the contract sued on the plaintiff was indebted to his said creditor in the amount alleged in the petition, and there being a substantial conflict in the evidence introduced by defendant to prove that a settlement had been made, and there being no evidence tending to show that the one with whom the settlement was claimed to have been made had authority to act for the plaintiff.

[Decided January 29, 1913.]   (129 Pac. 434.)

ERROR to the District Court, Big Horn County; HON. CARROLL H. PARMELEE, Judge.

The material facts are stated in the opinion.

R. B. West and *H. S. Ridgely,* for plaintiff in error.

The question to be here determined is whether or not the defendant proved the averments of his answer as to payment and settlement. The plaintiff introduced no evidence upon the question, and it is believed that a careful consideration of the evidence introduced by defendant fully establishes the payment and settlement alleged in the answer.

John P. Arnott, E. E. Lonabaugh and *Burke & Riner,* for defendant in error.

The defendant admitted the execution and delivery of the contract of sale, and, without pleading compliance therewith as to payment of the consideration, alleged payment to and settlement with the plaintiff. The defendant properly assumed the burden of proof upon the defense of settlement and payment, and offered evidence to sustain it. Owing to the conflict in the evidence given by the witnesses introduced by the defendant, and its generally unsatisfactory condition and lack of probative value, the trial court found against the defendant and rendered judgment for the plaintiff. Much of the evidence on the question consisted of mere statements of conclusions without the showing that a payment had in fact been made; and the legal effect of the testimony of the principal witness is that no settlement was made. A conflict of evidence may arise, not only where testimony is offered by both of the adverse parties, but also between the testimony of witnesses for the same party, when no two of them agree as to what was done. (Teske v. Teske, 1 Neb. (Unoff.) 365, 95 N. W. 685; Armstrong v. Ballew, 118 Ga. 68, 44 S. E. 996.) In such a case it would be more proper, perhaps, to designate the result as a failure of proof. Questions involving the credibility of witnesses, or a mere preponderance of evidence, will not be reviewed by the Appellate Court, where the trial court has passed on the facts, but some consideration must be given to the better position of the trial court to judge of the credibility of the witnesses and weigh their testimony. (Kelly v. Brown, (Cal.) 8 Pac. 38; Bettens v. Hoover, (Cal.) 107 Pac. 329.)

In order to establish a settlement of disputed accounts to be effective as a compromise or adjustment of conflicting claims there must at least exist the following state of affairs: The parties must arrive at an agreement, and they must agree as to a specific sum of money to be paid by one or the other, and a specific discharge of the obligations held by the payee against the payor. (Ry. Co. v. Haverstick, (Ind.) 77 N. E. 34; Barrett v. Kern, (Mo.) 121 S. W. 774.) As to what constitutes an accord and satisfaction see: 1 Words & Phrases, pp. 81, 82 and 83; Harrison v. Henderson, (Kan.) 72 Pac. 875; Hennessy v. Ry. Co., (Minn.) 67 N. W. 635.) The payment of a smaller sum than the admitted amount of an obligation does not constitute satisfaction thereof. (Ins. Ass'n. v. Wickham, 141 U. S. 564, 35 L. Ed. 860; Peachy v. Witter, 131 Cal. 316, 63 Pac. 468; Boston v. Gibson, 111 Ill. App. 457; Rauen v. Prudential &c. Co., 129 Ia. 725, 106 N. W. 198; Upton v. Dennis, 133 Mich. 238, 94 N. W. 728; 1 Ency. Law, 413; 1 Words & Phrases, 83.) The party claiming a settlement has the burden of proving that a full and fair settlement was made. (Schisler v. Null, 91 Mich. 321, 51 N. W. 900; Baumier v. Auteau, (Mich.) 44 N. W. 939; 8 Cyc. 538.) The language of the answer setting up the affirmative defense amounts only to a plea of payment, and did not authorize proof of accord and satisfaction.

BEARD, JUSTICE.

The defendant in error, T. A. Carrothers, brought this action against the plaintiff in error, W. J. Chapman, in the District Court of Big Horn County to recover the amount alleged to be due on a certain written contract. A jury was waived and the cause tried to the court. The court found in favor of Carrothers in the sum of $829.55, and rendered judgment against Chapman for that amount and costs. Chapman brings the case here on error.

The contract sued on bears date September 9, 1902, and recites that Carrothers had on that date sold and delivered to Chapman his stock of wines, liquors and cigars, and the saloon furnishings and fixtures, together with the good will of the saloon business conducted by him in the town of Cody; and as a part of the consideration of such sale Chapman assumed and agreed to pay all of the debts and liabilities of Carrothers to E. C. Enderly and Stein, Block and Company on account of said saloon business, amounting in all to the sum of five hundred dollars, more or less.

The petition is separated into paragraphs which are numbered. In the first paragraph the sale and delivery of the property is alleged. The second alleges that at the date of the sale and prior thereto Carrothers was justly indebted to E. C. Enderly on account of said saloon business in the sum of $523.25. The third alleges that Chapman had failed and refused to pay any part of said indebtedness except $62.00 paid to Carrothers April 27, 1905, and that on the last mentioned date Carrothers was compelled to pay and did pay said Enderly said indebtedness with interest amounting in all to the sum of $629.25. The fourth pleads the contract. The fifth alleges the failure of Chapman to pay to Carrothers any part of said sum except the $62.00. The prayer is for judgment for $567.35 with interest from April 27, 1905.

The answer admits the allegations of paragraphs one, two and four of the petition, denies the allegations of the third paragraph, and alleges "that on or about April 26, 1905, defendant had a full and complete settlement with plaintiff and fully paid him all of the consideration of the contract sued upon, and that he does not owe the plaintiff the sum of $667.35, or any sum whatever." And denies the allegations of the fifth paragraph of the petition. The reply denies the new matter pleaded in the answer.

The only ground for a reversal of the judgment urged by counsel for plaintiff in error is that the finding and judgment of the District Court are not supported by the evidence. It being admitted by the answer that on September.

9, 1902, the date of the contract sued on, Carrothers was
justly indebted to said Enderly in the sum of $523.25, coun-
sel for plaintiff in error very properly concede that the
burden rested upon the defendant below to prove settlement
and payment as alleged in the answer.

The evidence is very unsatisfactory. The defendant below testified in substance that a settlement was made between
himself and Carrothers in Mr. Zaring's law office (in Basin,
the county seat of Big Horn County) and that he signed a
check, leaving the amount blank, and delivered it to his attorney, Mr. Walls; that they did not know the amount and
for that reason the check was so made; that Walls was to
fill in the amount and pay it to Carrothers; that the check
was paid and the amount was $300.00 or $350.00; that it
had been mislaid and that he did not know whether it was
endorsed by Carrothers or not; that the check was given to
settle his contract between Carrothers and himself; that he
signed the check and left it with Walls, telling him he did
not know exactly what it was, but about $300.00; that he
signed the check and Walls filled it out; that at the time of
the settlement there were present in Mr. Zaring's office, Mr.
Zaring, Carrothers, a fellow they called Frenchy, and himself. Mr. Walls testified in substance that he was acting as
attorney for Chapman in his absence; that Chapman and
Carrothers arranged between themselves that one Fenton
was to receive certain moneys in behalf of Carrothers from
him; that at the time they did not know what the amount
would be; that Chapman made a check payable to his
(Walls') order, leaving the amount to be filled in by him;
that he ascertained the amount, wrote it in the check, got it
cashed and paid the money over to Fenton and took his
receipt therefor and afterwards delivered the receipt to
Chapman; that it ran in his mind that the amount was
around $111.00, but he would not undertake to testify to the
exact amount; that the money paid by him to Fenton was
in full settlement of all the difficulties between Carrothers
and Chapman. The receipt was not produced or offered in

evidence, and Chapman testified that he did not have it as he supposed the matter was settled and he never paid any attention to it. Mr. Arnott testified that in the early part of 1903 he had for collection an account in favor of E. C. Enderly and against T. A. Carrothers for $523.25 for cigars and liquors sold by Enderly to Carrothers for the saloon purchased by Chapman; that on April 16, 1903, he took a note for that amount in favor of Enderly, signed by Carrothers and wife and secured by mortgage and sent the note and mortgage to Enderly. Mr. Zaring testified to remembering Carrothers and Chapman being in his office in April, 1905, and it was his understanding that they were making a settlement of some differences, and he understood a settlement was made, but knew nothing of the details; that he then had for collection the note mentioned by Mr. Arnott and collected the amount including interest, $629.35, from Carrothers the next day. The note was put in evidence and is marked "Paid in full April 27-05. C. A. Zaring." Neither Carrothers nor Fenton testified in the case, and the foregoing is substantially all of the evidence in the case. Carrothers having paid that amount, he was entitled to recover the same from Chapman with legal interest from the date of payment, unless Chapman sustained his plea of settlement and payment. We think it is clear that the parties did not agree upon the amount to be paid, the undisputed evidence being that they did not then know the amount. There is no evidence tending to prove any authority of Fenton to make any agreement for Carrothers with Walls, or that he did do so in fact. How Walls ascertained the amount he inserted in the check does not appear. There is no evidence showing it to have been by any agreement between him and Carrothers or any one else having authority to do so. There is also a substantial conflict in the testimony between Chapman and his attorney as to the amount of the check, neither of them states the amount definitely, and they vary widely in their recollections or impressions on this important matter in the case and which could have been learned by referring to the books of the bank on which the check was drawn and where it was paid; especially is this the case when the record discloses that a part of the evidence was taken October 13, 1909, at which Chapman testified the check had been mislaid, and the cause was then continued over the term and the remaining evidence taken September 28, 1910. On the evidence presented, we think the District Court was correct in its conclusion that the evidence was insufficient to sustain the defense of settlement and payment pleaded in the answer, and that the record presents no error entitling the plaintiff in error to a reversal of the judgment. The judgment of the District Court is affirmed. *Affirmed.*

SCOTT, C. J., and POTTER, J., concur.

WEAVER v. RICHARDSON.
(No. 732.)

EJECTMENT—TRIAL—QUESTION FOR JURY—DIRECTING VERDICT.

1. When a case is tried to a jury, controverted questions of fact upon which there is substantial conflict in the evidence should be submitted to the jury for its determination.

2. In an action for the possession of real estate it was for the jury, and not the court, to weigh the conflicting evidence with reference to a contract under which defendant claimed right of possession, and determine whether or not the defense was established by a preponderance of the evidence; and it was error for the court to direct a verdict for the plaintiff on the ground that defendant had failed to show a contract of sale.

[Decided February 11, 1913.]   (129 Pac. 829.)

ERROR to the District Court, Albany County, HON. CARROLL H. PARMELEE, Judge.

The material facts are stated in the opinion.

V. J. Tidball and *N. E. Corthell*, for plaintiff in error.

The evidence tending to show an authorized or ratified contract of sale was sufficient for submission to the jury, and the court therefore erred in directing a verdict for the plaintiff. Where an oral contract for the sale of real estate has been made, and in pursuance thereof the vendee has gone into possession, paid a part of the purchase price, and made valuable and lasting improvements, the contract will be enforced in equity. (Sedgwick & Wait on Trial of Title to Land, 321-a.) Possession alone without payment is held in England sufficient to constitute part performance of such a contract, and take the case out of the statute of frauds. (36 Cyc. 652.) To the same effect, Kirk v. Hamilton, 102 U. S. 79; and the same rule is maintained by the courts in several states. (Calanchini v. Bransteter, (Cal.) 24 Pac. 149; Andrew v. Babcock, (Conn.) 26 Atl. 715; Robinson v. Thrailkill, (Ind.) 10 N. E. 647; Baldwin v. Baldwin. (Kan.) 84 Pac. 568; Coggswell & Co. v. Coggswell, (N. J.) 40 Atl. 213; Horton v. Stegmyer, 175 Fed. 736, 20 Ann. Cas. 1134; Hubbard v. Slavens, (Mo.) 117 S. W. 1104.) But the rule is general that possession and payment in full or in part is sufficient to take the contract out of the statute. (36 Cyc. 654; Jerman v. Misner, (Or.) 108 Pac. 179; Houston &c. R. Co. v. Wright, (Tex.) 38 S. W. 836.) And by other cases it is held that possession accompanied by the making of valuable improvements is sufficient to take the contract from the operation of the statute. (36 Cyc. 655; 26 Ency. Law, 57; O'Hara v. O'Hara, 16 O. C. C. 367; Pennington v. Pennington, (S. C.) 71 S. E. 825; Moulton v. Harris, 29 Pac. 706; Mudgett v. Clay, (Wash.) 31 Pac. 424; Smith v. McCorkle, (Mo.) 16 S. W. 602; Newkirk v. Marshall, (Kan.) 10 Pac. 571; Henrikson v. Henrikson, (Wis.) 127 N. W. 962; Ganes v. Kendall, (Ill.) 52 N. E. 141; Townsend v. Vandewerker, 160 U. S. 173; Metcalf v. Hart, 3 Wyo. 513.) There was error in the assessment of the amount of recovery, since no consideration was given to the cost or value of the defendant's improvements upon the property.

Frank E. Anderson, for defendant in error.

In the making of the alleged contract of sale Mrs. Weaver was dealing with an agent having limited authority, and she was bound to know the extent of such authority. Mrs. Richardson was not aware of any offer for the property made by Mrs. Weaver until several months after the latter had taken possession, and any notice of that possession which the alleged agent may have had could not have bound Mrs. Richardson, unless she had expressly accepted the offer. It is plain from the testimony that she did not accept the offer. The burden was upon the defendant to show the alleged contract, and having failed in that the court very properly directed a verdict for the plaintiff; the amount of damages and rent having been agreed upon by stipulation. The evidence did not show the necessary elements to make a good contract of sale. (Brown v. Grady, 16 Wyo. 151; Breckinridge v. Croker, 21 Pac. 179; Mieux v. Hogue, (Cal.) 27 Pac. 745.)

The evidence as to the alleged contract of sale did not bring it within the rule authorizing the enforcement of such a contract where the vendee has entered into possession, paid part of the purchase price and made valuable and lasting improvements. (O'Brien v. Foulke, 69 Kan. 475, 77 Pac. 103; Mieux v. Hogue, *supra;* Guthrie v. Anderson, 30 Pac. 6; Lamme v. Dodson, (Mont.) 2 Pac. 298.) The improvements made by Mrs. Weaver, if any were made, were made after she had written her letter stating that she would stay upon the place until Mrs. Richardson had made some other disposition of it, and after another letter written by her indicating that she knew her offer to buy had not been accepted.

BEARD, JUSTICE.

The defendant in error, Annie F. Richardson, brought this action in the District Court of Albany County against the plaintiff in error, Adelaide J. Weaver, to recover the possession of certain real estate situated at Tie Siding in said county, and for damages for the alleged unlawful detention of the possession of the same by plaintiff in error. The cause was tried to a jury and at the conclusion of the evidence, at the request of the plaintiff below, the court instructed the jury to return a verdict in favor of said plaintiff. Judgment was entered on said verdict, and defendant below brings the case here on error.

For convenience the defendant in error will be referred to as plaintiff, and the plaintiff in error as defendant. The answer denied the allegations of the petition, and for a second defense alleged in substance that about October 28, 1909, the plaintiff and defendant entered into an agreement by which the plaintiff agreed to sell to defendant said premises for the sum of $500, and that defendant deposited with one Ada Ulen, the agent of both parties, $20, in escrow as part of the purchase price of said premises; that said $20, together with the balance of said purchase price was to be paid to plaintiff when she should execute and deliver to defendant a good and sufficient warranty deed conveying to defendant a clear title to said premises; that defendant should take immediate possession and hold the same until such deed was executed and delivered; that relying on said agreement, and with the consent of plaintiff, the defendant entered into the possession of the premises and has since been in the quiet possession thereof, believing the same to be her property, and with the knowledge and consent of plaintiff has made valuable and lasting improvements thereon; and alleged that plaintiff had failed to keep and perform said agreement on her part. The reply admitted that defendant entered into possession of the premises at the time stated in the answer, and denied the other allegations therein contained.

For the trial of the issues of fact thus joined the plaintiff demanded a jury. On the trial it appeared that the agreement, if any, was made between the defendant and Mrs. Nally, the daughter of plaintiff, and her authority to enter into any contract as agent for her mother, as well as what

the agreement was, was in dispute. Also under what conditions or agreement the defendant entered into possession
of the premises; what improvements defendant had put
thereon, and whether the same were made in good faith relying on the contract; whether the plaintiff, with knowledge
of what her daughter had done in the matter, had been ratified by her, were all controverted questions of fact upon
which the evidence was in direct conflict. It would serve
no useful purpose and would unnecessarily lengthen this
opinion to set out herein the evidence showing such conflicts.
We deem it sufficient to say that upon each of the questions
above stated there was a direct conflict in the testimony of
one or more witnesses on each side, with more or less cor-
roborating or contradictory evidence in letters introduced in
evidence and in the substance of other correspondence which
it was testified had been destroyed and could not be produced. The case being tried to a jury it was not for the
court to determine on which side the evidence preponder-
ated, or which witnesses were most worthy of credence.
Had the case been tried to the court without a jury and the
court had found for the plaintiff on the conflicting evidence,
an entirely different question would be presented. But when
a case is tried to a jury it is the duty of the court to submit
to the jury for its determination controverted questions of
fact upon which there is a substantial conflict in the evidence. In this case it is not claimed that if the facts are
as the evidence on the part of the defendant tends to prove
they would not constitute a good defense to the action and
that for that reason it was proper for the court to take the
case from the jury.

The motion made in the District Court for an instruction
directing the jury to return a verdict for plaintiff was: "The
plaintiff moves the court to instruct the jury to return a
verdict for the plaintiff upon the ground that no contract for
the sale of said property has been shown, and that there has
been an absolute failure on the part of the defendant to
show any agency authorized by the plaintiff, Mrs. Richard-

son, or which could in any wise be binding upon her." That motion was sustained by the court; and counsel for defendant in error says in his brief: "The court sustained the motion, holding that the burden shifted to the defendant below to show a contract of sale, and that she had failed to do this." This, we think, was clearly an invasion by the court of the province of the jury. It was for the jury, and not the court, to weigh the conflicting evidence and determine whether or not the defense was established by a preponderance of the evidence. For the error in directing a verdict for the plaintiff the judgment of the District Court is reversed and the case remanded for a new trial   *Reversed.*

SCOTT, C. J. and POTTER, J., concur.

CARNEY COAL COMPANY v. BENEDICT.*
(No. 720.)

MASTER AND SERVANT—INJURIES IN COAL MINES—ASSUMED RISK—EVIDENCE—BELIEF OF SERVANT AS TO SAFETY OF PLACE OF WORK—ADMISSIBILITY—INEXPERIENCE OF SERVANT—DUTY OF EMPLOYER TO WARN—OBVIOUS DANGER—PROXIMATE CAUSE OF INJURY—DIRECTING VERDICT.

1. In an action for an injury to a coal miner, where defendant's liability was claimed upon the theory that the injured workman was inexperienced, and that the defendant knowing that fact had failed to instruct or warn him of the danger incident to the employment, and that the injury was the proximate cause of such failure of duty on the part of defendant, *Held*, that evidence of the plaintiff's acts just before and at the time of the injury was competent as a part of the *res gestae* and as bearing on the question whether as a reasonably prudent man, he ought, under the circumstances, to have appreciated the danger.

---

*An order was entered June 20, 1913, on the petition of defendant in error, granting a rehearing in this case.

2. In such an action evidence tending to show the skill and ability of the plaintiff as a coal miner to discover danger and how to avoid it was competent as bearing on the question whether he acted as a reasonably prudent man similarly situated should and ought to have acted.

3. The plaintiff was properly permitted to state, when examined as a witness on his own behalf, what his belief was just prior to the injury as to whether or not he was working in a safe place, and that he believed he was working in a safe place free from danger, and that there was nothing to indicate that he was in any presence of danger.

4. In an action by an alleged inexperienced coal miner to recover for injuries received in the mine by the falling of a lump of coal, where the plaintiff was permitted without objection to state as a witness in his own behalf that he did not appreciate the danger of the falling coal from which he was injured, the question whether such testimony was subject to proper objection was not before the appellate court for consideration.

5. Where the plaintiff, in an action brought for injuries received when working in a coal mine by coal falling upon him, testified without objection that he did not appreciate the danger of the falling coal from which he was injured, *Held*, that the jury were not concluded by such testimony of the plaintiff, but were required to find from all the evidence whether as a reasonably prudent man he ought to have appreciated the danger or was able to form a judgment with respect to it as to whether or not he was in danger at and just prior to his injury; the defendant's liability being claimed upon the theory that the plaintiff was inexperienced, and that the defendant knowing that fact failed to instruct and warn him of the danger incident to his employment, and how to discover and avoid such danger.

6. Notwithstanding that there was evidence in the action aforesaid, to the effect that plaintiff had worked and received wages as a miner while working with his father in mining coal in another coal mine, and also that he had previously been employed in and about the defendant's coal mine as a car driver, such evidence would not of itself relieve the defendant of the duty of warning the plaintiff of the dangers incident to his occupation as a coal miner, if in fact plaintiff was inexperienced, and the defendant had knowledge of that fact.

7. In an action for personal injuries brought by an injured employee against the employer, whether the danger was obvious to the plaintiff is ordinarily a question of fact for the jury, and in determining that question the jury may and should take into consideration the nature of plaintiff's employment in which the injury occurred, his experience and capacity to understand and appreciate the danger of his employment, and how to avoid such danger.

8. Although the plaintiff, in an action against an employer for personal injuries received when working in the employer's coal mine, may have been inexperienced as alleged, and although the defendant, as alleged, may not have instructed and warned the plaintiff how to discover and avoid danger of falling coal by what is known as the "sounding test," the plaintiff could not recover unless the failure of the defendant to so instruct and warn him was the proximate cause of the injury.

9. Plaintiff, a young man without experience, as alleged in his petition, was employed by the defendant as a coal miner. He and the one working with him, after having fired a shot to loosen the coal, discovered a crack on one side of a large projecting lump of coal, and inserted a bar in the crack in an attempt to pry down such lump, but being unable to get it down in that manner, plaintiff concluded that there was no immediate danger of its falling and proceeded with the work of loading the coal which had fallen after the firing of the shot, and while so working the said lump fell, injuring plaintiff's foot and ankle, necessitating amputation. *Held*, that plaintiff was charged with knowledge of the law of gravitation, that the risk of injury from the fall of said lump of coal was obvious, and, therefore, the plaintiff could not complain of failure on the part of the defendant to instruct and warn him of the danger incident to his employment, or how to discover and avoid such danger.

10. The evidence aforesaid to the effect that the plaintiff attempted to pry down the coal which subsequently fell and injured him for the purpose of avoiding danger from its falling showed that he appreciated the danger and concluded him upon that question, and, therefore, any failure of the defendant company to instruct and warn the plaintiff as an inexperienced miner was not the proximate cause of the injury, and, since the only ground for a recovery upon the petition and evidence would have been such

failure on the part of the company to instruct and warn, the motion of the defendant to direct a verdict in its favor should have been sustained.

[Decided February 17, 1913.]   (129 Pac. 1024.)

ERROR to the District Court, Sheridan County, HON. CARROLL H. PARMELEE, Judge.

Charles R. Benedict brought the action against the Carney Coal Company to recover for personal injuries received while working for the defendant in its coal mine as a coal miner. A peremptory instruction for the defendant was denied, and there was a verdict and judgment for the plaintiff. The defendant brought error. The material facts are stated in the opinion.

Enterline & LaFleiche, for plaintiff in error.

It was improper to permit the plaintiff to testify over objection that he believed immediately prior to his injury that the place wherein he was working was safe. Whether or not it was a reasonably safe place was for the jury to decide. The undisputed evidence discloses that the plaintiff was of mature years, of average intelligence, in the possession of all his faculties, and that his injury was caused by a condition made by himself and was so open, patent, obvious and apparent that no experience was required to appreciate the danger. The evidence also establishes that the plaintiff knew of the existence of the danger. Therefore, whether or not he was inexperienced became wholly immaterial. Error was committed in the admission of opinion evidence as to matters which were for the jury alone to decide, and examples of these are found in the questions calling for opinions as to whether the experience required to discover the dangers of mining coal could be acquired by one driving a car in the mine, and the questions asking for the opinion of the witness as to whether it would be necessary for a miner to have either experience or suitable warning or instruction in order to detect the danger of falling coal.

The fact that the lump of coal which fell and injured the·
plaintiff was liable to fall, appears from the evidence to have
been so obvious that any reasonably prudent person would
have appreciated the danger, and that danger was so obvious
that the case is brought within the authorities denying the
right to recover where the risk was obvious and ought to
have been fully appreciated by the party injured. (Maki v.
Coal Co., 187 Fed. 389, 109 C. C. A. 221; 1 Labatt's Master
& Servant, Sec. 238; Simms v. So. Car. R. Co., 2 S. E.
486; Bjbjian v. Rubber Co., 41 N. E. 265; Hathaway v.
Mich. C. R. Co., 16 N. W. 634; Houston &c. R. Co. v.
Strycharski, 26 S. W. 253, 642; Findlay v. Foundry Co.,
66 N. W. 50; Connolly v. Eldredge, 36 N. E. 469; Yeager
v. Burlington &c. R. Co., 61 N. W. 215; Hogle v. Wilson,
31 Pac. 469; Railsback v. Wayne &c. Co., 38 N. E. 221;
Dougherty v Iron & Steel Co., 60 N. W. 274; East Tenn.
&c. Co. v. Turvaville, 12 So. 63; Ill. Cent. R. Co. v. Price,
18 So. 415; Kean v. Detroit C. & B. Mills, 33 N. W. 395;
Campbell v. Mullen, 60 Ill. App. 497; Vilas v. Vanderbilt,
44 N. Y. Supp. 267; DeSouza v. Stafford Mills, 30 N. E. 81;
Casey V. Paving Co., 47 Atl. 1128; Cunningham v. Bridge
Works, 47 Atl. 846.) All employment in a coal mine is
dangerous and is generally so understood by everyone,
whether experienced or not. As to the plaintiff, who was a
man of mature years and had worked in the mine, there is
no reason for applying the rule which would govern in the
case of a minor or a person not in the possession of all his
faculties. Notwithstanding plaintiff's testimony, that he did
not appreciate the danger, the court should have directed a
verdict and not have permitted the jury to speculate upon
the question. The admission of plaintiff's testimony to the
effect that he did not understand or appreciate the danger,
which we contend was error, makes more apparent the error
in submitting the case to the jury. (Over v. Mo. K. & T.
R. Co., 73 S. W. 535.) It should have been held by the
court as a matter of law that the plaintiff was bound to
know, appreciate and understand the danger which resulted

in his injury. The sole purpose of requiring warning by an employer is to give information of unknown or unappreciated dangers, so that when the servant knows and appreciates the hazards of his employment no warning or instruction is required. (Cudahy Packing Co. v. Marcan, 45 C. C. A. 515.) Not only was the danger obvious, but it was one created by the plaintiff himself, and no warning or instruction is required under such circumstances. (1 Bailey's Pers. Inj., Secs. 298, 301, 304, and cases cited.) The plaintiff was bound to take notice of the ordinary operation of familiar natural laws and govern himself accordingly. (Swanson v. Ry. Co., 70 N. W. 978; Walsh v. Ry. Co., 27 Minn. 367, 8 N. W. 145; Olson v. McMullen, 34 Minn. 94, 24 N. W. 318; Pederson v. Rushford, 41 Minn. 289, 42 N. W. 1063; Quick v. Iron Co., 47 Minn. 361, 50 N. W. 244; Hardy v. Ry. Co., 115 N. W. 8; Thurman v. Copper Co., 108 Pac. 588; Paule v. Mining Co., (Wis.) 50 N. W. 189; Cole v. Ry. Co., (Wis.) 114 N. W. 84; White on Pers. Inj. in Mines, Sec. 41; 4 Thomp. on Neg., Sec. 4063; Coal Co. v. Barringer, 75 N. E. 900.)

The court erred in refusing instructions "A" and "B" requested by the defendant. The master is not liable for an injury received by reason of change of conditions made by the servant; and that rule is particularly applicable where the danger thus created is obvious and observed by the servant. Instruction "C" requested by the defendant should have been given. It seems to be the universal rule that where a man of mature years and average intelligence solicits a particular employment, he thereby holds himself out to the employer as qualified to perform the task, and the master may assume that he is qualified and experienced. Instructions "F" and "H" requested by the defendant should have been given, as well as instructions "I" and "K." Instruction "K" stated that if the jury should find that the plaintiff, either by himself or in conjunction with his fellow servant, set the blast in the face of the vein in which they were engaged at work, so that the blast cracked and loosened pieces of coal in the vein, and that plaintiff knew, or in the exercise of reasonable care could have known, that detached or loosened pieces of coal were liable to fall after having been so detached and loosened, the plaintiff could not recover. That instruction, we think, stated the law correctly. An instruction given stated to the jury unequivocally as a matter of law that a legal duty rests upon the master to warn and instruct his servant in any event, without mentioning any exception to the rule requiring such warning and instruction. That instruction, which was numbered "3," was, we maintain, error. The trial court attempted by instruction number "4" to define the law respecting open, visible and obvious danger, but the instruction embraced exceptions and qualifications such as to convey an entirely different direction than was warranted by the record in this case. The instruction was confined to dangers which are "visible and obvious to the comprehension of the servant, considering his years, experience and understanding." The other instructions that were given are subject to a similar objection.

Burgess & Kutcher, for defendant in error.

It was proper to permit the plaintiff to testify that he believed that at the time of his injury no danger existed. His testimony as to what he did or did not know and comprehend was competent and admissible. (Stewart v. Copper Co., (Mont.) 111 Pac. 723.) The fact that the plaintiff created the danger in the progress of the work is true in nearly all cases of this character. The very object of warning and instruction is to enable the servant to avoid the danger which he, himself, creates. Whether the danger was obvious or not was a disputed fact and was properly left to the jury, and by the verdict the jury found that the danger was not open, patent or obvious. The opinion of an experienced coal miner concerning whether one inexperienced could discern whether a large piece of coal, behind which there was a crack, was dangerous, was certainly admissible. (Texas &c. R. Co. v. Douglas, (Tex.) 11 S. W. 333; R. Co. v. Kennedy, 82 Fed. 158, 27 C. C. A. 136.) Likewise it was proper for such a witness to give his opinion, and the reason for it, that the driving of a mule in hauling cars in a mine would not give one experience in the actual operation of mining coal. An expert may testify concerning the dangers of a machine, what precautions are necessary to avoid them, and that before men are set to work they are carefully instructed in the use of the machine. (Biscuit Co. v. Rouss, 74 Fed. 608, 20 C. A. A. 555.)

Where one hires another to perform work which will expose him to danger known to the employer, but which the servant does not know, or, knowing in a general way, does not understand or appreciate by reason of his inexperience, it is the duty of the employer, if he has notice of such facts, to give such warning and instruction as is reasonably required to enable the one so employed, in the exercise of ordinary care, to understand and appreciate the danger and guard against it. (26 Cyc. 1165; White's Pers. Inj. in Mines, Secs. 392, 456; 4 Thompson on Neg. Sec. 4055; 1 Labatt on Master & Servant, Sec. 235.) The question whether the danger is obvious and apparent must be considered with reference to the age, experience and capacity of the servant. (4 Thompson on Neg., Sec. 4061; 26 Cyc. 1176; Cudahy Pack. Co. v. Marcan, 45 C. C. A. 515; Maki v. Coal Co., 109 C. C. A. 221.) A servant does not assume any risk which he does not know, or knowing in a general way, does not understand or appreciate on account of inexperience. (26 Cyc. 1196; White's Per. Inj. in Mines, Secs. 179, 180, 182; Stewart v. Copper Co., (Mont.) 111 Pac. 723; Delbusso v. Am. &c. Co., (Mich.) 130 N. W. 702.) The same rule applies to contributory negligence. (26 Cyc. 1236; 5 Thompson on Neg., Sec. 5339; 1 Labatt, Secs. 319, 320; White's Per. Inj. in Mines, Secs. 255-283.) These well settled rules, when applied to the facts of this case, clearly entitle the plaintiff to recover.

The danger of the falling of the particular lump of coal which did fall is not shown by the evidence to have been open, obvious and easily visible to the naked eye, nor was it obvious that the lump of coal was loose, nor is it shown that the plaintiff knew it to be loose. On the contrary, the evidence shows that the danger was not apparent except to one with knowledge sufficient to examine for and discover it; that so far as the plaintiff knew, the coal was not loose, but appeared to be solid; and the crack behind it was not a large one extending back of the lump, but a small crack indicating no particular evidence of danger. The projecting lump was obvious and the crack was visible, but not the danger of the coal falling. As in the case of a machine, the machine is visible, and the wheels, cogs and knives are open and obvious, but to an inexperienced and uninstructed employe the danger is unappreciated in the sense of knowing how to guard against it. Upon the facts in this case it was properly submitted to the jury. A directed verdict for the defendant would have been error. (Paving Co. v. Hudson, 52 N. E. 256; Sidwell v. Coal Co., 130 N. W. 729; Hosking v. Cleveland I. Min. Co., 128 N. W. 777; Hanley v. Cal. B. & C. Co., (Cal.) 59 Pac. 577; Larsen v. Magne-Silica Co., (Cal.) 111 Pac. 119; Daly v. Keil, (La.) 30 So. 254; 4 Thomp. on Neg., Sec. 4065; Olson v. Tel. Co., (Neb.) 127 N. W. 916; Gill v. Homrinhausen, (Wis.) 48 N. W. 862.) The controlling fact in the case with reference to the obviousness of the danger was plaintiff's inexperience. An experienced miner might have known that the body of coal was liable to fall, and yet it might be apparently safe to one without experience. An experienced miner assumes the ordinary and usual risks of his employment; but this rule does not apply to one who is inexperienced, respecting dangers he does not know or appreciate, while exercising reasonable care.

SCOTT, CHIEF JUSTICE.

The defendant in error as plaintiff, and who will be referred to as the plaintiff, brought this action in the District Court of Sheridan County against the Carney Coal Company as defendant, which will be referred to here as the defendant, to recover damages for a personal injury alleged to have been sustained while mining coal in defendant's coal mine. The case was tried to a jury which found for the plaintiff and assessed his damages at the sum of $1,000. A motion for a new trial was filed by the defendant and submitted to the court, which motion the court overruled, and judgment having been rendered upon the verdict, the defendant brings the case here on error.

(1) It is urged that the court erred in the admission and exclusion of certain evidence over defendant's objection; (2) that the petition failed to state facts sufficient to constitute a cause of action; (3) that the evidence was insufficient to support a judgment, and (4) that the court erred in refusing to instruct the jury to find for the defendant. The first three of these alleged errors are grouped and discussed together in plaintiff in error's brief, and for convenience the four may be here considered together.

The case was brought and tried upon the theory that the plaintiff, who was twenty-three years of age at the time of the injury, was inexperienced in coal mining, which fact was well known to the company, and that the company failed to instruct or warn him of the danger incident to his employment and put him to work with a man who was unable to talk or converse in the English language, and which language was the only one in which plaintiff could converse, and that the injury was the proximate cause of the failure of the company to warn and instruct him of the danger and how to discover and avoid such danger. That upon the day of the accident he and his co-employee in the room in which they were engaged in mining drilled a hole in the vein of coal and put in a charge which they fired for the purpose of loosening and throwing down the coal. The shot threw down some of the coal, after which they discovered a large piece of coal partially loosened with a crack in the vein, and inserted an iron tamping bar in the crack and tried to pry the coal down, but being unable to do so they proceeded with their work and while so working the piece of the coal fell and injured plaintiff's foot and ankle so that the same had to be amputated.

The plaintiff, over the objection of the company, was inquired of as to what his belief was just prior to the injury as to whether or not he was working in a safe place and answered that he believed he was working in a safe place, free from danger, and that there was nothing to indicate that he was in the presence of any danger. His acts just before and at the time of the injury were competent as a part of the *res gestae* and as bearing on the question as to whether as a reasonably prudent man he ought, under the circumstances, to have appreciated the danger. Evidence tending to show his skill and ability as a coal miner to discover danger and how to avoid it, was competent as bearing on the question as to whether he acted as a reasonably prudent man should or ought to have acted when similarly situated.

The case of Stewart v. Pittsburg & Montana Copper Co., 42 Mont. 200, 111 Pac. Rep. 723, was an action for personal injury. In that case Stewart was injured in emptying a slag pot while executing the order of a superior to enter into a dangerous place, and while acting under the personal direction of his employer. He was permitted, over objection, to testify that he did not appreciate the danger into which he was ordered by Zachman, the shift boss. The court say: "Contention is made that the witness was thus called upon to determine for himself the very question which it was the duty of the jury to decide; but with this we cannot agree. The question for determination at the trial was not whether plaintiff appreciated the danger, but whether, as a reasonably prudent person, under the circumstances he ought to have appreciated it. The standard in all such cases is that of a reasonably prudent person similarly situated. The plaintiff might say that he did not appreciate the danger, and yet his answer would not avail him if the jury concluded from all the facts and circumstances that, as a reasonably prudent person, he ought to have appreciated it; and the fact that plaintiff prevailed indicates that his lack of appreciation of the danger was deemed by the jury no greater than that of the average prudent person similarly situated. All the facts and circumstances were before the jury: A description of the place, the character of the work, the abnormal condition prevailing with respect to this particular slag pot, and the experience or inexperience of the plaintiff.

"We think the evidence was properly admitted. The manifest purpose of the question was to negative the idea that the plaintiff assumed the risk when he went into the place and attempted to pry out the contents of the slag pot. We have repeatedly said that it is not sufficient that plaintiff knows of the risk; he must appreciate the danger as well. O'Brien v. Corra Rock-Island Min. Co., 40 Mont. 212, 105 Pac. 724; Hollingsworth v. Davis-Daly Estates Copper Co., 38 Mont. 143, 99 Pac. 142; Stephens v. Elliott, 36 Mont. 92, 92 Pac. 45.

"What, then, is meant by saying that plaintiff appreciates the danger? In McKee v. Tourtellotte, 167 Mass. 69, 44 N. E. 1071, 48 L. R. A. 542, the court said: 'When we say that a man appreciates a danger, we mean that he forms a judgment as to the future, and that his judgment is right.' If this be correct, and we think it is, how, then, may the jury know whether the plaintiff appreciated the danger or formed a judgment with respect to it, except by the answer he gives to the direct question asked him? As said before, his answer is not controlling upon the jury. It indicates his state of mind at the time he acted; but it is still for the jury to say whether, as a reasonably prudent person, he ought to have reached a conclusion that the place into which he was ordered was dangerous, when considered in the light of the surrounding circumstances."

In the case here plaintiff in addition to the foregoing testimony was permitted, without objection, to say in answer to a direct question that he did not appreciate the danger of the falling coal from which he was injured. The jury were not concluded by the answer, but were required to find from all the evidence whether as a reasonably prudent man he ought to have appreciated the danger, or was able to form a judgment with respect to it as to whether or not he was in danger at and just prior to his injury. As there was no objection to this question or the answer we here express no opinion as to whether it was open to objection or not.

It is here urged, and the evidence tends to show, that the company's pit boss who employed the plaintiff at the time plaintiff commenced mining coal in its mine knew that he was inexperienced, and notwithstanding such knowledge failed to warn him of the dangerous character of the work, or instruct him, or to place an experienced miner with him in the room where he worked and where he was injured. In so far as the alleged inexperience of Rotolo and his inability to converse, and with whom plaintiff was directed to work by the pit boss, is concerned, the plaintiff testified that he discovered that he was unable to converse with him at the time he first went to work and on the second day thereafter and before he was injured he became convinced that Rotolo was inexperienced as a miner. If, therefore, the company was negligent in failing to place an experienced miner to work with him, that fact became apparent and was known to plaintiff before the injury occurred, and notwithstanding such knowledge the plaintiff continued to work in the room with Rotolo up to the time of the injury. The question, however, as to Rotolo's inexperience as a coal miner and his inability to speak the English language, and all evidence bearing thereon, was withdrawn from the jury. It is alleged in the petition, and there is evidence to the effect that plaintiff worked and was paid miner's wages while working with his father in mining coal in another coal mine during the summer of 1903, and also as to his previous employment in and about the defendant's mine as a car driver, but it may be said that of itself did not relieve the company with knowledge of his inexperience if in fact he was inexperienced, from the duty of warning him when he changed his occupation from car driving to mining. (Thompson on Negligence, Vol. 4, Sec. 4065; Olson v. Neb. Tel. Co., 87 Neb. 593, 127 N. W. 916.) It is said in 26 Cyc., at page 1165, as follows: "It is the duty of the master to warn and instruct his servant as to defects and dangers of which he knows or ought, in the exercise of reasonable care and diligence, to know, and of which the servant has no knowledge, actual or constructive." Following this paragraph on page 1167, id., the following language is used, viz.: "The duty of warning and instructing a servant is a primary duty of the master, and the delegation of such duty to another servant, whether higher or lower in the scale of employment than the one exposed to danger, cannot relieve him of the responsibility imposed on him by law." On page 1169, id., it is further said: "To be sufficient, a warning or instruction must be so plain and explicit that the servant will understand and appreciate the danger and know how to avoid it by the exercise of due care. * * * In an action for personal injuries alleged to have resulted from the failure of the master properly to warn and instruct the servant, a recovery can only be had when the master's negligence was the proximate cause of the injury." See Bell v. N. P. Ry. Co., 112 Minn. 488, 128 N. W. 829; Sidwell v. Economy Coal Co., (Iowa) 130 N. W. 729; Jones v. Florence Min. Co., 66 Wis. 268, 28 N. W. 207, 57 Am. Rep. 269; Hosking v. Cleveland Iron Min. Co., 163 Mich. 538, 128 N. W. 777; Hanley v. California Bridge & Cons. Co., 127 Cal. 232, 59 Pac. 577, 47 L. R. A. 597. When the employment is changed the same rules obtain. (Thompson on Negligence, Vol. 4, Sec. 4065; Olson v. Neb. Tel Co., supra.)

It is here urged that the danger was not latent, but was obvious, and brought about by the act of plaintiff in the course of his work, and for that reason the plaintiff was charged with knowledge of the danger. Whether the danger was obvious to the servant is ordinarily a question of fact for the jury, and in determining that question the jury could and should take into consideration the nature of his employment, his experience and capacity to understand and appreciate the danger of his employment, and how to avoid such danger. It is conceded that there was danger accompanying the plaintiff's work, and the evidence tends to show that plaintiff realized the hazard of his employment, for both he and his father told the agent of the company who employed him that he had never had experience in mining coal. On the day of the injury after the shot was fired the crack in the face of the coal vein was obvious to the plaintiff and his co-employee and an attempt was made to pry down the coal by inserting an iron bar in the crack. Evidence was introduced tending to show that a test unknown to plaintiff and used by experienced miners would have disclosed liability and danger of the coal falling. It is contended that this test was not resorted to by reason of plaintiff's inexperience. It is known as the sounding test, and by which, as the evidence tends to show, an experienced miner by tapping the coal can tell from the sound whether the coal is firm or liable to fall. Plaintiff was not instructed and was ignorant of such test. Conceding these facts to be true, still the plaintiff could not recover unless the failure of the company to so instruct him was the proximate cause of his injury. It is said in 26 Cyc., at page 1170, that "Although a master is negligent in not giving instructions as to the dangers of his employment, if the servant receives such information from other sources, whether from other persons or from his own observation, and is thereafter injured, the master is not liable, since his negligence is not the proximate cause of the injury. When, however, the servant has knowledge of the facts, but is entirely ignorant of the risks involved, it is the duty of the master to warn him."

There is nothing in the evidence tending to show that had the sounding test been used it would have enabled an experienced miner to discover more than the fact that the coal had been loosened by the blast and the crack, which was apparent to the naked eye, and known to plaintiff and Rotolo, his co-employee, showed that fact. The block of coal which fell was variously estimated to be from 600 to 2,500 pounds in weight. Unless supported it would be dangerous for any one to work close to or under it. This fact, we think, was appreciated by the plaintiff, for he testified that one of the reasons for attempting to pry it down was to protect himself from its falling. The crack was large enough, as testified to by him, to insert the tamping bar which he and Rotolo used in their attempt to pry down the coal, and Rotolo testified that the crack was about three inches wide. Such a crack must, we think, be deemed to have been notice that the block of coal had become at least partially detached from the vein and its support necessarily weakened. It is not shown that the sounding test would have discloseed more than the existence of the crack to an experienced miner, nor is it shown that the crack would have failed to indicate danger to a reasonably prudent man similarly situated. If the sounding test had been known and used, and would have indicated to a reasonably prudent man that the block of coal was partially detached from the vein and its support weakened, knowledge that it would be liable to fall would be imputed to plaintiff, for every one is supposed to know the law of gravitation. In Swanson v. Great Northern Ry. Co., 68 Minn. 184, 70 N. W. 978, it is said to be the universal rule "that in performing the duty of his place a servant is bound to take notice of the ordinary operation of familiar natural laws, and to govern himself according. Failing to do so he takes the consequences. He can not charge such consequences upon the master, when he can see that which is open and apparent to a person of ordinary intelligence." The condition was obvious and discernible by the plaintiff. He was not in a position to complain that he was not instructed by the company how to detect such condition, for he had discovered and upon his own evidence sought to protect himself from the falling of the coal in the attempt to pry it down. The danger would be predicated upon the condition and such condition as here shown was obvious and not latent. (26 Cyc., 1179, 1180.) It is said in Labatt on Master and Servant, Vol. 1, p. 531, Sec. 238, as follows: "The juridical consequences of constructive knowledge being the same as those 'of actual knowledge, it follows that no duty to instruct a servant can be predicated in a case in which the instruction will not add to the knowledge which, under the circumstances, is attributed to him. In other words, the master is not required to point out dangers which are readily ascertainable by the servant himself if he makes an ordinary careful use of such knowledge, experience and judgment as he possesses. The failure to give instruction, therefore, is not culpable where the servant might, by the exercise of ordinary care and attention, have known of the danger, or, as the rule is expressed, where he had all the means necessary for ascertaining the actual conditions, and there was no concealed danger which could not be discovered." It would make this opinion unnecessarily long to discuss at length the cases illustrating the rule as announced by that learned author as to what danger is open, obvious, or apparent, or plainly visible to a servant who is an adult and presumed to be sound physically and mentally and is chargeable with knowledge of the danger. As satisfying that rule, the following have been held sufficient, viz.: "Dangers which the servant can at a glance observe for himself. (Simms v. South Carolina R. Co., 26 S. C. 490, 2 S. E. 486). "Elements of the danger so obvious to a careful person of average intelligence that ordinary prudence should make him avoid them without warning." (Bjbjian v. Woonsocket Rubber Co., 164 Mass. 214, 41 N. E. 265); "Dangers so simple that it can as well be ascertained at a single view as at many." (Hathaway v. Mich. Cent. R. Co., 51 Mich. 253, 16 N. W. 634, 47 Am. Rep. 569); "Dangers which the servant may see and guard against as well as could the master himself, if present, or any one else deputed by him." (Houston & T. C. R. Co. v. Strycharski, 6 Tex. Civ. App. 555, 26 S. W. 253, 642);

"Dangers obvious to even a casual observer." (Findley v. Russell Wheel & Foundry Co., 108 Mich. 286, 66 N. W. 50); "Dangers obvious to any one of ordinary capacity." (Connolly v. Eldredge, 160 Mass. 566, 36 N. E. 469.) We refer in this way to only a few of the cases cited by plaintiff in error in its brief.

In Montgomery Coal Co. v. Barringer, 218 Ill. 327, 75 N. E. 900, the court refused the company's request for a peremptory instruction to the jury to find in its favor, and the Supreme Court speaking of assumed risks say: "The theory * * * is that when the servant had full and complete knowledge of the condition of * * * the place in which he is doing work, and no special knowledge is required on his part to apprise him of the danger which he incurs while * * * working in such place, he will be presumed to have assumed the risk of being injured * * * while working in such place, and that in case of injury the master, by reason of such assumption of risk, is not liable. In the case at bar the defect was obvious and open to the observation of every person of ordinary intelligence who would take the pains to observe the conditions which the appellant knew to exist. The appellee had full opportunity for such observation and, in the language of the Wilson Case (Lake Erie & Western Railroad Co. v. Wilson, 189 Ill. 89, 59 N. E. 573) this was 'sufficient to charge him with knowledge' of the defect and its attendant danger, and he was therefore barred, by reason of such knowledge, from a recovery." It is also said in 26 Cyc., at page 1170, that, "Although a master is negligent in not giving his servant instructions as to the dangers of his employment, if the servant receives such information from other sources, whether from other persons or from his own observation, and is thereafter injured, the master is not liable, since his negligence is not the proximate cause of the injury."

The danger being obvious, the question recurs, what would a reasonably prudent man similarly situated have or

ought to have done under like circumstances? Not alone
what plaintiff did, but whether he acted as a reasonably
prudent man would or ought to have acted when similarly
situated. It is here urged that although the danger was
obvious the question of whether the plaintiff appreciated
the danger was one which ought to have been, as it was,
submitted to the jury. It may be conceded that the question as to whether the danger is obvious is ordinarily one
for the jury, but in the absence of a showing a presumption
obtains in this class of cases that the servant is possessed of
a sound mind and body. It was not pleaded, nor is there
any showing or attempted proof that plaintiff was an exception to the rule in this respect other than by inference
by reason of want of instruction as to how to avoid the
danger. He was an adult twenty-three years of age. In
Maki v. Union Pacific Coal Co., 187 Fed. 389, 109 C. C. A.
221, an order of the U. S. Circuit Court of this state
dismissing the case on the ground that the plaintiff in the
opening statement of his counsel to the jury failed to state
facts expected to be proven which, taken together, would
be sufficient upon which to predicate a recovery, the court
say: "Finally, attention is called to the rule that a recovery
may sometimes be had where the risk is obvious, but the
danger is not fully appreciated by the party injured; and
counsel argue the question whether or not the decedent appreciated the danger, should have been submitted to the
jury. But the decedent was a man presumably possessing
the ordinary faculties of an adult who has a sound mind
and body. It is true that he was a Finlander; but the
statement of his counsel contained no intimation that he
could not see these engaging wheels, or could not understand or know that they would crush a human being drawn
between them, that a person upon the revolving horizontal
wheel might be caught between them and that the clothes
of one caught between the engaging cogs would draw him
between the wheels; and in the absence of any claim or
declaration that he had not the ordinary intelligence, ability

and prudence of men in like situations, he must be presumed to have been a Finlander of ordinary prudence and intelligence. And one cannot be heard to say that he did not know or appreciate a danger, whose knowledge and appreciation were so unavoidable that a person of his prudence and intelligence could not have failed to perceive and appreciate it."

The plaintiff is presumed to have known the law of gravitation—that the coal would fall of its own weight if its support was removed, and that if it fell on him it would cause injury. (Swanson v. Great Northern Ry. Co., *supra;* Walsh v. Ry. Co., 27 Minn. 367, 8 N. W. 145; Olsen v. McMullen, 34 Minn. 94, 24 N. W. 318; Pederson v. City of Rushford, 41 Minn. 289, 42 N. W. 1063; Quick v. Iron Co., 47 Minn. 361, 50 N. W. 244.) In Thurman v. Pittsburg and M. Copper Co., 41 Mont. 141, 155, 108 Pac. 588, 591, the Supreme Court of Montana say: "While under the general rule it is the duty of the master to use ordinary care to furnish a reasonably safe place to work, and while this duty can not be delegated, in mining one of the necessary incidents of the employment of the servant is the making of the place in which he works; and any danger arising from the work as it progresses, caused by changing conditions, or the making of dangerous places safe, is assumed by the employee." In the case here there is no question that the room in which plaintiff was put to work was safe at the time he went to work. The conditions changed as the work of himself and Rotolo progressed, and such conditions so changed as a necessary incident of their work. The plaintiff and his co-employee tried to pry down the coal by inserting the iron bar in the crack. Prudence dictated to them the necessity of so doing, just as any reasonably prudent man would have done under like circumstances in order to avoid the danger of falling coal. True, plaintiff testified that he did not appreciate the danger of falling coal. His testimony must be considered in the light of his conduct and other evidence given by him as to what occurred at the time. His attempt to pry down the coal must have been for some reason. Of course it was primarily for the purpose of loading it, and in doing so it was also necessary to get it down safely and without injury to anyone. He testified that the attempt to pry down the coal was for two purposes, (1) to get the coal down so as to load it, and (2) to avoid the danger of its falling, and further testified that it was a part of their duty after firing a shot to clean up, remove loose pieces of coal, and smooth off the face of the vein. The burden was upon the plaintiff to show that he did not appreciate the danger from the, coal falling. His own evidence to the effect that he attempted to pry it down for the purpose of avoiding danger from its falling, showed, we think, that he did so appreciate the danger and concluded him upon that question, or at least would not support a finding that he did not appreciate the danger, otherwise it would be necessary for the jury to disregard his evidence.

Defendant contends and its theory is that upon the allegations of the petition and the evidence it was an assumed risk on the part of the plaintiff. Such risk is not assumed by a servant when the latter is inexperienced and his employer, knowing that fact, has failed to warn and instruct him of the danger from latent defects in the place of the employment and the method of detecting and avoiding the same, and such failure is the proximate cause of injury to such servant. Such is the established rule. The issue of negligence here tendered cast the burden upon the plaintiff to prove that he was not only inexperienced, uninstructed and not warned under such circumstances as to constitute negligence on the part of his employer, but that such negligence was also the proximate cause of his injury. If it was not the proximate cause of his injury then the failure to warn and instruct the servant was not actionable negligence and as already stated we think the plaintiff failed to prove that the company's negligence, if any, was the proximate cause of his injury. We deem it unnecessary to discuss at length the sufficiency of the petition, for if it be sufficient as stating a cause of action the failure in the proof as already indicated would be fatal to the judgment.

Other specific assignments of error are presented, but in view of what we have already said we consider it unnecessary to discuss them other than to say that we have examined and considered the alleged errors in refusing to instruct the jury, as requested by defendant, and in giving instructions over defendant's objection, and find as to them no prejudicial error, and but for the failure of proof as indicated the instructions would have fairly presented the case to the jury. For such failure of proof the defendant was entitled to the peremptory instructions requested by it for a finding in its favor, and the court erred in overruling its motion for a new trial upon that ground. The judgment will be reversed and the case remanded for further proceedings in the lower court.   *Reversed and remanded.*

POTTER, J. and BEARD, J., concur.

EVANS v. CHEYENNE CEMENT, STONE & BRICK COMPANY.

(No. 673.)

WORK AND LABOR—ASSUMPSIT—SUFFICIENCY OF PETITION—QUANTUM MERUIT — EXPRESS CONTRACT — APPEAL AND ERROR — CONFLICTING EVIDENCE—REVIEW.

1. A petition in an action to recover the alleged value of work and labor and materials furnished *held* sufficient; the petition alleging the corporate capacity of the plaintiff, that the plaintiff, at defendant's request, furnished materials and labor and constructed a sidewalk around defendant's property, described as situated at the northeast corner of certain streets in a certain city named, that the labor and material so furnished and the sidewalk so constructed were of the reasonable value of $163.28, and that said sum was due and unpaid.

2. Where plaintiff sued for work and labor performed and materials furnished at defendant's request, in the construction of a sidewalk, and alleged in the petition the reasonable value of the labor and materials and the sidewalk as constructed, and that the amount thereof was due and unpaid, the fact that it appeared,' as alleged in the answer, that there was an express contract between the parties for the construction of the sidewalk, stating the price to be paid therefor, did not bar plaintiff's right to recover the contract price.

3. In an action for work and labor and materials furnished, where the petition is upon a *quantum meruit*, proof of a special contract fixing the price to be paid for said labor and the furnishing of the materials will not necessarily defeat the plaintiff's recovery, but the contract price becomes the *quantum meruit* in the case.

4. Where the evidence on several questions of fact was conflicting, but there was sufficient evidence on each of them to support the findings, *Held*, that the judgment would not be reversed on the ground that it was not sustained by the evidence.

[Decided March 24, 1913.]   (130 Pac. 849.)

Error to the District Court, Laramie County; Hon. Charles E. Carpenter, Judge.

The Cheyenne Cement, Stone and Brick Company brought the action against David P. Evans to recover the alleged value of the labor and materials furnished in the construction of a sidewalk. The answer alleged that the work was done under a special contract, and that it failed to comply with the contract in certain particulars. Judgment was rendered for the plaintiff, and the defendant brought error. The other material facts are stated in the opinion.

Ray E. Lee and *Charles F. Mallin*, for plaintiff in error.

The petition is insufficient to authorize a recovery. (2 Ency. Pl. & Pr. 1010; 6 id. 643; 15 Ency. Law, 1007; Bannister v. Coal & Coke Co., 61 S. E. 338; Bushnell v. Cogshall, 62 Pac. 1101.) It should have alleged that the defendant had accepted the work as done and promised to pay for it. The work having been done under a special contract the plaintiff could not recover the reasonable value thereof, except by proving substantial compliance with the contract, or that the defendant had accepted the work; and the burden of proof was upon the plaintiff to show that the contract was abandoned in order to recover another measure of value than that agreed upon by the parties to the contract. (Clark v. Smith, 14 Johns. 326; Peoria v. Fruin-Bambrick Co., 169 Ill. 36; Denmead v. Coburn, 15 Md. 29; Dermott v. Jones, 2 Wall. 1; Eckel v. Murphy, 15 Pa. St. 488; Elliott v. Caldwell, 43 Minn. 357; Fogg v. Rapid Trans. Co., 90 Hun, 274; Lumber Co. v. Sahrbacher, 38 Pac. 635; Harris v. Sharpless, 202 Pa. St. 243; Hart v. Mfg. Co., 221 Ill. 444; Hood v. Smiley, 5 Wyo. 70; Houlahan v. Clark, 110 Wis. 43; Jennings v. Camp., 13 Johns. 94; Perry v. Quackenbush, 38 Pac. 740; Smith v. Brady, 17 N. Y. 173; Turner v. Wills, 64 N. J. L. 269; Zottman v. San Francisco, 20 Cal. 96.)

The evidence discloses that the defendant did not accept the work, and therefore the plaintiff could not recover upon his petition, unless upon showing performance according to the contract. (Bozarth v. Dudley, 44 N. J. L. 304; Johnson v. Feshefeldt, 20 L. R. A. (N. S.) 1069; Denmead v. Coburn, *supra;* Dermott v. Jones, *supra.*) The contract was not complied with, since the sidewalk area had not been graded, as required by the city specifications, which were made a part of the contract. The sidewalk was constructed below grade. The approval of the City Engineer was required by the contract; this being shown by the proposal made by the plaintiff and accepted by the defendant; by the permit for the construction of the sidewalk issued by the engineer; and by the ordinances of the city. The plaintiff was not entitled to recover without showing such approval by the engineer or an excuse for not obtaining it. (Ashley v. Henahan, 50 O. St. 559; Beck v. B. & L. Co., 85 N. Y. Supp. 323; Diehl v. Schmalacker, 57 id. 244;

Guthat v. Gow, 95 Mich. 527; Hennessy v. Metzger, 152 Ill. 505; Cement Co. v. Beifeld, 173 Ill. 179; McAlpine v. Trustees, 101 Wis. 468; McNamara v. Harrison, 81 Ia. 486; Michaelis v. Wolf, 136 Ill. 68; Mundy v. L. & N. R Co., 67 Fed. 633; Hardware Co. v. Berghoefer, 103 Wis. 359; Schmidt v. North Yakima, 12 Wash. 121; Smith v. Brady, 17 N. Y. 173; Vincent v. Stiles, 77 Ill. App. 200; Wendt v. Voegel, 87 Wis. 462; Pope v. King, 16 L. R. A. (N. S.) 489.)

The plaintiff having been guilty of a breach of the special contract, and having attempted to abandon it without completing the work, cannot disregard it and recover the reasonable value of the work performed. (Barkstrom v. Ryan, 122 N. Y. Supp. 878; Clark v. Smith, 14 Johns. 326; Carpenter v. Gray, 12 R. I. 306; Ginther v. Schultz, 40 O. St. 104; Kennelly v. Walker, 107 N. Y. Supp. 95; Marshall v. Jones, 11 Me. 54; Maxwell v. Moore, 50 So. 882; Oakley v. Morton, 11 N. Y. 25; Tinley v. Van West, 104 N. Y. Supp. 3.) The law will not imply a contract to build a sidewalk in a manner forbidden by the city ordinances. (Cundell v. Dawson, 4 Man. G. & S. 375; U. S. v. Dietrich, 126 Fed. 671; Church v. Ga. Light Co., 6 A. & E., 864; Brady v. Mayor &c., 16 How. Pr. 432; Cope v. Rowlands, 2 M & W. 149; People v. Metz, 24 L. R. A. (N. S.) 201; Yount v. Denning, 35 Pac. 207.) The finding of substantial compliance with the contract without a finding of the defects and the reasonable damage caused thereby is insufficient. (Manitowoc &c. Co. v. Glue Co., 97 N. W. 515; Norton v. U. S. &c Co., 85 N. Y. Supp. 886; Spence v. Ham, 163 N. Y. 220.) The finding as to the reasonable value of the sidewalk was based on an improper measure of damages. (Hayward v. Leonard, 7 Pick. 181; Bell v. Fox, 123 N. Y. Supp. 310.) The finding that defendant had accepted the work is contrary to the evidence, since such acceptance could not be inferred from the fact that the defendant permitted the sidewalk to remain and made use of it without objection. (Gwinnup v. Shies, 161 Ind. 500; Hahl v.

Deutsch, 94 S. W. 443; Halleck v. Bresnahen, 3 Wyo. 73;
Land Co. v. Brewer, 51 So. 559; Marchland v. Perrin, 124
N. W. 1112; Church v. Cement Co., 66 Md. 598.) The
finding that the sidewalk had not been condemned by the
city engineer is against the evidence, the city engineer having testified that he refused to approve the sidewalk because it did not comply with the city specifications; that
he condemned a part of the material and ordered the work
to stop two or three different times for the reason that the
ingredients were not being properly mixed.

Marion A. Kline, for defendant in error.

No objection was raised to the petition in the Justice
Court and it could not, therefore, be objected to on the
trial in the District Court. (Comp. Stat. 1910, Sec. 5264.)
Pleadings in justice courts are to be construed liberally.
(Hudson Coal Co. v. Hauf, 109 Pac. 21; Everett v. Irwin,
(Ind.) 94 N. E. 352; Brown v. Thompson, (Ind.) 90 N.
E. 631; Costello v. Ten Eyck, (Mich.) 49 N. W. 153; 22
Ency. Pl. & Pr. 1365.) By filing an answer the defendant
was estopped to deny that he did not know the nature of
the action, or that he was unable to make an intelligent
defense. (Sinkling v. Ill. Cent. R. Co., (S. D.) 74 N. W.
1029.) The objection to the petition having been made
during the trial in the District Court by objecting to the
introduction of any evidence, the most liberal construction
will be given to the petition in order to sustain it. (1 Bates
Pl. & Pr. 458, 459; Wilkins v. Stidger, 22 Cal. 232; Hudson Coal Co. v. Hauf, *supra.*)

There is no authority under the code of procedure in
this state for a non-suit against the consent of the plaintiff;
but if a non-suit is ever authorized any error in refusing it
was cured by the evidence subsequently introduced. (Comp.
Stat. 1910, Sec. 4610; Byrd v. Blessing, 11 O. St. 364;
Stockstill v. R. Co., 24 O. St. 83; N. P. R. Co. v. Mares,
123 U. S. 713; Hopkins v. Clark, 158 N. Y. 304, 53 N. E.
27; Iron Co. v. Brown, 171 N. Y. 488, 64 N. E. 194; Lynch
v. Johnson, 109 Mich. 640, 67 N. W. 908; Chicago &c. R.

Co. v. Wedel, 144 Ill. 9, 32 N. E. 547; Chamberlain v.
Woodin, (Ida.) 23 Pac. 178; Runkle v. Burnham, 153 U.
S. 222; Ry. Co. v. Snyder, 152 U. S. 683; Denver &c. R.
Co. v. Smock, (Colo.) 48 Pac. 681; Gilmer v. Inv. Co.,
(Wash.) 79 Pac. 1103; Sigafus v. Porter, 179 U. S. 116;
Denver &c. R. Co. v. Robinson, (Colo.) 40 Pac. 840; Ry.
Co. v. Jones, (Md.) 50 Atl. 423; Keener v. Baker, 93 Fed.
377; Ratliff v. Ratliff, 131 N. C. 425, 63 L. R. A. 963;
United Rys. &c. v. State (Md.), 49 Atl. 923; Lowe v. Ry.
Co. (Cal.), 98 Pac. 675; Burnham v. R. Co. (N. H.), 45
Atl. 564; Thompson v. Avery (Utah), 39 Pac. 831; Horn v.
Reitler (Colo.), 25 Pac. 502; Taylor v. Taylor (Or.), 103
Pac. 537; Yergy v. Helena &c. Co. (Mont.), 102 Pac. 316;
Elmensorf v. Golden (Wash.), 80 Pac. 266; Weil v. Nevitt
(Colo.), 31 Pac. 488; Bopp v. Electric &c. Co. (N. Y.), 69
N. E. 122; Bostwick v. Willett (N. J.), 60 Atl. 398; Esler
v. Ry. Co. (N. J.), 58 Atl. 113; Dimuria v. Transfer Co.
(Wash.), 97 Pac. 657; Ryan v. Lambert (Wash.), 96 Pac.
232; Curtin v. Lumber Co. (Wash.), 91 Pac. 956; Trickey
v. Clark, 50 Ore. 516, 93 Pac. 457; Ry. Co. v. Henderson
(Colo.), 13 Pac. 910; Barton v. Kane, 17 Wis. 38; Ingalls
v. Oberg (Minn.), 72 N. W. 841; Carey v. Packet Co. (N.
J.), 60 Atl. 180; Jones v. Ry. Co., 46 N. Y. Supp. 321;
Ayres v. Ins. Co. (Ia.), 85 Am. Dec. 559; Weinhard v.
Bank (Or.), 68 Pac. 806.)

The court found that the defendant had accepted the sidewalk, "and is now enjoying the use and benefits of the same."
That finding was based upon competent evidence, and is,
therefore, binding upon the appellate court. The court further found that the contract did not require an approval of
the work by the city engineer. That finding was also supported by the evidence. The city specifications were not before the trial court, and, therefore, the finding as to the
necessity for approval by the engineer must be accepted as
final. All the evidence with reference to the grading of the
sidewalk area is outside the issues in this case. But the court
found that, although a part of the sidewalk was not upon the

established grade, neither the engineer nor the defendant offered any objection to its being constructed on the grade on
which it was constructed. Further, it was shown by the
evidence that temporary grades were allowed by the engineer upon demand of the owner.

The plaintiff was entitled to recover the contract price,
notwithstanding that he had sued for the reasonable value of
the work and materials. (Hecht v. Stanton, 6 Wyo. 84, 43
Pac. 508.) There was sufficient competent evidence to support every finding of fact, and that being true the appellate
court will not disturb the findings. (Slothower v. Hunter,
15 Wyo. 189, 88 Pac. 36; Riordan v. Horton, 16 Wyo. 363,
94 Pac. 448; Schiller v. Blyth &c. Co., 15 Wyo. 304, 88 Pac.
648; State v. Bridge Co. (Ind.), 97 N. E. 803; Hafel-
finger v. Perry (Colo.), 121 Pac. 1021; Hausam v. Parker
(Okla.), 121 Pac. 1063; 3 Cent. Dig., Sec. 3983, App. &
Error; 2 Dec. Dig., Sec. 1010, App. & Error; Kenck v.
Deegan (Mont.), 122 Pac. 746.) The defendant did not assert any damages nor ask for any finding for any supposed
breach of the contract, and, therefore, he cannot complain
that no such finding was made. (Leeds v. Little (Minn.),
44 N. W. 310; Heckmann v. Binkney, 81 N. Y. 214; Bader
v. N. Y. City, 101 N. Y. Supp. 351; Walstrom v. Constr.
Co., 161 Ala. 619.) Under the evidence the plaintiff could
have recovered upon the contract or upon a *quantum meruit.*
(30 Ency. Law, 1221, 1224; Roskilly v. Steigers, 96 Mo.
App. 576; Katz v. Bedford (Cal.), 19 Pac. 524; Pinches v.
Church, 55 Conn. 183, 10 Atl. 264; Blakeslee v. Holt, 42
Conn. 226; Hayward v. Leonard, 7 Pick. 181; Davis v.
Badders, 95 Ala. 348, 10 So. 422; Cigar Co. v. Wall. P. Co.
(Ala.), 51 So. 263; Lumber Co. v. Cook, 42 So. 838; School
Dist. v. Boyer, 26 Kan. 484; Gilman v. Hall, 11 Vt. 510, 34
Am. Dec. 700; Keeler v. Herr (Ill.), 41 N. E. 750; Glacius
v. Black, 50 N. Y. 145; Crouch v. Guttman, 134 N. Y. 45,
31 N. E. 271; Lynch v. Elevator Co., 80 Tex. 23, 15 S. W.
208; Flaherty v. Miner, 123 N. Y. 382, 25 N. E. 418; Gal-

lagher v. Sharpless, 134 Pa. St. 134; Wagner v. Allen (Mass.), 55 N. E. 320; Oberlies v. Bullinger (Ill.), 30 N. E. 999; City v. Stookey, 154 Fed. 775; Harlan v. Stufflebeam (Cal.), 25 Pac. 686; Anderson v. Harper (Wash.), 70 Pac. 965; Evans v. Howell (Ill.), 71 N. E. 854; Palmer v. Meriden Co. (Ill.), 59 N. E. 253; 6 Cyc. 86; Blood v. Wilson, 141 Mass. 25; Moore v. Carter, 146 Pa. St. 492; Taylor v. Renn, 79 Ill. 186; Fuller v. Rice (Mich.), 18 N. W. 204; Mosaic Tile Co. v. Chiera (Mich.), 95 N. W. 537; Smith v. Packard, 94 Va. 739; Goldsmith v. Hand, 26 O. St. 105; Becker v. Hecker, 9 Ind. 499; Moffit v. Glass, 117 N. C. 142; Dixon v. Gravely, 117 N. C. 84; Hattin v. Chase (Me.), 33 Atl. 989; Bozarth v. Dudley, 44 N. J. L. 304; School Dist. v. Lund (Kan.), 33 Pac. 596; Bush v. Finucane (Colo.), 6 Pac. 514; Hunt v. Elliott (Cal.), 20 Pac. 132; Foulger v. McGrath (Utah), 95 Pac. 1006; Comm'rs. v. Gibson (Ind.), 63 N. E. 983; McDonough v. Marble Co., 112 Fed. 637; Britton v. Turner, 6 N. H. 481; Bedow v. Tonkin (S. D.), 59 N. W. 223; Parcell v. McComber (Neb.), 7 N. W. 529; McKinney v. Springer, 3 Ind. 59; Major v. McLester, 4 Ind. 591; Tandy v. Hatcher, 9 Ky. L. Rep. 150; Powell v. Howard, 109 Mass. 192; Gove v. Island City Co. (Or.), 24 Pac. 521; Deposit Co. v. Burke, 88 Fed. 630; Orem v. Keelty, 36 Atl. 1030; Gross v. Creyts, 90 N. W. 689; Coal Co. v. Coal Co., 51 W. Va. 474; Edmunds v. Welling (Or.), 110 Pac. 533.) Even though there is a provision in the contract requiring an architect's certificate before payment, that will not prevent a recovery on a *quantum meruit* where such certificate has not been obtained. (Everroad v. Schwartzkopf (Ind.), 23 N. E. 969; Munk v. Kanzler, 58 N. E. 543; Davis v. Badders, 95 Ala. 348; Adams v. Crosby, 48 Ind. 153; Linnenkohl v. Winkelmeyer, 54 Mo. App. 570.) The work having been under the observation of the city engineer, and no complaint having been made during its progress, the objection that it was not properly constructed cannot now be raised. (Laycock

v. Parker (Wis.), 79 N. W. 327; Evans v. Howell, 111 Ill.
App. 171; S. C. 71 N. E. 854.) Whether there was a substantial compliance with the terms of the contract was a
question of fact for the trial court. (Harlan v. Stufflebeam,
25 Pac. 687; Nolan v. Whitney, 88 N. Y. 648; Phillips v.
Gallant, 62 N. Y. 264.) The conclusion of the trial court is
clearly and manifestly just upon the evidence, and, therefore,
any technical objection as to the findings ought not to be regarded with favor. (Pasha v. Bohart, 122 Pac. 284.)

BEARD, JUSTICE.

This case was brought by the defendant in error as plaintiff against the plaintiff in error as defendant in justice
court to recover the amount claimed to be due from said
defendant to the plaintiff for the construction of a cement
sidewalk. The case was tried to a jury in justice court resulting in a verdict and judgment in favor of plaintiff and
against the defendant for $163.25 and costs. The defendant,
Evans, appealed the case to the District Court of Laramie
County, where the case was tried *de novo* to the court, without a jury, and judgment was again rendered for the plaintiff and against defendant for the sum of $163.28 and costs,
and defendant brings error.

The plaintiff in its petition filed in the justice court, after
alleging the corporate capacity of plaintiff, alleged in substance that between the 14th and 28th days of September,
1908, plaintiff, at the request of defendant, furnished materials and labor and constructed a cement sidewalk around
defendant's property situated at the southeast corner of
House and Twenty-third streets, in the City of Cheyenne.
That the labor and materials so furnished and the sidewalk
so constructed were of the reasonable value of $163.20.
That said sum was due and unpaid.

The defendant filed an answer denying each and every
allegation of the petition; and for a second defense alleged
in substance that the plaintiff made and entered into the
following contract or agreement with defendant, to-wit:

"Cheyenne, Wyoming, Sept. 14, 1908.

"Mr. D. P. Evans, Cheyenne, Wyo.

"Dear Sir:—We propose to construct a cement sidewalk one hundred eight (108) feet long and five (5) feet wide along the west side of your residence, more fully described as No. 301 E. 23 street. Will furnish all labors and material, and put in same according to the city specifications, and guarantee a first-class job in every respect for the sum of $70.20.   Cheyenne Cement, Stone & Brick Co.

"By D. E. Clark, Treasurer."

That defendant accepted the terms of said agreement and plaintiff proceeded to lay sidewalk, but did not do so in accordance with the terms of said agreement, in that it did not lay said walk on the grade established by the city engineer, and failed to make the walk of the required thickness and did not properly mix the materials used in its construction. That under an oral agreement between the parties plaintiff constructed a walk on another side of said premises on the same terms; and alleged the same defects as stated above. Plaintiff replied orally, denying the new matter set up in the answer.

On the trial in the District Court the court found generally for the plaintiff, and also found that plaintiff had substantially complied with the conditions of its contract with defendant; that the walk is of the thickness required by the city specifications; that the materials used were of the proper kind and were properly mixed; that while part of said sidewalk is not on the established sidewalk grade of the city, the city engineer and the defendant both saw it while it was being constructed and made no objections to its being constructed on the grade on which it was being constructed; that neither the city or its engineer has condemned the walk or ordered its removal, although it has been laid for nearly two years; that defendant expressed himself satisfied with the walk and willing and ready to pay therefor upon the approval of the city engineer; that after the construction of the 108 feet of the walk the par-

ties entered into a new contract for the construction of the
remainder of the walk (on the other side of the lot). That
the contract did not require that the walk be approved or
accepted by the city engineer; and that defendant accepted
said walk and has enjoyed the use and benefit of the same
and that it is of substantial benefit and value to the premises. That it is of the reasonable value of $163.28.

Beside the contention of counsel for plaintiff in error that
the findings of the court are not sustained by the evidence,
it is contended that the court erred in several particulars,
which we will notice briefly. It is urged that the petition
does not state a cause of action. But we think the objection
is not well taken. The petition is substantially in the form
approved in Whittaker's Code Forms, page 26; Bradbury's
Rules of Pleading, page 865, Form No. 172; and 3 Sutherland's Code Pleading, Practice and Forms, Section 5185,
Form No. 1464. It is also contended that as the petition
claims on a *quantum meruit* the plaintiff must recover on
his *quantum meruit* or not at all. That question was passed
upon in Hecht v. Stanton, 6 Wyo. 84, on page 91 (42 Pac.
749, 43 Pac. 508), where in the opinion on petition for a rehearing, page 91, the court said: "As we understand the argument on behalf of plaintiff in error, the position is taken
that defendant in error must recover upon his *quantum meruit* or not at all, although the evidence may show that he is
entitled to recover under the contract set up by plaintiff in
error in his defense. We cannot agree to this proposition.
Neither do the authorities cited sustain it. The contract might change the amount of recovery, but could not
preclude an inquiry as to whether anything was due to
defendant in error or not." In that case the cause of
action stated in the petition was that the plaintiff had
at the instance and request of defendant made, excavated
and constructed an irrigating ditch and in so doing had necessarily removed 29,432 cubic yards of stone, gravel and
earth, which was reasonably worth ten cents per cubic yard,
or a total sum of $2,943.20, and admitted payment of $1,659.

Defendant answered denying performance of the work as alleged, and as a separate defense averred that plaintiff had commenced the construction of the ditch, that the work so commenced was not done upon any promise of defendant to pay the reasonable value of the work, but that it was done under an express contract in writing. The terms of the contract were set out, and the failure of plaintiff to construct the ditch according to the terms of the contract was alleged. In the present case the plaintiff alleged that it constructed the walk at the request of defendant and that the labor and materials were reasonably worth so much—the price mentioned in the contract pleaded by defendant—and that defendant had failed to pay therefor. Defendant denied generally those allegations and averred that the work was done under a special contract and that the work failed to comply with the contract in three particulars, viz.: 1. The materials were not properly mixed; 2. The walk was not of the required thickness; and 3. That it was not on the established grade. The two cases are alike in principle and the same rule applies to each. "It is settled law that where the contract has been fully performed by the plaintiff, and nothing remains to be done but the payment of the money by the defendant, it is not necessary to set out or declare upon the special contract, but the liability of the defendant may be enforced under a count for the reasonable value of the services." (E. D. Metcalf Co. v. Gilbert, 19 Wyo. 331, 340, 116 Pac. 1017, 1020.) "Where the complaint is upon a *quantum meruit*, proof of a special contract for a given price does not necessarily defeat the plaintiff's recovery, but the price fixed by the contract becomes the *quantum meruit* in the case." (22 Ency. P. & P. 1378.) In the case at bar the walk had been completed, and the defendant was not misled by the form of the pleading, and he had the opportunity to make and did make his defense under the contract pleaded by him. He failed, in the judgment of the court, to sustain his defense, but was not prejudiced by the form of plaintiff's pleading. On a number of questions of fact in the case the evidence was conflicting; but there was sufficient evidence on each of them to support the findings; and under the well settled rule when such is the case the judgment will not be reversed on the ground that it is not sustained by the evidence. We find no prejudicial error in the record, and the judgment of the District Court is affirmed.   *Affirmed.*

Scott, C. J., and Potter, J., concur.

THOMSON v. STATE.
(No. 712.)

Criminal Law—Larceny—Horse Stealing—Trial—Verdict—Failing to State Value of Property Stolen.

1. The statute (Comp. Stat. 1910, Sec. 6252), which provides that when an indictment charges an offense against the property of another by larceny, embezzlement or obtaining under false pretenses, the jury, on conviction, shall ascertain and declare in their verdict the value of the property stolen, embezzled or falsely obtained, is mandatory, and applies where the accused is charged with stealing a horse, although horse stealing is declared by statute to be a felony regardless of the value of the animal stolen.

[Decided March 24, 1913.]   (130 Pac. 850.)

Error to the District Court, Weston County; Hon Carroll H. Parmelee, Judge.

Daniel Thomson was charged by information in the District Court with stealing one horse alleged to be "of value" and "the property of James Ryan." The trial resulted in a verdict finding him guilty "as charged in the information," and the defendant was sentenced to a term in the penitentiary. The other material facts are stated in the opinion.

A. H. Beach and *Camplin & O'Marr,* for plaintiff in error.

The motion of the defendant below for a postponement of the trial on account of the absence of a witness for whom a subpoena had been duly issued, but who could not be found in the county by the sheriff, as shown by his return on the subpoena, should have been sustained under the provisions of Section 5139, Compiled Statutes, 1910, since the state did not agree that such absent witness would, if present, testify to the facts stated in the affidavit in support of said motion. The court also erred in permitting the filing by the prosecution of counter-affidavits opposing the motion and affidavit for continuance. (Comp. Stat. 1910, Secs. 5139-5141; Hair v. State, 14 Neb. 503; Newman v. State, 22 Neb. 355; Gandy v. State, 27 Neb. 707; State v. Abshire (La.), 17 So. 141; State v. Dakin, 52 Ia. 395; Terr v. Kinney, 9 Pac. 599.)

The court should have charged the jury to declare in their verdict the value of the property taken. (Comp. Stat. 1910, Sec. 6252.) And the jury having failed by their verdict to ascertain and declare such value, the verdict is insufficient. (Armstrong v. State, 21 O. St. 357; Holmes v. State, 58 Neb. 297, 78 N. W. 641; McCoy v. State, 22 Neb. 418, 35 N. W. 202; Fisher v. State, 52 Neb. 531, 72 N. W. 954; Bartley v. State, 53 Neb. 310.) Horse stealing is larceny, and the language of Section 6252 is clearly broad enough to embrace that offense. Defendant's motion for a directed verdict in his favor should have been sustained. A criminal charge must be proved as laid, and all essential elements of the charge must be established beyond a reasonable doubt. Where the accused is charged with larceny, if it appears that he came into possession of the property honestly, he is entitled to the benefit of such proof. (Conkwright v. People, 35 Ill. 204; People v. Miller, 11 Pac. 514.) Where the defendant has given a reasonable explanation of his possession, showing that he came by the property honestly, the burden is on the prosecution to prove the falsity thereof. (Powell v. State, 22 Tex. App. 447, 35 S. W.

737; Jones v. State, 30 Miss. 653; Johnson v. State, 12
Tex. App. 385.) There was no proof of asportation nor
of any felonious taking. Nor was there any proof of criminal intent, or of venue. The verdict is not sustained by
sufficient evidence. (Dean v. State, 41 Fla. 291, 26 So. 638;
Long v. State, 44 Fla. 134, 32 So. 870.)

D. A. Preston, Attorney General, for the State.

There was no effort made to procure the presence of the
defendant's alleged absent witness until some time after the
convening of the term at which the case stood for trial and
was tried. At the time the subpoena was issued the defendant knew that the witness was beyond the jurisdiction of the
court, and the affidavit for continuance stated that he was
a resident of North Dakota. The statute provides for taking the deposition of a non-resident witness by the defendant in a criminal case, but no effort was made by this defendant to procure the deposition of his said witness. The
application for a continuance, therefore, did not show due
diligence in procuring the presence or testimony of the witness. (Keffer v. State, 12 Wyo. 49; State v. Farrington,
90 Ia. 673; State v. Lewis, 56 Kan. 374; State v. McCoy,
11 Mo. 517; People v. Oh Lee Doom, 97 Cal. 171; Haile
v. State, (Tex.) 43 S. W. 999.)

Section 6252, Comp. Stat. 1910, requiring the jury to
ascertain and declare in their verdict the value of the property stolen, was enacted in 1869, when the penalty for larceny depended upon the value of the property stolen. But
when the value of the property stolen does not affect the penalty the provision of said section does not apply. (Hoge v.
State, 117 Ill. 35; Woodring v. State, 14 Okl. 250; Shepherd v. State, 42 Ala. 531.) Section 5832, a subsequent
statute, makes the stealing of a horse a felony regardless of
value. Therefore, it was not necessary to allege or prove
. the value of the horse described in the information as having been stolen. (Chestnut v. People, 21 Colo. 512; State
v. Young, 13 Wash. 584; State v. Washing, 36 Wash. 485.)
The defendant was found guilty as charged in the informa-

tion. The offense charged was a felony, and no essential right of the defendant was affected by the omission of the jury to find by their verdict the value of the stolen property. (Cook v. State, 49 Miss. 8; Bryant v. State, 5 Wyo. 377; Mason v. People, 2 Colo. 373; Schoonover v. State, 17 O. St. 294; State v. White, 25 Wis. 359; U. S. v. Tyler, 7 Cranch, 285.) A general verdict of guilty is a finding upon all material averments of the indictment, including the value of the property charged to be stolen. (Chitwood v. State, 44 Tex. Cr. 439; Woodring v. Terr. *supra.;* Hoge v. People, *supra;* Wolverton v. Comm. 75 Va. 909; Koolenberger v. People, 9 Colo. 233; Elphege v. State, 31 La. Ann. 717; Burgess v. State, 33 Tex. Cr. 9.)

An examination of the evidence will fully disclose it to be sufficient and the justness of the verdict. The court will not substitute its judgment for that of the jury upon the facts. (Horn v. State, 12 Wyo. 120.) Upon conflicting evidence the verdict will not be disturbed. (Joseph v. State, 47 Ind. 255; Turner v. State, 36 S. W. 87; Wright v. State, 144 Ind. 210.) The assignment of error that the verdict is contrary to law, without stating any reason therefor, presents no question for consideration. (Dickerson v. State, 18 Wyo. 440; Miller v. State, 3 Wyo. 657.) Where no objection was made to the giving of an instruction it cannot be considered on error. (2 Sackett on Inst. 2059; Meerschat v. State, (Tex.) 57 S. W. 955.)

Admitting that it is within the discretion of the trial court to direct a verdict of acquittal, yet it is an established rule that a motion to direct such a verdict will be entertained only where the trial judge can clearly see from the evidence that it would be his duty to set aside a conviction. (Clark's Cr. Proc. 469; State v. Cady, 82 Me. 426; State v. Jones, 18 Ore. 256; State v. Collins, 24 R. I. 242; Breese v. U. S., 106 Fed. 680.) The assignments of error with reference to the admission and exclusion of evidence do not point out the evidence admitted or excluded, and hence present no question for consideration here. (Foster v. State, 59 Ind.

481; Walrath v. State. 8 Neb. 80; Edmonds v. State, 34 Ark. 724; Anderson v. Terr, (N. M.) 13 Pac. 21; Sweat v. State, 90 Ga. 315; Grant v. Westfall, 57 Ind. 121; Benson v. State, 119 Ind. 488.) A party cannot complain on error of the giving of a single instruction, where the only reference thereto in the motion for new trial was as one of a group, and one or more of such instructions appear to be correct. (Dickerson v. State, 18 Wyo. 444.)

BEARD, JUSTICE.

The plaintiff in error, Daniel Thomson, was informed against, tried and convicted in the District Court of Weston County, of the crime of stealing a horse, and was sentenced to a term in the penitentiary. He brings the case here on error, seeking a reversal of that judgment.

The information was filed under the provisions of Section 5832, Comp. Stat. 1910, which provides, "Whoever steals any horse, mule, sheep or neat cattle, of value, * * * shall be deemed guilty of a felony, and upon conviction thereof shall be imprisoned in the penitentiary not less than one year nor more than ten years." The information charged the defendant below, Thomson, with stealing one horse (describing it) of value the property of James Ryan. On the trial the jury returned the following verdict: "We, the jury being lawfully impaneled and duly sworn in the above entitled cause, do find the defendant guilty as charged in the information." The sufficiency of the verdict to support the judgment is the important question in the case. The statute provides, "When the indictment charges an offense against the property of another by larceny, embezzlement, or obtaining under false pretenses, the jury, on conviction, shall ascertain and declare in their verdict the value of the property stolen, embezzled or falsely obtained." (Sec. 6252, Comp. Stat. 1910.) The Attorney General argues that this section of the statute does not apply to the case at bar, for the reason that horse stealing is declared to be a felony, regardless of the value of the animal stolen, and for the further reason that at the time Section 6252, *supra,* was adopted horse stealing was included in the statute defining larceny generally, and to be a felony the value must be twenty-five dollars or more, and if below that amount it would be a misdemeanor only; and that in that state of the law it was necessary for the jury to ascertain and return in their verdict the value of the property stolen in order to determine the grade or degree of the crime, and that it is necessary for the jury to do so only in those cases in which the value determines the degree of crime. He has cited a number of authorities to the effect that where the statute makes the stealing of a particular article or kind of property a felony without regard to its value, it is not necessary, in the absence of a statute requiring it, to allege or prove any particular value or for the jury to find and return the value in their verdict, and that a general verdict of guilty as charged in the indictment or information would support the judgment. In none of the states from which decisions have been cited by the Attorney General and numerous others which we have examined, and which so hold, do we find a statute like ours. So far as we have been able to discover, Ohio and Nebraska are the only states having such a statute, and in each of them the language is identical with that of the section above quoted. In Armstrong v. State, 21 O. St. 357, this section of the statute and the precise question involved in the present case was decided. It was there held that the statute was peremptory and applied to horse stealing, which was a felony, whatever the value of the animal stolen. The court said: "Horse stealing is larceny, and the language employed in the 167th section of the code (our section 6252, *supra*), is clearly broad enough to embrace that offense. It expressly includes in its provisions the offense of obtaining property by false pretenses, and the grade of punishment affixed to this offense by the statute, like that of horse stealing, does not depend upon the value of the property obtained. Since then the section applies expressly to one of these offenses, we cannot well hold that it has no application to the other, for there is no reason for applying it in one case that is not equally strong in the other. The determination of the grade of punishment is not, then, the only reason for this provision of the code. Although the value of the property stolen in one case, or falsely obtained in the other, may not affect the grade or kind of penalty imposed for these offenses, it may influence the degree of punishment to be inflicted. The statute gives a wide discretion to be adjudged, on conviction. In this view, it may have been regarded as material to the substantial rights of the defendant, that the actual value of the property stolen, or falsely obtained, should be ascertained and returned in the verdict, and that it should not be left, as on a general verdict of guilty, according to respectable authority it might be, (Bish. Crim. Proc., Sec. 719,) to be implied to be the amount stated in the indictment. But whatever reasons may have induced the enactment of the section, its terms are such, we are constrained to hold, that the offense for which the defendant was tried, was embraced in its provisions. To hold the reverse would virtually be a judicial repeal of the section. The verdict was not, therefore, in accordance with the express requisition of the statute, and should have been set aside on the motion of the defendant made for that purpose. It follows that the judgment must be reversed, and the cause remanded for a new trial."

The Code of Criminal Procedure containing what is now Section 6252, Comp. Stat. 1910, was adopted by the First Territorial Legislature of Wyoming and was approved December 10, 1869. (Sec. 156, Ch. 74, Title 13, Laws 1869.) The Crimes Act passed by the same legislature and approved on the same day did not make the stealing of a horse of less value than twenty-five dollars a felony, but did make the obtaining of property, of whatever value, by false pretenses, a felony. (Sec. 139, Ch. 3, Title 10, Laws 1869.) So that what is said, in the above quotation, by the Supreme Court of Ohio applies with equal force to our statute and need not be repeated.

In Holmes v. State, 58 Neb. 297, 78 N. W. 641, (a case of larceny from the person) the court, after quoting at length from Armstrong v. State, *supra*, said: "We are entirely satisfied with the reasoning employed in the opinion from which we have just quoted, and think it states the correct rule. In McCoy v. State, 22 Neb. 418, (35 N. W. 202), the prisoner was tried on the charge, and declared guilty by general verdict, of the crime of larceny as bailee and no value of the property was stated in the verdict. In an opinion of this court it was said, after quoting Section 488 of the Criminal Code (same as our Sec. 6252): 'This provision of the Code, although clearly applicable to the case at bar, was wholly ignored. Its provisions are mandatory and cannot be evaded. The verdict, therefore, conferred no authority upon the trial court to enter a judgment or sentence by which plaintiff in error was convicted of felony.' " The judgment was reversed and the cause remanded. See also Fisher v. State, 52 Neb. 531, 72 N. W. 954; McCormick v. State, 42 Neb. 866, 61 N. W. 99. In the case at bar the information clearly charges an offense against the property of another by larceny, and in our opinion comes within the provisions of Section 6252, *supra*, and that they are mandatory; and for that reason the judgment of the District Court will have to be reversed. Were it not for the express command of the statute we would not feel inclined to do so; but whatever may have been the reasons which induced the Legislature to make the provision, it has done so, and we agree with the Ohio court, that "to hold the reverse would virtually be a judicial repeal of the section."

The giving of certain instructions to the jury and the refusal to give others requested by defendant are assigned as error. We have considered the instructions given and think they fairly presented the law of the case to the jury on the evidence, with the exception that the jury should have been instructed that, if they found the defendant guilty they should ascertain and declare in their verdict the value of the property stolen. Other errors assigned are not likely to occur on another trial of the case and need not be considered.

For the reasons stated the judgment of the District Court is reversed and the case remanded for a new trial.

Reversed.

Scott, C. J., and Potter, J., concur.

[April Term, 1913.]

GROVER IRRIGATION AND LAND COMPANY v. LOVELLA DITCH, RESERVOIR AND IRRIGATION COMPANY.

(No. 705.)

Appeal and Error—Ruling on Demurrer—Exception—Necessity of Bill of Exceptions—Pleadings—Demurrer—Waiver—Pleading—Petition—Insufficiency—Objections—Defective Petition—Raising Question First Time on Appeal—Demurrer—Review of Order Overruling Demurrer—Admission of Facts by Demurrer—Answering Over—Effect of—Eminent Domain—Definition—Exercise of Power—Use in Another State—Taking Land for Irrigation Purposes—Land in Another State—Statutes—Construction.

1. Under the statute (Comp. Stat. 1910, Sec. 4597) providing that when a decision objected to is entered on the record and the grounds of the objection appear in the entry, exception may be taken by the party causing it to be noted at the end of the entry that he excepts, the grounds of objection sufficiently appear in an entry showing a ruling upon a demurrer to a pleading, either sustaining or overruling it, and an exception thereto is properly taken by causing it to be noted at the end of the entry that the objecting party excepts to the ruling; the demurrer constitutes the objection, and, since it is a part of the record proper, a statement of the grounds thereof in the entry showing a ruling upon it is unnecessary, within the meaning of said statute, to

authorize an exception thereto by noting the same at the end of the entry.

2. Where an entry upon the court journal shows that a demurrer to the petition was overruled, and that such ruling was excepted to, a bill of exceptions is not necessary to present such ruling for review.

3. Where the petition fails to state the substance of a good cause of action the defect is not waived by failure to demur, or by answering over after demurrer filed and overruled, unless the defect be aided or cured by the answer or the subsequent proceedings.

4. Where a petition in a condemnation proceeding was demurred to on the ground that it totally failed to state the substance of a good cause of action, the defect was not waived by answering after the demurrer was overruled and the ruling excepted to.

5. While a verdict may aid a defective statement of a cause of action, it will not aid a statement of a defective cause of action, and an intendment which is inconsistent with the allegations on the record will not be made after verdict in support thereof.

6. A pleading of fact, such as an answer, ·does not admit the sufficiency in law of the facts adversely alleged in a prior pleading.

7. Where a pleading is insufficient in substance, the opposite party may, without demurring, generally avail himself of such insufficiency by objecting to the introduction of evidence at the trial, by motion in arrest of judgment, by motion for judgment *non obstante veredicto,* or by proper proceeding in error.

8. An objection to a petition on the ground of a defect in substance may be made for the first time on appeal, but in such case the pleading objected to will be construed liberally and supported by every legal intendment, and it will be upheld if the necessary facts are fairly to be inferred from the allegations; this rule excluding objections relating merely to the form or manner in which the cause of action is stated.

9. Although a defendant has demurred to a petition on the ground that it is defective in substance, and the demurrer has been overruled, he does not lose the right, which would be his without demurring, to object to the petition on that ground on appeal.

10. An appellate proceeding cannot be taken from an order overruling a demurrer, but only from a final judgment rendered thereon when the party stands on his demurrer
without pleading further, or from a final judgment rendered in the cause after the trial of the issues of fact
where there has been further pleading presenting issues
of fact, but, when reviewing a judgment rendered upon a
trial involving issues of fact presented by subsequent pleadings, it is the long established practice in this court held
to accord with the intent and spirit of the code to consider
an exception to an order overruling a general demurrer.

11. Where an order overruling a demurrer is treated, as in this
state, as interlocutory merely, and not, therefore, an order
authorizing the immediate taking of an appeal or proceeding
in error, and the objection is either that the pleading, if a
complaint or petition, fails to state facts sufficient to constitute a cause of action, or that there is a want of jurisdiction of the subject matter, the general rule that error in
overruling a demurrer is waived by pleading over does not
apply.

12. Where, as in this state, an appeal or proceeding in error can
only be taken from a final order or judgment in the case
and the party is permitted to except to the overruling of
his demurrer and then plead over, it is not necessary that
a demurrer be withdrawn upon pleading over, or that it be
treated as withdrawn.

13. A demurrer does not admit the allegations of the pleading
demurred to except for the purposes of the demurrer, the
effect of which is merely to deny the legal sufficiency of
the facts alleged, so that on the overruling of the demurrer
the demurring party may then plead to the facts, and the
demurrer, though remaining on the record, will not after
such subsequent pleading be regarded as an admission of
the facts necessary to be proved to establish the cause of
action or defense upon the trial of the issues of fact.

14. Since the code allows a proceeding in error only from a final
judgment, that judgment, when rendered after the trial of
an issue of fact arising upon a pleading filed after the
overruling of a demurrer, is to be regarded as rendered
upon all the issues in the cause—the issue of law as well
as the issue of fact—or, at least, as a final judgment authorizing an appellate proceeding to question the correctness of
the decision on the issue of law as well as the issue of fact.

15. Although by pleading over after the overruling of a demurrer and going to trial upon the merits, the party who demurred takes the chances of the suggested defect in the pleading being aided or cured by the subsequent pleadings or proceedings, he retains the benefit of a proper exception taken by him to the ruling on the demurrer.

16. Under the statute (Comp. Stat. 1910, Sec. 4436) providing that after the overruling of a demurrer the party may plead further if the court is satisfied that he has a meritorious defense or claim, and did not demur for delay, when such leave to further plead is given it is full and complete, and upon pleading over after such leave granted the withdrawal of the demurrer will not be implied, where the ruling upon it was excepted to.

17. Eminent domain is the right or power of a sovereign state to appropriate private property to particular uses for the purpose of promoting the general welfare. It embraces all cases where, by authority of the state and for the public good, the property of the individual is taken, without his consent, for the purpose of being devoted to some particular use, either by the state itself or by a corporation, public or private, or by a private citizen.

18. Respecting eminent domain the several states are distinct and independent of each other, respectively possessing and exercising the power for their own purpose or their own public welfare.

19. If the particular improvement or use for which land is sought to be taken under the power of eminent domain will be of sufficient benefit to the people of the state to authorize an exercise of the power, it will not be prevented by the fact that the people of another state will also be benefited.

20. Under the power of eminent domain a state cannot take or authorize the taking of property or rights in property situated in another state.

21. Under Section 32, Article 1, of the Constitution of the State, which provides that private property shall not be taken for private use unless by consent of the owner, except for private ways of necessity, and for reservoirs, drains, flumes or ditches on or across the lands of others, for agricultural, mining, milling, domestic or sanitary purposes, nor in any case without due compensation, a private use for any of the purposes mentioned is given the same force and effect as a public use, but no greater.

22. The exercise of the power of eminent domain for the purpose of irrigation and reclamation of land is founded upon the conditions and necessities of the state where the power is to be exercised, and does not rest upon the necessities or the physical conditions of another state.

23. Where land in this state situated near the boundary line between this state and Colorado was sought to be condemned for a headgate and part of a ditch of an irrigation system to irrigate lands in Colorado near such boundary line, the fact that the irrigation and the reclamation of such land might indirectly benefit some of the people of this state, and that settlers on said lands in Colorado might purchase their supplies from a neighboring city in this state, is not such a benefit to the public of this state as to authorize the taking of the desired land in this state under the power of eminent domain; the only use which could support the exercise of the power will occur not in this state, nor for any purpose of this state, but in the other state where the water is to be applied and the land to be irrigated is located.

24. Under the conditions stated in the last preceding paragraph, it appearing that no land in this state will receive for its reclamation or cultivation any of the water to be diverted or distributed by means of the ditch, but the water is to be entirely devoted to the irrigation of land in another state, the use will be in and for that state—for its use and purpose, and not in this state or for any of its purposes. and, therefore, the principle is applicable, that the power of eminent domain will not be exercised by a state for the use of another state.

25. Another state cannot exercise.the power of eminent domain in this state, and any authority conferred by its laws to do so would be void, for the sovereignty of any government is limited to persons and property within the territory it controls.

26. The laws of a state have no extra territorial effect, and it is not necessary for a state statute to contain words expressly confining its operation within the state, since it is generally understood that it is so confined.

27. The statute (Comp. Stat. 1910, Sec. 3874) conferring authority to appropriate and condemn land for a right of way for a ditch for agricultural purposes is intended to be confined not only to a right of way within the state, but also to agricultural purposes within the state; such

authority is conferred to encourage agriculture within the
state, and if the legislative power exists to make the authority broader than that, and extend it to agricultural
purposes beyond the state boundaries, it should be so extended, if at all, by the legislature, and by words clearly
showing an intention to do so.

28. Where it was sought to condemn land in this state for a
headgate and ditch to be used to divert and conduct water
into the State of Colorado solely for the purpose of irrigating and reclaiming lands situated in that state, near the
southern boundary line of this state, *Held*, that a right to
condemn the land in this state was not shown, since no
part of the use which would support the right to condemn
was to occur in this state, or for any of the purposes of
this state.

[Decided April 7, 1913.]   (131 Pac. 43.)

Error to the District Court, Laramie County;   Hon.
Roderick N. Matson, Judge.

This was a proceeding for the condemnation of certain
land in this state for a headgate and part of an irrigation
ditch brought by the Lovella Ditch, Reservoir and Irrigation
Company against the Grover Irrigation and Land Company.
Judgment was rendered in favor of the petitioner and the
defendant brought error. The material facts are stated in
the opinion.

Clark & Clark, for plaintiff in error.

The only points desired to be presented arise upon the
demurrer to the amended petition. The contention that said
petition is insufficient is based upon two grounds: 1. Because the plaintiff acquired no permit from the state engineer authorizing the diversion of any water. 2. Because the
proposed use is not public with respect to this state. It is
not the law in this state that the necessity of an appropriation of land is left to the decision of the condemning party,
nor has that been determined by the Legislature. It is provided by statute (Comp. Stat. 1910, Sec. 3874) that a corporation requiring a way of necessity for an irrigation ditch
may condemn so much land as is "necessary therefor." The

petition in a condemnation proceeding must allege the "immediate necessity for the appropriation." (Sec. 3876.) Before commissioners can be appointed to appraise the damages the court must hear the allegations and proofs touching "the immediate necessity of the appropriation," and that question must be determined in favor of the plaintiff. (Id. Sec. 3879). No such showing as that required by the sections of the statute cited can be made in the case of an irrigation ditch in the absence of a valid permit from the state engineer authorizing the construction of a ditch and the diversion of water through it. (Id., Secs. 727, 730.) The right to condemn property is not inherent in any person or corporation; it is a matter of grace on the part of the sovereign, which may refuse it altogether, or in granting it, may annex conditions to its exercise. The right can be exercised only where the proposed use will constitute a public benefit, although it may not be necessary that it be a public use. The digging of a ditch is not a public benefit; the public benefit is found in the irrigation of lands. The party seeking to take property for an irrigation ditch must therefore establish his right to divert water through it. (Castle Rock Irr. C. & W. P. Co. v. Jurisch, 67 Neb. 377, 93 N. W. 690.) The petition does not show the securing of the necessary permit for the construction of the ditch and the appropriation of the water. It shows certain applications and the action taken thereon by the engineer, but it is contended on behalf of plaintiff in error that those proceedings did not amount to such an approval of the application as to give the defendant in error any right whatever. No indorsement made by the engineer upon either of the applications contains the essential elements of an affirmative indorsement specified in Section 732. If it should be held that by the engineer's indorsement the application of the defendant in error was approved, then the question arises whether the engineer has authority under our statutes to issue a permit for the diversion of water in this state to be used for irrigating lands in another state. The authority of the engineer to issue a permit may be attacked collaterally, since the only right to an appeal is given to the applicant for a permit. (Sec. 733.) Therefore, if the authority to issue a permit can be questioned at all it must be done collaterally.

The proposed use is not public with respect to Wyoming, and will not justify the condemnation of land in Wyoming. The only justification for extending the power of eminent domain to a private use is found in the resulting benefit to the state as a whole. The irrigation of lands in Colorado is in no sense a benefit to this state authorizing the taking of land in this state. (Lewis on Em. Dom., Secs. 1, 282, 310, 315; Mining Co. v. Sewell, 11 Neb. 394; Strickley v. Highland Boy Co., 200 U. S. 527; Potlach Lumber Co. v. Peterson, 12 Ida. 769, 88 Pac. 426; Healy Lumber Co. v. Morris, 33 Wash. 490, 74 Pac. 681; Columbus W. W. Co. v. Long, 121 Ala. 243, 25 So. 702.) In the last case cited it was said to be an admitted fact generally that the power of eminent domain inheres in a state for domestic uses only, to be exercised for the benefit of its own people, and cannot be extended merely to promote the public uses of a foreign state. Citing that case it is said in Lewis on Eminent Domain: "The public use for which property may be taken is a public use within the state from which the power is derived." (Sec. 310.)

Kinkead & Mentzer, for defendant in error.

The defendant below having answered after the overruling of its demurrer and allowed the trial to proceed on the merits there can be no review of the ruling upon the demurrer. (Griffin v. Wattles, (Mich.) 78 N. W. 122; 2 Cyc. 646; Wheeler v. Baker, (Neb.) 71 N. W. 750; Prosser v. Chapman, 29 Conn. 515; Love v. Johnson, 34 N. C. 367; Jordan v. Wickham, 21 Mo. App. 536; Ry. Co. v. Murray, 87 Fed. 647; Davis v. Lumber Co., 14 Wyo. 517; Johnston v. Irrigation Co., 4 Wyo. 164; Perkins v. McDowell, 3 Wyo. 328.) If the plaintiff might have amended its petition, if amendment was necessary, so as to support the judgment, the defendant could not have been prejudiced by the overruling of the demurrer, even though such amendment was not filed. (Ry. Co. v. Pollock, 16 Wyo. 321; Kuhn v. McKay, 7 Wyo. 42.)

There was no proper exception to the decision upon the demurrer; the entry showing the ruling not containing the grounds of the objection, and there being no bill of exceptions. (Comp. Stat. 1910, Secs. 4594, 4595, 4597-9, 5107, 5109; Burns v. Ry. Co., 14 Wyo. 498.)

The validity of a water right cannot be questioned in an action to condemn a right of way for the ditch. (Schneider v. Schneider (Colo.), 86 Pac. 347; Denver P. & I. Co. v. Ry. Co. (Colo.), 69 Pac. 568.) A lawful appropriation of water is not under the law of this state a condition precedent to acquiring a right of way for a ditch by purchase nor to the right to construct a ditch. Hence, if the defendant by its conduct in this case has acquiesced in the condemnation proceedings by stipulating that the question of damages which it would sustain by reason of the taking should be submitted to the court for adjudication, it could not repudiate its own act. The allegations of the petition upon which the final judgment was rendered alleges the facts as to the applications filed in the engineer's office and the official action taken thereon, and that a right to construct the ditch and divert water was acquired. Whether such right was acquired was a question of fact in the case, and that question was finally decided against the defendant by the lower court upon the evidence submitted, and as the evidence is not before this court, the decision of the trial court upon the question is not here for consideration. The pleadings show the necessary affirmative action by the state engineer upon the application of the plaintiff, defendant in error here, and is thus sufficient to sustain the judgment. The acts of public officers are presumed to be legal and regular until the contrary affirmatively appears. (Cicero v. Ry. Co. (Ind.), 97 N. E. 389.) The case cited by opposing counsel (Castle Rock &c. Co. v. Jurisch, 93 N. W. 690) is not in point, for the reason that in that case the petitioner in the condemnation proceeding had been refused a permit to appropriate water for its proposed ditch. The state is the only party competent to question the acts of the engineer in the exercise of the power granted him by the constitution and statutes to supervise the waters of the state and their distribution. (Water Works v. Peralta (Cal.), 45 Pac. 169; Quigley v. Birdseye (Mont.), 28 Pac. 741.) The state engineer has the power to approve an application for and thereby to permit the diversion of water in this state for the purpose of irrigating lands lying wholly within a neighboring state. (Willey v. Decker, 11 Wyo. 496; Bean v. Morris, 221 U. S. 485; Atchison v. Peterson, 20 Wall. 507; Basey v. Gallagher, id. 681; Kansas v. Colo., 206 U. S. 46; Rickey L. & C. Co. v. Miller, 218 U. S. 258; Morris v. Bean, 146 Fed. 423; Bean v. Morris, 159 Fed. 651; Hoge v. Eaton, 135 Fed. 411; Anderson v. Bassman, 140 Fed. 14; Howell v. Johnson, 89 Fed. 556; Const., Art. I, Sec. 31; Art. VIII, Secs. 1, 2, 3, 5; Farm Inv. Co. v. Carpenter, 9 Wyo. 110; Cline v. Stock (Neb.), 98 N. W. 454; Brown v. Cunningham, 82 Ia. 512, 48 N. W. 1042; Rosmiller v. State, 89 N. W. 839; Perkins Co. v. Graft, 114 Fed. 441.) From a review of the authorities cited it is apparent that where, as appears in this case, the legitimate demands of this state as to the waters of Crow Creek having been satisfied, the State of Colorado and this plaintiff have the right to insist upon the natural flow of the surplus waters of the stream into Colorado. Plaintiff's diversion being at a point below any possible subsequent diversion for useful purposes within this state, and the plaintiff having lawfully appropriated and acquired the right to divert such waters at a point just over the line in the other state, its taking of the water in this state as desired is merely taking that which already belongs to it by virtue of its appropriation under the laws of Colorado. In permitting such appropriation and diversion in this state the engineer guarded every interest, and followed the spirit and plain intent of the constitution.

Upon the facts alleged in the petition this state was required to permit the waters of the stream in question to flow in their natural channel, without further diminution, into the State of Colorado. (Coffman v. Robbins, 8 Or. 278.) One who is entitled to a given quantity of the water of a stream may take the same at any point on that stream, and may change the point of diversion at pleasure, if the rights of others be not injuriously affected thereby. (Hobart v. Wicks, 15 Nev. 418; Kidd v. Laird, 15 Cal. 162; Davis v. Gale, 32 Cal. 26; Junkans v. Bergin, 67 Cal. 267; Ramelle v. Irish, 96 Cal. 214; Coffin v. Ditch Co., 6 Colo. 444; Sieber v. Frink, 7 Colo. 148; Strickler v. Colo. Springs, 16 Colo. 62; Woolman v. Garringer, 1 Mont. 535; Kinney on Irr., Secs. 233, 248; Black's Pom. on Water Rights, Sec. 69; Gould on Waters, Sec. 237; Anderson v. Bassman, 140 Fed. 21.)

If the contention that this plaintiff in its petition has shown a right to divert the water in this state is correct, then it must follow that it has the right to condemn land for a right of way for its ditch. The constitution and the statute give it that right. (Const., Art. 1, Secs. 32, 33; Comp. Stat. 1910, Sec. 3874.) An irrigation ditch serves a public purpose, and although it is constructed for a private use the right to condemn a right of way therefor is given by the constitution. The Legislature may vest the power of eminent domain in a company, whose purpose it is to irrigate lands in a neighboring state. The language of the statute above cited is general and does not withhold the power of condemnation from this plaintiff. The requirements as to public use are met when the taking will tend to enlarge the resources, increase the industrial energies, and promote the productive powers of any considerable part of the state. As found by the trial court, the reclamation of the land in question in the adjoining state just beyond the boundary line of this state will be of material and substantial benefit to a considerable part of the individuals of a section of this state, and "indirectly contribute to the prosperity of the whole community." The *obiter dictum* found in the Alabama case of Water Works Co. v. Long, 25 So. 702, is cited as the sole authority for the text in Lewis on Eminent Domain, and is neither controlling nor applicable here, for the reason that with reference to an irrigation ditch it is the public benefit, irrespective of the character of the use, which furnishes the foundation for the right of eminent domain. The right claimed in this case is supported by the authorities cited as to the right to appropriate water for use in another state, and particularly by the case of In re. Townsend, 39 N. Y. 175, which involved the right of a canal company to condemn lands in New York which would be flooded by the construction of a reservoir for supplying water to the canal of the petitioner in the State of New Jersey. (See also Gilmer v. Lime Point, 18 Cal. 229.)

Clark & Clark, for plaintiff in error, in reply.

In this state no appeal can be prosecuted until after final judgment, but a defendant whose demurrer is overruled may either stand thereon and submit to judgment and then appeal from the judgment, or may save his exception to the order overruling the demurrer, answer over, go to trial, and then appeal from an unfavorable judgment, and thereby secure a review of the order overruling the demurrer. (Perkins v. McDowell, 3 Wyo. 328; Dobson v. Owens, 5 Wyo. 85; Mo. Pac. Ry. Co. v. Webster, 3 Kan. App. 106, 42 Pac. 845.) No bill of exceptions is necessary to present for review a ruling upon a demurrer to a pleading. (Perkins v. McDowell, *supra;* Dobson v. Owens, *supra.*) The entry in which the ruling upon the demurrer appears states the exception of the defendant thereto. It was unnecessary for the entry to state any further grounds of objection in the entry. There can be no question as to the power of this state to prohibit, limit or condition the right of any person to divert public waters within the state. (Kirk v. Board (Neb.), 134 N. W. 167.) When the plaintiff comes into this state to make its diversion it subjects itself to all the statutory limitations imposed by this state. An examination

of the petition as finally amended will show that the various
applications and official indorsements with reference to the
right to construct the ditch and appropriate the water in
this state are set out in full, for the very purpose of raising
the legal question as to whether the action of the engineer
constituted an approval, and the answer put in issue that
question.   The general grant by statute of the power of
eminent domain to all corporations of a certain class or organized for certain purposes does not include foreign corporations.   (Lewis on Em. Dom., Sec. 374; Pyrites Co. v.
Mining Co., 119 Ga. 354, 100 Am. St. Rep. 174; Helena
&c. Co. v. Spratt, 35 Mont. 108, 88 Pac. 772; Postal Tel. C.
Co. v. Railroad, 94 Fed. 234.)   Although a foreign corporation may be authorized to do business in this state, the
courts will not permit it to exercise the power of eminent
domain unless the Legislature has clearly and expressly
granted that right to such a corporation.

POTTER, JUSTICE.

The Lovella Ditch, Reservoir and Irrigation Company, a
corporation organized under the laws of the State of Colorado, brought this proceeding in the District Court in Laramie County by filing a petition with the clerk of that court
to condemn certain land situated in this state owned by the
Grover Irrigation and Land Company, a corporation also
organized under the laws of Colorado, for the purpose of
locating and maintaining thereon the headgate and part of
the ditch of an irrigation system being constructed or about
to be constructed by the plaintiff to divert water from Crow
Creek and thereby reclaim 10,000 acres of land situated in
Weld County, in the State of Colorado.   It is alleged and
the fact is not disputed that Crow Creek is a natural stream
flowing through the land of defendant and into and through
the northern part of Colorado.   That stream has its source
in this state, and the land of defendant is located on or near
the southern boundary line of the state in township 12,
range 62.   The location of the proposed headgate and point
of diversion for the ditch in question is upon the east bank

of the stream in this state about 700 feet from the boundary line between this state and the State of Colorado.

An amended petition was filed as a substitute for and taking the place of the original petition. The defendant filed a demurrer to the amended petition stating the following grounds: (1) That said petition does not state facts sufficient to constitute a cause of action; (2) that it is insufficient in law, on its face, to authorize the appropriation of the land of the defendant as prayed for; (3) that it shows that the plaintiff is not entitled to appropriate the land of the defendant as prayed. The demurrer was overruled, and to that ruling the defendant excepted. Thereafter the defendant filed an answer putting in issue the necessity for taking the land described or locating the headgate in this state, and also the right of the plaintiff to locate the headgate, or construct the same or the ditch, or divert and appropriate the water of said stream in this state as proposed. A reply was filed denying some of the allegations of the answer which relate to matters not necessary to be considered.

Before the matter was submitted to the District Court for final determination an application made by the plaintiff for an order authorizing it to take immediate possession of the land upon executing a good and sufficient bond with sureties to be approved as provided by law was heard and granted, to which the defendant objected and excepted. It appears that upon the hearing of that application evidence was introduced by both parties, and the cause was finally submitted upon that evidence and the pleadings and record. The court found specifically, among other things, that the plaintiff has a right to divert the water of the stream aforesaid within this state for the purpose of irrigating about 10,000 acres of land situated in the northern part of the State of Colorado; and that in the construction of plaintiff's said irrigation system and its headgate it is necessary for it to have, own and control the said land of the defendant, the same being described by metes and bounds. And it was thereupon ordered, adjudged and decreed that the plaintiff "be and is hereby authorized to permanently appropriate" the said land "for the purpose of constructing its said irrigation system," and commissioners were appointed to determine the compensation to be paid for the taking or injuriously affecting such lands. The facts found, the conclusions, and the order, including the appointment of commissioners, are all embraced in the same entry, and at the end thereof appears the following: "to all of which the defendant, The Grover Irrigation and Land Company, at the time duly excepted and excepts." The commissioners so appointed subsequently filed their report showing that they had met, qualified and organized as required by law, and certifying the amount of land necessary to be taken and the damages accruing to the owner thereof. It was stated in said report that the commissioners had appointed a time and place for hearing, notified the parties thereof, and met at the time so appointed, that the said defendant did not appear, and that after viewing the premises and hearing the proofs offered by the plaintiff, the damages to be paid to the defendant had been assessed in the sum of $84. The defendant, as permitted by statute, filed a written exception to the report of the commissioners, thereby excepting to said report on the ground "that the plaintiff herein has shown no right to appropriate for the uses and purposes set forth in the amended petition herein any of the land owned by this defendant as prayed in said petition." Upon the exceptions so filed the report was reviewed by the court, no demand being made by either party for a jury trial, and the same was confirmed, and it was ordered that the title to the land in question be confirmed in the plaintiff, it being recited in the order that the amount of the compensation assessed by the commissioners had been paid to the clerk of the court for the use and benefit of the defendant. To all of that order also, as recited therein, the defendant duly excepted.

A petition in error has been filed in this court by said defendant for the review of the proceedings, assigning as error the overruling of the demurrer to the amended and substituted petition, the overruling of the exceptions to the report of the commissioners, and the making and entering of the several orders and judgment above referred to, complaining of the judgment and each of said orders on the ground that the same is contrary to law. A motion to dismiss was filed by counsel for defendant in error, and the cause was argued and submitted upon such motion and also upon the merits without a waiver of the motion.

1. The motion to dismiss is based upon these facts: That there is no bill of exceptions in the record, that after the demurrer was overruled the defendant filed an answer and permitted a hearing upon the merits, and has brought this proceeding for a review of the final judgment. It is contended in support of the motion that without a bill of exceptions the exception to the ruling upon the demurrer is not properly preserved and cannot, therefore, be considered, and, further, that by filing the answer and permitting a trial upon the merits the demurrer was waived and also the error, if any, in overruling it. And it seems to be assumed in so contending that by waiving the demurrer the objections therein stated would also be waived. In view of the character of the objections urged against the amended petition as ground for reversal, it may not be very important in this case whether the plaintiff in error is in a position permitting it to assign as error the order overruling the demurrer. But it is not improper to consider and decide that question, and, since counsel for defendant in error have earnestly contended for a rule as to the necessity of a bill of exceptions to present for review on error a ruling upon a demurrer to a pleading in conflict with the previous decisions and the uniform and hitherto unquestioned practice in this court, we think it advisable, particularly as to that question, that the law upon the subject as we understand it should be again stated, and the reasons therefor more fully explained, especially with reference to certain statutory provisions relating to exceptions relied on by counsel in support of the

motion. Properly construed and understood, there should
be no confusion in applying those provisions.

Originally, at common law only the errors apparent on
the face of the record proper were reviewable on a writ of
error, that record consisting of the pleadings, process, verdict, and judgment. To remedy that condition of the law a
statute was enacted permitting a bill of exceptions. A bill
under that statute was described as founded on some objection in point of law to the opinion and direction of the court,
upon a trial at bar, or of the judge at *nisi prius,* either as to
the competency of witnesses, the admissibility of evidence or
the legal effect of it, or for overruling a challenge, or refusing a demurrer to evidence, or some matter of law arising
upon facts not denied, in which either party is overruled by
the court. (2 Tidd's Pr. 862; Wheeler v. Winn, 53 Pa.
St. 122, 91 Am. Dec. 186.) It was always held that the
statute contemplated a bill for the purpose and as the only
means of bringing upon the record objections or points of
law ruled upon by the inferior court, and that it did not affect or apply to any matter that would be shown by the
record proper, since the only reason for allowing or providing for a bill of exceptions was that the ruling excepted to
could not otherwise appear upon the record. Referring to
the English statute, Judge Tilghman, in Downing v. Baldwin, 1 S. & R. 300, said: "The statute does not say that a
writ of error shall lie on the bill of exceptions. But, inasmuch as a writ of error lies at common law, and the
effect of it is to bring the record before the superior court,
the judges, finding the bill of exceptions upon the record,
are bound to take notice of it." In Wheeler v. Winn, *supra,*
after quoting and referring to the remarks of Judge Tilghman, and speaking of a state statute which required, when
requested by counsel, that the opinion of the court with the
reasons therefor be reduced to writing and filed "of record
in the cause," the court said: "The judges, on return of a
writ of error, finding upon the record palpable errors in a
charge written and filed under the statute, are equally bound

to take notice of them as if they were contained in a bill of exceptions." Since the Appellate Court must necessarily take notice of the record, and certain papers and proceedings in a cause either by the common law or statute constitute the record without a bill of exceptions, including by statute in this state the pleadings, as well as the judgment and orders proper to be entered upon the journal of the court, and the sole purpose of a bill of exceptions is to bring upon the record and before the court facts and proceedings which otherwise would not appear of record, a bill is unnecessary where all the facts and proceedings upon which error is alleged are shown by the record proper, and that is the firmly established rule. (3 Ency. Pl. & Pr. 404-406; 2 Cyc. 1076; 4 Standard Proc. 293, 298.) In line with the general ruling upon the subject this court has held that it is unnecessary and improper to incorporate the pleadings and journal entries in a bill, although when that is done it will not invalidate the bill or prevent that properly within it from becoming part of the record. (Sawin v. Pease, 6 Wyo. 91, 42 Pac. 750; see also 3 Ency. Pl. & Pr. 404-406.) With these principles in mind there cannot be much difficulty, we think, in construing the statutory provisions on the subject, notwithstanding that they may seem to contain some confusing expressions. The provisions are found in Sections 4597 and 4598, Compiled Statutes, 1910, the latter prescribing when it is, and the former when it is not, necessary to reduce exceptions to writing and have them allowed and signed by the court or judge. We quote all of Sec. 4597 and the material part of Section 4598.

"Sec. 4597. When the decision objected to is entered on the record, and the grounds of objection appear in the entry, the exception may be taken by the party causing it to be noted at the end of the entry that he excepts."

"Sec. 4598. When the decision is not entered on the record, or the grounds of objection do not sufficiently appear in the entry * * * the party excepting must reduce his exception to writing and present it to the court, or to the judge * * * within the time given for allowance."

Following the generally accepted rule above stated, it has been the practice in this court from the beginning when considering an error alleged in the sustaining or overruling of a demurrer to a pleading to do so upon the record proper, without requiring the ruling and exception to be shown by a bill of exceptions. A few cases only will be cited. In some, perhaps a majority of those cited, the fact that the hearing was had upon the record without a bill is not stated, but it appears inferentially at least in most of them, and in none does it appear that the exception was preserved by bill, or that a bill was deemed necessary for that purpose. (U. P. R. R. Co. v. Byrne, 2 Wyo. 109; Commissioners v. Johnson, 2 Wyo. 259; Perkins v. McDowell, 3 Wyo. 328, 23 Pac. 71; Wheaton v. Rampacker, 3 Wyo. 441, 26 Pac. 912; France v. Connor, 3 Wyo. 445, 27 Pac. 569; Cone v. Ivinson, 4 Wyo. 203, 212, 33 Pac. 31, 35 Pac. 933; State v. Commissioners, 4 Wyo. 313, 33 Pac. 992, 35 Pac. 929; Commissioners v. Atkinson, 4 Wyo. 334, 340, 33 Pac. 995; Dobson v. Owens, 5 Wyo. 85, 37 Pac. 471.) It was held in Railroad Co. v. Byrne, *supra,* and in Dobson v. Owens, *supra,* that a bill was not necessary to present the exceptions. In the first of these cases Judge Peck said: "This is an action of assumpsit for merchandise sold and delivered by Byrne to the Company. The latter duly excepted, and duly presents to us under Section 302 of the Civil Code, an exception to an order of the District Court, overruling its demurrer to the petition; but the exception has no merit." The section referred to, found on page 71 of the Compiled Laws, 1876, is now Section 4597 above quoted. The opinion clearly discloses that the demurrer and exception thereto were not shown by bill of exceptions. That it was intended by the learned judge to construe the section in accordance with the general rules above stated as to the purpose and necessity of a bill fairly appears from his dissenting opinion in Johns v. Adams Bros., 2 Wyo., at page 203. He there said: "The record defined by Section 387, (the section stating from what the record shall be made up, now Section 4630 Comp. Stat.) embraces exceptions that are preserved under 302 and 303 (now Sections 4597 and 4598, Comp. Stat.) These two sections intended only to put the record of the District Court, in respect to exception, into condition for review here; but are wholly distinct from, and independent of each other—each applying to a class of cases essentially different from that to which the other applies; and, when either has been complied with, and the other appellate provisions have been observed, the exception secures to the party the right to a review here of whatever the exception presents. The first (302) provides for only exceptions which relate to matters originating in—have their basis in the record—and are perfected, by being in the first instance entered there; the second (303) for only exceptions which' relate to matters not originating in—have their basis not of the record—and are perfected upon, and become a part of it only through a bill of exceptions." In Dobson v. Owens, Chief Justice Groesbeck, delivering the opinion, it was held that although the bill of exceptions was defective and, therefore, could not be considered, the ruling upon the demurrer to the answer which was excepted to was open to consideration, since the transcript of the record outside the bill showed such ruling and exception, and the ruling was assigned as error, the court saying: "This is sufficient to confer jurisdiction upon this court, without regard to the matters presented in the bill of exceptions." And a motion to dismiss on the ground that the bill of exceptions was defective was denied. In Perkins v. McDowell, it appears that an order overruling a demurrer to the petition was reviewed upon the record proper, Chief Justice Van Devanter delivering the opinion.

Counsel for defendant in error cite the case of Johnson v. Irrigating Co., 4 Wyo. 164, 33 Pac. 22, as authority for the proposition that a bill is required to preserve and present an exception to the ruling upon a demurrer. But the point was not involved in that case. It was a proceeding conducted under a statute for an adjudication of priorities of water rights, and came to the District Court on appeal from the State Board of Control. Motions to dismiss the appeal were sustained on the ground of the insufficiency of the notice of appeal, and a motion for leave to file an amended notice was overruled. The cause came to this court on error without any bill of exceptions, and it was held that no question was presented for review, in the absence of a bill showing the exceptions to the ruling on the motions and the facts explaining the same; and a reference to the argument of counsel published in the report of the case shows that the point made in that respect was that the motions aforesaid were not part of the record without a bill. That we think was the point decided with reference to the necessity of a bill. The case does not hold that a matter otherwise of record must also be presented by a bill of exceptions. Other cases decided by this court might be cited which hold that a bill is not required as to matters fully shown by the record proper, but those above cited are sufficient to show that the question has for many years been definitely and conclusively settled by this court, and we think without doubt that it has been correctly settled.

It is provided in Section 4598 that when the bill has been allowed and signed it shall be filed *with the pleadings as a part of the record,* thus recognizing the purpose of the bill to bring something into the record, and that the pleadings constitute a part of the record. A demurrer is a pleading under the code. (Comp. Stat. 1910, Sec. 4378.) If there is any expression in either section at all confusing it is that which refers to the grounds of objection appearing or not appearing in the entry. But when the object of a bill is considered, it is clear that in connection with the demurrer already a part of the record, the grounds of objection sufficiently appear in an entry showing a ruling upon the demurrer, either sustaining or overruling it. The purpose, and the only purpose, of the provisions of the two sections is to have a record showing and explaining the exception. The cases from Ohio, from which state our code was taken, so far as they touch upon the matter, show that the rule there observed is that a bill is required only in respect of matters not shown by the record proper. (Goyert v. Eicher, 70 O. St. 30, 34, 70 N. E. 508; Howell v. Fry, 19 O. St. 556; Harner v. Batdorf, 35 O. St. 113; Lockhart v. Brown, 31 O. St. 431.) And in Commercial Bank v. Buckingham, 12 O. St. 402, referring to the provisions covering the matter of exceptions, it is said that these provisions are found in the title which treats of and regulates the trial of causes, "and they manifestly relate to decisions which are made by the court, upon questions of law which arise during the progress of the trial." And it was held that they did not relate to the final judgment, the court saying further: "If the record shows such final judgment to be erroneous, it is the right of the party aggrieved to have it reversed, vacated, or modified, on petition in error, to the proper reviewing court. To note an exception to a final judgment, in the court which renders it, after the controversy is there ended. would seem to be utterly futile." That decision was cited and followed by this court in Nichols v. Com'rs., 13 Wyo. 1, 76 Pac. 681, 3 Ann. Cas. 543, as to the necessity for noting an exception to the final judgment.

In Indiana the code provisions respecting this matter are expressed in the same language as that found in our statute, and they have been construed by the Supreme Court of that state as to their effect upon an exception to a ruling upon a demurrer. Referring to the provision that where the decision objected to is entered on the record, and the grounds of objection appear in the entry, the party may cause it to be noted at the end of the entry, that he excepts, and that such entry shall be sufficient, it is said in Matlock v. Todd, 19 Ind. 130: "Now pleadings must be entered of record. The complaint, answers, demurrers, etc., must be filed by the clerk, and they constitute a part of the record proper. The journal entry, by the clerk, of their filing, is, also, necessarily a part of the record. And where a demurrer is filed to a pleading, the demurrer, as we have said, is a natural part of the record; the entry, by the clerk, of its filing, is so also; and so is the action of the court in sustaining or overruling it. And as the demurrer must assign causes, the ground of the decision of the court upon it appears necessarily, as a general rule, in such cases, in the entry of the decision by the clerk, considered in connection with the demurrer. Hence, a bill of exceptions, in such cases, is not necessary. It is only necessary that the party cause it to be noted that he excepts." The same principle is announced and applied in Lucas v. Waynetown, 86 Ind. 180; Redinbo v. Fretz, 99 Ind. 458, and Lindley v. Kelley, 42 Ind. 294. In the case last cited, after quoting the two sections like our own under consideration, the court say: "The above quoted sections do not introduce any new practice, but simply re-enact the law as it has existed since bills of exception were introduced by statute in England." (See also Elliott's App. Proc. Secs. 783, 797; Phillips on Code Pl., Sec. 528.) In Kansas under a statutory provision like our own, as to an exception where the grounds of objection appear in the entry, it was uniformly held that a bill of exceptions was necessary only to make a record of what would not otherwise appear in the record . In Burns v. Burgett, 19 Kan. 162, it was said that a bill should be confined to its legitimate purpose of only stating matters which would otherwise not be incorporated in the record. And in that state it was also held that neither a bill of exceptions nor an exception is necessary to present for review an error apparent upon the record. (Est. of Shaffer v. McKanna, 24 Kan. 22; Wooley v. Van Volkenburgh, 16 Kan. 20; McKinstry v. Carter, 48 Kan. 428, 29 Pac. 597; Nute v. Am. Glucose Co., 55 Kan. 225, 40 Pac. 279; Burdick on New Tr. & App., Secs. 191-193.) A bill of exceptions, if prepared to show an exception to a ruling upon a demurrer to a petition would necessarily and only recite the filing of the petition and demurrer, setting them out in full, the ruling upon the demurrer and the exception.

All that appears by the record proper. None of that requires the additional authentication of the certificate and signature of the judge. To require a bill in such case would be worse than useless. The record entry of the decision and exception necessarily shows that the demurrer was sustained or overruled. The exception, if one is noted, is to that decision; the demurrer constitutes the objection. And where the entry states that the ruling was upon the demurrer, a paper which is of record in the cause, the grounds of the objection sufficiently appear in the entry, and with the same force and effect as a record as though the cause or the several causes assigned for the demurrer were copied at length in the journal entry recording the decision. But in the case at bar the entry is not confined to a statement of the decision, as it might have been, but preceding the order overruling the demurrer it recites that the court finds that the petition states a cause of action, clearly indicating thereby the ground of the objection urged against the petition. In accordance with the previous decisions of this court, therefore, we hold that the exception to the ruling upon the demurrer sufficiently appears upon the record, if under the circumstances of the case, that ruling may properly be considered in reviewing the final judgment.

2. A waiver of the demurrer would not be ground for dismissal without also a waiver of the defects suggested by the demurrer. The grounds of objection stated in the demurrer and here urged do not relate to the form of the statement of the cause of action, but the effect thereof is to charge a total failure to state the substance of a good cause of action, and that the petition is therefore insufficient to support the judgment. Such a defect is never waived either by failure to demur or by answering over after demurrer filed and overruled, unless the defect be aided or cured by the answer or the subsequent proceedings.

At common law, after the enactment of the statutes of amendments and *jeofails,* a general demurrer was limited to defects in substance, and by pleading over, without de-

murring specially, defects of form were waived or cured.
Defects of substance, which might be taken advantage of
by general demurrer, such as want of jurisdiction of the
subject matter, or the failure to allege sufficient facts, the
defect not being merely in the form of the statement, were
not waived or cured by pleading over without demurring.
On the contrary such defects could be taken advantage of
at any subsequent stage of the proceedings, as by objecting
to the introduction of evidence, by motion in arrest of judgment, by motion for judgment *non obstante veredicto,* or by
writ of error. There were certain exceptions to this rule.
A defect in a pleading even as to matter of substance might
be aided or cured. by the pleading of the adverse party, as
where the answer supplied a necessary fact omitted from
the declaration. And the defect might be aided or cured
by the verdict, that is to say, by intendment after verdict,
the doctrine in that respect being that where a defect in a
pleading would have been a fatal objection upon demurrer,
yet if the issue joined be such as necessarily required, on the
trial, proof of the facts defectively or imperfectly stated or
omitted, and without which it is not to be presumed that
either the judge would direct the jury to give, or the jury
would have given, the verdict, such defect, imperfection or
omission is cured by the verdict; but the thing presumed
to have been proved must be such as can be implied from the
allegations, by fair and reasonable intendment. (1 Chitty's
Pl., 16th Am. Ed., 705.) The main rule on the subject is,
as said by Chitty, that a verdict will aid a defective statement of title, but will never assist a statement of a defective
title, or cause of action. (Id. 713.) The courts will never,
in order to support a verdict, made an intendment which is
inconsistent with the allegations on the record. (Id. 712:
Stephen's Pl., 3rd Am. Ed., 164; Andrews' Stephen's Pl.,
2nd Ed., Sec. 142.)

The reason for the rule that a defect in substance is not
waived except under the conditions stated is, that a pleading
of fact, such as an answer, does not admit the sufficiency in

law of the facts adversely alleged in a prior pleading. If a pleading does not state a cause of action or a defense, there is none to be maintained by the proof. It follows, therefore, as said in Phillips on Code Pleading, "that where a pleading is insufficient in substance, the opposite party may, without demurring, generally avail himself of such insufficiency. He may do this in various ways, such as by objecting to the introduction of evidence at the trial, by motion in arrest of judgment, by motion for judgment *non obstante veredicto,* or by writ of error." (Sec. 304.) Some defects of form which at common law are grounds for special demurrer are objected to under the code practice only by motion. The various grounds of·demurrer stated in the code include want of jurisdiction of the subject of the action, and that the petition does not state facts sufficient to constitute a cause of action. (Comp. Stat., Sec. 4381.) And the demurrer is required to specify the grounds of objection, although it is declared that if the grounds are not specified, it shall be regarded as objecting only that the petition does not state facts sufficient to constitute a cause of action, or that the court has no jurisdiction of the subject matter. (Id., Sec. 4382.) Since these two defects are those reached by general demurrer at common law, a demurrer specifying those grounds is usually referred to as a general demurrer, though that term is not employed in the code. It is further provided in the code as to these two substantial defects as follows: "When any of the defects enumerated in Section 4381 do not appear upon the face of the petition, the objection may be taken by answer, and if no objection be taken either by demurrer or answer, the defendant shall be deemed to have waived the same, except only the objection to the jurisdiction of the court, and that the petition does not state facts sufficient to constitute a cause of action." (Sec. 4383.) And by Section 4624 it is provided: "When, upon the statements in the pleadings, one party is entitled by law to judgment in his favor, judgment shall be so rendered by the court, although a verdict has been found against such party." This provision, it is said by the Supreme Court of Ohio, carries into the code the substance of what was theretofore known as a motion *non obstante veredicto* and a motion in arrest of judgment. (McCoy v. Jones, 61 O. St. 119, 55 N. E. 219.)

The code, therefore, follows the rule at common law, that a defect in substance is not waived by failure to demur, and that is the rule generally prevailing under code practice. In accordance with this is the further rule prevailing in most jurisdictions, that for such a defect in substance the objection may be made for the first time on appeal, the rule excluding, of course, objections relating merely to the form or manner in which the cause of action is stated, and requiring that the pleading be construed liberally and supported by every legal intendment, and therefore upheld if the necessary facts are fairly to be inferred from the allegations. (2 Ency. Pl. & Pr. 541-542, 365-366, 373; 2 Cyc. 691; 2 Standard Proc. 250; Phillips on Code Pl., Sec. 304; Elliott's App. Proc. 471; Chicago v. Lonergan, 196 Ill. 518, 63 N. E. 1018; Kellogg v. School Dist., 13 Okla. 285, 74 Pac. 111; Trimble v. Doty, 16 O. St. 119; Dalles L. Co. v. Urquhart, 16 Or. 71, 19 Pac. 78; Hartford Fire Ins. Co. v. Kahn, 4 Wyo. 364, 34 Pac. 895; Nichols v. Com'rs., 13 Wyo. 1, 76 Pac. 681, 3 Ann. Cas. 543.) In the last case cited, it was said by this court to be the established rule that a judgment obtained on a petition which fails to state a cause of action will be reversed, though no objection was made thereto in the lower court. Dalles L. Co. v. Urquhart, *supra*, was like this case in this, that the question was whether on the pleadings condemnation was authorized.

The principles above stated apply as well where a demurrer has been filed and overruled, for nothing can be clearer than that a party cannot by demurring lose the right which is his without demurring. As said in Colorado, "Having demurred (although no exception was taken to the ruling), appellant is not in any worse position than if no demurrer had been filed." (Board &c. v. Leonard, 26 Colo.

145, 57 Pac. 693.) This is, indeed, clearly implied by the provisions of Section 4383, *supra*, for it could not be intended that a defect not waived by failing to take the objection by demurrer or answer would be waived when the objection is so taken. If the demurrer remains on the record for consideration on appeal, together with the exception to the ruling thereon, then surely the objection is not waived by demurring, and if the demurrer is waived by pleading over after it is overruled, then it goes out of the record and cannot be considered for any purpose, for the theory upon which the courts adopting the rule hold that a demurrer when overruled is waived by pleading over is, that either expressly or impliedly the demurrer is withdrawn or abandoned by filing the subsequent pleading of fact, and when so withdrawn or abandoned the case stands as though no demurrer had been filed. Formerly, at common law, when a demurrer to the declaration was overruled, the facts were deemed to be established as alleged, and judgment was entered thereon, as is now done when a defendant stands on his demurrer, refusing to further plead. When the practice was adopted of allowing the defendant to plead after the demurrer was overruled, he was required to withdraw his demurrer, and thereafter the case was treated the same as if there had been no demurrer. It passed out of the record and judgment thereon was avoided. By the modern practice, where the rule prevails that by pleading over after the overruling of a demurrer the latter is waived, it is not usual to require a formal withdrawal of the demurrer, but it is so treated and ceases to be considered as on the record, and the parties are left in that respect in the same situation as if the demurrer had not been filed. (Phillips on Code Pl., Sec. 307; Bliss on Code Pl., Sec. 417; Nordhaus v. R. R. Co., 242 Ill. 166, 89 N. E. 974; Wales v. Lyon, 2 Mich. 276.) Therefore, for clear and obvious reasons, whether the position be taken that the ruling on the demurrer is open to consideration when reviewing the final judgment, or that it is not, in either case the objection is not waived by filing a demurrer that has been overruled, where it would not be waived by failing to demur. This is recognized by all the authorities, as will be disclosed by reference to the cases decided in those states where the demurrer and the specific error, if any, in overruling it is held to be waived by pleading over, as well as where the contrary is the accepted rule. (Wheelock v. Lee, 74 N. Y. 495; Sullenberger v. Gest, 11 Ohio, 205; City of Plankinton v. Gray, 63 Fed. 415, 11 C. C. A. 268; Marske v. Willard, 169 Ill. 276, 48 N. E. 290; Chicago v. Lonergan, *supra;* Catron v. La Fayette Co., 106 Mo., 659, 17 S. W. 577; Haase v. Distilling Co., 64 Mo. App. 131; Wilson v. Ry. Co., 67 Mo. App. 445; Goodrich v. Com'rs., 47 Kan. 355, 27 Pac. 1006, 18 L. R. A. 113; Sanford v. Weeks, 39 Kan. 649. 18 Pac. 823; Fordyce v. Merrill, 49 Ark. 277, 5 S. W. 329; White v. Stokes, 67 Ark. 184, 53 S. W. 1060; Cox v. Peoria Mfg. Co., 42 Neb. 660, 60 N. W. 933; Hopewell v. Mc-Grew, 50 Neb. 789, 70 N. W. 397; Bank v. Pence, 59 Neb. 579, 81 N. W. 623.)

It follows that it would be necessary to deny the motion to dismiss, whether the ruling on the demurrer may properly be considered or not, for upon the record, without regard to the demurrer, but treating it as never filed or withdrawn, the question is presented by the petition in error whether the petition upon which the judgment was rendered states facts sufficient to constitute a cause of action or to support the judgment. A consideration of the ruling on the demurrer as an alleged ground for reversal would not change the situation, or the rules to be applied in reviewing the judgment, for any error or defect in the pleadings or proceedings not affecting the substantial rights of the adverse party must be disregarded; and the defendant having answered and gone to trial upon the issues of fact, the plaintiff would be entitled at this stage of the case to the benefit of anything in the proceedings subsequent to the overruling of the demurrer that may have aided the defect in the petition, if any, under the rules above adverted to. (Davis v. Lumber Co., 14 Wyo.

517, 85 Pac. 980; Nott v. Johnson, 7 O. St. 270.) In this case there is nothing in the intermediate proceedings that can aid the petition, if the objections are well taken. Aside from the mere technicality involved in the question, therefore, it is immaterial whether the assignment of error based upon the overruling of the demurrer be considered, or the other assignments under which it is also claimed that the judgment is erroneous because unsupported by any facts alleged in the petition. And that, we think, might be a sufficient reason for disregarding the strict and technical rule at common law that the effect of answering over is to abandon or withdraw the demurrer, at least where there is no right of appeal directly from the order overruling the demurrer, but only from a final judgment rendered thereon, or from the final judgment rendered in the cause. But the practice has been long established in this court of considering an exception to the order overruling a general demurrer, when reviewing a judgment rendered upon a trial involving issues of fact presented by subsequent pleadings. This is shown by many cases, some of them being cited in that part of this opinion discussing the matter of exceptions, and among others that might be cited are the early cases of Insurance Company v. Pierce, 1 Wyo. 45, and Ivinson v. Althorp, 1 Wyo. 71; and the later case of Davis v. Lumber Co., 14 Wyo., 517, 85 Pac. 980. We should hesitate in refusing to follow a practice so long established without the most urgent reasons for doing so. But we are convinced that it accords with the intent and spirit of the code and is sustained by its provisions. As frequently decided by this court an appellate proceeding cannot be taken from the order overruling the demurrer, but only from a final judgment rendered thereon when the party stands on his demurrer without pleading further, or from a final judgment rendered in the cause after a trial of the issues of fact where there has been further pleading presenting issues of fact.

Where the order overruling a demurrer is treated as interlocutory merely and not, therefore, an order authorizing the

immediate taking of an appeal or proceeding in error, and
the objection is either that the pleading, if a complaint or
petition, fails to state facts sufficient to constitute a cause of
action, or that there is a want of jurisdiction of the subject
matter, the general rule that error in overruling a demurrer
is waived by pleading over does not apply. (6 Ency. Pl. &
Pr. 365; 1 Bates Pl. Pr. Par. & F. 423-424; Teal v. Walker,
11 U. S. 242, 4 Sup. Ct. 420, 28 L. Ed. 415; Bauserman v.
Blunt, 147 U. S. 647, 13 Sup. Ct. 466, 37 L. Ed. 316; Trimble v. Doty, 16 O. St. 119; Coal & Car Co. v. Norman, 49
O. St. 598, 32 N. E. 857; O'Donohue v. Hendrix, 13 Neb.
255, 13 N. W. 215; U. P. Ry. Co. v. Estes, 37 Kan. 229,
15 Pac. 157; Mo. Pac. Ry. Co. v. Webster, 3 Kan. App.
106, 42 Pac. 845; Cox v. Peoria Mfg. Co., 42 Neb. 660,
60 N. W. 933; Schofield v. Terr., 9 N. M. 526, 56 Pac. 306;
Fletcher v. Dunbar, 21 La. Ann. 150; Hunter's App., 71
Conn. 189, 41 Atl. 557; Zieverink v. Kemper, 19 Wkl. L.
Bull. (Ohio) 270.) It is said in Kansas that the only effect
of filing the answer and participating in the trial is that the
question of error in the ruling on the demurrer cannot be
taken to the reviewing court until the remainder of the case
is so taken. (Ry. Co. v. Webster, *supra.*) And it is held
in that state that a defendant whose demurrer has been
overruled may elect to stand on the demurrer and at once
take the case to the Appellate Court; or, an answer may be
filed, and when the case is finally tried, if it is tried on the
original petition, the case may then be taken to the Appellate
Court by the party demurring, and the ruling on the demurrer will be passed on there. (Ry. Co. v. Estes, *supra.*)
The rule is clearly stated by the Supreme Court of the
United States in Teal v. Walker, *supra,* as follows: "The
writ of error is not taken to reverse the judgment of the
court upon the demurrer to the complaint, for that was not
a final judgment, but to reverse the judgment rendered upon
the verdict of the jury. The error, if it be an error, of overruling the demurrer could have been reviewed on motion
in arrest of judgment, and is open to review upon this writ

of error. When the declaration fails to state a cause of action, and clearly shows that upon the case as stated the plaintiff cannot recover, and the demurrer of the defendant thereto is overruled, he may answer upon leave and go to trial, without losing the error in overruling the demurrer. The error is not waived by answer, nor is it cured by verdict. The question, therefore, whether the complaint in this case states facts sufficient to constitute a cause of action, is open for consideration."

The same rule is announced in the Connecticut case above cited, the court so holding on the ground that by statute the defendant had an absolute right to plead over after demurrer overruled, and, therefore, the right to take every objection open to him in one and the same suit, without being compelled to elect between matters of law and matters of fact in presenting the issues to be tried and determined. In Zieverink v. Kemper, *supra,* decided on error by the Superior Court of Cincinnati, where a demurrer on the ground that it appeared on the face of the petition that the action was barred by the statute of limitations was filed and overruled, and after the demurrer was overruled an answer was filed which did not plead the statute, it was held that the error in overruling the demurrer was not waived, and the provisions of the code requiring that judgment be rendered in favor of the party entitled thereto upon the statements in the pleadings, notwithstanding a verdict against him, was referred to as sufficient to sustain the decision. It was further held that having raised the question of the bar of the statute by demurrer, the facts appearing by the petition, it was not necessary to tender the same defense a second time by answer after it had been decided adversely to the defendant. The judgment was reversed for the error in overruling the demurrer.

The reasons for requiring a demurrer to be withdrawn upon pleading over, or treating that as done, do not exist where an appeal or proceeding in error can only be taken from a final order or judgment in the case, and a party is

permitted to except to the overruling of his demurrer and
then plead over. Where that practice is provided for it is
clearly intended that after the issue of law is determined
by the decision of the court adversely to the demurrant, he
may then tender an issue of fact before the rendition of final
judgment upon the issue of law, without waiving the error,
if any, in the decision on that issue. Otherwise an election
between the issue of law and a proposed issue of fact would
be required without the right to present the issue of fact
if electing to stand upon the demurrer, or to have the demurrer passed on by the reviewing court if electing to submit an issue of fact; that this was not intended is disclosed
by the various provisions of the code relating to the pleadings, the trial, and proceedings in error. One of the reasons
assigned for a withdrawal of the demurrer upon pleading
over is that a demurrer admitting the facts and an answer
denying them are totally inconsistent with each other and
cannot stand together. (Pickering v. Telegraph Co., 47 Mo.
457.) But it is not true in fact that a demurrer admits the
allegations of the pleading demurred to, for nothing is thereby affirmatively or expressly admitted. It merely denies the
legal sufficiency of the facts alleged, and hence such facts
are said to be admitted, and, impliedly, they are admitted,
but solely for the purpose of testing their sufficiency in law.
When the demurrer is overruled the implied admission has
served its purpose. (Brewing Ass'n. v. Bond, 66 Fed. 653,
13 C. C. A. 665; Belden v. Blackman, 124 Mich. 667, 83 N.
W. 616; Donovan v. Boeck, 217 Mo. 70, 116 S. W. 543;
Bliss on Code Pl., Sec. 418.) It thereafter remains on the
record as an overruled demurrer, at least when an exception
is noted to the ruling, if it continues on the record at all, and
when permitted to so remain it cannot be regarded as an
admission and therefore evidence of the facts necessary to
be proved to establish the cause of action or defense upon the
trial of the issues of fact arising upon subsequent pleadings.
Since the code allows a proceeding in error only from the
final judgment, that judgment, when rendered after a trial

of an issue of fact arising upon pleadings filed after the overruling of the demurrer, is to be regarded as rendered upon all the issues in the cause—the issue of law as well as the issue of fact, or, at least, as a final judgment authorizing an appellate proceeding to question the correctness of the decision on the issue of law as well as the issue of fact, for the code contains nothing disclosing an intent to deprive a party of the right to challenge by a proceeding in error the correctness of the decision of the trial court upon both issues, or an issue of fact as well as an issue of law. (Mechanics Bank v. Woodward, 74 Conn. 689, 51 Atl. 1084.) Of course by pleading over and going to trial upon the merits the party takes the chances of the defect in the pleading being aided or cured, under the rules above explained. But as he cannot appeal from the mere ruling on the demurrer and, believing that he has a good claim or defense upon the facts, may be unwilling to sacrifice the right to present an issue thereon by standing on his demurrer and allow judgment to be then rendered, the only proper and logical view, we think, is that through the remainder of the proceedings, when he has answered over, he retains the benefit of his exception to the ruling on the demurrer. Thus the same right is accorded him that would be his if allowed an appeal from that ruling, though the result may be somewhat affected by the rules for aiding or curing the alleged defect.

Unlike the statute in Connecticut our code does not expressly confer upon a party an absolute right to further plead after his demurrer has been overruled, but it does provide that he may do so if the court is satisfied that he has a meritorious claim or defense, and did not demur for delay. (Comp. Stat. 1910, Sec. 4436.) And the prevailing practice here under that provision is to grant the leave almost as a matter of course upon a mere request. Although the matter is discretionary with the court, when the leave is given it is full and complete, and no reason is perceived for applying a rule different from that which would prevail under a statute giving an absolute right without requesting leave. The code

does not expressly, at least, require a withdrawal or abandonment of the demurrer or the exception to the ruling
thereon on requesting leave to plead further, nor is such
withdrawal or abandonment mentioned as a condition upon
which the leave may be granted. Giving effect to the various provisions of the code, no substantial reason is perceived
for implying the withdrawal of a demurrer by pleading over
after it is overruled and the ruling excepted to, or that the
statute so requires. We think it proper, therefore, to follow
the practice hitherto established, which permits a consideration of the ruling on the demurrer when duly excepted to
and assigned as error, upon a review of the final judgment.
For the several reasons stated the motion to dismiss must be
denied.

3. Whether the assignment of error based upon the overruling of the demurrer be considered or either of the other
assignments, the same question is presented, viz: the sufficiency of the facts alleged to entitle the plaintiff below to
appropriate the property of the defendant through the power
of eminent domain. In addition to the facts previously
stated, it is alleged that the plaintiff has accepted the constitution of this state and complied with the laws thereof with
reference to foreign corporations doing business in this
state, and is duly and legally authorized to transact business
here. That the land to be irrigated and reclaimed situated
in Weld County, Colorado, was granted by the United States
prior to the adoption and ratification of the constitution of
this state, and a large part of such land is now owned by the
plaintiff. That in July, 1910, the plaintiff was granted the
right and authority by the State Engineer of Colorado to
divert and appropriate water from Crow Creek for the purpose of irrigating said lands and that it has the right to divert
and appropriate the unappropriated water of said stream for
that purpose. That it is impracticable and impossible to construct a headgate and divert the water of the stream within
the State of Colorado to irrigate and reclaim said lands, "because of the lay of the land and the condition of the soil":

and that there is a suitable location for the headgate for plaintiff's irrigation system on the land of defendant in this state, and about 700 feet from the southern boundary line thereof. Certain applications alleged to have been filed by the plaintiff in the office of the State Engineer of this state for a permit to divert and appropriate water from Crow Creek in this state for the purpose aforesaid are set out in full, together with alleged indorsements thereon and correspondence relating thereto, whereby it is claimed and alleged that plaintiff acquired a right to so construct the headgate, and divert and appropriate water of said stream not theretofore appropriated. It appears to have been stated in one of said applications filed as an amendment, and it is alleged in the amended petition, that the proposed point of diversion is below any diversion from said stream previously authorized, or that could be made for any beneficial use within this state; that such proposed diversion will not interfere with or injuriously affect any prior appropriation within this state, nor in any way result to the detriment of the public interest or welfare; and that there is ample unappropriated water going to waste each year in said stream during flood time, which can be diverted through plaintiff's irrigation and reservoir system to annually irrigate and successfully reclaim all the lands proposed to be irrigated and reclaimed by the means of that system.

If the purpose for which the headgate and ditch is proposed to be constructed is such as would authorize the condemnation of land in this state, the question of the necessity for locating the headgate and part of the ditch on the land in controversy and taking the land sought to be condemned is eliminated from the case by the manner in which the record comes to this court, and such necessity stands established by the judgment, in case a right to condemn for the proposed use is shown by the facts alleged. We understand it to be admitted that the amended petition states all the facts that could be stated or shown to justify condemning the land, and that they were fully and particularly stated in order that the legal issue might be fairly and clearly presented by demurrer.

Two points are urged against the right to condemn. First, that land in this state cannot be taken by condemnation where the only proposed use, as in this case, is the irrigation of lands in another state; second, that to condemn land required for an irrigating ditch or irrigation purposes it is necessary to show a right or permit to divert and appropriate water therefor, and that the amended petition fails to show that such a right or permit was acquired by the plaintiff in this state. It is argued in support of the second proposition that it is beyond the authority of the State Engineer to grant a permit or authorize the diversion and appropriation of water in this state for the irrigation of land outside the boundaries of the state, and, further, that had he such authority the facts alleged do not show that a permit was granted or that the proposed diversion and appropriation by the plaintiff was authorized.

It will not be necessary to consider the second proposition or either of its divisions suggested by the argument, for in the view we take of the case the fact that all the water to be diverted by means of the headgate and ditch is to be used exclusively for the irrigation of land in another state is sufficient to cause a reversal of the judgment. Eminent domain is generally defined as the right or power of a sovereign state to appropriate private property to particular uses, for the purpose of promoting the general welfare. "It embraces all cases where, by authority of the state and for the public good, the property of the individual is taken, without his consent, for the purpose of being devoted to some particular use, either by the state itself or by a corporation, public or private, or by a private citizen." (1 Lewis on Em. Domain, 3rd Ed., Sec. 1.) In this respect the several states are distinct and independent of each other, respectively possessing and exercising the power for their own purposes or their own public welfare. "The eminent domain in any sovereignty exists only for its own purposes."

(Trombley v. Humphrey, 23 Mich. 471, 476, 9 Am. Rep. 94.) "It means nothing more or less than an inherent political right, founded on a common necessity and interest, of appropriating the property of individual members of the community to the great necessities of the whole community." (Bloodgood v. R. R. Co., 18 Wend. (N. Y.) 9, 31 Am. Dec. 313.) "The proper view of the right of eminent domain seems to be, that it is a right belonging to a sovereignty to take private property for its own public uses, and not for those of another. Beyond that, there exists no necessity; which alone is the foundation of the right." (Kohl v. U. S., 91 U. S. 367, 23 L. Ed. 449.)

If the particular improvement or use will be of sufficient benefit to the people of the state to authorize an exercise of the power, it will not be prevented by the fact that the people of another state will also be benefited. (Gilmer v. Lime Point, 18 Cal. 229; Washington Water Power Co. v. Waters, 19 Idaho, 595, 115 Pac. 682; Columbus W. & W. Co. v. Long, 121 Ala. 245, 25 So. 702.) It was said in the California case, that it is not essential that the use or benefit should be exclusively for the people of the state, or exclusively for even a portion of those people, "that the people of California have no right to complain that the people of Oregon are also benefited by a public improvement," and that such improvement would be none the less a public use in California because it was also useful elsewhere. And in the Idaho case it was said: "but where the use for which condemnation is sought is a public use in this state, and will serve the citizens of this state—their demands, necessities and industries—the fact that it may incidentally also benefit the citizens and industries of a neighboring state will not defeat the right of condemnation."

There is some conflict in the authorities as to the right of a state to exercise its power for the benefit of the United States government. That right was denied in Michigan. (Trombley v. Humphrey, *supra.*) It was upheld in California. (Gilmer v. Lime Point, *supra.*) But it was conceded in the Michigan case, and is now well settled, that for its own purposes the general government possesses the power of eminent domain and may acquire land by condemnation in any state, such right being sustained upon the ground that property required for the purposes of the national government, being for the use of the people of all the states, is as well for the use of the people of that state where it is located. (1 Lewis on Em. Dom., 3rd Ed., Sec. 309; Cooley's Const. Lim. 526; Reddall v. Ryan, 14 Md. 444, 74 Am. Dec. 550.) The Maryland case involved the taking of land in that state for an aqueduct to supply water to the City of Washington, the same having been authorized not only by an act of Congress, but also by an act of the Legislature of Maryland. It was contended that the use was not a public use in Maryland, and an elaborate argument was made upon that proposition. The court held to the contrary, giving as one of its reasons that Maryland was one of the states of the Union, and, as such, "in some sense, an integral part of the great public, interested in and constituting a part of the general government," and could, therefore, lawfully enact the statute authorizing the condemnation proceedings. And it was said that the words "public use" in the provision of the constitution of the state requiring just compensation to be made for property taken therefor, "do not mean merely a use of the government of Maryland, or of the State of Maryland, and its inhabitants as such, but, in our opinion, they embrace within their scope a use of the government of the United States." It was also said in the case that by its cession of the District in which the City of Washington was situated Maryland had not intended to abandon all interest in that District, and, therefore, the relation between the District and the State was more intimate and close than that which it bears to any other state.

It will be noticed that in the cases cited it was deemed necessary to sustain the exercise of the power that the particular use have some substantial relation to a public pur-

pose and the public interest and welfare of the state wherein
the land to be taken is located. And this thought runs
through all the cases discussing the question of public use,
or a use permitting or justifying the taking of private property by eminent domain. That is true in the case of In re.
Townsend, 39 N. Y. 171, upon which counsel for defendant
in error, plaintiff below, strongly rely in support of the
judgment. That case demands more than a passing notice,
for upon the facts it seems to us to be the only one that
might be supposed to lend some support to the theory. upon
which the right of condemnation is claimed in the case at
bar. It does not, we think, support the right claimed in this
case, for the statute authorizing the taking was upheld on
the ground that the improvement, a canal in New Jersey,
served the State of New York and contributed to the welfare of its people in precisely the same way that it benefited
the people of New Jersey, or as though it had been built
within the limits of New York. The canal company was
incorporated in New Jersey to construct a canal to unite the
Delaware River, near Easton, in the State of Pennsylvania,
with the tide waters of the Passaic, in New Jersey, and was
subsequently authorized to continue the canal to the waters
of the Hudson, at or near Jersey City. It was declared in the
act incorporating the company, that when completed the
"canal shall forever thereafter be esteemed a public highway,
free for the transportation of any goods, commodities or
produce whatsoever on payment of tolls." It was a canal
for transportation purposes. At the outlet of a lake situated
partly in New York, but mostly in New Jersey, a dam was
built by the company to form a reservoir as a feeder for the
canal, and thereby some of the land of the appellant in the
case situated on the margin of the lake in New York was
flooded. By an act of the Legislature of New York the
company was authorized to acquire title to any land injuriously affected by the dam or reservoir by the appointment of
commissioners to appraise the compensation. The principal
question in the case was whether the taking was for a public

use, in view of the fact that the canal itself was not located within the limits of the State of New York. A few quotations from the opinion, and also from the opinion of one Justice who dissented from the conclusion only upon other questions in the case, will serve to show clearly that the New York statute was sustained on the ground that the benefits accruing to the people of New York were of the same character as though the canal had been constructed within the limits of that state. In the opinion of the court it was said:

"It does not follow, because the canal is outside the state limits, that its construction and maintenance are not for a public use, within the meaning of our Constitution. If it were within our limits, what are the public benefits to result from its construction? Not merely that our citizens may use it for transportation and travel. Providing transportation to market and facilitating intercommunication are some of the public purposes of such improvements; but communication between our chief cities and the productive regions which lie outside our state, and intercourse with those who dwell there, are as truly objects of public interest and advantage as between two sections of the state itself. Besides, the court cannot say that the Morris canal does not run within the reach of a portion of our own citizens, and directly aid them in the conduct of their intercourse with our Eastern border, or the counties along the Hudson river to which it runs."

In the dissenting opinion the fact is referred to that the canal terminates directly opposite the city of New York, "where concentrates, not only the internal trade and business of all the States of the Union, but, to a considerable extent, the trade and commerce of the whole world. * * * Every avenue opened for the accommodation of those who have occasion to contribute to its augmenting inland trade, or facilitate the transportation of the vast amount of merchandise which is disposed of within its limits, or the entrance or departure of those who may have occasion to visit or to leave it, is of paramount importance. * * * Suppose the depot of the Morris Canal Company had been located immediately across and adjoining the boundary line of the State of New Jersey, and within the limits of New York; could there be any doubt that the land taken for such a purpose would be for the public use? Most certainly there would not. It does not, then, alter the case, because the Hudson river separates the terminus of the canal company from immediate connection with the State of New York. It accommodates the citizens of New York precisely as much, and the public are equally benefited, and, as such, interested, as if the depot was located on the opposite side of the river, and it is quite as much for the public use." Reference is made in both opinions to the railroads of other states which are authorized to construct a part of the line in New York. And the right of condemnation appears, we think, to have been sustained on the same ground and for the same reason that the right of a railroad company is sustained whose road is mainly in another state, to condemn land in the state for a part of the line or terminal station inside the state limits. Throughout both opinions the principle is recognized that the term public use in connection with eminent domain has reference to the state or government within whose territorial limits is situated the land proposed to be taken, and by whose authority the same must be taken, if at all. And that principle is, we think, to be deduced from all the authorities, although distinctly stated in but few, for, as above suggested, in every case where the use as a justification for the proceeding has been questioned, the inquiry in that respect has been confined to the interest and welfare of the state or sovereignty within whose limits or jurisdiction the land sought to be condemned is located. This does not mean the interest or welfare dependent upon or affected by development and growth in another state. In the case cited and quoted from, the benefit to the people of New York held sufficient to support condemnation was not the interest or advantage to be derived from the upbuilding of the industries or development of the resources of the neighboring state of New Jersey, but the benefit to arise directly from service rendered in the operation of the canal. The canal itself would serve the people of New York, and was, therefore, held to be a public use in and of that state.

In Lewis on Eminent Domain, it is said: "The public use for which property may be taken is a public use within the State from which the power is derived." (Sec. 310.) The Supreme Court of Alabama say: "It seems to be an admitted fact generally, that the power inheres in a State for domestic uses only, to be exercised for the benefit of its own people, and cannot be extended merely to promote the public uses of a foreign State." But it was held that the right is not to be denied where public uses are subserved in the State granting condemnation, because in connection therewith public uses in another state may likewise be promoted. And the principle was applied in favor of a corporation engaged in supplying water to two cities in Alabama and to one city in Georgia, the court saying: "While a State will take care to use this power for the benefit of its own people, it will not refuse to exercise it for such purpose, because the inhabitants of a neighboring state may incidentally partake of the fruits of its exercise." (Columbus W. W. Co. v. Long, 121 Ala. 245, 25 So. 702.)

In the Idaho case of Washington Water Power Co. v. Waters, 19 Idaho, 595, 608, 115 Pac. 682, 686, above cited, the same doctrine was stated, and while the fact that another state might be incidentally benefited was not deemed sufficient to deny condemnation for an improvement which would be a public use in Idaho, it was said: "Condemnation could evidently not be had in this state for the purpose alone of serving a public use in another State." (115 Pac. 682, 686. See also Walbridge v. Robinson, 22 Idaho, 236, 125 Pac. 812.) The same principle is suggested in the recent case of Thayer v. California Development Co., (Cal.) 128 Pac. 21, where it was said as to a water or irrigation company diverting water in California, conducting it into Mexico and back again into California: "The fact that that company is carrying on a public service in Mexico and has devoted some water to public use there does not affect the water carried into the United States nor the character of the use thereof in California," and, though it was not a condemnation case, but one involving the question whether the company had appropriated and was engaged in conducting water in its canal or canals for public use, it was said that the company in California did not possess the power of eminent domain.

It is said in Nichols on the Power of Eminent Domain: "It has been intimated that one State cannot condemn property within its limits for the use of another State (citing Kohl v. U. S. *supra*), and a taking for such a purpose has never received the sanction of the courts." (Sec. 22.) In the same section Townsend's Case, *supra,* is referred to as furnishing no exception to the proposition, the author saying that the statute considered in that case was sustained on the ground that the canal was of great benefit to New York as well as New Jersey, and "if this feature had been lacking the decision would probably have been otherwise, as there would have been no use, public to New York, to be subserved." It is also well settled that a State cannot take or authorize the taking of property or rights in property situated in another State. (Nichols on Em. Dom., Sec. 19; 1 Lewis on Em. Dom., 3rd Ed., Sec. 385: 10 Ency. L., 2nd Ed., 1051; Crosby v. Hanover, 36 N. H. 404; U. S. v. Ames, 1 Woodb. & M. 76, Fed. Cas. No. 14,441; Ill. State Trust Co. v. St. Louis T. M. & S. Ry. Co., 208 Ill. 419, 70 N. E. 357.) "One state cannot expropriate for its public purposes property within the territory of another state." (McCarter v. Hudson W. Co., 70 N. J. Eq. 695, 65 Atl. 489, 14 L. R. A. (N. S.) 197, 207, 118 Am. St. 754, 774, 10 Ann. Cas. 116, 125.) "The question has arisen whether, by virtue of the right of eminent domain, one state can take, or subject to public use, land in another state, and the decisions have naturally been against such a power." (Holyoke W. P. Co. v. Conn. R. Co., 52 Conn. 570, 575; s. c. (C. C.) 20 Fed. 71, 79.)

The principles above stated seem to have been recognized by the trial court in this case, if we may refer to a quotation from the opinion of the learned judge found in the brief of counsel for defendant in error, for the ground of the decision seems to have been that the proposed irrigation of the lands, which lie just over the line of this state in the State of Colorado, will be of material benefit to a considerable part of the inhabitants of a section of this state, since it may lead to the growth of towns and the creation of new channels for the employment of capital and labor. And counsel argue that such a benefit is sufficient. In the part of the opinion of the trial court found quoted in the brief it was said that "the court will take judicial notice of the fact that the city of Cheyenne and several incorporated towns of Wyoming are located so near the lands, which it is proposed to irrigate, that such lands may be considered tributary thereto, and that the development and settlement of these lands would be of considerable benefit to the citizens of this State residing in said city and towns. It may be that in the future a town may be located within the State of Wyoming, and within but a few hundred feet of these lands, and even should such town, or the immediate trading point for the future settlers upon these lands, be located within the State of Colorado, the central trading point for wholesale purposes, and for the larger wants of the settlers of these lands, would be the City of Cheyenne. Therefore, it cannot be said that the ultimate purpose of the exercise of eminent domain in this case would not result in benefit to the people of this state. Unquestionably, the developing and settling of several miles of the northern portion of Colorado, immediately adjacent to Wyoming, would be of great benefit to the citizens living just over the line in Wyoming." This line of argument is not without some force, but we think it disregards or misconceives the theory or public interest supporting the exercise of eminent domain for irrigation works or the irrigation of land, and would, in effect, if sustained, permit the exercise of eminent domain in this state by the State of

Colorado, or any other state, for its own uses and purposes.

We are not required in this case to discriminate between a public use and a private use with reference to the taking of property under the power of eminent domain, for, whether our constitution is to be understood as authorizing such taking for a use distinctively private, as distinguished from a public use, when the purpose thereof is irrigation, or as declaring that any taking for irrigation purposes is for a public use, it clearly authorizes a taking for such purpose. It is provided in the Constitution as follows: "Private property shall not be taken for private use unless by consent of the owner, except for private ways of necessity, and for reservoirs, drains, flumes, or ditches on or across the lands of others for agricultural, mining, milling, domestic or sanitary purposes, nor in any case without due compensation." (Art. 1, Sec. 32.) "Private property shall not be taken or damaged for public or private use without just compensation." (Art. 1, Sec. 33.) It was said in Washington, referring to a provision like that contained in Section 32: "Here is an inference so strong as to amount almost to an affirmative declaration that private property may be taken for private use when the use is confined to the purposes enumerated in the provision, one of which is ditches on or across the land of others for agricultural purposes; and it is no strained construction of the provision to say that this includes ditches for irrigation purposes, in view of the vast extent of arid land within our state and the benefits of irrigation thereto in the increase of its productiveness and value. The very thought of agriculture in connection with this vast arid portion of our state suggests irrigation in connection therewith." (State v. Superior Court, 59 Wash. 621, 110 Pac. 429, 140 Am. St. 893.) It is, however, proper that we consider the use for such a purpose in its relation to the necessities and welfare of the state, to ascertain the reason for the provision found in Section 32 and what was thereby intended to be accomplished, or what interest of the people was intended to be served, for it is not to be supposed that

the intention or purpose was to take the property of one
and give it to another, even upon the payment of just compensation, without some public necessity or advantage. Nor
is it to be supposed that it was intended to authorize a taking
for private use, which would not be a public use when participated in by all or many who could and might desire to
be accommodated by the proposed reservoir, flume or ditch.
If a reservoir or ditch constructed for irrigation purposes
and to furnish water to any who might apply therefor
within the district proposed to be irrigated would not, when
considered as a public use, authorize a taking of property in
this state, such taking would not be authorized for a private
use covering the same district. In this respect under the
constitutional provisions aforesaid there is no difference
between a public use and a private use. A private use for
any of the purposes mentioned in Section 32 is given the same
force and effect as a public use, and no greater. In State v.
Superior Court, *supra,* the court say: "We have quoted the
constitutional provision which clearly indicates that property
may be taken under the power of eminent domain for certain
enumerated private uses, among which are ways for ditches
for agricultural purposes. While this provision in terms
seems to give the power for private use, it was evidently
adopted upon the theory that the public would be sufficiently
benefited by the taking for such a purpose to warrant the
taking; that is, though it be seemingly called a private use
by these words of the constitution, it is also in effect a public
use in view of the necessities of a state like ours having
·vast areas of arid land." Even without such constitutional
provision the taking of land for an irrigating ditch in the
Western States where the lands are arid or semi-arid has
been upheld as for a public use, regardless of the number of
acres or distinct tracts or farms to be irrigated or the number of independent owners, such taking being held permissible for the purpose of irrigating land owned by a single
individual. (Oury v. Goodwin, 3 Ariz. 255, 26 Pac. 377;
Nash v. Clark, 27 Utah, 158, 75 Pac. 371, 1 L. R. A. (N. S.)

208, 101 Am. St. Rep. 953, 1 Ann. Cas. 300; Clark v. Nash,
198 U. S. 361, 25 Sup. Ct. 676, 49 L. Ed. 1085, 4 Ann. Cas.
1171; Fallbrook Irr. Dist. v. Bradley, 164 U. S. 112, 17
Sup. Ct. 56, 41 L. Ed. 369.)

What, then, we inquire, is the public necessity, benefit or
advantage that justifies the taking of land for an irrigating
ditch or other irrigation works?   Mr. Kinney, in his work
on Irrigation and Water Rights, says that the reclamation
of lands in the Western States has been declared a public
use, in the aid of which the right of eminent domain may be
exercised, upon the theory that although it may benefit the
individual directly, the indirect benefit to the general public
is greater by permitting the upbuilding and settlement of the
country." (Vol. 2, 2nd Ed., Sec. 1066.)   And again, referring to the line of authorities as to what constitutes a
public use holding that a private individual or corporation
may condemn rights of way for ditches where the sole use
of the water is by the individual or corporation, that author
says: "This is upon the theory that the physical and climatic conditions of the State are such that the promotion of
any great industry, such as irrigation, * * * is of sufficient importance in the upbuilding of the country and the
developing of its natural resources, that such a use is a public
benefit to the community at large, and, therefore, it is a
public use, even if the more direct benefit is to a private individual or corporation." (Id. Sec. 1069.)   Speaking on
this question another author refers to the fact that where the
State is dependent for its prosperity on the irrigation of its
arid lands as a whole, it is held immaterial whether one or
many proprietors are benefited by a particular enterprise.
(Nichols on Em. Dom. Sec. 253.)   And, referring to the
case of Fallbrook Irr. Dist. v. Bradley, *supra*, it is said that
the court rested its decision on the ground that in a state,
like California, embracing millions of acres of arid lands
which when left in their original condition would present an
effectual obstacle to the advance of a large portion of the
state in material wealth and prosperity, irrigation thereof

would benefit the public of the whole state, and was, therefore, a public use. (Id. Sec. 252.) In the case so referred
to, Mr. Justice Peckham, delivering the opinion of the court,
said on this subject: "While the consideration that the work
of irrigation must be abandoned if the use of the water may
not be held to be or constitute a public use is not to be regarded as conclusive in favor of such use, yet that fact is
in this case a most important consideration. Millions of
acres of land otherwise cultivable must be left in their
present arid and worthless condition, and an effectual obstacle will therefore remain in the way of the advance of a
large portion of the State in material wealth and prosperity.
To irrigate and thus bring into cultivation these large masses
of otherwise worthless lands would seem to be a public
purpose and a matter of public interest, not confined to the
landowners, or even to one section of the State."

In the case of Nash v. Clark, *supra,* the Supreme Court
of Utah sustained the right of eminent domain in cases of
this character solely on the ground that the irrigation of the
arid lands of the State is a public benefit. The court, speaking by Mr. Justice McCarty, say: "In view of the physical
and climatic conditions in this state, and in the light of the
history of the arid West, which shows the marvelous results
accomplished by irrigation, to hold that the use of water for
irrigation is not in any sense a public use, and thereby place
it within the power of a few individuals to place insurmount-
able barriers in the way of the future welfare and prosperity
of the State would be giving to the term 'public use' altogether too strict and narrow an interpretation." The case
was affirmed by the Supreme Court of the United States.
(Clark v. Nash, *supra.*) The rule of that case, that private
enterprise may constitute a public use, is summarized in
Wiel on Water Rights (2nd Ed., Sec. 263) as follows:

"The situation of a State and the possibilities and necessities for the successful prosecution of various industries,
and peculiar condition of soil or climate or other peculi-
arities, being general, notorious and acknowledged in the

State so as to be judicially known and exceptionally familiar to the courts without investigation—such conditions justify a State court in upholding a statute authorizing the taking of another's private property by one individual for his own enterprise, where it believes, *by reason of the above,* that such a taking will, through its contribution to the growth and prosperity of the State, constitute a public benefit, and the Supreme Court of the United States will follow the decision of the State court in such a case."

Stating the reason and the necessity causing the enactment of statutes and the adoption of the rule in the other arid land states permitting the exercise of eminent domain for the purposes of irrigation, and applying the rule in Nebraska, the Supreme Court of that state say:

"Nor were the conditions surrounding the people of the Pacific states, when the foundation was laid for the body of their laws upon the subject, materially different from those which today confront the western half of our own state. We behold what was but yesterday the public domain, occupied to the western limit of the rain belt, so called, and settlers eagerly seeking for homes in the semi-arid region beyond. We behold thousands of acres of fertile land in the valleys of the Platte, the Loups, the Elkhorn, and the Republican rivers, practically worthless under existing conditions for the purpose of agriculture, but which by application of the waters of those streams may be made most productive, thus not only supporting the rapidly increasing population of that region, but adding largely to the wealth and material prosperity of the state. That an undertaking so important can be prosecuted alone through the agency of the state none can doubt. The reclamation of a region so vast, equal in extent to more than one State of the Union, is surely a legitimate function of government. And the exercise of the reserve power of the state in the promotion of an enterprise so beneficial is not even in a technical sense violative of the restrictive features of, the constitution." (Paxton & Hershey Irr. Co. v. Farmers & Merchants Irr.

Co., 45 Neb. 884, 64 N. W. 343, 29 L. R. A. 853, 50 Am.
St. Rep. 585.)

So in the Washington case above cited (State v. Superior
Court) it is said: "The benefit to the public which supports
the exercise of the power of eminent domain for purposes
of this character is not public service, *but is the development
of the resources of the state,* and the increase of its wealth
generally, by which its citizens incidentally reap a benefit.
Whether such development and increased wealth comes from
the effort of a single individual, or the united efforts of
many, in our opinion does not change the principle upon
which this right of eminent domain rests."

Expressions similar to those contained in the cases above
quoted from are found in all the cases relating to the exercise of the power of eminent domain for rights of way for
irrigating ditches, whenever stating the principle upon which
the exercise of that power for such purpose rests. In none
is the exercise of the power for such a purpose based upon
the necessities, or the physical and climatic conditions of
another state. But it is founded upon the conditions and
necessities of the State where the power is to be exercised.
And that is true also as to other purposes more or less
analogous. Where the development of mines is held to be
a public use, it is because of the public necessity of developing the mining resources of the State and the public benefit
resulting from such development. (Dayton Min. Co. v.
Seawell, 11 Nev. 394; Butte &c Ry. Co. v. Montana U. Ry.
Co., 16 Mont. 504, 41 Pac. 232, 31 L. R. A. 298, 50 Am. St.
508.) The building of grain elevators was held to be public
use in Minnesota on the ground of public necessity in view
of the magnitude of the agricultural interests of that State.
(Stewart v. Great Nor. Ry. Co., 65 Minn. 517, 68 N. W.
208, 33 L. R. A. 427.) And in sustaining a statute as a proper
exercise of the power of eminent domain, which authorized
the taking of a right to flow land for mill purposes without
the landowner's consent, but upon making due compensation
to be assessed in a proceeding provided for that purpose,

the court referred to the interest of the State in the improvement of her water powers and the prosperity arising to the State from the development of those natural resources. The court said: "No State of the Union is more interested than ours in the improvement of natural advantages for the application of water power to manufacturing purposes. * * * The present prosperity of the State is largely due to what has already been done towards developing these natural advantages." And again: "The business of manufacturers and mechanics in this State is largely dependent on the use of the water power. To create a water power in a large stream sufficient for manufacturing on an extensive scale, it is generally necessary to dam the water in the stream itself, and also to raise and retain it in natural or artificial reservoirs connected with the stream. * * * In most cases, to do this, the right to flow the land of numerous proprietors must be obtained; and an individual, or a few individuals, might defeat or greatly embarrass the whole enterprise by an unreasonable and obstinate refusal to part with this right. In such a case can it be doubted that, to remove this obstacle to a great public improvement, in which large numbers are interested, would be, in the language of the constitution, 'for the benefit and welfare of the State.' and that a private right taken for that purpose would be taken for a public use within the legal meaning of that term." (Great Falls Mfg. Co. v. Fernald, 47 N. H. 444.)

The irrigation of land in a neighboring state, and so also the building of a railroad in that State, or the development of its mines or other natural resources, may no doubt result in some benefit to the people of this state, but only in the general way that one State is benefited by the growth in industrial activities, population and wealth of an adjoining State, or even of a more distant State or the Nation at large. To accept that, however, as a sufficient reason for taking land in this State under the power of eminent domain, if for the purpose of irrigation, would not tend to advance the interest of this State in the reclamation and cultivation of its lands, or the development of its natural resources, but the effect might be entirely the reverse, and it would abandon the principle upon which the right to exercise the power foʋ irrigation and other analogous purposes has been asserted and maintained. The headgate and ditch by which water for agricultural purposes is diverted and distributed is not the use for which land required for a right of way is taken; the use authorizing such a taking is the application of the water to the land. The use, whether public or private, therefore, occurs where the water is applied; that is, where the land to be irrigated is located. If located in another State the use is there, and that use must support the exercise of eminent domain for a right of way for the ditch, if it is to be supported. Since in this case it appears that no land in this State will receive for its reclamation or cultivation any of the water to be diverted or distributed by means of the ditch, but the water is to be entirely devoted to the irrigation of land in another State, the use will be in and for that State —for its uses and purposes, and not in this State or for any of its purposes. The principle above discussed, that the power of eminent domain will be exercised by a State for its own purposes, and not for the use of another State, seems, therefore, to be applicable. Clearly the State of Colorado cannot exercise the power in this State, and any authority conferred by its laws to do so would be void, for it is fundamental that the sovereignty of any government is limited to persons and property within the territory it controls. (Nichols on Em. Dom., Sec. 19; Trombley v. Humphrey, *supra*; Crosby v. Hanover, 36 N. H. 404; 1 Lewis on Em. Dom., (3rd Ed.) Sec. 385.)

While this State may be interested and even indirectly benefited in the manner above indicated by the reclamation and settlement of lands in another State, it would be difficult, we think, to uphold the exercise of emident domain in this State on the ground that such reclamation and settlement in another State is a necessity of the government of this state, in view of the fact that within its own boundaries and in all parts of the State there are vast areas yet uncultivated capable of irrigation and reclamation. And this power of eminent domain is founded upon the law of necessity, for "no government," says Judge Cooley, "could perpetuate its existence and further the prosperity of its people, if the means for the exercise of any of its sovereign powers might be withheld at the option of individuals." That eminent jurist further says that the power to appropriate must in any case be justified and limited by the necessity; "and whenever in any instance the government or its officials shall attempt to seize and appropriate that which cannot be needful to the due execution of its sovereign powers, or the proper discharge of any of its public functions, the same means of resistance and legal redress are open to the owner that would be available in case of a like seizure by lawless individuals." (Trombley v. Humphrey, *supra.*)

It is not necessary to rest our conclusion alone upon a consideration of these general principles, though we would feel content to do so, in the absence of authority upon the precise question here presented. With the exception of the statement found in the opinion in Thayer v. California Development Co., *supra,* to the effect that a public use in Mexico of water appropriated and diverted in California would not authorize the exercise of eminent domain in California, the specific question as to the right to condemn land in one State for a ditch to irrigate land in another State does not seem to have been decided or considered by any court, although we think the various judicial expressions and intimations are all against such a right. But the question as relating to other uses of the water of natural streams has been considered and the right to take land in one State under the power of eminent domain for an enterprise or use in another State has been denied by the courts of the State wherein the land was located. We refer to cases arising under the so-called "Mill Acts." Those statutes, and the provisions made by them, are too familiar to require extended explanation. It is sufficient to say that the purpose thereof is the encouragement of mills by authorizing their owners to erect a dam or dams and thereby overflow the lands of other persons, by paying such damages as may be assessed in the mode prescribed. The authorized proceeding in every material respect corresponds to a condemnation proceeding, and such statutes have been generally upheld as a rightful exercise of the power of eminent domain. (Ingram v. Water Co., 98 Me. 566, 56 Atl. 893; 1 Lewis on Em. Dom. (3rd Ed.) 280.) We have referred to a case decided in New Hampshire stating the ground upon which a taking for such a purpose has been sustained. Mr. Justice Clifford, in Holyoke Company v. Lyman, 15 Wall. 500, 507, 21 L. Ed. 133, alluded to the matter by saying: "Authority to erect dams across such streams for mill purposes results from the ownership of the bed and the banks of the stream, or the right to construct the same may be acquired by legislative grant, in cases where the legislature is of the opinion that the benefit to the public will be of sufficient importance to render it expedient for them to exercise the right of eminent domain and to authorize such an interference with private rights. Lands belonging to individuals have often been condemned for such purposes, in the exercise of the right of eminent domain, in cases where, from the nature of the country, mill sites sufficient in number could not otherwise be obtained, and that right is, even more frequently, exercised to enable mill-owners to flow the water back beyond their own limits, in order to create sufficient power or head and fall to operate their mills."

It is apparent that with respect to the question before us there is a close analogy between the taking of land under the mill acts, where the taking is caused or required by the necessity for flowing the land to furnish power for the mill below, and the taking of land to construct a ditch to carry water for irrigation. In two cases the question arose as to the right to have the damage for such taking for mill purposes assessed under the statute of the State in which the land flowed was situated, where the mill was located in an-

other State, and in both cases the right was denied.
(Wooster v. Great Falls Mfg. Co., 39 Me. 246; Salisbury
Mills v. Forsaith, 57 N. H. 124. See also Gould on Waters,
3rd Ed., Sec. 593; U. S. v. Ames, 1 Woodb. & Min. 76, Fed.
Cas. No. 14,441.) Referring to the statute of Maine the
court in the case cited from that state, say: "The dam
which causes the flowing—the mill for the benefit of which
such flowing is permitted, and the land overflowed, or the
property otherwise damnified by these erections, are assumed
to be within the boundaries of the State, and within legislative jurisdiction." And, stating the conclusion of the court,
it is said that "mills without the jurisdiction of the State, not
being subject to the terms, conditions and regulations of the
statutes, are not entitled to its benefits; and the common
law remedy remains unaffected by its provisions."

In the New Hampshire case of Salisbury v. Forsaith, it
was held that a mill owner having erected a dam on its land
in another State, whereby the water was set back upon land
in New Hampshire could not by petition have the damage
assessed, and the rights of flowage ascertained and fixed
under the New Hampshire statute for the encouragement of
manufactures. The opinion contains an interesting and able
discussion of the matter, and is particularly persuasive upon
the question as it arises in this case, for it answers the argument here made, and which was made in that case, that a
mill in the other State—Massachusetts would be a benefit to
New Hampshire. The court say: "In order that land may
be taken for this purpose against the owner's consent, the
committee, and ultimately the court, must be satisfied that
such taking is and may be of public use or benefit to the
people of this State. I agree with counsel for the defendant
that the act goes to the verge of the constitutional power of
the legislature, and I may say that, but for the authorities
by which the court thought they should be governed in the
late case of Amoskeag Co. v. Head (56 N. H. 386), I should
find great difficulty in sustaining it. But giving to the act
the widest scope and effect which have been thought ad-

missible under the constitution, I think it must be said that
the public use and benefit intended were those which would
arise from the erection of mills and the employment of our
water-power within our own limits, and not outside.   It
certainly may be, in one sense, of public use and benefit to
the people of this State to have so good and so rich a
neighbor on the south as our sister commonwealth of Massachusetts.   Doubtless it may be of benefit to our people that
every stream which flows from this State into that should be
skirted with manufacturing establishments from the point
where it leaves our borders to where it empties into the
ocean;   that thriving and opulent manufacturing town,
should spring up along the line, although upon the other
side; and that the industry, enterprise and thrift for which
the people of that State are so justly renowned should be
stimulated and encouraged by the exercise of a liberal comity
in the making and administration of our laws.   It may be
of public benefit to the people of this state that the City of
Chicago was rebuilt after the great fire which laid so large
a part of it in ashes in the autumn of 1871.   It perhaps would
not be difficult to show that no inconsiderable benefit has
resulted to our people from the rebuilding of the burnt district in Boston.   I do not see that these benefits differ at all,
unless it may be in degree, from those which would result
from the building of a dam and mills for the manufacture
of cotton and woolen goods just over the line in Massachusetts, and I do not think they are such as could have
been intended by the act."

Since the purpose is solely to irrigate lands in another
state, it is not material that the headgate is to be located
but a short distance above the southern boundary line of
this state, or that the lands to be irrigated are located just
over the line in the adjoining state.   It would make no difference in principle if it was proposed to divert the water
from some stream in the interior or elsewhere in our state
much farther removed from the lands to be irrigated, or if
it was proposed to irrigate lands in another state situated at

a greater distance beyond our territorial limits. Nor is the fact material that the diversion will occur below that of any previous appropriation, so far as the right of eminent domain is concerned. We are not here considering, and have not deemed it necessary to consider, the right to divert and appropriate water in this state for the purpose proposed.

The statute under which this proceeding to condemn for the right of way is brought prescribes that "Every person, association of persons, company or corporation (the word 'corporation' including a municipal corporation wherever appearing in this chapter), organized or hereafter organized under the laws of this state, or under the laws of any other state, and legally doing business under the laws of this state, who shall in the course of their business require a way of necessity for reservoirs, drains, flumes, ditches, canals, or electric power transmission lines, on or across lands of others for agricultural, mining, milling, domestic, electrical power transmission, municipal or sanitary purposes, shall have power and are authorized" * * * (Comp. Stat., Sec. 3874.) The authority given is to enter upon any land for the purpose of examining and making surveys for the purposes mentioned, and to hold and appropriate so much real property as may be necessary for the location, construction and convenient maintenance and use of such reservoir, drain, flume, ditch, canal, or electric power transmission line, and the procedure is prescribed in succeeding sections for the appropriation and condemnation of the land so required. It is a familiar elementary principle that the laws of a state have no extra-territorial effect. And it is not necessary for a state statute to contain words expressly confining its operation within the state. That it is so confined is generally understood. It is therefore not a strained construction of the statute conferring authority to appropriate and condemn land for a right of way for a ditch for agricultural purposes, that it is intended to be confined not only to a right of way within the state, but as well to agricultural purposes within the state. The authority is no doubt conferred to encourage agriculture within the state. If the legislative power exists to make the authority broader than that, and extend it to agricultural purposes beyond the boundaries of the State, it should be so extended, if at all, by the legislature, and by words clearly showing an intention to do so. In a concurring opinion in Salisbury Mills v. Forsaith, *supra*, it was said: "It is one of the plainest elementary rules, that no legislature can extend its laws to territory beyond the borders of its own state. How, then, can the courts of this state have any jurisdiction over dams and mills in another state?" And in Wooster v. Great Falls Mfg. Co., *supra*, it was said by the court: "All legislation is necessarily territorial. The statutes of a state are binding only within its jurisdiction. The legislature cannot, if they would, authorize acts to be done in a foreign territory. * * * They cannot affect or control property elsewhere, and it is not to be presumed they intended to exceed their jurisdiction." Mr. Justice Story, in Farnum v. Blackstone Canal, 1 Sumner, 62, Fed. Cas. No. 4,675, remarked: "Every legislature, however broad may be its enactments, is supposed to confine them to cases or persons within the reach of its sovereignty."

Again, it might be difficult to find authority in this statute to condemn land for the benefit of the business of a foreign corporation conducted exclusively in another state. What is meant by the words, "who shall in the course of their business require a way of necessity," &c., in immediate connection with the provision authorizing the taking of land for a reservoir or ditch for agricultural purposes by a foreign corporation "legally doing business under the laws of this state"? Was it intended or not that the right of way should be required only in the course of the business legally done, or to be legally done, by the foreign corporation under the laws of the state? Our laws do not control the affairs of a foreign corporation within the state where it is incorporated, but only its business within this state. The construction and maintenance of the ditch in this state by the petitioner would seem to be merely incidental to its business of irrigating and cultivating lands for agricultural purposes in Colorado. Is that, then, a business to which the statute refers in authorizing the taking of land for a right of way in this state when required by a foreign corporation in the course of its business, in view of the provision of the section extending the authority to a foreign corporation "legally doing business under the laws of this state," or is that authority conferred upon such corporation for any business wherever carried on? These questions seem to be pertinent, but we need not do more than suggest them, for we are satisfied upon the other grounds above stated that the petitioner has shown no right under the Constitution or statutes of this state to condemn the land in controversy. For that reason the demurrer should have been sustained, and for the same reason the facts stated in the amended petition are insufficient to support the judgment. The judgment, therefore, must be reversed, and the cause will be remanded with directions to vacate the order and judgment confirming the report of the commissioners and granting the right to take and use the land of the defendant below for the purpose specified in the amended petition, and enter the proper order or judgment denying that right in accordance with the views and conclusions herein expressed.   *Reversed.*

Scott, C. J., and Beard, J., concur.

FREMONT LODGE NO. 11, INDEPENDENT ORDER OF ODD FELLOWS v. BOARD OF COMMISSIONERS OF FREMONT COUNTY.

(No. 716.)

APPEAL AND ERROR—TIME FOR PROCEEDING IN ERROR—LIMITATION.

1. Under the statute (Comp. Stat. 1910, Sec. 5122) prescribing a limit of one year after the rendition of the judgment for bringing a proceeding in error, or, where the person entitled to such proceeding is an infant, a married woman, a person of unsound mind, or in prison, then within one year, as aforesaid, exclusive of the time of such disability, and providing for an extension of time by the trial court upon a sufficient showing that the party will be unavoidably prevented from instituting a proceeding within the time specified, such period of limitation is to be computed from the date of the actual rendition of the judgment, where no motion for new trial was filed in the court below, and the case does not fall within any of the exceptions mentioned in the statute, or no application, as therein provided, was made to the trial court for an extension of time.

[Decided April 7, 1913.]   (131 Pac. 62.)

ERROR to the District Court, Fremont County; HON. CHARLES E. CARPENTER, Judge.

The action was brought by Fremont Lodge No. 11, of the Independent Order of Odd Fellows, against the Board of the County Commissioners of the County of Fremont, and was heard in the court below upon an agreed statement of facts resulting in a judgment entered of record on January 16, 1911, in favor of the defendant. The plaintiff brought error.

E. H. Fourt, for plaintiff in error.

R. B. Landfair, County and Prosecuting Attorney of Fremont County, for defendant in error.

(An abstract of the briefs is omitted for the reason that they were confined to a discussion of the question raised by the pleadings in the cause and presented by the agreed statement of facts, and, without considering that question, the proceeding in error was dismissed because not brought within the time limited by the statute, and the Appellate Court was therefore without jurisdiction.)

SCOTT, CHIEF JUSTICE.

The plaintiff in error seeks by proceedings in error to reverse a judgment filed and entered of record on January 16, 1911, in the District Court of Fremont County.

It does not appear from the record here presented that there was any motion for a new trial filed or presented to the court below, and it follows that the judgment in so far as proceedings in error are concerned became final on the date above mentioned. (Conradt v. Lepper, 13 Wyo. 99, 78 Pac. 1, 3 Ann. Cas. 627.) The petition in error was filed in this court on April 16, 1912, or one year and three months after the judgment was rendered. Section 5122, Compiled Statutes, 1910, provides that "No proceeding to reverse, vacate, or modify a judgment or final order shall be commenced, unless within one year after the rendition of the judgment, or the making of the final order complained of; or, in case the person entitled to such proceeding is an infant, a married woman, a person of unsound mind, or in prison, within one year, as aforesaid, exclusive of the time of such disability; *Provided, however,* That the court rendering such judgment or making such final order, upon application of the party desiring to institute such proceeding and upon making to said court a sufficient showing that said party will be unavoidably prevented from instituting such proceeding within said time, shall, by an order duly entered of record, give to said party a reasonable extension of time, not exceeding eighteen months, within which to institute such proceeding." It does not appear from the record that this case falls within any of the exceptions contained in that section, or that there was any application made to the trial court for an extension of time within which to institute proceedings in error as therein provided. Upon this state of the record this court is without jurisdiction to entertain the attempted proceedings in error and the petition will be dismissed.   *Dismissed.*

POTTER, J. and BEARD, J., concur.

HAMILTON v. DIEFENDERFER.
(No. 676.)

HAMILTON v. DIEFENDERFER.
(No. 677.)

BILLS AND NOTES—NEGOTIABLE INSTRUMENTS—CHATTEL MORTGAGES—
SUFFICIENCY OF EVIDENCE TO SHOW PAYMENT AND CANCELLATION—
ASSIGNMENT OF MORTGAGE—ADMISSIBILITY AND EFFECT OF DECLA-
RATION OF PAYMENT BY HOLDER OF NOTE AND MORTGAGE PRIOR TO
ASSIGNMENT—CONSIDERATION—RIGHT OF JUNIOR LIENOR TO QUES-
TION CONSIDERATION OF ASSIGNMENT OF SENIOR MORTGAGE—ADMIS-
SIONS—WEIGHT AS EVIDENCE.

1. By statute (Comp. Stat. 1910, Sec. 3182) a promissory note
   negotiable in form is deemed prima facie to have been issued for a valuable consideration.
2. By his indorsement of a negotiable promissory note the payee
   and holder thereby impliedly warrants that it is in all respects genuine; that it is the valid instrument it purports
   to be; that such indorser has lawful title to it; and that it
   is a valid and subsisting obligation.
3. Where, in an action of replevin brought by the assignee of a
   chattel mortgage covering the property, there was evidence
   to the effect that the assignor had stated to the defendant,
   a subsequent mortgagee, and others a short time before the
   assignment that the mortgage was paid and she had neglected to cancel it, and it also appeared that at the time of
   the assignment the assignor had the note in her possession,
   which was not due or marked paid or otherwise canceled,
   and that she had indorsed and delivered it to the plaintiff
   for a valuable consideration, and signed and acknowledged
   the assignment of the mortgage, which at the time remained on the record uncanceled, *Held,* that such facts
   were in direct conflict with the statements of the assignor
   as to the payment of the note and mortgage and the war-
   ranties implied by the indorsement of the note, and justified a finding that the defense of payment had not been
   established by a preponderance of the evidence.
4. It being determined that the negotiable promissory note secured by the senior chattel mortgage had not been paid,
   and it appearing that whatever admissions were made by
   the assignor as to payment were made after the defendant
   had taken the subsequent mortgage and extended the credit
   secured thereby, the rights of the defendant under his subsequent mortgage were not affected, and he was not placed

in any worse position by the assignment of the senior mortgage, but the latter remained a prior and superior lien and enforceable while it remained in the hands of the mortgagee named therein, and was thereafter equally valid and enforceable by the assignee; and it was, therefore, immaterial whether or not the assignee was a bona fide purchaser.

ON PETITION FOR REHEARING.

5. Where, in an action by the assignee of a chattel mortgage against a subsequent mortgagee to recover possession of the mortgaged property, evidence was admitted to the effect that the assignor had stated prior to the assignment and the indorsement of the note secured by the mortgage, that the note and mortgage were paid, *Held*, that, conceding the admissibility of such statements, they were not conclusive in favor of the subsequent mortgagee, whose mortgage was taken long prior to the making of the statements, and who had not acted upon them.

6. The only evidence to sustain the defense in such action that the note and mortgage under which the plaintiff claimed had been paid consisted of admissions of payment by the assignor, while all the other facts in the case tended to show non-payment. *Held*, that the trial court was not only' as well able as the appellate court to determine the weight to be given to the alleged statements of the assignor, but in a better position to do so.

7. The weight to be given to admissions of payment by the assignor of a chattel or contract is to be determined by the jury, or by the court where the case is tried without a jury, and though they may amount to satisfactory proof, even when verbally made, they are to be weighed with caution when unaccompanied by other facts or evidence.

8. Though the price of a thing sold or assigned may be inadequate, and that fact may be considered in determining the question of good faith, it may nevertheless be a valuable consideration within the meaning of that term, as where money is paid, whether the amount be large or small.

9. Where a senior chattel mortgage was valid and had not been paid, the consideration for an assignment thereof was immaterial, as against the junior mortgagee, and the latter could not impeach such assignment on the ground of the insufficiency of the consideration to constitute the assignee a purchaser for value.

[Decided April 7, 1913.]   (131 Pac. 37.)
[Rehearing denied July 19, 1913.]   (133 Pac. 1081.)

ERROR to the District Court, Sheridan County; HON. CARROLL H. PARMELEE, Judge.

Each of the actions was replevin brought by Alf Diefenderfer against L. P. Hamilton. From a judgment in favor of the plaintiff in each case the defendant brought error. The material facts are stated in the opinions.

Metz & Sackett, for plaintiff in error.

The evidence seems to be undisputed that the indebtedness secured by the mortgage assigned to Diefenderfer had been paid and satisfied prior to the asisgnment, since no evidence was produced to contradict the admissions of John Schmitt, the mortgagor, and Marie Schmitt, the mortgagee, made prior to the assignment. Such admissions were admissible, not only against the party making them, but against subsequent purchasers from such party. (1 Ency. Ev. 510, note 73; Williams v. Judy, 3 Gilm. 282, 44 Am. Dec. 699; Horton v. Smith, 8 Ala. 73.) The burden of proving consideration was upon plaintiff. (Lane v. Starky (Neb.), 18 N. W. 47.) The note and mortgage were executed by husband to wife. and therefore presumed to be fraudulent, it appearing that the husband was insolvent.

It was necessary that Diefenderfer should show a purchase of the note and mortgage in the usual course of business, and that he received the same for a valuable consideration. It was also necessary for him to show that the purchase was made without notice of defendant's claim, or the invalidity of the debt and mortgage. We regard it as clear from the evidence that the assignment was not taken in the usual course of business. Diefenderfer was not a bona fide purchaser. (Tiedeman on Comr. Paper, Secs. 290, 291; Dewitt v. Perkins, 22 Wis. 474; Fuller v. Goodnow, 62 Minn. 163, 64 N. W. 161; Proctor v. Cole, 104 Ind. 373, 3 N. E. 106; Schmueckle v. Waters, 125 Ind. 265, 25 N. E. 281: Hodson v. Glass Co., 156 Ill. 397, 40 N. E. 971; Loftin v. Hill, (N. C.) 42 S. E. 548; Pelletier v. Bank, (La.) 38 So. 132; Hunt v. Sandford, 6 Yerg. (Tenn.) 387; Gould

v. Stevens, 43 Vt. 125; Bank v. Bennett, 8 Ind. App. 679, 36 N. E. 551; Lytle v. Lansing, 147 U. S. 59, 37 L. Ed. 78; Roberts v. Hall, 37 Conn. 205, 9 Am. Rep. 308.) It was not necessary that Diefenderfer should have had notice of any particular equity. A notice of some equity, illegality, defect, or defense is sufficient. (Bank v. Marcy (Ark.), 95 S. W. 145; Hodson v. Glass Co., *supra*.) The burden was upon him to show good faith, since the evidence was conclusive as to the payment of the note and mortgage. (Vette v. Sacker, 114 Mo. App. 363, 89 S. W. 360; Hodson v. Glass Co., *supra;* Loftin v. Hill, *supra*.).

(In support of petition for rehearing.) While commercial paper is presumed to have been given for a valuable consideration, it should not be permitted to prevail against the repeated admissions of payment by the holder. The statements, acts and conduct of Marie Schmitt at the time she indorsed the note and assigned the mortgage to Diefenderfer were competent only for the purpose of showing the circumstances surrounding the transaction on the question of the good faith of Diefenderfer; they were not competent to show title in the assignor or the validity of her claim. (1 Ency. Ev. 357, 383, note 62, 385; Nutter v. O'Donnell, 6 Colo. 253; Lewis v. Adams, 61 Ga. 559; Wilson v. Patrick, 34 Ia. 362; Wescott v. Wescott, 75 Ia. 628, 35 N. W. 649; Royal v. Chandler, 79 Me. 265, 9 Atl. 615; Hunt v. Roylance, 11 Cush. 117; Comm. v. Goodwin, 14 Gray, 55; Blake v. Everett, 1 Ala. 248; Baxter v. Knowles, 12 Ala. 114; Pickering v. Reynolds, 119 Mass. 111; Hayden v. Stone, 121 Mass. 413; Turner v. Belden, 9 Mo. 787; Criddle v. Criddle, 21 Mo. 522; Clark v. Huffaker, 26 Mo. 264; Hurlburt v. Wheeler, 40 N. H. 73; Warring v. Warren, 1 John. 340; McPeake v. Hutchinson, 5 S. & R. 294; Patent v. Goldsborough, 9 S. & R. 47; Galbraith v. Green, 13 S. & R. 85; Crooks v. Bunn, 136 Pa. 368, 20 Atl. 529.) The note and mortgage were not transferred for value. (Alger v. Scott, 54 N. Y. 14; Williams v. Walker, 18 S. C. 577; Nelson v. Searle, 4 M. & M. 795; Tiedeman on Com. Paper,

Sec. 157.)   A "good" consideration is not alone sufficient
for commercial paper.   (Tiedeman, Sec. 159; 9 Cyc. 319.)
A promise to do that which the promisor is already bound
to do is no consideration.   (9 Cyc. 347-351; Havana P. D.
Co. v. Ashhurst, 148 Ill. 115, 35 N. E. 873; Beaver v. Fulp,
136 Ind. 595, 36 N. E. 418; Ellison v. Water Co., 12 Cal.
542; Johnson v. Seller, 33 Ala. 265; Merrick v. Giddings,
1 Mackey, 294; Schuler v. Myton, 48 Kan. 282, 29 Pac. 163;
Putnam v. Woodbury, 68 Me. 58; Ecker v. McAllister, 54
Md. 362, 45 Md. 290; Gordon v. Gordon, 56 N. H. 170;
Arend v. Smith, 151 N. Y. 502, 45 N. E. 872; Robinson v.
Jewett, 116 N. Y. 40, 22 N. E. 224; Vanderbilt v. Schreyer,
91 N. Y. 392; L' Amoreux v. Gould, 7 N. Y. 349, 57 Am.
Dec. 524; Alley v. Tuck, 8 App. Div. (N. Y.) 50, 40 N. Y.
Supp. 433; Hanks v. Barron, 95 Tenn. 275, 32 S. W. 195;
Kenighberger v. Windgate, 31 Tex. 42, 98 Am. Dec. 512;
Davenport v. First. Con. Soc. 33 Wis. 387.)

Enterline & LaFleiche, for defendant in error.

The indorsement and delivery of the Schmitt note to the
plaintiff would have carried with it the mortgage securing it
without a formal assignment.   (Graham v. Blinn, 3 Wyo.
746.)   The defendant was not in a position to complain even
if it should be assumed that the mortgage assigned to plaintiff had been executed for the purpose of defrauding his
existing creditors.   The defendant extended credit after the
mortgage in question had been executed and he therefore
had constructive notice of such mortgage.   (Bump on Fraudulent Conveyances, Sec. 462; Gentry v. Lanneau, 54 S. C.
514, 71 Am. St. 814; Wilson v. Stevens, 129 Ala. 630, 29
So. 678, 87 Am. St. 86; Seed v. Jennings (Or.), 83 Pac.
872; Schreyer v. Scott, 134 U. S. 405, 33 L. Ed. 955; Todd
v. Nelson, 109 N. Y. 316, 16 N. E. 360; Cole v. Brown, 114
Mich. 396, 72 N. W. 247; Treblicock v. Big Mo. Min. Co.,
9 S. D. 206, 68 N. W. 330; Smith v. Vodges, 92 U. S. 183,
23 L. Ed. 481; Moore v. Page, 111 U. S. 117, 28 L. Ed.
373; Jones v. Clifton, 101 U. S. 225, 25 L. Ed. 908; Hager-
man v. Buchanan, 45 N. J. Eq. 292, 14 Am. St. 732.)   The

authorities cited by counsel for plaintiff in error upon the proposition that the plaintiff was not a holder in due course are not in point, in view of the provisions of Sections 3210, 3214, 3215 and 3217, Comp. Stat. 1910. The meager testimony introduced as to the declarations of Marie Schmitt, who transferred the note and mortgage, is not sufficient to establish that the note and mortgage were invalid or had been paid. A married woman may mortgage, pledge or transfer her own property for the purpose of securing or satisfying her husband's debts. (King v. Hansing (Minn.), 93 N. W. 306; Sigel-Campion L. S. Com. Co. v. Haston (Kan.), 75 Pac. 1028; Fiske v. Osgood (Neb.), 78 N. W. 124; Hallowell v. Daly (N. J.), 56 Atl. 234; Holmes v. Hull (Neb.), 70 N. W. 241; Just v. Bank (Mich.), 94 N. W. 200; Goldsmith v. Lewine (Ark.), 68 S. W. 308.)

BEARD, JUSTICE.

The defendant in error, Diefenderfer, commenced these two actions against the plaintiff in error, Hamilton, to recover the possession of certain personal property, and for damages for the alleged wrongful taking and detention of the same. The cases involve the same questions and were consolidated for the purpose of trial and were tried to the court without a jury, and in each case the court found that the plaintiff below was entitled to the possession of the property and that he had sustained damages in the sum of ten dollars and rendered judgment accordingly. From those judgments the defendant below brings error. The cases have been submitted together in this court, and one opinion will cover both cases.

The property in question was owned by one John Schmitt, who on February 21, 1907, executed a chattel mortgage thereon to Marie Schmitt, his wife, to secure two notes of $500 each, one due January 1, 1908, and the other due January 1, 1909. The mortgage was filed in the office of the County Clerk and duly indexed February 23, 1907. On December 3, 1908, Marie Schmitt assigned the mortgage to Diefenderfer, which assignment was duly filed and indexed

on the same day, and at the same time the note due January
1, 1909, was indorsed and delivered by her to Diefenderfer.
The consideration as recited in the assignment of the mortgage being one dollar and other valuable considerations.   It
appears by the evidence that Diefenderfer had, on September
23, 1908, signed a note, as surety for John Schmitt, to the
Sheridan National Bank for $690, due ninety days after
date; and that at the time the note and mortgage were so
transferred to him by Marie Schmitt, he agreed with her to
pay the note to the Bank on which he was surety for John
Schmitt, and that he did pay it on December 11, 1908, before
it was due.   John Schmitt had absconded a few days before
Diefenderfer procured the note and mortgage from Marie
Schmitt, and on the day he procured the same he took possession of the mortgaged property, deeming himself insecure.
On July 18, 1908, John Schmitt executed a chattel mortgage
on the property to the plaintiff in error, Hamilton, to secure
a note of that date for $600, due Nov. 18, 1908, which mort-
gage was duly filed and indexed and renewed from time to
time by affidavits.   A few days after Diefenderfer took possession of the property Hamilton took possession of a part
of it and Diefenderfer replevied it, and soon afterwards
Hamilton took possession of the balance of it; hence the
two suits.

It is not claimed that if the mortgage held by Diefenderfer
was a valid and subsisting lien upon the property it would
not be superior to the lien of the Hamilton mortgage.   The
defenses to it pleaded in the answer are, that it was given
without consideration; that it was given to hinder, delay
and defraud the creditors of John Schmitt; that the notes
secured by it had been paid; and that Diefenderfer was not
a bona fide purchaser.   The first two defenses are not seriously contended for by counsel for plaintiff in error.   The
note was negotiable in form and by our statute is deemed
prima facie to have been issued for a valuable consideration,
(Sec. 3182 Comp. Stat. 1910) and there was no evidence
offered to rebut this presumption; and the evidence fell far

short of proving that the mortgage was given for the purpose or with the intent of hindering, delaying or defrauding the creditors of John Schmitt. These matters were referred to briefly in the brief of counsel for plaintiff in error, but were practically abandoned in a supplemental brief filed after oral argument, by agreement of counsel and leave of court, in which they say: "The brief of plaintiff in error filed in the above case was confined to two questions, namely: That the mortgage, while in the hands of Marie Schmitt, was satisfied, paid, and should have been cancelled, and that Diefenderfer was not a bona fide purchaser." In view of that statement of counsel we deem it unnecessary to further discuss the questions previously referred to.

On the question of the payment of the note held by Diefenderfer, while in the hands of Marie Schmitt, the only evidence was that she had stated to Hamilton and others a short time before she assigned the note and mortgage to Diefenderfer, in substance, that it was paid; that she thought it was paid; that there was nothing to it; that Hamilton's mortgage was first; that it was no good; that she had neglected to cancel it; and that she would go to the court house and cancel it as soon as her condition would permit. Each and all of these statements testified to as having been made by Marie Schmitt, were made within two or three weeks before she assigned the note and mortgage to Diefenderfer and long after Hamilton took his mortgage, and there is no evidence that Diefenderfer had any knowledge at or before the time he took the assignment that she had made any such statements. On the other hand it appears that she had the note in her possession, it was not yet due, was not marked paid or otherwise cancelled, she indorsed and delivered it to Diefenderfer for a valuable consideration and signed and acknowledged an assignment of the mortgage which remained uncancelled on the record. By her indorsement of the note she engaged or impliedly warranted that it was in all respects genuine; that it was the valid instrument it purported to be; and that she had lawful title to it (1 Daniel on

Negotiable Instruments (5th Ed.), Sec. 669a) ; and that it
was a valid and subsisting obligation.   (Idem. Sec. 673; 7
Cyc. 831 ; and Sec. 3224, Comp. Stat. 1910.)   All of these
things are in direct conflict with the statements which it is
testified she made a short time before as to payment. Assuming, but without deciding, that the statements of Marie
Schmitt were competent and admissible evidence of payment, her acts and the circumstances of the transactions are
so conflicting with those statements that the court may well
have concluded that the defense of payment had not been
established by a preponderance of the evidence.   The findings of the court are general and we cannot say that they
were not based upon that ground, which to our minds was
a reasonable conclusion considering all of the evidence and
the circumstances surrounding the transaction.   If the note
was not paid, the lien of the mortgage remained a prior and
superior lien to that of the Hamilton mortgage and could
have been enforced by Marie Schmitt had it remained in her
hands, and was equally valid and enforceable in the hands
of her assignee.   Hamilton's rights were not affected and he
was placed in no worse position by reason of the assignment.
The evidence being sufficient to sustain the findings and
judgment of the District Court on this branch of the case,
and as the judgment must be affirmed for that reason, the
other question, namely: whether or not Diefenderfer was
a bona fide purchaser, becomes immaterial and will not
therefore be considered.   The judgment of the District Court
in each case is affirmed.   *Affirmed.*

SCOTT, C. J., and POTTER, J., concur.

ON PETITION FOR REHEARING.

POTTER, JUSTICE.

A petition for a rehearing has been filed in each of these
cases which, as stated in the former opinion, were submitted
together, and had been consolidated in the District Court
for the purpose of trial.

The only points discussed in the brief in support of the
petition for rehearing are those mainly relied upon by the

plaintiff in error at the time the cases were originally submitted, viz.: that the mortgage assigned to Diefenderfer had
been paid, and should have been cancelled, while it remained
in the hands of the assignor, Marie Schmitt, and that the
assignment was without consideration. It is argued at some
length that the statements made by Mrs. Schmitt to Hamilton
and others before she assigned the mortgage, to the effect
that it was paid, or she thought it was paid, and that she
had intended to cancel it but had neglected to do so, were
admissible in evidence, and a number of authorities are cited
upon that proposition. The statements were admitted in evidence and, without deciding the question, it was assumed in
the former opinion that the statements were admissible, notwithstanding that the note was indorsed and the mortgage
securing it assigned to Diefenderfer before maturity, it being
found unnecessary to determine whether or not the assignee
was a bona fide holder. But counsel erroneously assumes
that the statements so made were conclusive in favor of
Hamilton and against Diefenderfer. They might have been
conclusive in favor of one who had acted upon them, if the
assignee was not a bona fide holder for value under circumstances protecting him against such admissions. Not having been acted upon by Hamilton, whose mortgage was taken
long prior to the making of the statements, it would have
been competent to prove the untruth of the statements, and
to prove by Mrs. Schmitt that although she made the statements they were untrue in fact. The principle is stated in
Greenleaf on Evidence:

"These admissions by third persons, as they derive their
value and legal force from the relation of the party making
them to the property in question, and are taken as parts of
the *res gestae*, may be proved by any competent witness who
heard them, without calling the party by whom they were
made. The question is, whether he made the admission, and
not merely, whether the fact is as he admitted it to be. Its
truth, where the admission is not conclusive (and it seldom
is so) may be controverted by other testimony; even by call-

ing the party himself, when competent." (Redfield's Ed.,
Vol. I, Sec. 191.) "Admissions, whether of law or of fact,
which have been acted upon by others, are conclusive against
the party making them, in all cases between him and the
person whose conduct he has thus influenced." (Id., Sec.
207.) "On the other hand, verbal admissions which have not
been acted upon, and which the party may controvert, without any breach of good faith or evasion of public justice,
though admissible in evidence, are not held conclusive
against him." (Id., Sec. 209. See also Bigelow on Estoppel,
p. 480 *et seq.*) It is said in Encyclopedia of Evidence (Vol.
I, 612-613) to be the general rule that admissions are not ·
conclusive, but may be disproved by other evidence, the exceptions being judicial admissions and those which were intended to be and have been so acted upon as to give rise
to the doctrine of estoppel.

The weight to be given to such admissions is to be determined by the jury, or by the court where the case is tried
without a jury. (I Ency. Ev. 612; I Ency. Law, (2nd
Ed.) 724.) Though verbally made, they may amount to
satisfactory proof, but when unaccompanied by other facts
or evidence are to be weighed with caution. (I Ency. Ev.
611; I Ency. Law, 723.) The only evidence that the note
and mortgage had been paid consisted of testimony showing
the admissions aforesaid of Mrs. Schmitt. That testimony
was not corroborated by any other fact in the case. On the
contrary, all the other facts tended to show non-payment.
The trial court was as well able as this court would be to
determine the weight to be given to the alleged statements
of Mrs. Schmitt, if not, indeed, in a better position to do so.
Counsel complains of the statement in the opinion that the
mortgage was assigned for a valuable consideration. That
remark had reference only to the acts of Mrs. Schmitt
seemingly in conflict with her alleged statements. The
assignment executed by her recited that it was made in
consideration of one dollar in hand paid "and other valuable
considerations;" and it was shown that she was actually

paid the sum of money stated at the time of executing the assignment. Nothing was said in the opinion concerning the adequacy or sufficiency of the consideration to constitute the assignee a bona fide holder, but the court refrained, as stated in the opinion, from deciding that question, deeming it unnecessary, for the reason that Hamilton was not in a position permitting him to question the consideration. Though the price be inadequate, and that fact may be considered in determining the question of good faith, it may nevertheless be a valuable consideration within the legal meaning of that term, as where money is paid, whether the amount be large or small.

Having concluded that the evidence was sufficient to sustain a finding that the mortgage and the note which it secured had not been paid, the consideration for the assignment became immaterial in this case, for it did not concern Hamilton, the junior mortgagee, whether there was any consideration for the assignment of the senior mortgage. (1 Jones on Mort., Sec. 788; Jones on Chat. Mort., 5th Ed., Sec. 502; 2 Ency. Law, 2nd Ed., 1073, 1075; 20 Id. 920-921; 4 Cyc., 31-32; 7 Cyc., 58; 27 Cyc., 1284; Beach v. Derby, 19 Ill. 617; Briscoe v. Eckley, 35 Mich. 112; Whittaker v. Johnson County, 10 Ia. 161; Norris v. Hall, 18 Me. 332; Pugh v. Miller, 126 Ind. 189, 25 N. E. 1040; Sammis v. Wightman, 31 Fla. 10, 12 So. 526; Deach v. Perry, 53 Hun, 638, 6 N. Y. Supp. 940; Anderson v. Maynard, 1 Colo. App. 1, 27 Pac. 168; Rue v. Scott, (N. J.) 21 Atl. 1048.)

In Beach v. Derby, *supra,* the court say, concerning the assignment of a chattel mortgage: "Nor do we think the court erred in ruling out the evidence offered, tending to show that Derby paid no consideration to Graves for the assignment of the mortgage. That was no business of the creditors of the mortgagor." In 27 Cyc., page 1284, it is said: "But the consideration of the transfer is in general no concern of the mortgagor, and he cannot be permitted to impeach it, nor can a junior mortgagee do so." In Jones on Mortgages (Vol. 1, Sec. 788) it is said: "Whether the assignee of a mortgage has paid value for it or not does not concern the mortgagor, except in reference to his interposing an equitable defense in way of payment or set-off." We quote the following from Am. & Eng. Ency. of Law (2nd Ed.), Vol. 2, page 1075): "In an action by the assignee of a chose in action against the debtor, it is in general no defense that the assignment was made without consideration, as the matter in no way affects his liability." It is well settled also that one who has taken an assignment of a mortgage for less than its value or the amount secured is not limited in his recovery to the amount actually paid, but may recover the whole amount due. (Rue v. Scott, *supra*; Jones on Chat. Mort., 5th Ed., Sec. 502.)

While we have rested our decision upon the well established principles above stated, we might add that the difficulty, if any, in holding the consideration for this assignment to be sufficient to constitute the assignee a bona fide holder for value seems much less to us than it does to counsel. The point urged against the sufficiency of the consideration is that the assignee's promise to pay the note of John Schmitt at the bank was merely a promise to perform an existing obligation, since he was liable thereon as surety, and hence did not constitute in law a consideration for the assignment. In that respect the chief difficulty, we think, would be in determining the effect of the evidence relating to the agreement between the assignor and assignee for the payment of the note. It might reasonably be concluded from that evidence, in our opinion, that Diefenderfer's agreement was to pay and discharge the debt of his principal, and not merely perform his obligation as surety. In other words, that his agreement was to make the debt his own and pay it as such, thereby assuming the obligation of the principal to the holder of the note, and releasing the obligation of the principal to him as surety.

While it is true that before the mortgage was assigned to Diefenderfer he was bound as surety upon the note which he agreed to pay as a part of the consideration for the assignment, he was bound only as surety, with all the rights and entitled to all the remedies allowed a surety, including the statutory remedy of an action aided by attachment to obtain indemnity. (Comp. Stat., Secs. 5030, 5031.) Having signed the note as surety the principal might at any time thereafter indemnify him, the obligation assumed by the surety being a sufficient consideration, especially where the surety upon receiving such indemnity agrees to pay the note. This is well settled law. It is said in Brandt on Suretyship (Vol. 1, 3rd Ed., Sec. 239): "The liability of a surety or guarantor for the debt of his principal before he has made any payment on account thereof is a sufficient consideration for the execution of a mortgage or trust deed for his indemnity, and such mortgage or trust deed will take precedence of any subsequent lien upon the property encumbered thereby. A promissory note for the payment of a certain sum of money executed for the purpose of indemnifying the payee against his liability as a surety for the maker of an administration bond, and to enable him to secure himself by an attachment of the property of the maker, is valid, notwithstanding the payee at the time of its execution has not been damnified. The existing liability with an implied promise to pay that amount upon the principal indebtedness, forming a sufficient consideration for the note, the note will be enforced against the objections of other creditors." The following authorities also sustain and illustrate the general proposition above stated, and some of the cases cited sustain as to consideration an instrument executed by a third person to indemnify the surety, where the latter has agreed to pay the debt, or relinquished some right, upon receiving the indemnity. (Swift v. Crocker, 21 Pick. (Mass.) 241; Osgood v. Osgood, 39 N. H, 209; Cushing v. Gore, 15 Mass. 69; Stevens v. Bell, 6 Mass. 339; Hamaker v. Eberley, 2 Binn. (Pa.) 506, 4 Am. Dec. 477; Bank v. Jefferson, 101 Wis. 452, 77 N. W. 889; Harris v. Harris, 180 Ill. 157, 54 N. E. 180; Coal Co. v. Blake, 85 N. Y. 226; Hapgood v. Wellington, 136 Mass. 217; 1 Page on Contracts, Sec. 276; 6 Ency. Law, (2nd Ed.) 709; Carroll v. Nixon, 4

W. & S. 517; Carman v. Noble, 9 Pa. St. 366; Gladwin v.
Garrison, 13 Cal. 331; Goodwin v. McMinn, 204 Pa. St.
162, 53 Alt. 762; Steen v. Stretch, 50 Neb. 572, 70 N. W.
48; Williams v. Silliman, 74 Tex. 626, 12 S. W. 534; Ellis
v. Herrin, (N. J.) 24 Atl. 129; Willis v. Heath, (Tex.)
18 S. W. 801; Landigan v. Mayer, 32 Or. 245, 51 Pac.
649, 67 Am. St. Rep. 521.)

Where a married woman may contract and convey her
property in the same manner as if she were unmarried, as
she may do under the laws of this state, what would prevent
her from paying the note of her husband, or conveying her
property for that purpose, if such act is not fraudulent as to
creditors? Assuming that a new consideration would be
necessary to sustain a mortgage or other conveyance, or an
agreement by a third person, indemnifying one who has
already become a surety and obligated as such, and that is
said to be the rule in Jones on Mortgages (Vol. 1, Sec.
615), the surety's agreement to waive a valuable right, or
to assume and pay the debt of the principal might, perhaps,
be found to be a sufficient consideration. (Pollock on Contracts, 8th Ed., 201-203; Wright v. McKitrick, 2 Kan. App.
508, 43 Pac. 977; Judy v. Louderman, 48 O. St. 562, 29
N. E. 181; Harris v. Harris, 180 Ill. 157, 54 N. E. 180;
Hamaker v. Eberley, 2 Binn. (Pa) 506, 4 Am. Dec. 477;
Rockafellow v. Peay, 40 Ark. 69.) But deeming it not involved in this case, we do not decide the question of the
sufficiency of the consideration as between the assignee of
the mortgage and the assignor, or her creditors.

The assignor is not a party, nor is it sought to defeat the
assignment in her interest. The plaintiff in error was not
a creditor of the assignor, and no such creditor is here attempting to impeach the assignment. Indeed, it does not
appear that Mrs. Schmitt had any creditors. Under such
circumstances the question of consideration is not important.
As an executed transfer it might, therefore, be sustained
and enforced as a gift, if not otherwise. Rehearing will be
denied.

SCOTT, C. J., and BEARD, J., concur.

JUSTICE ET AL. v. BROCK.
(No. 721.)

FACTORS—DUTIES AND LIABILITY—NEGLIGENCE—SUIT FOR ADVANCES—INSTRUCTIONS—TRIAL—BURDEN OF PROOF—ARGUMENT—RIGHT TO OPEN AND CLOSE.

1. A factor is not obliged to sell at the request of his principal at a price which would be less than his lien for advances, commission, and just charges, unless the principal pays or tenders such advances and charges, but he is bound to the exercise of ordinary care, skill and diligence to obtain the market value of the consigned property, and may not withhold the same from the market against the directions of the principal, without incurring liability for damages resulting therefrom, if the exercise of ordinary care, skill and diligence would have resulted in a sale at a price which would have been satisfactory to the principal and sufficient to pay the factor's advances and charges.

2. Upon a simple consignment of wool to be sold on commission, without any instruction, direction, or advice communicated by the principal to the factor at the time of the consignment, the principal had the right to say when the wool should be sold, and at what price, so long as it did not impair the factor's right to reimbursement out of the proceeds for all his advances and charges.

3. The rule requiring a factor to exercise ordinary care, skill and diligence to obtain the market value of the consigned property refers to a market available to the factor.

4. The fact that property like that consigned and of the same or higher quality may have been sold at the market quotations furnished from time to time by the factor to the principal will not of itself be sufficient to entitle the principal to recover damages for the failure of the factor to sell the consigned property, where it appears that the factor was diligent and in good faith endeavoring to sell.

5. A factor is not an insurer of sale or price and does not agree that he will commit no error, but is liable only for negligence, bad faith or dishonesty.

6. An instructed factor who has in good faith held the consigned property for a rise in price, will not be liable for damages resulting from the fact that the market weakened thereafter, if he was diligent and faithful in trying to sell at a satisfactory price and sufficient to pay his advances and charges, for, under the circumstances, the principal will be presumed to have approved the factor's conduct in

so holding the property, and at most, the failure to sell prior to such weakening of the market would only be a mistake in judgment on the part of the factor made in good faith.

7. Wool was consigned in September to factors who made an advance at the time of the consignment, without any instruction or direction at the time of the consignment as to selling, and in the following February the principal wrote the factors to the effect that he would like to have the wool closed out and to get his returns by April first if that could be done without too much of a sacrifice, and early in March following also wrote referring to the February letter and stating that he saw no reason why the future market would be any better than it was then and that he was willing to sell on present market quotations received from the factors. *Held,* that, treating the two letters as a positive instruction to sell, the factors were not authorized to sell below the market quotations, and were not required to sell at a price insufficient to reimburse and recompense them for their advances and just charges, in the absence of any tender or a satisfactory offer to pay the same.

8. In an action by factors to whom wool was consigned to recover advances, the defendant alleged in his answer that the plaintiffs were negligent in failing to sell at the market price of the wool in the market at Philadelphia, to which place the wool had been consigned, and that if plaintiffs had complied with the terms of the contract and had sold the wool at the best or average market price obtainable on the Philadelphia market, the defendant would have received much more than the amount of the advances and charges of the factors, and prayed judgment for damages. *Held,* that the issues tendered by the answer were that the wool could have been sold at the quoted or average market price at Philadelphia by the exercise of ordinary care, skill and diligence, and that the failure to exercise such ordinary care, skill and diligence to sell the wool upon that market resulted in damage to the defendant; that the consignment was general and to a specified market, and the plaintiffs were not bound to look for any other market than the one to which the wool was consigned; and that the evidence as to sales and prices in other markets was not material and was improperly admitted, since, although such evidence, under some circumstances, might be admissible as tending to show the market price at the place where the wool was

to be sold, and the want of care or diligence of the factor in selling the wool at the best available price, no circumstances of that nature were disclosed as would take it out of the general rule.

9. In an action by factors for advances, where defendant counter-claimed, setting up a loss alleged to have occurred through the negligent failure of the factors to sell at the market price, an instruction that the factors were under obligations to carry out any and all positive instructions of the defendant with reference to the property consigned was erroneous because disregarding the lien of the plaintiffs for advances and their right to reimbursement out of the proceeds of the sale.

10. An instruction in such action that if the jury should find that any latitude was given to the factors then they should consider whether the factors had acted in good faith and according to their best judgment in carrying out the instructions of the principal so as best to preserve his rights, was erroneous because of the absence of any evidence challenging the good faith of the plaintiffs.

11. The defendant had the right to open and close the argument to the jury where, in an action for advances by factors, the defense was a counter-claim by way of confession and avoidance alleging a loss occasioned by the negligent failure of the factors to sell at the market price, and the court properly instructed the jury that there was no dispute in the evidence as to the right of the plaintiffs to recover, unless the defendant had established his counter-claim by a preponderance of the evidence, and that the burden of proof rested upon the defendant.

ON PETITION FOR REHEARING.

12. In an action by factors for advances, where the defendant has counter-claimed alleging a loss occurring through the negligent failure of the factors to sell, if there is evidence which may properly be understood as showing a long delay by the factors in selling during a falling market, it may to that extent tend to show lack of diligence sufficient to justify the submission of the matter to the jury, and if unexplained may be sufficient to justify a finding of negligence; but, in applying that principle in the case stated, the rule concerning the duty of a factor who has made advances should be considered, and the jury properly instructed with reference thereto.

[Decided April 7, 1913.]   (131 Pac. 38.)

[Rehearing denied August 2, 1913.]   (133 Pac. 1070.)

ERROR to the District Court, Sheridan County, HON. CARROLL H. PARMELEE, Judge.

The action was brought by Theodore Justice, Henry Justice, William Warner Justice, James Bateman and Henry K. Kenderdine, co-partners doing business under the firm name and style of Justice, Bateman and Company, against A. L. Brock. From a judgment in favor of the defendant the plaintiffs brought error. The material facts are stated in the opinion.

Enterline & La Fleiche, for plaintiffs in error.

The wool having been consigned without instructions or directions to the plaintiffs, who made large advances thereon, the defendant was not in a position authorizing him to control absolutely the sale by the factor or direct the time of sale and price, nor did his letters introduced in evidence amount to a positive direction that the wool be sold without further delay. (Heffner v. Gwynne-Treadwell Cotton Co., 87 C. C. A. 606; Drumm-Flato Com. Co. v. Union Meat Co., (Tex. Civ. App.) 77 S. W. 634; Poels v. Wilson, (Neb.) 108 N. W. 153; Poels v. Brown, (Neb.) 111 N. W. 798; Gordon v. Cobb, 60 S. E. 821; Brown v. McGram, 14 Pet. 479; 12 Ency. Law, (2nd Ed.) 646; Sturtevant Co. v. Dugan, 14 Ann. Cas. 675; Field v. Farrington, 10 Wall. 141; Wynne et al. v. Schnabaum, (Ark.) 94 S. W. 50.) To authorize a recovery by the defendant it was necessary that he should allege and prove that the failure to sell the wool at the best market price obtainable was due either to the fraud of the plaintiffs, or their failure to exercise ordinary care, skill and diligence, and that as a consequence he suffered the damage complained of. And the burden of proof was upon the defendant to establish those facts, if alleged. But the answer is defective in failing to properly allege these material matters.

A factor, as shown by the cases cited, and others, is only bound to exercise ordinary and reasonable care, skill and diligence in selling the consigned commodity at or within

. the market to which it is shipped for sale. Proof of sales made by the same or other parties, even though it be within the same market, does not of itself establish negligence on the part of the factor. It was error to permit the introduction of evidence as to the sale of wool by other parties in Philadelphia and elsewhere. (Pugh v. Porter Bros. Co., 50 Pac. 772; Lockett v. Baxter, 19 Pac. 23; Patterson v. Whaley, (Ga.) 66 S. E. 804.) The furnishing of market quotations by the plaintiffs to the defendant did not affect the matter in issue, for such quotations did not represent the price that wool could be sold for on the market each week. Market quotations may be based on sales actually made, few or many, and they are also given in the absence of any sales and based merely upon prices asked. The quotations furnished therefor were in no respect evidence of negligence on the part of the plaintiffs.

The defendant was given the privilege of opening and closing the argument. That was prejudicial to the rights of the plaintiffs. (Comp. Stat. 1910, Secs. 4391, 4499.)

Metz & Sackett, for defendant in error.

The evidence clearly sustains the verdict by showing that the failure of the plaintiffs to sell defendant's wool was caused solely by their negligence. The lowest price during all the time in controversy for the grade .of wool consigned was much greater than that for which it was subsequently sold, and enough to pay all advances and charges and the amount now demanded by the defendant as damages. The contract of consignment included a guaranty of sale. Such a guaranty we believe to mean a sale within reasonable time at the then market price. The February letter of the defendant requesting that his wool be sold, but not at too much of a sacrifice, is to be regarded as a direction to sell, even though at some sacrifice. An agent cannot put himself in an antagonistic relation to his principal and may not deal for his own benefit respecting the business of the agency. (Mechem on Agency, Secs. 454-457.) It was a question for the jury whether or not the plaintiffs refused to follow the

defendant's instruction, and made the sales that were made
because of the advances, or because of negligence. (Butterfield v. Stevens, (Ia.) 13 N. W. 751.) The plaintiffs are
not in a position to now take advantage of any error in the
instructions complained of for the reason that the case was
not tried upon the theory now advanced, and no instructions
were requested upon any such theory. (Bunce v. McMahon,
6 Wyo. 24; Cosgriff v. Miller, 10 Wyo. 190; McKnight
v. R. R. Co., 44 Minn. 141; Mullen v. Wilson, 44 Pa. St.
413; Simms v. R. R. Co., 3 S. E. 301; Schuman v. Johnson, 66 Tex. 70; Sutherland v. Shelton, 59 Tenn. 374;
Knoxville v. Bell, 80 Tenn. 157; Cook v. Wootters, 42 Tex.
294; Ins. Co. v. Ice Co., 64 Tex. 578; Ins. Co. v. Tile Co.,
43 N. E. 41; Hindman v. Timme, 35 N. E. 1046; Mackie
v. Cent. R. R. Co., 6 N. W. 723; McQuillan v. Seattle, 13
Wash. 600, 43 Pac. 893; Barton v. Grey, 24 N. W. 638;
Schroeder v. Webster, 88 Ia. 627, 55 N. W. 569.) Where
a party wishes more specific instructions, the instructions
given being correct so far as they go, he must request the
giving of them. (Northern Pac. R. Co. v. Mares, 123 U.
S. 710; Burlington R. Co. v. Schluntz, 14 Neb. 425, 16 N.
W. 439; Eppert v. Hall, 133 Ind. 417, 31 N. E. 74; Wimer
v. Allbaugh, 78 Ia. 79, 42 N. W. 587; Haymaker v. Adams,
61 Mo. App. 581; Kelly v. Houghton, 59 Wis. 400, 18 N.
W. 326; Sudlow v. Warshing, 15 N. E. 532; Burkholder
v. Stahl, 58 Pa. 371; Wiggins v. Guthrie, 101 N. C. 661,
7 S. E. 761.)

The admission of evidence as to sale and price at other
places than Philadelphia was not prejudicial or erroneous,
for the reason that it appeared by the testimony of the plaintiffs that wool prices within this country are based upon
the Philadelphia market.

The rule of Brown v. McGram, 14 Pet. 479, and other
decisions following that case, does not apply to this case.
That was a case where the consignor attempted to delay
sales by the factor, the latter claiming that it was necessary
for him to sell to protect the advances made. The question

is a different one, however, where the instructions are to
sell, and where, if sales are made according to the instructions, the advances made will be fully protected. The factor
has no right to disobey the instructions of his principal except where it becomes necessary to protect his interest in
the consigned property. If the property will bring the
advances made by the factor, then the general rule is the
same as though no advances had been made. (Butterfield
v. Stevens, 13 N. W. 751; Weed v. Adams, 37 Conn. 378;
Phillips v. Scott, 43 Mo. App. 86, 97 Am. Dec. 369; Rice
v. Brock, 20 Fed. 611; Spruell v. Davenport, (N. C.) 20
S. E. 1022; Johnson v. Wade, 61 Tenn. 480; Howland v.
Davis, 40 Mich. 545.) Where there is no attempt, either in
the pleadings or during the trial, to show that the failure
to obey the instructions of the principal was necessary to
protect the advances, the question cannot thereafter be
raised. (Benedict v. Inland Grain Co., 80 Mo. App. 449;
Phillips v. Scott, *supra*; Weed v. Adams, *supra;* Rice v.
Brock, *supra*; Butterfield v. Stevens, *supra*.) The evidence was sufficient to sustain the verdict. (Benedict v.
Grain Co., *supra*; Field v. Farrington, 10 Wall. 141; Atchison v. Burton, 67 Ky. (4 Bush) 299; Linsly v. Carpenter,
27 N. Y. Super. Ct. 200; Usborne v. Stephenson, 48 L. R.
A. 432; Burnett et al. v. Hockaday, 61 Mo. App. 628;
Howland v. Davis, *supra*.) It is the duty of the factor as
a general rule to sell at the market price. (12 Ency. Law,
(2nd Ed.) 658, 659; Davis v. Cotton Mills, 178 Fed. 784;
Bigelow v. Walker, 24 Vt. 149, 58 Am. Dec. 156.) It is
contended by counsel for plaintiffs that the weekly market
quotations furnished by the defendant to the plaintiffs were
not competent evidence of their contents, or as to market
prices. That is not the law. (Sisson v. R. R. Co., 14 Mich.
489; Kibler v. Caplis, 140 Mich. 28, 103 N. W. 531, 112
Am. St. 388; C. B. & Q. R. Co. v. Todd, 74 Neb. 712,
105 N. W. 83; Tex. Cent. Ry. Co. v. Fisher, 18 Tex. Civ.
App. 78, 43 S. W. 584; Aulls v. Young, 98 Mich. 231, 57 N.
W. 119; Bank v. City, 56 N. E. 288.) A part of said re-

ports were introduced by the plaintiffs and the remainder by the defendant, and all are in the record without objection. The following are additional authorities supporting the proposition that the plaintiffs cannot now change the theory upon which they transacted the business, prepared the pleadings and conducted the trial: 2 Cyc. 670, 671; 3 Cyc. 243; Aaron v. Holmes, (Utah) 99 Pac. 450; Silver Peak Mines v. Judicial Dist., (Nev.) 110 Pac. 103; Bank v. Ketchum, (Neb.) 96 N. W. 614; Parker v. Ins. Co., (Neb.) 97 N. W. 280; Rutter v. Carothers, (Mo.) 122 S. W. 1056; Zeller & Co. v. Vinardi, (Ind.) 85 N. E. 378; Lesser Cotton Co. v. R. R. Co., 114 Fed. 133.

On petition for rehearing it was contended that the delay in sales was some evidence of negligence which might well have been submitted to the jury, and that since the case must be tried again the attention of the court was called to certain language of the opinion to the effect that there was no evidence of negligence which would seem to foreclose the defendant from .presenting his case according to the view well sustained by the authorities that a long delay upon a falling market tends to show lack of diligence and care on the part of the factor, and is sufficient when unexplained to sustain a verdict in favor of the consignor.

SCOTT, CHIEF JUSTICE.

The plaintiffs in error as co-partners brought this action in the court below as plaintiffs to recover from the defendant in error as defendant upon an alleged balance on an account for advances made by them as factor upon a consignment of wool, interest on such advances, and commission on the sale. The case was tried to a jury and a verdict returned in favor of the defendant for the sum of $2,000 upon his counter-claim for damages for an alleged failure to sell the wool at the market price and as directed by the defendant. A motion for a new trial was overruled, judgment was rendered upon the verdict, and the plaintiffs bring error.

1. It is assigned as error that the verdict is unsupported by the evidence and that the trial court erred for that reason in denying a motion for a new trial. The plaintiffs were commission merchants residing and doing business as such in the City of Philadelphia in the State of Pennsylvania. On September 21, 1907, the defendant consigned to them as factor 45,852 pounds of his own wool and 10,345 pounds known as the J. O. Morgareidge wool, in all 56,197 pounds. Concurrent with the consignment and shipment he drew on plaintiffs as his factor, a sight draft for advancement on the wool so consigned for the sum of $7,535.77, which, by agreement bore interest at the rate of 6 per cent per annum until paid. The following letter was received by the defendant from plaintiffs through due course of mail:

"JUSTICE, BATEMAN & Co.

WOOL

122 South Front Street, Philadelphia.

Sept. 25th, 1907.

Mr. A. L. Brock, Buffalo, Wyoming:

DEAR SIR:—We will receive and sell your wool for the commission of one and one-quarter cents per pound. Interest on advances at the rate of six per cent per annum; no other charges after arrival of wool in store.

Our Commission includes Fire Insurance, premium, Storage and Labor for any period not exceeding six months after arrival of wool, and also Guarantee of Sales.

While we do not guarantee insurance Companies, we make ourselves responsible to keep your wool insured in first class Foreign and Domestic Companies.

Yours truly,

(Signed)   JUSTICE, BATEMAN & Co."

On the same day the following letter was written by plaintiffs and sent to defendant by due course of mail:

"Philadelphia, September 25, 1907.

Mr. A. L. Brock, Buffalo, Wyoming:

DEAR SIR:—We have received through Mr. Charles T. Lee invoice of your 155 bags of wool, which shall have our best attention on arrival. We note that you wish the 30 bags of the J. O. Morgareidge clip accounted for separately.

The wool market is quiet at present, but we look for a better demand shortly, when we think manufacturers will find it easier to get money to finance wool purchases.

Very truly yours,

(Signed)   JUSTICE, BATEMAN & Co.

Charles S. Haight."

Thereafter plaintiffs as factor sent to defendant by due course of mail the following letter:

"Philadelphia, October 4, 1907.

Mr. A. L. Brock, Buffalo, Johnson Co., Wyoming:

DEAR SIR:—We today paid your draft for $7,535.77.

Very truly yours,

(Signed)   JUSTICE, BATEMAN & Co.

Childs."

The plaintiffs as factor received the wool, stored, exhibited it for sale and sent weekly market quotations on that market to the defendant. The market quotations furnished on January 28 and February 4, 1908, were the same. On February 8, following, the defendant wrote plaintiffs to close out his wool so he could get his returns by April 1st following, if it could be done without making too much sacrifice. On March 5, 1908, he again wrote plaintiffs as follows: "I wrote you sometime ago in regard to my wool. *I wrote you to sell my wool as I will want the money April 1,* and I really fail to see any reason why the future market will be any better than it is now. One of my neighbor sheep men recently made a good sale of 25 cents. I am willing to sell on present market quotations I received from you. * * *" The wool was classified by the plaintiffs and of the amount so consigned, 47,996 pounds, was classified, graded and sold as fine and fine medium, and the price for that grade of wool, according to the market quotations furnished from time to time between the consignment on Sept. 21, the day of shipping, until April 1, 1908, following, was not less than 19 cents per pound. The balance of the wool was also graded and sold according to its grade. In the account rendered only 970 pounds out of the total of 56,197 pounds consigned, was sold prior to April 4, 1908, and the balance was sold from time to time after that date until November 18, 1908, when the wool was finally closed out. The total gross amount for which plaintiffs sold the wool was $9,113.18, receiving for defendant's share the amount of $7,426.40. It is alleged that had plaintiffs sold defendant's wool independent of the Morgareidge lot as directed by defendant it would have brought $9,535.00 net, and defendant testified that plaintiffs would have received $9,170.40 therefor, which sum would have been sufficient to have paid the draft, interest thereon, commission and all charges for shipping and handling the wool, leaving a balance of $2,000 due defendant.

The plaintiffs alleged that after receiving and making the advances on the consignment they were unable to sell the wool at the market quotations or otherwise than at the times and prices received for it, and that their lien for advances could not have been realized had they sold at a greatly reduced price, which would have been necessary. Their evidence tends to support these allegations with the exception that the market was a little firmer in the early part of October, 1907, when the wool was received, up to the time of a financial panic which occurred soon after and during that month, and thence on through the year following the wool market was dull. The defendant gave no positive instructions to sell prior to his letter of February 8, 1908, supplemented by his letter of March 5, 1908, but up to that time had left price and time of sale to the judgment of the plaintiffs. It is the general rule that a factor is not obliged to sell at a price which would be less than his lien for advances, commission and just charges at the request of his principal unless the latter pays or tenders such advances and charges. (Heffner v. Gwynne-Treadwell Cotton Co., 160 Fed. 635, 87 C. C. A. 606.) The evidence, however, tends to show that had the factor here sold as instructed at the market quotations furnished their principal there would have been $2,000 realized from the sale over and above what was necessary to have paid such factor all advances, interest, commissions and charges. The plaintiffs were bound to exercise ordinary care, skill and diligence to obtain the market value of the wool, but could not withhold the wool from the market against the directions of the defendant if such ordinary care, skill and diligence would have resulted in a sale at a price that would have secured them in their charges, and been satisfactory to the defendant. There was nothing but a simple consignment of the wool to be sold on commission, without any instruction, direction or advice whatsoever communicated by the defendant to plaintiffs at the time. The defendant had the right to say when the wool should be sold and at what price so long as it did not impair the factor's right to reimbursement out of the proceeds for all his advances and charges. (19 Cyc. 126, 127, 128; Heffner v. Gwynne-Treadwell Cotton Co., *supra*.) Under such circumstances the lien would be paid and the factor could not dictate to his principal when the wool should be sold, or impose on him the hazard of a falling market. When we say market, we mean such a market as was available to the plaintiffs. We can not go further than that within the issues in this case for there is no allegation in defendant's answer or counter claim that plaintiff's failure to sell the wool at the market quotations was the result of fraud. We think the issue of failure to exercise ordinary care, skill and diligence and that as a consequence the defendant suffered the damage complained of was the only one fairly made by the pleadings. Drum-Flato Commission Co. v. Union Meat Co., 33 Tex. Civ. App. 587, 77 S. W. 634, was a case somewhat similar on the facts to the one here. There the principal shipped cattle to its factor who, it was claimed, wrongfully sold them on a low classification. The court said that at the market to which the cattle were shipped it was the invariable custom "for the factors to whom they were consigned to exhibit them in the market for sale, and sell them

at the highest price that can be obtained. The great preponderance of the evidence shows that this method of sale
was adopted by the defendant, the cattle exhibited to the
buyers, due care and diligence taken and good faith exercised, by the defendant, to sell them at the highest market
price obtainable, and after the exercise of such care and
diligence they were sold at the best price that could be obtained." In the case before us the evidence shows that the
method of selling the wool was to exhibit it to proposed
buyers and that this was done. There is no evidence of
want of diligence in this respect. There may have been wool
of the same or higher quality sold at the market quotations
but that fact of itself would not be sufficient to entitle the
defendant to recover if the factor was diligent and in good
faith endeavoring to sell defendant's wool. In Commission
Co. v. Union Meat Co., *supra*, the following instruction to
the jury was upheld, viz.: "If defendant's agent exercised
ordinary care, skill, and diligence to obtain the fair market
value of the cattle" defendant was entitled to a verdict,
"although the jury may have believed from the evidence that
the cattle were sold for less than their market value." As
is said by Judge Cooley: Whoever bargains to render
services for another undertakes for good faith and integrity,
but he does not agree that he will commit no error. For
negligence, bad faith, or dishonesty he would be liable to
his employer, but if he is guilty of neither of these, the
master or employer must submit to such incidental losses as
may come in the course of the employment, because there
are incidents to all avocations, and no one by any implication of the law ever undertakes to protect another against
them." It was further said in that case that "Because the
verdict on the question of negligence finds no support in the
evidence the judgment is reversed and the cause remanded."
The plaintiffs here were bound under their contract to exercise ordinary care, skill and diligence to obtain the fair
market value of the wool. We look in vain to find any evidence in this record showing, or tending to show, negligence

in that respect on the part of the plaintiffs. They were not insurers of sale or price. The record is silent as to whether they could have sold the wool prior to the panic in October, 1907, and at the market quotations. Assuming that they could have done so, yet they were not instructed to sell at that time, and being agents for selling the wool without such instructions from their principal the latter will be presumed to have approved the action of the former in not selling at that time. In such case he took the risk of any loss by reason of the market becoming demoralized, and could not be heard to complain of the failure to sell at that time and the resulting loss after it had occurred. At the most upon the evidence the failure to sell at that time would only be a mistake in judgment made in good faith which would not render plaintiffs liable provided always they were diligent and faithful in trying to effect a sale. (Lesesne v. Cook, 16 La. 58; Savage v. Birkhead, 20 Pick. (Mass.) 167; 19 Cyc. 119.) It is true that the market quotations purported to show the price of wool on the Philadelphia market from time to time, but the plaintiffs' evidence is undisputed to the effect that such quotations after the said panic in October, 1907, until after the Presidential election in November, 1908, were merely nominal and the prices at which sellers were offering their wool, but that there were few buyers and scarce sales at such prices, and further that the manufacturers or customers owing to difficulty in getting money to finance purchases were buying such small quantities of wool as would enable them to fill their contracts and, owing to the unsettled financial condition, were not stocking up for future orders. On November 18, 1908, plaintiffs wrote defendant that there had been a better demand for wool and that they had closed out his wool at the prices appearing in the account rendered, a part of the fine and fine medium grade at 16 cents, and a part at 16½ cents per pound, and the other grades at the prices therein stated. The market quotations theretofore furnished had written across their face, "Market quiet. Medium wool slow of sale," and similar notations. Defendant's letter of February 8, 1908, hereinbefore referred to, indicates that he understood the difficulty of selling wool at the market quotations. He says in that letter: "I would like to have you close my wool out so I can get my returns by April first *if you can do so without too much of a sacrifice,* as I will be needing some money at that time. While I have always left the time for selling with you heretofore I would rather sell now on the market as it is than to borrow money to meet my demands on April first." The letter of March 5th, following, from defendant to the plaintiff and heretofore quoted, may be deemed to have changed the condition contained in the former with reference to selling the wool, and the two letters considered together constituted the first positive direction to sell. The plaintiffs treated these letters as a direction to sell the wool on the market quotations as of those dates. Their efforts and diligence in that respect were unavailing. In order to sell at all concessions from the quoted price had to be made and the direction to sell was at the quoted price. Plaintiffs' undisputed evidence tends to show that they were endeavoring all the time to sell by exposing the wool to their customers, and were for the reasons stated only able to sell small quantities from time to time. Upon the pleadings their good faith is not questioned, and the question of the amount of sacrifice to be made in selling the wool as contained in defendant's letter of February 8, 1908, until the receipt of the letter of March 5, 1908, lodged in the plaintiff a discretionary power as to when and for what price to sell. Treating the two letters as a positive instruction to sell, plaintiffs were not authorized to sell below the market quotations, nor as already said, were they required to sell at a price insufficient to reimburse and recompense them for their advances and just charges, in the absence of any tender or a satisfactory offer to pay the same by defendant. The undisputed evidence, notwithstanding the market quotations furnished, shows that they used due diligence and were unable to find a purchaser who would pay the market quotations for the wool or sufficient to reimburse them for their advances and charges.

2. The defendant was permitted, over objection and which is here assigned as error, to introduce evidence as to the price of wool at markets other than that to which he shipped his wool. It was within the purview of the contract that the wool should be sold upon the Philadelphia market. It was shipped to that market and it was the failure to sell upon that market of which defendant complained. He alleges in his amended answer "that the market price obtainable for said wool upon the said market at Philadelphia during the spring and summer of 1908 averaged about 20 cents per pound. That the said plaintiffs wholly neglected and failed and refused to sell the said wool at said market price above mentioned, but disposed of said wool, a part thereof, at 10 cents per pound, and other portions thereof at 16 cents per pound. Defendant alleges that if the said plaintiffs had complied with the terms of said contract and sold said wool at the best market price, or at the average price obtainable on said market in Philadelphia, that this defendant would have received $9,535.00 net." The issue was thus squarely tendered, (1) that the wool could have been sold by the plaintiffs at the quoted or average market price at Philadelphia by the exercise of ordinary care, skill and diligence, and (2) that their failure to use such ordinary care, skill and diligence to so sell the wool upon that market resulted in damage to the defendant. If upon those issues and the evidence the plaintiffs did exercise ordinary care, skill and diligence to obtain the quoted or average market price for wool at that market, then under the rule announced in Commission Co. v. Union Meat Co., *supra*, they would be entitled to a verdict even though the jury may have believed from the evidence that the wool was sold for less than the quoted or average market price. The consignment was general and to a specified market and the plaintiffs were not bound to look for any other market than the one to which the wool was consigned (Kingston v. Wilson, 14 Fed. Cas.

No. 7,823, 4 Wash. C. C. 310.) The defendant selected the
market upon which the wool was to be sold (Davis v. Kobe,
36 Minn. 214, 30 N. W. 662, 1 Am. St. Rep. 663) and he
assumed the risk of plaintiffs being unable by the exercise ·
of ordinary care, skill and diligence to sell it upon that
market. It was held in Phillips v. Scott, 43 Mo. 86, 97 Am.
Dec. 369, that under a general consignment such as here the
factor had no authority to ship the goods to another market,
and it was held in Phy v. Clark, 35 Ill. 377, that if he does
so he is liable for loss incurred from selling at a less price
than he could have obtained in the market where he had
authority to sell. Applying these rules to the case here it
follows that plaintiffs were not bound within the terms of
the contract to sell the wool other than on the Philadelphia
market. In that view evidence of the price of wool in other
markets was not material or germane to the issue and the
court erred in admitting it over objection, for the plaintiffs
were under no obligation to sell on those markets. That
evidence under some circumstances might perhaps be admissible as tending to show the market price at the place
where the wool was to be sold, and the want of care or
diligence of the factor in selling the wool at the best available price, but no such circumstances are disclosed in this
case as would take it out of the general rule.

3. The court, over plaintiff's objection, instructed the
jury without qualifications that the plaintiffs "were under
obligations to carry out any and all positive instructions of
his (the defendant) with reference to the property consigned to them. If you find that any latitude was given to
the said agents in regard to their handling of the property
entrusted to them, then, I charge you, you should consider
whether they acted in good faith and according to their best
judgment in carrying out such instructions so as best to
preserve the rights and interests of their principal." This
instruction was erroneous for two reasons; first, it disregarded plaintiff's lien for advances made on the consignment and their right to be reimbursed out of the proceeds

of the sale; and, second, the absence of any evidence in the record upon which the good faith of plaintiffs could be challenged. Both of these questions have hereinbefore been discussed on the sufficiency of the evidence and need not be further referred to.

4. It is urged that the court erred in permitting the defendant over objection to open and close the argument to the jury. The defense was a counter claim by way of confession and avoidance and the court correctly instructed the jury that there was no dispute in the evidence as to the plaintiff's right to recover unless the defendant had established his counter claim by a preponderance of the evidence, and that the burden in this case rested upon the defendant. That being the situation, the defendant had the right to open and close the argument to the jury.

Other alleged errors have been presented, but as the judgment must be reversed for the errors hereinbefore discussed we assume that they are not likely to occur upon a new trial. The judgment will be reversed and the cause remanded for a new trial.   *Reversed.*

POTTER, J., and BEARD, J., concur.

ON PETITION FOR REHEARING.

PER CURIAM.

The defendant in error has filed a petition for rehearing, but takes exception only to certain language in the former opinion used in discussing the sufficiency of the evidence, and does not question the correctness of the conclusions reached upon the other points discussed in the opinion. Exception is taken particularly to the following language of the opinion: "The plaintiffs here were bound under their contract to exercise ordinary care, skill and diligence to obtain the fair market value of the wool. We look in vain to find any evidence in this record showing, or tending to show negligence in that respect on the part of the plaintiffs. * * * The undisputed evidence, notwithstanding the market quotations furnished, shows that they used due diligence and were unable to find a purchaser who would pay the market quotations for the wool, or sufficient to reimburse them for their advances and charges." In the brief supporting the petition for rehearing it is conceded that the judgment must be reversed upon other grounds stated in the opinion and not now contested, but it is contended that there was evidence in the case tending to show that the plaintiffs below held the consigned wool for several months during a falling market, and that such evidence was not only competent, but was proper to go to the jury, and sufficient *prima facie* to show negligence or lack of diligence on the part of the plaintiffs. And it is said that the language above quoted from the former opinion ignores such evidence, and unless modified will have the effect upon a new trial of preventing the submission of such evidence to the jury.

In stating that "We look in vain to find any evidence in this record showing, or tending to show negligence in that respect on the part of plaintiffs," and that "The undisputed evidence * * * shows that they used due diligence," &c., reference was had to the whole of the evidence, and it was not intended as an assertion that there was no evidence tending to show lack of diligence. If there was evidence in the case which might properly be understood as showing that there had been a long delay during a falling market, or if upon another trial evidence to that effect is introduced, then to that extent the evidence tended, or may tend, to show lack of diligence, and sufficient to justify the submission of the matter to the jury, and if unexplained might be sufficient to justify a finding of negligence. (Field v. Farrington, 10 Wall. 141, 19 L. Ed. 923.) It was not the intention by the use of the language above quoted to foreclose or embarrass the defendant below, plaintiff in error here, in the proof of his defense upon another trial. It must be remembered that advances had been made by the factors in this case, and in view of such fact, and the failure, as it seemed to the court, to show that the wool could have been sold at an earlier date for a sufficient amount to reimburse the factors for their advances, and all the evidence bearing upon the question, the court was of the opinion, intended to be expressed by the language now criticized, that upon the whole evidence negligence had not been shown. The above explanation of the language used in expressing that opinion will, we think, obviate any danger of its misconstruction upon another trial. We repeat that it was not intended to deny the admissibility of evidence showing long delay in selling the wool during a falling market, nor its sufficiency, in the absence of satisfactory explanation, to show negligence, but in applying that principle where advances have been made, the rule concerning the duty of a factor under such circumstances should be considered, and the jury properly instructed with reference thereto. Having thus explained the language excepted to, a rehearing is deemed unnecessary and will be denied.

WHEELOCK v. CLARK.
(No. 743.)

INSURANCE—APPLICATION FOR LIFE INSURANCE—RIGHT OF APPLICANT TO CANCEL BEFORE ACCEPTANCE—PREMIUM NOTE.

1. An application for life insurance is a mere proposal to enter into a contract and until accepted there is no contract and the applicant may prior to acceptance withdraw his proposal, notwithstanding that he may have given a promissory note for the payment of the first premium.

2. An applicant for life insurance was not liable upon the promissory note given by him to the soliciting agents of the insurance company for the amount of the first premium and indorsed by the payees and forwarded to the general agent who sued thereon, where it appeared that before acceptance of the application the applicant notified the company to cancel it and return the note, and after such notice a policy was issued at the request of the general agent, the latter stating that he would have the matter taken up with the applicant, and thereafter the applicant refused to accept the policy when forwarded to him and returned it to the company.

[Decided April 14, 1913.]   (131 Pac. 35.)

ERROR to the District Court, Fremont County, HON. CHARLES E. CARPENTER, Judge.

The action was brought by Jesse M. Wheelock against William Scott Clark upon a promissory note given at the time of an application for life insurance for the amount of the first annual premium. From a judgment for the defendant the plaintiff brought error. The other material facts are stated in the opinion.

E. H. Fourt, for plaintiff in error.

It is the duty of the court to give such instructions upon the law as may be necessary, and that duty is not excused by the failure of counsel to request specific instructions good in law and applicable to the evidence. (Comp. Stat. 1910, Sec. 4499; U. P. R. R. Co. v. Jarvi, 3 Wyo. 375.) Special findings control the general verdict. (Comp. Stat. 1910, Secs. 4511, 4512.)

The applicant was insured from the time of the application. The contract was that if the premium was paid at the time of the medical examination the insurance should date from that time upon the acceptance of the application, and the note in suit was given in payment of that premium. The applicant was insured from the time the policy was applied for, and the policy was delivered to him by mail within a short time of the date of the application. He retained the receipt given to him for the first premium, and cannot be heard to say that he did not receive value, or that the terms of the contract were not fully complied with by the company. (McFarland v. Ry. Officials &c., 5 Wyo. 126; Summers v. Mut. L. Ins. Co., 12 Wyo. 369; Tayloe v. Ins. Co., 9 How. (U. S.) 390; Eams & Cooley v. Ins. Co., 4 Otto, 621, 24 L. Ed. 298; Ins. Co. v. Ins. Co., 19 How. (U. S.) 518.) The condition set up to avoid the payment of the note is a condition subsequent, and not sufficient to invalidate the contract. (Belo v. Ry. Co., 62 Pac. 295; Cotton v. Fid. & Cas. Co., 41 Fed. 506; Nachez v. Ins. Co., 42 Fed. 169.)

The fact that it was the defendant's purpose to use the proceeds of the note to pay the premium is foreign to the controversy. He might have borrowed the money from the bank and paid the premium with the proceeds. Had he done so and then withdrawn his application before the completion of a contract he might have recovered the premium from the company, but that would not be a defense to a suit upon the note. The fact that the payees were the agents of the company is immaterial. They did not take the note as company agents, but in their individual capacity. They were not authorized to take a note for the company. The premium was paid to the company by the payees at the instance and request of the defendant, and it does not matter whether they paid the money directly, or whether it was charged against their commissions. Such payment of the premium was an actual payment to the company at the request of the insured. (Mooney v. Ins. Co., 80 Mo. App. 192; Ins. Co. v. Curtis, 32 Mich. 401; Miller v. Ins. Co., 12 Wall. 285; Reppond v. Ins. Co., 100 Tex. 519, 101 S. W. 786.) The note was not a premium note, but was a personal note given to the payees named therein as evidence of an indebtedness to them. (Ins. Co. v. Parker, 66 Neb. 359, 62 L. R. A. 390; Griffith v. Ins. Co., 101 Cal. 627, 40 Am. St. 96; Ins. Co. v. Curtis, *supra*; Mooney v. Ins. Co., *supra*; Reppond v. Ins. Co., *supra*; Griffith v. Ins. Co., *supra*; Ins. Co. v. Hoover, 113 Pa. St. 591.) The payment of premiums by an agent out of his own funds is a valid consideration for a note to him by the insured for the amount advanced, or which he has agreed to advance, and recovery may be had upon the note although the insured might be entitled to recover the premiums from the company. (White v. McPeck, 185 Mass. 451, 70 N. E. 463; Hudson v. Compere, 94 Tex. 449, 61 S. W. 389; Rafferty v. Romer, 122 Ill. App. 57.)

Ralph Kimball, for defendant in error.

The plaintiff is not a bona fide holder for value because (1) He took the note from his agent, who acquired it in the regular course of his business as such, and the agent's knowledge is imputed to the principal. (Tiffany on Agency, Sec. 59; Perry v. Archard, 1 Ind. Ter. 487, 42 S. W. 421; Shedden v. Heard, 110 Ga. 461, 35 S. E. 707; Battanier v. Smith, (Ia.) 105 N. W. 999, 5 L. R. A. (N. S.) 628.) (2) The plaintiff had actual knowledge of the consideration. (Heard v. Shedden, 113 Ga. 162, 38 S. E. 387; Suhr v. Hoover, 15 O. C. C. Rep. 690.) (3) If he had no knowledge of the consideration when taking the note, he did have knowledge before parting with any value therefor. (Thompson v. Bank, 150 U. S. 231, 37 L. Ed. 1063.) (4) The evidence does not show any sale of the note to plaintiff. The payees seem to have treated the note as the plaintiff's, though taken in their names.

There was no consideration for the note unless a contract of insurance was consummated. (Summers v. Mut. Life Ins. Co., 12 Wyo. 369; Whitman v. Milwaukee F. Ins. Co., 128 Wis. 124, 107 N. W. 291; Ins. Co. v. Young, 23 Wall. 85, 23 L. Ed. 152; Frank v. Stratford-Handcock, 13 Wyo. 55; Life Ins. Co. v. Babcock, 104 Ga. 67, 30 S. E. 273, 69 Am. St. 134, 42 L. R. A. 88; Travis v. Nederland Life Ins. Co., 104 Fed. 486; Morstadt v. Mut. Life Ins. Co., 115 Fed. 81; Northwestern Mut. L. Ins. Co. v. Neafus, 145 Ky. 563, 140 S. W. 1026, 36 L. R. A. (N. S.) 1211; Ins. Co. v. Levy, 122 Ky. 457, 92 S. W. 325, 5 L. R. A. (N. S.) 739; Union Central L. Ins. Co. v. Robinson, 148 Fed. 358; 8 L. R. A. (N. S.) 883.) The premium if paid could have been recovered from the company. (Ins. Co. v. Felix, 73 O. St. 46; Mahoney v. Ins. Co., 76 Am. Rep. 458; Ins. Co. v. Pyle, 44 O. St. 19, 4 N. E. 465; 25 Cyc. 758; Ins. Co. v. Bowser, 20 Ind. App. 557, 50 N. E. 86.) A premium note given in advance may be cancelled, or its payment refused, if it has not come into the hands of a bona fide holder. (27 Cyc. 2764; Van Arsdale v. Young, (Okl.) 95 Pac. 778; Travis v. Ins. Co., supra.)

Where a letter is shown to have been stamped and mailed, the presumption is that it was received by the party to whom addressed in due course of mail. (Jones on Evidence, Sec. 52.) Courts will take judicial notice of distances between cities and the rate of speed of trains. (Id. Sec. 127.) Nondirection of the jury is no ground for a new trial, unless correct instructions are asked and refused. (Hay v. Peterson, 6 Wyo. 419.) Since the court would have been justified in directing a verdict for defendant, there can be no prejudicial error in refusing any or all of the instructions requested by the plaintiff. The general verdict is consistent with the special findings, but this question is not raised in the motion for new trial.

The contention that the note sued on is not a premium note, but was given by the defendant for moneys loaned him by the agents, and that the premium was paid to the insurance company by the payees of the note at the request of the defendant, is not the theory advanced by the pleadings nor raised by the evidence, nor suggested by the instructions given or refused. That is not the issue made by the pleadings. The defendant's answer stated that the note was given as security for the payment of the first premium to be due when the contract was perfected and the policy issued and accepted. The reply alleged that the consideration was a perfected insurance contract made on the date of the note. The issues were made up and the case submitted upon the theory that a contract of insurance was the sole consideration for the note, so that the question was whether or not there was such a contract. The evidence does not show that any money was loaned to the defendant by the payees named in the note, or that they paid the amount of the note to the company "at the special instance and request of the defendant." No money was loaned to the defendant for any purpose, and it was not claimed on the trial that there was any such loan; nor was it claimed that the payees had paid anything to the company either at defendant's request or otherwise. If the plaintiff, after receiving the note, paid anything to the company, he did not make the payment for the defendant nor at his instance or request, but contrary to his expressed desire and request. The cases cited in the opposing brief upon this question are all distinguishable from the case at bar.

A party is restricted on appeal to the theory adopted at the trial. (Dean v. Oil Co., (Wyo.) 128 Pac. 881; Smith v. Colson, (Okl.) 123 Pac. 149; Normile v. Thompson, (Wash.) 79 Pac. 1095; Sanders v. Stimson Mill Co., (Wash.) 75 Pac. 974; Durfee v. Harper, (Mont.) 56 Pac. 582; Tibbet v. Zurbuch, (Ind. App.) 52 N. E. 816; Ry. Co. v. Stephens, (Ill.) 51 N. E. 69.) By returning a verdict for the defendant the jury found that the consideration for the note was the contemplated contract of insurance and that no contract was completed or entered into. These findings are supported by the evidence, and the verdict should not be disturbed.

BEARD, JUSTICE.

The plaintiff in error, Wheelock, brought this action in the District Court of Fremont county against the defendant in error, Clark, on a promissory note. There was a trial to a jury resulting in a verdict for defendant, judgment was entered on the verdict, and Wheelock brings error.

The undisputed facts are that Wheelock was the general agent at Denver, Colorado, of the Northwestern Mutual Life Insurance Company of Milwaukee, Wisconsin, and that Allen & Galloway, the payees of the note, were the special agents of the plaintiff for soliciting applications for life insurance for said company under the direction and control of Wheelock. That on Nov. 10, 1909, Allen & Galloway procured from the defendant, Clark, an application for insurance on his life in said company in the sum of $10,000, and at that time they took defendant's note for the amount of the first annual premium, which note is as follows:

"$401.70.   4694-1.   Lander, Nov. 10, 1909.

Nov. 11th, 1910, after date I promise to pay to the order of Allen & Galloway, at Noble, Lane & Noble Bank, Lander, Wyo., Four hundred one and 70-100 Dollars, Value received, with interest at the rate of eight per cent. per annum, from maturity until paid, and to pay all legal expenses and attorneys fees which may be incurred in the collection of the same. This note is given for money loaned and advanced by said payee to satisfy the premium on my policy No..... issued by the Northwestern Mutual Life Insurance Company, and as a collateral security for the payment hereof it is agreed that the owner of this note, or the debt represented by it, shall have a lien upon such policy and its proceeds until this note, or such debt shall be paid, and for such purpose said policy is hereby assigned to said payee.

William Scott Clark, Insured.
No....... Due 11-11.   ....Beneficiary."

At the same time said agents, Allen & Galloway, executed and delivered to Clark a receipt as follows:

"No other form of receipt for advanced premiums will be recognized by the Company.

An application for a $10,000.00 policy having been made by Wm. Scott Clark to The Northwestern Mutual Life Insurance Company, there has been collected of him Four hundred one and 70-100 Dollars, to be considered the first annual premium on said policy, provided the application is approved by the Company at its home office, and in that event the insurance as applied for will be in force from the date of the medical examination. If the application is not approved, the sum collected will be returned. Lander, Nov. 10, 1909.

Allen & Galloway, Agents.

767437. If the premium is paid in advance this receipt must be completed and given to the applicant; if the premium is not paid the receipt must not be detached."

On the same day the applicant was examined by the company's local medical examiner, and Allen & Galloway indorsed the note and forwarded it together with the application and medical examiner's report to Wheelock, who forwarded said application and report to the home office of the company at Milwaukee, where they were received Nov. 15, and were in the hands of its medical director on the same day. Nov. 16 Clark telegraphed the company as follows:

"Northwestern Life Ins. Co., Milwaukee, Wis. Cannot accept policy applied for agent Allen & Galloway. Have written. William Scott Clark. 553 P." In the letter referred to in the telegram and mailed the same day and addressed to the Secretary of the company, he said: "Confirming my telegram to you of this date I wish to reiterate, that after more mature deliberation, I·have determined that my circumstances at the present will not permit of my accepting the policy applied for some days ago in your company through your agents, Mess. Galloway & Allen, and I will ask you to cancel the application and advise your agents to return my note for $401.70, to the Noble, Lane & Noble bank here, when settlement receipt No. 767437 will be immediately forwarded to you or them." Nov. 17 the company's medical director wrote Wheelock: "We are just in receipt of a telegram from Mr. William Scott Clark advising that he cannot accept his policy. Will you kindly advise us further relative to the case and oblige." To which Wheelock replied Nov. 19: "We have yours of the 17th in reference to a telegram from William Scott Clark that he cannot accept policy for which he recently applied. We would ask that you kindly issue the policy as applied for, and our agents will take the matter up with Mr. Clark." The application was not acted upon, approved or accepted by the company until Nov. 23, when it was approved, and on Nov. 26 a policy was issued and dated Nov. 10, 1909, and was forwarded to Clark, who refused to accept it and returned it to the company.

The facts being as above stated, we have no hesitancy in holding that no contract of insurance was entered into between Clark and the company. His application was a mere proposal to enter into a contract, and until accepted by the company no contractual relations existed between them, and until such acceptance he had a perfect right to withdraw his proposal. In Travis v. Nederland Life Ins. Co., 104 Fed. 486, 43 C. C. A. 653, the Circuit Court of Appeals (Eighth Circuit) speaking through Judge Sanborn, said: "An application for life insurance is not a contract. It is only a proposal to contract on certain terms which the company to which it is presented is at perfect liberty to accept or reject. It does not in any way bind the company to accept the risk proposed, to make the contract requested, or to issue a policy. * * * Until the meeting of the minds of the parties upon the terms of the same agreement is effected by an acceptance of the proposition contained in the application, or of some other proposition, each party is entirely free from contractual obligations. The applicant may withdraw his application and refuse to take insurance on any terms. * * * Nor is the freedom of the parties to retire from the negotiations or to modify their proposals, at any time before some proposition has been agreed upon by both, ever lost or affected by the fact that the applicant accompanies his proposal or application with a promise to pay the premium in the form of promissory notes, or even by an actual payment thereof. Until his application is accepted, such a promise or payment is conditional upon the acceptance, and his application is still no more than a proposition to take and pay for the insurance if the company accepts his terms.". (Citing many cases.) See also The Northampton Mutual Live Stock Ins. Co. v. Tuttle, 40 N. J. Law, 476; Insurance Co. v. Johnson, 23 Pa. St. 72; Globe Mutual Life Ins. Co. v. Snell, 19 Hun (N. Y.) 560; John R. Davis Lumber Co. v. Scottish Union & National Ins. Co., 94 Wis. 472, 69 N. W. 156: and 1 Cooley's Briefs on Law of Insurance, 416. In the case from which we have quoted, Travis at the time he made the application gave to the soliciting agent his notes for the premium, and the agent sent the notes to the general agents who used them as collateral and reported that the premium was paid. The court said: "Could the company or the agents have enforced the collection of the notes which Travis gave them for the premium in this state of facts, after the agents had received his withdrawal of his original application, and after they had thus declined his new proposition? The question is susceptible of but one true answer. Would it not have been a perfect defense to those notes, in the hands of the company or its agents, that he had withdrawn his first application before it was accepted, and had made a new one, which they had declined to accept? Neither the agents nor the company could have overcome such a defense. The truth is that the minds of the parties to this negotiation never met upon the terms of any contract, and neither the notes nor the policy ever became effective." In that case Travis notified the agents before his application was acted upon and accepted that he would not accept the policy if the company was to have another medical examiner in his town, he being its medical examiner at the time he made the application. This was held to be a withdrawal of his original application, and the company not having accepted the new terms he proposed the minds of the parties had never met on the same terms and hence there was no contract, and that the policy could not be enforced. In the case at bar, Clark withdrew his application before it was accepted by the company, but offered no new terms; but the rule of law is equally applicable to each case. The condition on which the note in suit should become effective was that a contract of insurance should be entered into between Clark and the company, in which case the note should be considered as payment of the first annual premium on the policy. It was for the purpose of paying such premium and for no other purpose that the note was given. But as no contract was ever consummated, no premium ever accrued or became due or payable by the applicant or any one else. Wheelock knew the purpose for which the note was given when he received it, and that it would become effective only if the application was accepted by the company; and he must be held to have known that Clark had the right to withdraw his application at any time before it was accepted by the company at its home office. The application was approved, and the policy issued at the request of Wheelock, after both he and the company had notice that the application was withdrawn. He took the chance of being able to induce Clark to accept it, but because he failed to do so gave him no just cause to complain. His contention is, that by the receipt given by Allen & Galloway to Clark, Clark was insured from the date of the medical examination, and that he could not rescind that contract without the consent of the company. But as we have shown that contention is not tenable, and the point was directly decided adversely to such contention in Northwestern Mutual Life Ins. Co. v. Neafus, 145 Ky. 583, 140 S. W. 1026, 36 L. R. A. (N. S.) 1211. In that case the receipt given to the applicant by the agent was in the identical language of the receipt in this case.

It is further contended by counsel for plaintiff in error that the court erred in refusing to give to the jury certain instructions requested by plaintiff. Those instructions were based on the theory that the application and receipt constituted a contract of insurance which Clark could not rescind without the consent of the company. They were not applicable to the facts as shown by the evidence, and were properly refused. On the facts as shown by the record, the court would have been warranted in instructing the jury to return a verdict in favor of the defendant. No prejudicial error being made to appear, the judgment of the District Court is affirmed.   *Affirmed.*

SCOTT, C. J., and POTTER, J., concur.

RYAN v. ROGERS, SHERIFF.
(No. 752.)

EXTRADITION—DUTY OF GOVERNOR RECEIVING REQUISITION—EXTRADITION WARANT—PRESUMPTION AS TO SUFFICIENCY OF PROOF TO AUTHORIZE ITS ISSUANCE—HABEAS CORPUS—PROPER PROCEEDING TO QUESTION LAWFULNESS OF ARREST UPON EXTRADITION WARRANT—SCOPE OF HEARING—SUFFICIENCY OF CHARGE OF CRIME—ALIBI—FOR WHAT PURPOSE DEFENSE OF ALIBI MAY BE CONSIDERED—EFFECT OF CONFLICTING EVIDENCE—PROOF NECESSARY TO AUTHORIZE DISCHARGE—SUFFICIENCY OF EVIDENCE.

1. A person charged with crime against the laws of a state who, after committing the crime, flees from justice—that is, leaves the state—in whatever way and for whatever reason, and is found in another state, may, under the authority of the constitution and laws of the United States, be brought back to the state in which he stands charged with the crime, to be there dealt with according to law.

2. When the executive of the state wherein a crime was committed makes a demand upon the executive of a state where the one charged with the crime is found, as authorized by Section 5278, U. S. Rev. Stat., producing at the time a copy of the indictment, or an affidavit certified as authentic and made before a magistrate charging the demanded person with a crime against the laws of the demanding state, it becomes the duty of the executive of the state where the fugitive is found, to cause him to be arrested, surrendered, and delivered to the appointed agent of the demanding state to be taken to that state.

3. The executive of a state may decline to issue an extradition warrant, upon the demand of the executive of another state for an alleged fugitive from justice, unless it is made to appear to him by competent proof that the accused is substantially charged with crime against the laws of the demanding state, and is in fact a fugitive from the justice of that state.

4. Whether an alleged criminal for whom a requisition is issued and presented is or is not a fugitive from the justice of the demanding state may, so far as the constitution and laws of the United States are concerned, be determined by the executive upon whom the demand is made in such way as he deems satisfactory, and he is not obliged to demand proof of the fact apart from proper requisition papers from the demanding state.

5. When it is determined by the executive of a state upon whom a demand is made that the alleged criminal is such fugitive from the justice of another state, and a warrant of arrest is issued after such determination, the warrant is to be regarded as making a prima facie case in favor of the demanding state and as requiring the removal of the alleged criminal to the state in which he stands charged with crime, unless in some appropriate proceeding it is made to appear that he is not a fugitive from the justice of the demanding state.

6. A proceeding by habeas corpus in a court of competent jurisdiction is appropriate for determining whether one accused of crime in another state and arrested upon an extradition warrant is subject, under such warrant of arrest, to be taken as a fugitive from justice from the state in which he is found to the state whose laws he is charged with violating.

7. One arrested and held upon an extradition warrant as a fugitive from justice is entitled, of right, upon habeas corpus, to question the lawfulness of his arrest and imprisonment, showing by competent evidence, as a ground for his release, that he was not, within the meaning of the constitution and laws of the United States, a fugitive from the justice of the demanding state, and thereby overcoming the presumption to the contrary arising from the face of an extradition warrant.

8. A requisition for one Charles T. Crane, otherwise known as James Ryan, was accompanied by an indictment charging the commission of a crime in the demanding state by Charles T. Crane, and also by an affidavit referring to said Charles T. Crane as "otherwise known as James Ryan," which affidavit purported to state some of the facts of the alleged crime, that the one indicted had fled the jurisdiction of the demanding state and was under arrest in the other state as such fugitive from justice. *Held*, that the charge of crime sufficient to authorize the requisition was contained in the indictment, and it was not necessary that said affidavit should have been sworn to before a magistrate; it appearing that the affidavit was presented to the executive of the demanding state for the purpose of showing the presence in that state of the one indicted at the time of the commission of the crime, and that he had fled from the state, and also the good faith of the request for the extradition.

9. Under the statute of Illinois providing that every person who shall obtain from any other person or persons, any money or property, by means or by use of any false or bogus checks, or by any other means, instrument or device, commonly called the confidence game, shall be imprisoned in the penitentiary, &c., and the statute providing that it shall be a sufficient description of such offense in any indictment to charge that the accused did unlawfully and feloniously obtain from the person defrauded his money or property by means and by use of the confidence game, an indictment charging that the accused on a date named unlawfully, fraudulently and feloniously did obtain from a person named a large sum of money, goods and personal property described, the property of said person, by means and by use of the confidence game, contrary to the statute and against the peace and dignity of the people of the State of Illinois, sufficiently charged accused with said crime to justify a requisition for his arrest in another state and return as a fugitive from justice; an indictment so charging the offense being held sufficient by the decisions of the Supreme Court of Illinois.

10. Where the legality of an arrest under an extradition warrant is questioned on habeas corpus, the question of the plaintiff's guilt or innocence of the crime charged is not involved, and it is therefore unnecessary that an affidavit accompanying the extradition papers intended to establish the identity of the accused with the person charged in the indictment shall allege all the facts or elements of the crime charged, and hence it is not a ground for the discharge of the person arrested that the facts stated in such affidavit do not show the charge in the indictment to be well founded.

11. A requisition for an alleged fugitive from justice named him as "Charles T. Crane, otherwise known as James Ryan," and was accompanied by an indictment charging the commission of a crime in the demanding state by Charles T. Crane. The warrant of arrest issued by the executive of the state upon whom the demand was made also named the one to be arrested as "Charles T. Crane, otherwise known as James Ryan." *Held*, on habeas corpus, where the legality of the arrest was questioned, that it was unnecessary to decide whether the facts shown made it proper to embrace in the requisition and the warrant an alias name, for, even if the insertion of the alias name in the requisition and warrant was unauthorized, that would not affect

the regularity of the papers, and would not be material in
the habeas corpus proceeding, if in fact the person arrested
and seeking to be discharged was the identical person intended to be named and charged by the indictment.

12. When a person is held in custody as a fugitive from justice
under an extradition warrant in proper form, and showing
upon its face all that is required by law to be shown as a
prerequisite to its being issued, he should not be discharged
from custody on habeas corpus, unless it clearly and satisfactorily appears that he is not a fugitive from justice
within the meaning of the Constitution and laws of the
United States; in such a case the question is not one
merely of preponderance of evidence.

13. Habeas corpus is not the proper proceeding to try any
question as to the guilt or innocence of a petitioner arrested and held upon an extradition warrant, or to try
the question of alibi so far as it relates to his guilt or
innocence; but where the same evidence that might be
used to establish the defense of alibi on his trial tends
also to prove that he is not a fugitive from justice it is
proper to consider it in determining that question in a
habeas corpus proceeding, wherein the legality of his arrest is questioned, and the fact that he is a fugitive from
justice is denied.

14. The mere fact that in such a proceeding the evidence is
conflicting as to the identity of the one arrested with the
person charged in the indictment will not justify the discharge of the petitioner, for the extradition papers are
entitled to some consideration, and it is incumbent upon
the person in custody to do more than produce evidence
possibly sufficient to raise a doubt as to his identity; the
evidence that he is not the person charged and demanded
must be clear and satisfactory.

15. On habeas corpus, where the plaintiff questioned the legality of his arrest under an extradition warrant, claiming
that he was not the person named in the indictment and
charged with the crime in the demanding state, *held*,
upon an examination of the evidence, that it did not
clearly and satisfactorily show that the plaintiff was not
the person charged, or that he was not within the demanding state at the time of the commission of the alleged
crime.

[Decided May 3, 1913.]   (132 Pac. 95.)

ORIGINAL proceeding on habeas corpus.

The material facts are stated in the opinion.

W. B. Ross and *Ray E. Lee,* for plaintiff, contended that the identification of the plaintiff as the person indicted was not sufficient, and that the requisition papers were insufficient to justify the arrest, citing the following: State ex rel. v. Richardson, 24 N. W. 354; Ex parte Powell, 20 Fla. 806; Ex parte Hart, 63 Fed. 249; Ex parte Smith, 22 Fed. Cas. No. 12,968; Ex parte Morgan, 20 Fed. 298; 8 Am. & Eng. Ann. Cas. 1068; Pierce v. People, 81 Ill. 98; People ex rel. v. Byrnes et al., 33 Hun, 98; Barnes v. Nelson, 121 N. W. 89; Johnson v. Riley, 13 Ga. 97; State v. Bates, 102 Minn. 104, 112 N. W. 1026; 15 Fed. Cas. No. 8,162.

D. A. Preston, Attorney General, and *George C. Bliss* of Chicago, Illinois, Assistant State's Attorney, for defendant, contended that the identification of the plaintiff was sufficient; that the requisition papers were in proper form and sufficient to justify the arrest of the plaintiff and his return to the demanding state, citing the following: Laws of Illinois, Secs. 98, 99; Dubois v. People, 200 Ill. 157; People v. Weil et al., 244 Ill. 176; In re Keller, 36 Fed. 681; Ex parte Reggel, 114 U. S. 642; Roberts v. Riley, 116 U. S. 80; Pierce v. Texas, 155 U. S. 311; Munsey v. Clough, 196 U. S. 364; Pierce v. Creecy, 210 U. S. 387; People v. Baker, 127 N. Y. Supp. 382.

POTTER, JUSTICE.

This is an original proceeding in habeas corpus involving the arrest and imprisonment of the plaintiff, James Ryan, by the sheriff of Niobrara county in this state.   Upon the presentation of the petition to one of the Justices of this court the writ was allowed and made returnable to the court. The officer's return to the writ, as well as the petition, shows that the plaintiff was arrested and is held by said sheriff by virtue of a warrant issued by the Governor of this state upon a requisition from the Governor of the State of Illinois,

commanding that one Charles T. Crane, otherwise called
James Ryan, be arrested, safely kept, and delivered to the
agent named by the Governor of Illinois in said requisition.

The requisition of the Governor of Illinois directed to the
Governor of this state, omitting the caption, attestation and
signatures, is as follows: "Whereas, it appears by the papers
required by the statutes of the United States, which are
hereunto annexed, and which I certify to be authentic and
duly authenticated in accordance with the laws of this state,
that Charles T. Crane, otherwise called James Ryan, stands
charged with the crime of Confidence Game, which I certify
to be a crime under the laws of this state, committed in the
county of Cook in this state, and it having been represented
to me that he has fled from the justice of this state and has
taken refuge in the state of Wyoming; Now, Therefore,
pursuant to the provisions of the Constitution and Laws of
the United States in such case made and provided, I do
hereby require that the said Charles T. Crane, otherwise
called James Ryan, be apprehended and delivered to William Murvane, who is hereby authorized to receive and convey him to the State of Illinois, there to be dealt with according to law." Accompanying and annexed to said requisition is a certified copy of an indictment presented by the
grand jurors at the April Term, 1913, of the Criminal Court
of Cook County in said State of Illinois, charging that one
Charles T. Crane, late of the County of Cook, on the 3rd day
of March, 1913, in said county and state, unlawfully, fraudulently and feloniously did obtain from Hope L. McEldowney a large amount of money, goods and personal property
(describing the same), the goods, money and personal property of Hope L. McEldowney, by means and by use of the
confidence game, contrary to the statute, and against the
peace and dignity of the people of the State of Illinois. A
second count is contained in the indictment charging the said
Charles T. Crane with the crime of grand larceny, alleging
the same money and property as that described in the first
count, of the value of $15,500, to have been stolen, taken

and carried away by the said Charles T. Crane on the date and in the county aforesaid. Annexed to said requisition is also a petition by the State's Attorney for Cook County, Illinois, directed to the Governor of that state, stating that Charles T. Crane, otherwise called James Ryan, stands charged "by the accompanying certified copy of indictment and affidavit with the crime of Confidence Game, committed in the County of Cook and State of Illinois, on or about the 3rd day of March, 1913; that on or about the 3rd day of March, 1913, the said Charles T. Crane, otherwise called James Ryan, fled from the State of Illinois, and is now, as your petitioner verily believes, in the County of Converse and State of Wyoming, fugitive from the justice of this state, and the grounds of such belief are as follows: Telegram from A. C. Jones that Charles T. Crane is under arrest by A. R. Rogers, Sheriff, Lusk, Wyoming. Therefore, your petitioner prays that a requisition may issue upon the Governor of the said State of Wyoming and that William Murvane of the City of Chicago, County of Cook, and State of Illinois, may be appointed messenger of the State of Illinois to go after, receive and return the said fugitive to the County of Cook, State of Illinois, for trial. Your petitioner further certifies that in his opinion the ends of public justice require that the said Charles T. Crane, otherwise called James Ryan, be brought to this state for trial at the public expense, and that he believes he has sufficient evidence to secure his or her conviction." An affidavit appears as a part of that petition signed and sworn to by Hope L. McEldowney, stating that the facts set forth in the petition are true, and that the requisition for the fugitive named therein is not sought for the purpose of collecting a debt, to allow any person to travel at the expense of the state, or to answer any private end whatever, and shall not be used for any of said objects. Said affidavit was sworn to April 18, 1913, before the Clerk of the Criminal Court of said Cook County, Illinois, the same appearing to be duly attested and authenticated. Also annexed to said requisition appears an affidavit in words and figures as follows:

"STATE OF ILLINOIS,⎫
    COUNTY OF COOK,   ⎰ SS.

IN THE CRIMINAL COURT OF COOK COUNTY.

The People of the State of Illinois⎫
            vs.   ⎬ Confidence Game.
Charles T. Crane, otherwise called⎱
    James Ryan.

In the matter of the extradition of⎫
    Charles T. Crane, otherwise called⎪
    James Ryan, defendant mentioned⎬
    in the above entitled cause, and⎪
    fugitive from justice.   ⎭

Affidavit of Hope L. McEldowney, prosecuting witness in
aid of the petition for extradition:

Hope L. McEldowney, being first duly sworn, according
to law, deposes and says that she resides at 2969 Michigan
avenue, City of Chicago, County of Cook and State of Illinois, and that she is acquainted with the said Charles T.
Crane, otherwise known as James Ryan, and knows of her
own knowledge that the said Charles T. Crane, otherwise
known as James Ryan, was personally present in the City of
Chicago, county and state aforesaid, on the 3rd day of
March, 1913.

Affiant further says that on or about the 3rd day of
March, A. D. 1913, the said Charles T. Crane, otherwise
known as James Ryan, suggested to this affiant that she
ought to put her money in railroad bonds, and told this affiant that Great Northern Railroad bonds would be a good
investment for her and that he would gladly aid this affiant
in helping her to invest her money; that thereupon this
affiant, believing in the honesty and integrity of the said
Charles T. Crane, otherwise known as James Ryan, and believing in the representations made by the said Charles T.
Crane, otherwise known as James Ryan, that he would invest this money for her as he stated that he would, gave to
the said Charles T. Crane, otherwise known as James Ryan,
the sum of $15,500. Affiant further says that the said

Charles T. Crane, otherwise known as James Ryan, having obtained the $15,500 above mentioned, immediately left the city of Chicago and fled the jurisdiction of Illinois and is now a fugitive from justice under arrest at Lusk, Wyoming, as this affiant is informed and believes from a telegram from A. C. Jones, Cheyenne, Wyoming, that the said Charles T. Crane, otherwise known as James Ryan, is under arrest at Lusk, Wyoming.

Affiant further says that the said Charles T. Crane, otherwise known as James Ryan, did not invest the said sum of money of $15,500 in any railroad bonds for her and that she did not receive any bonds at all from the said Charles T. Crane, otherwise known as James Ryan; nor has the said Charles T. Crane, otherwise known as James Ryan, returned to her the said sum of $15,500, or any part thereof.

Affiant further says that this prosecution is not brought for the purpose of collecting any debt nor to enable any one to ride free at the expense of the State, but is bona fide in every respect, and when the said Charles T. Crane, otherwise known as James Ryan, is returned to the County of Cook and jurisdiction of Illinois, this affiant will appear in the Criminal Court to testify against said defendant in the cause therein pending against him, as will more specifically appear from the attached copy of indictment, which are made a part of this affidavit.

And further affiant saith not.

(Signed)   Hope L. McEldowney.

"STATE OF ILLINOIS,⎱ ·
      County of Cook,   ⎰ ss.

Hope L. McEldowney being first duly sworn according to law, deposes and says that she has read the foregoing affidavit, by her subscribed, and knows the contents thereof, and that the same is true in substance and in fact, except as to the matters and things which are therein stated to be upon information and belief, and as to such matters she believes them to be true.

(Signed)   Hope L. McEldowney.

Subscribed and sworn to before me, this 18th day of April, A. D. 1913.   (Signed)   FRANK J. WALSH,
(Seal)   Clerk of the Criminal Court."

The warrant of the Governor of this State issued upon said requisition recites as follows: "Whereas, it appearing from the requisition of His Excellency, the Governor of the State of Illinois, bearing date April 19, 1913, and from papers thereto attached duly authenticated, that Charles T. Crane, otherwise called James Ryan, stands charged with the crime of Confidence Game committed in the County of Cook in the year 1913 in said State, and that said Charles T. Crane, otherwise called James Ryan, is a fugitive from justice and has taken refuge in this state. And, Whereas, the said Requisition requests that the said Charles T. Crane be apprehended and delivered to William Murvane, who is the duly appointed agent and authorized to receive and convey him to the State of Illinois to be dealt with according to law." Following such recitals the warrant commands any and every sheriff, in whose hands soever the writ may be placed, to arrest the said Charles T. Crane, otherwise called James Ryan, and to safely keep and deliver to said William Murvane, agent as aforesaid.

It is alleged in the petition for this writ of habeas corpus that the plaintiff is a resident of this state and has resided therein for a period of about three years last past; that he is unlawfully imprisoned and restrained of his liberty by the defendant, the sheriff of Niobrara County; that the cause or pretense of such restraint and imprisonment is the requisition and warrant above referred to; that the requisition was honored and allowed by the Governor of this state without receiving any evidence on behalf of the plaintiff to disprove any of the facts stated in the affidavit in support of the requisition pretending to identify the plaintiff with Charles T. Crane, the person named in the indictment; that said indictment does not charge the plaintiff with the commission of any crime or offense, and does not charge one Charles T. Crane with any crime or offense; that said plaintiff is not said Charles T. Crane, has never been known by that name, and has never pretended or assumed to be Charles T. Crane; that each and every statement of fact contained in the affidavit charging the plaintiff with the commission of the pretended crime or offense is false and untrue, and that each and every statement contained in said affidavit charging that plaintiff is Charles T. Crane, or that he is a fugitive from justice is false and untrue; that the plaintiff is not a fugitive from justice, and that he is not guilty of either of the pretended crimes or offenses alleged in said indictment. It is further alleged that the legality of the restraint and imprisonment of said plaintiff has been adjudged upon a proceeding for a writ of habeas corpus before the District Court of the First Judicial District sitting within and for Niobrara County; that upon such hearing it was adjudged that said plaintiff was lawfully restrained and imprisoned by said defendant; that said court refused to grant sufficient time within which the plaintiff could bring his appeal to this court, and that had he attempted to complete said appeal he would have been delivered to said William Murvane and transported to the State of Illinois before the same could have been commenced; that the plaintiff feels that he has been wronged and aggrieved by the said decision of said District Court. It is further alleged that the Governor of this State had no jurisdiction to issue the warrant because no competent evidence was before him that plaintiff was or is a fugitive from justice from the State of Illinois; or that the plaintiff and said Charles T. Crane are one and the same person.

The return or answer of the defendant to the writ of habeas corpus states that he has the plaintiff in his custody, and produces him in court, and that the cause of his detention is a certain warrant issued by the Governor of this state and a certain order of the District Court of the First Judicial District, in and for Niobrara County, copies of which are attached to and made a part of the answer. The nature, recitals and command of the Governor's warrant are above set forth. The order of the District Court appears to have been made in the habeas corpus proceeding in that court and states the finding of the court that the plaintiff is lawfully held by the defendant under and by virtue of the Governor's warrant issued upon the requisition of the Governor of Illinois, and that it is ordered and adjudged that the petition of the plaintiff be denied, that he be remanded to the custody of the defendant, and that said defendant deliver the plaintiff to William Murvane, the messenger of the Governor of Illinois, on April 30th, 1913, at two o'clock p. m. In passing it may be said that before the hour named in said order for the delivery of the plaintiff to the messenger from Illinois, the writ in this case was allowed. The plaintiff has filed a reply to said answer whereby it is denied that the answer states any cause or facts sufficient to warrant the defendant in holding the plaintiff, that the plaintiff is the person known or described in the alleged requisition, or named in the warrant issued thereon; or that he is a fugitive from justice charged with any crime or offense under the laws of the State of Illinois or under the laws or Constitution of the United States; or that any charge, indictment or affidavit such as is required by the Act of Congress under the Constitution of the United States has been filed in any court of competent jurisdiction within the State of Illinois charging the plaintiff with the commission of any crime or offense against the laws of that state. And the plaintiff alleges by his reply that he is a resident of this state and re-alleges each and every allegation and statement of fact in his petition filed herein. The pleadings are respectively verified, the answer being verifiied by the oath of the defendant and the reply by the oath of the plaintiff.

In addition to the requisition papers and the warrant upon which the plaintiff was arrested, counsel representing the sheriff and also the demanding state produced as a witness Mrs. Hope L. McEldowney to identify the plaintiff as the person demanded by the requisition and named in the indictment annexed thereto, the court having suggested in response to an inquiry as to the necessity for additional evidence that since the name of the accused was stated in the indictment merely as Charles T. Crane, and the prisoner had denied under oath that he is or has ever pretended or assumed to be Charles T. Crane, some evidence should be produced identifying the plaintiff as the person indicted. (See Barnes v. Nelson, 23 S. D. 181, 121 N. W. 89, 20 Ann. Cas. 544.) Upon further consideration of that matter, in view of the affidavits attached to the requisition supporting the request of the State's Attorney therefor referring to the person indicted by the name stated in the indictment and also as otherwise known as James Ryan, we entertain some doubt as to whether it was necessary for the production of anything more than the warrant and requisition papers, if regular in form, to make out a prima facie case warranting the holding of the plaintiff, unless overcome by competent evidence on his behalf. But we shall leave the question undecided, deeming it immaterial to a determination of the case as finally presented.

Mrs. McEldowney not only positively identified the plaintiff as the person indicted by the name of Charles T. Crane, testifying that she appeared before the grand jury in Cook County, Illinois, at the April term this year, that her testimony resulted in the indictment aforesaid, that as such witness she testified against this plaintiff, whom she had known in Chicago as Charles T. Crane, with reference to the crime charged in the indictment, and that the plaintiff is the identical person so indicted and intended to be indicted, but she further testified in substance that she knew the plaintiff as Charles T. Crane, that she first met him in Chicago, Illinois, on January 18, 1913, and saw him in that city after that date nearly every day until March 3, 1913, that being the last day she saw him there, and that on that date he obtained from her the money mentioned in the indictment, stating that it was in the form of a draft; the fact of his so obtaining the money being brought out on cross-examination. That on that day he came to her apartments at 2507 Michi-

gan avenue in Chicago to "get this draft, this money from
me." That when she first saw the plaintiff it was at his
office, 204 North State Street, in Chicago, where, from his
advertisements, he was conducting a business described as
clairvoyancy, palmistry and investments. That after the day
she first saw him at his said office she saw him there about
six times, and also several times at restaurants and theatres,
having been with him at those places; that she was with him
at different restaurants about twenty-five times, and had
also taken automobile rides with him. When asked if she
saw in the court room the man to whom she referred as
Charles T. Crane, as the one whom she had seen and been
with as above stated, and, if so, to point him out, she pointed
out the plaintiff, stating positively that she knew him to be
the man. She further testified that when she saw him enter
the court room at Lusk at the time of the recent hearing
there she was then also positive that he was the same man
Charles T. Crane, the person she knew in Chicago by that
name; and that she was the same Mrs. McEldowney whose
name appears in the indictment, and who swore to an affidavit before the Clerk of the Criminal Court about this
matter, referring to Charles T. Crane as otherwise known as
James Ryan.

The plaintiff testified as a witness in his own behalf, stating in substance that he resided at Manville, near Lusk, in
Niobrara County in this state (formerly a part of Converse
County) and had resided there about three years last past.
That he had never lived in Chicago, was not in that city on
March 3rd, 1913, and had not been there more than two
days at any one time, and then only as he was passing
through the city. That he had never seen Mrs. McEldowney
in Chicago, or until he saw her at Lusk at the time of the
habeas corpus hearing there, and that she had never seen
him in Chicago. That his name was James Ryan; that he
had never gone by the name of Charles T. Crane, and had
never received any money, draft, or other property from
Mrs. McEldowney. He testified in detail respecting where

he had been from the time he left his place of residence in this state about the 1st of October, 1912, until his return about the 20th of March, 1913, stating that he first went to Syracuse, New York, his former home, where he remained until the third day of January of the present year; that he then went to New York City where he remained until about the middle of March, when he returned to this state. That on his return he came through Chicago without stopping there, thence to Kansas City, and from that place to his home in this state. Mrs. Ryan's testimony corroborated that of the plaintiff to the effect that he went to Syracuse upon leaving his home at Manville about the 1st of October, 1912, and then went to New York City early in January, 1913. She testified that she went to New York City about January 20th and remained there with the plaintiff for one week, then returning to Syracuse, and that she also went to New York about the 20th of February and was with the plaintiff there for four or five days or nearly a week, and upon her return to Syracuse received a letter from him March 2, 1913, sent to her from New York City. That on that date she left Syracuse for Manville, arriving there the 18th day of March, and that she was accompanied by a younger brother of the plaintiff named Charles, and another young man by the name of Bartholomew. She also testified that the plaintiff had never been known as Charles T. Crane to her knowledge.

The Constitution of the United States, in Section 2 of Article IV, provides for inter-state extradition as follows:

"A person charged in any state with treason, felony, or other crime, who shall flee from justice, and be found in another state, shall on demand of the executive authority of the state from which he fled, be delivered up to be removed to the state having jurisdiction of the crime." And by Section 5278 of the Revised Statutes of the United States it is provided: "Whenever the executive authority of any State or Territory demands any person as a fugitive from justice, of the executive authority of any State or Territory to which

such person has fled, and produces a copy of an indictment
found or an affidavit made before a magistrate of any State
or Territory, charging the person demanded with having
committed treason, felony, or other crime, certified as authentic by the governor or chief magistrate of the State or
Territory from whence the person so charged has fled, it
shall be the duty of the executive authority of the State or
Territory to which such person has fled to cause him to be
arrested and secured, and to cause notice of the arrest to
be given to the executive authority making such demand, or
to the agent of such authority appointed to receive the fugitive, and to cause the fugitive to be delivered to such agent
when he shall appear. If no such agent appears within six
months from the time of the arrest, the prisoner may be
discharged. All costs or expenses incurred in the appre-
hending, securing, and transmitting such fugitive to the
State or Territory making such demand, shall be paid by
such State or Territory."

Referring to these provisions it was said by the Supreme
Court of the United States in McNichols v. Pease, 207 U.
S. 100, 28 Sup. Ct. 58, 52 L. Ed. 121, that the following
principles are to be deduced from previous decisions of that
court, citing the cases:

"1. A person charged with crime against the laws of a
State and who flees from justice, that is, after committing
the crime, leaves the State, in whatever way or for whatever reason, and is found in another State, may, under the
authority of the Constitution and laws of the United States,
be brought back to the State in which he stands charged with
crime, to be there dealt with according to law.

"2. When the Executive authority of the State whose
laws have been thus violated makes such a demand upon
the Executive of the State in which the alleged fugitive is
found as is indicated by the above Section (5278) of the
Revised Statutes—producing at the time of such demand a
copy of the indictment, or an affidavit certified as authentic
and made before a magistrate charging the person demanded

with a crime against the laws of the demanding State—it becomes, under the Constitution and laws of the United States, the duty of the Executive of the State where the fugitive is found to cause him to be arrested, surrendered and delivered to the appointed agent of the demanding State, to be taken to that State.

"3. Nevertheless, the Executive, upon whom such demand is made, not being authorized by the Constitution and laws of the United States to cause the arrest of one charged with crime in another State unless he is a fugitive from justice, may decline to issue an extradition warrant, unless it is made to appear to him, by competent proof, that the accused is substantially charged with crime against the laws of the demanding State, and is, in fact, a fugitive from the justice of that State.

"4. Whether the alleged criminal is or is not such fugitive from justice may, so far as the Constitution and laws of the United States are concerned, be determined by the Executive upon whom the demand is made in such way as he deems satisfactory, and he is not obliged to demand proof apart from proper requisition papers from the demanding State, that the accused is a fugitive from justice.

"5. If it be determined that the alleged criminal is a fugitive from justice—whether such determination be based upon the requisition and accompanying papers in proper form, or after an original, independent inquiry into the facts —and if a warrant of arrest is issued after such determination, the warrant will be regarded as making a prima facie case in favor of the demanding State and as requiring the removal of the alleged criminal to the State in which he stands charged with crime, unless in some appropriate proceeding it is made to appear that he is not a fugitive from the justice of the demanding State.

"6. A proceeding by habeas corpus in a court of competent jurisdiction is appropriate for determining whether the accused is subject, in virtue of the warrant of arrest, to be taken as a fugitive from the justice of the State in which

he is found to the State whose laws he is charged with violating.

"7.   One arrested and held as a fugitive from justice is
entitled, of right, upon habeas corpus, to question the lawfulness of his arrest and imprisonment, showing by competent evidence, as a ground for his release, that he was not,
within the meaning of the Constitution and laws of the
United States, a fugitive from the justice of the demanding
State, and thereby overcoming the presumption to the contrary arising from the face of an extradition warrant."

In this cause the plaintiff questions the legality of his
arrest and imprisonment upon two principal grounds: 1.
That the papers accompanying the requisition are insufficient to show that the plaintiff, James Ryan, is charged with
having committed a crime in the State of Illinois, or that
Charles T. Crane is so charged.   2. That if the requisition
papers be deemed sufficient to show that Charles T. Crane
is charged with having committed a crime in Illinois, the
plaintiff is not Charles T. Crane, or the person so charged,
and was not in the State of Illinois at or about the time
when such crime is charged to have been committed.   In
support of the proposition that the papers are insufficient
to show a charge of crime authorizing the arrest or demand
for extradition, it is contended in the first place that the
affidavit of Mrs. McEldowney is the only paper accompanying the requisition which purports to charge the commission
of crime by James Ryan, and that said affidavit is insufficient
for the reason that it does not appear to have been made
before a magistrate, and for the further reason that the facts
stated therein do not show the commission of any crime.
That affidavit appears to have been made before the clerk
of the Criminal Court of Cook County, Illinois, and is entitled in that court in the case of the People of the State of
Illinois vs. Charles T. Crane, otherwise called James Ryan;
and in the matter of the extradition of Charles T. Crane,
otherwise called James Ryan, "defendant mentioned in the
above entitled cause, and fugitive from justice."   It does not

appear that any warrant from said court was issued or ordered to be issued upon that affidavit. If that was the only paper to show a charge of crime as authority for the extradition of the person named therein, we should doubt its compliance with that provision of the statute permitting the charge of crime to be shown by affidavit made before a magistrate. But it is apparent, we think, that this affidavit was not filed for the purpose, independently of any other proceeding, of charging the commission of a crime by Charles T. Crane, otherwise called James Ryan, but to be presented to the Governor of Illinois together with a copy of the indictment against Charles T. Crane to show that the accused was personally present in the State of Illinois at the time of the commission of the crime, and had fled from that state, and also the good faith of the request for the extradition of the accused, which we believe customary in such cases. The charge of crime is contained in the indictment, a copy of which duly authenticated accompanies the requisition, and its allegations must control in determining the legal question whether it is shown that the person named therein is charged with the commission of a crime. By the statutes of Illinois, which were introduced in evidence, and the decisions of its Supreme Court, a crime appears to be sufficiently charged by the indictment. It is provided by statute in that state as follows: "Every person who shall obtain, or attempt to obtain, from any other person or persons, any money or property by means or by use of any false or bogus checks, or by any other means, instrument or device, commonly called the confidence game, shall be imprisoned in the penitentiary not less than one year nor more than ten years," and in the succeeding section it is provided as follows: "In every indictment under the preceding section, it shall be deemed and held a sufficient description of the offense, to charge that the accused did, on, etc., unlawfully and feloniously obtain, or attempt to obtain (as the case may be), from A B (here insert the name of the person defrauded or attempted to be defrauded), his money (or

property, in case it be not money), by means and by use of
the confidence game." In referring to the crime so charged
and the necessity of setting forth in an indictment the elements constituting the offense it is held by the Supreme
Court of Illinois that an indictment charging the offense in
the manner in which it is charged in this indictment is sufficient (Morton v. People, 47 Ill. 468; Maxwell v. People,
158 Ill. 248, 41 N. E. 995.) In Morton v. People, the court
said: "The nature and character of the so-called confidence
game has become popularized in most of the cities and large
towns, and even the rural districts of this broad Union, and
is well understood, and this defendant was distinctly ap-
prized by the indictment of what he was called upon to
defend. The accusation is sufficiently identified by the name
of the victim. This name must appear in every indictment
on this statute, and appearing there, no second indictment for
the same offense could be successfully prosecuted. * * *
We are of the opinion that the offense is so set forth in the
indictment that the accused can be at no loss to know what
it is with which he is charged, and can so prepare his defense." And again, referring to the section defining the
crime called "confidence game," it was said in the same case:
"Now, as these devices are as various as the mind of man
is suggestive, it would be impossible for the legislature to
define them, and equally so, to specify them in an indictment; therefore the legislature has declared, that an indictment for this offense shall be sufficient if the allegation is
contained in it that the accused did, at a certain time and
place, unlawfully and feloniously obtain or attempt to obtain the money or property of another by means and by use
of the confidence game, leaving to be made out by the proof
the nature and kind of the devices to which resort was had."
    In Maxwell v. People, *supra*, the court said that it was
difficult to give a definition of what is commonly called the
confidence game, and, after quoting from Morton v. People,
supra, it was further said: "The popular idea of the confidence game, as understood 'in most of the cities and large

towns, and even in the rural districts' of the Union, is best expressed in the definition thereof in Webster's International Dictionary, and is as follows: 'Confidence game is any swindling operation in which advantage is taken of the confidence reposed by the victim in the swindler.' " In view of these decisions based upon the statutory provisions aforesaid, it is clear that the indictment before us must be considered as charging the commission of the crime of confidence game, and sufficient, so far as a charge of crime is concerned, without regard to the second count charging the crime of larceny, to justify the requisition, and the warrant of the Governor of this State, for the arrest of the accused, if found in this State, and his surrender to the agent named in the requisition. There seems to be some contention that the facts stated in the affidavit above referred to show that the charge in the indictment is not well founded. But the question of the guilt or innocence of the accused is not involved in this proceeding, and it was not necessary to state in the affidavit all the facts or elements of the crime charged, nor does it appear that it was intended to do'so.

Since the indictment does not mention any *alias* of the person charged it may be doubtful whether the words "otherwise known as James Ryan," following the name Charles T. Crane, were properly inserted in the requisition and governor's warrant. We expressed some doubt about that matter when orally announcing our conclusion to remand the plaintiff, stating, however, that we deemed it to be immaterial for the reason that the name stated in the indictment is also in the requisition and warrant, so that if the insertion therein of the *alias* was unauthorized it would not constitute a fatal objection to the arrest and detention of the plaintiff, though his true name may be James Ryan, if he is the identical person indicted and intended to be indicted by the name of Charles T. Crane and demanded by the requisition, since he may have been known in the State of Illinois by that name, or, if he committed the crime charged may have assumed that name. At the time of writing this opinion the doubt concerning the authority to insert in the requisition and in the warrant the words above mentioned as further describing the person therein named has been somewhat removed. The petition of the State's Attorney stating that the party charged by the indictment is a fugitive from justice, and the supporting affidavit each refers to the party indicted as "otherwise known as James Ryan," and in such a manner, we think, as to inform the Governor of the State of Illinois that Charles T. Crane, the person who stands charged with the crime by the indictment, is in fact otherwise known as James Ryan, and we are now inclined to think that this might be sufficient to authorize such a description in the requisition of the accused and alleged fugitive from justice, and likewise in the governor's warrant, though we do not decide that question.

Where a requisition by the Governor of Pennsylvania had demanded one Robert J. Williams, charged with having committed the crime of forgery in that state, and the Governor of Georgia, to whom the requisition was directed, had by his warrant ordered the arrest of Robert J. Williams (alias Spencer Riley) it was held in Johnston v. Riley, 13 Ga. 97, 136, that the insertion of the alias name in the warrant of arrest was unauthorized. That was an action for false imprisonment, and, answering the argument made upon the proposition that there was no authority to issue a warrant for Spencer Riley upon the requisition for Robert J. Williams, the court said: "As a distinct legal proposition, it is undoubtedly true, that the Governor of Georgia had no such right; but the error was committed by him in doing that which he believed to be a faithful discharge of his constitutional duty towards the State of Pennsylvania. The insertion of the alias was not necessary in our judgment, to have authorized the arrest of Riley, if, indeed, he was the same individual who committed the forgery, under the assumed name of Robert J. Williams. Had Riley been arrested under the warrant issued for the arrest of Williams, without the insertion of the alias, and been carried to the

State of Pennsylvania, and put upon his trial in the court in which the indictment was found, as the defendant named therein, and had pleaded in abatement that his name was not Robert J. Williams, the person named in the indictment, but that his name was Spencer Riley, a different person, it would have been competent for the prosecutor to have replied, that he was the identical person who committed the crime, and that he was as well known by the name of Robert J. Williams as that of Spencer Riley; or that, at the time of committing the crime, he represented his name to be Robert J. Williams, and upon proof of the facts contained in such replication he might have been properly convicted. (Citing authorities.) But the party making the arrest would have taken the responsibility of proving the identity of the person so arrested." And further on in the opinion it was said: "Had the defendant plead the warrant under which the arrest was made, and the other proceedings under which it was founded in justification, and had further alleged in his plea that the defendant was as well known by the name of Robert J. Williams, as Spencer Riley; that at the time the offense was committed in Philadelphia, the plaintiff represented his name to be Robert J. Williams, and was in fact the same identical person who assumed the latter name at the time, we should have held such plea upon principle to have been good. Upon such plea having been filed, it would have been competent for the defendant to have requested the court, to have instructed the jury, at the trial, that if they believed, from the evidence, that the plaintiff was the same person, who, under the assumed name of Robert J. Williams, committed the forgery in Philadelphia, they should find a verdict for the defendant."

In ex parte Glucksman, (C. C.) 189 Fed. 1016, which was a proceeding in habeas corpus and certiorari pending application for extradition, it appeared by the extradition papers that in the summer of 1910 a forgery was uttered by a leather merchant residing at Lodz in Russia, named Leiba Gliksman; that Leibel Pincusov Glucksman, a leather merchant formerly living at Lodz, Russia, arrived at the Port of New York early in August, 1910. That the person so arriving in New York, except in the matter of age, answered the description sent from Russia of the person who forged the instruments; that a photograph attached to the papers sent from Russia was a photograph of the prisoner. The name of the prisoner given in the habeas corpus proceeding seems to have been Leibel Pincusov Glucksman. The court after remarking that it attached very little importance to the fact that the name of the prisoner was spelled differently in the various papers, said: "In the Russian papers it is spelled Leiba Glicksman and in the papers written in the English language it is frequently spelled Lewek Glucksman, the difference, it is thought, being largely attributable to whether Polish, Russian or Yiddish is used. In any event, it is immaterial; if the prisoner be the person who committed the forgery he may be held under an alias, without any knowledge of his true name."

In Tiberg v. Warren, 192 Fed. 458, 112 C. C. A. 596, it appeared that the complaint attached to the requisition charged the commission of crime by Johan Tiberg. It does not appear from the opinion whether an alias name was contained in the requisition. But a habeas corpus proceeding to determine the legality of the arrest upon a warrant issued upon the requisition was brought by "Johan Tiberg, also known as Edwin Johansen." There seems to have been no question made in the case with reference to the name of the person charged.

There is this difference between the facts in this case and those considered in Johnston v. Riley, *supra*: the requisition, as well as the governor's warrant, describes the person demanded by the name stated in the indictment and also by the alias, that is to say, by the words "otherwise known as James Ryan." And he is described in the same manner in the petition of the State's Attorney for the extradition, and in the affidavit appearing to have been presented with it, each referring to the indictment and the party thereby charged with crime. But, as above indicated, it is unnecessary here to decide whether such facts would make it proper to embrace in the requisition and the warrant issued thereon an alias name or other words more particularly describing the person charged and intended to be charged with crime by the indictment and alleged to be a fugitive from justice. The requisition and warrant each names Charles T. Crane, and even if the insertion of the alias name in the requisition and warrant should be held to be unauthorized, that would not affect the regularity of those papers, and is not material in this proceeding, if in fact the person arrested, the plaintiff here, is the identical person intended to be named and charged by the indictment. The witness, Mrs. McEldowney, positively identified him as the one against whom she testified before the grand jury and the one named in the indictment, and testified that, known by the name stated in the indictment, he was personally present in the City of Chicago in the State of Illinois, at the time the crime charged is alleged to have been committed. With this testimony, if not without it, the showing was sufficient prima facie to justify the arrest and detention of the plaintiff for the purpose of delivering him into the custody of the duly appointed agent of the State of Illinois. (In re Leary, 10 Ben. 197, 15 Fed. Cas. 106 (No. 8162) ; Barnes v. Nelson, *supra*; McNichols v. Pease, *supra*.)

To overcome this the plaintiff and his wife testified as above set forth, the testimony of the plaintiff directly contradicting that of Mrs. McEldowney, so far as it related to his presence in the State of Illinois and being known there by the name of Charles T. Crane. The testimony of Mrs. Ryan cannot be considered as tending much to reduce the effect of this conflict, or to dispute the testimony of Mrs. McEldowney, for it is not impossible that the plaintiff may have been in New York City when his wife was there in the latter part of January for about a week, and four or five days the latter part of February, and also in Chicago on January 18, and the next day, and March 3, and at the several other times when, according to the testimony of Mrs. McEldowney, she saw him there. We are not required to determine the mere preponderance in this evidence and discharge or remand accordingly, for in a proceeding of this character, where the prisoner is held under an extradition warrant, a different rule of decision prevails.

The latest expression of the Supreme Court of the United States relative to the evidence necessary to overcome a prima facie case made by the extradition papers, when in proper form, is found in McNichols v. Pease, *supra,* where it is said: "When a person is held in custody as a fugitive from justice under an extradition warrant, in proper form, and showing upon its face all that is required by law to be shown as a prerequisite to its being issued, he should not be discharged from custody unless it is made clearly and satisfactorily to appear that he is not a fugitive from justice within the meaning of the Constitution and laws of the United States." Following the statement thus quoted it is , further said, "that a faithful, vigorous enforcement of the constitutional and statutory provisions relating to fugitives from justice is vital to the harmony and welfare of the states, and that 'while a state should take care, within the limits of the law, that the rights of its people are protected against illegal action, the judicial authorities of the Union should equally take care that the provisions of the Constitution be not so narrowly interpreted as to enable offenders against the laws of a state to find a permanent asylum in the territory of another State.' "

In a previous decision of that court (Munsey v. Clough, 196 U. S. 364, 25 Sup. Ct. 282, 49 L. Ed. 515) it was said: "When it is conceded, or when it is conclusively proved, that no question can be made that the person was not within the demanding State when the crime is said to have been committed, and his arrest is sought on the ground only of a constructive presence at that time, in the demanding state, then the court will discharge the defendant. But the court will not discharge a defendant arrested under a governor's warrant where there is merely contradictory evidence on the subject of presence in or absence from the State, as habeas corpus is not the proper proceeding to try the question of alibi, or any question as to the guilt or innocence of the accused." In that case no evidence was given other than the papers before the governor and it was not, therefore, a case involving conflicting evidence concerning the presence of the accused in the demanding state. For that reason the statement quoted was referred to in People ex rel. Genna v. McLaughlin, 145 App. Div. (N. Y.) 513, 130 N. Y. Supp. 458, as dictum and therefore not controlling, and the rule announced in McNichols v. Pease, *supra,* above quoted, was referred to as the reasonable as well as the controlling rule where the so-called question of alibi arises in a habeas corpus proceeding instituted by one arrested upon an extradition warrant. The New York case cited was heard upon appeal from an order of the court at special term refusing to discharge the petitioner on the ground that although it had been completely and satisfactorily established by the evidence that the person was not in the demanding state at the time of the commission of the crime charged in the indictment, there was a conflict of testimony upon the point, and therefore it was not within the power of the court to determine that the prisoner was not in the demanding state when the crime was committed; the court declaring that it felt bound to ignore the complete and satisfactory proof of an alibi because a matter of defense at the trial and not proper to be used for the purpose of defeating extradition. The Appellate Court considered that proposition at some length and held that if the so-called alibi be of such nature as to establish the absence of the prisoner from the demanding state when the crime was committed, it must be considered on the question of the jurisdictional fact, not whether the prisoner be guilty or innocent, but whether he is in fact a fugitive from justice, and said: "Any expression of opinion to the contrary has no longer any basis of authority either in the Federal courts or in the courts of this State," basing that statement principally upon the case of McNichols v. Pease, *supra*. Referring to the opinion of the court at special term that the proof of an alibi could not be considered, and the reason given for it, the Appellate Court said: "It seems to us that this reasoning is clearly unsound. An alibi in its general features consists of proof that the defendant was not at the scene of the crime at the time of its commission. Proof that the prisoner was not in the demanding State at the time of the commission of the crime is necessairly proof that he was not at the scene of the crime. But the question involved in extradition proceedings is not whether the defendant was at the scene of the crime at the time of its commission, but whether he was anywhere within the demanding State when the crime was committed. This latter question had nothing to do with guilt or innocence, but it has all to do with the question whether the prisoner has fled from the demanding State and is, therefore, a fugitive from justice." The order dismissing the writ of habeas corpus was reversed and the case remanded for a determination of the question whether the prisoner be actually a fugitive from justice either on the proofs already taken or upon such further proofs as either party might see fit to offer, the specific ground of such reversal being that when the court declared that it was satisfied that the prisoner had not been in the demanding State at the time of the commission of the crime, it became its duty to discharge him.

In a later New York case decided by the same court, where there was conflicting testimony upon the question, involving the identity of the prisoner with the person charged with crime in the demanding State, an order discharging the prisoner on habeas corpus was reversed, upon the ground that the proof offered to overcome the presumption arising from the official documents was not sufficient to clearly and satisfactorily show that the one in custody was not a fugitive from justice. In the opinion it was said to be a rule laid down by high authority that "mere evidence of an alibi, or evidence that the person demanded was not in the state as alleged, would not justify his discharge, where there was satisfactory evidence on the other side, as habeas corpus was not the proper proceeding to try the question of the guilt or innocence of the accused." (People ex rel. Edelstein v. Warden of City Prison, 154 App. Div. 261, 138 N. Y. Supp. 1095.) In that case the extradition warrant directed the arrest and delivery of Morris Edelson to the agent of the demanding State. The petitioner, Morris Edelstein, testified that he had never been known by the name of Edelson, and that he had never been in the city in the demanding State where it was alleged the crime had been committed. His wife also testified that he had never gone by the name of Edelson. Two witnesses, however, positively identified the petitioner as having been at or near the scene of the crime at the time mentioned. The court said that it appeared from the papers that the petitioner was known to the authorities of the demanding state as Edelson, alias Edelstein, and the positive identification by two witnesses as having been at or near the scene of the crime at the time mentioned, in connection with his denial that he was ever there, indicates plainly that the relator was the person charged with the crime, "and the mere fact that his name is misspelled in the papers before the court is not a sufficient justification for discharging the relator in a proceeding of this character." And again the court say: "The question is: Is this the person who has been charged with a crime in the State of New Jersey, and who has fled to this state?"

It is true that habeas corpus is not the proper proceeding to try any question as to the guilt or innocence of a petitioner arrested and held upon an extradition warrant, or to try the question of alibi so far as it relates to his guilt or innocence. But where the same evidence that might be used to establish the defense of alibi on his trial tends also to prove that he is not a fugitive from justice, that is to say, that he was not in the demanding State when the alleged crime was committed, it is proper, we think, to consider it in determining that question in a habeas corpus proceeding, wherein the

legality of his arrest is questioned and it is denied that he is
a fugitive from justice. In the case of McNichols v. Pease,
supra, the evidence offered upon the question was considered
and held to be insufficient to overcome the prima facie case
made by the official documents. The mere fact that the evidence is conflicting will not justify the discharge of the petitioner, for the extradition papers are entitled to some consideration, and it is incumbent upon the person in custody
to do more than produce evidence possibly sufficient to raise
a doubt as to his identity. The evidence that he is not the
person charged or demanded must be clear and satisfactory,
and in this case we are unable to say that a clear and satisfactory showing has been made that the plaintiff is not a
fugitive from justice. Aside from the improbability that
the witness upon whose testimony before the grand jury this
indictment was found and presented could be mistaken in
her identification of this plaintiff as the person so indicted,
considering the number of times that she saw him and was
in his company so recently as the period from January 18
to March 3 of the present year, certain facts were brought
out upon the cross-examination of the plaintiff and his wife
which would cause us to seriously hesitate in declaring that
even the preponderance of the evidence is with the plaintiff,
much less that it clearly or satisfactorily establishes the fact
that he was not in the demanding state, is not Charles T.
Crane, and not the person charged with crime by this indictment. Mrs. McEldowney testified that she saw in the plaintiff's office in Chicago a man whom the plaintiff represented
to be his brother, and who resembled him. Mrs. Ryan testified that when she returned from Syracuse to Manville she
went through Chicago and Kansas City, and was accompanied (but from what point she does not state) by her
brother-in-law, Charles—the plaintiff's brother, and a friend
of his named Oscar Bartholomew. The plaintiff testified
that his brother was a young man twenty-four years of age.
Either the plaintiff or his wife testified on cross-examination
that both these young men who had accompanied Mrs. Ryan

to Manville when she returned in March, left that place after the plaintiff's arrest, and no further explanation is given of their departure except that plaintiff testified that his brother went to New York. On cross-examination of the plaintiff he was asked about a man who had been sent here in his behalf, as he testified, and who was previously unknown to him. We quote from his testimony: "Q. How long have you known him? A. Since the—— I have only known him since this trouble came up. Q. Where did you first meet him? A. At Lusk, Wyoming. Q. You didn't know him before that? A. No, sir. Q. Had you heard of him before that? A. No, sir. Q. You didn't know Mr. Moses until after he came up here after your arrest? A. Never saw him; no, sir. Q. How did he happen to come up here? A. He was sent here in my behalf. Q. He was sent here in your behalf from where? A. I don't know, sir. Q. Don't know where he was sent from? A. No, sir. Q. Know where he is from, don't you? A. Kansas City, he came from." The fact of the departure after his arrest of the plaintiff's brother and his friend without any explanation or attempted explanation thereof, when the plaintiff was intending to question the legality of his arrest and deny his identity with that of the person charged with crime in Illinois, and the plaintiff's failure to explain more definitely the circumstances connected with sending here after his arrest a man entirely unknown to him, are facts tending to create an unfavorable impression. That a stranger might be sent to assist him, after his arrest, by someone interested in his welfare, would not ordinarily be a matter to excite doubt or suspicion. But if there was nothing about the facts to conceal, it would seem that they might have been fully explained. We have also considered the fact that upon a similar hearing in the District Court, the learned judge refused to discharge the plaintiff.

The only question in the case upon which there can be any doubt, in our opinion, is that of identity. We cannot say upon the evidence that the plaintiff has clearly and satisfactorily established the fact that he is not the person indicted by the name of Charles T. Crane, and is therefore not a fugitive from justice. The necessary conclusion, therefore, is that the court must refuse to discharge the plaintiff, and it is ordered that he be remanded to the custody of the sheriff to be dealt with according to law and the directions contained in the governor's warrant.

BEARD, J., concurs.

SCOTT, C. J., did not sit.

LOBELL v. STOCK OIL COMPANY.
(No. 729.)

APPEAL AND ERROR—BRIEFS—FAILURE TO FILE—DISMISSAL.

1. Where, without presenting any excuse therefor, plaintiff in error has failed to file briefs, and no extension of time therefor was applied for or granted, a motion to dismiss for that reason must be granted.

[Decided May 24, 1913.]   (132 Pac. 433.)

ERROR to the District Court, Natrona County, HON. DAVID H. CRAIG, judge.

William H. Martz, for plaintiff in error.

Norton & Hagens, for defendant in error.

PER CURIAM.

The petition in error in this case was filed August 28, 1912. No brief on behalf of plaintiff in error was ever filed as required by Rule 15 of this court, nor was any extension of time therefor applied for or granted. March 7, 1913, defendant in error filed a motion to dismiss the proceedings in error for the failure of plaintiff in error to file briefs as required by said rule. It is provided by Rule 21, (104 Pac. XIV.): "When the plaintiff in error or party holding the affirmative has failed to file and serve his brief as required by these rules, the defendant in error or party holding the negative may have the cause dismissed, or may submit it, with or without oral argument." No excuse has been presented in this case for the failure to file briefs as required by the rule. The motion to dismiss will have to be granted and the cause dismissed, (Small v. Savings Bank, 16 Wyo. 126, 92 Pac. 289) and it is so ordered.

Dismissed.

WEAVER v. RICHARDSON.
(No. 709.)

APPEAL AND ERROR—ORDER DENYING TEMPORARY INJUNCTION—RE-VIEW—RESTRAINING ORDER BY APPELLATE COURT PENDING PROCEED-ING IN ERROR—JURISDICTION—INJUNCTION PENDENTE LITE—DIS-CRETION OF COURT—REVIEW—PRESUMPTION AS TO GROUND FOR DENIAL OF TEMPORARY INJUNCTION—RIGHT OF DEFENDANT TO INJUNCTION PENDENTE LITE—PLEADINGS—ANSWER DEMANDING AFFIRMATIVE RELIEF—EJECTMENT—INJUNCTION TO PROTECT POS-SESSION OF VENDEE UNDER CONTRACT OF SALE PENDING ACTION FOR SPECIFIC PERFORMANCE.

1. An order granting or refusing an injunction as a provisional remedy in a pending cause is an order affecting a substantial right in a special proceeding, and therefore a final order subject to review on error.

2. After the commencement of a proceeding in error to review an order denying a motion for injunction *pendente lite* the Supreme Court is authorized to issue a restraining order pending the proceeding in error.

3. The granting or refusing of an injunction *pendente lite* is a matter resting largely in the discretion of the court, to be exercised so as to prevent injury, considering the situation of the parties, and the appellate court will not interfere with or control the action of the court below in such case. unless it has been guilty of a clear abuse of discretion; abuse of discretion, within the meaning of that rule, mean-ing an error of law committed by the court.

4. Where the defendant in an action for the recovery of land claimed under an alleged contract of sale and asked for its specific performance and moved for an injunction *pendente lite* to prevent plaintiff from forcibly removing defendant and her property from the premises, *Held*, that

the exclusion of evidence relating to the contract of sale as immaterial on the hearing of the motion for the injunction rendered it proper to assume that such motion was not denied on the ground that defendant's claim appeared to be doubtful.

5. Defendant's answer in an action for the recovery of land which demands judgment for damages for the breach of an alleged contract for the sale of the premises, or, in the alternative, for specific performance of the contract, is in that respect an answer in the nature of a counter-claim under the code and entitles the defendant to apply for an injunction *pendente lite* to protect his possession; and it is immaterial that the part of the answer setting forth the facts upon which the affirmative relief is demanded is not styled a cross-petition or named a counter-claim.

6. A defendant in an action for the recovery of land, upon filing an answer in the nature of a counter-claim or cross-petition praying for specific performance of an alleged contract for the sale of the premises is entitled to have his possession protected by an injunction pending the action.

7. In an action for recovery of land in which the defendant asked for specific performance of an alleged contract for a sale of the premises and moved for an injunction to protect her possession *pendente lite, Held,* that the motion was improperly denied, where the effect of such denial was to recognize a right in the plaintiff to retake the property in controversy by force, and to continue to enjoy, as a result of that act, what rightfully belonged to the defendant, if the allegations of the answer were true.

[Decided June 2, 1913.]   (132 Pac. 1148.)

ERROR to the District Court, Albany County, HON. CHARLES E. CARPENTER, Judge.

The action was brought by Annie F. Richardson against Adelaide J. Weaver to recover possession of certain real estate. It was alleged in the answer as a separate defense that the plaintiff and defendant had entered into an agreement for the sale of the premises by the plaintiff to the defendant and that defendant should take immediate possession of the premises, and the prayer was for judgment for damages for the failure of the plaintiff to comply with the contract, or, in the alternative, for specific performance thereof.

A motion of the defendant for an injunction to protect her possession pending the action was denied, and from such order denying the injunction the defendant brought error. The other material facts are stated in the opinion.

N. E. Corthell and *V. J. Tidball,* for plaintiff in error.

Although a party is not entitled to an injunction in a case of a single trespass unaccompanied by force or involving any other element of equitable jurisdiction, it is well established that injunction is an appropriate remedy for a trespass committed with force, or for a continuing trespass or repeated trespasses. (Martin v. Sheep Co., 12 Wyo. 432; 3 Pomeroy's Eq. Juris. 1357; 1 High on Inj. 356; 28 Ency. Law, 595; R. R. Co. v. Fiske, 123 Fed. 760; King v. Stuart, 84 Fed. 546; Nichols v. Jones, 19 Fed. 855; Smith v. Bivens, 56 Fed. 352; Ry. Co. v. McConnell, 82 Fed. 65; Tie Co. v. Stone, (Mo.) 117 S. W. 604; O'Brien v. Murphy, (Mass.) 75 N. E. 700; Pollock v. Ship Bldg. Co., 56 O. St. 655; 47 N. E. 582; Wilson v. Harrisburg, (Me.) 77 Atl. 787; Rhoades v. McNamara, (Mich.) 98 N. W. 392.) The right to the remedy is incidental to possession. (38 Cyc. 1014, 1018-1019; Tobin v. French, 93 Ill. App. 18; Holland v. San Antonio, (Tex.) 23 S. W. 756; Beaufort Land & I. Co. v. Lumber Co., (S. C.) 68 S. E. 637; Kellogg v. King, (Cal.) 46 Pac. 166; La Chapelle v. Bubb, (Wash.) 69 Fed. 481.) This remedy is peculiarly applicable for the purpose of preserving the condition of the title and occupancy pending litigation. (22 Cyc. 821; Cohen v. Delavina, 104 Fed. 946; Newton v. Levis, 79 Fed. 715; R. R. Co. v. U. S. 124 Fed. 156; Ry. Co. v. Carolina C. & I. Co., 151 Fed. 477.) It has frequently been granted to protect the rights of a party in possession under a contract of sale. (Hadfield v. Skelton, 66 Wis. 634, 29 N. W. 639; Hornung v. Herring, 74 Neb. 637, 104 N. W. 1071; Carter v. Warner, 2 Neb. 688, 89 N. W. 747.) And in cases to protect the actual possession of a party against forcible intrusion by another. (Heaton v. Wireman, 74 Neb. 817, 105 N. W.

634; W. U. Tel. Co. v. Ry. Co., 3 Fed. 430; Zimmerman v. McCurdy, (N. D.) 106 N. W. 125.)

In this case the court was proceeding in the usual and ordinary way to determine the facts disputed by the pleadings, and the plaintiff undertook by force to retake possession of the property. It would be difficult to conceive of a stronger case for injunction. (Hinckel v. Stevens, 45 N. Y. Supp. 678; Pokegama S. P. Co. v. Lumber Co., 86 Fed. 528; McHugh v. Bridge Co., (Ky.) 65 S. W. 456.) A party is not deprived of the remedy because the wrongful act has been already committed; the injunction will be mandatory to the extent necessary to restore the status of the parties, and put the injured party in the position occupied before the commission of the wrongful act. (22 Cyc. 742; Clock Co. v. Kochersperger, (Ill.) 51 N. E. 629; Wheelock v. Noonan, 108 N. Y. 179; U. S. v. Brighton Ranch Co., 26 Fed. 218.)

Frank E. Anderson, for defendant in error.

Whether a temporary injunction shall be granted, or, having been granted, whether it shall be dissolved, are matters resting in the sound discretion of the court, and that discretion will not be interfered with unless it clearly appears to have been abused. (Collins v. Stanley, 15 Wyo. 282, 88 Pac. 620, 123 Am. St. Rep. 1022; Anderson v. Englehart, 108 Pac. 977; Stowe v. Powers, (Wyo.) 116 Pac. 576; Williams v. Los Angeles R. Co., (Cal.) 89 Pac. 330.) The granting of an injunction is the exercise of original and not appellate jurisdiction. (1 High on Inj., Sec. 42.) A court of last resort is not allowed to enlarge or extend its jurisdiction to the granting of injunctions pending in inferior courts where the power is not granted by the Constitution. (Id.) No injunction had been granted by the District Court, and it is not a writ necessary to the complete exercise of the appellate and revisory jurisdiction of this court. Further, the denial of the injunction was not a judgment or final order of the District Court, and hence this court had no jurisdiction to grant the injunction pending the proceeding in error.

The motion for injunction and the affidavit supporting it are insufficient. There was no supplemental answer or cross-petition filed in the case in the nature of a counter-claim, so as to entitle the defendant to an injunction under the statute. (Comp. Stat. 1910, Sec. 4913.) The pleadings do not show that the defendant counter-claimed for specific performance. It is not sufficient in an application for injunction in case of trespass to allege merely the absence of an adequate remedy at law and that the damage will be irreparable, but facts must be stated to enable the court to determine those matters. (Indian River &c. Co. v. Trans. Co., 28 Fla. 387, 29 Am. St. Rep. 263.) Neither the motion nor the affidavits show that the defendant below had any title to the property or any right to the possession, nor is it shown that the plaintiff below is unable to respond in damages for the injury complained of. The only allegation tending to show injury is the statement in the affidavit in support of the motion that personal property of the defendant was removed. An injunction will not be granted in the first instance except upon a prima facie case and upon positive averments of the equities of the applicant. (1 High on Inj. Sec. 34; 16 Ency. Law, (2nd Ed.) 360-361; 10 Ency. Pl. & Pr. 951-953; Randall v. Freed, (Cal.) 97 Pac. 669; Tifft Co. v. Med. Inst. (Wash.) 101 Pac. 1081.) It is necessary to warrant the injunction that the title of the applicant be established, or at least a right to possession superior to that of the adverse party, and if the title is in doubt, the injunction, if granted, should be only temporary until the title can be determined at law. (1 High on Inj., Sec. 70; Caldwell v. Bush, 6 Wyo. 342; State v. McGlynn, 20 Cal. 233, 81 Am. Dec. 131.) A mere naked trespasser will not be protected by a restraining order. (Central Trust Co. v. Wabash &c. Co., 25 Fed. 1; Waring v. Munson, 17 N. W. 745; Woodford v. Alexander, (Fla.) 17 So. 658.) The facts given in evidence upon the hearing of the motion did not entitle the defendant to the remedy sought. It is not the function of an injunction to take the premises from the peaceable and quiet possession of the owner, and place the same in the possession of a mere trespasser. (1 High on Inj. Sec. 355; Williams v. Long, 129 Cal. 229, 61 Pac. 1087; Arnold v. Bright, 41 Mich. 210; 2 N. W. 17; Ry. Co. v. R. R. Co., 61 Mich, 9, 27 N. W. 715; Flood v. Goldstein Co. (Cal.) 110 Pac. 916.) The defendant in error had a right to enter the premises at any time she saw fit, and since she entered them peaceably the possession should not be taken from her by injunction.

POTTER, JUSTICE.

This is a proceeding in error for the review of an order denying a motion for injunction *pendente lite.* The action was brought to recover possession of real esate and damages for withholding the same, and the defendant applied by motion supported by affidavit for an injunction restraining the plaintiff from interfering with the defendant's possession of the property during the pendency of the action. At the time the motion was filed and heard the pleadings in the cause consisted of an amended petition, an amended answer, and a reply. By the amended petition the plaintiff, Annie F. Richardson, alleged that she was the owner of and entitled to the immediate possession of the property, and that the defendant, Adelaide J. Weaver, had unlawfully kept her out of possession and excluded her from the rents, issues and profits of the premises since the 20th day of April, 1910. It was alleged in the amended answer "as a second defense" that on or about October 28, 1909, the plaintiff and defendant entered into an agreement as follows: "Said plaintiff agreed for the sum of $500 to sell said premises, for which this action is brought, to said defendant, and said defendant agreed to purchase said premises for said price. That thereupon said defendant delivered to Adda Ulen, who was the duly authorized agent of both plaintiff and defendant for the purpose of this sale, $20 in escrow as part purchase price of said premises. That by the terms of said agreement the balance of said purchase price amounting to the sum of $480 was to be paid when said plaintiff should furnish a clear title to said premises and execute and deliver a good and sufficient warranty deed conveying said premises to said defendant, and that said $20 should be held in escrow by Adda Ulen until such time as said deed should be furnished. That it was further agreed between plaintiff and defendant that defendant should take immediate possession of said premises under said agreement and should hold possession thereof until plaintiff should convey said premises to her by said deed above mentioned." It was further alleged that, "thereupon this defendant, relying upon the agreement above set out, without fraud or collusion on her part, and with the full knowledge and consent of plaintiff, and at plaintiff's request, entered into and took quiet and peaceable possession of said premises, believing, because of the representations and promises aforesaid of plaintiff, that she was the owner of said premises; and this defendant has since taking possession of said premises, been in quiet possession thereof and lived thereon, believing them to be her property." That with the knowledge and consent of the plaintiff and without objection on her part the defendant has made various and sundry valuable and lasting improvements upon the property in good faith, of the reasonable value of $206.30; that none of said improvements can be detached from the premises and would be valueless except as used in connection therewith: that the plaintiff has never carried out said contract on her part; that she has never furnished evidence of clear title to the property; and has never made, executed, and delivered any deed conveying the premises to the defendant, to the defendant's damage in the sum of $206.30. It was also alleged that "during all of said time defendant was, and now is, ready and willing to comply with said agreement on her part and to pay the balance of the purchase price for said premises upon the delivery of the deed above mentioned." By said amended answer defendant prayed judgment for the sum of $206.30, "the reasonable value of said improvements, her damages sustained by reason of the failure of the plaintiff to comply with the terms of said contract in defendant's answer, set up or, in the alternative, that the

court order and adjudge that the plaintiff perform the contract specifically by conveying the said property to this defendant upon payment of the residue of the purchase price
and for all other proper relief."

The reply admitted that defendant entered into possession
of the premises at the time mentioned in the second defense
of the answer, and denied each and every other allegation
contained in that defense.   On December 30, 1911, the cause
being then pending and undetermined upon the issues raised
by the pleadings, the defendant filed her said motion, supported by her affidavit stating in addition to the fact that the
defendant had been in continuous possession since about
October 28, 1909, that she had been put in possession by the
plaintiff under a contract made between the parties as set
forth in the amended answer; that on or about November
25, 1911, the plaintiff wrongfully and unlawfully entered
the premises with force, and by intimidation and threats excluded the defendant therefrom, and since said date has
wrongfully continued to occupy the premises and to exclude
the defendant therefrom; and that the plaintiff intends and
threatens to continue her wrongful acts, and by force, intimidation and threats to exclude the defendant permanently
from the enjoyment of the premises; and since taking
possession of the premises the plaintiff has threatened to remove the defendant's personal property from the premises
and unless restrained will remove and destroy defendant's
said property.   Upon the presentation of said motion it was
ordered that it be set down for hearing on January 4, 1912,
and that until said hearing and the further order of the
court, the plaintiff, her agents, servants, and all persons acting in aid of her, be restrained from removing or in any
manner interfering with the personal property of the defendant on the premises in controversy, and that if any of
such property shall have been removed by the plaintiff that
she forthwith restore the same in the said buildings on the
premises; said restraining order to become operative upon
the defendant giving a bond in a sum stated in the order.

The plaintiff filed a counter affidavit stating therein that she had never contracted to sell the premises to the defendant; that the latter had unlawfully retained possession until about November 20, 1911, at which time the plaintiff found the premises unoccupied and took peaceable possession thereof. On January 5, 1912, the motion came on for hearing before the District Court and evidence was introduced by both parties. It appears that a house, referred to in the evidence as a hotel, is located on the premises, and it was not disputed that the defendant occupied the house and was in possession of the property from the latter part of October, 1909, until on or about November 25, 1911. What occurred then is stated by defendant in her testimony in substance as follows: That on the morning of that date she went to her ranch, intending to come back the same evening if possible, but was delayed until the next morning. That she left the front door of the house bolted, and all the other doors locked, and when she returned she found the plaintiff in the house, who had entered by pushing the front door away from the bolt, splitting the door in doing so "from the top down." That she asked the plaintiff what she was doing there and what right she had to come there in that way, and that the plaintiff replied, she had every right and was told by her attorney to break in if necessary, and that she would not leave. The defendant further testified that she also remained in the house or occupied a room therein two days, and was then called away on business, and although she went back three times she was not again allowed to enter the house. It seems from the evidence that the plaintiff's personal property had been returned to the house and remained therein. The plaintiff admitted in her testimony that she had gone into the house and taken possession during defendant's absence at the time stated by the defendant, but did not explain how she obtained an entrance. There appears to be some dispute in the testimony as to when and by whom the front door was broken, whether by the plaintiff or by someone assisting her when she entered the house, or by the defendant, or a man who accompanied her when she returned, but that is immaterial, for it is clear enough that defendant's absence was merely temporary and that she had not vacated or abandoned the premises, and also that the plaintiff used such force as was necessary in gaining an entrance into the house. It appears by the bill of exceptions that at the conclusion of the testimony the court stated that the parties might consider the pleadings in the case and the order dismissing the jury as received in evidence. Thereupon the motion of the defendant for the injunction was denied and the order excepted to.

To reverse the order denying defendant's said motion, a petition in error was filed in this court January 16, 1912, and upon the application of the defendant, after a hearing at which both parties were represented, an order was entered enjoining the defendant in error, plaintiff below, her agents and servants, and all persons acting in aid of her, from trespassing upon or in any manner interfering with the possession of plaintiff in error in and to the premises aforesaid during the pendency of the proceeding in error in this court, upon the plaintiff in error giving an undertaking with sufficient sureties in a stated amount, "conditioned that the said Adelaide J. Weaver shall pay to the said Annie F. Richardson the damages she may sustain if it be finally decided that the injunction ought not to have been granted." It appears that such undertaking was given and filed with the papers in the cause in this court.

1. Counsel for defendant in error contends, *inter alia,* that the order complained of is not reviewable, and that therefore this court is without jurisdiction in the matter and was also without jurisdiction to issue the restraining order pending the proceeding in error. But in Anderson v. Englehart, 18 Wyo. 196, 105 Pac. 571, Ann. Cas. 1912c, 894, upon a full consideration of the question, such an order was held to be reviewable. And therefore the order of this court granting the injunction during the pendency of the proceeding in error was authorized by that provision of the Consti-

tution conferring upon the court the power to issue writs
necessary and proper to the complete exercise of its appellate
and revisory jurisdiction. (Const., Art. V, Sec. 3.)   It was
held in the case cited that an order granting or refusing an
injunction as a provisional remedy in a pending cause is an
order affecting a substantial right in a special proceeding, and
therefore a final order subject to review on error, and it
was said: "Although injunction allowed as a provisional
remedy is collateral to the pending cause, it is nevertheless
a proceeding in that cause, and after a hearing upon an application for such remedy, or on a motion to dissolve, the
order which disposes of the application or motion, and grants
or denies it, is final, so far as that particular proceeding is
concerned, and settles the right to the provisional remedy,
until at least another hearing upon a renewal of the application or motion."

2.   The granting or refusing of an injunction *pendente lite*
is a matter resting largely in the discretion of the court, to
be exercised so as to prevent injury, considering the situation
of the parties.   (Collins v. Stanley, 15 Wyo. 282, 88 Pac.
620, 123 Am. St. Rep. 1022.)   And the Appellate Court will
not interfere with or control the action of the court below
in such case unless it has been guilty of a clear abuse of
discretion.   By abuse of discretion within the meaning of
that rule is meant an error of law committed by the court.
(Anderson v. Englehart, 18 Wyo. 409, 108 Pac. 977.)   In
Joyce on Injunctions (Vol. 1, Sec. 118), it is said: "Sound
discretion consists in an observance of the rules and considerations which have generally guided the courts in granting preliminary injunctions.   In any given case such discretion is shown in the steady judgment with which the judge
applies the general rules to the particular facts with which
he has to deal.   The granting of an injunction is matter of
grace in no sense except that it rests in the sound discretion
of the court, and that discretion is not an arbitrary one.   If
improperly exercised in any case, either in granting or refusing it, the error is one to be corrected on appeal.   Such

discretion will often be influenced by a consideration of the
relative injury and convenience likely to result to the parties
from granting or refusing the injunction." As above recited
it appears in the bill of exceptions that the court announced
at the conclusion of the testimony that the pleadings in the
cause and the order of the court dismissing the jury would
be considered as received in evidence. The pleadings above
referred to are in this record, but we do not find in the bill,
or in the record proper, any order dismissing a jury in the
cause prior to the hearing upon this motion, although there
is in the record what purports to be a certified copy of all
the journal entries in the cause. Whether, therefore, such
an order, if any was made, could have materially affected the
decision of the court in denying the motion, does not definitely appear. If there had been a trial of the cause and it
appeared that the only facts in dispute upon the trial were
those set up in the second defense of the answer above referred to, and the jury had disagreed and had been dismissed for that reason, the court might, perhaps, have considered the order of dismissal under such circumstances as
showing the defendant's claim to be doubtful. But it is
shown by the bill of exceptions that evidence relating to the
contract of sale alleged in the answer was excluded as immaterial upon the hearing of the motion, and we think it
proper, therefore, to assume that the motion was not denied
upon the ground that defendant's claim appeared to be
doubtful. Moreover, it does not appear that if there was a
former trial resulting in the disagreement of the jury the
pleadings were the same upon that trial as they appear in
this record.

The code provides that the injunction provided thereby
may be the final judgment in an action, or may be allowed
as a provisional remedy, and that when so allowed it shall be
by order. (Comp. Stat., 1910, Sec. 4897.) It is provided in
Section 4898 that when it appears by the petition that the
plaintiff is entitled to the relief demanded, and such relief,
or any part thereof, consists in restraining the commission

or continuance of some act, the commission or continuance of which, during the litigation would produce great or ir- reparable injury to the plaintiff, or when, during the liti- gation, it appears that the defendant is doing, or threatens, or is about to do, or is procuring or suffering to be done, some act in violation of the plaintiff's rights, respecting the subject of the action, and tending to render the judgment ineffectual, a temporary order may be granted restraining such act. And by Section 4913, found in the same chapter of the code, it is provided that a defendant may obtain an injunction upon an answer in the nature of a counter-claim, and that he shall proceed in the same manner prescribed in that chapter. A defendant may set forth in his answer as many grounds of defense, counter-claim, and set-off as he has, whether they are such as were formerly denom- inated legal or equitable, or both. (Comp. Stat., Sec. 4390.) And the counter-claim thus permitted must be one arising out of the contract or transaction set forth in the petition as the foundation of the plaintiff's claim, or connected with the subject of the action. (Id. Sec. 4391.) When affirma- tive relief is demanded in an answer it may be styled cross- petition. (Id. Sec. 4378.) The answer in this cause de- mands affirmative relief, viz: judgment for damages for breach of the contract alleged, or in the alternative, for spe- cific performance of the contract. In that respect it is an answer in the nature of a counter-claim under the code. (Bliss on Code Pl., 2nd Ed., Sec. 368; Pomeroy's Rem., Secs. 737, 742; G. & H. Mfg. Co. v. Hall, 61 N. Y. 226, 19 Am. Rep. 278.) And it is immaterial that the part of the answer setting forth the facts upon which the affirmative relief is demanded is not styled a "cross-petition," or named a "counter-claim." (Klonne v. Bradstreet, 7 O. St. 323; Bartholomew v. Lutheran Church, 35 O. St. 567; Pome- roy's Rem., Sec. 748.) "It must be indicated that a coun- ter-claim or set-off is intended, either by naming the plead- ing or praying affirmative relief or both. * * * If the facts are stated it is immaterial whether the plaintiff call his pleading a defense or a counter-claim; the use of the right term is immaterial; the facts determine the character." (1 Bates Pl. Pr. Par. & F. 386.) In Klonne v. Bradstreet, *supra*, the court say: "If, on inspection of a defendant's answer, it shall be found to contain a prayer for judgment, and the necessary averments to show the party's right to relief, under the proceedings instituted against him, the court will not require the filing of a cross-petition, in form, but will treat such answer as equivalent to a petition of that kind, and grant whatever relief the party may show himself entitled to receive."

If the facts alleged in the answer as to a contract for a sale of the premises to the defendant and the latter's possession under that contract are true, then the plaintiff could not maintain her action for possession, and the defendant would be entitled to enforce specific performance of the contract. "Ejectment is not maintainable by a vendor against his vendee in possession under an executory contract of sale who is not in default in the performance of his contract, or who has performed it and is in a position to demand a deed, or who seasonably and in good faith offers to comply with the terms of his purchase, and continues ready to comply with them. To a vendee in possession under such circumstances the contract will avail him as a defense to an action of ejectment, or as a cross-action in equity to enforce a trust against his vendor, or to obtain a specific enforcement of the contract." (2 Warvelle on Vendors, Sec. 886.) And a vendee who is in peaceable possession under his contract is entitled to an injunction to protect his possession pending his action for specific performance. (1 High on Inj., 4th Ed., Sec. 356; Hadfield v. Bartlett, 66 Wis. 634, 29 N. W. 639; Doane v. Allen (Mich.), 138 N. W. 228.) In Hadfield v. Bartlett the court say: "Most clearly the defendant did a great wrong in intruding into the possession of said barn and premises after commencement of the suit for specific performance of the contract. The merits of that suit cannot be determined on this ap-

peal. * * * What the plaintiff may be able to prove on
the trial cannot yet be known. It would seem to have been
a most proper case where the matters ought to have remained *in statu quo* after the suit was brought until its determination." (See also Glasco v. Sch. Dist., 24 Okl. 236,
103 Pac. 687.)

We think it apparent that upon the answer in the nature
of a counter-claim or cross-petition praying for specific performance, the defendant would be entitled to have her possession protected by injunction pending the action, the same
as a plaintiff in her situation who brings an action for specific performance. (Johnson v. Hall, 83 Ga. 281, 9 S. E.
783; Horton v. White, 84 N. C. 297.) In the case last
cited, the plaintiff brought an action for the recovery of
land claiming to be the owner thereof. The answer denied
plaintiff's allegations of title, and averred title in some of
the defendants, and that the others were tenants under
them. While the action was pending the plaintiff, through
an agent, entered into and took possession of an unoccupied
house on the premises in controversy, and resisted the re-
occupation thereof by the defendants. Thereupon the defendants applied for and obtained a temporary restraining
order against further interference by the plaintiff until the
hearing of the case upon its merits. On appeal the granting
of the restraining order was sustained.

Upon the pleadings and the evidence taken at the hearing
of the motion a very proper case was presented for an injunction, and we are unable to see any substantial reason
for a denial thereof, or to say that the discretion of the
court was properly exercised in refusing it. The plaintiff
would have been protected by bond, and a refusal to protect
the alleged right of the defendant until the matter in dispute could be determined in the pending action would seem
to recognize a right in the plaintiff to retake by force the
property in controversy, and to continue to enjoy as the
result of that act what rightfully belonged to another, if
the allegations of the defendant's answer are true. It was

said by Judge McCrary, in a case where an injunction was granted to prevent the forcible seizure of property in violation of the terms of a contract which the defendants claimed to be void: "If they have the right to seize this property by force, upon the ground that they hold the contract void, according to the same reasoning the plaintiff would have the right to adjudge the contract valid, and by force retake the property. In other words, force and violence would take the place of law, and mobs would be substituted for the process of courts of justice. * * * Such a doctrine, if recognized by the courts as a proper mode of adjusting disputes concerning property rights, would lead at once to anarchy." (W. U. Tel. Co. v. St. J. & W. Ry. Co., 3 Fed. 430, 434.) We know, of course, that upon a subsequent trial of the cause the plaintiff recovered a verdict and judgment, for an appeal was taken from the judgment resulting in its reversal. (Weaver v. Richardson, 129 Pac. 829.) That appeal and this were submitted at the same time, but when deciding the former we inadvertently neglected to dispose of this appeal from the order denying the injunction. Our conclusion is that prejudicial error was committed by the denial of the defendant's motion. The order will be reversed, and the District Court directed, if there has not been a final disposition of the cause, to enter the proper order restraining the plaintiff below from interfering with the possession of the defendant during the pendency of the action and until the respective rights of the parties are determined therein, upon the giving of an undertaking or bond as provided by statute in an amount to be fixed by said court deemed sufficient to protect the interest of the plaintiff if she shall finally succeed in the action.

SCOTT, C. J., and BEARD, J., concur.

STATE EX REL. JAMISON v. FORSYTH, STATE AUDITOR.

(No. 751.)

STATUTES—APPROVAL BY GOVERNOR—APPROPRIATIONS—GENERAL APPROPRIATION BILL—POWER OF GOVERNOR TO DISAPPROVE PART AND APPROVE PART OF A DISTINCT ITEM.

1. Without deciding whether the governor is authorized to disapprove part and approve part of a distinct item in a general appropriation bill, under Section 9 of Article IV of the Constitution conferring power upon him to disapprove of any item or items or part or parts of any bill making appropriations of money embracing distinct items, *held,* as to a bill presented to the governor on the last day of the session of the legislature and not acted upon by him until after adjournment, that if he has such power his disapproval of part only of the amount of a distinct item would leave the remainder appropriated, and if such power is not conferred his act in disapproving a part and approving a part of the item would be invalid and a nullity, and the entire amount of such item would be appropriated and available for the purpose declared by the bill, since under Section 8 of Article IV of the Constitution, to prevent a bill so presented and not acted upon until after adjournment, or any of the items thereof, from becoming a law, the Governor would be required to expressly disapprove the same by filing the bill with his objections in the office of the Secretary of State within fifteen days after the adjournment of the legislature.

2. The provision of Section 8 of Article IV of the Constitution that any bill not returned by the governor within three days (Sundays excepted) after its presentation to him shall be a law, unless the legislature by its adjournment prevent its return, in which case it shall be a law, unless he shall file the same with his objections in the office of the Secretary of State within fifteen days after such adjournment, applies to the general appropriation bill as well as to other bills.

3. Where the general appropriation bill contained among other distinct items of appropriation to pay the necessary contingent expenses of state and district officers, employes, boards and commissions, an item of $15,000 for the office of state geologist, and said bill was presented to the governor on the last day of the session of the legislature,

and within fifteen days thereafter the governor signed the bill, stating above his signature: "This act is approved save and except the items or parts of items specially noted herewith as being disapproved and as shown by accompanying communication. * * * See also notations on margin"; and on the margin of the item appropriated for said office was the following notation: "$10,000 of item approved. $5,000 of item disapproved"; and in the accompanying communication it was stated by the governor that he approved of so much of the item as appropriates $10,000, and withheld his approval from $5,000, leaving the appropriation $10,000; said bill so signed and with the accompanying communication being filed with the Secretary of State within said period; *held,* that the action of the governor as to said item of appropriation was not an objection to or a disapproval of the entire item, and if the authority is not conferred upon him to disapprove a distinct item in part and approve it in part, his act in attempting to do so would be a nullity, and ineffectual for the purpose intended, or for any other purpose; that at least the sum of $10,000 was appropriated for said office, and that being sufficient to pay the claim for which mandamus was sought against the auditor, which was conceded to be the first claim, if not the only one, presented for allowance out of said appropriation, it would be unnecessary to decide whether said action of the governor lawfully reduced the appropriation to the amount approved.

4. By "objections" or "disapproval," as those terms are employed in the Constitution with reference to the veto power of the governor, is meant objections or disapproval within the authority of the governor, and expressed in the manner provided by the Constitution.

5. Under Section 8 of Article IV of the Constitution, providing that a bill received by the governor too late to be returned to the legislature within a specified time will become a law unless disapproved by the governor within the period limited for that purpose after adjournment, an unauthorized disapproval will not defeat the bill.

6. Where an affirmative approval of the governor is not required to a general appropriation bill becoming a law, but the bill or the items contained therein will become law unless disapproved, an unauthorized disapproval will be ineffectual. (Beard, J., dissenting.)

[Decided June 16, 1913.]   (133 Pac. 521.)

Original proceeding in mandamus.

The action was brought in the name of the state on the relation of Claude E. Jamison against Robert B. Forsyth, State Auditor, to require the payment of a claim of the relator out of an alleged existing appropriation for the office of state geologist. The case was heard upon a demurrer to the petition, it being conceded that all facts were fully and correctly set forth therein. The material facts are stated in the opinion.

D. A. Preston, Attorney General, for respondent, in support of demurrer, cited Commonwealth v. Barnett, 199 Pa. 161; Fulmore v. Lane, (Tex.) 140 S. W. 405; State v. Holder, (Miss.) 23 So. 643; Porter v. Hughes, (Ariz.) 32 Pac. 165; Oklahoma v. Trapp, 113 Pac. 910, 28 Okl. 83.

C. L. Rigdon, for relator, *contra.*

Potter, Justice.

The original jurisdiction of this court is invoked in this case. It is an action seeking a peremptory writ of mandamus requiring the defendant as State Auditor to allow the bill and voucher of the relator for the sum of five dollars and issue to the relator a warrant for that amount upon the State Treasurer in payment of said bill. The case has been presented upon a demurrer to the petition and it is conceded that all the facts have been fully and correctly set forth in the petition. The question involved is the effect of the action of the Governor in approving a part of an item in the general appropriation bill passed at the recent session of the Legislature, and disapproving the remainder of that item.

The facts are, as set forth in the petition, that the relator, Claude E. Jamison, is the duly and regularly appointed, qualified and acting State Geologist of the State of Wyoming, and was such on the first day of April, 1913. That biennially there is appropriated by the legislature out of funds in the state treasury not otherwise appropriated a certain sum of money to pay the necessary contingent expenses of the State Geologist. That on the last day of the session, viz.: February 22, 1913, the Twelfth Legislature passed an act making appropriations of money embracing distinct items, entitled: "An Act making appropriations for salaries and contingent expenses of State and District offcers and employees, and the various State Boards and Commissions, for the two years ending March 31st, 1915, including * * * ." That among the distinct items of appropriation enumerated in Section 3 in said act to pay the necessary contingent expenses of State and District officers and employees, and the various State Boards and Commissions from March 31, 1913, to and including March 31, 1915, is one which reads as follows: "For the office of State Geologist, fifteen thousand dollars." That on the 8th day of March the Governor signed the said act and approved the said item of appropriation for the contingent expenses of the office of State Geologist to the extent of ten thousand dollars, and disapproved of five thousand dollars thereof in words and figures to-wit: "This act is approved save and except the items or parts of items specially noted herewith as being disapproved and as shown by accompanying communication. March 8, 1913, 6 p. m. See also notations on margins. Joseph M. Carey, Governor." That on the margin of the item "For the office of State Geologist, fifteen thousand dollars," is the following notation: "$10,000 of item approved, $5,000 of item disapproved. J. M. C., Governor." That the accompanying communication of the Governor appended to said act and explaining his action thereon is in words and figures as follows (omitting everything not pertaining to this particular item of appropriation):

"March 8, 1913.

Hon. Frank L. Houx,
    Secretary of State,
        Cheyenne, Wyo.

Sir:—I herewith file with you Enrolled Act No. 93 (O. H. B. No. 266), House of Representatives, entitled: 'An

Act making appropriation for salaries and contingent expenses * * * ' etc., etc., said act being what is known as the General Appropriation Act. I have approved this act except where specifically noted hereinafter. . * * * Section 3, the paragraph reading 'For the office of State Geologist, fifteen thousand dollars.' I approve of so much of this item as appropriates $10,000, and withhold my approval from $5,000, leaving the appropriation $10,000. The State Geologist's office had an appropriation of $5,000 for the biennial period just passing. I believe double this appropriation ought to be more than sufficient to carry on the work of his office for the next two years. * * *

Very truly yours
Joseph M. Carey,
Governor."

That on the 1st day of April, 1913, the relator presented to the defendant as State Auditor his bill and voucher in due form against the state for the sum of $5, an amount due and payable as an expenditure necessarily made by the relator in the performance of the duties imposed by law upon him as State Geologist. That the Auditor, questioning the legality of the said item of appropriation for the contingent expenses of the office of the State Geologist, has refused a warrant for the said bill and voucher, or any other amount. The petition, after setting forth the said facts, alleges: "That in and by said Section 3 of said Act the sum of ten thousand dollars, or so much thereof as may be necessary, is appropriated by law to pay the necessary contingent expenses of the State Geologist from March 31st, 1913, to and including March 31st, 1915, and so said petitioner represents that an amount of money sufficient to pay said expenditure due to said relator as set forth in said bill and voucher is in the treasury of the state, and has been duly and regularly appropriated by law."

As above suggested, the question presented by the demurrer is whether, as a result of the Governor's approval of part and disapproval of part of the item appropriated for the contingent expenses of the State Geologist's office, there is an appropriation of any amount for that purpose.

Counsel for relator does not contend that the Governor is without authority to disapprove a part only of a distinct item in a general appropriation bill and approve the remainder of such item, but has assumed that the Governor possesses such authority, insisting, however, that whether the Governor is vested with that authority or not, at least the sum of $10,000 remains appropriated for the payment of the contingent expenses of the Geologist's office. The position of the Auditor, as explained by the Attorney General, is that the authority of the Governor to disapprove of a part of an item in an appropriation bill containing distinct items has been doubted, leaving the result of such action on has part also in doubt, that is to say, whether it has resulted in destroying the entire appropriation for said contingent expenses of the Geologist's office or in an appropriation by law of the amount as reduced by the Governor or as passed by the legislature.

The provisions of the Constitution applicable to the question thus submitted are as follows:

Art. III, Sec. 24. "No bill, except general appropriation bills and bills for the codification and general revision of the laws, shall be passed containing more than one subject, which shall be clearly expressed in its title; but if any subject is embraced in any act which is not expressed in the title, such act shall be void only as to so much thereof as shall not be so expressed."

Art. III, Sec. 34. "The general appropriation bills shall embrace nothing but appropriations for the ordinary expenses of the legislative, executive and judicial departments of the state, interest on the public debt, and for public schools. All other appropriations shall be made by separate bills, each embracing but one subject."

Art. III, Sec. 35. "Except for interest on public debt, money shall be paid out of the treasury only on appropriations made by the legislature, and in no case otherwise than upon warrant drawn by the proper officer in pursuance of law."

Art. IV, Sec. 8. "Every bill which has passed the legislature shall, before it becomes a law, be presented to the governor. If he approve, he shall sign it; but if not, he shall return it with his objections to the house in which it originated, which shall enter the objections at large upon the journal and proceed to reconsider it. If, after such reconsideration, two-thirds of the members elected agree to pass the bill, it shall be sent, together with the objections, to the other house, by which it shall likewise be reconsidered, and if it be approved by two-thirds of the members elected, it shall become a law; but in all such cases the vote of both houses shall be determined by yeas and nays, and the names of the members voting for and against the bill shall be entered upon the journal of each house respectively. If any bill is not returned by the governor within three days (Sundays excepted) after its presentation to him, the same shall be a law, unless the legislature by its adjournment, prevent its return, in which case it shall be a law, unless he shall file the same with his objections in the office of the secretary of state within fifteen days after such adojurnment."

Art. IV, Sec. 9. "The governor shall have power to disapprove of any item or items or part or parts of any bill making appropriations of money or property embracing distinct items, and the part or parts of the bill approved shall be the law, and the item or items and part or parts disapproved shall be void unless enacted in the following manner: If the legislature be in session he shall transmit to the house in which the bill originated a copy of the item or items or part or parts thereof disapproved, together with his objections thereto, and the items or parts objected to shall be separately reconsidered, and each item or part shall then take the same course as is prescribed for the passage of bills over the executive veto."

A provision similar to that contained in Section 9 of Art.
IV, allowing the Governor to disapprove of any item or
part of a bill appropriating money containing distinct items
is found in the constitution of many of the states. (See
note to the case of Commonwealth v. Barnett, 55 L. R. A.
882.) But the authority under such provision to disapprove
of part only of an item and approve the remainder of the
item does not seem to have been positively decided except in
one case, where it was held, one justice dissenting, that the
power to so act was conferred upon the governor, so that
he could by approving a part and disapproving a part of an
item, reduce the amount thereby appropriated for a specific
purpose. (Commonwealth v. Barnett, *supra,* officially reported in 199 Pa. St. 161, 48 Atl. 976, 55 L. R. A. 882.)
Expressions to the contrary are, however, to be found in
at least two cases, the right to so reduce an item being distinctly denied in the opinion of one of the justices in the
Texas case of Fulmore v. Lane, 140 S. W. 405, 423, although
the other justices concurring in the disposition made of the
case do not seem to have rested their conclusion upon that
ground.

It appeared in the Pennsylvania case that the general appropriation act, containing distinct items of appropriation,
embraced one item of $11,000,000 for the support of the
public schools, and that the governor approved such item of
appropriation to the extent of $10,000,000 and disapproved
$1,000,000 thereof. The veto message explaining the rea-
sons for the disapproval of the item in part concluded as
follows: "The authority of the governor to disapprove part
of an item is doubted, but several of my predecessors in
office have established a precedent by withholding their approval from a part of an item and approving other parts of
the same item. Following these precedents, and believing
that the authority which confers the right to approve the
whole of an item necessarily includes the power to approve
part of the same item, I, therefore, approve of so much of
this item which appropriates $5,000,000 annually, making

$10,000,000 for the two years beginning June 1, 1899, and withhold my approval from $500,000 annuallly, making $1,000.000 for the two school years beginning June 1, 1899." The provisions of the Constitution of Pennsylvania which were considered in the case cited, are very much like our own. It provides that where a bill which has been presented to the governor cannot be returned to the house in which it originated with the governor's objections thereto because of the adjournment of the legislature, it shall become a law unless the governor shall file the same with his objections in the office of the secretary of the Commonwealth, and give notice thereof by public proclamation within thirty days after such adjournment. The governor is also given "power to disapprove of any item or items of any bill making appropriations of money, embracing distinct items," and it is declared in the same section that "the part or parts of the bill approved shall be the law, and the item or items of appropriation disapproved shall be void, unless repassed according to the rules and limitations prescribed for the passage of other bills over the executive veto."

The reasons given by the court, in the opinion delivered by Mr. Justice Mitchell, for declaring the power conferred upon the governor to disapprove of part and approve part of the same item are substantially as follows: That the disapproval by the governor, commonly known as a veto, is essentially a legislative act; and that the fact that the governor is limited to negation or concurrence and cannot affirmatively initiate or amend legislation, does not take away the legislative character of his act. That the presumption is that within its limited sphere of negation the power applies to every branch and subject of the bill to which the legislative powers of the two houses apply. That the veto power as originally confined to approval or disapproval of an entire bill as presented was found to be inadequate to the accomplishment of its full purpose, and that the legislature in framing and passing a bill had full control over every subject and every provision that it contained, and the governor as a co-

ordinate branch of the law-making power, was entitled to
at least a negative of the same extent. That by joining a
number of different subjects in one bill, the governor was
compelled to accept some enactments that he could not approve, or defeat the whole, including some that he thought
desirable or even necessary. That such bills, popularly
called "omnibus" bills, became an evil which the later
changes in the constitution were intended to remedy. That
omnibus bills were done away with by the amendment to the
constitution that no bill shall contain more than one subject
which shall be clearly expressed in its title, but excepting appropriation bills, as to which it seems to be convenient or
necessary that distinct items may be contained therein, although the various items may be so diverse as to come within the description of different subjects. That the constitution meets that difficulty by providing that the general appropriation bill shall embrace nothing but appropriations
for the ordinary expenses of the executive, legislative and
judicial departments of the commonwealth, interest on the
public debt, and for public schools; and that all other appropriations shall be made by separate bills each embracing
but one subject, and granting to the governor the power to
disapprove of any item or items of any bill making appropriations of money, embracing distinct items. That such
provisions distinctly recognize the legislative character of the
governor's part in the passage of bills, and show a purpose
to increase the power and scope of his veto. That "item"
and "part" are used interchangeably in the same sense in the
section granting the power to disapprove of any item or
items of the bill, and declaring that the part or parts of the
bill approved shall be law, and the item or items disapproved
shall be void; that "if any special or different meaning was
attached to the word 'item' the natural mode of expression
would have been to use that word throughout the section,
but for the sake of euphony and to avoid the repetition of
the same word three times in the same sentence, the
draughtsman used the word 'parts' as an evident synonym."

That in ordinary bills the single subject is a unit which admits of approval or disapproval as a whole, without serious inconvenience, even though some of the details may not be acceptable; but that every appropriation, though it be for a single purpose, "necessarily presents two considerations almost equally material, viz.: the subject and the amount. The subject may be approved on its merits, and yet the amount disapproved as out of proportion to the require-- ments of the case, or as beyond the prudent use of the state's income." That the legislature has full control of the appropriation in both its aspects, and the plain intent of the constitution was to give the governor the same control as to disapproval, over each subject and each amount; that a contrary construction would destroy the usefulness of the constitutional provision; and that "if the legislature by putting purpose, subject and amount inseparably together and calling them an item, can coerce the governor to approve the whole or none, then the old evil is revived which this section was intended to destroy." That the practice adopted by the governor was not new in the state, but that in a number of instances parts of appropriation bills had been vetoed by other governors. As to that practice and its effects the court say: "Appellant has argued at some length that none of these instances was actually like the present, and as to the details that much may be conceded. But they all rest on the same principle, the right of the governor in the exercise of his independent legislative judgment to approve an appropriation in part, by reducing the amount fixed by the legislature. As to that principle the executive practice must be considered as settled. While the executive interpretation of his own powers is not binding on the judiciary, it has always been considered as persuasive and entitled to great respect. And where, as in this instance, the practice has been frequent and acquiesced in without objection for a number of years, it should be very clearly shown to be unconstitutional to justify the courts in declaring against it."

The majority of the court appear to have entertained the view that if the constitution should be construed as not authorizing the disapproval of a part of the item, then there would be no appropriation at all for the support of public schools, and thereby the express provision of the constitution would be defeated or violated which requires that the legislature "shall appropriate at least one million dollars each year" for that purpose, for it is said in the opinion of the court, after referring to that constitutional provision: "The appellants have entirely overlooked or misconceived the effect of a partial veto such as was given in the present case. If the disapproval of part and the approval of the rest were not valid acts, then there was no appropriation at all, and the money already received by the schools was illegally paid. For there was no executive approval of an appropriation of $11,000,000." And we suppose that to have been one of the grounds, locally applicable to that state, upon which the provision for the disapproval of an item was construed to authorize the disapproval of part of an item.

Mr. Justice Mestrezat, in a dissenting opinion, referred to the reason for the adoption of the section in question as follows: "Prior to the adoption of the present constitution, the governor was compelled to approve or disapprove the entire appropriation bill, and could not give his consent to some of the items, and withhold it from others, embraced in the bill. This frequently led to the executive being coerced to approve many unwise and improper appropriations, as public necessity would not permit him to disapprove the whole bill. To remedy this evil, the veto power was extended by Section 16 of Article IV so that he might strike out such items of an appropriation as were improper and permit the others to become effective. The section must be construed in the light of the purpose for which it was adopted, and the people did not intend to go further than was necessary to effect that object when they made it a part of the constitution. Whatever veto authority the governor possesses, be it legislative or executive in its character, is, as has been said, conferred upon him by the constitution, and when he claims the right to exercise this power, it is incumbent upon him to show that the people have clearly delegated it to him. The grant of the power must be strictly construed."

Discussing the meaning of the section it was said in the dissenting opinion: "Section 16 confines the use of the veto power to bills making appropriations of money containing more than one item. Such bills are the only ones that may contain 'more than one subject.' As the school appropriation is, by the constitution, required to be embraced in the general appropriation bill, it is 'one subject' of the many that the bill may contain. This could not be reached by the general veto power conferred on the governor. * * * That will authorize him to veto the whole bill, but not a single item of the bill. He must, therefore, resort to the power given him in Section 16. The bill of 1899 'embraces distinct items,' and therefore this provision of the constitution applies to it. The governor could under this authority disapprove of 'any item or items' of the bill. By reference to the act it appears that the appropriations made for the several departments of the government, except that for the support of the public schools, are each divided into, and composed of, several items. The executive may, therefore, in his discretion, disapprove one or more of the items in each or all of the several appropriations. The part or parts of the bill composed of entire items, and not the part or parts of entire items, he may approve and thus make them the law. In other words, the executive has authority to select such of the many items contained in a general appropriation bill as he may desire and disapprove them, and the parts of the bill embracing separate and entire items, which he approves, shall be the law. Item, as used in the constitutional provision, signifies a specific sum appropriated to a specific purpose, and not a fractional part of said sum thus appropriated. Such is the plain language of the instrument, and in its interpretation there is no necessity for resorting to any technical rules of construction or to the exposition of it by former executives. * * * The executive, how-

ever, maintains that his authority to veto is not confined to
'any item or items' of the bill, but that he may disapprove
a 'part of an item,' and such is the argument here by the attorney general for the respondent. This, as we have seen,
is not the plain, obvious meaning of the language used in the
instrument itself. To sustain the position it is argued for
the respondent that, unless his construction be given the
section, and the executive be thereby permitted to annul its
requirements, the governor cannot obey the 4th section of
Article IX and keep the appropriation within the revenues
of the state. This interpretation may appeal strongly to the
lay mind and convince the over-burdened taxpayer that the
executive is enforcing the constitution by violating it, but it
will find no support in the well established canons of constitutional construction. * * * But is such power necessary
to prevent the state from becoming involved beyond its
revenues? Clearly not. The executive has the authority to
veto the whole of any item of, or an entire bill making an
appropriation. Aside from the school fund, he could, therefore have destroyed the entire appropriations if he had so
desired and the emergency had required it. But it may be
suggested that this would have stopped the wheels of government, and would have been a violation of the constitution. Concede it. The executive would then have been
placed in a position of violating another part of the constitution instead of infringing Article IV, Section 16. The
difference is only as to what part of the instrument shall be
violated, and in bestowing upon the governor the authority
to determine which part of the organic law he will enforce
and what part he will annul. Such a construction is not in
consonance with any rule in the books. It is contended by
the respondent that because the governor may disapprove
of a distinct item of an appropriation bill, he may reduce
that item to any sum he may desire to approve. The practical operation of such a construction of his veto power
would be to annul Section 1 of Article II of the constitution
which provides: 'The legislative power of this common-

wealth shall be vested in a general assembly.' It is well known that most of the appropriation bills are passed upon by the governor after the legislature has adjourned. * * * He could, therefore, under the authority claimed by respondent, determine the amount of every appropriation by reducing the various items embraced in general appropriation bills. This is solely a legislative function under the constitution which in no form is granted to him in that instrument. It places the legislature in the position of being able to fix the maximum of an appropriation to any object, subject, however, to the will of the governor whether he will permit the members of that body to exercise their judgment as to the amount of the item appropriated. Such was clearly not the intention of the people who adopted the constitution. The executive may, for any reason deemed sufficient by him, deprive the beneficiary of the item of appropriation, unless subsequently passed over his veto, but he is not empowered to take from the legislature its constitutional prerogative of fixing the amount of the item to be appropriated. That is purely a legislative and not an executive function under the constitution of Pennsylvania."

Referring to the proposition that former governors had interpreted the constitution as conferring authority to veto a part of a single item of an appropriation, the dissenting justice further said: "When the language is plain and the intent of the provision is clearly deducible, extrinsic circumstances and practical construction are not permitted to have any force in its interpretation: (Story on Const. Sec. 407; Cooley's Const. Lim., 84.) The rule, therefore, can not be invoked to aid in the construction of this section of the constitution. I think the section in question is not ambiguous nor susceptible of two interpretations, and hence its language is the sole guide to its construction. However, an examination of the veto messages referred to in the respondent's brief shows that all of them do not support his construction of the constitutional provision in question. Some have no application by reason of dissimilar facts, others suggest ne-

cessity as the basis of their action and interpretation, while
others distinctly recognize the lack of authority in the executive to disapprove of a part of an item.   Such construction
is worthless as a precedent to a court of justice in the interpretation of a constitutional provision."

We have referred to and quoted from the opinions in the
Pennsylvania case so fully for the reason that it is the only
one in which the question as to the authority of the executive to veto a part of a distinct item in a general appropriation bill has been directly decided by any court of last resort, and for the further reason that the opinions forcibly
present the arguments for and against a construction of the
constitutional provision so as to include such authority, and
the grounds upon which the power was maintained and upheld.

In the Texas case of Fulmore v. Lane, *supra,* Mr. Justice
Ramsey, dissenting in part but concurring in the result, said:
"An effort was made in argument to sustain the governor on
the theory that under the constitution he has the right to
reduce any part of an item.   To this contention and claim
we can never give our assent.   If this were conceded, then
it would be within the power of the governor to reduce any
appropriation, where the amount sought to be appropriated
was not fixed in the constitution.   It would authorize, in
respect to the health department, to the comptroller's department, our educational institutions, our eleemosynary institutions, and every department of the state government,
that the governor, when the legislature had properly passed
on the matter and probably adjourned, might reduce and
tear down the appropriations made for the administration
of the affairs of the state in such a way as to beggar and
bankrupt all of them and to deny the representatives of the
people of the state, the legislature duly assembled, any authority or participation whatever in the money mills of the
commonwealth.   Such a proposition involves such intolerable
tyranny and hurtful usurpation as not to be entertained for
one moment.   Nor, it should be said, was the action of the

governor based on this principle, nor does he seem to entertain this belief."

The provision of the constitution of Texas, considered in the case cited, as quoted in the opinion of Mr. Justice Dibrell is as follows: "If any bill presented to the governor contains several items of appropriation, he may object to one or more of such items and approve the other portion of the bill. In such case he shall append to the bill, at the time of signing it, a statement of the items to which he objects, and no item so objected to shall take effect. If the legislature be in session, he shall transmit to the house in which the bill originated a copy of such statement, and the items objected to shall be separately considered. If, on reconsideration, one or more of such items be approved by two-thirds of the members present of each house, the same shall be a part of the law, notwithstanding the objection of the governor." After quoting that provision Judge Dibrell proceeds to say: "As provided for in the foregoing section of the constitution, where any bill providing for several items of appropriation is presented to the governor for his approval, he may object to one or more of such items, which items shall not take effect, unless passed by both houses by two-thirds of the members thereof. If the appropriation for the attorney general's department contained one item of appropriation only, then the governor's veto struck out the whole of the appropriation; but, if the appropriation contained more than one item, the veto struck out only a part of such appropriation. It will therefore be necessary to determine, as a matter of law, whether the appropriation contains one or more items. Having determined that issue, we will then proceed to determine whether the veto of the governor struck out the whole or a part of the appropriation."

The case involved an objection by the governor to an appropriation made for the attorney general's department for two years, viz.: the sum of $83,160, or, as stated in the appropriation act, $41,580 for each of the two years. The governor vetoed the lump sum of $83,160 appropriated for the two years, and also the appropriation of one-half of that sum for the second year, leaving or intending to leave untouched by the veto the sum of $41,580 for the first year. In the veto message the governor stated that the amount which he had not objected to would be subject to the use of the attorney general for the two fiscal years named. It was held by a majority of the court that the appropriation for the attorney general's department, notwithstanding the mention in the act of the aggregate appropriation for the two years contained two distinct items, viz.: $41,580 for each year, authorizing the governor to disapprove of one of them as a separate and distinct item, and allowing the other item to remain appropriated; and that the amount so appropriated was sufficient for the payment of the amount alleged to be due, for which a writ of mandamus was asked against the comptroller.

It is provided in the constitution of Mississippi as follows: "The governor may veto parts of any appropriation bill, and approve parts of the same, and the portions approved shall be law." Referring to that provision it was said in State v. Holder, 76 Miss. 158, 23 So. 643, that it relates to general appropriation bills, or those containing several items of distinct appropriations, and that it applies to such as are made up of parts and consist of portions separable from each other as appropriations; and, further, that it was framed with a view of guarding against the evils of omnibus appropriation bills, securing unrighteous support from diverse interests, and to enable the governor to approve and make law some appropriations, and to put others to the test of securing a two-thirds vote of the legislature as the condition of becoming law. And the true meaning of the section was said to be that "an appropriation bill made up of several parts—that is, distinct appropriations, different, separable, each complete without the others, which may be taken from the bill without affecting the others, which may be separated into different parts complete in themselves—may be approved and become law in accordance with the legislative will, while others of like character may be disapproved and put before the legislature again, dissociated from the other appropriations." Again, in the same connection, the court said: "To allow a single bill entire, inseparable, relating to one thing, containing several provisions, all complementary of each other and constituting one whole, to be picked to pieces and some of the pieces approved and others vetoed, is to divide the indivisible, to make one of several, to distort and pervert legislative action, and by veto, make a two-thirds vote necessary to preserve what a majority passed allowable as to the entire bill, but inapplicable to a unit composed of diverse complementary parts, the whole passed because of each." The particular question as to the power to disapprove of a part of a distinct item of appropriation and approve the remainder was not presented in that case, but it involved the disapproval of certain provisions in a bill appropriating money for a College, to be complied with as conditions before the money appropriated would become available for some of the purposes for which the appropriation was made, and such disapproval was held not to be authorized by the constitutional provision above quoted. But the court's explanation of the true meaning of the provision seems to conflict with the decision in the Pennsylvania case construing words of similar import, and might be held, we think, to deny the power to split a distinct item by disapproving a part of it, for a part of the item would not be "different, separable," and "complete" * * * "which could be taken from the bill without affecting" any other part.

It will thus be observed that there is not a concurrence of judicial opinion respecting the power of the governor to disapprove part of an item under a constitutional provision authorizing him to disapprove an item or items, or part or parts, of an act appropriating money. Some of the grounds of the decision in the Pennsylvania case would not be applicable here. We do not have the practice of former executives showing an interpretation of the constitution favoring the right to disapprove part of an item, but, so far as we are advised, the practice has been the reverse of that, and it has not been suggested that any executive has heretofore assumed the power of reducing an item by approving a part and disapproving a part thereof. Not only is there a conflict in the authorities respecting the interpretation of such a constitutional provision, but judicial opinion differs concerning the effect, as an aid to interpretation, of the former practice of executives, no matter how long continued, in assuming and exercising a veto power, when the right is once questioned. That was considered in the case of May v. Topping, 65 W. Va. 656, 64 S. E. 848, where it was held, under the constitution of West Virginia, that after the legislature has adjourned the governor is without authority to disapprove of an appropriation bill, or of items therein, but must so act, if at all, before adjournment, and communicate his disapproval, with his reasons therefor, to the house in which the bill originated. Answering the argument that it had been the custom to approve appropriation bills, or to disapprove some item therein, within five days after an adjournment of the legislature, and that such custom had never been questioned, the court said: "Such custom, if it has existed as alleged, has been directly contrary to the constitutional provision. No affirmative approval of a general appropriation bill is required, and no disapproval of such bill, or any item therein, is effective, if expressed after adjournment. The rule of contemporaneous or practical construction is sought to be invoked. We are cited to Lewis's Sutherland on Statutory Construction, Sec. 472 *et seq.* This celebrated authority does not justify the position, nor does any authority, in this case. The rule applies only where there is ambiguity and doubt. * * * The rule cannot be applied to overthrow an unambiguous mandate of the law. * * * It was reasonably supposed when these provisions were adopted that they would be fairly dealt with, appropriately and usefully applied, and quite as fairly, appropriately and usefully interpreted by those to whom direction is given thereby. That the section has not hitherto received such interpretation is no reason why it should not in the future. 'Two wrongs cannot make a right.' " Again, the statement in the court's opinion in the Pennsylvania case to the effect that if the acts of the governor in disapproving a part and approving the rest of the item were not valid, then they destroyed the entire appropriation, is contrary to the other decisions and judicial expressions on the subject, where an absolute approval is not essential to the bill becoming a law.

So far, therefore, as a determination of the right of the governor to disapprove part of a distinct item may depend upon authorities, the question appears to be at least a doubtful one. But the conclusion we have reached in this case renders it unnecessary to determine that matter, and, hence, we ought not to assume the delicate responsibility of deciding whether the governor, in this instance, has or has not acted, or attempted to act, in excess of the authority conferred by the constitution. It is clear that if the governor possesses the power, then there is at least the sum of $10,000 appropriated for the contingent expenses of the office of the State Geologist for the two years beginning April 1, 1913, and ending March 31, 1915, and we understand it to be conceded that the expenditure here involved is the first, if not the only one, which has been presented to the auditor for allowance and the issuance of a warrant. And we think it equally clear that if the power is not conferred upon the governor to thus disapprove of a part of an item and approve a part, the action of the governor would be invalid and a nullity, and the entire amount of the appropriation as passed by the legislature for such contingent expenses would be appropriated and available. Hence in either case it would be the duty of the respondent, as state auditor, to allow the bill of the relator, if otherwise proper and regular, and issue a warrant upon the treasurer for the payment thereof.

The appropriation bill in question might have become a law without the affirmative approval of the governor, under the provision found in Section 8 of Article IV, that any bill

not returned by the governor within three days (Sundays
excepted) after its presentation to him shall be a law, unless
the legislature, by its adjournment, prevent its return, in
which case it shall be a law, unless he shall file the same with
his objections in the office of the secretary of state within
fifteen days after such adjournment.   The bill was presented
to the governor on the last day of the session, and to prevent it, or any of the items therein contained, from becoming
law, he would be required to expressly disapprove the same
in the manner provided by the constitution, viz.: by filing
the bill with his objections in the office of the secretary of
state within said period.   Any item not so disapproved,
therefore, became part of the law. We think it clear that
the·above mentioned provision of Section 8 applies as well
to the general appropriation bill as to other bills, for the
section provides that *"every bill* which has passed the legislature" shall, before it becomes a law, be presented to the
governor; and the latter part of the section referring to
"any bill" not returned by the governor, must be given the
same inclusive effect, for it cannot be doubted that it refers
to and is intended to include every bill which is required to
be presented to the governor.   It is evident that the governor
did not intend to veto or disapprove of the entire item of
the appropriation made for the contingent expenses of the
office of the State Geologist, and that he did not, by his indorsement upon the bill, or his communication appended to
it, express a disapproval of the entire item.   Over his official signature attached to the bill it is stated: "This act is
approved save and except the *item or parts of items* specially
noted herewith as being disapproved and as shown by accompanying communication."   Opposite and on the margin
of the item appropriating the sum of $15,000 for the con-
tingent expenses of the office of the State Geologist the following is noted: "$10,000 of item approved, $5,000 of
item disapproved. J. M. C. Governor." And in the communication addressed to the secretary of state and appended
to the enrolled act it is stated by the governor that he ap-

proves of so much of the item referring to the contingent expenses of the geologist's office "as appropriates $10,000," and withholds his approval from $5,000, "leaving the appropriation $10,000." The mere fact that he considered the amount of $15,000 appropriated by the act to be excessive, or beyond the needs of the office of the State Geologist for the ensuing two years, does not amount to a disapproval of the item. Notwithstanding that fact he might have approved the item, explaining, however, in his communication that he considered it to be excessive. We find it impossible to construe the action of the governor with reference to that item as an objection to or a disapproval of the entire item, but on the contrary, it seems to us, that to hold his act to amount to a disapproval of the entire item would distort his language used in explaining his approval and disapproval and in noting upon the margin of the item his approval of part and disapproval of part. Further, if he was without authority to thus split the amount appropriated by that item in the act, then to say that by doing so he has disapproved the entire item would be to give effect to an invalid act and permit it to accomplish the purpose of a disapproval, without which the appropriation would become law. If the authority to disapprove an item in part and approve it in part is not conferred upon the governor, his act in attempting to do so would be a nullity, and necessarily ineffectual for the purpose intended, or any other purpose, for, being unauthorized, it would be void, and entitled to no consideration whatever. The effect would be the same, necessarily, we think, as if no such partial disapproval, or other disapproval, had been attempted. Either the governor's signature to the bill would stand without any qualification as to such an item, or the item would have force as law without approval because not disapproved. By "objections" or "disapproval" is meant lawful objections or disapproval—objections or disapproval within the authority of the governor, and expressed in the manner provided by the organic law. By "objections" to a bill when returned to the house in which it originated, or when filed with the secretary of state after adjournment, is meant an expression of disapproval. The word is used in the sense of disapproval. That the governor did not intend or propose to object to, disapprove of, or veto the entire item seems to us to be unquestionable. He stated, indeed, that he approved of the larger part of the amount appropriated for the purpose, and expressly confined his disapproval to a part only of the amount. If it be assumed that the power of such a disapproval is not conferred upon him, then it would be no disapproval at all. The principle thus stated, seems to us not only to be sound, but we believe it to be well settled by the authorities.

In the case of Porter v. Hughes, 4 Ariz. 1, 32 Pac. 165, a case cited perhaps more than any other upon this question, it appeared that an item in the general appropriation act appropriating money for "territorial salaries of the district judges, as provided by law," was attempted to be disapproved by the governor by stating in signing the act that the same was approved, "except as to sub-division 17 of Section 1, which applies to appropriations for salaries of judges of the District Court." And the veto was sustained by the body in which the act originated. The question considered in the case was whether said item became a law at the time the governor affixed his signature to the act, notwithstanding his attempt to except the item from his approval of the bill as a whole. The court said: "What is commonly known as the 'veto power' was conferred upon the governor of the Territory by the Act of Congress of July 19, 1876. By the terms of this act the governor, in exercising the power, is limited to one of the following courses of action: First, if he approve a bill, he shall sign it; second, if he shall not approve it he shall return it, together with his objections, to the house in which it originated; third, he may retain a bill presented to him for his approval until it becomes a law by the expiration of ten days after said presentation, provided the assembly shall not have adjourned *sine die* during the ten days, in which case it shall not become a law. By the organic act referred to, whatever the governor may do in the premises has reference to a bill in its entirety, and not to any of its parts. A bill is approved as a whole. The signature of the governor affixed to the bill is the evidence of his approval. In the case of the act in question, it being admitted that the governor affixed his signature to the same, this action of the governor, being in full compliance with the organic act, must be taken, therefore, as an approval of the whole bill as passed by the assembly, and as presented to him for his official action. It becomes immaterial what the governor may have done thereafter in the way of adding his objections to any part of said bill, for he had already exercised the full measure of his power in respect thereto." The court held that the item in question was valid and that the plaintiff, one of the parties for whose benefit the appropriation was made, was entitled to a peremptory mandamus upon the auditor to issue a warrant for the amount so appropriated and at the time payable. The same comments might be made with reference to the item involved in this case should the governor be without authority to disapprove it in part, for each of the distinct items in the bill. as to approval and disapproval, by reason of Section 9 of Article IV, could be separately considered, the same as though each constituted a separate bill. More than that, under our constitution, the disapproval of part being unauthorized, it would be ineffective, and the item would become law, without the governor's signature approving the act or any part of it. In the dissenting opinion in Commonwealth v. Barnett, *supra,* after declaring the executive to have been without authority to disapprove a part of the item appropriated by the legislature for the support of the public schools, it was said: "The bill having been approved by the governor, and the exception therefrom of a part of the school fund item being void, the entire amount became effective for the purpose for which it was appropriated."

In May v. Topping, *supra,* wherein it was held that the governor was without authority to disapprove an item in an appropriation bill after the adjournment of the legislature, as he had attempted to do, it was said that disapproval in any other form or manner than that authorized by the constitution would not affect an appropriation act or an item therein.   And again, "No disapproval of such bill, or any item therein, is effective, if expressed after adjournment." And concluding, the court said: "It appearing that the governor did not disapprove the item * * * within the time prescribed by the constitution, and in the manner therein directed, the writ will be awarded."   The case was one for a peremptory mandamus to compel the certification of a copy of the act and to include in such copy the item which the governor had attempted to veto.   It appears that the constitution permitted the governor in the case of a bill making appropriation of money, embracing distinct items, to disapprove the bill, or any item or appropriation therein, and it required him to communicate such disapproval with his reasons therefor to the house in which the bill originated, and that "all items not disapproved shall have the force and effect of law according to the original provisions of the bill," and that "any item or items so disapproved shall be void unless re-passed by a majority of each House according to the rules and limitations prescribed in the preceding section in reference to other bills."   The court said that it was the action in communicating such disapproval, with the reasons therefor, to the house in which the bill originated, that consummates and effects a veto of the item, and that the communication of the governor's disapproval, with his reasons therefor, is the disapproval itself.   Discussing the meaning of the words "so disapproved" in the provision that an item so disapproved shall be void unless re-passed, etc., the court say: "Clearly they relate not simply to disapproval in the mind of the governor, but to some act of disapproval, some manner of disapproval.   That act or manner of disapproval, provided for just above those words, and to which 'so disapproved' clearly relates, is by communication with reasons to the house in which the bill originated."   The same principle was again announced in Woodall v. Darst, (W. Va.) 77, S. E. 264, the court saying, in conclusion: "The veto in the present case was ineffectual to defeat the passage of the special appropriation in favor of relator."

In the Texas case of Fulmore v. Lane, *supra*, it appeared that, following the statement in the act of the total amount appropriated for the attorney general's department for two years, and the amount appropriated for each year, was a paragraph referred to in the opinion as the "guidance clause" making certain provisions concerning the expenditure of the sum or sums appropriated. This paragraph or clause was stricken out by the governor and he stated in his communication to the secretary of state explaining his action upon the bill that he disapproved the said paragraph, giving the reasons therefor. It was held that the governor was without authority to veto that part of the bill which directed the method of the expenditure of the money appropriated, and further, that, since the disapproval was unauthorized, it was not effective for any purpose, and that the paragraph so attempted to be stricken out remained as a part of the act. In the opinion of Mr. Justice Dibrell it is said: "It follows conclusively that where the veto power is attempted to be exercised to object to a paragraph or portion of a bill other than an item or items, or to language qualifying an appropriation or directing the method of its uses, he exceeds the constitutional authority vested in him, and his objection to such paragraph, or portion of a bill, or in qualifying an appropriation, or directing the method of its use, becomes noneffective. So that we are constrained to hold that that portion of the veto message contained in sub-division 3 of the statement of objections appended to the appropriation bill and filed in the office of the secretary of state was unauthorized, and therefore non-effective, and the paragraph so attempted to be stricken out will remain as a part of the appropriation bill." In the opinion of Mr. Justice Ramsey, who stated his judgment to be that the appropriation in question consisted of a single item, and, therefore, beyond

executive veto, unless vetoed in its entirety, it was said that
all of the justices had agreed that the "guidance clause"
must remain as a part of the law.

In the Mississippi case of State v. Holder, *supra*, it appeared that the governor had expressed his approval of that
part of the bill which included the appropriation, but had
disapproved part of the section declaring certain conditions
upon the expenditure of the money. The constitution provided: "If any bill shall not be returned by the governor
within five days (Sundays excepted) after it has been presented to him, it shall become a law in like manner as if he
had signed it, unless the legislature, by adjournment, prevent
its return, in which case it shall be a law unless sent back
within three days after the beginning of the next session of
the Legislature. No bill shall be approved when the Legislature is not in session." It was held that the bill in question
was an entire thing, inseperable in its provisions and to be
approved or disapproved as such, and not having been signed
as a whole, was not made law by the partial and qualified
approval which it received. It will be observed that by the
constitutional provision above quoted a bill would not become
a law when not signed by the Governor, and its return was
prevented by adjournment, until there was an opportunity to
return it within three days after the beginning of the next
session of the Legislature, but that such a bill would become
a law "unless sent back within three days after the beginning
of the next session." Since, in order to make a bill a law
immediately, it was necessary that it be lawfully approved,
the court held that as the bill had not been approved as a
whole it did not become a law even in part, and that "the
bill, in legal contemplation, must be held to be yet in the
hands of the Governor, and may become law unless sent
back by him within three days after the beginning of the
next session of the Legislature." As we understand the
decision, therefore, the court held not only that the qualified
approval was not an approval authorized by the constitution,
but that the disapproval was not authorized or lawful, for

which reason the bill would become law unless sent back within three days after the beginning of the next legislative session. Applying that principle to the case in hand, it would follow under our constitution, which provides that a bill received too late to be returned to the Legislature within the specified time will become a law unless disapproved within the period limited for that purpose after adjournment, an unauthorized disapproval would not defeat the bill.

The same principle, or one controlled by the same reasons, was announced in Oklahoma in the case of Regents of the State University v. Trapp, Auditor, 28 Okl. 83, 113 Pac. 910. It appears from the opinion in that case that the constitution of Oklahoma provides that, "If any bill or resolution shall not be returned by the Governor within five days (Sundays excepted) after it shall have been presented to him, the same shall be a law in like manner as if he had signed it, unless the Legislature shall, by their adjournment, prevent its return, in which case it shall not become a law without the approval of the Governor. No bill shall become a law after the final adjournment of the Legislature, unless approved by the Governor within fifteen days after such adjournment." And the court say: "By reason of that section no bill which is sent to the Governor less than five days before the adjournment of the Legislature can become a law without the approval of the Governor, unless passed over his veto; and it cannot become a law with his approval, unless approved by him within fifteen days after such adjournment." It appears also that the constitution contains a provision authorizing the Governor to disapprove any item contained in a bill making appropriations of money embracing distinct items. The bill there under consideration, in the first section thereof, appropriated a certain sum for the support and maintenance of the State University for the ensuing two years. In Section 2 the amount so appropriated was apportioned for the various purposes of the university. The Governor approved the bill except as to certain items contained in Section 2, each of which, with a single exception, he reduced. The court held that the bill did not embrace distinct items of appropriation, but a single item, with direction how that item shall be expended, together with direction as to how other items of appropriation made by other acts of the Legislature shall be apportioned and expended; that, therefore, the bill did not come within the section permitting the Governor to disapprove of a distinct item in an appropriation bill; and that having approved the bill in part and disapproved it in part, without authority so to do, his sanction of the parts of the bill approved was ineffectual to give those parts the force of a law. There, an affirmative approval was essential to the bill becoming a law, and the approval being a qualified one, and unauthorized in that form, it was held not to amount to an approval at all within the meaning of the constitution, and not effectual for any purpose. If that be true, we think the same reasons require it to be held that where an affirmative approval is not required, but the bill or the items contained therein will become law unless disapproved, an unauthorized disapproval will be ineffectual. Conceding that where an approval is required to give the act force as law, words qualifying the approval, showing a purpose to approve it only in part, will nullify the approval and render it ineffectual, it does not, we think, reasonably follow that similar words qualifying an approval and showing a purpose to disapprove in part, will amount to a disapproval of the entire bill, or of an item in it affected by the attempted disapproval, where such partial disapproval is unauthorized by the constitution, and the bill or the particular item would become a law unless disapproved.

We conclude for the above reasons that there is at least $10,000 appropriated for the contingent expenses of the office of the State Geologist for the two years ending March 31, 1915, and a peremptory writ will be awarded requiring the allowance of the claim of the relator and the issuance of a warrant upon the State Treasurer for the payment thereof. Whether or not the entire amount as passed by the Legislature is appropriated, we find it unnecessary to decide, and, therefore, refrain from doing to.

Scott, C. J., concurs.

BEARD, JUSTICE (dissenting).

There are three ways and only three ways by which any bill can become law. (1) By being passed by the vote of a majority of the members elected to each house and the approval of the Governor. (2) By being passed by the Legislature over the Governor's veto. (3) By being passed by the Legislature and retained by the Governor without action thereon for the length of time prescribed in the constitution. On the other hand, no bill becomes a law which has been returned by the Governor with objections thereto to the house in which it originated, without further action by the Legislature; or when he has filed it in the office of the Secretary of State, with objections thereto, within fifteen days after the adjournment of the Legislature. It is the same identical bill, in the same language and containing the same terms and conditions, which, to become law, must be adopted by each house and be either expressly approved by the Governor, or to which he has waived his right to object by retaining it without action thereon beyond the time fixed by the constitution. It appears clear to my mind that no bill can become law to which the Governor has filed objections, whether those objections are sent to the house in which the bill originated, or are filed with the bill in the office of the Secretary (unless in the former case the bill is reconsidered and passed over the veto), any more than it can become law by the concurrence of one house and the Governor, without the assent or over the objection of the other house. In the present case it is conceded that the part or item of the general appropriation bill under consideration, making an appropriation for the office of State Geologist, is a "distinct item" within the meaning of the constitution, and as such could be vetoed by the Governor without disturbing the other items of appropriation embraced in the bill. And I think it must also be conceded that the Governor has the power to veto a bill appropriating money, or a distinct item of the general appropriation bill, for the reason that in his judgment the amount appropriated is too large, as well as for any other reason.

We must then look to the action taken by the Governor on
this item and determine its effect; and in so doing must consider what he wrote on the bill itself and what he said in his
communication to the Secretary of State. In signing the
general bill he expressly excepted certain "items or parts of
items specially noted herewith as being disapproved," so
that it cannot be said that in so signing the general bill he
intended to, or did in fact, approve the excepted items,
among which was the one here in question. On the margin
opposite this item he wrote "$10,000 of item approved,
$5,000 of item disapproved." There is but one construction,
in my opinion, that can be put upon that language, and that
is, that it was a disapproval of the item as it was written
and passed by the Legislature. In his communication accompanying the bill he says: "I approve so much of this
item as appropriates $10,000, and withhold my approval
from $5,000, leaving the appropriation $10,000." That was
also clearly a disapproval of the item as written and passed
by the Legislature, and a positive objection to the item becoming law in form and substance as it was presented to
him and to which both houses had agreed. The reason for
the objection and why he would not permit it to become law
was that the amount appropriated was, in his judgment, too
large—a good and valid objection if standing alone. But
how did the statement that it was $5,000 too much lessen or
remove the force of the objection to the item as presented to
him? It is true, he undertook to approve or make an appropriation of $10,000; but such a bill never passed either
house. In this instance the amount of the appropriation
was the principal question for consideration by the Legislature. The office was created by the constitution and the
salary of the officer had been fixed by law, so that the amount
to be appropriated for the contingent expenses of the office
was the chief matter to be determined and fixed in the item.
If any other amount either greater or less than $15,000 was
considered at any time during the pendency of the bill in
either house it was not agreed to; but $15,000 was the

amount that received the vote of a majority of the members elected to each house. No other amount ever received such vote, and could not, therefore, become law under the plain provisions of Section 25, Article III, of the constitution, which provides, "No bill shall become a law, except by a vote of a majority of all the members elected to each house," etc. And in Section 1 of the same article it is written, "The legislative power shall be vested in a Senate and House of Representatives," etc. These measures the people of the state in their sovereign capacity adopted and declared to be the supreme law of the state, binding upon and to be observed and obeyed by all and by every department of the state government. The constitution is a limitation upon the powers of the Legislature; but the authority therein given · to the Governor to veto an act of the Legislature is a grant of power. It is negative, not affirmative, destructive, not creative. He can by virtue of the power so granted prevent an act of the Legislature becoming law except by the vote of an increased majority of each house; but he cannot alter the language or terms of an act and make that law to which the Legislature has not given its assent. He cannot make that conditional which the Legislature has declared shall be unconditional, or the converse. Either would be legislation by the Governor without the consent of the Legislature. Let us suppose that the general appropriation bill embracing the item in question had been passed and presented to the Governor more than three days (Sundays excepted) before its adjournment and he had returned a copy of this item to the house in which it originated with exactly the same indorsements thereon and the same objection contained in his communication transmitting it to the Secretary of State. Would it have become the law appropriating $10,000 or $15,000, or at all, without further action by the Legislature? I think not. The effect of the objection is the same in each case, and I am unable to discover any provision of the constitution to the contrary. As I understand it, a veto is an objection by the Governor to a bill as written and passed by the Legislature becoming law, whatever his objection or the reasons therefor may be. As above stated, it is the bill as written and presented to him that is or is not to become law, and no other. If it is permissible for him to change the amount of an appropriation, why may he not by the same authority change the objects, terms or conditions of the bill and make it a valid enactment without further action by the Legislature? The provisions of Section 9, Article IV, of the constitution were evidently intended to and do give to the Governor exactly the same right, neither greater nor less, to object to any "distinct item" of the general appropriation bill that is granted to him by Section 8 of the same article with respect to a separate bill; and that is to approve it in its entirety or to object to it. The objection may go only to some condition or term contained in the bill which causes him to withhold his approval of it in its entirety; but whatever the objection may be, if made, it prevents the bill from becoming law until passed over the objection, or it is changed to conform to the wishes of the Governor by the Legislature—the only body empowered by the constitution to make or change the statute law. To construe the constitution as granting to the Governor the power to reduce the amount of an appropriation made by the Legislature and make it valid for the reduced amount, is to limit the powers of the Legislature to determining the purposes for which public funds shall be appropriated and fixing the maximum amount of such appropriations, leaving the amount to be fixed by the Governor, and thus substituting his judgment for that of the Legislature. In the present case the Governor objected to the appropriation as made by the Legislature because in his judgment it was too large. That, in my opinion, was an objection to the item *as it was written* becoming law, and constituted a veto of the item; and the attempt of the Governor to make an appropriation for a different amount without the consent of the Legislature was beyond his constitutional authority and void. With all due respect for the opinion of my associates, I am constrained to differ from them, and believe the writ should be denied.

FOURT v. EDWARDS ET AL.

(No. 717.)

TRUSTS—SALE OF LAND BY TRUSTEE—LIABILITY—DUTY TO ACCOUNT.

1. Where one holding the legal title to land in trust for the joint use and benefit of himself and another has sold and conveyed the land without the knowledge and consent of the other party, the latter is entitled to recover from such trustee the value of his interest in the land, or the amount for which it was sold if the value is not shown to exceed that amount.

2. In an action to recover the alleged value of an undivided one-half interest in and to a certain tract of land, it was alleged that the legal title was held by the defendant in trust for the joint use and benefit of himself and plaintiff, and that without the knowledge or consent of the plaintiff the defendant conveyed the same, together with other land in which the plaintiff had no interest, for a stated amount. It appeared on the trial that the defendant had sold the land in which plaintiff was interested, together with other adjoining land, at an agreed price of forty dollars per acre for the entire tract, that the land was of little value for agricultural purposes, and if of greater value than the amount received it was because of its value as oil land; but the land was undeveloped, and no discovery of oil had been made thereon, though it included the south end of an oil dome upon which producing wells had been drilled at a distance of from three-quarters of a mile to a mile therefrom, and it was not shown that the plaintiff or the trustees could have obtained more than the latter received for it, nor that there was an opportunity to sell it for a greater price than that for which it was sold. *Held,* that the value based upon its supposed character as oil land was speculative, and that the plaintiff was properly limited in his recovery to the amount for which his interest was sold.

[Decided June 20, 1913.]   (132 Pac. 1147.)

ERROR to the District Court, Fremont County; HON. CHARES E. CARPENTER, Judge.

The material facts are stated in the opinion.

E. H. Fourt, for plaintiff in error.

The findings of the trial court as to the value of the property in question, and the value of the one-half interest of the plaintiff is against the weight of the evidence. The only evidence worthy of consideration shows that the value of the tract in which plaintiff was interested was from $250 to $500 per acre.

The defense was that the agreement entered into between the parties for the purpose of filing land scrip to secure title to the land in question was to obtain title to public lands, and was a fraud upon the government and could not be enforced. This filing was contested and the location was sustained because there had been no discovery of oil upon the land. And it is settled that such a location is valid if made before discovery of oil, although the parties may have believed that oil might be discovered within the boundaries of the land. (Olive L. & D. Co. v. Olmstead, 103 Fed. 568.) Mere surface indications do not constitute a discovery of oil, and will not support an oil location. (Bay v. Oklahoma &c. Min. Co., 73 Pac. 936.) Where parties to a suit had agreed to file land scrip upon certain public lands, and the case was brought in equity to determine the rights of the parties to the lands so obtained, it was held that the lands were not fraudulently taken, and that the court would afford relief. (Keeley v. Gregg, 83 Pac. 222.) No valid right to public lands by merely locating them as mineral lands can be secured until a discovery is made. (Whiting v. Straup, 95 Pac. 849; Phillips v. Brill (Wyo.), 95 Pac. 856.) And under the public land laws land is not held to be mineral land until there has been a discovery. (Belk v. Meagher, 104 U. S. 279; Atherton v. Fowler, 96 U. S. 513; S. N. Oil Co. v. Holden Oil Co., 98 Fed. 673.) Courts of equity will follow trust property into the hands of the trustee or those of his assigns who have notice of the trust, and if the property has been sold the *cestui que* trust may elect to follow the property or have personal judgment against the trustee. (Olive v. Piatt, 3 How. (U. S.) 622; Seymour v. Freer, 8 Wall. 202; Wylie v. Coxe, 15 How. (U. S.) 416.)

No brief for defendant in error.

SCOTT, CHIEF JUSTICE.

The plaintiff in error, who was the plaintiff below, brought this action in the District Court of Fremont County against Edwards, one of the defendants in error, as a defendant, to recover the alleged value of an undivided one-half interest in and to the southwest quarter of the northeast quarter of section twenty-four, township thirty-two north, of range ninety-nine west, in Fremont County, Wyoming, legal title of which is alleged to have been held by defendant Edwards in trust for the joint use and benefit of himself and the plaintiff. It is alleged that the defendant Edwards, without the knowledge or consent of plaintiff, conveyed the property, together with other property in which the plaintiff had no interest, to Richard C. Adams for the agreed price of $8,800, of which sum $1,000 was paid in cash and a note for the sum of $7,800, dated September 10, 1908, secured by mortgage on the real estate mentioned, together with other real estate, was given to secure the balance of the purchase price. It is further alleged that afterwards and on May 22, 1909, the defendant Oliver C. Edwards, without the knowledge and consent of plaintiff, entered into a contract with defendant Power to transfer and convey to him the said promissory note and mortgage so executed as aforesaid for the sum of $7,800 for the consideration of $6,800, and that at the time of making this contract Power paid $2,000 cash to defendant Edwards and the balance of said note, amounting to $4,800, was by its terms due and payable on or before September 15. 1909. That, upon demand duly made, defendant Edwards has refused to account to plaintiff for his share of the proceeds received by him for the trust property, that he is insolvent, has converted such proceeds to his own use, and that unless Powers be enjoined from paying to Edwards and the latter be enjoined from receiving the balance to be paid on such note the plaintiff will be irreparably injured and without remedy. A temporary injunction was issued. The case was tried to the court and the court found that the trust relation existed and sale made as alleged in the petition; that defendant refused to account for the plaintiff's interest in the property, and assessed plaintiff's damages at the sum of $800, for which amount judgment was rendered and the injunction made perpetual. The plaintiff moved upon the evidence to vacate the judgment and for judgment awarding him the sum of $4,800. This motion was overruled and the plaintiff brings error.

The amount to which plaintiff was entitled to recover is the sole question presented by this record. It was alleged in the petition that the value of plaintiff's interest in the land in controversy was $4,800. The defendant alleged that plaintiff had no interest whatever in the land. There was also a general denial. Upon the pleadings and issues thus presented, if the plaintiff prevailed as he did in establishing a trust in his favor, then he was entitled to recover the value of his interest in the land. The case was tried upon the theory that the land was valuable because of the oil which it was supposed to contain. It was sold by Edwards, the trustee, to Adams as a contiguous part of a 220-acre tract at the agreed price of $40 per acre for the entire tract. There is no controversy in the evidence that the land was of little value for agricultural purposes, and if valuable at all it was for oil purposes. The evidence upon the question of value was directed to that question and the stratification, geological formation, development of oil in the vicinity, and that the land included the south end of an oil dome upon which though farther north producing wells had been drilled at a distance of three-fourths of a mile to a mile, and plaintiff's evidence as to its value was based upon the asserted mineral character of the land and was to the effect that it was worth $250 per acre. The land was undeveloped and no discovery of oil had been made thereon. It was not known whether it was valuable as oil land or not. It was not shown that plaintiff or the trustee could obtain more than the latter received for it, nor that there was an opportunity to sell it for a greater price than that for which the trustee sold it. One of plaintiff's witnesses said there was no market value or price for such land, but that it was worth just what one could get for it. In this state of the evidence we are of the opinion that, in the absence of any evidence that he could obtain more, the value claimed by the plaintiff was purely speculative and that the court correctly found for him in the sum of $800, that being the amount for which plaintiff's one-half interest in the tract was sold. We discover no error in the record and the judgment will be affirmed.   *Affirmed.*

Potter, J., and Beard, J., concur.

McINTOSH ET AL. v. WALES.
(No. 708.)

Malicious Prosecution—Elements of Action—Termination of Prosecution—Probable Cause—Evidence—Malice—Inference—Witnesses — Competency — Damages — Counsel Fees—Reasonableness—Punitive Damages—Appeal and Error—Joint Assignment of Error.

1. The necessary elements to support an action for malicious prosecution are the institution of the proceedings without probable cause, with malice, that they have terminated in plaintiff's favor, and that plaintiff has been damaged.

2. Where defendants furnished a justice of the peace information and signed and made oath to the complaint upon which a warrant was issued charging plaintiff with stealing cattle, the fact that they took no further part in the prosecution and that it was dismissed by the justice at the request of the prosecuting attorney without the submission of any evidence did not relieve the defendants from liability in a civil action for damages, if their acts were malicious and without probable cause.

3. Such dismissal by the prosecuting attorney constituted a termination of the proceedings in favor of the plaintiff so as to enable plaintiff to maintain an action for malicious prosecution.

4. Where plaintiff was actually arrested and held under a warrant issued under a complaint sworn to by defendants, the

fact that such complaint did not state a criminal offense was no defense to an action for malicious prosecution.

5. While the dismissal of the criminal prosecution complained of at the instance of the prosecuting attorney without submitting any evidence was admissible and sufficient to show a termination of the proceeding alleged to be malicious, such act of the prosecuting attorney was not evidence against the defendants in an action for malicious prosecution upon the issue of want of probable cause in commencing the prosecution, nor was it evidence of malice.

6. Probable cause, to justify a criminal prosecution, may exist, even though the prosecuting witness acts maliciously if the charge be true; and, even if the charge be not true, if such witness acts honestly and in good faith, basing his charge upon facts which he in fact believes to be true, but which afterwards turn out to be false, he cannot be said to have acted without probable cause.

7. The dismissal of the prosecution at the request of the prosecuting attorney by the justice, who was acting in taking the complaint and issuing the warrant as a magistrate vested with authority to hold a preliminary examination and commit upon finding that there was probable cause to believe that a crime had been committeed and that the one charged therewith was guilty, was not a judicial determination by said justice of the existence of probable cause for the institution of the criminal proceeding, nor evidence thereof in an action for malicious prosecution subsequently instituted and based upon such proceeding.

8. The verdict of the jury in an action for malicious prosecution being general was a finding upon all the issues in favor of the plaintiff.

9. Malice necessary to be shown in an action for malicious prosecution may be inferred from a showing of want of probable cause, but want of probable cause will not be inferred from proof of malice alone.

10. Where, in an action for malicious prosecution, based upon the arrest of the plaintiff under a warrant issued upon a complaint sworn to by the defendants charging the plaintiff with stealing cattle, the plaintiff testified that she never stole any cattle from the defendants or either of them, and was permitted to and did introduce as part of her affirmative case proof of her general good character or reputation for honesty and integrity in the vicinity in which she lived, and one of the defendants was her uncle and had known her in the community where she lived from

childhood, *held*, that said acquaintance was sufficient to raise a presumption of his knowledge of her good reputation, and such proof was sufficient *prima facie* to show want of probable cause.

11. The defendants in an action for malicious prosecution, to show that they acted upon probable cause in instigating the criminal proceeding upon which the action was based, introduced evidence tending to show that plaintiff's reputation for honesty and integrity was bad, and evidence of different circumstances of which defendants had knowledge prior to the prosecution. *Held*, that, conceding that such information standing alone, if honesty believed, would be sufficient to raise in the mind of a reasonably prudent man ·a well grounded suspicion that plaintiff had at various times prior to the prosecution been guilty of the crime charged against her, and might constitute probable cause for the prosecution, the testimony as to the circumstances aforesaid having been denied by the plaintiff, causing a direct conflict in the evidence as to the facts relied upon to constitute probable cause, the question was one for the jury.

12. In an action for malicious prosecution the fact that by her arrest plaintiff's credit at a bank was injured could be· proven by her testimony, as well as by the officials of the bank, for it would be a fact within her knowledge, but whether evidence of such fact was competent was not decided, the only objection to the evidence having been that the best evidence would be that of the bank or persons connected with it.

13. In an action for malicious prosecution where plaintiff prayed for punitive damages, evidence of the financial condition of one of the defendants and the extent of his land holdings was admissible, not only upon the question of punitive damages, but as bearing upon the question of the motive of said defendant in instituting the prosecution claimed to have been malicious, plaintiff claiming that said defendant had joined in instituting the prosecution to get her and her husband out of the country and so have freer access to a range for his cattle.

14. In an action for malicious prosecution plaintiff was entitled to recover a reasonable attorney's fee for services in procuring her release from the prosecution alleged to have been instituted maliciously and without probable cause.

15. Where plaintiff, in an action for malicious prosecution, and her husband had been arrested for stealing cattle in the

prosecution complained of, and the hearing was held in a country precinct eighty miles from the county seat where the attorneys for the plaintiff resided, without railroad connection, an attorney's fee of $250 paid by plaintiff and her husband for representing her at said hearing to procure her release would not be held unreasonable, though there was no testimony upon the question as to the reasonableness of said amount.

16. There being evidence of actual malice on the part of the defendant punitive damages are recoverable in an action for malicious prosecution.

17. Where, to reverse a judgment in an action against several defendants for malicious prosecution which included punitive damages, all of said defendants joined in assigning error, and it appeared that actual malice warranting the recovery of punitive damages had been proved against one of said defendants, the other defendants were not in a position to complain of the allowance of such damages.

[Decided June 20, 1913.]   (134 Pac. 274.)

Error to the District Court, Fremont County; Hon. Charles E. Carpenter, Judge.

The material facts are stated in the opinion.

M. C. Brown, for plaintiffs in error. (*Ben Sheldon,* of Counsel.)

An action for malicious prosecution cannot be maintained upon an arrest made upon a complaint charging no crime, or where the alleged complaint was prepared by the justice of the peace and only signed by the parties giving the information to the justice, and said parties took no part thereafter in the arrest or proceeding. The complaint upon which this action was based lacked the necessary elements to charge a crime. (Comp. Stat. 1910, Secs. 5827, 5829, 5830-5832.) It was proper for the Prosecuting Attorney to dismiss such prosecution, for there was nothing to prosecute. No judgment could have been lawfully entered even upon a plea of guilty. The proceeding was entirely void and, therefore, cannot be held sufficient to support an action for malicious prosecution by the prosecuting attorney. Even if the warrant of arrest had been lawfully issued, it furnished no ground whatever for an action for malicious prosecution and did not indicate want of probable cause. (Fleckinger v. Wagner, 46 Md. 480; Yocum v. Polly, 36 Am. Dec. 583; Cockfield v. Braveboy, 39 Am. Dec. 123; Joiner v. Steamship Co., 86 Ga. 238; Purcell v. McNamara, 9 East, 361; Green v. Vochran, 43 Ia. 544; Goring v. Fraser, 76 Me. 37; Parker v. Farley, 10 Cush. 279; Stewart v. Sonneborn, 8 Otto, 25 L. Ed. 117; Baird v. Householder, 32 Pa. St. 168; Perker v. Huntington, 2 Grey, 128; Brown v. Lackanan, 12 Cush. 482; Halburstadt v. Ins. Co., 195 N. Y. 1; Davis v. McMillan, 142 Mich. 391.) Many cases hold that where the committing magistrate discharges the accused, such discharge, or the failure of the grand jury to indict, does not show a want of probable cause, and such dismissal of an action will not alone be sufficient to sustain an action for malicious prosecution. (Thompson v. Rubber Co., 56 Conn. 493; Heldt v. Webster, 60 Tex. 207; Ganea v. So. Pac. R. R. Co., 51 Cal. 140; Froman v. Smith, 12 Am. Dec. 265; Stant v. Van Bethuysen, 36 La. Ann. 476; Apgar v. Woods, 43 N. J. L. 57; Davis v. McMillan, *supra*.) The dismissal of the prosecution was by a public officer, and the defendants had nothing to do with it. They cannot be held in anywise responsible for it, and hence such action of dismissal cannot be deemed as evidence of want of probable cause. (Stewart v. Sonneborn, 98 U. S. 187.) Under the circumstances of this case the question of probable cause was a question for the court. (Id.) There is nothing to be found in the entire testimony of the plaintiff to show want of probable cause. While evidence might have been received of the financial condition of the defendant Johnson, evidence merely that he owned land without showing anything as to value was inadmissible. There is no suggestion in the case as to the relevancy of that testimony. That there was probable cause for the complaint made before the justice seems to have been abundantly established by the confession of the plaintiff herself to one of the defendants and others that she had stolen a calf belonging to another party. There is nothing in

the evidence showing the good reputation of the plaintiff or
that the fact of such reputation ever came to the knowledge
of the defendants, appellants here, and hence that evidence
does not tend to show want of probable cause.

To authorize punitive damages it must be shown that a
defendant acted with malice or wrong motive. (12 Ency.
Law, 23; Tracy v. Swartwort, 10 Pet. (U. S.) 80; Bennet
v. Smith, 23 Hun, 50.) Where there is no evidence warranting punitive damages the court should instruct that they
are not recoverable. (R. R. Co. v. Bridges, 86 Ala. 448,
11 Am. St. Rep. 58.) It is error to submit the question of
punitive damages to a jury in the absence of any requisite
elements for the application of the rule allowing them. (12
Ency. Law, 53; R. R. Co. v. Arms, 91 U. S. 489; R. R. Co.
v. Hall, 87 Ala. 708, 13 Am. St. Rep. 84; Paine v. R. R. Co.,
45 Ia. 569; R. R. Co. v. McGinnis, 46 Kan. 109; Caldwell
v. Steamboat Co., 47 N. Y. 282.) The question may be for
the court if there is no disagreement on any circumstances
materially bearing on the principle of exemplary damages.
(R. R. Co. v. Scurr, 59 Miss. 456.) The damages allowed
are excessive. Damages for injury to credit is too remote,
uncertain and speculative. (Dorr Cattle Co. v. Bank, 127
Ia. 153.)

Both malice and want of probable cause must concur to
support an action for malicious prosecution. In such an
action there must be more than malice in the ordinary sense
of the word. With reference to such an action it means
"such a state of mind as leads to the intentional doing of
some wrongful act knowing it to be without just cause or
legal excuse." (Noble v. White, 103 Ia. 361; Biering v.
Bank, 69 Tex. 599.) A prosecution for the purpose of
making an example of the accused for the benefit of the
public is not malicious. (Coleman v. Allen, 79 Ga. 637, 11
Am. St. Rep. 449.) Evidence of the existence of dislike
or ill will on the part of defendant towards the plaintiff
is not enough to show legal malice in an action for malicious
prosecution. (Lalor v. Byrne, 51 Mo. App. 578; Peck v.

Chonteau, 91 Mo. 138.) Generally malice is a question of
fact for the jury, but whether there is any proof of malice
is first for the court to determine, malice in law being a
question of law and fact. (Coal Co. v. Mores, (Ky.) 40
S. W. 681; Halliday v. Sterling, 62 Mo. 321; Sharp v.
Johnson, 76 Mo. 660; Reed v. State, 29 Tex. App. 449.)
Where there is no evidence of malice the question should
not be left to the jury. (Brown v. Hawkes, 65 L. T.
(n. s.) 108.) The inference of malice or want of probable
cause is not one of law or of necessary presumption, but is
merely a presumption of fact which may or may not be indulged by the jury. (Stanton v. Goshorn, 94 Fed. 56.) Probable cause is entirely independent of plaintiff's innocence.
The question in that respect is this: Considering all the
facts before the defendants, that is, of which they had been
informed when they signed the complaint, had they reasonable ground to believe the defendant guilty of the matter
alleged. It is believed there can be but one answer to this
question, viz.: the defendants were warranted, as reasonable men, in making the complaint. (Chisman v. Carney,
33 Ark. 316; Fadner v. Filer, 27 Ill. App. 506; Hays v.
Blizzard, 30 Ind. 457; Center v. Spring, 2 Ia. 393; Philpot
v. Lucas, 101 La. 478; Scatten v. Longfellow, 40 Ind. 23;
Lytton v. Baird, 95 Ind. 349; Widmeyer v. Felton, 95
Fed. 926; Ins. Co. v. Williams, 60 Miss. 916.) Public
policy favors prosecution for crime, and requires that a
person who, in good faith and upon reasonable grounds in-
stitutes such a prosecution shall be protected. (Teal v.
Fissell, 28 Fed. 351; Richey v. McBean, 17 Ill. 63; Girob
v. Graham, 41 La. Ann. 511; Stone v. Crocker, 24 Pick.
81; Cole v. Curtis, 16 Minn. 182.)

Stone & Winslow, for defendant in error.

It is no defense to this action that the criminal complaint
was not sufficient as a charge of a crime. It is not necessary, to sustain an action for malicious prosecution, that the
affidavit on which the prosecution was based properly
charged an offense. (Randall v. Henry, 5 Stew. & P. 367;

Ewing v. Sanford, 19 Ala. 605; Schattgen v. Holnback, 149 Ill. 646; Stancliff v. Palmeter, 18 Ind. 321; Streight v. Bell, 37 Ind. 550; Shaul v. Brown, 28 Ia. 37; Parli v. Reed, 31 Kan. 534; Bell v. Keepers, 37 Kan. 64; Potter v. Gjertsen, 37 Minn. 386; Mask v. Rawls, 57 Miss. 270; Stocking v. Howard, 73 Mo. 25; Malone v. Huston, 17 Neb. 107; Vennum v. Huston, 38 Neb. 293; Humphrey v. Ins. Co., 62 Hun, 618; Lueck v. Heisler, 87 Wis. 644.) Upon the trial the plaintiff, to show want of probable cause, introduced her own positive testimony and the evidence of numerous witnesses to negative any guilt on her part in connection with the matters charged in the criminal complaint, and also evidence of actual malice by expressions of threats and statements by the defendants. The defendants wholly failed to establish the commission of any crime by the plaintiff or any other person, or that any crime had been committed by anyone. By the great weight of authority the dismissal of the criminal proceeding by the prosecuting attorney constituted a termination of the proceeding such as to enable this plaintiff to maintain her action for malicious prosecution. The rule is that a prosecution is to be regarded as terminated, for the purposes of such an action, when it has been so disposed of that it cannot be revived, or that if the prosecutor intends to further prosecute new proceedings must be commenced. (Graves v. Scott, 104 Va. 372: Bell v. Mathews, 37 Kan. 686; see note to Graves v. Scott, *supra,* in 7 Ann. Cas. 482; Fox v. Smith, 26 R. I. 1, 3 Ann. Cas. 110; 19 Ency. Law, 655; 26 Cyc. 87.) The instructions given to the jury fairly stated the law and followed leading authorities upon the subject, viz.: Baker v. Hornik, 57 S. C. 213, 35 S. E. 524; 1 Brickwood's Sackett on Instr. 851, Sec. 1284; Wright v. Fansler, 90 Ind. 492. Probable cause is something more than mere ground for suspicion or even reasonable ground therefor. It was for the jury to determine whether or not probable cause existed. They found against the defendants on the question and their verdict is sustained by the evidence.

SCOTT, CHIEF JUSTICE.

The defendant in error as plaintiff recovered judgment for the sum of $500 and costs against the plaintiffs in error as defendants in the District Court of Fremont County for an alleged malicious prosecution. A motion to set aside the verdict and for a new trial was filed, which the court overruled and the defendants bring error.

There are two separate counts contained in the petition, but the court withdrew the first and the issue as finally submitted to the jury was upon the second count and the evidence directed thereto. It is alleged in the second count as follows:

"And the said plaintiff, Nancy Wales, further complains of the said named defendants, P. J. McIntosh, Jesse Johnson, and Donald A. Beaton, and each of them, and for her second cause of action alleges and says that on the 30th day of May, A. D. 1910, the said named defendants, and each of them, wrongfully, falsely and maliciously, and without probable cause, before Emil Jamerman, a Justice of the Peace in and for the County of Fremont in the State of Wyoming, charged that this plaintiff did, on the 22nd day of May, A. D. 1910, and during the last five years prior to said date, in Rongis, in the County of Fremont, State of Wyoming, unlawfully, maliciously and feloniously steal unbranded calves from the range adjacent to the ranch of this plaintiff and adjacent to the ranches of John Wales and William Johnson, and thereupon prayed and demanded that this plaintiff be forthwith apprehended on the said charge of the said defendants, and said defendants caused this plaintiff to be wrongfully arrested, detained and deprived of her liberty and be brought before the said magistrate and be arraigned to plead to the said charge on the said 30th day of May, A. D. 1910.

"That this plaintiff was so wrongfully detained, imprisoned and deprived of her liberty for the space of about five hours and was compelled to leave her home and work and be taken under arrest a distance of about eight miles and to be taken before the magistrate in the presence of a large number of the friends and neighbors of this plaintiff and accompanied by the defendants as complainants, and the said defendants there caused and procured the said magistrate to order this plaintiff to give bond and this plaintiff was then and there compelled to give bond in the sum of $500.00 for her further appearance before the said magistrate at a time fixed by him, and in default of said bond that she stand committed to the County Jail in said County of Fremont, that plaintiff was afterwards required without her consent and against her will to be and appear before the said magistrate on the 15th day of June, A. D. 1910, and again on the 25th of June, A. D. 1910, to answer said charge.

"That afterwards, on the 25th day of June, A. D. 1910, the said cause came on for hearing before Emil Jamerman, Justice of the Peace, and John Dillon, County and Prosecuting Attorney for the said County of Fremont, appeared on behalf of the prosecution of said cause, and after inquiry and investigation, said John Dillon as such Prosecuting Attorney failed and refused to prosecute said charge and the said charge against this plaintiff was without the consent of the said named defendants herein dismissed and this plaintiff was acquitted of said charge and then released from custody, and said prosecution is now ended and wholly determined.

"And this plaintiff says that she was not guilty of the charge made by said defendants and was never before charged with being guilty of any crime whatever, and up to that time had always been esteemed a good and worthy citizen and respected by all her neighbors and acquaintances in the community where she resides, and the plaintiff further says that the charge was made by the defendants against this plaintiff and said arrest and detention of said plaintiff was made and caused without any probable cause to suspect the plaintiff guilty of the charge as made by said defendants, or of stealing any livestock whatever; **and the said** arrest of plaintiff was malicious and was caused and procured by the said defendants in furtherance of their expressed intention and design to prosecute and litigate this plaintiff and involve this plaintiff in expensive litigation until she would be forced to abandon her residence and home in the community and dispose of her holdings to the said defendants and those interested with them, to the end that the said defendants for their benefit and profit might have the fences removed from around the lands of this plaintiff and of her husband and permit the said defendants easy access to the open territory and stock range upon the mountain and beyond the holdings of this plaintiff and of her said husband.

"That by reason of the wrongful acts of the said defendants this plaintiff has been greatly injured and damaged in her credit, standing and reputation in the community where she resides, and has been brought into public scandal, infamy and disgrace, and has suffered great anxiety, mental anguish, great humiliation, shame and disgrace, and has been obliged to expend the sum of $100.00 in procuring her discharge from said prosecution and imprisonment.

"That the whole of said proceedings by said defendants against this plaintiff were unlawful, wanton and malicious, and have greatly distressed and humiliated plaintiff and injured her in her good name and reputation, and by reason of the premises plaintiff has been damaged in the sum of Ten Thousand Dollars.

"Wherefore, Plaintiff prays judgment against the said named defendants, P. J. McIntosh, Jesse Johnson, and Donald A. Beaton, and each of them, in the sum of Ten Thousand Dollars, and that Plaintiff may have and recover such other further or different relief as may be just and equitable."

The defendants answered jointly, denying generally and specifically each allegation of the petition, alleged that defendants stated the facts to the justice in good faith, for good cause believed to exist as a duty to the public and for no other reason whatsoever, and denied that they brought about her arrest without probable cause. The plaintiff filed her reply putting in issue the new matter alleged in the answer.

It is assigned as error (1) that the court erred in overruling defendant's demurrer to the second cause of action on the ground that it failed to state facts sufficient to constitute a cause of action; (2) that the court erred in refusing plaintiff's motion at the close of the testimony to instruct the jury to find for the defendants; and (3) that the evidence does not support the verdict and that the court erred in not granting the motion for a new trial. The essential elements necessary to be shown by the petition and evidence in an action for malicious prosecution are (1) the institution of the proceedings; (2) without probable cause; (3) with malice; (4) that the proceedings have terminated and in plaintiff's favor; (5) damage to plaintiff. (19 A. & E. Ency. of Law, 653, 13 Ency. Pl. & Pr. 427.) In the case here the evidence tends to support the allegations of the second cause of action contained in the petition and if sufficient to entitle the plaintiff to recover what we have to say on that question would be determinative of the sufficiency of the petition. It is urged that proof to the effect that the information which failed to charge plaintiff with the commission of an offense under the laws of this state and the warrant issued thereon were written and prepared by the justice of the peace, the defendants doing nothing more than signing the information and taking no part in the arrest or any other or further action after signing the information is not sufficient to maintain the action. It is also contended that the dismissal of the criminal proceeding by the justice of the peace at the request of the prosecuting attorney without submitting any evidence was not a termination of that proceeding in plaintiff's favor.

The argument as to the first contention is based upon a false premise. The evidence is undisputed that the defendants applied to the justice, furnished him the information, and subscribed to the complaint as the basis of the prosecution, but that they each made oath to the same. Whatever facts were stated in the information were supported by their oaths, and furthermore the jury had a right to presume that they made oath thereto to secure the issuance of the warrant upon which the plaintiff was arrested. The machinery of the law was intended to be put in motion and to all intents and purposes in so far as these defendants are concerned it was, and if their acts were malicious and without probable cause then they could not escape liability in a civil action for damages on the ground that they took no further part in the prosecution or proceedings after signing the complaint.

It may be conceded, as eminent counsel for the defendants claim, that the complaint or information filed before the justice of the peace and upon which the warrant issued did not state a criminal offense, and it may further be conceded that the courts are at variance as to whether an action for malicious prosecution upon such a complaint can be maintained. The great weight of authority supports the right and we think the better reasoning sustains that view. In Shattgen v. Holnback, 149 Ill. 646, 36 N. E. 969, it is said: "It is not necessary, in order to sustain an action for malicious prosecution, that the affidavit on which the prosecution was based properly charged the offense." It may be said that that court had reference to a defective description of an offense, but not where there is no offense charged in the criminal complaint. In Bell v. Keepers, 37 Kan. 64, 14 Pac. 542, it was held that "in an action for malicious prosecution it is no defense that the complaint upon which the warrant of arrest was issued did not state a criminal offense." The reasons for so holding were pointedly stated in that case as follows: "A warrant was issued substantially following the complaint, and it is now claimed that this complaint does not state a criminal offense, and for this reason plaintiff insists that no action for malicious prosecution can be maintained for the arrest made thereunder. This is no longer an unsettled question in this state. This court has repeatedly held that it could not protect a complainant after procuring a warrant to issue on his complaint, to say in answer to a charge of malicious prosecution, that the complaint charges no crime. A void process procured through malice, and without probable cause, is even more reprehensible, if possible, than if it charged a criminal offense. The wrong is not in the charge alone, but more in the object and purposes to be gained, and the intention and motive in procuring the complaint and arrest. The contents of the complaint, when maliciously made, without good cause, are of but little consequence and can give no protection."

In Mask v. Rawls, 57 Miss. 270, it is said that "trespass on the case lies for malicious prosecution, although the affidavit which was the commencement of the prosecution fails to charge an offense known to the law." To the same effect is Lueck v. Heisler, 87 Wis. 644, 58 N. W. 1101. In the note to Ross v. Hixon, 46 Kan. 550, 26 Pac. Rep. 955, 12 L. R. A. 760, 26 Am. St. 123, 129, Mr. Freeman says: "It may be that the charge as made does not constitute a public offense, or that for some other reason no conviction can be had under it, or though constituting some offense, it does not justify the proceeding taken or warrant issued by the magistrate, and cannot for that reason result in a conviction. In each of the instances supposed, there cannot, if the law is properly construed and applied, be any conviction, and on that account it has been insisted that there is no prosecution such as will sustain an action, though it is shown to be malicious and without probable cause. As we shall hereafter show, it is necessary, to maintain an action for malicious prosecution, that the defendant was guilty of malice and acted without probable cause in preferring the charge which he made. If both of these elements are shown to have been present, it is not material that the prosecutor, in the complaint which he made, did not state facts sufficient to constitute a crime, or that some irregularity of proceeding after the complaint was preferred made the arrest under it improper and unauthorized. Hence, if the charge as made was false, malicious, and without probable cause, the person prosecuted cannot be deprived of compensation for such injury as may have resulted to him from it, by proving that the affidavit or complaint was defective in not charging a criminal offense or that the proceedings were otherwise irregular."

As already stated there are courts which have held contrary to the views of Mr. Freeman as above expressed, and to those courts from whose opinions the above quotations are taken, but we think the better reasoning is with the courts which hold that the action can be maintained even though the affidavit upon which the warrant was issued failed to charge a criminal offense, provided the other necessary elements are present in order to make out a case. Indeed to hold otherwise, would, we think, be contrary to the policy of the law, for it would deprive the injured party of a remedy for what is usually a great wrong and far-reaching in its effect.

It is urged that the dismissal of the case by the justice of the peace at the request of the County and Prosecuting Attorney without the introduction of any evidence was not such a termination of the criminal proceeding as to enable plaintiff to maintain her action. In Graves v. Scott et al., 104 Va. 372, 51 S. E. 821 (2 L. R. A. (N. S.) 927, 113 Am. St. Rep. 1043, 7 A. & E. Ann. Cas. 480), the plaintiff was arrested on a warrant issued upon a criminal complaint charging him with obtaining goods under false pretenses. The complaint was dismissed at the time set for trial because of the failure of the prosecuting witness to be sworn and give evidence, and it was held that this was such a termination of the case as would support an action for malicious prosecution for the reason that the case had been disposed of in such a manner that any further action would have to be based upon a new complaint, or by proceedings *de novo*. The case is an interesting one both upon the law and facts and also because of the appended note as to when a criminal proceeding is terminated and the right to maintain an action for malicious prosecution accrues. In the case before us the dismissal of the proceedings at the request of the prosecuting attorney put an end to any further proceedings against the plaintiff upon the criminal complaint theretofore filed. Further proceedings upon that record could not be revived and were at an end, though such dismissal would be no bar to a prosecution for the same offense charged in a new and different complaint. That being so we are of the opinion that the better reasoning and great weight of authority sustains the view that the dismissal of the proceedings by the justice was a sufficient termination thereof to enable plaintiff to maintain the action. (19 A. & E. Ency. Law, 681 ; 26 Cyc. 58.)

It was necessary in order to maintain her action to prove that the defendants acted maliciously and without probable cause. It is urged that proof of the dismissal of the proceeding at the request of the county and prosecuting attorney without submitting any evidence to the justice before whom the proceedings were had was not proof of want of probable cause. As already stated, the evidence of dismissal was admissible as showing a termination of the proceeding, and while theoretically the county and prosecuting attorney was acting officially for all citizens, including the defendants, yet he was not their attorney. He was acting in his official capacity and for the state and not under employment or direction of the defendants. Had they employed a private attorney to draw up the complaint and file it, and such attorney had asked the dismissal, his action would be construed as their act, through their authorized agent, but we are unable to understand how the act of the public prosecutor in procuring the dismissal of the criminal complaint and proceedings which were not instituted by him or upon his advice without having produced any evidence in support of the charge would be evidence against the defendants upon the issue of want of probable cause in commencing the action. It should be remembered that the issue before the justice was not the guilt or innocence of the accused, but whether or not a crime had been committed, and if so, whether there was probable cause to believe that accused committed such crime. Probable cause to justify a criminal prosecution may exist even though the prosecuting witness acts maliciously if the charge be true, and even if the charge be not true, yet if such witness acts honestly and in good faith, basing his charge upon facts which he in good faith believes to be true, but which afterward turns out to be false, he cannot be said to have acted without probable cause. It was said in Philpot v. Lucas, 101 Iowa, 478, 70 N. W. 625, that "Probable cause does not depend upon the guilt or innocence of the accused party in fact, but upon the honest and reasonable belief of the party commencing the prosecution." If the .rule were otherwise every good citizen would expose himself to an action for malicious prosecution when in performing his duty to the state to assist in the suppression of crime he in good faith subscribed to an affidavit as the basis of a criminal prosecution or proceeding, if such prosecution or proceeding be dismissed without a judicial determination upon a hearing from the evidence upon the question of probable cause. In the case here the proceeding was dismissed by the magistrate, not upon a finding from the evidence upon that question, but upon motion of the prosecuting attorney. The distinction we think is clear between this and like cases and those where the question has been judicially determined by the committing magistrate from evidence before him. He could make no affirmative finding on that question in the absence of any evidence before him. The question is important as bearing on the sufficiency of plaintiff's evidence to make out a *prima facie* case. The burden was upon her to prove that the prosecution was without probable cause, and we are constrained to believe from an examination of the adjudicated cases that upon the facts here a dismissal of a criminal complaint in the absence of a waiver of a hearing be-

fore the committing magistrate upon motion of the prosecuting attorney, without any evidence having been submitted
to such magistrate, is not a judicial determination by such
magistrate of the existence of probable cause, nor evidence
thereof in an action for malicious prosecution subsequently
instituted and based upon such proceedings. In Davis v.
McMillan et al., 142 Mich. 391, 105 N. W. 862, (3 L. R. A.
(N. S.) 928, 113 Am. St. Rep. 585, 7 Ann. Cas. 854),
which was an action for malicious prosecution, the court
say: "We think it can safely be said that the weight
of authority deines the rule that discharge by a magistrate upon the request of the prosecuting attorney is *prima
facie* evidence of want of probable cause." The holding of the court in that case and as stated therein accords
with the great weight of authority. Such a dismissal can
not be said to be predicated upon the sufficiency or insufficiency of the evidence, but upon the expressed desire of
the state speaking through its prosecutor to abandon the
case without introducing evidence and invoking a finding
thereon.

The finding of the jury, the verdict being general, was a
finding upon all the issues in favor of the plaintiff. It is
contended that the verdict, unless the dismissal upon request of the State be deemed competent, finds no support
in the evidence that the prosecution was commenced without
probable cause. In this connection it may be said to be the
established rule that malice may be inferred from a showing of want of probable cause, but that want of probable
cause will not be inferred from proof of malice alone. (19
Cyc. 680.) Both elements are necessary to be shown to
warrant a recovery in this kind of an action, although malice
may be inferred from a showing of want of probable cause.
As to what evidence is admissible as showing want of probable cause, it is said in 19 Cyc., at page 698: "It has been
held that the plaintiff is entitled to introduce proof of his
general good character or reputation on the question of
want of probable cause for the prosecution, or the defend-

ant's belief in his guilt, and this as a part of the plaintiff's affirmative case and not merely in rebuttal of an attack upon his character by evidence on the part of the defense. But of course it should be shown in addition that the defendant had knowledge of the plaintiff's good reputation." In the case here the plaintiff testified that she never stole any calves from defendants, or either of them, off the range, or from any other place, and was permitted to and did introduce as a part of her affirmative case proof of her general good character or reputation for honesty and integrity upon the question of want of probable cause for the prosecution. A number of witnesses who had known her for many years in the vicinity in which she lived testified that her general reputation in that respect was good. The defendant Johnson was her uncle, and he had known her in that community from childhood, she being the daughter of his deceased brother. Such acquaintance, and for the length of time shown, we think raises a presumption of his knowledge of her reputation. (Woodworth v. Mills, 61 Wis. 44, 20 N. W. 728, 50 Am. St. Rep. 135.) In Olson v. Tvete, 46 Minn. 225, 48 N. W. 914, it appeared in evidence that a search warrant was issued and served at the instigation of the defendant, the premises searched and the property alleged to have been stolen and there concealed was not found and the officer who served the warrant so returned and it was further in evidence that the plaintiff had long borne a good reputation for honesty and integrity. At the close of plaintiff's case the court dismissed the action and upon appeal the judgment was reversed. The court say: "We think the proof made a *prima facie* case of want of probable cause, from which malice might be inferred, and that it was error to take the case from the jury. It is true that the burden of proof was upon the plaintiff to show that the proceeding was instituted without probable cause and with malice. But in such a case it must often be that the only proof possible from the plaintiff is of a negative character, and in reference to matters peculiarly within the knowledge of the defendant;

and hence less satisfactory and convincing proof is required
of the plaintiff to shift the burden on the defendant than
would otherwise be necessary. The proof of a thorough
search, and the official return to the warrant that the property was not found in the plaintiff's possession, was *prima
facie* proof that the property was not there, and that the
plaintiff was not guilty of concealing stolen goods, or of
larceny. Proof of the plaintiff's good reputation for many
years in the community went to show an improbability that
the plaintiff would be guilty of the conduct implied in this
charge, and of this the defendant may be presumed to have
been aware. (McIntire v. Levering, 148 Mass. 546, 20
N. E. Rep. 191, (2 L. R. A. 517, 12 Am. St. Rep. 594);
Israel v. Brooks, 23 Ill. 575; Blizzard v. Hayes, 46 Ind.
166, 15 Am. Rep. 291; Woodworth v. Mills, 61 Wis. 44,
20 N. W. Rep. 728, 50 Am. Rep. 135.) Such proof having
been made, it was fairly incumbent on the defendant to
show affirmatively, as he could easily do, the facts, if any
existed, justifying a belief on his part in the truth of the
allegations upon which the search-warrant was procured."

This decision is one of the many cited in Cyc. supporting
the text above quoted, and while it is the general rule as
therein stated, that one may not introduce evidence as to
his general reputation for honesty and integrity before his
character has been assailed in that respect, yet the courts
generally have made an exception in this class of cases, as
the burden is upon the plaintiff to negative the existence of
probable cause, or to show want of good faith on the part
of the defendant in the prosecution of the criminal charge.
Such a rule is founded in justice and gives the defendant no
shelter from his wrongful act, purposely and maliciously accomplished. The defendant is then given the fullest opportunity to show affirmatively in his defense that he acted
in good faith or upon probable cause. The defendants in
order to show that they acted upon probable cause in instigating the criminal proceeding, introduced evidence of different witnesses tending to show that plaintiff's reputation

for honesty and integrity was bad, and also evidence of different circumstances of which defendants had information prior to the prosecution. It may be conceded that such information standing alone, if honestly believed, would be sufficient to raise in the mind of a reasonably prudent man a well-grounded suspicion that plaintiff had at various times prior to the prosecution been stealing unbranded calves of these defendants and others from the range, and have constituted probable cause for the prosecution. The evidence upon the latter questions was denied by the plaintiff in her testimony. •There was, therefore, a direct conflict in the evidence as to the existence or non-existence of the facts relied upon to constitute probable cause and this question was properly one for the jury. We are of the opinion that the second cause of action as pleaded stated facts sufficient to constitute a cause of action in favor of the plaintiff and against these defendants, and that there was sufficient evidence to make out a *prima facie* case to go to the jury at the close of the testimony, and that the verdict is supported by the evidence.

The plaintiff testified that one of the effects of her being publicly arrested and taken before the justice of the peace was that it injured her credit at the First National Bank of Rawlins. The following inquiry was then made, viz.: "Just tell the jury the facts as to how it was hurt, and what the transaction was." The question was objected to as follows: "We object to this; the best testimony as to whether credit was refused would be that the bank itself." The court overruled the objection and such ruling is here assigned as error. It will be observed that the objection goes to the manner of proof and not to the competency of the evidence. If competent at all, and it was not objected to on that ground, the fact could be proved by her as well as by the bank officials, for it would be a fact within her knowledge. We express no opinion as to whether this evidence was competent for that question was not presented to nor ruled upon by the trial court in the first instance and consequently can not be raised for the first time in this court.

Plaintiff testified as to the land holdings and stock business of Jesse Johnson, one of the defendants. Afterwards the defendants made and the court overruled the following motion, viz.: "I move the court to withdraw from the jury all statements made by this witness as to the business of Jesse Johnson, the amount of land he holds, and any business matters that have been stated by the witness, on the ground that it does not tend to prove any issue in the case; is not relevant to any issue in the case; that the value of a man's property or the extent of his holdings is not a fact to be considered in sustaining the petition in the case. I make the motion at this time because it is sometimes held that we waive our right if we proceed with the cross- examination before making the motion." The action of the court in overruling this motion is here assigned as error. We do not think the motion was by its terms directed to anything other than evidence given by her with reference to the business and land holdings of defendant Jesse Johnson. The relative situation of his land and that occupied by plaintiff was illustrative and bore on the question of motive and interest to defendant Jesse Johnson to get her and her husband out of the country as alleged in the petition, so that he could have freer access to the range for his cattle; and further, as hereinafter stated, as punitive damages upon the facts shown were recoverable, evidence of defendant Johnson's financial condition was admissible. (19 Cyc. 700.)

Plaintiff was further permitted to testify over objection that she and her husband paid an attorney's fee to Stone & Winslow for attending the justice court in their behalf on June 25, 1910. While the ruling was not assigned as error the sufficiency of such evidence to warrant a recovery of attorney's fee may be considered under the general assignment (1) that there was error in the assessment of the amount of recovery, the same being too large. The right to recover a reasonable attorney's fee in a case of this kind is well established. Evidence that such a fee amounting to $250 had been paid by herself and her husband was proper to go to the jury as an item of expense if reasonable in amount, and it appearing that the hearing was held in a country precinct a distance of eighty miles from the county seat where her attorneys resided, without railroad connection, we think it may be assumed that the amount was reasonable although its reasonableness was not shown by testimony. (Waüfle v. McLellan, 51 Wis. 484, 8 N. W. 300.) There was evidence of actual malice on the part of the defendant Johnson which would warrant the recovery of punitive damages as against him, (Cosgriff v. Miller, 10 Wyo. 190, 68 Pac. 206, 98 Am. St. Rep. 977) and joint error being here assigned if the judgment be good as to him it is good as to all the defendants, and upon the record, the other defendants having joined with him in the assignments of error, they are not in a position to complain. (North Platte Milling Co. v. Price, 4 Wyo. 293, 306, 33 Pac. 664; Hogan v. Peterson, 8 Wyo. 549-564, 59 Pac. 162; Greenawalt et al. v. Imp. Co., 16 Wyo. 226, 92 Pac. 1008; Ditch Co. v. Peterson, 18 Wyo. 402, 108 Pac. 72.) The verdict was for $500, which we think reasonable upon the issues being found in favor of the plaintiff. There is no claim in her evidence that she paid or obligated herself to pay all of the attorney's fee. Her evidence was that "we" (meaning herself and her husband) "paid $250 to Stone & Winslow for their services." The jury had a right to award her a reasonable attorney's fee necessarily incurred or paid for her defense in the prosecution, whether paid by herself (19 Am. & Eng. Ency. Law, 703) or some one else for her (Krug v. Ward, 77 Ill. 603) and upon the record the verdict being general we cannot say in making up their verdict what amount the jury allowed her for attorney's fee. The amount of expenditure alleged in the petition to procure her discharge from the criminal prosecution was $100, but the jury may have allowed her less than that amount for attorney's fee and the balance of the verdict be for other items of expenditure and damage, which were alleged and in proof and also exemplary damages.

Errors are assigned as to the admission and exclusion of evidence over defendant's objection. We deem it unnecessary to discuss these questions in detail, as they are not so discussed in plaintiff in error's brief, nor are their prejudicial character, if any, pointed out in their brief. The attention of the court is called to these alleged errors in a general way, casting upon this court the burden of searching the record to ascertain if error was committed, a burden which rests in the first instance with the plaintiffs in error. We have, however, examined the record and discover no prejudicial error as to the rulings of the court in that respect.

Errors are assigned to the court's refusal to give certain instructions requested by defendants and to the giving of certain instructions over their objections. We have examined these questions and find that the refusal to give the instructions requested and the giving of the instructions objected to are complained of because contrary to the contention of defendants that there was a failure in proof to sustain the action. As we have already held that the proof was sufficient to make out a *prima facie* case sufficient to go to the jury we deem it unnecessary to discuss these questions further than to say that, in our opinion, the instructions fairly presented the law of the case to the jury. The judgment will be affirmed.   *Affirmed.*

POTTER, J., and BEARD, J., concur.

(IN RE ESTATE OF RODY THORNTON, DECEASED.)
MERRILL v. STATE ET AL.
(No. 731.)

WILLS—NUNCUPATIVE WILL—VALIDITY.

1. By the laws of this state a nuncupative will is not recognized as valid, and is not entitled to be admitted to probate.
[Decided June 30, 1913.]   (133 Pac. 134.)

ERROR to the District Court, Uinta County, HON. DAVID H. CRAIG, Judge.

Proceeding brought in the District Court of Uinta County for the probate of an alleged nuncupative will of Rody Thornton, deceased. Objections were filed and a judgment was entered refusing to admit the instrument to probate, whereupon the petitioner brought error. The other material facts are stated in the opinion.

A. B. Gough and *Clark & Budge,* for plaintiff in error.

The right to dispose of one's property is not a constitutional right, but one depending entirely upon the sanction of the legislature, and subject to the restrictions which the law-making power may see fit to impose. (Page on Wills, Sec. 21.) Prior to the enactment of 32 Henry VIII, known as the statute of wills, such intsruments were not expressly recognized in England. That statute provided that lands might be devised by an instrument in writing, and thereafter oral wills of real estate were not approved except in certain localities in England, where by special custom such a practice was in vogue. At an early period, however, nuncupative wills of personal property were recognized; it not being considered that such testaments were affected by the statute of wills. (Page on Wills, p. 255.) Such verbal or oral wills were considered as valid as written wills. (30 Ency. Law, (2nd Ed.) 560). With the development of the law, and the growth of learning, nuncupations gradually fell into disfavor, and it came to be the practice that only such nuncupative wills as were made when the testator was *in ex-*

tremis, were held to be valid; they being justified only upon the plea of necessity. (30 Ency. Law, 2nd Ed., 560; Page on Wills, 255; Prince v. Hazelton, 20 Johnson, 502, 11 Am. Dec. 307.) And as to personalty, nuncupations made *in extremis* were commonly recognized by the courts in England, but upon the passage of the Statute of Frauds, it became necessary that the declaration of the testator should be made in the presence of three witnesses, and it was further necessary that such will should be made at the time of the testator's last sickness, and in the house of his or her habitation or dwelling, or where he or she had been resident for ten days or more next before the making of such will, except where such person was surprised or taken sick when away from home, and died before he returned to the place of his or her dwelling. Thus the law remained until the independence of this country. (Page on Wills, 255, 256.)

The meaning of Section 3588 of Wyoming Compiled Statutes is not quite clear. It seems to adopt the common law and declaratory and remedial acts or statutes in aid of such common law existing prior to the fourth year of James I, yet it may mean the common law of England as it now exists, and in addition thereto those declaratory and remedial acts passed prior to the fourth year of James I. But in either event it would seem that the statute of frauds, which was passed many years after the fourth year of James I, is not included in the terms of adoption, and that, therefore, the restrictions which the statute of frauds placed upon the execution of nuncupative wills, do not obtain in Wyoming, so that in this state the common law of England giving the unrestricted right to dispose of personal property by nuncupative will is now the law, unless it is modified or changed by some statute. Nuncupative wills are clearly recognized by the statutes of this state. (Comp. Stat. 1910, Secs. 5436-5438, 5410.) If the section of the statute (Sec. 5397, Comp. Stat. 1910) requiring that all wills to be valid must be in writing, witnessed by two competent witnesses,

and signed by the testator or some person in his presence
and by his express direction, is to be construed strictly
without regard to other sections of the code, the court might
hold a nuncupative will to be invalid; but such a decision
would abrogate the other sections which refer to nuncupative wills. The court will not lend itself to such a result
unless it is unavoidable, but will, if possible, harmonize the
seemingly inconsistent provisions that all may be effective.
(Humphries v. Davis, 100 Ind. 274; State v. Givens, 48
Fla. 165; Cahill v. State, (Ind.) 76 N. E. 182.) This rule
of statutory construction is universally accepted, making it
unnecessary to cite further authorities in its support. We
submit that Section 5397 has no application to nuncupative
wills. That section was enacted in 1882, and while it was
in force the legislature enacted what are now Sections 5410,
5437-5438, Comp. Stat. 1910. Why should the legislature
provide for admitting to probate nuncupative wills if it did
not intend that they should be considered as an exception
to the requirement of the then existing statute that all wills
must be in writing, &c.? These later provisions must be
considered as stating an exception to the earlier statute.
(Cincinnati v. Holmes, (Ohio) 46 N. E. 513; State v. Mc-
Gregor (Ohio), 10 N. E. 66; Carland v. Comm'rs., (Mont.)
6 Pac. 24; Ex-parte Turner, 24 S. C. 211.) The several
statutes on this subject should be harmonized and each construed in connection with the other statutes on the same
subject. (36 Cyc, 1146, 1147; State v. Boswell, (Ind.) 4
N. E. 675; Minnich v. Packard, (Ind.) 85 N. E. 787.)
The facts as to the making of this nuncupative will are
such as to render it valid, if such a will is valid at all in this
state. (In re Megary's Est. 25 Pa. Super. Ct., 243; In re
Grossman's Est. 75 Ill. App. 224; Mellor v. Smyth, (Pa.)
69 Atl. 592; Baird v. Baird, (Kan.) 79 Pac. 163; In re
Miller's Est. (Wash.) 91 Pac. 967.)

The statutes relating to nuncupative wills do not limit
their operation to personal property, and while it may be
conceded that at common law such wills were not effectual

to dispose of real estate, it appears that the legislature of
this state had no intention of thus restricting their effect.
We contend, therefore, that as to the personal property of
the deceased the nuncupative will is valid, both by virtue
of the common law and by the statutes of this state, and
that the will should also be held valid as to the real estate,
since there is no statute prohibiting the devise of real estate
in that manner, but on the contrary a general statute recognizing the validity of such a will.

John R. Arnold and *Baily D. Berry*, for defendant in
error Arnold, as Administrator.

The alleged nuncupative will does not meet the legal requirements of the definition of such a will. (5 Words &
Phrases, 4869; Ex parte Thompson, 4 Bradf. Sur. 154, 155;
Shouler on Wills, 2nd Ed., Sec. 361.) One of the essential
elements of such a will is that the testator shall declare the
same to be his will and call upon a sufficient number of witnesses to witness the fact that he proposes to make his will,
disposing of his property and naming his executor; not
that he shall merely state in casual conversation that he
would like to make a particular disposition of his property,
nor that when prompted by the beneficiary to do so, he stated
to him that he would leave him all his property. The reason
for these restrictions is apparent, and on account of the op-
portunities for mistake and fraud the modern practice re-
gards a nuncupative will with disfavor, and holds the pro-
pounders of such a will to the strictest requirement of the
law for the establishment and probate of nuncupative wills.
(30 Ency. Law, 2nd Ed., 566.)

The so-called nuncupative will of this decedent is not entitled to probate because there is no complete statute of this
state outlining the method of probating such oral testamentary declarations. At no place in the statute is the
number of witnesses specified. Even in the absence of Section 5397 it would be improper to probate any oral testamentary declarations, except the same be hedged about by
such other restrictions and qualifications as are laid down

by the common law. Again there is a direct conflict between the provisions of Section 5436 and Section 5397. These statutes cannot be harmonized. (26 Ency. Law, 2nd Ed., 656; Hilburn v. Ry. Co., 23 Mont. 241.) In most states nuncupative wills are now invalid, and generally regarded with disfavor. This fact was fully recognized by this court by the case of Neer v. Cowhick, 4 Wyo. 49, 31 Pac. 862. We believe it is admitted by practically all law writers that real estate never passed under the provisions of a nuncupative will. (30 Ency. Law, 2nd Ed., 562.)

John R. Arnold and *C. P. Arnold,* for heirs at law of decedent.

The fact that the sections of the statute which relate to and control the execution of wills, viz.: Sections 5394 and 5397, and the sections relating to the probating of wills, viz.: Sections 5410, 5436, 5437 and 5438, appear as of equal dignity, force and effect in the compilation is misleading. Prior to 1882 Wyoming had no statute covering the subject of the execution of wills, other than the act of 1869 adopting the common law. An act of 1882 provided for the manner of executing wills. Section 5494, Comp. Stat. 1910, appears in that act, and also Section 5397, with the exception of a subsequent amendment thereto authorizing a will to be typewritten as well as written. No change was made in the legislation upon either the subject matter of wills or their probate until the act of 1890-91 establishing the present probate code. In this act are to be found the provisions relating to the proving of nuncupative wills. The present probate code was a substantial adoption of the probate code of California, but the legislature did not appropriate or adopt the California statute creating the right to make nuncupative wills. Had such further provision of the statute of California been adopted prescribing the essentials for making a nuncupative will there would have been harmony in our legislation respecting the execution and the probating of wills. And the supposed will in question, lacking as it does every element of a valid nuncupation, would have been

rejected for probate had it been offered. In 1892 the case
of Neer v. Cowhick was decided by this court wherein it
was held that an olographic will was not provided for by
the statutes of this state, notwithstanding that the probate
code declared that "an olographic will may be proved in
the same manner as other private writings are proved." In
1895 a new act was passed upon the subject of the execution of wills, which was an amendment of the section of
the Revised Statutes of 1887, prescribing the manner of executing a valid will. The law now stands as it stood with
the passage of that act. All wills must be in writing and
signed by the testator, and with the exception of an olographic will, which was excepted from the provisions of
the act of 1895, all wills must be witnessed by two competent witnesses signing in the presence of the testator and
by his express direction. The statutes thus brought into
consideration, and which it is contended should be construed together as in *pari materia,* do not come within the
rule which is invoked, for the reason that they do not cover
the same subject nor have the same general purpose. They
are inconsistent and are in conflict. Only statutes are in
pari materia which are consistent, which can stand together,
and which relate to the same subject, though enacted at different times. (Sutherland on Stat. Constr., Secs. 283, 284;
Linton's Appeals, 104 Pa. St. 228; 4 Words & Phrases,
3478; Waterford v. People, 9 Barb. 161; 26 Ency. L., 2nd
Ed., 622; Wheelock v. Myers, 64 Kan. 47, 67 Pac. 632;
Salers v. Barber Asphalt Co., 160 Mo. 671, 66 S. W. 979.)
Where two statutes in *pari materia,* originally enacted at
different periods of time, are subsequently incorporated in
a revision and re-enacted, the times when they first took effect will be ascertained and effect will be given to that
which was the latest legislative declaration, if they are not
harmonious. An existing statute is not to be considered as
original because embodied in a revision, and therefore is
not to be construed on the theory that none of its provisions
had previously been in effect. (Suth. Stat. Constr., Sec.

161; Judd v. State, 62 S. W. 543, 25 Tex. Civ. App. 418;
Braun v. State, 49 S. W. 620, 40 Tex. Cr. App. 236; Louis-
ville v. Louisville P. W. Co., 53 S. W. 291, 107 Ky. 184;
Inhabitants &c. v. Rockland, 89 Me. 43, 35 Atl. 1033; Cape
Girardeau v. Riley, 52 Mo. 424, 14·Am. Rep. 427.)

Even under the facts and the authorities cited by plaintiff
in error this proposed will must be rejected. The decedent
asked no one to bear testimony that he was making a will.
He called no witnesses. It was not a case of sudden death.
An essential element recognized by the common law to the
validity of a nuncupative will was that the testator should
have called witnesses in a solemn manner to witness the
nuncupation, and requested them expressly to bear witness
to his act.

BEARD, JUSTICE.

The plaintiff in error, J. G. Merrill, filed a petition in
the District Court of Uinta County, alleging in substance
that one Rody Thornton died at Bennington, Idaho, on the
4th day of May, 1912, and that at the time of his death he
was a resident of Uinta County, Wyoming; and that he
left in said Uinta County an estate consisting of personal
and real property. That the real estate left by the deceased
was of the estimated value of $30,000, and the personal
property of the value of about $40,000. That deceased left
a nuncupative will in which the petitioner is named as the
sole legatee; that deceased died without issue and was an
unmarried man, and that there are no heirs resident in the
State of Wyoming or elsewhere so far as petitioner knows.
The writing alleged to be the nuncupative will of said deceased, and which the petitioner prayed might be admitted
to probate as the last will and testament of said Rody
Thornton, deceased, is in words and figures as follows,
to-wit:

"In the matter of the nuncupative will of Roda Thornton, deceased. On the 4th day of May, 1912, at Bennington, in Bear Lake County, Idaho, Roda Thornton of Mid-
way, Uinta County, Wyoming, being in the immediate ex-

pectation of death from hemorrhage of the lungs due to Pulmonary Tuberculosis, and being there and then informed by his attending Physician that he could live but a short time, and there and then not being physically able to make and execute a written will, in the presence of the undersigned subscribers, did declare his last will and wishes concerning the disposition of his property, in the following words, or substance thereof, viz.: 'I desire that J. G. Merrill of Bennington, Idaho, have all of my property and estate, and I give and will it all to him.' At the time the said Roda Thornton stated the foregoing as his will, he was of sound mind and memory, and not under any restraint, and he at that time desired us to bear witness that such was his wish, desire and will. Reduced to writing and sealed by us this 7th day of May, 1912."

(Signed)   "DR. D. W. POYNTER (S)"
"SAMUEL R. HALL."

(This instrument is referred to in the findings of the court as Exhibit 1.)

The Attorney General, on behalf of the State of Wyoming, filed objections to admitting said alleged will to probate on the grounds that said deceased left no heirs at law so far as known. That the instrument purporting to be a nuncupative will was no will at all. That the same was not made, attested and executed as required by the laws of Wyoming, in this: "that said instrument was not made in writing or typewritten; that said instrument was not witnessed by two competent witnesses; that said instrument was not signed by the deceased nor by a person in his presence, by his express direction."

Upon the trial the court found the facts to be, and stated its conclusions of law as follows:

"First: That Rody Thornton died at Bennington, Bear Lake County, Idaho, on the 4th day of May, A. D. 1912, and that at the time of his death he was a resident of Uinta County, Wyoming, and left in said county and state an estate consisting of real and personal property.

Second: That the said Rody Thornton left no heirs within the State of Wyoming, or elsewhere, so far as known.

Third: That a few hours before his death on the said 4th day of May, A. D. 1912, the said Rody Thornton called to his bedside one Samuel R. Hall and made the following declaration and statement to said Hall, and to Dr. D. W. Poynter, then and there present, to-wit:

'I desire that J. G. Merrill have all of my property, and I will it to him.' That at the time said statement and declaration was made, said Thornton was in imminent danger of death, and made said statement with the understanding that he could not live.

Fourth: That at the time said statement was made by said Thornton he was of sound and disposing mind.

Fifth: That the said declaration and statement of the said Rody Thornton so made to said Samuel R. Hall and Dr. D. W. Poynter, was thereafter within three (3) days after the death of the said decedent, to-wit: on the 7th day of May, A. D. 1912, reduced to writing and signed by the said Hall and Poynter, and is identified herein as petitioner's Exhibit No. 1, offered for probate as the nuncupative will of the said Rody Thornton, deceased.

Sixth: That the statement and declaration offered for probate, purporting to be the last will and testament of the said Rody Thornton, deceased, was not made in writing nor typewritten; that the said statement and declaration was not witnessed by two competent witnesses; that said statement and declaration so offered was not signed by the deceased, nor by a person in his presence, at his express direction, at or prior to the time of his death.

As a conclusion of law, from the foregoing facts, the Court finds that said instrument purporting to be the last will and testament of the said Rody Thornton, deceased, does not conform to Chapter 355, and particularly to Section 5397 of the Revised Statutes of Wyoming and is not such an instrument as complies with the requirements of said chapter and section aforesaid, and cannot be admitted to probate, and the court therefore rejects and denies the application and petition of said J. G. Merrill, filed herein for the probate of said will."

From the judgment of the court refusing to admit to probate the instrument presented as the nuncupative will of said Rody Thornton, deceased, the proponent brings error.

It appears from the record filed in this court that after the decision of the District Court refusing to admit to probate said instrument as the will 'of said Rody Thornton, deceased, certain persons claiming to be heirs at law of said deceased appeared and petitioned the court for the removal .of James W. Chrisman, who had been appointed as administrator of said estate, and for the appointment of John R. Arnold as such administrator; and that such proceedings were had that said Chrisman was removed and said Arnold appointed as such administrator. That he duly qualified, and on motion in this court it was ordered that he be substituted as defendant in error in this action in the place of said Chrisman.

It is conceded by counsel for plaintiff in error that the right to dispose of one's property by will "is not a constitutional right, but one depending entirely upon the sanction of the legislature, and subject to the restrictions which the law making power may see fit to impose." It is contended, however, that by Ch. 26, Comp. Laws 1876, now Section 3588, Comp. Stat. 1910, the common law of England, which recognized nuncupative wills as valid as to personal property, was adopted by that section of our statutes and that such wills are valid in this state at least to that extent. The section reads as follows: "The common law of England as modified by judicial decisions, so far as the same is of a general nature and not inapplicable, and all declaratory or remedial acts or statutes made in aid of or to supply the defects of the common law prior to the fourth year of James the First, (excepting the second section of the sixth chapter of forty-third Elizabeth, the eighth chapter of thirteenth Elizabeth, and ninth chapter of thirty-seventh Henry Eighth) and which are of a general nature, and not local to England, shall be the rule of decision in this territory when not inconsistent with the laws thereof, and shall be considered as of full force, until repealed by legislative authority." For the purposes of this case it may be conceded that if there is no statute of this state inconsistent with the common law as adopted by the above quoted section, then a nuncupative will is valid in this state for all the purposes that it would have been valid at common law. But by an act approved February 8, 1882, entitled, "An act to provide the manner in which wills shall be executed in the Territory of Wyoming and for other purposes," it was provided: "All wills to be valid must be in writing, witnessed by two competent witnesses, and signed by the testator or by some person in his presence and by his express direction," etc. (Sec. 4, Ch. 107, S. L. 1882.) Since the passage of that act it cannot be reasonably maintained that the common law with respect to nuncupative wills is still in force in this state, unless that statute has been modified or repealed by subsequent legislation. It declares in no uncertain terms that *all* wills *must* be in writing and *signed* by the *testator* or by some person in his presence and by his express direction. No statute of the territory or state mentioned a nuncupative will prior to the act of 1891; and it is upon that act that counsel for plaintiff in error chiefly rely. That act was approved January 10, 1891, and is entitled, "An act providing for probate jurisdiction and procedure, and prescribing the duties of courts and the officers in connection therewith." That act relates solely and exclusively to probate procedure. It provides how wills shall be proved; but not one word can be found in the entire chapter (covering seventy-five pages of the Session Laws) prescribing in any form the requisites of a will, who is competent to make a will, or what property may be devised or bequeathed thereby. There is nothing in the act which would enable the court to determine whether or not the instrument propounded for probate was in law a valid will; and recourse would necessarily have to be had to the statute prescribing what persons are competent to make a will and the formalities necessary to be employed in its execution; and these we find in a separate and distinct part of the statutes. The provisions of the act relied upon to sustain the contentions of plaintiff in error are found in Chapter 70, sub-Chapter 4, Secs. 5, 6 and 7, S. L. 1890-91, entitled as above, and are as follows: "Sec. 5. Nuncupative wills may, at any time within six months after the testamentary words are spoken by the decedent, be admitted to probate, on petition and notice, as provided herein for the probate of other wills. The petition, in addition to the jurisdictional facts, must allege that the testamentary words, or the substance thereof, were reduced to writing within thirty days after they were spoken, which writing must accompany the petition." "Sec. 6. The court, or judge thereof in vacation, must not receive or entertain a petition for the probate of a nuncupative will, until the lapse of ten days from the death of the testator, nor must such petition at any time be acted on until the testamentary words, or their substance, is reduced to writing and filed with the petition, nor until the surviving husband or wife (if any) and all other persons resident in the state or county interested in the estate, are notified as hereinbefore provided." "Sec. 7. Contests of the probate of nuncupative wills and appointments of executors and administrators of the estates devised thereby must be had, conducted and made as hereinbefore provided in cases of the probate of written wills."

These provisions, and in fact the entire chapter in which they appear, were taken almost literally from the Code of California, and seem to have been adopted by the Legislature without discovering that the laws of that state on the subject of wills provided for nuncupative wills as follows: "A nuncupative will is not required to be in writing, nor to be declared or attested with any formality."

"To make a nuncupative will valid, and to entitle it to be admitted to probate, the following requisites must be observed: 1. The estate bequeathed must not exceed in value the sum of one thousand dollars. 2. It must be proved by two witnesses who were present at the making thereof, one of whom was asked by the testator, at the time, to bear witness that such was his will, or to that effect. 3. The decedent must, at the time, have been in actual military service in the field, or doing duty on shipboard at sea, and in either case in actual contemplation, fear, or peril of death, or the decedent must have been, at the time, in expectation of immediate death from an injury received the same day." (Cal. Civ. Code, Secs. 1288 et seq.) Such a will being provided for in the substantive law of that state, the rules of procedure for its proof have something to act upon; but not so here, where our statute contains no such provision. In the case of Neer v. Cowhick, 4 Wyo. 49, 31 Pac. 862, 18 L. R. A. 588, the olographic will of Cowhick was offered for probate. It was not witnessed; but it was contended by the proponant that by another provision of the chapter we are now considering, viz: "An olographic will may be proved in the same manner as other private writings are proved," the will was valid although not witnessed. The court said: "This act repeals in express terms many provisions of the former law made obsolete under the constitutional provision conferring the powers and jurisdiction of probate courts under the territorial regime upon district courts. The former statute relating to the competency of testators, the devises of lands, the passing of after acquired property by the will, and the provisions relating to the execution and attestation of such instruments were not repealed, although a number of sections relating to the proof of wills succeeding these sections of the Wills Act were repealed expressly. There is no general repeal of inconsistent laws, and the intent of the Legislature is plain to preserve unimpaired Section 2237 of the Revised Statutes (now, as amended, Section 5397, Comp. Stat. 1910), requiring all wills to be in writing, signed by the testator or by some person in his presence by his express direction and by two competent witnesses."

And it was held that because the will was not witnessed it was invalid. If this provision relating to the proof of olographic wills did not repeal the former act requiring all wills to be witnessed, it would seem to imply that the provision we are considering did not repeal the requirement of the former act that "all wills must be in writing and signed by the testator," etc. But if it be assumed that the act of 1891 validated nuncupative wills, being the later expression of the legislative will, what is the situation? In 1895 the Legislature passed an act which was approved February 6, 1895, entitled, "An act to amend section two thousand two hundred and thirty-seven (2237) of the Revised Statutes of Wyoming, relating to wills." Which act is as follows:

"Section 1. That Section 2237 of the Revised Statutes of Wyoming is hereby amended so that it shall read as follows. Section 2237. All wills to be valid must be in writing, or typewritten, witnessed by two competent witnesses, and signed by the testator or by some person in his presence and by his express direction, and if the witnesses are competent at the time of attesting the execution of the will, their subsequent incompetency, from whatever cause it may arise, shall not prevent the probate and allowance of the will. No subscribing witness to any will can derive any benefit therefrom unless there be two disinterested and competent witnesses to the same, but if without a will such witness would be entitled to any portion of the testator's estate, such witness may still receive such portion to the extent and value of the amount devised.

"Sec. 2. Any typewritten wills which may have been executed prior to the passage of this act, shall be admitted to probate, notwithstanding the fact that they are typewritten, if in all other respects they are legally executed.

"Sec. 3. This act shall not apply to olographic or holographic wills.

"Sec. 4. This act shall take effect and be in force from and after its passage."

We have set out this act in full for the reason that it is the latest legislation on the subject of wills, and to clearly show that if the former Wills Act was modified by the Probate Procedure Act of 1891, that act was again modified by the act of 1895, and since that date all wills are governed by its provisions. We are clearly of the opinion that at least since the taking effect of the act of February 6, 1895, nuncupative wills are not recognized as valid wills by the laws of this state, and that the instrument offered for probate as the will of said Rody Thornton, deceased, was invalid as a will, and that the District Court committed no error in refusing to admit it to probate as such. The judgment of the District Court, therefore, is affirmed.   *Affirmed.*

SCOTT, C. J., and POTTER, J., concur.

POOL v. POOL, AS ADMINISTRATOR.
(No. 728.)

ESTATES OF DECEDENTS—CLAIMS AGAINST ESTATE—SERVICES OF SON DURING DECEDENT'S LIFETIME—CONTRACT FOR—FAILURE OF DECEDENT TO PERFORM—RECOVERY OF VALUE OF SERVICES UPON THE QUANTUM MERUIT.

1. In an action against an administrator by a son of the decedent upon a claim for work and labor performed during the father's lifetime and at his request, *held,* that the evidence stated showed an intention on the part of the deceased and an understanding between him and his son, the plaintiff, that the latter should be compensated for his services, and that the services were rendered in pursuance of such understanding, rendering it sufficient to support a verdict in plaintiff's favor.

2. Where a father agreed to give his son practically all of his property at the time of his death in consideration for his services in working upon and caring for the farm owned by the father, and upon which he resided, and failed to do so because of the loss or destruction of a will making the agreed disposition of his property, *held,* that the value of the son's services rendered under the contract could be recovered upon the *quantum meruit* in an action against the administrator of his father's estate.

3. The petition alleging the understanding between the father
   and son, the performance of the services, the value thereof,
   and the loss or destruction of a will made by the father
   devising practically all his property to the plaintiff, was
   sufficient to permit proof of the reasonable value of the
   plaintiff's services, and sufficient to state a cause of action.
[Decided June 30, 1913.]   (133 Pac. 372.)

ERROR to the District Court, Johnson County; HON. CAR-
ROLL H. PARMELEE, Judge.

The material facts are stated in the opinion.

Metz & Sackett, for plaintiff in error.

Failing to allege any specific promise of the decedent to
pay the plaintiff for his services, the petition is insufficient.
Where one performs services for another, living in and as
one of the family of the latter, being provided with food,
clothing, lodging and care as one of the family, and there is
no contract relating or providing for compensation for the
services, no action can be maintained therefor. (Hay v.
Peterson, 6 Wyo. 419.) There should have been a verdict
for the defendant, for the evidence fails to show any contract. A son cannot recover for services performed on his
father's farm while residing with and making his father's
home his own home, without a specific agreement and promise to pay him wages. The jury were instructed that no
specific promise was necessary, but that a mere intention, or
an implication of an intention on the part of the father that
the son should receive some compensation was all that was
necessary to bind the father's estate. This is not the law.
(Robinson v. Cushman, 2 Denio, 149; McGarvey v. Roods,
35 N. W. 488; Hinkle v. Sage (Ohio), 65 N. E. 999; Bash
v. Bash, 9 Pa. 260; Duffey v. Duffey, 42 Pa. 399; Zimmerman v. Zimmerman, 129 Pa. 227, 15 Am. St. 720, 18 Atl.
129; Hall v. Finch, 29 Wis. 278, 9 Am. St. 559; Schmidt's
Est., 93 Wis. 120, 67 N. W. 37; Coller v. Patterson, 137
Ill. 403, 24 N. E. 604; Desbrow v. Durand, 54 N. J. L. 343,
24 Atl. 545, 33 Am. St. 678; Wood on Mast. & Servt., Secs.
72, 75; Thorpe v. Patterson, 37 Mich. 68; James v. Gillen

(Ind.), 30 N. E. 9; Starkey v. Perry, 71 Cal. 495, 12 Pac. 508; Gerber v. Baurline, 19 Pac. 849; Mobley v. Webb, 3 So. 812; Daubson v. Austin, 9 Pa. St. 309; Barhite's App., 126 Pa. St. 404, 17 Atl. 617; Ryan v. Lynch, 9 Mo. App. 18; Williams v. Williams, 132 Mass. 304; Smith v. Johnson, 45 Ia. 308; Wyley v. Bull, 41 Kan. 206, 20 Pac. 855.)

Enterline & LaFleiche, for defendant in error.

Although the plaintiff below was a son of the decedent, he was not a member of his family during the period for which he claims compensation for his services, in the sense in which that term is employed in the cases cited by opposing counsel. This case is not like Hay v. Peterson, 6 Wyo. 419. Ample evidence was introduced in this case to sustain the verdict. There is overwhelming testimony to the effect that the deceased had promised to compensate his son by giving him all of his property. The case is narrowed down to the question whether the recovery was proper upon a *quantum meruit.* We think clearly that the question is to be answered in the affirmative. (Norton's Est. v. McAllister, 123 Pac. 963.) The decedent having agreed to compensate his son in the manner suggested, the contract could not be avoided even though he destroyed the will which he made devising the property to the son. By the instructions the issue was squarely submitted whether or not there was an intention on the part of the decedent and the plaintiff that the labor of the latter and money expended by him should be paid for. The jury was properly instructed in that respect, and must have found such an intention to have existed. The fact that the decedent made a will in favor of his son tends to rebut the presumption that the latter was working for his father gratuitously. (Loper v. Sheldon's Est. (Wis.), 97 N. W. 524; 35 N. W. 496 (Iowa); Ridler v. Ridler (Ia.), 72 N. W. 671; Winkler v. Killian (N. C.), 54 S. E. 540; Williams v. Barnes, 14 N. C. 348; Parker v. Parker, 33 Ala. 459; Steel v. Steel, 12 Pa. 64; Page on Contracts, 778-782; Hokler v. Van Slambrook (Mich.), 86 N. W. 402; Fry v. Fry, 94 S. W. 990; App. of Huntington,

73 Conn. 582, 48 Atl. 766; Nelson v. Masterton, 2 Ind.
App. 524, 28 N. E. 731; Purviance v. Shultz, 16 Ind. App.
94; Griffith v. Robertson, 73 Kan. 666, 85 Pac. 748; Mc-
Guire v. McGuire, 74 Ky. (11 Bush.) 142; Williams Est.,
106 Mich. 490, 64 N. W. 490; Shane v. Shearsmith's Est.,
137 Mich. 32, 100 N. W. 123; Cullen v. Wolverton, 65 N.
J. L. 279, 47 Atl. 626; Gall v. Gall, 27 App. Div. (N. Y.)
173, 50 N. Y. Supp. 563; Leahy v. Campbell, 77 App. Div.
(N. Y.) 127, 75 N. Y. Supp. 72; In re Wescott, 34 App.
Div. (N. Y.) 239, 54 N. Y. Supp. 545; Bair v. Hager, 90
N. Y. Supp. 27; In re Funk's Est., 98 N. Y. Supp. 934, 49
Misc. Rep. 199; Waddell v. Waddell, 42 S. W. 46.) The
above cases fully sustain the right of the son in this case to
recover.

SCOTT, CHIEF JUSTICE.

It is alleged in the petition filed in the court below and
the evidence adduced upon the trial tends to show that
Daniel J. Pool died intestate on October 3, 1911, and that
during his life time he owned and resided on a farm in
Johnson County, Wyoming, which he sold in August, 1910,
receiving therefor $6,000, and removed to California. He
had raised a family of children, all of whom were adults and
all of whom had departed from the parental roof and were
in business for themselves. Becoming old and by reason
of the infirmity of age, he solicited his son, W. B. Pool, the
defendant in error, to give up his business in Sheridan
County in 1903 and come and work for him on the farm
and relieve his father and mother, both of whom are now
deceased, the wife and mother having died first on or about
January 7, 1910, of the duties and cares of conducting the
farm in pursuance of a contract between them that if his
son would come and work upon the place and take care of
the father and mother during their lifetime that the father
would pay him by giving him all the property he had at his
death. Such offer had been made to other members of his
family, but had been refused. The defendant in error gave
up his business, returned and brought with him some

money of his own, which he expended in improvements on
the farm, and worked upon the farm and continued to do so
up to one year prior to the time of the decease of his father,
when the farm was sold, appropriating, as it is alleged, the
proceeds of the farm or the rent received therefrom during
the last few years prior to his father's death, and caring for
his father and mother during that time, and up to the time
his father died. The father made a will devising all of his
property to the defendant in error, with the exception of
$25 to each of his other children, and reciting therein the
reason why he so disposed of his property. This will was
either lost or destroyed, but the scrivener who wrote it testified to its contents as above, and the reasons given by testator, in conversation at the time of writing the will, for the
manner of his disposition of the property. Upon the decease of the father, George H. Pool procured himself to be
appointed administrator of the estate, and his brother, the
plaintiff, filed his claim, duly verified, for the sum of
$3,579.27, for work and labor performed at the request of
and during his father's lifetime at the rate of $40 per month,
and for items of expenditure, which claim was disallowed
by the administrator, whereupon this action was commenced upon a *quantum meruit*. The case was tried to a
jury and a verdict was rendered for the sum of $2,000 in
favor of W. B. Pool, plaintiff below and defendant in error
here, and judgment rendered thereon for said sum and
costs. The administrator brings error.

It is assigned as error that the petition does not state facts
sufficient to constitute a cause of action, and that the proof
is insufficient to warrant a recovery. It is contended by the
administrator that the case upon the facts falls within the
rule announced by this court in Hay v. Peterson, 6 Wyo., at
page 423, 45 Pac. at page 1073, 34 L. R. A. 581, and which
is as follows: "If the person performing such services lives
in and is one of the family of the other, for whom the services are performed, being provided with food, clothing,
lodging and care as one of the family, and doing labor and

work for such other person, and, as a matter of fact, there is no contract between them relating to or providing for any compensation to be paid for such work and labor, then no action can be maintained." The inapplicability of the rule to the facts here is apparent. Here an express contract was proven, that is to say, if the son would return to the parental roof, and work for his father and mother during their lifetime, then the father would give him all of his property at the time of his death. Upon this question the scrivener who wrote the will at the request of decedent testified to a conversation had with him at the time he made the will, as follows:

"Q. You may state to the jury whether or not at that time you had any conversation with Daniel James Pool relative to any work, labor, or moneys that the plaintiff had advanced in relation to work or labor performed on the deceased's ranch and improvements made thereon?

"A. I had such a conversation with him.

"Q. What did he say to you about that?

"A. He said that some five or six years previous to this conversation, his son, W. B. Pool, had come to work for him upon his place. That his coming had been in pursuance of a contract between them, to the effect that if the son would come and work upon the place, for the father and mother during their lifetime, that he would pay him by giving him all he had at his death. He said that he had made this offer to the other members of the family and that the offer had been refused. He said that in pursuance of this offer the boy had left his business in Sheridan County, and had come to live with him on the place, and had at that time worked for him about four, or five, or six years. That in addition to the work of caring for the place the boy had put some of his own money into certain improvements upon the place; that he was growing old and that certain troubles in the family had emphasized the necessity of concentrating the understanding and contract between himself and his son and that he desired to make a will whereby his son would

inherit his real and personal property at his death. He said
with reference to his other children that it was his understanding of the *law* that they should be left some portion of
his estate else the will would be illegal. I told him I knew of
no law that would render the will illegal for that reason, but
he insisted that the will should be so drawn that the children
should be mentioned individually and that the sum of twenty-five dollars should be left to each of them and that the
remainder of the estate, both real and personal, of every
kind and nature, should go to his son, William B. Pool. He
further requested that an explanation should be entered in
the will of why he did this, explaining at the same time that
he had had an understanding with the other children that
this should be the manner of the disposition of his property.
I made the will in conformity with this request. He read
it over and signed it, expressing an earnest desire that there
should be no trouble about it. He asked me if it would
stick. I told him I thought it would. I then explained to him that it had to be witnessed by someone and
he went out and was gone some few minutes and came back .
with Richard M. Kennedy and J. M. Sonnamaker and they
signed as witnesses to the will. After the signing of the will
I put it in an ordinary envelope and he said, 'What must I
do with this?' I said do whatever you please; we have a
place here to keep it or you can take it anywhere you want
to. 'Well,' he says, 'now I have a little package down at the
bank with Mr. Thom, will that be all right?' I said I think
so, so he took it away. He didn't speak to me about this
matter after that until some time during February, March,
or possibly April, of 1910; he then spoke to me again in the
store of Mr. Adams and Young and in that conversation he
said 'Do you remember making a will for me?' Yes, I do.
'Do you remember in that will that my wife was spoken of—
that the boy should keep her upon the ranch and maintain
her in the manner in which she has been maintained in case
I preceded her to the grave?' I said, Yes, I remember that,
and he said 'Is there any change necessary in that now she

has gone? She has passed away,' and I said, Yes, I understand she is dead, Mr. Pool, but I don't think any change
is necessary on that account, and that's about all I now
recollect in regard to the matter."

There is other evidence in the record showing the intention of the father to compensate his son, the defendant in
error, for his services. On March 20, 1907, the son married and took his wife to live on the farm where they lived
until August 10, 1910, with the exception of from December 17, 1907, until May 1, 1908, during which time they
were in California on account of the wife's health. They
then returned to the farm in response to a telegram from
the young wife's father saying that both Daniel J. and his
wife were ill. Helen Pool, the son's wife, testified that she
had several conversations with her husband's father as to
how her husband was to be compensated for his work. That
the father had said her husband had left his interests, his
own work, and came there to take care of him and his
mother, to run the ranch, and he didn't have any way of
paying him, and he was going to pay him when he was gone
by giving him his property. That afterward there was
trouble in the family and she wanted to leave and he said
"No, that we must stay there and take care of him, that
that was our home.

Q. "Did he at that time or any time later say anything
about payment?

A. "He often spoke about paying my husband by leaving
him his property.

Q. "Did he, in course of the conversation, Mrs. Pool,
ever tell you when it was—or how long your husband had
worked for him?

A. "He didn't tell me the year. He said that when he
left Prairie Dog he came there to live."

A week after the ranch was sold in August, 1910, the
plaintiff, his wife and Daniel J. Pool removed to California,
where they resided until the death of the latter on October
3, 1911. Charles A. Buel, who was sworn and testified as

a witness in behalf of W. B. Pool that his daughter was the wife of the plaintiff; that she came over to his home one day during 1908 and he went over to Mr. Pool's; and also as follows:

Q. "Go on and state what conversation you had with Mr. Pool, at the time after your daughter came home and you went to see him.

A. "He said they couldn't agree in the house and 'It is hard for me to live here alone without her. I didn't want her to go away,' he said, 'I have a hard time.' I will express it just as he said it. He always called his wife, to me, the old woman. I don't like to use the expression but that is the words he used. He said 'I had a hard time to get the old woman to live in the building, but,' he says, 'we finally prevailed upon her to live there. 'Now,' he says, 'Willie has got married and they don't agree to living here. Now, if you will get them to come back and stay here I will build them another house to live in.'

Q. "Go on and state the conversation.

A. "He said, 'I owe all I have got to Willie. He has taken care of me. He has come here and took care of me and done what I asked him to do without compensation; I owe it to him. I owe it to him and the only way that I have got to pay him is to keep him here. If he will stay here and take care of me and the old woman as long as we live he shall have this property. That is the only way I can pay him.' * * *

Q. "I omitted to ask you also, Mr. Buel—I don't know whether you had any conversation with the old man—did he give you any reason at the time you had the conversation with him why he wanted to compensate Will and give him his property?

A. "For staying there and taking care of him and working the place he said. He said he owed it to him.

Q. "Did he say anything about the others?

A. "He said there didn't any of the rest of them want to live with him.

Q. "And meaning the other relatives?

A. "I suppose that is what he meant. That is the words he used."

Mr. Ed Kelle was sworn and testified as a witness on behalf of the plaintiff that in the fall or early winter of 1909 he had a conversation with the deceased relative to his paying the plaintiff and as to when the plaintiff came from Sheridan County to work on the ranch, and further testified as follows:

Q. "Now, tell the jury just what the old gentleman said to you about these matters?

A. "Mr. Daniel Pool and I were very much attached to one another and visited quite often together. That is, when we were alone and he often told me about his affairs there and asked me not to speak to anybody about them, because he didn't care to have them public, and I would also tell him about a case I had and we would speak about our cases amongst one another, and he told me that he didn't know what he would do if it wasn't for his son helping him on the place. He said his son lived on Prairie Dog and he didn't have anybody there and it was hard to have any hired man come and take care of the place the way it should be, and he had asked his son to come and help him, and his son gave up his place and came and helped him and he also said he expected to pay his son very well for helping him on the ranch.

Q. "Now did he say, Mr. Kelle, he expected to pay his son?

A. "Well, he said he expected, the way that Willie had worked there, that he expected to pay him by letting him have the place and that was the only way that he could pay him for what he had done for him.

Q. "When you speak of the old gentleman speaking about his son, to which one did he refer?

A. "He referred to Willie Pool.

Q. "The plaintiff in this suit?

A. "Yes, sir.

Q. "In the course of your conversations with him, Mr. Kelle, did he state anything about the other children, that he could, or could not get along with them, and why he wanted to pay Willie?

A. "He said that Willie was the only one that would come and take care of him and he was his favorite in that way; that he would sooner have Willie come and take care of him than any of the rest as he had asked the rest and they had refused and he had asked Willie to come and he had quit his place and had come and took care of him and had took care of the place for him. * * *

Q. "What did he say in reference to having made his will, if anything, and concerning the payment, and how it was to be made to the plaintiff for his work and labor?

A. "Well, he said he had made out a will and that he had made it out mostly to his boy Will, as Will had worked there on the place and that he had put his money into the place and he wanted to repay him by the will.

Q. "That is, give his property to him?

A. "Yes, sir. * * *

Q. "I want you to give his language. Give what he said?

A. "That is what he said.

Q. "Give his words, now, just as though it was Mr. Pool speaking?

A. "He said I have made out a will, and, he said I have made it out mostly to the boy for the work he has done here on the place, to repay him for the money he had put into the place."

This evidence clearly shows an intention upon the part of the deceased and an understanding between him and his son William B., the plaintiff, that the latter should be compensated for his services, and that the services were rendered in pursuance of such understanding, and we are of the opinion that there was sufficient evidence to support the verdict. It is however urged that no recovery could be had upon *quantum meruit*, but should if at all be by and through the will. The evidence tends to show that the will upon being executed was deposited in the bank by deceased where he kept his private papers, and that during his lifetime the will was known to exist until a short time before he sold the farm and departed for California, when it disappeared. The inference is that the decedent upon the sale of the land destroyed the will. Conceding that to be the fact, there was then no will to probate, but that did not relieve the father from the duty of compensating his son as he had agreed to do. The fact was amply proven that the defendant in error did abandon his private interests at the request of his father and returned to the family homestead for the purpose of managing his father's farm and working for his aged parents, and he was the only one of the children who would do so. In Hay, executor, v. Peterson, *supra*, there was no blood relation between the testator and Peterson, who sued the executor for services rendered to Strom, the testator, during his lifetime. There was a claim that Peterson was a member of Strom's family, clothed and subsisted as such without any promise to pay for his services. This claim was not sustained by the evidence. Upon the facts here the right to recover upon a *quantum meruit* is supported by authority. In Norton's Estate v. McAlister, 22 Colo. App. 293, 123 Pac. 963, the deceased hired his niece to care for him during his declining years, and agreed to compensate her at his death by giving her certain named real estate which he failed to do, and it was held that she was entitled to maintain an action on the *quantum meruit* for the value of her services. So in the case at bar the deceased agreed to give his son practically all of his property at the time of his death in consideration for his services, and having failed to do so the value of such services so rendered under the contract could be recovered upon the *quantum meruit* under the rule announced by the court in Norton's Estate, *supra*. It would indeed be a harsh rule to hold that after defendant in error had performed his part of the contract and nothing was left but to pay him in property, that because of the failure of the decedent to make provision for his payment as he had agreed, the defendant should be barred from recovery. The case was tried upon the theory that the services were rendered in pursuance of an express contract and there was evidence sufficient to go to the jury as to the existence of such contract and having found that such contract existed but was unperformed by the father, the son was entitled to maintain this action as upon *quantum meruit*. Of course the father did not agree to pay his son at the rate of $40 per month for his services, but the law in such case, the decedent having failed to carry out his part of the agreement during his lifetime, permits a recovery for the value of the services rendered. (Norton's Estate, *supra*.) The allegations of the petition were sufficient to permit of such proof and for that reason stated facts sufficient to constitute a cause of action in favor of the plaintiff and against the defendant. The jury were instructed in accordance with the theory upon which the case was tried. We discover no error in the record and the judgment will be affirmed.   *Affirmed.*

POTTER, J., and BEARD, J., concur.

DEMPLE v. CARROLL.
(No. 734.)

EVIDENCE—PAROL EVIDENCE—CONTRACT—PLEADING—AMENDMENT— NEW TRIAL—SURPRISE—NEWLY DISCOVERED EVIDENCE—ABSENCE OF WITNESS—PETITION—SUFFICIENT STATEMENT OF CAUSE OF ACTION.

1. The law excludes, as incompetent, parol testimony to vary the terms of a written instrument, or to prove a parol contemporaneous agreement at variance from the writing, in the absence of fraud, accident, or mistake.

2. The rule stated applied, where defendant, who had purchased plaintiff's interest and stock in a corporation and as part of the consideration agreed in writing to assume

"all" of the plaintiff's "obligations of the" corporation, alleged and sought to show by parol testimony, in an action by plaintiff to recover an obligation entered into by the plaintiff for the corporation and not paid by defendant, that the agreement was for the assumption by defendant of certain specified obligations not including the one in suit.

3. It was not error during the trial for the court to refuse permission to the defendant to amend his answer so as to allege that his signature to the contract was procured by fraud, deceit and false representations.

4. Having permitted the defendant to introduce his evidence as to fraud, deceit and false representations subject to the plaintiff's objection, it was not error at the close of the evidence to exclude all such evidence, since its purpose was to alter or vary the terms of the written contract, and was inadmissible under the pleadings.

5. Aside from the statute (Comp. Stat. 1910, Sec. 4437) providing that a party applying to amend a pleading during the trial shall be required to show that the amendatory facts were unknown to him prior to the application, unless the court in its discretion shall relieve him from so doing, the general rule is that it is not an abuse of discretion to refuse to allow on the trial an amendment which materially changes the cause of action or defense.

6. That a witness did not testify to certain matters does not entitle the party complaining thereof to a new trial on the ground of surprise, where it appears that the witness was not interrogated as to such matters, for it cannot be assumed that he would not have so testified had he been examined as to them.

7. That a witness who had been summoned did not appear at the trial on account of a death in his family is not a ground for new trial where no continuance of the case or postponement of the trial was asked for on that ground.

8. It was not error to refuse defendant's motion for a new trial on the ground of newly discovered evidence where it appears that the alleged new evidence consisted of the testimony of persons who were interested in the corporation before, at the time of, and subsequent to the transaction between plaintiff and defendant, and what could be shown by the books of the company, and it not appearing that defendant had consulted said persons about the matter, or examined the books of the company before the trial, or that any effort was made to produce such evidence on the trial.

9. A party cannot neglect to exercise such reasonable diligence in the preparation of his case as the circumstances would reasonably suggest and as will enable his attorneys to take the necessary steps to procure the evidence, go to trial without it, and when defeated, be entitled to a new trial for the lack of evidence which could have been produced had proper diligence been exercised.

10. Referring to the petition set out in the opinion it is held to have stated facts sufficient to constitute a cause of action.

ON PETITION FOR REHEARING.

11. The plaintiff having advanced to the corporation the sum of money sued for prior to the sale of his interest and stock to the defendant upon the latter assuming the payment of the plaintiff's obligations for the company, the fact that the plaintiff was a stockholder of the company did not make the company any less his debtor or entitle the defendant to a reduction in the amount of recovery proportionately to plaintiff's stock ownership in the action against defendant for the payment of an obligation assumed by him.

12. Where defendant as a part of the consideration for the purchase of the interest and stock in a corporation assumed. all of plaintiff's obligations for the corporation, and in an action by the plaintiff upon that contract to recover the amount of an obligation so assumed it was not set up in the answer that defendant was merely acting as an agent for another person with the knowledge of the plaintiff, that issue was not presented by the pleadings and was not a question in the case on error.

[Decided June 30, 1913.]   (133 Pac. 137.)
[Rehearing denied September 29, 1913.]   (135 Pac. 117.)

ERROR to the District Court, Sheridan County, HON. CARROLL H. PARMELEE, Judge.

The material facts are stated in the opinions.

Camplin & O'Marr, for plaintiff in error.

The petition fails to state a cause of action and therefore the court should have sustained the objection to the introduction of any evidence by the plaintiff. No authority is shown for the borrowing of money for the company by the plaintiff. It is not alleged that demand was ever made

by the plaintiff on the corporation for the money so borrowed or advanced or that the corporation refused to pay
the amount. And the facts alleged are insufficient to show
that plaintiff's individual note was an obligation of the
corporation or that it was one of its obligations at the time
it was paid by the plaintiff.

It was error to deprive the defendant of the right to
cross-examine the plaintiff as to the consideration for the
sale of his stock to the defendant. If the writing relied on
by the plaintiff is a contract at all it is nothing more than
a simple contract importing no consideration. The denial
of defendant's motion to dismiss at the close of plaintiff's
testimony was error, for the reasons above stated, and for
other reasons as follows: 1. Because it appeared that
Demple was not acting for himself, but as agent for another, a fact known to the plaintiff at the time. 2. Because of the variance between the so-called written contract
and the testimony of the plaintiff as to the consideration
for the sale of his stock to the defendant. 3. Because the
suit is not against the company, and no recovery is sought
upon any claim against the company assumed by defendant;
whether or not the plaintiff is a creditor of the company
or could sue and recover from it is not the question here,
because the note was not an obligation of the company, but
in order to make it appear to be a company obligation the
plaintiff alleged that the company agreed to pay it. 4. Because the plaintiff owned one-half of the stock of the company and the money was borrowed for his benefit as much
as for that of the company. The defendant should have
been permitted under the denial in his answer to show a
different consideration from that alleged in the petition, or
that there was no consideration at all. (4 Ency. Pl. & Pr.
928, 930, 946; 1 Andrews' Am. L. (2nd Ed.) 718-719, and
cases cited.)   Any evidence was admissible that would
show an absence of consideration. (3 Ency. Ev. 373, 384,
388; Culver v. Bank, 78 Ill. 625; Peabody v. Dewey, 153
Ill. 657; Julliard v. Chaffee, 92 N. Y. 529.) The effect

of the evidence offered by defendant was not to vary the
writing but merely to vary its construction and to ascertain
the true meaning and intention of the parties. (Cain v.
Hagenbaith, 106 Pac. 945; Gardiner v. Corson, 15 Mass.
500; 1 Andrews' Am. L., 743.) There is only one party
to the contract and therefore it is not a contract at all. It
can be considered only as a naked promise to answer for
the debt of another. It fixes no time for the performance
of anything. It appears to be indeed a bill of sale from
Carroll to Demple with a clause that the vendee is to assume
&c., and it is then signed by Demple. Considered as a bill
of sale, if there had been verbal reservations, oral evidence
thereof would be admissible. (Hecht v. Johnson, 3 Wyo.
277.) The evidence of the defendant which was stricken
out shows that in the negotiations between the parties the
only "obligations" mentioned or discussed were direct obligations of the company, and, therefore, the natural conclusion of Demple would be that his assumption was merely
to relieve Carroll of any company obligations, and that the
word "obligations" had no reference to the individual notes
of Carroll, though executed for or on behalf of the company. The oral evidence was admissible. (Lattimer v.
Buxton, 40 N. Y. Supp. 1033; 9 Ency. Ev. 418; 1 Elliott
on Ev., 579-582.) It was admissible to explain this contract which is clearly ambiguous and uncertain. (Julian v.
Oil Co., 109 Pac. 969, 111 Pac. 445; Manvell v. Weaver,
102 Pac. 36; Whipple v. Lee, 108 Pac. 601; Phoenix P.
Co. v. Humphrey-Ball Co., 108 Pac. 952.)

This note was signed by another party as well as the
plaintiff. It is elementary that where a joint note is declared on the declaration will not be sustained by proof of
an individual note. The defendant was entitled to a new
trial on the ground of newly discovered evidence. The
new evidence shown by the affidavit in support of the motion would establish a clear case of fraud on the part of
the plaintiff, for it would show that the note was not an
obligation of the corporation.

H. W. Nichols, for defendant in error.

Under the pleadings and the evidence no valid defense to the action was shown. The meaning of the contract is clear. It was sought by the defendant by the introduction of evidence which was finally stricken out to vary the terms of the contract. The evidence was clearly inadmissible. (George v. Emery, 18 Wyo. 352; Grieve v. Grieve, 15 Wyo. 358; Stickney v. Hughes, 13 Wyo. 257.) The plain intent of the contract is that Demple agreed to assume all the personal obligations or debts that Carroll had incurred in behalf of the company. And the petition alleged that the amount sued for was an indebtedness of the plaintiff incurred in behalf of the company. The note given by him was merely an evidence of the debt, and it is immaterial whether that note was itself an obligation of the company or not. It is also immaterial that the plaintiff was not the only person who had signed the note. He was called upon to pay it and he did pay it. It was his note and it was clearly admissible to show in connection with other evidence that it was a debt incurred by him. Demple did not sign the contract as an agent, but as acting for himself. If he was in fact acting for another person, he is liable since the principal was not disclosed. However, the evidence shows that Demple was acting for himself in making the purchase and contract. There was no proper showing in the motion for new trial to entitle the defendant to a new trial on the ground of newly discovered evidence.

BEARD, JUSTICE.

The defendant in error, George G. Carroll, brought this action in the District Court of Sheridan County, against the plaintiff in error, Peter Demple, to recover the sum of one thousand dollars and interest alleged to be due on a certain written agreement. The case was tried to the court without a jury, and judgment rendered against the defendant below (Demple), and he brings error.

The plaintiff, Carroll, alleged in his petition, in substance, that prior' to May 16, 1911, he was the owner of a large

interest in, and a large part of the capital stock of the Sheridan Manufacturing Company, a Wyoming corporation, engaged in the business of purchasing wheat from farmers
and others and manufacturing it into flour; that on said
date he sold his interest and stock in said company to the
defendant, Demple, for the consideration of $1,000 cash
and the assumption by the defendant of all the obligations
incurred by plaintiff for and on behalf of said company,
and as evidence of such sale and agreement the defendant
executed the following written contract.

"This 16th day of May, 1911, know all men by these
presence, that said G. G. Carroll has this day sold unto
Peter Demple his right, title and interest in the Sheridan
Manufacturing Company for the sum of (one thousand
dollars) $1,000.00 cash. Said Peter Demple agrees to as-
sume all of said G. G. Carroll obligations of the Sheridan
Mfg. Co. (Signed) "PETER DEMPLE."

That one of the obligations incurred by the plaintiff for
and in behalf of said company and which was unpaid and
owing at the time said contract was made was the sum of
$1,000, and interest which had been advanced by plaintiff
for said company about December 7, 1908, in payment for
wheat sold and delivered to said company by W. S. Metz;
which sum the plaintiff borrowed from the First National
Bank of Sheridan on his personal note. That defendant
had failed and refused to pay said note in accordance with
his contract, and that plaintiff was compelled to and did
pay said note. Alleged the payment of the $1,000 cash.

The defendant in his answer admitted the purchase of
the interest and shares of stock in the company; that he
paid plaintiff $1,000, as part of the consideration therefor;
and that he signed the instrument set out in the petition.
Alleged "that at the time of making the contract and agreement set out in paragraph one of said petition and the purchase by defendant from plaintiff, plaintiff's interest and
stock in said Sheridan Manufacturing Company it was
fully agreed, understood and intended by the plaintiff and

defendant, that, as part of the consideration for such sale, the defendant was to assume and pay certain debts and obligations of plaintiff and the said Sheridan Manufacturing Company, which were at said time specified and agreed upon by the parties, which said specified debts and obligations are as follows, to-wit: one note given to Citizens State Bank of Sheridan, Wyo., in the amount of $1,200.00; one note given to the Bank of Commerce of Sheridan, Wyoming, in the amount of $1,400.00; and small quantities of flour due various persons who had furnished wheat to said Sheridan Manufacturing Company's mill and were to receive flour in return therefor. That by said agreement in said petition set forth it was agreed, understood and intended by the parties thereto, the plaintiff and defendant herein, that the above debts and obligations were the only debts and obligations to be assumed by said defendant; that the defendant did not at the time of signing said agreement know of the existence of the obligation of plaintiff to the First National Bank of Sheridan, Wyoming, mentioned in said petition, and that defendant did not at said time, or at any time, agree with plaintiff that he, the said defendant, would pay or assume the payment of the said obligation of plaintiff to said First National Bank; that it was fully understood, agreed and intended by the parties to this suit that the full and complete consideration for the sale of plaintiff's interest and stock in the said Sheridan Manufacturing Company was the sum of $1,000.00 and the assumption of the specified debts and obligations hereinabove set forth." The other allegations of the petition were denied. A reply was filed denying the new matters set up in the answer.

We have set out at length the allegations of the answer containing what the defendant sought to prove by way of an affirmative defense to the action, in order that the rulings and decision of the court may clearly appear. We think it clearly appears by the answer and the defendant's evidence that the obligation sued upon was one of the class or character of debts and obligations a part of which defendant admits he was to assume and pay as a part of the consideration for the transaction. The answer contains no allegations of any false or fraudulent representations with respect to, or fraudulent concealment of the debts or obligations to be assumed by the defendant, made by the plaintiff to induce, or which did induce the defendant to sign the agreement which he admits in his testimony he read before he signed it. The defendant sought to prove by parol testimony that the contract was different from that contained in the writing. This the court refused to permit, and rightly so under the pleadings. No rule of law is better settled than the one which excludes, as incompetent, parol testimony to vary the terms of a written instrument, or to prove a parol contemporaneous agreement at variance from the writing, in the absence of any allegation of fraud, accident or mistake. On the trial and while the defendant was introducing his evidence, he asked leave to amend his answer and be permitted to plead that defendant's signature to the agreement was procured by fraud, deceit, and false representations made by plaintiff. The court refused to permit the amendment to be made, but stated, in substance, that he would permit the defendant, subject to the objection of plaintiff, to introduce his evidence on that matter. We think there was no abuse of discretion on the part of the court in refusing leave to so amend the answer at that stage of the case. To have done so would have introduced a new and important element of defense not pleaded in the answer upon which the case went to trial, and a defense which the defendant must necessarily have known to exist, if it did exist, at the time he filed his answer; and no showing was made excusing the failure or neglect to so plead in the original answer, or that the amendatory facts were unknown to the defendant prior to the application. The statute, Sec. 4437, Comp. Stat. 1910, provides, "The party applying to amend during the trial shall be required to show that the amendatory facts were unknown to him prior to

the application, unless in its discretion the court shall relieve him from so doing." Aside from the statute the rule
is quite uniform that it is not an abuse of discretion for
the court to refuse to allow an amendment on the trial
which materially changes the cause of action or defense.
(Gale, Adm'r. v. Foss, 47 Mo. 276; Wixon v. Devine, 91
Cal. 477, 27 Pac. 777; Pierce v. Bruman, 88 Minn. 50, 92
N. W. 507; Moyers v. Fogarty, 140 Ia. 701, 119 N. W.
159; Barrett v. Kansas & T. Coal Co., 70 Kan. 649, 79
Pac. 150; Phenix Ins. Co. v. Stocks et al., 149 Ill. 319, 36
N. E. 408; Deline v. Ins. Co., 70 Mich. 435, 38 N. W. 298.)

While the court refused to allow the defendant to amend
his answer, he did permit him to introduce his evidence tending to prove fraud and misrepresentations on the part of
the plaintiff as to the indebtedness of the company, and
tending to prove that he was only to assume certain specified debts. But on those matters the evidence was conflicting and to our minds was insufficient to sustain the charge
of fraud or misrepresentations had the amendment been
allowed. At the close of the evidence the court, on motion
of plaintiff, excluded all testimony offered by defendant attempting to alter or vary the terms of the written agreement. In this there was no error. Under the pleadings
such testimony was clearly inadmissible. Many rulings of
the court sustaining objections to testimony are assigned as
error in the motion for a new trial, but as they related to
the testimony offered to vary the terms of the writing need
not be considered separately. It is also assigned as error
that the court excluded the testimony of one Whitney, a
witness for defendant. Counsel are mistaken in this. The
record shows that but one question asked this witness was
objected to by counsel for plaintiff and that objection was
overruled, and at the end of his examination in chief counsel for plaintiff moved to strike out all of his testimony as
incompetent, irrelevant and immaterial, which motion was
denied. It is also made a ground in the motion for a new
trial, that defendant was surprised that this witness did not

testify to certain matters which it is stated in the affidavit in support of the motion he had said he would testify to; but he was not interrogated as to those matters, and it cannot be assumed that he would not have so testified had he been examined as to them. A new trial is also urged for the reason that one Traphagen, a witness for defendant, and who had been summoned, did not appear at the trial on account of a death in his family. But no continuance of the case or postponement of the trial was asked for that reason and in those circumstances it was too late to complain after judgment. Another ground of the motion for a new trial is alleged newly discovered evidence. This new evidence consists of the testimony of persons who were interested in the company before, at the time of, and subsequent to the transaction and what could be shown by the books of the company. Some of this evidence would be inadmissible under the pleadings and much of it merely cumulative. In preparing his case for trial it was the duty of defendant to make inquiry of those persons whom he knew would be most likely to know the facts necessary to establish his defense. It does not appear that these persons were consulted about the matter, or the books of the company examined before the trial, nor is any reason for the failure to do so stated, or that any effort was made to produce such evidence on the trial. A party cannot neglect to exercise such reasonable diligence in the preparation of his case as the circumstances would reasonably suggest and as will enable his attorneys to take the necessary steps to procure the evidence, go to trial without it, and when defeated be entitled to a new trial for the lack of evidence which could have been produced had proper diligence been exercised.

It is further contended that the court erred in permitting the plaintiff to introduce any evidence for the reason that the petition did not state facts sufficient to constitute a cause of action. With that contention we do not agree. The substance of the petition is set out at the beginning of this opinion and we think it unnecessary to discuss that question more at length. We think the case was fairly tried upon the issues presented by the pleadings, and a correct judgment entered on the evidence.

Finding no prejudicial error in the record the judgment is affirmed.   *Affirmed*.

SCOTT, C. J., and POTTER, J., concur.

ON PETITION FOR REHEARING.

BEARD, JUSTICE.

Plaintiff in error has filed a petition for a rehearing in which it is claimed we did not give proper consideration to the alleged errors assigned in the motion for a new trial. The main contention now is that we did not consider the objection that the judgment was excessive and should have been for only $500, if for any amount, for the reason that Carroll was the owner of one-half of the capital stock of the Sheridan Manufacturing Co. The claim of plaintiff below, as we understand the pleading, was that the company was indebted to Metz in the sum of $1,000, and not having the money to pay Metz, Carroll advanced it for the company; that the company failed to repay him and still owed him that amount when Demple executed the instrument sued on. It was the company (a corporation) which was his debtor and not the stockholders, and the fact that he was a stockholder did not make the company any less the debtor and him its creditor than if he had been an outside party. It was the debt of the company to him that Demple assumed. The fact that he borrowed the money and when he renewed the note another stockholder became surety on the note did not change his liability, or the company's obligation to him; and the evidence sufficiently shows that he paid the full amount. The amount of the company's indebtedness to him at the time of the transaction with Demple and at the time of the trial was $1,000, which Demple had assumed. The judgment therefore was not excessive.

In the brief in support of the petition for rehearing it is stated, "Although the contract set out in the petition signed by Demple appears to be the transaction of Demple, it is disclosed from the testimony of Demple that he was acting as agent for another person in the purchase, and from the testimony of the plaintiff, Carroll, it also appears that he was aware of that fact, and from the testimony of both, it is disclosed that Demple was not the real party in interest." On that question it is sufficient to say, that no such issue was presented by the pleadings; and we have again carefully reread the entire testimony of Demple and no such condition is even suggested. He repeatedly stated that he made the contract, and in answer to the following question propounded by his own counsel, "Did you examine the books since?" answer, "No, because I sold out that stock again right the day after that you know. I am not interested in the mill at all." His own testimony would have effectually disposed of any question of agency had such an issue been presented by the pleadings. Not only so, but in the first paragraph of the answer it is admitted "that defendant, on or about the 16th day of May, 1911, purchased from plaintiff plaintiff's interest and shares of stock in the Sheridan Manufacturing Company."

Other questions with reference to the alleged newly discovered evidence, the exclusion of certain testimony, and the refusal of the court to permit the defendant to amend his answer during the trial, have been argued in the brief on petition for rehearing. They were considered and decided in the opinion (133 Pac. 137), and on a re-examination of the record the views expressed in the opinion are adhered to. As was there said, we think the case was fairly tried upon the issues presented by the pleadings, and the judgment sufficiently supported by the evidence. A rehearing will therefore be denied.   *Rehearing denied.*

SCOTT, C. J., and POTTER, J., concur.

J. J. CRABLE & SON v. O'CONNOR.
(No. 715.)

Appeal and Error—Conflicting Evidence—Sufficiency of Evidence—Partnership—Parol Evidence That Contract of Partner Was Partnership Contract—Admissions by Partner—Attachment—Motion to Quash Writ—Motion to Strike Part of Affidavit—Practice—Appeal Bond—Stay of Execution.

1. In an action to recover from a partnership the rent of certain teams of horses and mules, the evidence examined and held sufficient to justify a finding that the contract relied on by the plaintiff was made for the benefit of the partnership, although made in the name of and signed by one partner.

2. The trial court having found that the teams were leased for the partnership and for its benefit, and there being a conflict in the evidence on the subject, the finding of the court will not be disturbed on error, it appearing that the evidence is sufficient to justify the finding.

3. It is competent to show by parol evidence that a party who is named in and has signed a contract as one of the parties thereto was an agent for another, and acted as such agent in making the contract, so as to give the benefit of the contract to, and charge with liability, the unnamed principal, whether the unnamed principal was or was not disclosed or known to the other party to the contract at the time it was made. And this rule applies to a contract made and executed by one partner, when acting for the firm and within the scope of the partnership business.

4. Where the fact of a partnership is shown by other evidence, the conversations between the parties to a contract are admissible to show that although made in the name of and signed by one of the partners, it was made for the benefit of the partnership.

5. It would not be proper to strike out statements contained in an affidavit for attachment, upon a motion alleging that the statements are immaterial or disclose no ground for attachment; *so held* where a motion was made to strike out a statement of the non-residence of one of the defendants.

6. A judgment having been entered for the plaintiff, in an action wherein the property of the defendants had been attached, an order was entered after judgment upon the application of the defendants that upon their giving bond as provided by law for stay of execution in a sum fixed

by the order, to be approved by the clerk of the court, execution should be stayed for a stated period as to the parties giving the bond, and that the attached property be released, the order providing that such bond should be given under the statute relating to appeals; the bond was given and the attached property released. *Held,* that without anything appearing in the record to show that the bond was merely a forthcoming bond, it was the privilege and duty of the court to assume that it was a bond authorized by the said order of the court, viz.: a bond to stay execution pending proceedings in error, obligating the parties to pay the judgment if affirmed, thereby taking the question as to the validity of the attachment or the correctness of the ruling of the court refusing to quash it out of the case, the attachment being unnecessary to give the court jurisdiction of the person of either of the defendants, the personal appearance of each of them having been entered in the cause.

[Decided June 30, 1913.] (133 Pac. 376.)

ERROR to the District Court, Big Horn County, HON. CARROLL H. PARMELEE, Judge.

The material facts are stated in the opinion.

James M. Workman and *William C. Snow,* for plaintiffs in error.

Parol evidence is inadmissible to contradict the terms of a written instrument. (21 Ency. Law, (2nd Ed.) 1078.) Such evidence is inadmissible to show that a third party is interested in the contract as a partner, thereby contradicting the terms of the instrument. (Chambers v. Brown, 69 Ia. 213, 28 N. W. 561.) The parol admission of a party made *in pais* is competent evidence only of the facts which may be lawfully established by parol evidence. (Greenleaf on Ev., Sec. 203; 1 Ency. L. (2nd Ed.) 716.) A person contracting with an agent, who has full knowledge of the principal, but extends credit to the agent exclusively, cannot thereafter resort to the principal, and the latter is not bound, although the agent acted in the course of his employment and for the benefit of his principal. (31 Cyc.

1570; Ford v. Williams, 62 U. S. 287, 16 L. Ed. 36; 1
Ency. L., (2nd Ed.) 1138; Henderson v. Mayhew, 2 Gill.
(Md.) 393, 41 Am. Dec. 434; Peterson v. Roach, 32 O.
St. 374, 30 Am. Rep. 607; Holmes v. Burton, 9 Vt. 252,
31 Am. Dec. 621; Mechem on Agency, Sec. 558.) The
usual and decisive indication of an exclusive credit to the
agent is where the creditor knows that there is a principal,
but makes the charge against the agent. It is a question of
intention. (Taintor v. Prendergast, 3 Hill, 72, 38 Am. Dec.
618; 1 Bates on Partnership, Sec. 446-447; 22 Ency. Law,
(2nd Ed.) 163; Mechem on Agcy., Sec. 446.) Agency
cannot be proved by the declarations of the one assuming
to act as agent. (1 Ency. L., (2nd Ed.) 690; Mechem on
Agcy., Sec. 100; Blake v. Bremyer, 84 Kans. 708, 115
Pac. 538.) One dealing with an agent as principal who
afterwards discovers the concealed principal may then elect
to hold one or the other, but he cannot hold both, and such
election must be within a reasonable time after discovering
the principal. (Mechem on Agcy., 698, 699; 1 Ency. L.,
. (2nd Ed.) 1139; Gay v. Uren, (Minn.) 26 L. R. A. 742.)
The fact that a partnership has received the benefit of merchandise purchased by one partner on his individual credit
does not entitle the creditor to look to the firm for payment
unless the partner acted as agent in making the purchase.
(22 Ency. L., (2nd Ed.) 164; 1 Bates on Partnership, Sec.
446.) The acceptance of a note of an individual with full
knowledge of the firm or principal discharges the latter.
(Paige v. Stone, 10 Metc. (Mass.) 160, 43 Am. Dec. 420.)
Where at the time of dealing with an agent the principal
is not concealed, the act of giving credit to the agent constitutes an election. (Morrell v. Kenyon, 48 Conn. 314,
40 Am. Rep. 174; 1 Ency. Law, (2nd Ed.) 1139, note 1.)
The testimony of the attorney who drew the contract
was inadmissible because it contradicted the written instrument, and also because agency cannot be shown in that manner so as to bind the partnership who was not named in and
did not sign the contract. The plaintiff was not entitled

to recover against the partnership for the reason that when he signed the contract he had full knowledge of the partnership and elected to give credit to the partner with whom he contracted. The evidence, we think, establishes that the teams were leased by E. A. Crable individually and upon his own responsibility, and not for the firm.

The court erred in overruling the motion to quash the writ of attachment. There is no evidence to sustain any of the allegations of the affidavit concerning fraud. The allegation that one of the defendants, J. J. Crable, was a non-resident, afforded no ground for attachment. No claim was made against him as an individual. The partnership was a resident of the state, notwithstanding the fact that one of its members was not. The firm was doing business and one of the partners resided here, and the property was attached as the property of the firm, and it was shown that it belonged to the firm.

C. A. Zaring and *Thomas M. Hyde,* for defendant in error.

The testimony of the attorney who drew the contract was competent to show that E. I. Crable when he signed the contract was acting as a member of the firm of J. J. Crable & Son, and for their benefit. Parol evidence is admissible to show the capacity in which a person acts, the actual relation of parties to a writing, and that persons not named therein are in fact interested. (Jones on Ev., (2nd Ed.) par. 452 and cases cited; Curran v. Holland, 75 Pac. 46; Exchange Bank v. Hubbard, 62 Fed. 116.) A written contract is binding on a firm, although signed by one of the partners only instead of in the firm name, when it is shown that it was made in a firm transaction and intended as an obligation of the partnership. (30 Cyc, 485; Brewing Co. v. Hawke, (Utah) 66 Pac. 1058.)

In the affidavit supporting the motion to quash the attachment the averment that J. J. Crable was a non-resident of the state was not denied. Upon a motion to dissolve an attachment on the ground that the allegations in the affidavit for attachment are untrue all of the allegations must be traversed. (Bank v. Latham, 8 Wyo. 316.) The court therefore properly overruled the motion to dissolve the writ.

Potter, Justice.

The defendant in error was plaintiff in the court below and brought this action against J. J. Crable, E. I. Crable and J. J. Crable & Son, plaintiffs in error here, to recover a sum of money alleged to be due as rent for certain teams delivered to J. J. Crable & Son by the plaintiff pursuant to a written contract set out in the petition as follows:

"This agreement made this 5th day of September, 1910, between Pat O'Connor, of Thermopolis, Wyoming, party of the first part, and E. I. Crable of Thermopolis, Wyoming, party of the second part.

"Witnesseth, that the said party of the first part, for and in consideration of the agreements hereinafter contained, to be kept and performed by the party of the second part, does hereby lease unto the party of the second part eleven two-horse teams composed of horses and mules, for and during three months from date hereof.

"And the party of the second part, for and in consideration of the agreements herein contained by the party of the first part, does hereby agree that he will pay the said party of the first part for the use of said property the sum of $330 per month, same being $30.00 per team, that he will keep the said mules and horses well fed and well cared for and in a first-class and healthy condition, and that he will exercise every care and diligence in the proper care of the same; that he will pay the value of all animals lost, destroyed or injured in any way by reason of his negligence or the negligence of his employees, and that at the termination of this lease he will re-deliver the said property to the party of the first part at Thermopolis, Wyoming, in as good condition as when received by him.

"It is further understood and agreed that the said rental shall be due and payable by the second party to the first party on the 25th day of each month hereafter.

"In witness whereof the parties hereto have hereunto set their hands and seals this 5th day of September, 1910.

"PAT O'CONNOR.

"E. I. CRABLE."

The petition alleges that J. J. Crable & Son is a partnership composed of J. J. Crable and E. I. Crable; that the defendant E. I. Crable, while acting as a member of said firm, entered into the said contract with the plaintiff for and in behalf, and for the use and benefit, of said partnership; that pursuant to the contract the plaintiff delivered to said firm of J. J. Crable & Son eleven teams, "which were thereupon taken to a certain railroad grade between Scribner and Fromberg, Montana, and there used for a period of about three months by said J. J. Crable & Son in working upon their contract in the construction of a certain grade between the places above mentioned." That subsequent to the execution of the contract it was adopted and ratified and the proceeds and benefits thereof were taken and enjoyed by said firm. The petition contains an itemized statement of the amount claimed to be due for the rental of said teams, showing that amount to be $1,136.25, and also a statement of additional items amounting to $79.35, including charges for rent of three carts, and certain property claimed in the testimony of the plaintiff to have been delivered with the teams and not returned, making a total alleged indebtedness of $1,215.60, on which a credit of $212.75 is allowed by the petition for hay furnished the teams, explained in plaintiff's testimony to be for hay furnished after defendants had ceased to use the teams, the net amount alleged to be due, and for which judgment is prayed, being $1,002.85.

An answer was filed by E. I. Crable admitting the execution of the written contract and that he is indebted to the plaintiff under the same in the sum of $990, and denying each and every other material allegation in the petition. He alleged by way of set-off that the plaintiff was indebted to him in the sum of $80.30 for the care and feed of the teams

after the written contract had expired. J. J. Crable filed
an answer denying each and every material allegation in
the petition. J. J. Crable & Son filed a separate answer
alleging that at the time the contract was entered into between the plaintiff and E. I. Crable the partnership existing
between the latter and J. J. Crable had been dissolved by
mutual consent, and denying each and every other material
allegation of the petition. Replies were filed denying the
new matter contained in the separate answers. The case
was tried to the court, without the intervention of a jury,
whereupon the court found that the plaintiff should have
and recover of the defendants and each of them the sum of
$1,073.30, and entered judgment for that amount, together
with costs. It appears that an order of attachment had
been issued in the cause and that certain horses and mules
were attached as the property of J. J. Crable & Son. Motions
to dissolve the attachment were filed, and they were heard
at the same time the cause was tried upon its merits, and the
judgment entry embraced an order that the motions to dissolve the attachment be overruled, and that the attached
property be sold by the sheriff as under execution. It was
further ordered by the judgment that the sheriff exhaust
the property in his hands belonging to the partnership before proceeding against the individual property of the defendants. A motion for a new trial was filed and overruled,
and the case is here upon a petition in error, assigning error
in overruling the motions to dissolve the attachment and
the motion for a new trial.

Parol evidence was admitted, over the objection of the
defendants, to sustain the averments of the petition to the
effect that in making the contract with the plaintiff for the
lease of the teams E. I. Crable acted as a member of and
for the firm of J. J. Crable & Son, and that it was in fact
a partnership contract. It is contended that this ruling was
error for the reason that it violated the principle that parol
evidence is inadmissible to vary or contradict the terms of
a written instrument. It is unnecessary to rehearse all the

testimony on that subject, which to some extent is conflicting.   The plaintiff testified in substance, concerning the
making of the contract, that he knew the firm of J. J. Crable
& Son and the business conducted by the firm; that E. I.
Crable was a member thereof, and that the other member
was his father, J. J. Crable, and that the firm had a contract
for construction work on the railroad grade mentioned in
the petition.   That he had done business with the firm prior
to the making of this contract, having loaned them some
money when they were engaged in other construction work;
that he rented the teams for E. I .Crable and his father to
work on the contract they had on the Frannie-Fromberg
cutoff.   That J. J. Crable was not at the time in Thermopolis, where the contract was made, but that he was up
on the construction work, and Ed came down to get the
teams, "to make arrangements to get them."   He testified
specifically with reference to renting the teams, after referring to the contract of J. J. Crable & Son on the said
railroad grade, "I was renting them to the Crables for that
contract.   I knew he and his father had a contract up on
the cutoff.   And I rented them for that work."   He also
testified, as well as the attorney who drew the contract,
concerning the directions given respecting it and the parties
to it, the effect of their testimony being that the teams were
to be leased to J. J. Crable & Son.   The matter was explained by said attorney as follows:

"Mr. O'Connor and Mr. E. I. Crable met me one morning
in front of my office, and Mr. O'Connor said they wanted
me to draw up a little memorandum for them, and the conversation was to this effect: That Mr. O'Connor wished to
rent certain horses and mules to the firm of Crable & Son
—I cannot state the initials or the name of the other Crable.
* * *   I informed them that the best way for them to
execute this contract was to have all the parties involved
sign the contract; that is, all the members of the partnership.   They explained to me there was a partnership.
* * *   That the other member of the firm was absent and

could not sign at that time, that they wanted this deal closed
at once, or they wanted it fixed up, so I understood. I told
them if it suited them that way it was all right with me,
and therefore I drew the contract." He further testified
that he thought it was not drawn on that day, but probably
the next day, and that he drew it in accordance with the
conversation the parties had with him.

It was shown that the teams were taken to the railroad
grade referred to and that some of them were used on the
firm's construction contract, with the knowledge of J. J.
Crable, who also seems to have known of the contract with
plaintiff, and that others were hired out to brothers of E. I.
Crable, mostly for use on other portions of the grade. E. I.
Crable, maintaining that he alone made the contract with
plaintiff, testified that he rented the teams which he did
not use to his brothers. It may be said here that if the
teams were rented by him for the firm, his act in subletting
them may also have been for the firm. It is not disputed
that as to the construction work in which E. I. Crable was
then interested, a partnership existed between him and his
father, J. J. Crable, under the firm name and style of J. J.
Crable & Son. Indeed, they testified that the partnership
continued as to that work, but that prior to the making of
this contract with plaintiff the partnership had been dissolved, so far as the partnership property was concerned,
E. I. Crable having surrendered his interest in that property to his father. There was no proof of any other work
or business conducted by either J. J. Crable or E. I. Crable
during the time they worked on this grade, or the time for
which the teams in question were rented or used. Counsel
for defendants contend not only that plaintiff's evidence on
the subject of the parties to the contract was inadmissible,
but that "the effect of this testimony is not to show that
Crable acted as agent for the firm when he signed, but to
show that the parties at the time of ordering the contract
drawn intended to have it run to the partnership," and that
"what the parties did, however, was to make a contract run-

ning to the individual." And counsel contend that there is nothing in the testimony to contradict the presumption that the contract correctly represents the intention of the parties when it was signed. The court must have found that the teams were leased for the partnership and for its benefit, and there being a conflict in the evidence we cannot, under the familiar rule, disturb the court's finding, for we are satisfied that the testimony above recited, with the other evidence in the case relating to the matter, is sufficient to justify the finding.

The law is well settled, both in England and this country, that it is competent to show by parol evidence that a party who is named in and has signed a contract as one of the parties thereto was an agent for another, and acted as such agent in making the contract, so as to give the benefit of the contract to, and charge with liability, the unnamed principal; and this is so, whether the unnamed principal was disclosed or known to the other party to the contract at the time it was made or not, although there is an occasional opinion to the contrary where the unnamed principal was known to the other party at the time. (Higgins v. Senior, 8 M. & W., 834; Jones on Ev., (2nd Ed.) Sec. 452; 9 Ency. of Ev., 404-405; Story on Agency, (7th Ed.) Sec. 270; 4 Wigmore on Ev., Sec. 2438; Curran v. Holland, 141 Cal. 437, 75 Pac. 46; Briggs v. Partridge, 64 N. Y., 357, 21 Am. Rep. 617; Byington v. Simpson, 134 Mass. 169, 45 Am. Rep. 314.) It is said in Story on Agency: "There is no doubt that parol evidence is admissible, on behalf of one of the contracting parties, to show that the other was an agent only in the sale, although contracting in his own name, so as to fix the real principal. It has been well observed that, in cases of this sort, the liability of the principal depends upon the act done; and not merely upon the form in which it is executed. If the agent is clothed with the proper authority, his acts bind the principal, although executed in his own name. The only difference is that, where the agent contracts in his own name, he adds

his own personal responsibility to that of the principal, who
has employed him."

In the section in Wigmore on Evidence, above cited, the
general state of the law on the subject is said to be sufficiently outlined in the following passage quoted from the
decision of Wolverton, J., in Barbre v. Goodale, 28 Or.,
465, 38 Pac. 67, 43 Pac. 378: "The question is here presented whether it is competent to show by parol testimony
that a contract executed by and in the name of an agent is
the contract of the principal, where the principal was known
to the other contracting party at the date of its execution.
There are two opinions touching the question, among
American authorities—the one affirming, and the other denying; but the case is one of first impression here, and we
feel contsrained to adopt the rule which may seem the more
compatible with the promotion of justice, and the execution
of honest and candid transactions between individuals. The
English authorities are agreed that parol evidence is admissible to show that a written contract executed in the
name of an agent is the contract of the principal, whether
he was known or unknown; and the American authorities
are a unit, so far as the rule is applied to an unknown principal, but disagree where he was known at the time the contract was executed or entered into by the parties. All the
authorities, both English and American, concur in holding
that, as applied to such contracts executed when the principal was unknown, parol evidence which shows that the
agent who made the contract in his own name was acting
for the principal does not contradict the writing, but simply
explains the transaction; for the effect is not to show that
the person appearing to be bound is not bound, but to show
that some other person is bound also. And those authorities
which deny the application of the rule where the principal
was known do not assert or maintain that such parol testimony tends to vary or contradict the written contract, but
find support upon the doctrine of estoppel; it being maintained that a party thus dealing with an agent of a known

principal elects to rely solely upon the agent's responsibility, and is therefore estopped to proceed against the principal. The underlying principle, therefore, upon which the authorities seem to diverge, is the presumption created by the execution of the contract in the name of the agent, and the acceptance thereof by a party, where the principal is known. Is this presumption conclusive, or is it disputable? Without attempting to reconcile the decisions, we believe the better rule to be that the presumption thus created is a disputable one, and that the intention of the party must be gathered from his words, and the various circumstances which surround the transaction, as its practical effect is to promote justice and fair dealing. The principal may have recourse to the same doctrine to bind the party thus entering into contract with his agent. Parol evidence, however, is not admissible to discharge the agent, as the party with whom he has dealt has his election as to whether he will hold him or the principal responsible."

Where it was known at the time that a party contracted as the agent of another, the rule was applied in Byington v. Simpson, *supra*. We quote from the opinion of the court delivered by Holmes, J., for it is particularly applicable to the facts in this case, and answers some of the arguments made here: "The argument is, that, inasmuch as the plaintiffs knew of the existence of a principal before the contract was made, and then were contented to accept a written agreement which on its face bound the agent, they must be taken to have dealt with, and to have given credit to the agent alone; just as, upon a subsequent discovery of the undisclosed principal, they might have determined their right to charge him by a sufficient election to rely upon the credit of the agent. We are of the opinion that the plaintiff's knowledge does not make their case any weaker than it would have been without it. Whatever the original merits of the rule, that a party not mentioned in a simple contract in writing may be charged as a principal upon oral evidence, even where the writing gives no indication of an intent to bind any other person than the signer, we cannot reopen it, for it is as well settled as any part of the law of agency. (Citing cases.) And it is evident that words which are sufficient on their face, by established law, to bind the principal, if one exists, cannot be deprived of their force by the circumstance that the other party relied upon their sufficiency for that purpose. Yet that is what the defendant's argument comes to. For the same parol evidence that shows the plaintiff's knowledge of the agency may warrant the inference that the plaintiffs meant to have the benefit of it and to bind the principal. The only reasons which have been offered for the admissibility of oral evidence to charge the alleged principal confirm this conclusion. * * *. The most that could fairly be argued in any case would be, that, under some circumstances, proof that the other party knew of the agency, and yet accepted a writing which did not refer to it, and which in its natural sense bound the agent alone, might tend to show that the contract was not made with anyone but the party whose name was signed; that the agent did not sign as agent, and was not understood to do so, but was himself the principal. But these are questions of fact, and, as a matter of fact, it is obvious, and it is found, that the defendant was the principal, and that the contract was made with her. The objection that two persons cannot be bound by the same signature to a contract, if sound, would be equally fatal when the principal was not known. There is a double obligation, although there can be but one satisfaction. Our decision is in accordance with a thoroughly discussed case which went to the Exchequer Chamber, and with the statement of the law by Mr. Justice Story there cited. (Calder v. Dobell, L. R. 6 C. P. 486; Story Agency, Sec. 160a.)"

That the rule applies to a contract made and executed by one partner, when acting for the firm and within the scope of the partnership business, is equally well settled. (30 Cyc. 485; 9 Ency. of Ev., 473; Brewing Co. v. Hawke, 24 Utah, 199, 66 Pac. 1058; Dreyfus & Co. v. Union Nat. Bank, 164

Ill. 83, 45 N. E. 408; Carson et al. v. Byers et al., 67 Ia. 606, 25 N. W. 826; Kitner v. Whitelock, 88 Ill. 513; White Mountain Bank v. West et al., 46 Me. 15; Beckwith v. Mace, 140 Mich. 157, 103 N. W. 559; Berkshire Woolen Mills v. Juillard, 75 N. Y. 535, 31 Am. Rep. 488; Stillman v. Harvey, 47 Conn. 26; 22 Ency. Law, (2nd Ed.) 161-164.) It is contended that the conversations at the time the contract was made were inadmissible, on the ground that agency on the authority of an agent cannot be proved by the declarations of the alleged agent. But it was competent to prove the transaction, to ascertain whether E. I. Crable acted for the firm or on his own behalf. Whether there was a firm, and whether E. I. Crable had authority to act for it, "would, perhaps," as said in the Michigan case of Beckwith v. Mace, *supra,* "affect the validity of his attempt to bind others, but the evidence offered was admissible to show the nature of the contract actually agreed upon." In that case the evidence had been excluded, and for that reason the judgment was reversed. Here the evidence was admitted, and properly so, for it explained the transaction and tended to show that the contract was made for the partnership. The fact of the partnership was shown by other evidence, and this contract was such as to come clearly within the partner's authority.

As above indicated, we think the evidence sufficient to justify the trial court in finding that E. I. Crable, in making the contract for the use of the teams, was acting for the firm of which he was a member, that it was a partnership contract, and created a firm obligation. The amount of the judgment indicates that the plaintiff was only allowed the rent of the teams, with interest, after deducting the credit given for the hay.

The only other question in the case relates to the attachment proceedings. As grounds for attachment it was stated in the affidavit "that the defendants are about to remove their property out of the jurisdiction of the court, with intent to defraud their creditors; that defendants are about to dispose of their property, with the intent to defraud their creditors; that defendants fraudulently contracted the obligation for which suit is about to be brought; and that defendant, J. J. Crable, is a non-resident of the State of Wyoming."

E. I. Crable and J. J. Crable filed separate motions to quash the writ of attachment, supported by their respective affidavits, denying the truth of the grounds mentioned in the affidavit for attachment, except the non-residence of J. J. Crable. As to that ground it was moved that the allegation of non-residence be stricken from the affidavit as immaterial. It would certainly be an unusual proceeding to strike from a party's affidavit any matter therein contained. An entire affidavit might, perhaps, be stricken from the files, good and sufficient reasons appearing therefor, and it is proper to move for the discharge of an attachment on the ground that the affidavit is insufficient. But we do not understand it to be proper to strike out the statements contained in the affidavit, or any of them, for the reason that they are immaterial or disclose no ground for attachment. It is probable, however, that the question was presented upon the motions to discharge the attachment, whether the non-residence of one of the partners, the other being a resident, constituted a ground for attachment of the property of the partnership, or the individual property of the non-resident partner. Counsel for plaintiffs in error state in their brief that the question was presented.

The evidence shows that J. J. Crable was a non-resident of the state, and it is not contended that the evidence sustains either of the other alleged grounds for attachment. It is contended for defendants, plaintiffs in error here, that the non-residence of J. J. Crable was not a sufficient ground for attaching either his individual property or the property of the partnership, since he was only liable, if at all, as a member of the partnership. We think it unnecessary to decide that question, for it appears that after the judgment was rendered an order was entered upon the application of the defendants, J. J. Crable & Son and J. J. Crable, that upon their giving a bond as provided by law for stay of execution, in the sum of $2,700, to be approved by the clerk of the court, execution on said judgment be stayed for ninety days as to the parties giving the bond, and that the property attached be released; the order providing that such bond should be given under the statute relating to appeals. It is stated in the brief·of counsel for plaintiffs in error that after the judgment had been entered the attached property was released upon bond being given. If the bond was given as provided in the order authorizing it, it would bind the parties to pay the amount of the judgment and costs, if the judgment be affirmed in whole or in part, or if the proceedings in error be dismissed. (Comp. Stat., 1910, Secs. 5116 and 5117.)

It would not be a forthcoming bond provided for in Section 4855 Compiled Statutes. That section requires the sheriff to deliver the property attached to the person from whose possession it was taken, upon his executing, with sufficient surety, of an undertaking to the plaintiff, to the effect that the parties to the same are bound in double the appraised value of the property, that the property or its appraised value in money shall be forthcoming to answer the judgment of the court in the action. The statute relating to stay of execution in case of appeal provides that no proceeding to reverse, vacate or modify a judgment of the District Court shall operate to stay execution until the party against whom the judgment was made shall file a written undertaking with sureties to be approved by the court, or judge, or the clerk of the court; that when the judgment directs the payment of money, the undertaking shall be in such sum as fixed by the court or judge to the effect that the plaintiff in error will pay the condemnation money and costs, if the judgment be affirmed in whole or in part, or if the proceedings in error be dismissed. (Comp. Stat., Sec. 5116.) And it is further provided that such undertaking shall operate as a stay of execution for the period of ninety days from the date it is filed in the clerk's office, whether any proceedings to reverse, vacate or modify the judgment shall have been taken or not, and, if within said period the party shall have commenced his proceedings in error, then the undertaking shall operate as a stay of execution until the cause is finally determined by the Supreme Court. (Id. Sec. 5117.) To give a mere forthcoming bond under Section 4855 no order of the court is necessary, nor is it necessary in such case for the court to fix the amount thereof; that is fixed by reference to the amount of the appraised value of the attached property. It appearing that a bond to stay execution under the statute relating to appeals was authorized by the order of the court, on the application of certain of the defendants, and that when given the attached property was ordered released, and, by admission of counsel, that a bond was given and the property released, without anything to show that it was merely a forthcoming bond, we are at liberty to assume, and must do so, we think, that the bond so given was that authorized by the court's order, viz.: a bond to stay execution pending proceedings in error, obligating the parties to pay the judgment, if affirmed. This seems to take every question as to the attachment out of the case. The attachment is not needed to confer jurisdiction of the person of J. J. Crable, for he entered his personal appearance in the cause by pleading to the merits, and participating in the trial. The discharge of the attachment is not necessary, for the property has been released upon the giving of the bond aforesaid; and to hold that the court erred in denying the motions to dissolve would not relieve the parties from the payment of the judgment, which we think must be affirmed, or their liability to pay the same under the bond given to stay execution. E. I. Crable disclaimed, upon the trial, any interest in the attached property, testifying that it all belonged to his father, J. J. Crable. So far as he is individually concerned, therefore, he is not interested at this time in the result of the attachment. There is nothing to show that the firm is not a party to the bond, and we have a right to assume that it is, since the court's order provided that upon the bond being given by the firm and J. J. Crable execution should be stayed and the attached property released, and it is admitted that upon giving bond the property was released. The plaintiffs in error are not in a position, therefore, at this time, to demand a consideration of the alleged error in refusing to dissolve the attachment.

For the reasons stated, the judgment will be affirmed.

SCOTT, C. J., and BEARD, J., concur.

NICHOLS v. HUFFORD.
(No. 714.)

WATER AND WATER RIGHTS—IRRIGATION—APPROPRIATION—PRIORITY— WATER RIGHT STATEMENTS—PURPOSE AND EFFECT—DATE OF APPROPRIATION—ADJUDICATION OF PRIOROTIES—AMOUNT ALLOWED FOR IRRIGATION—EVIDENCE—RECORD AS TO CERTAIN MATTERS IN STATE ENGINEER'S OFFICE—APPEAL AND ERROR—RECORD EVIDENCE—WITNESSES—OPINIONS.

1. The statute with reference to water rights enacted by the Territorial legislature in 1886 (Laws 1886, Ch. 61, Rev. Stat. 1887, Sec. 1331 *et seq.*), providing for the filing of statements by ditch owners or claimants, was enacted for the purpose of establishing a record of the claims of water users to protect them in their rights, assist in adjudicating the various priorities through the procedure provided by the act, and in the regulation by the proper officials for the use of the water. Such statements were intended merely to set forth, under oath, the claim of the party filing the same, and did not amount to a permit to appropriate the specific amount of water claimed regardless of the necessity therefor, nor was the recital in such a statement of a definite amount of water claimed controlling as to the amount of water to be adjudicated in favor of the party filing it.

2. Although it was provided in Section 13 of said act as to statements thereafter filed by a party intending to construct a ditch and to use or appropriate water for beneficial purposes that from the time of filing any such statement water sufficient to fill such ditch or ditches, and to sub-

serve a lawful or just use, shall be deemed and adjudged
to be appropriated, if the actual construction of the ditch
or ditches shall begin within sixty days after filing the
statement and be prosecuted diligently and continuously to
completion, the effect of the section, taken in connection
with the rest of the act, was merely to provide or declare
that when the work of constructing the ditch was commenced within the time specified and pursued diligently
and continuously to completion, the date of filing the
statement should be considered as the date of the appropriation.

3. No warrant is to be found in the section aforesaid, nor in
any other statute, for permitting or recognizing an appropriation of water not applied to a beneficial use, or intended to be so applied, or a greater quantity of water
than is reasonably required for such purpose.

4. Without deciding whether the provision of the statute
enacted by the first State legislature (Laws 1890-91, Ch. 8,
Sec. 25, Comp. Stat. 1910, Sec. 777), declaring that no
allotment of water for irrigation shall be made by the
board of control in adjudicating priorities exceeding one
cubic foot per second for each seventy acres of land, is
or is not a valid regulation as to appropriations made
prior to its adoption, the board and the courts may properly so limit the right of any appropriator when it is found
to be sufficient and adequate for the purpose of the appropriation.

5. Aside from the general information possessed by the board
of control concerning the requirements of various classes
of land in the state, the court may assume that some such
information as to land in controversy involved in an adjudication proceeding was of record in the office of the state
engineer, the contest before the court having been instituted and heard in the course of a proceeding for adjudication of priorities, and it being the duty of the engineer
or his assistant to make an examination of the stream, the
works diverting water therefrom, the carrying capacity of
the various ditches, an examination of the irrigated lands,
and an approximate measurement of the lands irrigated
or susceptible of irrigation from the various ditches, and
to make a record in his office of such observation and
measurements.

6. The statute requiring that on an appeal from an order of
the board of control adjudicating priorities to the right to
the use of water for irrigation or other beneficial purposes

shall file in the office of the clerk of the District Court to which the appeal is taken a certified transcript of the order appealed from, the records of the board relating to the determination, and the evidence offered before the board, including the measurements of streams, appropriations and ditches made by or under the supervision of the engineer as required by law, the court should hesitate to disturb the board's findings and determination, where the record of the board as to the measurements and examination so provided for by law has not been brought before the court by certified transcript or otherwise.

7. Whatever may be the effect of the statutory limitation upon the allotment of water for irrigation upon appropriations made prior to the enactment of the statute, the use may be limited in accordance with the statute where there is no evidence, or the evidence is insufficient, to establish the duty of water upon the lands in controversy.

8. The statutory provision limiting an allotment of water for irrigation to one cubic foot per second for each seventy acres of land for which an appropriation may be or has been made having remained unchanged for more than twenty years, it may be assumed that the maximum use thereby prescribed has been found at least generally to be sufficient, and, in the absence of other satisfactory evidence, the statute respecting the amount to be allotted should be followed.

9. It having been stated in the findings of the board adjudicating the priorities to the use of water upon a certain stream and its tributaries that the measurements of the duty of water in the state indicate that the maximum use prescribed by the statute is sufficient under the most extreme conditions, *held,* that whether said statutory limit as to maximum use is conclusive or controlling in any case or not, it is at least to be regarded as furnishing a standard, in the absence of competent or satisfactory evidence that the use thereby permitted is insufficient in a particular case, and the evidence to that effect should be reasonably clear and satisfactory to entitle an appropriator to an allotment exceeding the statutory limit.

10. A showing that all the water of the stream had at times been used or allowed to flow upon the land of a party does not necessarily prove an appropriation of all of it for a beneficial use, for an appropriation must be limited to the amount reasonably required for a proper and successful

cultivation of the land, or other use to which the land is
applied.

11. Upon the question of the quantity of water necessary to
irrigate a particular tract of land and whether the amount
of water allotted by statute per acre for irrigation purposes is sufficient for the irrigation of said tract the testimony of witnesses who were practical irrigators, but whose
testimony was confined to expressions of opinion based
upon the general gravelly character of the soil, causing it
to absorb more water than in the case of other kinds of
soil, without showing any tests or measurements, or particular examination of the soil, or a knowledge of the
quantity of water embraced in a flow of one cubic foot
per second, and very little, if any, acquaintance with the
method employed in irrigating the particular land, except
that ditches and laterals were used, *held,* to be unsatisfactory and not entitled to much weight in determining
the duty of water as applied to land in controversy; the
opinions of the witnesses, though honest, seeming to be
little more than conjecture or guesswork.

12. The record made by the examination and measurements of
the state engineer provided for by law (Comp. Stat.
1910, Sec. 776), cannot affect the question as to the time
or times when uncultivated lands may have been irrigated
and the extent of the appropriation therefor in respect to
the period of use.

13. On appeal from the state board of control adjudicating priorities of water rights, *held,* upon the evidence, that the
order of the board improperly restricted the use of water
found to have been appropriated by a party for uncultivated lands by denying his right to use such water during
the season when irrigation is more particularly required
for cultivated crops; but, it not appearing that those lands
had been irrigated when said party's cultivated lands were
being irrigated, he was not entitled to use at the same time
the water appropriated for his cultivated and uncultivated
lands, though when not engaged in irrigating his cultivated
lands, even during the irrigation season, he should be permitted to use the amount found to have been appropriated for the uncultivated or pasture lands.

[Decided June 30, 1913.]   (133 Pac. 1084.)

ERROR to the District Court, Uinta County, HON. DAVID
H. CRAIG, Judge.

The material facts are stated in the opinion.

H. E. & H. R. Christmas, for plaintiff in error.

The contestant, Hufford, failed to establish a right to the use of any of the water of the stream or any of the allegations contained in his contest affidavit. The testimony of the witnesses, all claiming to be experienced irrigators and ranchmen, established the fact that all the water of the stream at all times was used in irrigating the lands of the contestee, the plaintiff in error, thereby leaving no water to be appropriated by the contestant. Appropriators of water for irrigation purposes are allowed a reasonable time, after conducting water to the point of intended use, to apply it to the use intended. They may add to the acreage of cultivated land from year to year, and make application of water thereto for irrigation as their interests demand, or as their abilities may permit, until the entire amount of water at first diverted has been put by them to a beneficial use, provided that amount is required for the usual irrigation of the land. (Conant v. Jones (Ida.) 32 Pac. 250.) The first appropriator is entitled to use and enjoy the water to the full extent of his original appropriation, even though that includes all of the water of the stream. (Barnes v. Sabron, 10 Neb. 217; Nevada W. Co. v. Powell, 34 Cal. 109; Gale v. Toulumne W. Co., 14 Cal. 25; Hines v. Johnson, 61 Cal. 259; Hillman v. Hardwick, 2 Ida. 983; Huning v. Porter, 54 Pac. 584; Kirk v. Bartholomew, (Ida.) 29 Pac. 40; Geertson v. Barrack, 29 Pac. 42; Strickler v. Colo. Springs, 26 Pac. 313; Jennison v. Kirk, 98 U. S. 461; Roberts v. Arthur, 15 Colo. 456.) No public interest enters into this controversy, and therefore the declaration of the Constitution applies, that priority of appropriation for beneficial use shall give the better right. The statute limiting the quantity of water to be allotted an appropriator for irrigation purposes cannot apply to the appropriation of the plaintiff in error for the reason that his rights are to be controlled by the earlier statutes in force when his appropriation was made. It cannot be successfully contended that the predecessors of plaintiff in error could not assign or sell his rights

to them, for the question has been decided in favor of such
right of assignment. (Strickler v. Colo. Springs, *supra*.)
Not only the actual prior appropriations of water, but the
quantity of land and character of the soil are to be considered in determining the controversy as to water rights.
(Kinney on Irr., p. 386.)

The board of control improperly restricted the use by
plaintiff in error of some of the waters appropriated by
him to a certain period in the year, excluding the summer
season, and improperly limited his right to use water to the
maximum amount of one cubic foot for each 70 acres, thereby depriving him of a vested property right.

B. M. Ausherman, for defendant in error.

There is no conflict in the evidence as to the quantity of
water ordinarily in the stream. It is exceptional in this
respect that its normal flow seems to be constant or continuous. The fact that all of the water in the stream may
have been turned upon the land of the plaintiff in error does
not establish compliance with statutory regulations, or with
the principle of law that an appropriation of water shall be
actual and beneficial use. (Farm Inv. Co. v. Carpenter, 9
Wyo. 110, 61 Pac. 258; Johnston v. Little Horse Creek
Irrigation Co., 13 Wyo. 208, 79 Pac. 22.)

The mere filing of a statement of claim to a water right
under the statutes of the Territory did not constitute an appropriation of water. Neither the board nor the court can
make an allotment of water for irrigation beyond the amount
authorized to be allotted for that purpose by the statute.
(Comp. Stat. 1910, Sec. 777.) It is clear by the testimony
that little attention was paid by the plaintiff in error to the
proper distribution of water upon his lands to irrigate them
economically, but he allowed considerable water from time
to time to be wasted.

POTTER, JUSTICE.

This is a proceeding in error for the review of a judgment of the District Court sitting within and for the County
of Uinta, disposing of a contest on appeal from the State

Board of Control, involving the right of the plaintiff in error, Harry Nichols, to the use of the waters of Pine Creek, a tributary of Smith's Fork, a tributary of Bear River. The Board of Control having taken up the matter of the adjudication of the priorities of rights by appropriation to the use of the water of Bear River and its tributaries, and Harry Nichols having produced evidence before the Division Superintendent in support of his claim to all of the water in Pine Creek, Vaughn Hufford, who had been granted a permit to appropriate water from said stream, instituted a proceeding contesting the right of said Nichols to the amount of water claimed by him. That the right of Nichols to so much of the water as had been appropriated by him for irrigation was prior in point of time and superior to that which would be acquired by the contestant under his permit was not disputed, but the grounds of the contest were that Nichols was claiming to have irrigated much more land than had in fact been irrigated, and a greater quantity of water for that purpose than had in fact been beneficially used and appropriated. The evidence taken in the contest by the water division superintendent was transmitted to the Board of Control, and upon a hearing by the Board upon that evidence, which was conflicting as to the number of acres irrigated, and upon "the records of the office of the State Engineer," the Board allowed the contestee an appropriation for practically the entire acreage of land shown by his testimony to have been irrigated, viz.: 459 acres of cultivated land, and 296 acres of uncultivated land covered with a growth of sage brush, which had been irrigated at times when the water was not needed for the cultivated land, to increase the growth of the natural grasses for pasture purposes, but limited him as to all of the land to an appropriation of one cubic foot per second for each 70 acres, and to the use of water upon the uncultivated land during the period between September 15 and June 15, denying the right to use the water on that land during part of the irrigation season for cultivated crops, viz.: between June 15 and September 15. The Board stated in its findings, explaining the amount allowed for the cultivated land, as follows:

"That no reliable or accurate measurements have been made of the discharge of Pine Creek, that from the evidence it would seem that the normal flow of the stream during the late irrigation season does not exceed from six to eight cubic feet of water per second of time; that if the contestee estimates that his lands require more than one cubic foot of water per second for each seventy acres of land, this conception is due to an overestimate of the volume of water flowing in Pine Creek rather than because of the excessive demands of his lands and crops; that all of the measurements of the duty of water in Wyoming indicate that the maximum use, under conditions similar to those along Pine Creek, would require a total depth of water of 2.50 feet on the land irrigated during the irrigation season; that the average use requires a total depth of approximately 1.50; that the volume put on the lands at the rate of one cubic foot per second for each seventy acres would cover the land to a depth of 3.43 for an irrigation season of 120 days, which would be sufficient under the most extreme conditions; that the law and the practice of the Board of Control only fixes the maximum limit and the actual use is regulated thereunder by the water commissioner in accordance with actual needs; that there is no evidence in this case which would establish the duty of water for the lands along Pine Creek and all information available would show that the statutory limit would furnish a volume in excess of the actual needs of such lands."

With reference to the irrigation of the uncultivated land, it was said in the findings of the board: "The Goodell ditch (one of the ditches of contestee) follows a ridge enabling it to serve 287 acres of land because of the favorable southern slope, and quality, thus enabling cultivation to take place, and cultivated crops to be raised, and that other lands have, in a measure, been irrigated on the northern slope of said ridge. The testimony shows that lands on the said northern slope of the ridge, and which lie in a general northerly direction from the cultivated area, have been irrigated from time to time, after the cultivated crops have been served, for the purpose of increasing the growth of natural grasses. This area of land, still remaining uncultivated and covered with a growth of sage brush, has a total area of 296 acres. Such lands are reclaimed through the said Goodell Ditch with a priority relating back to the year 1887, but the record discloses that they have been irrigated at times when the cultivated crops do not need irrigation."

It was specified in the order or decree of the board that the contestee was found and adjudged entitled to water from Pine Creek as follows: By and through the Collett Ditch 2.47 cubic feet per second, for 172 acres, the same being particularly described, with a priority relating back to the year 1881. By and through the Goodell Ditch, 4.10 cubic feet per second, for 287 acres, particularly described, with a priority of appropriation dating back to 1887. By and through the said Goodell Ditch, with the same date of priority, 4.23 cubic feet per second of time, permitting the irrigation of 296 acres of uncultivated land. "These lands to have no right to irrigation between May 1st and September 15th of each year." This limitation as to the 296 acres is found in the tabulated statement contained in the order. But in a separate paragraph it was specifically ordered and adjudged that the use of water from the Goodell Ditch for said uncultivated land be confined to the period between the 15th day of September of each year and the 15th day of June of the following year, and that such lands be denied the right of irrigation during that period of each year commencing with June 15th and ending with September 15th. It was also ordered that the proof submitted by said Nichols for the "Nichols Ditch" or "Pine Creek Falls Ditch" be rejected; and that all the appropriations of water thereby determined shall be limited to the needs of the land, and not to exceed in amount "one cubic foot of water per second for each 70 acres of land irrigated." The "Nichols" or "Pine Creek Falls Ditch," it appears, was intended by Nichols to carry water in the spring and fall to a certain tract referred to as a desert entry, but it was clearly shown by the testimony that said tract had not been irrigated; and it does not seem to be here contended that any error was committed in the denial of an appropriation for any land under that ditch. It was found by the Board that the permit held by the contestant, Hufford, had not expired, and that he had further time to complete his irrigation works and apply the water to a beneficial use.

The cause was heard in the District Court upon the evidence taken before the Division Superintendent, and without anything that appeared among the records in the office of the State Engineer not included in the evidence so taken. Upon consideration thereof the District Court, in its judgment order, approved and confirmed the findings and order of the Board of Control, "save and except its finding as to the measurement or normal flow of water in Pine Creek which the evidence and record in the case show to be sixteen to eighteen cubic feet of water per second of time instead of six to eight cubic feet as designated in said finding and order." And with that exception, the findings and order of the board were adopted, approved, confirmed and made the findings and order of the court. The evidence clearly showing that the normal flow of the stream is 16 to 18 feet per second, it is probable that the statement in the board's order that the same was 6 to 8 feet was the result of a clerical error. The court, therefore, modified the order in that respect, and in every other particular allowed it to stand as the order and judgment of the court. The appeal to the District Court was taken by the contestee, and he brings this proceeding in error.

It is not contended that the plaintiff in error was allowed an appropriation and priority for less land than he was entitled to, but that such appropriation for the cultivated lands was improperly limited as to amount, and for the uncultivated lands improperly limited as to the time when the water may be used. It is argued that his right to the water having been acquired when Wyoming was a Territory, and under Territorial laws, prior to the enactment of the statute fixing in effect the maximum of use at one cubic foot per second for each 70 acres, and all of the water of the stream having been used by him at times in the irrigation of his land, he thereby became entitled to all of such water at all times. Counsel is in error in supposing that under the territorial laws one who filed a statement claiming a water right thereby obtained a permit to appropriate the specific amount of water claimed in such statement, whether the same would or would not be required for the intended purpose, or that by reciting in such statement the quantity of water claimed to be appropriated or intended to be appropriated, his right to such quantity was conclusively established. The Act of 1886, which provided for the filing of statements by ditch owners or claimants, was enacted for the purpose of making a record of the claims of water users, to protect them in their rights, assist in the adjudication of the various priorities through the procedure established by the act, and in the regulation by public officials of the proper use of the water. Such statements were intended merely to set forth the claim of the party under oath, and, respecting the amount of water appropriated or intended to be appropriated, the act required only that there should be stated "the amount of water claimed by or under" the construction, enlargement or extension of the ditch. (Laws of 1886, Ch. 61, Sec. 10; Revised Statutes 1887, Sec. 1340.) It is true that in Section 13 of the Act (Rev. Stat. 1887, Sec. 1343) it was provided as to statements thereafter filed by a person intending to construct a ditch and to use or appropriate water for beneficial purposes, that "from the time of filing any such statement water sufficient to fill such ditch or ditches, and to subserve the use or uses aforesaid, if a lawful or just use, shall be deemed and adjudged to be appropriated; * * * Provided, * * * that such person

* * * shall within sixty days next ensuing the filing of
such statement, begin the actual construction of said ditch
or ditches, and shall prosecute the work of the construction
thereof diligently and continuously to its completion." The
effect of that section, taken in connection with the rest of
the act, was merely to provide that when the work was commenced within the time specified and pursued diligently and
continuously to completion, water sufficient, within the capacity of the ditch, to subserve the intended lawful and just
use, would be deemed and adjudged appropriated from the
time of filing the statement. In other words the date of
filing the statement in such case was declared to be the date
of the appropriation. No warrant can be found in that
section, or in any other statute, for permitting or recognizing
an appropriation of water not applied to a beneficial use,
or intended to be so applied, or a greater quantity of water
than is reasonably required for such purpose. Indeed it
was provided in the same act that the water commissioners
shall so divide, regulate and control the use of the water
of all streams within their respective districts, in such manner as will prevent unnecessary waste, and to that end that
such commissioners shall so regulate the headgate or gates
of all ditches that no more water will flow therein than is
actually required and will be used for the purpose for
which the water was appropriated. (Laws 1886, Ch. 61,
Sec. 29; Rev. Stat, 1887, Sec. 1359.) The recital of a
definite amount of water claimed would not, therefore, be
controlling as to the amount to be adjudicated in favor of
the party filing the statement.

It is no doubt true that when the appropriators were few,
and there was ample water for all, the law was not construed very strictly with reference to the amount of water
appropriated, either by irrigators in using the water, or the
courts in adjudicating priorities, more attention being paid
to the capacity of ditches than the quantity of water actually
required. And it was customary, in compliance with the
statute of 1886 as to the filing of statements, to claim in

such statement an amount for irrigation purposes equal to the capacity of the ditch, although that might exceed the quantity that could be economically or properly applied and used. But with the increase of the acreage under irrigation and the number of appropriators, requiring economy in the distribution and use of water to make it serve as much land as possible, there has been a gradual and persistent tendency to restrict the appropriation and use to an amount reasonably necessary when properly applied. Hence the enactment of our statute in 1890 by the first State Legislature, as the result, we suppose, of experience and measurements, declaring that no allotment of water for irrigation shall be made by the Board of Control, in adjudicating the various priorities, exceeding one cubic foot per second for each 70 acres of land. Whether that provision is or is not a valid regulation as to appropriations made prior to its adoption it is unnecessary in this case to decide. Without such provision in the statute, it is clear that the Board and the courts may properly so limit the right of any appropriator when it is found to be sufficient and adequate for the purpose. In this case the Board so found, stating in its order the general result of the measurements of the duty of water in this state, and that there was no evidence in the case establishing such duty for lands along Pine Creek, but that all available information shows that the statutory limit would furnish a volume in excess of the needs of such lands.

Aside from the general information possessed by the board concerning the requirements of various classes or kinds of land in the state, we may assume that some such information as to these lands was on record in the office of the state engineer, for this contest was instituted and heard in the course of a proceeding for the adjudication of the various priorities to the use of water from Bear River and its tributaries, and it was and is made the duty of the state engineer, or some qualified assistant, in such cases, to make an examination of the stream, the works diverting water therefrom, the carrying capacity of the various ditches and canals, an examination of the irrigated lands, and an approximate measurement of the lands irrigated, or susceptible of irrigation, from the various ditches and canals, "which said observation and measurements shall be reduced to writing, and made a matter of record in his office." (Comp. Stat. 1910, Sec. 776.) That section also requires that the state engineer shall make, or cause to be made, a map or plat on a scale of not less than one inch to the mile, showing with substantial accuracy, the course of said stream, the location of each ditch or canal diverting water therefrom, and the legal sub-divisions of land which have been irrigated, or which are susceptible of irrigation from the ditches or canals already constructed. It is made the duty of a party appealing from a determination of the board, within six months after the appeal is perfected, to file in the office of the clerk of the District Court a certified transcript of the order appealed from, the records of the board relating to such determination, and the evidence offered before the board, including the measurements of streams, tributaries and ditches provided for by Section 776. (Comp. Stat., 1910, Sec. 782.) The certified transcript of the order, and the evidence which was taken before the division superintendent, was so filed in this case, but the record made of the measurements and examination provided for in Section 776 do not appear in the record here by any certified transcript or otherwise. On that ground it appears that a motion was made in the District Court by the contestant, Hufford, to dismiss the appeal. That motion was denied and the contestee, the appellant, was given additional time within which to secure from the board and file in the office of the clerk such additional papers as are necessary to make complete the certified copy of all the records of the board relating to the determination. Counsel for defendant in error, in his brief, insists that by the failure of the plaintiff in error to file such additional papers the entire record upon which the matter was determined by the board is not here and was not before the District Court. So far as any such additional papers or record might affect the controversy, we should at least hesitate, in their absence, to disturb the board's findings and determination. And we think it possible, if not indeed probable, that the board may have had before it the record provided for in Section 776, showing an examination of the irrigated lands of the plaintiff in error, and the result thereof respecting their quality and character, enabling the board to arrive at a reasonable conclusion in the absence of other satisfactory evidence upon the subject as to the amount of water which would be sufficient for their proper and successful irrigation.

Again, if it should be conceded that the statutory limitation upon the use of water for irrigation would not necessarily control the allotment for an appropriation made or initiated prior to the enactment of the statute, we perceive no impropriety or injustice in limiting the use in accordance with the statute, where there is no evidence, or it is insufficient, to establish the duty of water upon the lands. The statutory provision has remained unchanged for more than twenty years, and we may suppose that the maximum use thereby prescribed has been found at least generally to be sufficient. Indeed in the absence of other satisfactory evidence there would seem to be no other course open than to follow the statute respecting the amount to be allotted. There was an attempt to show by the opinions of men having some acquaintance in a general way with the lands and were practical irrigators, that the lands of plaintiff in error required more water than one cubic foot per second for each 70 acres, and some witnesses produced by the contestee testified that all of the water normally flowing in the stream would be required to irrigate the 800 acres. But, aside from the statement that one cubic foot per second was insufficient, the amount that would be sufficient for the cultivated land was not stated, either exactly or approximately, and it appeared that the irrigation of the uncultivated land had occurred only when irrigation of the cultivated tracts was finished or unnecessary. It was shown clearly enough that at times all of the water in the stream was turned into the ditches of plaintiff in error and allowed to run upon his lands, though we think that appears to have been done without any great care to ascertain whether all of it was necessary at the time; and there is evidence to the effect that the attempt to use so much water resulted in waste, and to the detriment of the land. Mr. Hufford, the contestant, who testified that he was an engineer and had made a close study of irrigation for many years, and considered himself competent to determine when land is properly irrigated, and when it is not, and to judge the amount of water that different kinds of soil required, testified that at different times during the irrigating season he had examined and made a test of the soils from different locations upon the Nichols ranch, and that in his opinion too much water had been used upon the crops, the same standing in pools in some places, and that the soil is of such character that the legal allowance, or less than that, is sufficient to properly irrigate all of the land; that the soil generally is of a very good quality, gravelly loam, containing a light per cent of gravel, and has what is called a gravelly cement subsoil, which water will not penetrate. He further testified that he knew that Mr. Nichols had turned in his ditches and upon his lands more than the statutory allowance, but also knew that in doing so he had turned more water upon the ground than could be sufficiently or beneficially used, and that the amount of water so attempted to be used was detrimental to the crops and the lands.

The showing that all of the water of the stream had been at times used or allowed to flow upon the land does not necessarily prove an appropriation of all of it for a beneficial use, for the appropriation must be limited to the amount reasonably required for the proper and successful cultivation of the land, or other use to which the water is applied. (Little Walla Irr. Union v. Finis Irr. Co., (Or.) 124 Pac. 666; 2 Kinney on Irr., 2nd Ed., Sec. 885.) Beyond that it was attempted to show, as above stated, by the testimony of practical irrigators, that the amount of water allowed by statute to be allotted for irrigation purposes was insufficient for the irrigation of these lands. That testimony was confined to expressions of opinion, without showing any tests or measurements, or particular examination of the soil, but the opinions were based upon the general gravelly character of the soil, which would cause it to absorb more water than in the case of other kinds of soil, thereby requiring a greater amount of water for successful irrigation and cultivation. None of the witnesses appeared to know the quantity of water that would be embraced in a flow of "one cubic foot per second," and some of them had no acquaintance or very little with the method employed in irrigating these lands, except that ditches and laterals were used. One witness never saw the land irrigated. Another seemed to resent by disrespectful and even insolent answers the attempt by counsel on cross-examination to ascertain the extent of his knowledge of irrigation and his competency to testify concerning the needs of these lands, although the questions were courteous in form and appear to have been properly propounded for the purpose indicated. We are impressed, as the board must have been, with the unsatisfactory character of this testimony. The witnesses were no doubt honest in respectively stating their opinions, but such opinions seem to be little more than conjecture or guesswork, based solely upon the gravelly condition of the soil and the fact that they had seen all the water of the creek turned into the ditches or on the land. It is not the kind of testimony usually deemed necessary for the purpose of establishing the duty of water as applied to irrigation. As the result of the decisions it is stated in Wiel on Water Rights that in determining the duty of water in any particular case, evidence should be from actual experiment and measurement if possible; and that opinion evidence is of less value than experiment. (3rd Ed., Vol. 1, Sec. 487.) And in Kinney on Irrigation (Vol. 2, Sec. 916) it is said that the court should hear the evidence of persons who are competent to testify upon the subject, and who can do so, not from guesswork or hearsay, but from actual measurements and tests and the actual application of the water to the lands irrigated. Further, in Section 888, it is said that the courts hold "in order for a witness to be competent to testify as to the measurement and duty of water, he must have had experience and training along these lines."

In the case of Farmers Co-operative D. Co. v. Riverside Irrigation District, 16 Idaho, 525, 102 Pac. 481, the remarks in a former case were quoted as follows: "The law only allows the appropriator the amount actually necessary for the useful or beneficial purpose to which he applies it. The inquiry was therefore not what he had used, but how much was actually necessary," following which the court announced this principle: "In determining the duty of water, reference should always be had to lands that have been prepared and reduced to a reasonably good condition for irrigation. Water users should not be allowed an excessive quantity of water to compensate and counter-balance their neglect or indolence in the preparation of their lands for their successful and economical application of the water." And, further, that for the purpose of determining the question as to the duty of water for irrigation, "the court can hear evidence of persons who are competent to testify on the subject, and who can do so, not from guesswork or hearsay, but from actual measurements and tests and applications of the water to the lands irrigated." In Longmire v. Smith, 26 Wash. 439, 67 Pac. 246, 58 L. R. A. 308, the court said that "the Superior Court found that it could not determine from the evidence the quantity of water required for the irrigation of plaintiff's parcels of land. The evidence upon this issue is not sufficiently clear to set aside this finding. An examination discloses that a number of witnesses, when testifying, and while expressing opinions as to the number of inches of water required to irrigate the land, had not very definite ideas of the measurement of water; and the court was justified in attaching but little weight to such testimony." (See also Whitted v. Cavin, 55 Or. 98, 105 Pac. 396.) The board evidently adopted the view that the opinions of these witnesses were not entitled to much weight in determining the duty of water as applied to the lands in controversy, and the District Court no doubt took the same view. Without more minutely rehearsing this testimony we think it sufficient to say that it fails to satisfy us that the board and court erred in that particular.

It is stated in the findings of the board that all the measurements of the duty of water in this state indicate that the maximum use prescribed by the statute is sufficient under the most extreme conditions, thus showing the reasonableness of the statutory provision generally, at least. Whether it is conclusive or controlling in any case or not, we think it may at least be properly regarded as furnishing a standard in the absence of competent or satisfactory evidence that the use thereby permitted is insufficient in a particular case; and that the evidence to that effect should be reasonably clear and satisfactory to entitle an appropriator to an allotment exceeding the statutory limit.

That part of the findings and order confining the plaintiff in error to a certain period of the year for the use of the water upon his 296 acres of uncultivated land is complained of. As stated in the findings these lands appear to have been irrigated "after the cultivated crops have been served, for the purpose of increasing the growth of natural grasses"; and that "the record discloses that they have been irrigated at times when the cultivated crops do not need irrigation." The order limits the use of the water found to have been appropriated for such lands to the period between the 15th day of September of each year and the 15th day of June of the following year, the purpose evidently being to deny the right to use such water during the season when irrigation is more particularly required for the cultivated crops. While the testimony is not very clear as to whether it had been the custom of the plaintiff in error to irrigate the uncultivated land during the usual so-called irriga-

tion season, we think the evidence may reasonably be construed as showing that this irrigation may have occurred at
times during such irrigation season, but when water was not
being used upon the cultivated land. The plaintiff in error
testified in that respect as follows: "Q. How then do you irrigate your pasture land? A. When we are not using the
water on the alfalfa then we turn it out on the pasture.
Q. Then do you have men there to distribute it? A. We
change it as we need it from one place to another. Q. Do
you keep two men employed that way? A. Not all the
time. We change it as necessary." There is a discrepancy
between the tabulated statement of the priorities contained
in the findings and order, and the provisions of the order
following such statement, as to the period to which the use
of the water for the uncultivated land is limited. At the
foot of the tabulated statement it is stated that said lands
shall have no right to irrigation between May 1st and September 15th of each year. In the order, following the
statement, it is declared that the right of irrigation for such
lands is denied during the period each year commencing
June 15 and terminating September 15. The words contained in the latter provision of the order we think show
what was finally intended by the board, because they are
more specific, stating not only the period during which the
water may not be used, but also the period during which it
may be used; and the restricted period for using the water
under that order should be understood and held to be from
September 15 to the 15th day of June following, thus denying the right of use only during the period from June 15
in each year to September 15, and, so far as we shall affirm
the order, it will be affirmed with that modification. We
do not believe that the record made by the examination and
measurements of the State Engineer provided for in Section
776 of the Compiled Statutes could affect the question as to
the time or times when the uncultivated land may have been
irrigated, and the extent of the appropriation therefor in
respect of the period of use. It seems to us that upon the

evidence in the case the order of the board improperly restricts the use of the water found to have been appropriated for the uncultivated lands. Since it does not appear that those lands were irrigated or that the water was used therefor when the cultivated lands were being irrigated, we do not think the plaintiff in error is entitled to the right to use at the same time the water appropriated for the uncultivated lands and also that appropriated for the cultivated lands. But when not engaged in irrigating the cultivated lands, even during the irrigation season, we see no impropriety in permitting him to use the 4.23 cubic feet per second found to have been appropriated for said uncultivated or pasture lands. This would not permit the plaintiff in error to turn his aggregate appropriation for all the lands into his ditches at the same time, but when engaged in the irrigation of his 459 acres of cultivated lands he would only be permitted the use of the amount of the allotted appropriation for those lands; and when engaged at any time between June 15 and September 15 in irrigating 296 acres of uncultivated or pasture land, or any part thereof, he would only be permitted to turn into his ditch or ditches and use the amount of his appropriation for those lands, viz.: 4.23 cubic feet per second of time. We believe that this matter can be properly regulated by the water officials, to the end that no subsequent appropriator will be thereby injured. The order will, therefore, be further modified by adding to the paragraph declaring the restriction upon the use of the water for the 296 acres of unculitvated lands the following: "Provided that during the period commencing with said 15th day of June and terminating with said 15th day of September, in each year, whenever the said Harry Nichols, or his successors in the ownership of said lands, are not using, taking or diverting water from Pine Creek for the purpose of irrigating any of the cultivated lands described in the findings and tabulated statement, for which he is allowed an appropriation of 2.46, and 4.10 cubic feet per second of time respectively, the water allowed for said uncultivated lands may be used to irrigate the same; and whenever during that period the water shall be used for said 296 acres of land, or any part thereof, none of the water found to have been appropriated for the above described cultivated tracts shall be used, taken or diverted from said stream."

In all respects, except as modified by the District Court and by this court as above stated, the judgment will be affirmed.

SCOTT, C. J., and BEARD, J., concur.

CARLSON SHEEP COMPANY v. SCHMIDT, ET AL.
(No. 733.)

ANIMALS—SHEEP—TORTS—MIXING HERDS OF SHEEP—DAMAGES—EXEMPLARY DAMAGES—APPEAL AND ERROR—INSTRUCTIONS—PREJUDICIAL ERROR.

1. Where defendant's band of sheep was purposely driven so near a band belonging to plaintiffs with the intention of compelling the plaintiffs to move their sheep from the place on the public range where they were then being herded that the two bands became mixed, resulting in considerable damage to plaintiffs' sheep, including the loss of 38 head, a verdict allowing the plaintiff $750 actual damages and $250 exemplary damages was not excessive.

2. The extent of plaintiff's damages, if any, was a question for the jury upon consideration of all the evidence which was conflicting, and there being substantial testimony, if believed, to warrant the verdict, it will not be disturbed on the ground that it is not supported by sufficient evidence.

3. The evidence justified a finding that the defendant's acts were willful, and done with the intent and for the unlawful purpose of compelling the plaintiffs to cease grazing their sheep on that part of the public range where they were being herded and grazed, and upon the jury so finding it was proper to award exemplary damages.

4. In an action against a corporation for damages caused by the willful mixing of defendant's band of sheep with a band belonging to the plaintiffs, the court instructed the

jury that the rule making an employer responsible for a trespass by his employee while acting within the scope of his employment and in pursuance of the employer's business does not apply to or permit the recovery of exemplary damages for the willful and malicious acts of an employee of a corporation, except where the defendant corporation previously authorized or directed, or subsequently ratified or approved, such acts, or where it retained in its employ the one committing such act after knowledge of such willful and malicious conduct, or where, through its officers, it directly participated in, directed, authorized, approved or ratified such acts. *Held,* that evidence tending to show ratification by the vice-president and manager of the defendant was sufficient to go to the jury, rendering the instruction proper, but whether or not the instruction should have been refused on the ground that the evidence as to ratification was insufficient, it was not prejudicial, since it was stated in another instruction that even if the jury should find from a fair preponderance of the evidence that the employes of the defendant company willfully mixed defendant's sheep with those belonging to the plaintiffs, that would not authorize exemplary damages unless they should further find that the managing officer or foreman of the defendant company authorized or directed such employes to so willfully mix the sheep, or ratified such acts after they were done.

[Decided July 19, 1913.]   (133 Pac. 1053.)

ERROR to the District Court, Weston County, HON. CARROLL H. PARMELEE, Judge.

The action was brought by Charles Schmidt and others, doing business as Charles Schmidt & Sons, against the Carlson Sheep Company, a corporation. Upon a trial in the District Court judgment was rendered for plaintiffs and the defendant brought error. The material facts are stated in the opinion.

Enterline & LaFleiche, for plaintiff in error.

Conceding for the sake of argument that a willful trespass was committed by defendant's employes, the evidence of plaintiffs is wholly insufficient to show that they sustained $750 actual damages, or that 38 head of sheep were lost by reason of the mixing of the two bands. There is no evidence whatever authorizing the assessment of exemplary damages. Plaintiffs wholly failed to prove that defendant had authorized or directed the acts complained of in this case. (Hagan v. R. R., 3 R. I. 88; Warner v. So. Pac. Ry. Co., 113 Cal. 105; Ry. Co. v. Prentice, 147 U. S. 110.)

Metz & Sackett, for defendants in error.

Practically every question raised in the brief of the plaintiff in error has been settled by this court in Henderson v. Coleman, 19 Wyo. 183. There was ample evidence to support the verdict, both as to actual and exemplary damages. It is proper in assessing damages in a case of this character to consider the value of the animal before and after the injury. (Krouschnable v. Knoblauch, 20 Minn. 56; Shea v. Hudson, 165 Mass. 43, 42 N. E. 114; C. & N. W. Ry. Co. v. Calumet Farm (Ill.), 61 N. E. 1095; Ry. Co. v. Biggs, 50 Ark. 169, 6 S. W. 724; Montgomery St. Ry. Co. v. Hastings, 138 Ala. 432, 35 So. 412; Loomis v. Besse, (Wis.) 135 N. W. 123.)

BEARD, JUSTICE.

This action was brought by the defendants in error against the plaintiff in error to recover damages alleged to have been sustained by the mixing of the bands of sheep of the respective parties. The cause was tried to a jury and a verdict returned in favor of plaintiffs (defendants in error), and against defendant (plaintiff in error) for $1,000 damages. Judgment was entered accordingly. A motion of defendant for a new trial was denied, and defendant brings the cause here on error.

The substance of the material allegations of the pleadings necessary to an understanding of the issues are, that during the month of January, 1911, the plaintiffs were the owners of 1,004 head of sheep, which they were ranging and caring for on the public range in Weston county; that said band of sheep consisted of breeding ewes kept by plaintiffs for the purpose of raising lambs and wool and for market.

That defendant was engaged in the sheep business, ranging his sheep in the same vicinity. That on January 27, 1911, the defendant with the intention of injuring and damaging plaintiff's sheep, and with the willful, unlawful and malicious intent to drive the plaintiffs out of the country where they were ranging their sheep, and to injure and destroy their business, wilfully, unlawfully and maliciously drove a band of 3,000 sheep of defendant into the band of plaintiffs, to their actual damage in the sum of $1,500, and claiming exemplary damages in the sum of $1,500.

The answer admitted the corporate capacity of the defendant and denied the other allegations of the petition.

The verdict was as follows: "We the jury duly impaneled and sworn in the above entitled cause, to try the same, do find generally upon the issues in favor of the plaintiff, and against the defendant, and assess the damages of the plaintiff at the sum of One Thousand Dollars ($750.00 damages and $250.00 exemplary) against the defendant."

The only grounds relied upon for a reversal of the judgment and presented by the brief of counsel for plaintiff in error are: 1. That the damages awarded are excessive. 2. That exemplary damages were improperly awarded. And 3. That the court erred in giving instruction numbered 12. We shall not attempt to set out the evidence at length, as to do so would serve no useful purpose. The undisputed facts are that plaintiff was ranging and herding a band of about 1,000 head of sheep on the public range in Weston county, and that defendant was at the same time also ranging a band of about 2,220 head of sheep about a mile distant from plaintiff's band. That one Edlum was the range foreman of the defendant in charge of the camp-movers, herders and four bands of sheep, including the band mentioned. That as soon as Edlum learned the plaintiff's sheep were at or near where the mix occurred he directed the camp-mover and herder to take the band to the vicinity of plaintiff's sheep, as he did not want them to get all the feed. That in pursuance of his directions they were taken close

to plaintiff's sheep, to which plaintiffs objected.   That no
effort was made by defendant's herder or camp-mover to
prevent the mixing, and that the sheep became mixed.   The
camp-mover testified that what he did was by direction of
the foreman; that he was perfectly willing that the sheep
should mix up.   He further testified, speaking of the mixup:
"Q.   Why didn't you prevent it?   A.   Carl Schmidt was
in between them.   Q.   Did you go in between them?   A.
No, sir.   Q.   You took your rifle out to follow the sheep
that morning?   A.   Yes, sir.   Q.   You expected trouble?
A.   Yes, sir.   Q.   You took your rifle along for that purpose?   A.   Yes, sir.   Q.   You intended to go through with
it and back it up with a gun?   A.   Yes, sir."   And further
on in his testimony: "Q.   You wanted the Schmidt sheep
to be moved in that vicinity?   A.   Yes, sir.   Q.   That was
what you desired?   A.   Yes, sir.   Q.   That was the desire
of the foreman?   A.   I don't know.   Q.   Didn't you say
he expressed dissatisfaction about their being there?   A.
Yes, sir.   Q.   You knew it was his desire that they should
be gotten out?   A.   I supposed so.   Q.   You knew it was
the desire of your company?   A.   Yes, sir.   Q.   You went
there endeavoring to get the Schmidt sheep out of that section of the country?   A.   Not necessarily.   Q.   That was
part of the purpose?   A.   To get the feed and they would
have to get out.   Q.   You intended to get the feed anyway,
didn't you?   A.   Yes, sir.   Q.   You didn't care whether
the Schmidt sheep got any feed or not?   A.   No, sir."
Without further stating the testimony at length, it strongly
tends to show that defendant's sheep were purposely taken
so near plaintiff's band, if they were not actually driven into
it, that the result would be a mixup if plaintiffs did not
move from that locality, and that it was the defendant's intention in so doing to compel plaintiffs to move their sheep
from that place.   After the mixup, plaintiffs went away and
defendant took the sheep to a corral and separated them.
After being separated, the plaintiffs not being there to take
charge of them, and the defendant not having sufficient help

at hand to run the two bands separately, put them together and again separated them a few days later.

Plaintiff's sheep were in defendant's possession about seven days, and there was evidence tending to prove that thirty-eight head and a few lambs were lost and the sheep considerably damaged. There was also evidence on part of defendant that the sheep were but slightly damaged, if at all. The extent of the plaintiff's damages, if any, was a question for the jury on a consideration of all of the evidence, and as the evidence was conflicting and there being substantial testimony, if believed, to warrant the verdict, this court under the well established rule will not disturb the judgment on the ground that it is not supported by sufficient evidence. A careful reading of the evidence convinces us that the acts of the defendant were willful and done with the intent and for the unlawful purpose of compelling plaintiffs to cease grazing their sheep on that part of the public range. Such being the case, and if the jury so found, it was proper to award exemplary damages. The amount so awarded was not large, and evidently no more than the jury believed sufficient to admonish the defendant that in the future it should conduct its business with due regard for the rights of others.

By the twelfth instruction the court told the jury, in substance, that the employer is responsible for a trespass committed by the employee while acting within the scope of his employment and in pursuance of his employer's business. "But this instruction shall not apply to or permit the recovery of exemplary damages for the willful and malicious acts of such agents, servants or employees, except where the defendant corporation previously authorized or directed or subsequently ratified or approved such acts, or where it retained the agent, servant or employee committing such act, in its employ, after knowledge of such willful and malicious conduct, or where, through its officers, it directly participated in, directed, authorized approved or ratified such acts." It is argued that there was no evidence of ratification of the acts of the camp-mover and herder by the officer or officers of the company, to which the instruction was applicable.   We think, however, that there was sufficient evidence tending to show a ratification by Carlson, the vice-president and manager of the company, to go to the jury. But whether or not that instruction should have been refused on that ground, the giving of it was not in our opinion prejudicial to defendant; for by the ninth instruction given, to which no objection is here made, the jury was instructed, "that even if you should find from a fair preponderance of the evidence, that the employees of the company wilfully mixed the band of sheep, belonging to the defendant company, with those belonging to the plaintiffs, and that plaintiffs sustained damages thereby, this would not authorize you to assess exemplary damages, that is, damages in the way of punishment, unless you should further find from a further fair preponderance of the evidence, that the managing officer or foreman of the defendant company, authorized or directed such employees to so wilfully mix the sheep, or ratified such acts after they were done."   There was ample testimony given by defendant's witnesses alone tending to show that the acts of the camp-mover and herder were done by the express direction of the foreman of the defendant company, and the question of awarding exemplary damages was rightly submitted to the jury.   No prejudicial error being made to appear the judgment of the District Court is affirmed.   *Affirmed.*

SCOTT, C. J., and POTTER, J., concur.

CLAUSSEN v. STATE.
(No. 737.)

CRIMINAL LAW—TRIAL—MISCONDUCT—APPLAUSE BY AUDIENCE—
WHEN GROUND FOR NEW TRIAL—REVIEW—APPEAL AND ERROR—
QUESTIONS FOR REVIEW—INSTRUCTIONS—REASONABLE DOUBT—DEFI-
NITION—WORDS AND PHRASES—"DOUBT"—"REASONABLE."

1. Questions involving a consideration of the evidence cannot
   be considered on error where the bill of exceptions does
   not contain any of the evidence.

2. Although an applause by the audience in the court room
   during the trial of a criminal case is reprehensible, such
   conduct is not a ground for new trial unless it impedes
   the administration of justice or deprives the defendant of
   a fair trial.

3. Where the trial judge has promptly checked an applause by
   the audience and directed the jury not to be influenced by
   such conduct, his subsequent denial of a motion for a new
   trial on the ground of such misconduct of the audience
   will not cause a reversal where it appears that the opposing
   affidavits concerning the matter were conflicting, since the
   trial judge determined by denying the motion that the
   alleged misconduct did not impede the administration of
   justice or deprive the defendant of a fair trial, and he
   was better able than the Appellate Court to determine that
   matter because of his personal knowledge of what occurred
   at the time of the conduct complained of.

4. A motion in a criminal case made at the close of the case
   for the state to require the prosecution to elect upon which
   of two theories it would rely cannot be considered, where
   neither the motion nor the evidence is incorporated in the
   bill of exceptions.

5. A requested instruction to the effect that a reasonable doubt
   is that state of mind which, after a full comparison and
   consideration of all the evidence, leaves the minds of the
   jury in that condition that they cannot say that they feel
   an abiding faith amounting to a moral certainty that the
   defendant is guilty, is erroneous, since the state of mind
   produced by the evidence arises not alone "from a full
   comparison and consideration" of the evidence, but after
   a fair and impartial comparison and consideration of all
   the evidence.

6. Such instruction fails to define "reasonable doubt," or make
   its meaning any clearer to the jury than the phrase itself,
   and it was therefore properly refused.

7. The failure of the court in a criminal case to give an instruction defining "reasonable doubt" is not ground for reversal where no instruction is requested correctly defining the term.

8. The word "doubt" is plain and simple to understand; it means to question or hold questionable, and "reasonable" means having the faculty of reason; rational; governed by reason; being under the influence of reason; agreeable to reason; just.

9. Where none of the evidence is in the bill of exceptions the only question presented on error by objections to instructions is whether they would be proper under any possible phase of the evidence in the case.

[Decided July 19, 1913.]   (133 Pac. 1055.)
[Rehearing denied October 27, 1913.]   (135 Pac. 802.)

ERROR to the District Court, Sheridan County, HON. CARROLL H. PARMELEE, Judge.

Herman Claussen was charged with the crime of murder in the first degree, convicted of involuntary manslaughter, and prosecuted error. The material facts are stated in the opinion.

H. W. Nichols, for plaintiff in error.

A defendant in a criminal case has the right to be tried decently and in order, in an atmosphere unpolluted by the breath of hostile public sentiment. If he has not been so tried a new trial should be granted. (Comm. v. Hoover, (Pa.) 75 Atl. 1023.) If a person prescribes for, or treats another for an ailment, acting with an honest intention and expectation of curing, even if the effect of the treatment is death, he is not guilty of manslaughter or culpable neglect. (State v. Schulz, 55 Ia. 628, 8 N. W. 469; Comm. v. Thompson, 6 Mass. 134; Rice v. State, 8 Mo. 561; Robbins v. State, 8 O. St. 138.) The series of instructions to the effect that if the culpable neglect of the defendant in any way hastened the death of the deceased were too broad, in that the "hastening" was not qualified as to time. It is error to refuse instructions which are prepared in writing and presented to the court with the request that they be given, if they are relative to the issues, when no other instructions on the subject are given by the court. In a case charging manslaughter by culpable neglect, the neglect must be shown to have been the cause of death, and the defendant is entitled to an instruction to that effect. (State v. Lowe, 68 N. W. 1094.) The court having given two instructions for the state to the effect that they might believe the testimony of the defendant or not, it is error to refuse an instruction asked for by the defendant stating the proper rule as to disregarding his testimony. The defendant is entitled to have an instruction given defining "reasonable doubt" where a proper instruction stating such definition is presented and requested. A request to give a presented instruction should be granted, notwithstanding there may have been another instruction given respecting the matter, if the further instruction requested is deemed essential and is properly prepared and presented. (Bunce v. McMahon, 6 Wyo. 24; Smith v. State, 17 Wyo. 481.)

It appearing that the state was presenting its case upon two separate and distinct theories entirely inconsistent the motion to require the state to elect on which theory it would proceed was proper and should have been granted. (People v. Aiken, 11 Am. St. Rep. 512, 33 N. W. 821; Hamilton v. State, 37 S. W. 431.)

The defendant did not have a fair and impartial trial. The conduct of the audience shown by the affidavits in support of the motion for new trial demonstrates the unfairness of the trial. The record showing this conduct is contained in the motion for new trial and said affidavits. It clearly appears from the affidavits that during nearly all of the trial the court room and entrances were packed with spectators. The people were not attracted to the trial as in an ordinary murder case, but because of popular prejudice against the defendant among the people residing in the community where he lived. The opposing affidavits agree that the audience applauded at the end of the closing address of counsel for the prosecution, and that the court room was crowded during the trial. The affidavits disagree as to the sympathies and feelings of the audience and whether those matters were manifest to the jury. It is a matter of common knowledge that the feelings and attitude of an audience is soon manifested. It is submitted that the jury in this case must have realized or known what the feelings of the audience were, and that they were hostile to the defendant. Although the court orally instructed the jury not to pay any attention to the applause of the audience it is very doubtful if the effect of such applause could have been taken from the minds of the jurymen. (Hamilton v. State, 37 S. W. 431.) If there is any probability that any member of the jury was influenced by such conduct a new trial should be granted. (Id.)

D. A. Preston, Attorney General, for the State.

The trial court determined by denying the motion for new trial that the fact of the applause by the audience had not deprived the defendant of a fair and impartial trial, or impeded the administration of justice, and no prejudice from said misconduct appearing the judgment of the lower court should not be reversed. (State v. Larkin, 11 Nev. 314; Debney v. State, 45 Neb. 856.) The record does not show an objection or exception at the time of the alleged irregularity and therefore defendant is not in a position to urge a new trial. (12 Cyc. 718; State v. Floyd, 61 Minn. 467.) If the instructions given by the trial court over the objection of the defendant and the instructions requested by the defendant and refused were covered by other instructions, or if the action of the trial court in the giving and refusing instructions was correct under any state of facts, the errors complained of respecting the instructions cannot be sustained. (Downing v. State, 11 Wyo. 86; Hill v. State, 43 Ala. 335; State v. Kern, 127 Ind. 465; Koppala v. State, 15 Wyo. 398.)

There is no merit in the contention that the court erred in overruling the defendant's motion to elect upon which of its two theories the state would proceed. The information charged the defendant with the crime of murder in the first degree, and under it the defendant might be convicted of murder in the first or second degree or manslaughter. And evidence was admissible to show the unlawful killing of the deceased by the defendant by whatever means. The record does not show that the state was proceeding upon two theories as to the cause of the death of the deceased. While there is a statement in the record that the defendant moved at the close of the case for the state to require the state to elect upon which of two theories of the means used to produce death it would proceed, it cannot be said that any such state of facts developed upon the trial, for the evidence is not in the record. But if the evidence had disclosed two theories of the prosecution as to the means used by defendant in producing the death of the deceased, it would have been proper for the jury to consider the same. By its verdict of manslaughter the jury adopted the theory as to the means used to produce death most favorable to the defendant, and therefore if there was any merit in the error assigned, the error would be harmless.

Scott, Chief Justice.

The plaintiff in error was charged by information in the statutory form with the crime of murder in the first degree, tried and convicted of the crime of involuntary manslaughter and judgment pronounced against him upon the verdict, and he brings error.

The bill of exceptions contains none of the evidence produced upon the trial, and for that reason our consideration of the case will have to be confined to those questions which do not involve a consideration of the evidence.

1.   It is contended that there was misconduct of the audience during the trial, which was prejudicial to and prevented the defendant from having a fair trial. Upon this question the defendant presented affidavits in support of his contention, and the State presented affidavits in opposition thereto. The misconduct of the audience consisted in one or two outbursts of approval by the audience, which were promptly

checked by the judge who tried the case, and the threat was then made to clear the court room if there was a recurrence, and the court also directed the jury not to be influenced by such conduct. The matter was again brought to the attention of the trial court upon a hearing of the motion for a new trial and that court having upon the affidavits submitted and hereinbefore referred to, and in view of his personal knowledge of what occurred at the time of the conduct complained of was the better able to judge whether the conduct was prejudicial or not. While such conduct is reprehensible, it appears that the court pursued the right course, and if the conduct did not impede the administration of justice the defendant cannot complain. That it did not impede the administration of justice nor deprive defendant of a fair trial was determined by that court in view of its personal knowledge of the acts complained of, and from the conflicting affidavits submitted and we cannot say that the trial court erred in so finding.

2.   It is urged that the court erred in overruling defendant's motion made at the close of the State's case in chief to require the State to elect upon which of its two theories it would proceed, "whether (first) upon the theory that the defendant was guilty of causing the death of the deceased Elise Claussen by strangulation or suffocation, or (second) upon the theory that the defendant caused the death of the deceased Elise Claussen by culpable neglect." This quotation is from the motion for a new trial. Neither the motion to require the State to so elect nor the evidence is incorporated in the bill, and for that reason the motion is not properly before this court for consideration.

3.   The court gave no instruction to the jury defining reasonable doubt, although the defendant prepared and requested the court to instruct the jury "that reasonable doubt is that state of mind which after a full comparison and consideration of all the evidence, both for the State and the defense, leaves the minds of the jury in that condition that they cannot say that they feel an abiding faith amounting

to a moral certainty, from the evidence in the case, that the defendant is guilty of the charge as laid in the information. If you have such doubt—if your conviction of the defendant's guilt as laid in the information does not amount to a moral certainty, from the evidence in the case—then the court instructs you that you must acquit the defendant." It was not error to refuse this instruction. The state of mind produced by the evidence arises not alone from "a full comparison and consideration," but after a fair and impartial comparison and consideration of all the evidence. As to whether the court should have instructed as to what constituted reasonable doubt was discussed by this court in Smith v. State, 17 Wyo. 481, 101 Pac. 847, and we there said: "In the absence of the presentation, either orally or in writing, of an instruction correctly defining the term, we think there was no error in the court declining the attempt." The jury were properly instructed that they could not convict unless they were satisfied of defendant's guilt beyond a reasonable doubt, and that they should give him the benefit of such doubt. In our judgment there is no definition of reasonable doubt which would convey to a juror's mind any clearer idea than the term itself. The word *doubt* is plain and simple to understand. *To doubt,* as defined in Webster's New International Dictionary, means "To question or hold questionable," and the same author defines reasonable "as having the faculty of reason; rational; governed by reason; being under the influence of reason; thinking, speaking, or acting rationally, or according to the dictates of reason; agreeable to reason; just; rational." Courts have attempted in giving the definition of "reasonable doubt" to define the state of mind when a reasonable doubt may be said to exist. Every juror knows, or ought to know, what a doubt is, and the meaning of the word reasonable as applied to such doubt. Is it any clearer in meaning to say to a juror that if he be convinced from the evidence to a moral certainty of defendant's guilt then he has no reasonable doubt? What does moral certainty mean more than reasonable certainty or beyond a reasonable doubt? In State v. De Lea, 36 Mont. 531, 538, 93 Pac. 814, 817, the court say: "Every attempt to define the apparently simple phrase 'a reasonable doubt' has been attended with the greatest difficulty, and it may fairly be said that in a great majority of instances the definitions do not convey any more accurate idea than the phrase itself. So great is the difficulty that some courts hold that it is not error to decline any attempt at a definition." (12 Cyc. 623.) Our statute does not expressly require the definition of "reasonable doubt" to be given to the jury. We think the definition requested failed to define "reasonable doubt" or make its meaning any clearer to the jury than the phrase itself, and for that reason the court did not err in refusing to give it.

Objection was made to the giving of other instructions, some or most of which referred to definitions of the higher degrees of the crime of which defendant was convicted. As already stated, there is none of the evidence given upon the trial incorporated in the bill of exceptions. The only question presented then is whether these instructions or any of them would be improper under any possible phase of the evidence. (Downing v. State, 11 Wyo. 86, 70 Pac. 833, 73 Pac. 758.) We have examined the instructions in this view of the case and without further discussion find that plaintiff in error's contention in this respect is without merit. We find no error in this record, and the judgment will be affirmed.   *Affirmed.*

POTTER, J., and BEARD, J., concur.

ON PETITION FOR REHEARING.

PER CURIAM.

The plaintiff in error has filed a petition for a rehearing. No new point is raised and the motion is directed to matters discussed in his brief upon his petition in error and considered in the opinion. No good purpose would be subserved by a rediscussion of these assignments for after considering the petition and brief in support thereof we adhere to the opinion filed.   *Rehearing denied.*

BLONDE v. MERRIAM, ET AL.
(No. 735.)

APPEAL AND ERROR—NECESSITY OF MOTION FOR NEW TRIAL—NEW
TRIAL—TIME FOR FILING MOTION—EXTENSION OF TIME.

1. Where no ground for reversal is suggested that could not
have been properly assigned as ground for new trial, a
motion for new trial, the overruling thereof, and an exception thereto, is necessary to a consideration of the questions involved.

2. A motion for a new trial is not a pleading under the provisions of the code, and therefore the provision for extending the time to file a pleading does not apply to such
a motion.

3. Under the statute requiring an application for new trial to
be made within ten days after the verdict or decision is
rendered, unless such party is unavoidably prevented from
filing the same within such time, and except for the cause
of newly discovered material evidence which could not,
with reasonable diligence, have been discovered and produced at the trial, an order purporting to extend the time
beyond the ten-day period is ineffectual, where newly discovered evidence is not alleged, and where no showing
was made that the party would be or had been unavoidably prevented from filing his motion within such prescribed
period; and it appearing that the order was made without
such a showing upon an *ex parte* application, without notice
to or consent of the opposing party or his counsel, a
motion filed after the ten-day period, but within the time
as so extended, was properly stricken from the files.

[Decided July 19, 1913.]   (133 Pac. 1076.)

ERROR to the District Court, Fremont County, HON.
CHARLES E. CARPENTER, Judge.

The material facts are stated in the opinion.

V. H. Stone and *L. E. Winslow,* for plaintiff in error.

The striking of the motion for a new trial from the files
was equivalent to overruling and denying the same, so that
if the order striking the motion was error the court may
here consider the questions presented by said motion, under
the assignments of error. Since the decision of Kent v.
Upton, 3 Wyo. 43, holding that the time for filing motion
for new trial cannot be extended upon an *ex parte* applica-

tion without a showing that the party was unavoidably prevented from filing the same within the period then fixed by
statute therefor, there has been a material change in the
consideration of technical rules of practice not affecting the
substantial rights of the parties, and a change has also occurred in the statute with reference to the right of the court
to extend the time for filing pleadings. (Comp. Stat. 1910,
Sec. 4418.) This change in the statute has the effect of en-
larging the power of the court to extend the time. (Todd
v. Peterson, 13 Wyo. 513; Casteel v. State, 9 Wyo. 267.)
If additional time may not be had upon an *ex parte* showing
the provision of the statute is of little practical value, since
ordinarily when it appears necessary to apply for an extension of time there will not remain sufficient time before the
lapse of the statutory period within which to make a full
showing and give notice of the application to the adverse
party. In California the general statute for extending time
for filing pleadings is held to apply to motions for a new
trial. (Simpson v. Budd, 91 Cal. 488; Burton v. Todd, 68
Cal. 485; Harper v. Minor, 27 Cal. 113; see also Bailey v.
Drake, 12 Wash. 99.) Again, by Section 4438, Comp. Stat.
1910, it is required that in every action the court shall disregard any error or defect in the pleadings or proceedings
not affecting the substantial rights of the adverse party. In
the furtherance of justice it would seem that the plaintiff
in error was entitled to a hearing and determination of its
motion upon its merits; it having been filed within the time
granted by the court, and the order extending the time not
affecting the substantial rights of the adverse parties.

(It was further contended that the evidence and record
disclosed error requiring a reversal of the judgment.)

W. E. Hardin and *P. B. Coolidge,* for defendants in error.

The provision of the statute governing motions for new
trial in criminal cases is materially different from that providing for the filing of such motions in civil cases. In criminal cases the court is vested with some discretion in the
matter, and for good cause shown may grant additional time.

(Comp. Stat. 1910, Sec. 6287.)   A motion for new trial is
not a pleading and therefore the statutory provision for extending the time for filing the pleadings is not applicable.
(McDermitt v. Halleck, 65 Kan. 403, 69 Pac. 335.)   The
cases of Kent v. Upton, 3 Wyo. 43, and McLaughlin v.
Upton, 3 Wyo. 48, referred to with approval in Todd v.
Peterson, 13 Wyo. 513, are decisive of this case upon the
question presented by the order striking the motion for new
trial from the files.   The statute in force at the time of
those decisions is identical in all material respects with the
present statute.   There is no injustice in the statute prescribing the time for filing a motion for new trial, or in the construction thereof by the decisions in the cases cited.   Before
verdict or final judgment the statute is very liberal in allowing amendments to pleadings, and assisting litigants in arriving at and having determined the true issues involved;
after verdict or final judgment it has been deemed wise by
the legislature to eliminate all dilatory and uncertain tactics,
and requiring of litigants seeking to set aside a verdict or
final judgment a definite and exacting mode of procedure.

POTTER, JUSTICE.

The plaintiff in error, Charles E. Blonde, was the defendant in the District Court.   It appears that a partnership had
existed between him and the plaintiffs below, Edward Merriam and William Madden, and that the same had terminated, and the action was brought for an accounting and to
recover the amount which might be found to be due the
plaintiffs from the defendant, the petition alleging a stated
amount to be due.   Upon the evidence, which was taken
before a special master commissioner, and reported to the
court with the commissioner's findings, the defendant was
found by the court to be indebted to the plaintiffs, and judgment was rendered for the amount so found to be due.   This
proceeding in error is brought to reverse that judgment.   No
ground for reversal is here suggested that could not have
been properly assigned as ground for new trial, and, therefore, under the rule and decisions of this court the filing of

a motion for new trial, the overruling thereof, and an exception thereto, would be necessary to a consideration of the questions involved. A motion for new trial was filed by the defendant, but the court ordered it stricken from the files, on the motion of plaintiffs, on the ground that it was not filed within the time allowed by the statute. That order was excepted to and is assigned as error. The major portion of each brief is devoted to a discussion of that assignment, it being contended by counsel for plaintiff in error that the motion was timely filed, because within the time allowed by an order extending the time, and that the order striking it from the files is equivalent to an order overruling the motion, if it was filed in time. Opposing counsel, on the other hand, contend that the order extending the time was unauthorized and invalid, and that the motion was, therefore, not filed in time to entitle it to any consideration, and was properly stricken from the files.

A bill of exceptions is in the record showing the motion that was filed, the disposition made of it, and the facts relating thereto. The record discloses the following facts respecting the matter: The findings of the court and judgment were rendered July 15, 1911, that being one of the days of the May, 1911, term of the court. An order, appearing in form as a court order, was signed by the district judge, dated July 24, 1911, and filed July 29, 1911, reading as follows (omitting the caption, signature and date):

"Upon the application of the defendant, Charles E. Blonde, and for good cause shown, it is hereby ordered that the time for the filing of the motion for a new trial in the above entitled cause is hereby extended to and including the 1st day of August, A. D. 1911; and said defendant is now and hereby given to and including the 1st day of August, A. D. 1911, within which to prepare and file his motion for a new trial of said cause." On July 29, 1911, more than ten days after the rendition of the judgment, the defendant filed his motion for new trial. At the November term the motion was presented to the court and argued by counsel for defendant below, counsel for plaintiffs being present. Thereupon the argument was suspended at the court's suggestion and by agreement of the parties, to permit the preparation and filing of written briefs. On or about January 29, 1912, the defendant's attorneys filed with the judge of said court and served upon the attorneys for the plaintiffs their brief in support of the motion, the same being set out in full in the bill of exceptions, discussing the questions presented by the exceptions to the findings, and contending that the same were not supported by the evidence. On the 12th day of May, 1912, the attorneys for plaintiffs served upon the defendant's attorneys their written brief opposing the motion by a discussion of the questions thereby raised.

On May 14, 1912, while said motion for new trial was pending before the court, and, as stated in the bill, before the motion had been finally submitted, the plaintiffs made and filed their motion to strike the defendant's motion for a new trial from the files, on the ground that it was not filed in time, and, therefore, a nullity. The motion to strike recited the date of the judgment, the date when the motion for new trial was filed, the fact that it was not filed within ten days after the rendition of the judgment, and that it does not allege newly discovered evidence, or that the defendant was unavoidably prevented from filing the same within ten days from the rendition of the judgment; that no showing was made to the court prior to its filing that the defendant had been unavoidably prevented from filing the same within said ten days; and alleging that defendant was not unavoidably prevented from filing the motion within that time. It was recited also that an order of court had been filed in the cause on July 29, 1911, purporting to extend the time within which to file the motion for new trial to August 1, 1911; and it was alleged that said order was granted upon an *ex parte* application, that neither the plaintiffs nor their attorneys had any notice or knowledge that such an order would be applied for, or that the same had been entered until after it was filed as aforesaid, and that

said order was granted without any written application or
petition therefor, and was, therefore, ineffective. The motion to strike was supported by affidavits. On June 29,
1912, an order was made and entered sustaining the motion
to strike. That order recites that the motion of the plaintiffs
to strike defendant's motion for new trial came on for hearing; that the plaintiffs appeared in person and by attorneys,
and that the defendant appeared in person and by his attorneys, and also recites the dates respectively when the judgment was entered and the mation for new trial was filed;
and continues as follows:

"And it further appearing that the previous order of this
court purporting to extend the time for filing said motion
for a new trial to August 1st, 1911, was granted on an oral
and *ex parte* application of the defendant's attorneys, without any notice to the plaintiffs or either of them, or to their
attorneys or either of them, or without any showing to this
court that the defendant was or would be unavoidably prevented from filing said motion for new trial within the statutory period, and said order, for the reason aforesaid, being
ineffectual, and without warrant or authority of law; and
no showing having been made in said motion for a new trial,
or otherwise, that the defendant had been unavoidably prevented from filing a motion for a new trial within the statutory period; and it further appearing for the reasons aforesaid that this court is without jurisdiction to hear and determine said motion for a new trial, and the same should
be stricken from the files of this case and the records of this
court: It is therefore considered, ordered, adjudged and
decreed by the court that said motion to strike be and the
same is hereby sustained, and the defendant's said motion
for a new trial is hereby stricken from the files in this case
and the records of this court."

The defendant excepted to the above ruling and order.
Thereafter the defendant filed and presented a motion for a
new trial upon the motion to strike, which was also overruled, and the ruling excepted to. It appears that the judge

who presided when the motion for new trial was stricken from the files was the same judge who had signed the order extending the time. It does not appear that any evidence was produced by the defendant upon the hearing of the motion to strike, and, therefore, the only evidence that the court had before it at the time of that hearing consisted of the court records, and the affidavits filed in support of the motion to strike, the latter showing that neither the plaintiffs nor their counsel had any notice that an order to extend the time for filing a motion for a new trial would be applied for, and no knowledge that an order purporting to extend the time had been entered until long after the same had been filed, and that the extension order was secured upon an oral and *ex parte* application. The fact that the application for the order was oral and *ex parte* was probably also within the knowledge and recollection of the judge, as well as the fact that no showing had been made at that time that the defendant was or would be unavoidably prevented from filing the motion within the period prescribed by statute. The record does not disclose any written application for the order, or a showing by affidavit or otherwise of any necessity or cause therefor, nor does the motion itself make any showing in that respect.

The statutory provisions applicable to the above facts are found in Sections 4603, 4604, Compiled Statutes 1910. Section 4603 reads as follows:

"The application for a new trial must be made at the term the verdict, report or decision is rendered; and except for the cause of newly discovered evidence, material for the party applying, which he could not, with reasonable diligence, have discovered and produced at the trial, shall be made within ten days after the verdict or decision is rendered, unless such party is unavoidably prevented from filing the same within such time."

Section 4604 provides that the application must be by motion, upon written grounds, filed at the time of making the motion. These provisions of the statute are held to be mandatory. (Kent v. Upton, 3 Wyo. 43, 2 Pac. 234; Mc-

Laughlin v. Upton, 3 Wyo. 48, 2 Pac. 534; Boswell v.
Bliler, 9 Wyo. 277, 62 Pac. 350; Todd v. Peterson, 13 Wyo.
513, 81 Pac. 878; Casteel v. State, 9 Wyo. 267, 62 Pac.
348.) The very question here presented was considered and
determined upon facts somewhat like those in the case at
bar in Kent v. Upton and McLaughlin v. Upton, *supra*. At
the time of those decisions the motion was required to be
filed within three days after the verdict or decision was rendered, instead of within 10 days as the statute now provides,
but otherwise the provisions of the statute were substantially and practically the same. In the case of Kent v. Upton
it appeared that the verdict was rendered December 14,
1876; that on December 16, 1876, an order was entered by
the court, on the application of counsel for defendant, extending the time for filing a motion for new trial to the end
of the term; and that the motion for new trial was not filed
until February 16, 1877, presumably during the term. In
the McLaughlin v. Upton case it appeared that within three
days after the verdict was rendered a like order extending
the time was entered, on the application of counsel for the
party desiring to file the motion, the journal entry reciting
that the order was made "for good cause shown." It was
held in each case, that the order extending the time was invalid, for the reason that the court was without any power
to extend the time upon an *ex parte* application. It was
further held that a party desiring to file a motion for new
trial after the period has expired within which he might
have filed it as of right, must show that he was unavoidably
prevented from filing it within such period. The court said
in McLaughlin v. Upton: "We hold that every motion for
a new trial must be on written grounds, and that any party
coming in after his right to file his motion for a new trial
has expired must do so upon written grounds filed at the
time of coming in, and then showing how and in what manner he has been unavoidably prevented." Further it was
said: "To dispense with the requirement of being 'unavoidably prevented' something more is required than the mere
will of the judge, or the wishes of one party to the suit."

In Kent v. Upton, the case of Odell v. Sargent, 3 Kan. 80, was referred to and the following was quoted with approval from the opinion in that case: "When the motion is filed in writing after the three days during which the motion for new trial is a matter of right, it is equally clear that there must be affirmative matter in writing in the motion or accompanying it, showing that the party has been unavoidably prevented from earlier making such motion. And even then such affirmative showing that a party has been unavoidably prevented from making the motion within the statutory period is not to be taken as of course true, but may be traversed." In each of the cases cited the judgment was affirmed for the reason that the motion for new trial not having been filed within the time allowed by the statute, no question presented by the petition in error was before the court for consideration.

These cases determined by our own court are not only decisive upon the facts in this case, but they are sustained by the uniform holding in other states under similar statutory provisions. (Sedam v. Meeksback, 6 O. C. C. 219; Fox v. Meacham, 6 Neb. 530; Roggencamp v. Dobbs, 15 Neb. 621, 20 N. W. 100; Aultman, Miller & Co. v. Leahey, 24 Neb. 286, 38 N. W. 740; Davis v. State, 31 Neb. 240, 47 N. W. 851; McDonald v. McAllister, 32 Neb. 514, 49 N. W. 377; Neb. Nat. Bank v. Pennock, 59 Neb. 61, 80 N. W. 255; Odell v. Sargent, 3 Kan. 80; City of Osborne v. Hamilton, 29 Kan. 1; Schallehn v. Hibbard, 64 Kan. 601, 68 Pac. 61; Railroad Co. v. Holland, 58 Kan. 317, 49 Pac. 71; Joiner v. Goldsmith, 25 Okl. 840, 107 Pac. 733; Riely v. Robertson, 29 Okl. 181, 115 Pac. 877; Eggleston v. Williams, 30 Okl. 129, 120 Pac. 944.)

In Fox v. Meacham, *supra*, it was contended that the right to grant a new trial is an inherent power in the court, and hence the court might grant a new trial upon a motion filed at any time without regard to the statutory limitation as to time, but the court said: "Now the authority of the legislature to regulate by statute the application for a new trial will not be questioned; and as the legislature of our state

has, by a mandatory act, fixed the time within which the
application must be made, we think the court has no power
to disregard such law." In Aultman, Miller & Co. v. Leahey,
supra, it appeared that an amendment to the motion for
new trial was made the fourth day after the verdict was
rendered, the statute requiring the motion to be made within
three days after verdict, and it also appeared that the amendment was made "without the finding by the court that the
plaintiff was unavoidably prevented from a compliance with
the statute, as a palliation for the amendment." After stating these facts the court proceeded to show that without the
amendment the original assignments in the motion were incomplete and insufficient, and that the amendment comprised
substantially the whole of the error assigned, and then said:
"It does not seem, therefore, to have been competent for the
court to have extended the time limited by the code, by the
allowance of a substitute, as an amendment, after the expiration of the three days appointed, after the verdict. The
authority of the legislature to regulate, by the code, application for new trials, will not be disputed. It has done so
in a mandatory provision. This amendment is no less than
an infraction of it."

In the case of McDonald v. McAllister, *supra*, the court
say: "Where a motion for a new trial is filed out of time,
it must be supported by a showing excusing delay." And,
because the affidavit filed for the purpose of excusing delay
was found to be insufficient for that purpose, it was held
that no error was committed in striking the motion from the
files, the same having been filed after the expiration of the
three days provided by the statute. In Davis v. State, *supra*,
it is said: "The court has no power to extend the time for
filing such a motion beyond three days, except for newly
discovered evidence, unless the party was 'unavoidably prevented' from making the application in time. If the court
could grant an extension of one day, it can extend the period
for one month or six months." The motion in that case was
not filed until the fourth day after the verdict, and it was
not based on the ground of newly discovered evidence. It

is further said in the opinion: "No showing was made excusing the delay, nor is there any finding of the trial court that the defendant was unavoidably prevented from filing his motion before the time allowed him by law had expired. The errors assigned in the motion for a new trial could not be considered by the court below, and cannot be reviewed here."

In the Oklahoma case of Joiner v. Goldsmith, *supra*, the court say that the statute "requiring that the motion be filed within three days after the verdict is mandatory, and, in the absence of a showing that the party filing it has been unavoidably prevented from filing it within the time specified by the statute, this court cannot consider it or review the errors occurring upon the trial." In Kansas and Oklahoma it is held that the words in the statute "unless unavoidably prevented," apply as an exception to the provision requiring the motion to be filed during the term at which the verdict or decision was rendered, as well as to the provision requiring it to be filed within three days after verdict. (Schallehn v. Hibbard, *supra;* Riely v. Robertson, *supra*.) In the Kansas case of Schallehn v. Hibbard a new trial had been granted, but the record was silent as to whether a showing was made that the party was unavoidably prevented from filing it during the term. It was held by reason of the silence of the record on that matter that it should be presumed that the motion fell within the exception, and that the facts showing such to be the case were proven to the satisfaction of the trial court. The court say: "In this case the record shows that, although the motion for a new trial was not filed until after the adjournment of the term at which the verdict was given and the judgment rendered, yet that the court took up this motion and granted it. This the court might do if the party filing the motion out of time was unavoidably prevented from filing within the time. The failure to file within three days and within the term is not inexcusable. If a party is prevented from so doing by unavoidable circumstances, yet his motion may be heard. The court must determine whether such circumstances exist. In this case

the record is silent upon the question as to whether there was
sufficient excuse for not filing the motion within the term.
Nothing whatever is said upon the subject.   But all pre-
sumptions that are warranted by the record must be indulged
in to support the correctness of the ruling of the court, and,
so far as the record shows, abundant proof may have been
introduced to show that the party was unavoidably prevented
from filing his motion for a new trial within the term.   We
cannot presume error.   If this evidence was not before the
court, the record ought to have shown its absence in order
to show error.   It must be remembered that this case is one
where a new trial was granted, and not one where it was
refused.   In a number of cases this court has decided that a
trial court is justified in refusing a new trial where the
motion therefor was not filed within the time prescribed by
the section which we have cited."   In the Oklahoma case of
Riely v. Roberston, it appeared that the trial court had refused to strike the motion for new trial from the files.   The
court say: "Obviously the court found as a fact that the
plaintiff in error was unavoidably prevented from filing his
motion for a new trial at the term at which the verdict was
rendered and for that reason he refused to strike the motion
from the files.   We are not prepared to say that he erred,
as there was evidence reasonably tending to show the unavoidable prevention of its filing within time.   The motion
for new trial, however, failed to allege the unavoidable
casualty, but the defendant in error having of his own motion introduced evidence without objection, from which the
court evidently found the fact of unavoidable casualty, that
cured such defect."   The court further say: "We are of
the opinion where a party is prevented by an unavoidable
casualty from filing a motion for a new trial within the prescribed three days and at the term at which the verdict was
returned that under proper allegations, supported by proof,
a motion to vacate and set aside the judgment may be filed
after the close of the term, and that the conclusion reached
in Schallehn v. Hibbard, 64 Kan. 601, 68 Pac. 61, is correct.
This being in line with the adjudications of the same pro-

cedure in Kansas, and facilitating the ends of justice, we
follow the same."

In the case of Sedam v. Meeksback, *supra,* decided in one
of the Circuit Courts of Ohio, from which state our code
provisions were taken, it is said in the opinion: "The record
shows the filing of the motion for a new trial long after the
time fixed by the statute—and that as is claimed by counsel
for the defendant in error, no leave to do this by the court
is shown, and that there is no finding by the court on the
journal that the person moving for a new trial was unavoidably prevented from doing so within the three days allowed.
This, we think, is requisite, * * * ." In Indiana the
statute provided that the application for a new trial may be
made at any time during the term at which the verdict or
decision is rendered; and if the verdict or decision be rendered on the last day of the session of any court, or on the
last day of any term, then, on the first day of the next term
of such court, whether general, special, or adjourned. In
Evansville & Richmond R. Co. v. Maddux, 134 Ind. 571 (33
N. E. 345, 34 N. E. 511), it appeared that the verdict had
been rendered some time before the final adjournment of
the term, but the judgment was entered on the last day
of the term; that there was no offer to file a motion during
the term, nor until the first day of the next term. It was
held that the motion came too late. In McIntosh v. Zaring,
150 Ind. 301, 49 N. E. 164, it appeared that the verdict was
returned on the last day of the term, that an adjourned term
was called, and that the court allowed until the first day of
the "next term" to present a motion for new trial, "but without consent of or notice to" the other party. It appeared
also that the motion was not filed at the adjourned or special
term. It was held that the motion was carried forward to
the next term "whether general, special or adjourned," and
that whichever term, general, special or adjourned, came
next after the term in which the verdict was returned would
be the "next term" within the meaning of the statute, and
that, therefore, the application should have been made at the
adjourned term, and the court said: "The court had no right

to extend the time for filing the motion beyond the time fixed by law for filing the same, especially in the absence and without the consent of appellees." (See also King v. Gilson, 206 Mo. 264, 104 S. W. 52 ; 29 Cyc. 927-929.) Counsel for plaintiff in error has called attention to Section 4418, Compiled Statutes, 1910, which provides that the court, or a judge thereof in vacation, may, for good cause shown, extend the time for filing any pleading upon such terms as are just, and to the fact that when the Upton cases were decided the section provided only that time might be extended for filing a petition or answer. The provision is not applicable. A motion for a new trial is not a pleading under our code provisions, as we have frequently held, and as held in other states having the same code procedure. It clearly appears by this record that no showing was made at any time that the plaintiff in error, defendant below, would be or had been unavoidably prevented from filing his motion for a new trial within ten days after the decision was rendered. It also appears that the order purporting to extend the time was made upon an oral *ex parte* application, without notice to or the consent of the defendants in error, plaintiffs below, or their counsel. Such order was therefore ineffectual. Whether such an order might be made before presenting a motion, upon notice to and consent of the other party to the cause, and a satisfactory showing that the one desiring to file the motion would be unavoidably prevented from doing so within the statutory period, it is unnecessary to decide. An order extending the time would not be required, for it would be competent for the party to make the necessary showing that he had been unavoidably prevented upon coming in with his motion and asking leave to file the same. Defendant's motion having been filed when he had no right to file it, it was properly stricken from the files. (29 Cyc. 929.) He is here without a motion for new trial, and, for that reason, none of the errors assigned can be considered. The judgment must, therefore, be affirmed.   *Affirmed.*

SCOTT, C. J., and BEARD, J., concur.

INDEX

ATTACHMENT—*Continued.*

duty of the court to assume that it was a bond authorized by the said order of the court, viz.: a bond to stay execution pending proceedings in error, obligating the parties to pay the judgment if affirmed, thereby taking the question as to the validity of the attachment or the correctness of the ruling of the court refusing to quash it out of the case, the attachment being unnecessary to give the court jurisdiction of the person of either of the defendants, the personal appearance of each of them having been entered in the cause. Id.

BANKS AND BANKERS. See Negotiable Instruments, 6, 9; Pleading, 3.

BILL OF EXCEPTIONS.

1. While the statute respecting a bill of exceptions is to be liberally construed to the end that the bill, which the trial judge has deemed proper to be signed, may be sustained if possible, rather than defeated, the court cannot go so far as to disregard the plain provisions of the statute, and sustain a bill clearly not presented for allowance in time. Meadows v. Roberts, as executor, 43.

2. Time was given to reduce exceptions to writing and present them for allowance until and including the first day of the next regular term; a bill was presented for allowance on the first day of said next regular term, it appearing by the certificate of the judge thereto as follows: that the bill was not then complete, in that it did not contain the transcript of the testimony given upon the trial; that permission was then given to withdraw the bill and complete the same; that the facts respecting the completion of the bill were correctly stated in the affidavit of the court reporter appearing in the record; that the bill was several months afterwards and during a later term completed and presented to the judge; that a written objection to the allowance of the bill was thereupon filed supported by said reporter's affidavit. The objection was overruled and the bill as finally presented, containing a transcript of the evidence, was allowed and signed by the judge. The affidavit of the court reporter stated substantially that the party presenting the bill had notified said reporter a few days after the trial that a transcript of the evidence was desired, but that said party did not have the money to pay therefor; that thereafter and immediately prior to the opening of the second term of court following the trial,

BILL OF EXCEPTIONS—*Continued.*

one of the attorneys for said party informed the reporter that a transcript of the evidence was desired, and subsequently ordered such transcript; that pursuant thereto the evidence was then transcribed; and that had such transcript been ordered in time for that purpose the transcript would have been furnished prior to the time originally fixed for the presentation of the bill. *Held,* that, since a writing not containing the facts, or so much of the evidence as is necessary to explain the exception, is not such a bill of exceptions as the statute requires to be presented within the time allowed, the bill was not presented for allowance within the time allowed by law and fixed by the court, and that a motion to strike the bill from the record should be granted. Id.

See also Appeal and Error, 7.

BILLS AND NOTES. See Negotiable Instruments.

BRIEFS. Failure to file—Dismissal, see Appeal and Error, 11.

BURDEN OF PROOF. See Payment, 1.

CANCELLATION. Of state land lease. See Public Lands of the State.

CHANGE OF JUDGE. See Venue, 1, 2.

CHANGE OF VENUE. See Venue, 1, 2.

CHATTEL MORTGAGES.

1. It being determined that a negotiable promissory note secured by a senior chattel mortgage had not been paid, and it appearing that admissions made by the assignor as to payment were made after the junior mortgagee had taken his mortgage and extended the credit secured thereby, his rights under his subsequent mortgage were not affected, and he was not placed in any worse position by the assignment of the senior mortgage, but the latter remained a prior and superior lien and enforceable while it remained in the hands of the mortgagee named therein, and was thereafter equally valid and enforceable by the assignee; and it was, therefore, immaterial whether or not the assignee was a bona fide purchaser. Hamilton v. Diefenderfer, 266.

2. Where, in an action by the assignee of a chattel mortgage against a subsequent mortgagee to recover possession of the mortgaged property, evidence was admitted to the effect that the assignor had stated prior to the assignment and the indorsement of the note secured by the mortgage,

CHATTEL MORTGAGES—*Continued.*

that the note and mortgage were paid, *Held,* that, conceding the admissibility of such statements, they were not conclusive in favor of the subsequent mortgagee, whose mortgage was taken long prior to the making of the statements, and who had not acted upon them. Id.

3. The only evidence to sustain the defense in such action that the note and mortgage under which the plaintiff claimed had been paid consisted of admissions of payment by the assignor, while all the other facts in the case tended to show non-payment. *Held,* that the trial court was not only as well able as the appellate court to determine the weight to be given to the alleged statements of the assignor, but in a better position to do so. Id.

4. Where a senior chattel mortgage was valid and had not been paid, the consideration for an assignment thereof was immaterial, as against the junior mortgagee, and the latter could not impeach such assignment on the ground of the insufficiency of the consideration to constitute the assignee a purchaser for value. Id.

See also Payment, 3.

CHECK. Action against drawer. See Negotiable Instruments, 1-9; Pleading, 3.

CITIZENSHIP. Proof of, in adverse mining suit—Presumption. See Mines and Minerals, 15-18.

COAL MINES. Action for personal injuries. See Master and Servant, 1-10.

CONDEMNATION. See Eminent Domain.

CONSIDERATION.

1. Though the price of a thing sold or assigned may be inadequate, and that fact may be considered in determining the question of good faith, it may nevertheless be a valuable consideration within the meaning of that term, as where money is paid, whether the amount be large or small. Hamilton v. Deifenderfer, 266.

See also Chattel Mortgages, 4; Negotiable Instruments, 10; Pleading, 2.

CONTRACTS.

Admissibility of parol evidence to show that written contract of partner was made for the partnership. J. J. Crable & Son v. O'Connor, 460.

Sale of corporate stock—Assumption by purchaser of seller's obligations for the company—Action on the Contract—Amount of recovery. Demple v. Carroll, 447.

See also Consideration, 1; Insurance, 1, 2; Payment, 1, 2; Work and Labor, 2, 3.

CORPORATIONS.

1. There is a distinction in the rules of code pleading between an entire failure to state a cause of action and the statement of one in an imperfect and defective manner, but in an action by an objecting stockholder to set aside a sale of the assets of a corporation on the ground of fraud and misconduct on the part of the majority stockholders, where the defect of indefiniteness and uncertainty in the petition relates to material facts concerning which the averments ought to be reasonably definite and certain, it may amount to a failure to state a cause of action rendering the petition demurrable. Smith v. Stone et al., 62.

2. Where, in an action by a minority stockholder to set aside the sale of corporate assets pursuant to a resolution adopted at an annual meeting of the stockholders, it was contended as one ground for vacating the sale that the stockholders were without authority at such meeting to consider or adopt the resolution for the reason that the notice of the meeting did not specify that such matter would be considered, *Held*, that, since the statute provided as to notice of the annual meeting only that notice of the time and place of holding the same should be published, and it was provided by statute that the stockholders, or the trustees, if the certificate of incorporation so provides, shall have power to make by-laws as they shall deem proper for the management and disposition of the stock and business affairs of the company, not inconsistent with the laws of the state, and the petition did not show what provision, if any, was made in the by-laws with reference to the business that might be transacted at the annual meeting and the notice

CORPORATIONS—*Continued.*

property was sold, *Held,* that the petition was at least indefinite and uncertain as to who were meant by "all of the said parties," and that it ought not to be assumed on demurrer to the petition that any defendant, either individually or in combination with others, had a controlling or any other interest in the purchasing corporation, unless the fact was definitely alleged; and, hence, the averments to the effect that the purpose of the sale was to obtain the corporate property for less than its reasonable, fair, or market value, applied only to the said three defendants last specifically named. Id.

11. Where, in an action by a minority stockholder to set aside the sale of the corporate property to another corporation pursuant to a resolution adopted at the annual meeting of the stockholders of the selling corporation, it was alleged that objecting stockholders stated at the meeting that a much greater price could be obtained if an endeavor was made to do so, *Held,* that said allegation had no further effect than to show that said statement was made, and did not amount to an allegation that a greater price could in fact have been obtained; it not being alleged as a fact that a greater price could have been obtained for the property and that anyone was able, ready and willing to pay a greater price for it. Id.

12. In an action by a minority stockholder to set aside a sale of the corporate property on the ground of alleged fraud and misconduct of the majority stockholders, through the vote of whom at the annual meeting a resolution was adopted providing for the sale, *Held,* as to an allegation in the petition that objecting stockholders stated at the time of the adoption of the resolution that a much greater price than that named in the resolution could be obtained for the property if an endeavor was made to do so, that if the allegation should be considered as alleging as a fact that a "much greater" price could be obtained, said words were too indefinite under the circumstances upon which to base general charges of fraud, since, in addition to the possible natural increase in the value of the property, the words "much greater" might imply merely a fair and reasonable profit accruing to the purchaser. Id.

13. In the absence of fraud, the fact that a difference of opinion may have existed between the majority and minority stockholders respecting the propriety of selling the corporate property would not alone justify interference by a court of

CORPORATIONS—*Continued.*

18. There is no inflexible rule for determining what length of
    time will constitute unreasonable delay in bringing an ac-
    tion by an objecting stockholder to set aside the sale of
    corporate property, but whether the delay has been rea-
    sonable or unreasonable must depend upon the facts and
    circumstances of each case. Id.

19. In an action by a minority stockholder to set aside a sale
    alleged to have been made of all the corporate property
    on the ground of alleged fraud and misconduct on the
    part of majority stockholders and trustees, it appeared by
    the petition that the plaintiff was aware of the proposed
    sale and the circumstances and conditions thereof at the
    time of the annual meeting and the meeting of the trustees
    when the respective resolutions providing for the sale re-
    ferred to in the petition were proposed and adopted on
    October 2, 1906, and that he took no steps to prevent the
    sale until April 12, 1907, when he served upon each of the
    trustees a notice objecting to the sale, although in the
    meantime he had been informed that certain instruments
    had been executed by the president and secretary of the
    company pretending to convey the property to the proposed
    grantee, and that the possession of the same had been
    transferred, and the suit to set aside the sale was not
    commenced until July 29, 1909, the delay in bringing suit
    being explained merely by the statement that a suit in the
    same court upon the same cause of action had been
    brought by the plaintiff and another against all of the
    present defendants except one, and that said suit had been
    prosecuted until September 16, 1908, when it was dis-
    missed without prejudice, without stating the reasons for
    the dismissal thereof, and the defendant not a party to
    the previous suit was another corporation to whom the
    property was alleged to have been transferred by the or-
    iginal purchasing corporation, and further, that all of the
    property had been disposed of by the last purchasing cor-
    poration, the purchasers thereof not being made parties to
    the action nor their names disclosed by the petition. *Held,*
    that, whatever the right of the selling corporation may
    have been. or the plaintiff as a stockholder, to question
    the validity of the sale even to the extent of demanding
    its vacation, had the property remained in the possession
    and control of either of the purchasing corporations,
    neither the selling corporation nor the plaintiff suing on its

behalf would be entitled to a decree in the present action setting aside the sale to the original purchasing corporation or a subsequent sale by said purchaser, since the rights of other parties had intervened who presumably obtained the property in good faith, there being no averments to the contrary, and no decree could be entered which would affect their title. Id.

20. It further appearing that the debt of the selling corporation had been paid, and there being no offer to return the consideration paid for the property by the original purchasing corporation, nor the showing of any means by which it could be refunded or returned, it would be inequitable to declare the sale void or by a decree to set it aside; all of such conditions having resulted through the laches of the plaintiff, if at any time the corporation or the plaintiff might have sustained an action for such relief. Id.

21. An allegation in a petition by a minority stockholder to set aside the sale of corporate property on the ground of alleged fraud and misconduct on the part of majority stockholders, where the only allegation of profit received by any individual defendant was that the property was disposed of for a sum much greater than the debt of the company to pay which the property was sold, *Held*, that said allegation did not necessarily imply an unfair or unreasonable profit or condition, and was not sufficient to require an accounting by the purchaser or any of the individual stockholders who assented to the sale and were made defendants. Id.

22. In such an action sufficient facts not being shown to justify a decree setting aside the sale, the mere general allegation, under the circumstances, as to the difference between the selling price and the reasonable and market value of the property is not sufficient to require an accounting by either of the purchasing corporations. Id.

See also Contracts; Damages, 4.

COUNTERCLAIM. See Factors, 8-12; Injunction, 2-4.

CRIMINAL LAW.

1. Although an applause by the audience in the court room during the trial of a criminal case is reprehensible, such conduct is not a ground for new trial unless it impedes the administration of justice or deprives the defendant of a fair trial. Claussen v. State, 505.

CRIMINAL LAW—*Continued.*

2. Where the trial judge has promptly checked an applause by the audience and directed the jury not to be influenced by such conduct, his subsequent denial of a motion for a new trial on the ground of such misconduct of the audience will not cause a reversal where it appears that the opposing affidavits concerning the matter were conflicting, since the trial judge determined by denying the motion that the alleged misconduct did not impede the administration of justice or deprive the defendant of a fair trial, and he was better able than the Appellate Court to determine that matter because of his personal knowledge of what occurred at the same time of the conduct complained of. Id.

3. A motion in a criminal case made at the close of the case for the state to require the prosecution to elect upon which of two theories it would rely cannot be considered, where neither the motion nor the evidence is incorporated in the bill of exceptions. Id.

4. A requested instruction to the effect that a reasonable doubt is that state of mind which, after a full comparison and consideration of all the evidence, leaves the minds of the jury in that condition that they cannot say that they feel an abiding faith amounting to a moral certainty that the defendant is guilty, is erroneous, since the state of mind produced by the evidence arises not alone "from a full comparison and consideration" of the evidence, but after a fair and impartial comparison and consideration of all the evidence. Id.

5. Such instruction fails to define "reasonable doubt," or make its meaning any clearer to the jury than the phrase itself, and it was therefore properly refused. Id.

6. The failure of the court in a criminal case to give an instruction defining "reasonable doubt" is not ground for reversal where no instruction is requested correctly defining the term. Id.

7. The word "doubt" is plain and simple to understand; it means to question or hold questionable, and "reasonable" means having the faculty of reason; rational; governed by reason; being under the influence of reason; agreeable to reason; just. Id.

See also Extradition; Jury and Jurors, 4; Larceny.

DAMAGES.

1. Where defendant's band of sheep was purposely driven so near a band belonging to plaintiffs with the intention of compelling the plaintiffs to move their sheep from the

DAMAGES—*Continued.*

place on the public range where they were then being
herded that the two bands became mixed, resulting in considerable damage to plaintiffs' sheep, including the loss of
38 head, a verdict allowing the plaintiff $750 actual dam-
ages and $250 exemplary damages was not excessive. Carl-
son Sheep Co. v. Schmidt et al., 498.

2. The extent of plaintiff's damages, if any, was a question
for the jury upon consideration of all the evidence which
was conflicting, and there being substantial testimony, if
believed, to warrant the verdict, it will not be disturbed
on the ground that it is not supported by sufficient evidence. Id.

3. The evidence justified a finding that the defendant's acts
were willful, and done with the intent and for the unlawful purpose of compelling the plaintiffs to cease grazing their sheep on that part of the public range where
they were being herded and grazed, and upon the jury so
finding it was proper to award exemplary dagames. Id.

4. In an action against a corporation for damages caused by
the willful mixing of defendant's band of sheep with a
band belonging to the plaintiffs, the court instructed the
jury that the rule making an employer responsible for a
trespass by his employee while acting within the scope of
his employment and in pursuance of the employer's business does not apply to or permit the recovery of exemplary
damages for the willful and malicious acts of an employee
of a corporation, except where the defendant corporation
previously authorized or directed, or subsequently ratified
or approved, such acts, or where it retained in its employ
the one committing such act after knowledge of such
willful and malicious conduct, or where, through its officers, it directly participated in, directed, authorized, approved or ratified such acts. *Held,* that evidence tending
to show ratification by the vice-president and manager of
the defendant was sufficient to go to the jury, rendering
the instruction proper, but whether or not the instruction
should have been refused on the ground that the evidence
as to ratification was insufficient, it was not prejudicial,
since it was stated in another instruction that even if the
jury should find from a fair preponderance of the evidence
that the employes of the defendant company willfully
mixed defendant's sheep with those belonging to the
plaintiffs, that would not authorize exemplary damages
unless they should further find that the managing officer

EMINENT DOMAIN—*Continued.*

6. The exercise of the power of eminent domain for the purpose of irrigation and reclamation of land is founded upon the conditions and necessities of the state where the power is to be exercised, and does not rest upon the necessities or the physical conditions of another state. Id.

7. Where land in this state situated near the boundary line between this state and Colorado was sought to be condemned for a headgate and part of a ditch of an irrigation system to irrigate lands in Colorado near such boundary line, the fact that the irrigation and the reclamation of such land might indirectly benefit some of the people of this state, and that settlers on said lands in Colorado might purchase their supplies from a neighboring city in this state, is not such a benefit to the public of this state as to authorize the taking of the desired land in this state under the power of eminent domain; the only use which could support the exercise of the power will occur not in this state, nor for any purpose of this state, but in the other state where the water is to be applied and the land to be irrigated is located. Id.

8. Under the conditions stated in the last preceding paragraph, it appearing that no land in this state will receive for its reclamation or cultivation any of the water to be diverted or distributed by means of the ditch, but the water is to be entirely devoted to the irrigation of land in another state, the use will be in and for that state—for its use and purpose, and not in this state or for any of its purposes, and, therefore, the principle is applicable, that the power of eminent domain will not be exercised by a state for the use of another state. Id.

9. Another state cannot exercise the power of eminent domain in this state, and any authority conferred by its laws to do so would be void, for the sovereignty of any government is limited to persons and property within the territory it controls. Id.

10. The statute (Comp. Stat. 1910, Sec. 3874) conferring authority to appropriate and condemn land for a right of way for a ditch for agricultural purposes is intended to be confined not only to a right of way within the state, but also to agricultural purposes within the state; such authority is conferred to encourage agriculture within the state, and if the legislative power exists to make the authority broader than that, and extend it to agricultural

EMINENT DOMAIN—*Continued.*

purposes beyond the state boundaries, it should be so extended, if at all, by the legislature, and by words clearly showing an intention to do so. Id.

11. Where it was sought to condemn land in this state for a headgate and ditch to be used to divert and conduct water into the State of Colorado solely for the purpose of irrigating and reclaiming lands situated in that state, near the southern boundary line of this state, *Held,* that a right to condemn the land in this state was not shown, since no part of the use which would support the right to condemn was to occur in this state, or for any of the purposes of this state. Id.

See also Pleading, 8.

ESTOPPEL. See Corporations, 17.

EVIDENCE.

1. The law excludes, as incompetent, parol testimony to vary the terms of a written instrument, or to prove a parol contemporaneous agreement at variance from the writing, in the absence of fraud, accident, or mistake. Demple v. Carroll, 447.

2. It is competent to show by parol evidence that a party who is named in and has signed a contract as one of the parties thereto was an agent for another, and acted as such agent in making the contract, so as to give the benefit of the contract to, and charge with liability, the unnamed principal, whether the unnamed principal was or was not disclosed or known to the other party to the contract at the time it was made. And this rule applies to a contract made and executed by one partner, when acting for the firm and within the scope of the partnership business. J. J. Crable & Son v. O'Connor, 460.

3. Where the fact of a partnership is shown by other evidence, the conversations between the parties to a contract are admissible to show that although made in the name of and signed by one of the partners, it was made for the benefit of the partnership. Id.

See also Admissions, 1; Chattel Mortgages, 2; Factors, 8, 12; Malicious Prosecution, 12; Master and Servant, 1-4; Payment, 1-3.

EXCEPTIONS.

1. Under the statute (Comp. Stat. 1910, Sec. 4597) providing that when a decision objected to is entered on the record and the grounds of the objection appear in the entry, ex-

EXCEPTIONS—*Continued*.

    ception may be taken by the party causing it to be noted at the end of the entry that he excepts, the grounds of objection sufficiently appear in an entry'showing a ruling upon a demurrer to a pleading, either sustaining or overruling it, and an exception thereto is properly taken by causing it to be noted at the end of the entry that the objecting party excepts to the ruling; the demurrer constitutes the objection, and, since it is a part of the record proper, a statement of the grounds thereof in the entry showing a ruling upon it is unnecessary, within the meaning of said statute, to authorize an exception thereto by noting the same at the end of the entry. Grover Irr. and Land Co. v. Lovella Ditch, Reservoir & Irr. Co., 204.

    See also Appeal and Error, 2.

EXCEPTIONS, BILL OF. See Bill of Exceptions.

EXECUTORS AND ADMINISTRATORS. See Work and Labor, 4-6.

EXEMPLARY DAMAGES. See Damages, 1, 3-4.

EXTRADITION.

    1. A person charged with crime against the laws of a state who, after committing the crime, flees from justice—that is, leaves the state—in whatever way and for whatever reason, and is found in another state, may, under the authority of the constitution and laws of the United States, be brought back to the state in which he stands charged with the crime, to be there dealt with according to law. Ryan v. Rogers, Sheriff, 311.

    2. When the executive of the state wherein a crime was committed makes a demand upon the executive of a state where the one charged with the crime is found, as authorized by Section 5278, U. S. Rev. Stat., producing at the time a copy of the indictment, or an affidavit certified as authentic and made before a magistrate charging the demanded person with a crime against the laws of the demanding state, it becomes the duty of the executive of the state where the fugitive is found, to cause him to be arrested, surrendered, and delivered to the appointed agent of the demanding state to be taken to that state. Id.

    3. The executive of a state may decline to issue an extradition warrant, upon the demand of the executive of another state for an alleged fugitive from justice, unless it is made to appear to him by competent proof that the accused is substantially charged with crime against the laws of the

EXTRADITION—*Continued.*

demanding state, and is in fact a fugitive from the justice of that state. Id.

4. .Whether an alleged criminal for whom a requisition is issued and presented is or is not a fugitive from the justice of the demanding state may, so far as the constitution and laws of the United States are concerned, be determined by the executive upon whom the demand is made in such way as he deems satisfactory, and he is not obliged to demand proof of the fact apart from proper requisition papers from the demanding state. Id.

5. When it is determined by the executive of a state upon whom a demand is made that the alleged criminal is such fugitive from the justice of another state, and a warrant of arrest is issued after such determination, the warrant is to be regarded as making a prima facie case in favor of the demanding state and as requiring the removal of the alleged criminal to the state in which he stands charged with crime, unless in some appropriate proceeding it is made to appear that he is not a fugitive from the justice of the demanding state. Id.

6. A proceeding by habeas corpus in a court of competent jurisdiction is appropriate for determining whether one accused of crime in another state and arrested upon an extradition warrant is subject, under such warrant of arrest, to be taken as a fugitive from justice from the state in which he is found to the state whose laws he is charged with violating. Id.

7. One arrested and held upon an extradition warrant as a fugitive from justice is entitled, of right, upon habeas corpus, to question the lawfulness of his arrest and imprisonment, showing by competent evidence, as a ground for his release, that he was not, within the meaning of the constitution and laws of the United States, a fugitive from the justice of the demanding state, and thereby overcoming the presumption to the contrary arising from the face of an extradition warrant. Id.

8. A requisition for one Charles T. Crane, otherwise known as James Ryan, was accompanied by an indictment charging the commission of a crime in the demanding state by Charles T. Crane, and also by an affidavit referring to said Charles T. Crane as "otherwise known as James Ryan," which affidavit purported to state some of the facts of the alleged crime, that the one indicted had fled the jurisdiction of the demanding state and was under

EXTRADITION—*Continued.*

arrest in the other state as such fugitive from justice. *Held,* that the charge of crime sufficient to authorize the requisition was contained in the indictment, and it was not necessary that said affidavit should have been sworn to before a magistrate; it appearing that the affidavit was presented to the executive of the demanding state for the purpose of showing the presence in that state of the one indicted at the time of the commission of the crime, and that he had fled from the state, and also the good faith of the request for the extradition. Id.

9. Under the statute of Illinois providing that every person who shall obtain from any other person or persons, any money or property, by means or by use of any false or bogus checks, or by any other means, instrument or device, commonly called the confidence game, shall be imprisoned in the penitentiary, &c., and the statute providing that it shall be a sufficient description of such offense in any indictment to charge that the accused did unlawfully and feloniously obtain from the person defrauded his money or property by means and by use of the confidence game, an indictment charging that the accused on a date named unlawfully, fraudulently and feloniously did obtain from a person named a large sum of money, goods and personal property described, the property of said person, by means and by use of the confidence game, contrary to the statute and against the peace and dignity of the people of the State of Illinois, sufficiently charged accused with said crime to justify a requisition for his arrest in another state and return as a fugitive from justice; an indictment so charging the offense being held sufficient by the decisions of the Supreme Court of Illinois. Id.

10. Where the legality of an arrest under an extradition warrant is questioned on habeas corpus, the question of the plaintiff's guilt or innocence of the crime charged is not involved, and it is therefore unnecessary that an affidavit accompanying the extradition papers intended to establish the identity of the accused with the person charged in the indictment shall allege all the facts or elements of the crime charged, and hence it is not a ground for the discharge of the person arrested that the facts stated in such affidavit do not show the charge in the indictment to be well founded. Id.

11. A requisition for an alleged fugitive from justice named him as "Charles T. Crane, otherwise known as James Ryan,"

FACTORS—*Continued.*

to sell the wool upon that market resulted in damage to the defendant; that the consignment was general and to a specified market, and the plaintiffs were not bound to look for any other market than the one to which the wool was consigned; and that the evidence as to sales and prices in other markets was not material and was improperly admitted, since, although such evidence, under some circumstances, might be admissible as tending to show the market price at the place where the wool was to be sold, and the want of care or diligence of the factor in selling the wool at the best available price, no circumstances of that nature were disclosed as would take it out of the general rule. Id.

9. In an action by factors for advances, where defendant counter-claimed, setting up a loss alleged to have occurred through the negligent failure of the factors to sell at the market price, an instruction that the factors were under obligations to carry out any and all positive instructions of the defendant with reference to the property consigned was erroneous because disregarding the lien of the plaintiffs for advances and their right to reimbursement out of the proceeds of the sale. Id.

10. An instruction in such action that if the jury should find that any latitude was given to the factors then they should consider whether the factors had acted in good faith and according to their best judgment in carrying out the instructions of the principal so as best to preserve his rights, was erroneous because of the absence of any evidence challening the good faith of the plaintiffs. Id.

11. The defendant had the right to open and close the argument to the jury where, in an action for advances by factors, the defense was a counter-claim by way of confession and avoidance alleging a loss occasioned by the negligent failure of the factors to sell at the market price, and the court properly instructed the jury that there was no dispute in the evidence as to the right of the plaintiffs to recover, unless the defendant had established his counter-claim by a preponderance of the evidence, and that the burden of proof rested upon the defendant. Id.

12. In an action by factors for advances, where the defendant has counter-claimed alleging a loss occurring through the negligent failure of the factors to sell, if there is evidence which may properly be understood as showing a long delay by the factors in selling during a falling market, it may

ACTORS—*Continued.*

to that extent tend to show lack of diligence sufficient to justify the submission of the matter to the jury, and if unexplained may be sufficient to justify a finding of negligence; but, in applying that principle in the case stated, the rule concerning the duty of a factor who has made advances should be considered, and the jury properly instructed with reference thereto. Id.

INAL ORDER. See Appeal and Error, 8, 12.

RAUD. See Corporations, 1-22; Pleadings, 6.

UGITIVE FROM JUSTICE. See Extradition.

OVERNOR. Veto power. See Statutes, 2-7.

ABEAS CORPUS. See Extradition, 6, 10-15.

JUNCTION.

1. The granting or refusing of an injunction *pendente lite* is a matter resting largely in the discretion of the court, to be exercised so as to prevent injury, considering the situation of the parties, and the appellate court will not interfere with or control the action of the court below in such case, unless it has been guilty of a clear abuse of discretion; abuse of discretion, within the meaning of that rule, meaning an error of law committed by the court. Weaver v. Richardson, 343.

2. Defendant's answer in an action for the recovery of land which demands judgment for damages for the breach of an alleged contract for the sale of the premises, or, in the alternative, for specific performance of the contract, is in that respect an answer in the nature of a counter-claim under the code and entitles the defendant to apply for an injunction *pendente lite* to protect his possession; and it is immaterial that the part of the answer setting forth the facts upon which the affirmative relief is demanded is not styled a cross-petition or named a counter claim. Id.

3. A defendant in an action for the recovery of land, upon filing an answer in the nature of a counter-claim or cross-petition praying for specific performance of an alleged contract for the sale of the premises is entitled to have his possession protected by an injunction pending the action. Id.

4. In an action for recovery of land in which the defendant asked for specific performance of an alleged contract for a sale of the premises and moved for an injunction to protect her possession *pendente lite, Held*, that the motion was

MALICIOUS PROSECUTION.

1. The necessary elements to support an action for malicious prosecution are the institution of the proceedings without probable cause, with malice, that they have terminated in plaintiff's favor, and that plaintiff has been damaged. McIntosh v. Wales, 397.

2. Where defendants furnished a justice of the peace information and signed and made oath to the complaint upon which a warrant was issued charging plaintiff with stealing cattle, the fact that they took no further part in the prosecution and that it was dismissed by the justice at the request of the prosecuting attorney without the submission of any evidence did not relieve the defendants from liability in a civil action for damages, if their acts were malicious and without probable cause. Id.

3. Such dismissal by the prosecuting attorney constituted a termination of the proceedings in favor of the plaintiff so as to enable plaintiff to maintain an action for malicious prosecution. Id.

4. Where plaintiff was actually arrested and held under a warrant issued under a complaint sworn to by defendants, the fact that such complaint did not state a criminal offense was no defense to an action for malicious prosecution. Id.

5. While the dismissal of the criminal prosecution complained of at the instance of the prosecuting attorney without submitting any evidence was admissible and sufficient to show a termination of the proceeding alleged to be malicious, such act of the prosecuting attorney was not evidence against the defendants in an action for malicious prosecution upon the issue of want of probable cause in commencing the prosecution, nor was it evidence of malice. Id.

6. Probable cause, to justify a criminal prosecution, may exist, even though the prosecuting witness acts maliciously if the charge be true; and, even if the charge be not true, if such witness acts honestly and in good faith, basing his charge upon facts which he in fact believes to be true, but which afterwards turn out to be false, he cannot be said to have acted without probable cause. Id.

7. The dismissal of the prosecution at the request of the prosecuting attorney by the justice, who was acting in taking the complaint and issuing the warrant as a magistrate vested with authority to hold a preliminary examination and commit upon finding that there was probable cause to believe that a crime had been committed and that the

MALICIOUS PROSECUTION—*Continued.*

one charged therewith was guilty, was not a judicial determination by said justice of the existence of probable cause for the institution of the criminal proceeding, nor evidence thereof in an action for malicious prosecution subsequently instituted and based upon such proceeding. Id.

8. The verdict of the jury in an action for malicious prosecution being general was a finding upon all the issues in favor of the plaintiff. Id.

9. Malice necessary to be shown in an action for malicious prosecution may be inferred·from a showing of want of probable cause, but want of probable cause will not be inferred from proof of malice alone. Id.

10. Where, in an action for malicious prosecution, based upon the arrest of the plaintiff under a warrant issued upon a complaint sworn to by the defendants charging the plaintiff with stealing cattle, the plaintiff testified that she never stole any cattle from the defendants or either of them, and was permitted to and did introduce as part of her affirmative case proof of her general good character or reputation for honesty and integrity in the vicinity in which she lived, and one of the defendants was her uncle and had known her in the community where she lived from childhood, *held,* that said acquaintance was sufficient to raise a presumption of his knowledge of her good reputation, and such proof was sufficient *prima facie* to show want of probable cause. Id.

11. The defendants in an action for malicious prosecution, to show that they acted upon probable cause in instigating the criminal proceeding upon which the action was based, introduced evidence tending to show that plaintiff's reputation for honesty and integrity was bad, and evidence of different circumstances of which defendants had knowledge prior to·the prosecution. *Held,* that, conceding that such information standing alone, if honestly believed, would be sufficient to raise in the mind of a reasonably prudent man a well grounded suspicion that plaintiff had at various times prior to the prosecution been guilty of the crime charged against her, and might constitute probable cause for the prosecution, the testimony as to the circumstances aforesaid having been denied by the plaintiff, causing a direct conflict in the evidence as to the facts relied upon to constitute probable cause, the question was one for the jury. Id.

MASTER AND SERVANT—*Continued.*

defendant of the duty of warning the plaintiff of the dangers incident to his occupation as a coal miner, if in fact plaintiff was inexperienced, and the defendant had knowledge of that fact. Id.

7. In an action for personal injuries brought by an injured employee against the employer, whether the danger was obvious to the plaintiff is ordinarily a question of fact for the jury, and in determining that question the jury may and should take into consideration the nature of plaintiff's employment in which the injury occurred, his experience and capacity to understand and appreciate the danger of his employment, and how to avoid such danger. Id.

8. Although the plaintiff, in an action against an employer for personal injuries received when working in the employer's coal mine, may have been inexperienced as alleged, and although the defendant, as alleged, may not have instructed and warned the plaintiff how to discover and avoid danger of falling coal by what is known as the "sounding test," the plaintiff could not recover unless the failure of the defendant to so instruct and warn him was the proximate cause of the injury. Id.

9. Plaintiff, a young man without experience, as alleged in his petition, was employed by the defendant as a coal miner. He and the one working with him, after having fired a shot to loosen the coal, discovered a crack on one side of a large projecting lump of coal, and inserted a bar in the crack in an attempt to pry down such lump, but being unable to get it down in that manner, plaintiff concluded that there was no immediate danger of its falling and proceeded with the work of loading the coal which had fallen after the firing of the shot, and while so working the said lump fell, injuring plaintiff's foot and ankle, necessitating amputation. *Held,* that plaintiff was charged with knowledge of the law of gravitation, that the risk of injury from the fall of said lump of coal was obvious, and, therefore, the plaintiff could not complain of failure on the part of the defendant to instruct and warn him of the danger incident to his employment, or how to discover and avoid such danger. Id.

10. The evidence aforesaid to the effect that the plaintiff attempted to pry down the coal which subsequently fell and injured him for the purpose of avoiding danger from its falling showed that he appreciated the danger and concluded him upon that question, and, therefore, any failure

MASTER AND SERVANT—*Continued.*

of the defendant company to instruct and warn the plaintiff as an inexperienced miner was not the proximate cause of the injury, and, since the only ground for a recovery upon the petition and evidence would have been such failure on the part of the company to instruct and warn, the motion of the defendant to direct a verdict in its favor should have been sustained. Id.

See also Work and Labor, 4-6.

MINES AND MINERALS.

1. An essential requirement of a valid location of a mining claim is that there shall be a discovery of mineral upon the ground. Dean v. Omaha-Wyoming Oil Co., 133.

2. A discovery for the purpose of location of a mining claim must be within the limits of the claim sought to be located. Id.

3. While discovery of mineral is supposed to chronologically precede the acts locating a mining claim, such discovery may follow, instead of preceding, the acts of location, and will be good as against all who have not acquired intervening rights. Id.

4. In an adverse suit contesting the right to patent to an oil placer mining claim, whether or not defendant had made a discovery of oil within the limits of the claim was a question of fact, and the burden of proving such discovery was upon the defendant. Id.

5. In an adverse suit contesting the right to patent for an oil placer mining claim covering the northeast quarter of a certain section, where the defendant claimed discovery on said quarter section by a well alleged to have been sunk on the dividing line between said quarter section and the southeast quarter of the same section, *Held*, that the evidence of the county surveyor, who made a survey of the property after defendant's well had been sunk, tending to show that the stone marking the quarter corner on the west boundary of the section had been moved several feet south of its original location, and that said well by the government survey was several feet south of and off said northeast quarter of the section, was sufficient to support a finding in favor of plaintiff to the effect that defendant's discovery was not made within the boundaries of his claim. Id.

6. The evidence in an adverse suit *held* insufficient to show discovery by defendant, where the trial court had found

MINES AND MINERALS—*Continued.*

against him upon that issue, since it did not establish the fact that oil was found in the well sunk by defendant to the depth of 52 feet, or, if oil was found, that it was sufficient in quantity to constitute a discovery, instead of being mere seepage; there being a substantial conflict in the evidence as to the character of the substance found in the well. Id.

7. In an adverse suit, where it was claimed that defendant had not made a sufficient discovery, the question of the sufficiency of his discovery of mineral within the limits of the claim was for the trial court, and the evidence *held* sufficient to support a finding that discovery had not been made. Id.

8. Where, in an adverse mining suit, the trial court found upon sufficient evidence that the defendant had not made a discovery within the limits of the claim, the defendant was not entitled to affirmative relief establishing in him the right of possession to the land in dispute. Id.

9. Where the defendant in an adverse mining suit had made no discovery, *Held,* that he had acquired no intervening right which would prevent the plaintiff from filing an amended or additional certificate to the original location certificate of his claim. Id.

10. The original location certificate of a mining claim and an amended certificate, if one be filed, must be construed together, and, if sufficient when so construed, the location record will be valid, although neither standing alone would be sufficient. Id.

11. One who has succeeded to the interest of the original locators of a mining claim is permitted under Section 3459, Compiled Statutes, 1910, upon making discovery, to amend or file an additional certificate to show the date of discovery, and, having done so, will be entitled to the right of possession, where such amendment has not infringed upon rights of others existing at the time thereof. Id.

12. Where an oil placer mining claim when originally located was properly staked and named, and otherwise properly located, except that there was no discovery, and afterwards upon making discovery, an additional certificate of location was filed stating the date of discovery, *Held,* that it was not necessary before filing the amended certificate to restake and again name the claim. Id.

13. In an adverse mining suit, where the defendant, who was the applicant for patent, has not shown a discovery suf-

MINES AND MINERALS—*Continued*.

ficient to entitle him to the right of possession, the fact that there was no proof of the citizenship of the original locators of the plaintiff's claim did not entitle the defendant to affirmative relief. Id.

14. A recorded certificate of a mining location is prima facie proof of the facts therein contained, in an adverse proceeding, as well as proof of compliance with the law in making the record, and the date thereof. Id.

15. When the citizenship of the locator or locators of a mining claim is in issue in an adverse mining suit, it should be proven as any other fact in the case, and may be established by the affidavit of the party or a duly authorized agent. Id.

16. The recital in the certificate of location of a mining claim to the effect that the original locators were each citizens of the United States and over the age of 21 years, together with other facts, may raise a presumption of such citizenship. Id.

17. In an adverse mining suit the affidavit of plaintiff's agent to an additional certificate, which was filed after discovery to complete the record of plaintiff's claim, stated that the original locators of the claim were each citizens of the United States, and said affidavit was received in evidence without objection. *Held*, that said affidavit, in connection with the original and additional certificate, was prima facie proof of the citizenship of the original locators; the original and additional certificates together with said affidavit being the only evidence on the subject of said citizenship, and no objection having been made in the trial court that said locators were not citizens or that the fact of their citizenship was not shown. Id.

18. In an action in support of an adverse mining claim the objection cannot be raised for the first time on appeal that the citizenship of the original locators under whom plaintiff claimed was not shown. Id.

See also Master and Servant, 1-10.

MORTGAGES. See Chattel Mortgages.

NEGLIGENCE. See Master and Servant, 1-10.

NEGOTIABLE INSTRUMENTS.

1. Where a check for a sum certain, payable to the order of a payee named, contained the additional words: "For Wilkes," and the following at the bottom of the check: "This check may not be paid unless object for which

NEGOTIABLE INSTRUMENTS—*Continued*.

drawn is stated," and the check was signed in the name of a corporation by a person named, *held*, that the words "For Wilkes" did not import that the check was drawn otherwise than upon the general personal credit of the drawer, but, on the contrary, was merely a statement of the object for which the check was drawn, or the person or account to which the amount was to be charged, and did not impress upon the check any element of contingency or condition as to payment. Brown v. Cow Creek Sheep Co., 1.

2. A statement in or upon a bill, note, or check indicating the consideration or account to be charged with the amount, does not render the payment, promise, or order conditional or affect the negotiability of the instrument, there being a clear distinction between such a statement and an order or promise to pay out of a particular fund; such distinction being usually recognized in statutes defining negotiable instruments, and in the statute of this state by the provision that an order or promise to pay out of a particular fund is not unconditional, but that an unqualified order or promise to pay is unconditional, though coupled with an indication of a particular fund out of which reimbursement is to be made, or a particular account to be debited with the amount, or a statement of the transaction which gives rise to the instrument. (Comp. Stat. 1910, Sec. 3161.) Id.

3. Where a check for a sum certain, payable to the order of a payee named, contained the additional words: "For Wilkes," *held*, that the direction contained in the instrument was not to pay out of a particular fund, as distinguished from an order upon the general credit of the drawer. Id.

4. A "check" is usually defined to be a draft or order upon a bank for the payment, at all events, of a certain sum of money to a person or his order, or to bearer, and payable on demand; it is an evidence of indebtedness, and, as between drawer and payee, is equivalent to the drawer's promise to pay, although the latter may not be bound absolutely until payment has been duly demanded of the bank and refused. Id.

5. An action may be brought upon a check by the holder against the drawer to recover the amount thereof. Id.

6. The payment of a check may be stopped or countermanded at any time before it is actually presented and paid; but in doing so the drawer assumes the consequences of his act.

NEGOTIABLE INSTRUMENTS—*Continued.*

7. A check for a sum certain, payable to the order of a payee named, signed in the name of a corporation by a person named, contained the words in the body of the check: "For Wilkes," and also at the bottom of the check the following: "This check may not be paid unless object for which drawn is stated." *Held,* that, conceding the effect of the memorandum to be, as contended, to require that the object be stated, when the memorandum was complied with, the instrument, if otherwise in proper form and unqualified, would be a check, and necessarily an instrument for the unconditional payment of money, though subject to such defenses as may properly be interposed in a suit upon any instrument of that character in the hands of the one suing upon it; and that the words "For Wilkes" were to be regarded as having been written in the check for the purpose of stating the object. Id.

8. Any form of statement, however brief and indefinite, informing the drawer as to the matter, would be a sufficient compliance with a memorandum at the bottom of a check stating that the check may not be paid unless object for which drawn is stated. Id.

9. As a general rule a bank is not bound to take notice of memoranda upon the margin or in the body of the check placed there for the convenience of the drawer. Id.

10. By statute (Comp, Stat. 1910, Sec. 3182) a promissory note negotiable in form is deemed prima facie to have been issued for a valuable consideration. Hamilton v. Diefenderfer, 266.

11. By his indorsement of a negotiable promissory note the payee and holder thereby impliedly warrants that it is in all respects genuine; that it is the valid instrument it purports to be; that such indorser has lawful title to it; and that it is a valid and subsisting obligation. Id.

See also Insurance, 2; Payment; Pleading, 1-3.

NEW TRIAL.

1. That a witness did not testify to certain matters does not entitle the party complaining thereof to a new trial on the ground of surprise, where it appears that the witness was not interrogated as to such matters, for it cannot be assumed that he would not have so testified had he been examined as to them. Demple v. Carroll, 447.

2. That a witness who had been summoned did not appear at the trial on account of a death in his family is not a ground for new trial where no continuance of the case

NEW TRIAL—*Continued.*

or postponement of the trial was asked for on that ground. Id.

3. It was not error to refuse a motion for a new trial on the ground of newly discovered evidence where it appeared that the alleged new evidence consisted of the testimony of persons who could easily have been consulted about the matter as interested parties before the trial, and it not appearing that they had been consulted about the matter, or that any effort was made to produce the evidence on the trial. Id.

4. A party cannot neglect to exercise such reasonable diligence in the preparation of his case as the circumstances would reasonably suggest and as will enable his attorneys to take the necessary steps to procure the evidence, go to trial without it, and when defeated, be entitled to a new trial for the lack of evidence which could have been produced had proper diligence been exercised. Id.

5. A motion for a new trial is not a pleading under the provisions of the code, and therefore the provision for extending the time to file a pleading does not apply to such a motion. Blonde v. Merriam et al., 513. .

6. Under the statute requiring an application for new trial to be made within ten days after the verdict or decision is rendered, unless such party is unavoidably prevented from filing the same within such time, and except for the cause of newly discovered material evidence which could not, with reasonable diligence, have been discovered and produced at the trial, an order purporting to extend the time beyond the ten-day period is ineffectual, where newly discovered evidence is not alleged, and where no showing was made that the party would be or had been unavoidably prevented from filing his motion within such prescribed period; and it appearing that the order was made without such a showing upon an *ex parte* application, without notice to or consent of the opposing party or his counsel, a motion filed after the ten-day period, but within the time as so extended, was properly stricken from the files. Id.

For new trial for newly discovered evidence, see Appeal and Error, 4.

OIL. Placer claims—Discovery—Evidence—Amended location certificate—Adverse suit. See Mines and Minerals.

PARTIES. See Appeal and Error, 1.

PARTNERSHIP.

PAYMENT.

PLEADING—*Continued.*

pleading being aided or cured by the subsequent pleadings or proceedings, he retains the benefit of a proper exception taken by him to the ruling on the demurrer. Id.

18. Under the statute (Comp. Stat. 1910, Sec. 4436) providing that after the overruling of a demurrer the party may plead further if the court is satisfied that he has a meritorious defense or claim, and did not demur for delay, when such leave to further plead is given it is full and complete, and upon pleading over after such leave granted the withdrawal of the demurrer will not be implied, where the ruling upon it was excepted to. Id.

19. An amendment to the answer in an action on a contract so as to allege that the defendant's signature to the contract was procured by fraud, deceit and false representations was properly refused. Demple v. Carroll, 447.

20. Having permitted the defendant to introduce his evidence as to fraud, deceit and false representations subject to the plaintiff's objection, it was not error at the close of the evidence to exclude all such evidence, since its purpose was to alter or vary the terms of the written contract, and was inadmissible under the pleadings. Id.

21. Aside from the statute (Comp. Stat. 1910, Sec. 4437) providing that a party applying to amend a pleading during the trial shall be required to show that the amendatory facts were unknown to him prior to the application, unless the court in its discretion shall relieve him from so doing, the general rule is that it is not an abuse of discretion to refuse to allow on the trial an amendment which materially changes the cause of action or defense. Id.

See also Corporations, 1, 2, 5, 9-12, 15, 21, 22; Injunction, 2-4; Work and Labor, 1, 6.

PRACTICE. Submitting case to jury, see Trial, 1, 2.

PREMIUM NOTE. See Insurance, 2.

PRINCIPAL AND AGENT. See Evidence, 2, 3; Factors.

PUBLIC LANDS OF THE STATE.

1. Where, in a contest before the board of school land commissioners, the contestant sought the cancellation of a lease previously made by the board to another party, the contestant claimed to have acquired the right to a part of the land for a reservoir site; the land having belonged to the United States, and having been selected by the state in lieu of other lands, but the exact date of the state's selec-

PUBLIC LANDS OF THE STATE—*Continued.*

tion did not appear in the record of the cause on appeal; *Held,* 'that the state's selection of the land would be presumed to have been made prior to the date of the lease. Bucknum v. Johnson, 26.

2. An appeal to the District Court from the state land board is a proceeding purely of statutory origin, and brings into the District Court those questions which were or might have been raised before the board; the issues cannot be enlarged, nor can the action be transformed into an equitable or common law action. Id.

3. On an appeal from the state land board the District Court acts as a substitute for the board, and is limited to questions that had or may be presumed to have been passed upon by the board. Id.

4. The statute providing for. an appeal from the state land board authorizing the parties to conduct the appeal upon the original papers and affidavits or upon new and amended pleadings, and prescribing that the case shall stand for trial upon the evidence taken before the board, with a proviso that in the discretion of the court, additional evidence may be adduced on the trial, where the party desiring to introduce such evidence shall have given notice to the adverse party immediately after the perfection of the bill, of the offering of said evidence and the purport and nature thereof, and further prescribing that the case shall be heard and tried the same in all respects as civil cases are tried in said court; *Held,* that the trial upon the appeal includes the trial and determination of the issues of fact made by the pleadings, independent of the findings and determination of those issues by the board, whether such trial be had upon the evidence submitted to the board or upon new evidence as permitted by the statute. Id.

5. The jurisdiction of the District Court on an appeal from the state land board is to try the case *de novo* on the facts, and the judgment to be rendered is not one of affirmance, reversal or modification as upon review on error, but a judgment based upon the findings of the court upon the evidence, uncontrolled by the findings of the board. Id.

6. On an appeal to the District Court from a decision of the state board of school land commissioners in a contest seeking the cancellation of a state lease, the question to be determined by the court was the same as that which was presented to the board, viz: whether the state which had granted the lease should cancel it. Id.

PUBLIC LANDS OF THE STATE—*Continued.*

7. Where a contestant seeking the cancellation of a lease of state lands before the state land board claimed a prior vested right to a ditch and reservoir site upon the land prior to the issuance of patent to the state for the land; *Held,* that if the contestant had in fact such a vested right it would be no ground for setting aside the lease, in said contest proceeding, either by the board or by the court on appeal, for the lease would not be involved, but would be subject to such prior vested right, and would be limited to the title conveyed to the state; whether such vested rights existed might be litigated in a proper forum and proceeding. Id.

8. In the performance of its duties with reference to the leasing and disposal of state lands the state land board is not vested with either equitable or common law jurisdiction. Id.

9. Where there was but one applicant for a lease to state school lands at the time a lease thereof was granted, the board was not required to pass upon any question other than the form and information contained in the application and evidence in support thereof as bearing upon the right of the applicant to the lease. Id.

10. Where, in an application to lease state school lands, a question and the answer thereto appeared as follows: "State who, if anyone, occupies land within one mile of the tract applied for, giving section number, township and range? A. No one," and the undisputed evidence in a contest seeking a cancellation of the lease, which had been granted upon the application, showed that the homestead of another party, including buildings, were situated within one mile of each quarter section of the land covered by the lease; *Held,* that it was the duty of the applicant to place the board in possession of the facts called for by the application, showing the true situation with reference to the homestead of the other party, since such information might have an important bearing on the amount of revenue obtainable for the lease, and, further, that the lease appeared to have been granted upon incorrect information as to the occupancy of such homestead. Id.

11. The section of the statute (Comp. Stat. 1910, Sec. 618) which provides that any lease for state lands procured by fraud, deceit or misrepresentation, may be cancelled by the board upon proper proof thereof, is permissive and not compulsory, though it might be the duty of the board in a

PUBLIC LANDS OF THE STATE—*Continued*.

proper case to cancel a lease so procured. Id.

12. Where the cancellation of a lease of state school lands is sought in a contest before the state board of school land commissioners on the ground that the lease was procured by fraud, deceit, or misrepresentation, in that the lessee untruthfully stated in the application for the lease that no one occupied land within one mile of the tract applied for; *Held*, that upon the proof submitted the board acts in a judicial capacity, and is not required to cancel the lease unless damage to the state is shown to have been sustained in the way of rental or otherwise, where there had been no application of the contestant before the board to purchase or lease the land at the time the lease sought to be cancelled was granted. Id.

13. In a petition filed by a third party with the state board of school land commissioners to contest a lease previously granted, petitioner claimed a preference right to the land in part on the ground of a vested water right and reservoir site. *Held*, that in the contest proceeding whether the contestant had such water right and reservoir site was a question without the jurisdiction of the board; and, further, that the cancellation of the lease was not necessary to protect any such right of the contestant existing at the time the patent had issued to the state, since the patent would be subject thereto, and the lease would be limited to the state's title. Id.

14. Any vested right to a reservoir site upon public lands of the United States, acquired under Sections 2339 and 2340, Revised Statutes, U. S., and supplementary statutory provisions, prior to the selection and patent of such lands to the state would be protected by such statutes, independent of any recognition or want of recognition by the state land board, for the board could only deal with the title conveyed to it by the patent as construed and affected by the acts of Congress in effect at the time of the issuance of the patent. Id.

15. Although the information furnished the state board of school land commissioners in an application for the lease of school lands with reference to the occupancy of land by other parties within one mile of the tract applied for was untrue, the board was not required to cancel said lease in a contest proceeding brought for such cancellation, in the absence of a showing that the state had been damaged by such un-

STATUTES—*Continued.*

of the session of the legislature and not acted upon by him until after adjournment, that if he has such power his disapproval of part only of the amount of a distinct item would leave the remainder appropriated, and if such power is not conferred his act in disapproving a part and approving a part of the item would be invalid and a nullity, and the entire amount of such item would be appropriated and available for the purpose declared by the bill, since under Section 8 of Article IV of the Constitution, to prevent a bill so presented and not acted upon until after adjournment, or any of the items thereof, from becoming a law, the Governor would be required to expressly disapprove the same by filing the bill with his objections in the office of the Secretary of State within fifteen days after the adjournment of the legislature. State ex rel. Jamison v. Forsyth, State Auditor, 359.

3, The provision of Section 8 of Article IV of the Constitution that any bill not returned by the governor within three days (Sundays excepted) after its presentation to him shall be a law, unless the legislature by its adjournment prevent its return, in which case it shall be a law, unless he shall file the same with his objections in the office of the Secretary of State within fifteen days after such adjournment, applies to the general appropriation bill as well as to other bills. Id.

4. Where the general appropriation bill contained among other distinct items of appropriation to pay the necessary contingent expenses of state and district officers, employes, boards and commissions, an item of $15,000 for the office of state geologist, and said bill was presented to the governor on the last day of the session of the legislature, and within fifteen days thereafter the governor signed the bill, stating above his signature: "This act is approved save and except the items or parts of items specially noted herewith as being disapproved and as shown by accompanying communication. * * * See also notations on margin"; and on the margin of the item appropriated for said office was the following notation: "$10,000 of item approved. $5,000 of item disapproved"; and in the accompanying communication it was stated by the governor that he approved of so much of the item as appropriates $10,000, and withheld his approval from $5,000, leaving the appropriation $10,000; said bill so signed and with the accompanying communication being filed with the Secretary

STATUTES—*Continued.*

of State within said period; *held,* that the action of the governor as to said item of appropriation was not an objection to or a disapproval of the entire item, and if the authority is not conferred upon him to disapprove a distinct item in part and approve it in part, his act in attempting to do so would be a nullity, and ineffectual for the purpose intended, or for any other purpose; that at least the sum of $10,000 was appropriated for said office, and that being sufficient to pay the claim for which mandamus was sought against the auditor, which was conceded to be the first claim, if not the only one, presented for allowance out of said appropriation, it would be unnecessary to decide whether said action of the governor lawfully reduced the appropriation to the amount approved. Id.

5. By "objections" or "disapproval," as those terms are employed in the Constitution with reference to the veto power of the governor, is meant objections or disapproval within the authority of the governor, and expressed in the manner provided by the Constitution. Id.

6. Under Section 8 of Article IV of the Constitution, providing that a bill received by the governor too late to be returned to the legislature within a specified time will become a law unless disapproved by the governor within the period limited for that purpose after adjournment, an unauthorized disapproval will not defeat the bill. Id.

7. Where an affirmative approval of the governor is not required to a general appropriation bill becoming a law, but the bill or the items contained therein will become law unless disapproved, an unauthorized disapproval will be ineffectual. Id.

STATUTES, CITED OR CONSTRUED.

STATUTES, CITED OR CONSTRUED—*Continued.*

STATUTES, CITED OR CONSTRUED—*Continued.*

STATUTORY CONSTRUCTION. See Larceny, 1.

STOCKHOLDERS. Action to set aside sale of corporate property. See Corporations, 1-22.

TIME. For commencing proceeding in error, see Appeal and Error, 10—For filing petition for rehearing, see Appeal and Error, 5—Extending time for filing motion for new trial, see New Trial, 5, 6.

TRESPASS. By causing herds of sheep to mix, see Damages, 1-4.

TRIAL.

1. When a case is tried to a jury, controverted questions of fact upon which there is substantial conflict in the evidence should be submitted to the jury for its determination. Weaver v. Richardson, 158.

TRIAL—*Continued.*

2. In an action for the possession of real estate it was for the jury, and not the court, to weigh the conflicting evidence with reference to a contract under which defendant claimed right of possession, and determine whether or not the defense was established by a preponderance of the evidence; and it was error for the court to direct a verdict for the plaintiff on the ground that defendant had failed to show a contract of sale. Id.

See also District Court Commissioner, 1-4; Factors, 11; Jury and Jurors; Venue.

TRUSTS.

1. Where one holding the legal title to land in trust for the joint use and benefit of himself and another has sold and conveyed the land without the knowledge and consent of the other party, the latter is entitled to recover from such trustee the value of his interest in the land, or the amount for which it was sold if the value is not shown to exceed that amount. But the value based upon the supposed character of the land as oil land being speculative cannot be considered. Fourt v. Edwards, 393.

VENUE.

1. An affidavit filed by a party in a civil action, as permitted by Section 5142, Compiled Statutes, 1910, stating that said party believes that, on account of the bias and prejudice of the presiding judge of the court, he cannot obtain a fair trial, when called to the court's attention, divests the presiding judge of the court of further jurisdiction other than to call in another district judge to preside in the further proceedings and trial of the cause. Huhn v. Quinn, 51.

2. An application for change of judge includes the filing of the affidavit therefor and calling the attention of the court or judge thereto, and where the application has been so made the judge becomes thereby divested of further authority in the matter, except to act upon the application, grant it if properly made, and call upon some other district court judge to preside in the further proceedings and trial of the cause; said judge is not thereupon authorized to direct the district court commissioner to preside in the court and hear and determine the cause. Id.

VERDICT. In larceny, see Larceny, 1.

VETO. Governor's power as to appropriations, see Statutes, 2-7.

WATER AND WATER RIGHTS.

1. The state engineer may, by express provision of statute, require additional information before passing finally upon an application for permit to construct a reservoir. Laughlin v. State Board of Control et al., 99.

2. The time within which to furnish additional information requested by the state engineer upon the filing of an application for permit to construct a reservoir is not limited by statute, but such information should be furnished within a reasonable time. Id.

3. In the statute requiring the state engineer to reject an application for a permit to appropriate water when the proposed use conflicts with existing rights, the words "when the proposed use conflicts with existing rights" means rights which are prior in time to the use of the water. Id.

4. It was not necessary, under the provisions of Sections 743 and 744, Compiled Statutes, 1910, to set forth in an application for a permit to construct a reservoir filed May 14, 1908, or to show upon the map accompanying the application, the land intended to be irrigated from the reservoir, but if such application complied in form and contained the requirements of Section 743, it would be complete as a primary application to construct a reservoir; and if the source of supply of water was sufficient, and if the proposed use would not conflict with prior rights, or threaten to be detrimental to the public interest, the applicant would be entitled to a permit. Id.

5. Where an application for a permit to construct a reservoir, filed May 14, 1908, was returned to the applicant for additional information concerning the supply ditch, and requiring that if the ditch required enlargement for the purpose of filling the reservoir the written consent of the ditch owners be filed in the engineer's office before the application would be approved; that the outlet of the reservoir should be shown; and the land on which the water was intended to be used should also be filed upon, or, if filed upon, the number of the permit or the description of the land should be given, so that the reservoir can be tied to the lands for which the water is to be used, *Held*, that the information called for was not required by the statute to be stated in the application, and that the engineer could not properly require, as a condition to his approval of the application, that the land to be irrigated, or the title thereto be shown, since the necessity of such showing for primary permit was dispensed with by the provisions of

WATER AND WATER RIGHTS—*Continued.*

tended to be so applied, or a greater quantity of water than is reasonably required for such purpose. Id.

20. Without deciding whether the provision of the statute enacted by the first State legislature (Laws 1890-91, Ch. 8, Sec. 25, Comp. Stat. 1910, Sec. 777), declaring that no allotment of water for irrigation shall be made by the board of control in adjudicating priorities exceeding one cubic foot per second for each seventy acres of land, is or is not a valid regulation as to appropriations made prior to its adoption, the board and the courts may properly so limit the right of any appropriator when it is found to be sufficient and adequate for the purpose of the appropriation. Id.

21. Aside from the general information possessed by the board of control concerning the requirements of various classes of land in the state, the court may assume that some such information as to land in controversy involved in an adjudication proceeding was of record in the office of the state engineer, the contest before the court having been instituted and heard in the course of a proceeding for adjudication of priorities, and it being the duty of the engineer or his assistant to make an examination of the stream, the works diverting water therefrom, the carrying capacity of the various ditches, an examination of the irrigated lands, and an approximate measurement of the lands irrigated or susceptible of irrigation from the various ditches, and to make a record in his office of such observation and measurements. Id.

22. The statute requiring that on an appeal from an order of the board of control adjudicating priorities to the right to the use of water for irrigation or other beneficial purposes shall file in the office of the clerk of the District Court to which the appeal is taken a certified transcript of the order appealed from, the records of the board relating to the determination, and the evidence offered before the board, including the measurements of streams, appropriations and ditches made by or under the supervision of the engineer as required by law, the court should hesitate to disturb the board's findings and determination, where the record of the board as to the measurements and examination so provided for by law has not been brought before the court by certified transcript or otherwise. Id.

23. Whatever may be the effect of the statutory limitation upon the allotment of water for irrigation upon appropriations

WATER AND WATER RIGHTS—*Continued.*

made prior to the enactment of the statute, the use may be limited in accordance with the statute where there is no evidence, or the evidence is insufficient, to establish the duty of water upon the lands in controversy. Id.

24. The statutory provision limiting an allotment of water for irrigation to one cubic foot per second for each seventy acres of land for which an appropriation may be or has been made having remained unchanged for more than twenty years, it may be assumed that the maximum use thereby prescribed has been found at least generally to be sufficient, and, in the absence of other satisfactory evidence, the statute respecting the amount to be allotted should be followed. Id.

25. It having been stated in the findings of the board adjudicating the priorities to the use of water upon a certain stream and its tributaries that the measurements of the duty of water in the state indicate that the maximum use prescribed by the statute is sufficient under the most extreme conditions, *held,* that whether said statutory limit as to maximum use is conclusive or controlling in any case or not, it is at least to be regarded as furnishing a standard, in the absence of competent or satisfactory evidence that the use thereby permitted is insufficient in a particular case, and the evidence to that effect should be reasonably clear and satisfactory to entitle an appropriator to an allotment exceeding the statutory limit. Id.

26. A showing that all the water of the stream had at times been used or allowed to flow upon the land of a party does not necessarily prove an appropriation of all of it for a beneficial use, for an appropriation must be limited to the amount reasonably required for a proper and successful cultivation of the land, or other use to which the land is applied. Id.

27. Upon the question of the quantity of water necessary to irrigate a particular tract of land and whether the amount of water allotted by statute per acre for irrigation purposes is sufficient for the irrigation of said tract the testimony of witnesses who were practical irrigators, but whose testimony was confined to expressions of opinion based upon the general gravelly character of the soil, causing it to absorb more water than in the case of other kinds of soil, without showing any tests or measurements, or particular examination of the soil, or a knowledge of the quantity of water embraced in a flow of one cubic foot

WATER AND WATER RIGHTS—*Continued.*

per second, and very little, if any, acquaintance with the method employed in irrigating the particular land, except that ditches and laterals were used, *held,* to be unsatisfactory and not entitled to much weight in determining the duty of water as applied to land in controversy; the opinions of the witnesses, though honest, seeming to be little more than conjecture or guesswork. Id.

28. The record made by the examination and measurements of the state engineer provided for by law (Comp. Stat. 1910, Sec. 776), cannot affect the question as to the time or times when uncultivated lands may have been irrigated and the extent of the appropriation therefor in respect to the period of use. Id.

29. On appeal from the state board of control adjudicating priorities of water rights, *held,* upon the evidence, that the order of the board improperly restricted the use of water found to have been appropriated by a party for uncultivated lands by denying his right to use such water during the season when irrigation is more particularly required for cultivated crops; but, it not appearing that those lands had been irrigated when said party's cultivated lands were being irrigated, he was not entitled to use at the same time the water appropriated for his cultivated and uncultivated lands, though when not engaged in irrigating his cultivated lands, even during the irrigation season, he should be permitted to use the amount found to have been appropriated for the uncultivated or pasture lands.

See also Eminent Domain, 5-11.

WILLS.

1. By the laws of this state a nuncupative will is not recognized as valid, and is not entitled to be admitted to probate. Merrill v. State et al., 421.

WITNESSES. See New Trial, 1, 2.

WOOL. Consignment—Duty of Factors—Justice et al. v. Brock, 281.

WORDS AND PHRASES.

"CHECK." Brown v. Cow Creek Sheep Co., 1.

"DISAPPROVAL." State ex rel. Jamison v. Forsyth, 359.

"DOUBT." Claussen v. State, 505.

"EMINENT DOMAIN." Grover Irr. and Land Co. v. Lovella Ditch, Reservoir & Irr. Co., 204.

"OBJECTIONS." State ex rel. Jamison v. Forsyth, 359.

"REASONABLE DOUBT." Claussen v. State, 505.

WORK AND LABOR.

1. A petition in an action to recover the alleged value of work and labor and materials furnished *held* sufficient; the petition alleging the corporate capacity of the plaintiff, that the plaintiff, at defendant's request, furnished materials and labor and constructed a sidewalk around defendant's property, described as situated at the northeast corner of certain streets in a certain city named, that the labor and material so furnished and the sidewalk so constructed were of the reasonable value of $163.28, and that said sum was due and unpaid. Evans v. Cheyenne Cement, Stone & Brick Co., 184.

2. Where plaintiff sued for work and labor performed and materials furnished at defendant's request, in the construction of a sidewalk, and alleged in the petition the reasonable value of the labor and materials and the sidewalk as constructed, and that the amount thereof was due and unpaid, the fact that it appeared, as alleged in the answer, that there was an express contract between the parties for the construction of the sidewalk, stating the price to be paid therefor, did not bar plaintiff's right to recover the contract price. Id.

3. In an action for work and labor and materials furnished, where the petition is upon a *quantum meruit*, proof of a special contract fixing the price to be paid for said labor and the furnishing of the materials will not necessarily defeat the plaintiff's recovery, but the contract price becomes the *quantum meruit* in the case. Id.

4. In an action against an administrator by a son of the decedent upon a claim for work and labor performed during the father's lifetime and at his request, *held*, that the evidence stated showed an intention on the part of the deceased and an understanding between him and his son, the plaintiff, that the latter should be compensated for his services, and that the services were rendered in pursuance of such understanding, rendering it sufficient to support a verdict in plaintiff's favor. Pool v. Pool, as administrator, 435.

5. Where a father agreed to give his son practically all of his property at the time of his death in consideration for his services in working upon and caring for the farm owned by the father, and upon which he resided, and failed to do so because of the loss or destruction of a will making the agreed disposition of his property, *held*, that the value of the son's services rendered under the contract could be

WORK AND LABOR—*Continued.*

　　recovered upon the *quantum meruit* in an action against the administrator of his father's estate. Id.

6. The petition alleging the understanding between the father and son, the performance of the services, the value thereof, and the loss or destruction of a will made by the father devising practically all his property to the plaintiff, was sufficient to permit proof of the reasonable value of the plaintiff's services, and sufficient to state a cause of action. Id.

8/2/15

Lightning Source UK Ltd.
Milton Keynes UK
UKHW022156260219
338052UK00009B/377/P